Praise for

AMERICA, EMPIRE OF LIBERTY

"This is history as full-blown participatory democracy, where people who had been silenced or excluded are brought in by the bus load and given a voice and a vote . . . [Reynolds] has an enthralling tale to tell and he relates it in plain lively terms." —*Daily Telegraph* (London)

"Neatly written, nicely spiced with quotes and scandal, and with brief, telling glimpses of the set pieces of a bloody past." —MICHAEL PYE, *Scotsman* (Edinburgh)

"The author has a knack for making it all seem fresh." —RAYMOND SEITZ, *Literary Review* (London)

"Reynolds remains in awe of America as a great experiment founded on noble principles, even if its rulers haven't always lived up to them. His hugely impressive book lays the country bare in all its messy glory." —*Sunday Business Post* (London)

"The book is a gigantic refutation of the old canard that Americans have no history, and Reynolds's narratives of major events such as the Civil War, the first modern, industrialized conflict, and one that killed more Americans than both world wars combined are briskly and judiciously handled." —*Evening Standard* (London)

"A solid narrative history offering some provocative views." —*Booklist*

"In an animated overview up to the present time, Cambridge historian Reynolds (*In Command of History*) captures the sprawling chronicle of a nation forged from the fires of revolution, populated by immigrants and constantly evolving politically and culturally. . . . Most readers will find Reynolds's epic overview provocative and enjoyable." —*Publishers Weekly*

"Concise and still-inclusive . . . teeming . . . an evenhanded distillation of America's story from a singular outside observer." —*Kirkus*

AMERICA, EMPIRE OF LIBERTY

ALSO BY DAVID REYNOLDS

THE CREATION OF THE ANGLO-AMERICAN ALLIANCE:
A Study in Competitive Cooperation, 1937–1941

AN OCEAN APART:
The Relationship Between Britain and America in the Twentieth Century
(with David Dimbleby)

BRITANNIA OVERRULED:
British Policy and World Power in the Twentieth Century

THE ORIGINS OF THE COLD WAR IN EUROPE (editor)

ALLIES AT WAR:
The Soviet, American and British Experience, 1939–1945
(co-edited with Warren F. Kimball and A. O. Chubarian)

RICH RELATIONS:
The American Occupation of Britain, 1942–1945

ONE WORLD DIVISIBLE:
A Global History Since 1945

FROM MUNICH TO PEARL HARBOR:
Roosevelt's America and the Origins of the Second World War

IN COMMAND OF HISTORY:
Churchill Fighting and Writing the Second World War

FROM WORLD WAR TO COLD WAR:
Churchill, Roosevelt and the International History of the 1940s

SUMMITS:
Six Meetings That Shaped the Twentieth Century

AMERICA, EMPIRE OF LIBERTY

A New History of the United States

David Reynolds

BASIC BOOKS

A MEMBER OF THE PERSEUS BOOKS GROUP

New York

Books published by Basic Books are available at special discounts for bulk
purchases in the United States by corporations, institutions, and other
organizations. For more information, please contact the Special Markets
Department at the Perseus Books Group, 2300 Chestnut Street, Suite 200,
Philadelphia, PA 19103, or call (800) 810–4145, ext. 5000, or e-mail
special.markets@perseusbooks.com.

The Library of Congress has catalogued the hardcover as follows:
Reynolds, David, 1952–
    America, empire of liberty : a new history of the United States / David
Reynolds.
        p.   cm.
    Includes bibliographical references and index.
    ISBN 978-0-465-01500-9 (alk. paper)
        1. United States—History.   I. Title.
E178.R469 2009
973—dc22

                                                            2009017831

Paperback ISBN: 978-0-465-02214-4
e-book ISBN: 978-0-465-02005-8

10 9 8 7 6 5 4 3

Margaret—once again
Her history, our odyssey

&

Jim, Ellie, Lucy, and Maddy—
21st-century cousins
A past for their futures

CONTENTS

List of Maps   ix

Introduction   xi

PART I: LIBERTY AND SLAVERY

1 Natives and Europeans   3

2 Empire and Liberties   21

3 Independence and Republicanism   45

4 Liberty and Security   73

5 East and West   95

6 Slave or Free?   123

PART II: POWER AND PROGRESS

7 North and South   149

8 White and Black   177

9 Capital and Labor   197

10 Reform and Expansion   221

11 War and Peace   245

12 From Boom to Bomb   273

PART III: EMPIRE AND EVIL

13   Red or Dead?   307

14   Rights and Riots   335

15   The Impotence of Omnipotence   361

16   Détente and Discontent   389

17   Revolution and Democracy   417

18   Pride and Prejudice   441

     Conclusion   469

     Further Reading   479

     Notes   493

     Acknowledgments   547

     Index   549

MAPS

1. Westward Expansion   96

2. The Civil War, 1861–1865   150

3. Cold War Europe, 1949   308

INTRODUCTION

This is a deliberately unfashionable book. Such is the richness of America's past and the amount of research about it that most scholars of U.S. history specialize in a specific half-century, a single strand, such as gender history, or a particular region—the South, say, or the West. When syntheses are published, they often devote six or seven hundred pages to two or three decades, and most college textbooks on U.S. history are multivolume works co-authored by several specialists. For one person to write a single volume on the history of the American colonies and the United States therefore goes against the grain; indeed, it may seem almost an act of hubris.

Yet I believe it is justified and worthwhile, for several reasons. The proliferation of historical monographs and articles tends to increase knowledge at the expense of understanding. We lose the forest in the trees. This is especially true for general readers, who have neither the time nor the inclination to keep up with the minutiae of scholarship. Hence the value of an overview, drawing on some of the recent writing and the themes addressed therein but offering a personal interpretation of the whole.

This is also the view of an outsider, which has both disadvantages and benefits. Disadvantages, in that there will be specifics that I don't properly appreciate, detail that I haven't properly grasped. On the positive side, however, a foreigner may sometimes see the picture in a different way from the natives, tracing fresh connections or suggesting unfamiliar contexts. As a Brit who has visited the United States several times a year since 1973, has taught American history to British students for much of that time, but has nevertheless written on a broad range of international history, I think I have some credentials for the task.

This is also a narrative, a mode of writing not always favored by professional historians today. Much modern scholarship prefers to explore themes and analyze problems, often revealingly but sometimes losing touch with simple chronology. For me, history, like living, is rooted in time: Every day we tell stories about what has happened, giving narrative shape to the flux of events. I believe that if, as historians, we stray too far from the sequence of what happened, we are in danger of missing something fundamental. Most of the book follows this principle—apart from two overlapping chapters on what I call the "long 1960s" (a period of enormous importance for modern America, I believe, and one for which domestic and foreign policy need to be addressed separately).

This is also a history full of people. Sometimes academic scholarship strays into the abstract: Conscious of the big socioeconomic forces that shape history, scholars may lose sight of the human beings that actually constitute those "forces." I have therefore woven into the narrative the stories and voices of men, women, and children from America's past. They constitute the bright threads that give color and depth to the tapestry.

A tapestry needs a larger design, however. This book is in no sense a comprehensive portrayal of America's past, nor does it cover all aspects of American life; inevitably some readers will question my omissions. I have constructed the story around three themes that, in my judgment, are significant historically and also shed light on America's future: These I encapsulate as empire, liberty, and faith. Each one has proved richly, sometimes fatally, ambiguous.

What do I mean by these three themes? Empire, on the face of it, seems fairly simple.[1] Today it is a standard charge of critics that America is an imperialist nation—militarily through war in Iraq or economically through globalization. In the 1960s there were similar protests about the brutality of America's war in Vietnam and about how American multinational corporations were buying up Europe and the developing world.

Yet if we go back a bit further, imperialism is an accusation that would have seemed ridiculous to most Americans of the early twentieth century. In an era when European empires like Britain, France, and the Netherlands ruled much of Asia and Africa, Americans proudly presented themselves as the only nonimperialist great power. And not just Americans: When Ho Chi Minh proclaimed Vietnam's independence from the French empire in 1945, he invoked the preamble to America's Declaration of Independence from Britain in 1776. President Woodrow Wilson in World War I and Franklin Roosevelt in World War II envisioned these conflicts as a way of curbing not only German militarism but also the imperialism of America's European allies as an essential precondition of a new and better world.

If we journey further back, to the first century or so of America's history as a nation, we find its people engaged in a protracted battle against Britain's empire. Declaring independence was relatively simple; making it real was much harder. Although in 1783 Great Britain acknowledged U.S. independence, two decades later the new American government could not prevent British redcoats from burning Washington. Throughout the first half of the nineteenth century, America remained almost an economic colony of Britain, reliant on the mother country for manufactured goods and financial capital. In 1900, much of the American West was still owned by British investors. So, for roughly half of U.S. history, Americans self-consciously saw their country as an anti-empire, the flagship of the New World on a collision course with the imperialist values of the Old World.

Yet, in reality, America was already an empire. The thirteen colonies that broke with Britain in 1776 extended only a few hundred miles inland. Within thirty years, however, the United States stretched far beyond the Mississippi, across half this vast continent. Thirty years later, by the mid-nineteenth century, it ran from the Atlantic three thousand miles to the Pacific. For many Americans in the nineteenth century and since, this process was axiomatic—an expression of "Manifest Destiny"—yet, from a historical perspective, it is of dramatic significance. Transposed onto the map of Europe, the continental United States would take us from the Urals to the Pyrenees, which is the domain of half a dozen separate nation-states—countries, moreover, that spent much of the nineteenth and twentieth centuries fighting ruinous wars against each other. The fact that the most fertile and mineral-rich swathe of North America was under the control of one government was a development of world-historical importance.

Parts of the American continent were bought—the Louisiana Purchase, for instance—but ultimately this country the size of a continent was made by war. War against the European empires—France, Spain, and Britain—which had previously controlled or claimed much of the continent. War against neighboring independent states—particularly Mexico, from which Texas and California were wrested by force. War against the Native Americans, the original inhabitants, who were steadily driven west, corralled on reservations, and even reduced to bit parts in Hollywood movies. And, most devastatingly, war against fellow Americans in the South who, on the model of 1776, wanted to break away from the Union and form their own Confederate States of America.

This was truly imperialism, used as a neutral, historical term. At much the same time, during the nineteenth century, the Russians were similarly constructing their own continental empire as they pushed across Asia to the Pacific. But Americans would not have thought of themselves in the same vein, and with good reason. The founders of the nation did refer to themselves as a new empire—unlike their successors, they had no problem with that term—but theirs, in the words of Thomas Jefferson, was to be an "empire of liberty."[2]

Liberty is the second great theme that runs through my story. From the very start, North America was a continent of potentially greater opportunity than Europe because there was no entrenched aristocracy controlling land and politics. A new immigrant, though often obliged to work for others for a while, could aspire to own his own property on a scale impossible back home. The American colonies were only loosely controlled by Britain: Liberty and property were regarded as fundamental rights and when London tried to tighten up imperial administration and make the colonists contribute more to the costs of defending the empire, this sparked revolt and eventually independence. The ethos of the new nation was encapsulated in the state motto of New Hampshire: "Live Free or Die."

This concept of liberty remained fundamental to America's development as settlers spread out across the continent in the nineteenth century—farming the rich prairies, battling the windswept plains, surging to the mountains and the west coast in search of gold. Free movement of people was also central to America's industrial development. Immigrants flooded in from a Europe racked by war, poverty, and persecution. Germans and Irish, many of them Catholic; later, men, women, and children from Italy and the Hapsburg and Russian empires—often fleeing military conscription because the United States, unlike continental Europe, had no standing army in which all young men were obliged to serve.

Liberty was stitched into the fabric of American federalism. In a sense that is hard to appreciate today, throughout the nineteenth century the federal government had little impact on daily life, apart from the local U.S. Post Office. It was *local* government, town or county, that made most of the important decisions, raising money for schools, roads, and so on. Individual states, likewise, ran their own affairs, often with idiosyncratic practices—such as Nebraska's one-house legislature or the predominance of Roman law in Louisiana—as long as these practices did not violate the U.S. Constitution.

This ideology of local liberties was not swept away by industrialization. Even in the large cities such as New York and Chicago, where the gap between rich tycoons and poor workers became vast and union movements took hold, Americans did not embrace socialism and communism. These ideologies, which revolutionized European politics in the twentieth century, left America virtually untouched. Whereas, geographically, the United States spans an area the size of Europe, its mainstream politics fits onto only a fraction of the European spectrum, well to the right of center. This also helps to explain America's Cold War abhorrence of the Soviet Union and all it stood for, at a level of intensity not matched in Europe.

Yet, under the surface, the character of American government and the nature of American liberty have changed profoundly. Since the New Deal the federal government has become much more intrusive in daily life. Most U.S. citizens have been drawn into the federal nexus of taxes and benefits, their personal details recorded in the databases of its proliferating bureaucracies. World War II and the Cold War also created a permanent military establishment and, underpinning it, a military-industrial complex whose tentacles reach out into many areas of national life. America's great private universities, such as Stanford and MIT, could not have survived without lucrative contracts from the federal government; the vast network of interstate highways that allows motorists to crisscross the country was designed and funded by the federal government to move military equipment and manpower around in a Cold War crisis. Uncle Sam, as much as free enterprise, built modern America.

The Land of the Free therefore became the home of big government. And there is an even deeper paradox. Liberty for whites was made possible by the enslavement of millions of blacks. The booming economy of the nineteenth-century South, generating vast profits from tobacco, rice, and especially cotton, depended on forced black labor. The great spokesmen of American liberty, men such as Thomas Jefferson and George Washington, could not have enjoyed their comfortable estates without slaves. Their consciences were troubled but their lifestyles remained unchanged; they had become slaves to slavery. In the 1850s Abraham Lincoln warned that "a house divided against itself cannot stand," the United States could not remain "half slave and half free." It would, he predicted, "become all one thing, or all the other."[3]

Lincoln was right: The Union did survive and it became all free, but the war that eventually ended slavery cost 620,000 lives—more than the American death toll in World War I and World War II combined. Little wonder that the Civil War etched itself into American memory, especially in the defeated South. Yet it did not solve America's racial problem. Although slavery was abolished, African-Americans remained second-class citizens in much of the South—generally denied the vote, confined to separate parts of trains or buses, and obliged to use segregated eating areas or public toilets. These practices ended only in the 1960s, after a concerted campaign by the civil rights movement, which finally enlisted the power of the federal government to override the liberties of the states. Even so, economic and social discrimination against blacks remained, in the North as much as the South—in housing, employment, and health care. By the late twentieth century, of course, racial discrimination had become an issue in Europe as well, as millions of former colonial subjects in Africa and Asia migrated to Britain, France, the Netherlands, and other imperial homelands. America's racial question was, however, unique because of its scale and longevity. The legacy of slavery cast a dark, brooding shadow across the Land of the Free and that is why the election of an African-American as president in 2008 was of such transcendent historical significance.

Another legacy of the Civil War was the marginalization (partly self-imposed) of the ex-Confederate South from major currents of the nation's cultural and social life for much of the twentieth century. After the end of Reconstruction, the North allowed Southern whites to impose their own "racial etiquette" buttressed by the doctrine of "states' rights." The South also remained more agrarian than the rest of the country—more small-town—and particularly resistant to the march of modernity. A central bulwark of its conservatism was evangelical Protestantism, whose role in American life had changed markedly since the nineteenth century. This leads me to my third big theme—faith.

The United States is known the world over for its constitutional separation of church and state and for its pioneering commitment to religious freedom. The first article of the Bill of Right states that "Congress shall make no law respecting an establishment of religion, or prohibiting the free exercise thereof." This was affirmed in 1791 at a time when Britain, one of the most tolerant European states, still barred from political office Catholics, Jews, and also Protestants who were not members of the Church of England. In 1797 the U.S. government signed a treaty with the Muslim state of Tripoli containing this striking statement: "As the government of the United States of America is not in any sense founded on the Christian Religion . . . it has in itself no character of enmity against the laws, religion or tranquillity of Musselmen" [Muslims].[4]

Yet a secular state did not mean an irreligious nation. The Constitution simply prohibited the federal government from establishing a national church, and most Americans of the time believed that Protestant faith and morals were essential for public order. This belief owed something to the Puritans, who founded Massachusetts in the 1630s, saw their new community as the bastion of true religion against a neo-Catholic king, and regarded their experiment as an example to the world, a "city on the hill." Yet the Puritans were something of a dead end, historically: Their attempt to impose a church-dominated uniformity was short-lived. The religious groups who really shaped America were the Baptists, Methodists, and other sects, whose roving preachers set off a series of religious revivals that sparked and crackled across the country from the mid-eighteenth century right up to the Civil War. For these preachers and their followers, religion was an affair of the heart, rooted in a conversion experience and expressed in a rich, vibrant community of the faithful. These evangelicals broke the stranglehold of the older churches—Anglicans in the South, Congregationalists in New England—and made the United States a nation of sects rather than churches. They also generated much of the moral fervor behind progressive causes such as anti-slavery, temperance, and women's suffrage. America's religion was a product of evangelicalism more than of Puritanism.[5]

So a secular state went hand in hand, for many people, with a religious nation. But what kind of religion? The evangelicals were fervently Protestant and often viscerally anti-Papist, yet many of the immigrants on whom America's industrial prosperity was based were Catholics from Germany, Ireland, and Italy. Their struggle for full political and cultural rights was at the heart of politics for decades from 1850, fought out over issues of daily behavior such as not respecting the Sabbath and drinking in saloons. It was only in 1960 that a practicing Catholic, John F. Kennedy, was elected to the White House, and Jews remained the victims of insidious discrimination even though they were central to the nation's cultural life. Increasingly, in the twentieth century evangelical Protestantism became a conservative force, standing up for core "American" values not just on the matter of religious observance but also on wider cultural issues such as feminism, evolution, homosexuality, and especially abortion.

The South was the evangelical heartland, but the diaspora of southerners in recent decades, especially to the West, has helped energize and, in a sense, nationalize evangelical conservatism. This hit American politics with a vengeance in the Reagan era, generating a series of "culture wars" that continue to reverberate. The term itself echoes the *Kulturkampf* of the 1870s, waged by Germany's Chancellor Otto von Bismarck against the influence of the Catholic Church, but in contemporary America "culture wars" is shorthand for a whole range of "conservative" versus "liberal" struggles over core social values, in which evangelicals and Catholics are usually arrayed on the same side. In a larger sense, such struggles may be seen as an effort to halt the creeping tide of secularization, already triumphant in twentieth-century Europe. Whether the United States proves a distinctive exception to that pattern, or whether its own secularization was simply delayed by the long ghettoization of the South, is another interesting question for the future.

Faith has shaped U.S. history in larger ways as well. A religious sense of mission animated America in its Cold War struggle between the "free world" and what Ronald Reagan called the Soviet "evil empire." More recently, it inspired George W. Bush in his "war on terror," supposedly promoted by an "axis of evil" and orchestrated by Muslim fundamentalists. For many Americans, in fact, both foreign policy and domestic politics have been defined in bipolar terms—as nonnegotiable struggles of good against fundamental evils.

In a more general sense, faith—self-belief in America's mission—has powered America's engagement in the world since World War I.[6] In 1917 Woodrow Wilson spoke of making the world "safe for democracy"; in 1941 Franklin Roosevelt offered another war-torn world "four freedoms" on the American model. Yet that moral commitment also has an obverse side: When faith is overwhelmed by self-doubt, as happened during the Depression of the 1930s or after the debacle in Vietnam, the United States pulls back in on itself. The empire of liberty has been made and unmade by its faith.

Empire, liberty, and faith: Here are three big themes that reverberate throughout U.S. history, each full of contradictions. Exploring them, teasing out those contradictions, is the task of this book.

PART I

LIBERTY AND SLAVERY

There is not a more difficult subject for the under-standing of men than to govern a large Empire upon a plan of Liberty.

— EDMUND BURKE, 1766

[S]lavery is in retreat, but the prejudice from which it arose is immovable.

— ALEXIS DE TOCQUEVILLE, 1835

We hold these truths to be self-evident: that all men and women are created equal.

— DECLARATION OF RIGHTS
AND SENTIMENTS, 1848

NATIVES AND EUROPEANS

Many people around the world, and some in the United States, think that American history really begins with the first English settlers, particularly the intrepid Pilgrims on the *Mayflower* who in 1620 founded the town of Plymouth, south of what is now the city of Boston. After a grim winter, they reaped a bountiful harvest the following year, which Americans now celebrate on the last Thursday of November as Thanksgiving. But the Pilgrims and other English settlers such as the pioneers of Jamestown, Virginia, were not the first Americans. Nor does the story begin in 1492 with Christopher Columbus, or even with Leif Eriksson who established a Norse settlement called "Vinland" on the tip of Newfoundland around AD 1000. A search for the first Americans takes us back thousands of years before that.

This search matters because part of the *Mayflower* myth is that the first Europeans found virgin land, ripe for the taking and rich with potential for those savvy enough to exploit it. Like most myths, it is rooted in a substratum of truth. Geologically, the North American continent is blessed with fertile soils and vast reserves of coal, oil, and other minerals; its white settlers have skillfully developed the technologies to exploit those innate riches. Yet this was not virgin land: Its aboriginal inhabitants were gradually but brutally dispossessed by the invaders, and the settlers' intensive extraction of the earth's resources stood at odds with the more conservative, even conservationist, approach of some of the native tribes. The European exploitation of both people and land helped make modern America, but it also left scars that remain visible to the present day.

THE FOUNDERS

In 1811 Henry Brackenridge was astonished at what he saw in the heartland of North America. A lawyer turned travel writer, he crossed the Mississippi from St. Louis and pushed east through some woods into a broad open plain. After fifteen minutes, he wrote, "I found myself in the midst of a group of mounds, mostly of a circular shape, and at a distance, resembling enormous haystacks scattered through a meadow." Looking around, he counted forty-five of these mounds. Standing at the foot of the biggest, Brackenridge was "struck with a degree of astonishment, not unlike that which is experienced in contemplating the Egyptian pyramids. What a stupendous pile of earth! To heap up such a mass must have required years, and the labors of thousands."[1]

But who were the laborers? Nineteenth-century writers came up with various theories—the Phoenicians, the Vikings, even Welshmen led by the shadowy Prince Madoc. But almost all commentators had no doubt that these great earthworks, known as Cahokia, were built by a civilized people from across the Atlantic. Virtually no one imagined that the mound-builders were the despised Native Americans, the Indians. Indeed, many assumed that the Indians had been the people who destroyed the mounds. In 1832 the poet William Cullen Bryant wrote about

> the mighty mounds
> That overlook the rivers . . .
> A race, that long has passed away,
> Built them;—a disciplined and populous race.

But then, he went on,

> The red men came—
> The roaming hunter tribes, warlike and fierce,
> And the mound-builders vanished from the earth.
> . . . All is gone—
> All—save the piles of earth that hold their bones. [2]

Bryant was articulating the standard nineteenth-century belief that anything civilized in America must have come from Europe. So Henry Brackenridge was unusual in suggesting that Cahokia was indeed built by the Native Americans. But not the Indians whom Americans of the nineteenth century looked down on as savages—Brackenridge believed that "a very populous town had once existed here, similar to those of Mexico, described by the first conquerors. The mounds were sites of temples, or monuments to the great men. It is evident this could never have been the work of thinly scattered tribes."[3]

Brackenridge was proved right. Archaeologists now believe that Cahokia was virtually an Indian metropolis covering nearly six square miles, which flourished in the late eleventh century when the Normans were conquering England. Row houses and courtyard mansions lined streets that led to large public plazas. The huge platform mounds were capped by temples, tombs, or palaces—the top of the largest mound is the size of a soccer field—and Cahokia did not stand alone because satellite towns spread out across the fertile floodplain of the Mississippi. In fact, Cahokia is the biggest prehistoric earthwork still surviving anywhere in the Americas. It is now designated by the United Nations Educational, Scientific, and Cultural Organization (UNESCO) as a World Heritage Site, which places it on a par with Stonehenge and the Pyramids.

The builders of Cahokia were descendants of people who had settled in North America by around 12000 BC. They came not from Europe but from Asia and they traveled not by sea but over land. Today fifty-five miles of water separate Siberia from Alaska, known as the Bering Strait after an eighteenth-century Danish explorer. Yet in the last great Ice Age of the Pleistocene period, the sea level was maybe 300 feet lower, creating what is often described as a "land bridge" between the two continents.

"Bridge" is not really the right word because "Beringia," as geologists call it, was actually a vast expanse of land. Throughout the coldest period in the Pleistocene era it was iced over, like most of what is now western Canada. Many geologists believe that as temperatures rose, around 15,000 years ago, there was a relatively brief period when the ice sheets were receding but before Beringia became an oceanic strait. During this period the "bridge" became a desolate but passable steppe; an ice-free corridor also opened up southeast of the Rockies and the Great Plains.

Not all scholars accept this theory. Some believe that the main migration route was down the Pacific coast, with groups gradually hopping from one temperate refuge to another in primitive boats or moving on foot down coastal plains that were subsequently inundated by the rising sea. As evidence of this coastal progression, they cite the settlement found at Mount Verde, near the coast of Chile, which dates from 12,500 years ago.

The corridor-versus-coast debate among geologists and archaeologists rumbles on, but the big point is clear. Human beings crossed into America from Siberia, and the main movement occurred during a relatively short climatic window of opportunity. There were later migrations, of course: Forebears of the Inuit probably crossed the Bering Straits in boats about 5,000 years ago. Yet dental, genetic, and linguistic evidence suggests that most contemporary Native Americans may trace their ancestry back to a few hundred original settlers.[4]

These founding people, known to scholars as Palaeo-Indians, were hunters. But the end of the Pleistocene Ice Age about 12,000 years ago spelled death for much of their prey, including mammoths and mastodons. Horses and camels also died out in North America during this period, though the Spanish *conquistadores* later reintroduced the horse with a vengeance. Of the Pleistocene big game, only the bison survived, albeit in a smaller form adapted to grazing the grasslands that now emerged.

Humans also adapted. In the so-called Archaic period, from about 9,000 to 3,000 years ago, Indians supplemented hunting by harvesting nuts, berries, and tubers. They also learned to fish, sometimes on a very sophisticated scale. Under one of Boston's most prestigious tower blocks—500 Boylston Street—are the remains of an elaborate fish weir some 5,000 years old, constructed in what was then a shallow tidal backwater (the area is still known as Back Bay). At least 65,000 stakes, intertwined with branches and shrubs, were arranged in walls to trap the fish stranded twice daily by the ebbing tide. The enclosure also proved an effective oyster farm.[5]

Although the Americas were settled from north to south, the dynamic of their development ran from south to north. The most technologically advanced region was the area from Peru to Mexico, home to great empires that we know as the Incas and the Aztecs. When the Spanish adventurer Hernán Cortés reached Mexico in 1519, he was astonished at the sophistication of Aztec society, including monumental city architecture, an extensive road network, and compulsory teenage education. He wrote home that "these people live almost like those of Spain, and in as much harmony and order as there, and considering that they are barbarous and so far from the knowledge of God and cut off from all civilized nations, it is truly remarkable to see what they have achieved in all things."[6] Mexico was the heart of Indian civilization. Its relation to the Indian societies of North America has been likened to that between imperial Rome and northern Europe.[7]

It was probably from examples in Mexico that the Indians further north learned to build cities like Cahokia; just how many cities is unknown because they did not leave written records and along the Mississippi they built in wood. On the arid plateaus of the Southwest, however, among the Hohokam and Anasazi cultures in what are now the states of Arizona and New Mexico, the Indians built in adobe (dried mud) or sandstone blocks and much more of their work survived.

James Simpson, a U.S. army surveyor, was part of a detachment of soldiers sent out from Santa Fe in 1849 to reconnoiter Navaho Indian country. En route, Simpson and his companions looked over some ruins known locally as Pueblo Pintado, or the painted village, and "found them to more than answer our expectations," discovering in the masonry what he called "a combination of science and art which can only be referred [i.e., attributed] to a higher state of civilization and refinement than is discoverable in the works of Mexicans or Pueblos of the present day." Simpson estimated that there must have been at least three stories originally, built around a courtyard, each side being about 400 feet. On the ground floor he counted "fifty-four apartments, some of them as small as five feet square, and the largest about twelve foot by six feet," and also noted "three circular apartments sunk in the ground, the walls being of masonry," where, he reckoned, "the people held their political and religious meetings." Shards of pottery lay scattered around, "the colors showing taste in their selection and in the style of their arrangement."[8]

What Simpson stumbled on was an outlying settlement of Chaco Canyon—today listed as another World Heritage Site. When modern archaeologists got to work, they unearthed a series of Great Houses stretching ten miles along the floor of the shallow canyon. The whole complex, which like Cahokia dates from around the time of the Norman conquest of England, housed thousands of people and was linked to outlying settlements by hundreds of miles of roads. The inhabitants were technologically sophisticated—building dams to catch the water from desert thunderstorms and divert it along canals to gardens on the canyon floor. Their whole way of organizing society was intriguingly different from that in the modern Western world, being based on matriarchal principles as their descendants, the Hopi Indians, explained: "Among us the family traces its kin from the mother, hence all its possessions are hers. The man builds the house but the woman is the owner, because she repairs and preserves it; the man cultivates the field, but he renders its harvest into the woman's keeping, because upon her it rests to prepare the food, and the surplus of stores for barter depends upon her thrift. . . . Our fields and houses always remain with our mother's family."[9]

Chaco and Cahokia flourished about the same time, a millennium ago, but their heyday was brief and both sites were abandoned during the thirteenth century. We do not know why: Lacking documentary records, scholars have to make informed guesses from the archaeological evidence. It seems likely that these concentrations of population became too large for the resources available, even if carefully husbanded. The growing crisis of resources—exhausted soil, water shortages, lack of timber—probably exacerbated internal feuds and local revolts until these little empires fell apart. A few of the Indian "nations" that succeeded them were in their own way complex societies, such as the mound-building Natchez people on the Lower Mississippi, but most were small groupings without much sophistication.

So, when traders and settlers from across the Atlantic started to probe the North American continent during the sixteenth century, they were contemptuous of what they saw. Chaco and Cahokia were long gone: Indian houses of wood or mud were nothing compared to the buildings of Madrid or London, or the cities the Spanish had marveled at in Mexico and Peru. Yet we should not fall into the trap of thinking that the outcome of these encounters between Europeans and Indians was a foregone conclusion. Although the settlers came with firearms, their muskets were often far less accurate and quick-firing than an Indian bow. They had to adapt their agricultural practices to a very different environment, learning in the process from the natives, and Indian nations had a long history of trading with other peoples and playing off one enemy against another. The decisive factor in the European conquest was as much biological as technological, part of what has been called "the Columbian exchange."[10]

COLUMBUS—BEARER OF DEATH

In Fourteen hundred and ninety-two
Columbus sailed the ocean blue.

Not the most sublime poetry but millions of Americans have been brought up on this rhyme. Many of them regard the Italian-born Christopher Columbus as the "discoverer" of America, and his voyage is celebrated as one of the country's national holidays. Yet in many respects the concept of Columbus Day is deceptive. The natives had been on the North American continent for thousands of years and the Vikings were the first European visitors, so Columbus was a relative latecomer. What's more, he never actually set foot in what is now the United States: All his four voyages were to the Caribbean islands or Central America. So how did Columbus Day come to be celebrated across the United States every October?

It was President Franklin Roosevelt who made it official, and he did so to please Italian-Americans, who were important backers of his Democratic Party in the 1930s. Roosevelt held up Columbus as an exemplar of all-American values, calling him "a great Italian whose vision and leadership and courage pointed the way to this new world of ours. Once launched upon this great voyage, he did not turn back. There were those who offered him the counsel of despair. There were those who thought that the price they were paying was too great. But the valiant admiral, firm to his purpose, sailed on." It was in the spirit of Columbus, Roosevelt claimed, that intrepid pioneers went on to tame the American West: "You are scarcely removed one generation from men and women who, cast in the same mold, sought to conquer nature for the benefit of the Nation."[11]

Conquering nature for the benefit of the nation: Roosevelt encapsulated the belief of many Americans that their continent was originally virgin land, ripe for the taking by settlers from Europe. This was certainly Columbus's view. Coming ashore in the Caribbean in 1492, he considered the Americas a paradise and its natives a pushover. Thinking he had reached the Indies he called the natives "Indians" and that label stuck. Columbus told his patrons the king and queen of Spain that the lands were "so good and fertile" that there was "no one who could believe if he had not seen them." All that was lacking was "a settlement and the order to the people to do what is required." The natives, he went on, "have no arms, and are without warlike instincts; they all go naked, and are so timid that a thousand would not stand before three of our men. So that they are good to be ordered about, to work and sow, and do all that may be necessary, and to build towns, and they should be taught to go about clothed and to adopt our customs."[12]

Here already was a basic mission statement: Establish a colony, civilize the natives, and put them to work. Indian agriculture—structured around the basic crops of maize, squash, and beans—did not impress Europeans accustomed to logging the forests, putting land to the plough, milling grain to make bread, and using domesticated animals for meat and milk. To them that was real farming, whereas the natives seemed to be engaged in mere gardening.

Today, however, we may feel less superior. The Indians knew that maize, squash, and beans thrived best when raised together—hence the nickname "three sisters"— even though they did not understand the underlying chemistry of how nitrogen and phosphorus were shared through the root systems. The settlers by contrast exploited the land ruthlessly, cutting down the trees and exhausting the soil through intensive cultivation before moving on to pastures new. As we shall see, that became a refrain of American history—what Roosevelt later called conquering nature for the benefit of the nation.

Of course we should not romanticize Native Americans as protoenvironmentalists, in contrast to the ecologically destructive Europeans, but many of the more settled tribes did have a keen sense of their dependence on the natural order, which was expressed in their animist religion and in folk myths handed down to the present day. "The earth is alive. All things of value come out of the earth," runs one such story. "And yet here we are disturbing the earth, occupying it and planting on it all through our lives. Well, the earth can get annoyed because we disturb it. . . . We go back and forth to market on it, and we get drunk on it but we don't give the earth any beer . . . that is the reason that she forsakes us and doesn't want to produce." Corn was the most delicate crop of all. "Corn is our blood. How can we grab from the earth when it is our own blood that we are eating?"[13]

Corn, or maize, was one of the plants that Columbus brought back from the New World, together with kidney beans and potatoes. Later came pineapples, pumpkins, strawberries, tomatoes, and turkeys—to name but a few of the early exports from the New World to the Old. Many of these seemed pretty exotic at first. William Salmon, an eighteenth-century English quack, asserted that potatoes, when boiled, baked, or roasted, "encrease Seed and provoke Lust, causing Fruitfulness in both Sexes, and stop all sorts of Fluxes of the Belly."[14] Yet potatoes became a basic food for the Irish peasantry during the seventeenth century and then caught on throughout Europe.[15] Maize was grown mostly in warmer climes such as Spain, Italy, and the Balkans, but turkeys spread rapidly across Europe—at least on rich men's tables. William Strickland, a Yorkshire gentleman who went on voyages of exploration in his youth, is generally credited with their introduction to England. His coat of arms in 1550, showing "a turkey-cock in his pride proper," is one of the earliest European drawings of the bird.

Europeans therefore imported from the Native Americans what proved some of the most basic foodstuffs of the modern world. The new crops were much more productive than the traditional ones: Maize and potatoes, for instance, have about a 50 percent higher calorific yield per acre than wheat, oats, or barley. Over a couple of centuries these new foods played an important part in the dramatic growth in Europe's population.

The terms of trade were not, of course, entirely beneficial to the Old World. Among the imports one must include tobacco, which has accounted for millions of premature deaths over the centuries. As early as 1604 King James I uttered an official health warning, enjoining his subjects to "forbeare this filthy novelty . . . in your abuse thereof sinning against God" and "harming yourselves both in persons and goods." He called it "a custom loathsome to the eye, hateful to the nose, harmful to the brain, dangerous to the lungs, and in the black stinking fume thereof nearest resembling the horrible stygian smoke of the pit that is bottomless."[16] Also on the debit side is the possibility that Columbus and his sailors brought back syphilis from the New World (the first recorded European epidemic occurred in 1494–1495), but this remains a matter of dispute.[17] In any case, the impact of syphilis hardly compares with the diseases the Europeans took west across the Atlantic. Many Amerindian groups today regard Columbus as the inaugurator of wholesale genocide.

That side of the story begins with Columbus's second expedition in 1493, when he brought people and animals to populate his first colony, Hispaniola (present-day Haiti). During the voyage an infection, starting from the pigs, spread throughout the animals and crew. Probably influenza, it had a debilitating effect on the Spanish, many of whom died, but the disease absolutely devastated the local Taino Indians. With fewer hands to cultivate the crops, food supplies contracted and famine often ensued. The Taino, 300,000 strong in 1492, were virtually extinct fifty years later.

The story of Hispaniola, though extreme, was not an isolated incident. Subsequent waves of settlers brought new and even deadlier diseases, of which the most virulent were epidemics of smallpox and measles. These were still killers in Europe but most of the settlers had developed some degree of immunity, whereas the Indians had none. Within a decade of first contact with a new disease, about half the natives in that area died. Successive outbreaks allowed the Indians little chance to reproduce and recover.

The effects were particularly apparent in Central and South America, the heartland of Spain's New World empire. Disease—as much as firearms, steel swords, and horses—helps explain the astonishingly rapid collapse of the great Inca empire in what is now Peru. But the Spanish also probed north, carrying European diseases into Florida and the Mississippi valley, decimating the local Indian populations. French traders, fishing fleets, and settlers brought death to the St. Lawrence valley, killing off most of the Huron Indians and then the Iroquois during the seventeenth century. The English had a similar effect on parts of the Atlantic seaboard. The obliteration of the Indian village of Patuxet, on whose site the Pilgrims built their settlement of Plymouth, was part of a massive epidemic of smallpox and measles that swept along coastal New England in the mid-1610s.

Just occasionally, we find documentary evidence of Europeans deliberately practicing germ warfare, as in 1763 when British officers gave Indian chiefs on the Ohio infected blankets from a smallpox hospital. Sir Jeffrey Amherst, their commander, sent a message of approval, urging them "to try every other method that can serve to extirpate this execrable race."[18] For the most part, however, the Europeans brought death unwittingly; sometimes they even gave help to the natives. But, to the settlers, the epidemics were by no means unwelcome. Colonists, particularly from England, crossed the Atlantic with well-developed concepts of private property. Their claim to North America rested on the legal doctrine of *res nullius*, meaning a right to take land that was unoccupied or abandoned. The decimation of the Indians therefore paved the way legally and theologically for European settlement.

John Winthrop, the first governor of the Puritan colony of Massachusetts, wrote home in 1634 that "as for the natives, they are neere all dead of the small Poxe, so as the Lord hathe cleared our title to what we possess."[19]

The terms of the "Columbian exchange" were therefore very one-sided: mostly a matter of nutritious Indian crops in return for virulent European diseases. Just how many Native Americans died from these epidemics has been a matter of fierce debate among historians, with "low counters" accusing "high counters" of conjuring "numbers from nowhere."[20] An estimate midway between the extremes suggests that the Indian population of all the Americas declined from 50 million in 1492 to 5 million by 1650. On the assumption that about a tenth of the natives lived north of Mexico, this means that by the mid-seventeenth century the Indian population of what is now the United States and Canada was only about 500,000.[21] American nationalists often talked about their country as "virgin land," almost untouched by human beings, but given what we now know about its population history, the term "widowed land" seems more appropriate.[22]

None of this meant that the Indians disappeared as a major force in the shaping of colonial America. They still played off the rival European empires with considerable skill in the century after 1650. But the diseases brought by Columbus and his successors fatally reduced their numbers and their ability to resist European imperialism, particularly in North America. In Africa, by contrast, the balance of biological warfare was the other way around, with the invaders being decimated by native diseases, and that made it much harder to establish European hegemony. So it is easy to understand why many Native Americans today are not enthusiastic about celebrating the coming of Christopher Columbus. His forename literally means "bearer of Christ," but for millions of American Indians he was the bearer of death.

BORDERLANDS OF THE SPANISH SUPERPOWER

Central and South America were the sites of the most developed native empires and also the area where the Indians were most numerous. Relations between the Spanish and the Indians were consequently more balanced and more interactive than in North America, which, by contrast, was more backward and less populous. There the Indians were more on the margins of colonial life and relations with the Europeans were increasingly confrontational. In North America, moreover, unlike the South, the colonial era was defined by a long and bitter struggle between rival European empires, especially Spain, France, and Britain. This would have a lasting impact not just on the Indians but on the whole character of the future United States.

During the sixteenth century the Spanish were the leading imperial power in the Americas. In brutal and far-reaching campaigns they seized the most advanced and prosperous native empires of South America. In 1519–1521 Hernán Cortés defeated the Aztecs of Mexico. In 1532–1533 Francisco Pizarro overwhelmed the Inca empire in what is now Peru, and during the 1540s the Mayan peoples of Central America were gradually subdued. The Spanish Crown divided its vast new empire into two vice-royalties called "Peru," which included much of South America, and "New Spain," covering Mexico, Central America, and the Caribbean.

The Spanish sought to impose their culture, language, and Catholic faith on the subject peoples. This was a vast project, for two centuries far outstripping what the French and even the British achieved to the north: The National University of Mexico was founded in 1551, Harvard College not until 1636.[23] By the 1740s, Boston, the most substantial city in British America, had a population of 16,000. Eight cities in Spanish America were bigger, with the largest, Mexico City, boasting well over 100,000 inhabitants.[24]

The empire also proved phenomenally profitable. Although the Spanish farmed the land, by far their most lucrative American asset was silver. For most of the sixteenth, seventeenth, and eighteenth centuries, the silver mines of Peru and New Spain not only covered the costs of the American empire but also accounted for 15 to 20 percent of the Crown's annual income.[25] (British America, by contrast, was not self-supporting; as we shall see, London's efforts to generate the revenue to pay for its defense eventually provoked the colonists to revolt.) Spain's imperial surpluses also helped the Crown to finance repeated wars to expand its domains in Europe and to contain the Protestant Reformation. Many English Puritans hated Spain in the same way American Cold Warriors loathed the Soviet Union—as a predatory superpower and an evil empire.

The main thrust of Spain's American imperialism was in Central and South America, but the lure of gold and silver encouraged some Spaniards to try their luck to the north. Between 1539 and 1543 Hernando de Soto traversed what is now Florida, the Carolinas, and the lower Mississippi valley. In 1540–1542 Francisco Vásquez de Coronado explored the Gulf of California and penetrated the Great Plains. Spreading disease and destruction in their wake, neither found gold and, after their failures, the rulers of New Spain left the northern borderlands alone for a generation.

By the 1560s, however, such neglect no longer seemed wise. French and British privateers were taking a heavy toll of Spanish bullion fleets as they hugged the Florida coast before picking up the Gulf Stream and sailing back home. Indians were also looting Spanish vessels wrecked on the treacherous Florida Keys. And in March 1565 news reached King Philip II that French Huguenot Protestants had established a settlement in what is now northern Florida. Galvanized into action, he contracted a buccaneer named Pedro Menéndez de Avilés to conquer the peninsula. By the end of September Menéndez had founded his first town, San Agustín, and had destroyed the nearby French settlement, butchering the Huguenots. Convinced that their beliefs were similar to those of the Indians, probably Satanic in origin, he told the king that "it seemed to me that to chastise them in this way would serve God Our Lord, as well as Your Majesty, and that we should thus be left more free from this wicked sect."[26]

Within a couple of years Menéndez had established seven garrisons along the east coast of Florida and two on the west. He also sent out expeditions west in search of silver and north up the Atlantic coast, hoping to extend Spain's economic tentacles all the way to the fishing grounds of Newfoundland. But his men found no silver, the subsidies from the Crown dried up, and Menéndez's grand design crumbled even before he died in 1574. Twelve years later San Agustín was raided by the English buccaneer Francis Drake. He "took and sacked the town and burned the church with its images and crosses, and cut down the fruit trees, which were numerous and good," reported the governor of Florida to Madrid. Drake also "carried off the artillery and munitions and food supplies." The governor added plaintively: "We are all left with the clothes we stood in, and in the open country."[27]

The town was rebuilt and, as St. Augustine, still survives as the oldest continuously settled town of European origin in the United States. But Drake's raid prompted the Spanish to pull back in Florida and try instead to extend their empire northwest, enticed by reports of the rich Indian pueblos beyond the Rio Grande. This time the royal commission was given to Don Juan de Oñate, a Mexican-born aristocrat in his late forties. Like Menéndez, he talked big, promising "new worlds, new, peaceful and grand, to His Majesty greater than the good Marquis [Cortés] gave to him," even predicting a route to the Pacific.[28] In the summer of 1598 Oñate and some 500 followers, only 130 of whom were fighting men, staked out a new Spanish province called New Mexico.

But the Indians fought back, the most defiant being in the pueblo of Acoma, perched spectacularly on a sheer sandstone plateau 350 feet above the surrounding desert. When a group of Spaniards reached the top and demanded supplies, several of them were killed—among them Oñate's nephew—and their bodies thrown down the cliff. The captain of the ill-fated expedition told Oñate that the pueblo was so impregnable that the Indians living in it or seeking refuge there were confident they could "defend themselves and escape punishment for their misdeeds." The captain was sure that "if the pueblo is not levelled and its inhabitants punished, there will be no security in all of New Mexico, nor could it be settled, as the natives of the pueblos are watching what we do at Acoma and whether we punish them."[29]

So in January 1599 Oñate decided to make an example of Acoma in order to terrify the locals into cooperating. He could spare only seventy soldiers—hardly enough in view of the pueblo's superb defensive position—but the Spanish mounted a small feint attack from the north while most of their troops scaled the plateau from the south, carrying muskets and a few cannons. In the unequal battle that followed, several hundred Indians were killed and the rest surrendered. The survivors were tried under Spanish law and Oñate himself delivered the verdicts. Male prisoners over twenty-five had one foot cut off—an accepted Spanish punishment for criminals. Two Indians from a neighboring pueblo who had fought in the battle had their right hands cut off and were then set free "in order that they may convey to their land the news of this punishment."[30] A savage lesson and it worked: Acoma lay desolate for half a century.

So both Florida and New Mexico failed to fulfill the extravagant hopes of their founders, but they did act as buffer zones for the northern borders of New Spain. Franciscan friars became one of the main agents of Hispanicization. Building missions in the major pueblos and backed by a few soldiers, they brought not only Catholic rituals but also new crops, such as apples and wheat, and new animals including cattle, pigs, and mules. The Indians found it expedient to work with the newcomers and to utilize their innovations, but they usually observed the Catholic rituals in public while maintaining their own religious practices in private. Spanish-Indian relations were therefore negotiated rather than simply imposed. On their side, the Spaniards adopted many Indian practices such as growing maize, wearing moccasins, and using folk medicines. Because there was such limited migration into Florida and New Mexico, the Spaniards often took Indian wives, creating a mixed population known as *mestizos*.[31] In British America, as we shall see, intermarriage was much less common and the line between colonists and natives remained much more starkly drawn.

Just how tenuous was Spain's hold on the borderlands became clear in the 1680s as the Indians struck back and the French and English pressed south in earnest.

In New Mexico the crisis was triggered by persistent droughts and also frequent raids by Apaches and other nomadic Indian tribes. As the inhabitants of the pueblos starved, they began to doubt the potency of the Franciscans; more and more of them turned back to traditional priests and ceremonies. In the words of one Spanish report, the Indians were "saying that now God and Santa Maria were dead" and "that their own God whom they obeyed had never died."[32] A dynamic religious leader called Popé united many of the Pueblos in a coordinated revolt in August 1680. Most of the small, isolated Spanish communities were easily overwhelmed and, after fierce fighting, the Spanish had to abandon the main town, Santa Fe. It took them sixteen years to recover control of New Mexico.

In Florida the Indians lacked the power to act independently, but they were armed and supported by the English from the new colony of South Carolina. During the 1680s Carolinians and their Indian allies attacked Florida's northern missions. In the 1700s, during the War of the Spanish Succession, they ravaged farther south, butchering the Spanish and enslaving many of the mission Indians. By 1706 only St. Augustine and a few surrounding villages survived and, unlike New Mexico, there was no *reconquista*.

Worst of all, the French were now starting to colonize the rich delta lands of the Mississippi. This was a serious blow, which meant that the Gulf of Mexico was no longer a Spanish lake: Spain's two struggling colonies in Florida and New Mexico were separated not just by distance but by a new French colony, Louisiana. The governor of Florida warned the king in 1704: "If we do not make one kingdom of all this, nothing is secure."[33] Desperately the Spanish sent small groups of settlers, missionaries, and troops to start a new colony of their own on the Gulf Coast— Texas, formally established in 1716. Two years later they started a base and township at San Antonio, with its mission chapel known as the Alamo.

Florida, Texas, and New Mexico would all play their part in later American history. The Hispanic imprint survives to this day in places and buildings from St. Augustine to Santa Fe; some sites, such as the Alamo, are part of American folk-memory. The Spanish dollar, the main coin circulating in the British colonies, gave its name to the U.S. currency. And, although Spain's American colonies won independence in the nineteenth century, the Hispanic influence in culture and cuisine persists, especially via Mexico. The country's language is full of Hispanic words— such as "ranch" and "siesta," "tornado" and "chocolate"—and America's iconic musical instrument, the guitar, came north with Mexican cowboys. The recent mass migration north across the Mexican border is another reminder that the dynamic of American development has not simply surged from east to west. Today Latinos make up a larger percentage of the U.S. population than African-Americans.

But, despite these durable cultural influences, Spain's empire failed to realize the promise shown in the early sixteenth century. Florida, Texas, and New Mexico were isolated, defensive outposts on the margins of New Spain, rather than springboards for a Spanish empire in North America. Unlike South America, this would be the domain of other European powers.

NEW FRANCE ASTRIDE AMERICA'S HEARTLAND

The French had thrust down from the northeast. In 1541 the explorer Jacques Cartier established a settlement on the St. Lawrence river but it had to be evacuated after the first winter, ravaged by cold, disease, and the Indians. Cartier's main legacy is the name he used to refer to the St. Lawrence region—Canada (adapted from the local Indian word for "village"). For the rest of the sixteenth century the French concentrated on trade—fishing in the Gulf of Lawrence and bartering with the Indians for furs—but profitable commerce required secure communications and that eventually made settlements essential.

So the Company of New France, as the fur traders were known, tried again. In 1608 Samuel de Champlain located the mournful remains of Cartier's abortive settlement, identifying "what seems to have been a chimney" and "indications of there having been ditches surrounding their dwelling, which was small. We found, also, large pieces of hewn, worm-eaten timber, and some three or four cannon-balls."[34] On a point in the river nearby Champlain built a fortified trading post, calling it "Quebec" after an Indian word meaning "where the river narrows."

Champlain also forged alliances with the Indian tribes, particularly the Huron, thereby pitting the settlers against the Hurons' southern enemies, the Five Nation Iroquois. The Iroquois, in turn, secured supplies and firearms from the Dutch, who had pushed up the Hudson river and built a settlement on the site of the modern city of Albany. Thus began a recurrent pattern: The rival European powers formed alliances with rival Indian tribes who, in turn, attempted to set the Europeans against each other. As in the Spanish borderlands the frontier was porous; rather than a clear-cut divide, it has been more aptly described as "the middle ground."[35]

In New France, as in New Spain, empire was also sustained by faith. The Canadian equivalents of the Spanish Franciscans were the Jesuit missionaries—known to Indians as "Black Robes." The priests often won the respect of the natives because of their courage and austerity but, as in New Mexico, the Indians combined public conformity to Catholicism with private adherence to their own religious practices. And they tended to judge religion by its results: The epidemics of smallpox and measles that ravaged the Hurons in the 1630s raised suspicions that the priests were really sorcerers.

In the middle of the seventeenth century New France was still a struggling colony and the French Crown demanded a more aggressive policy of colonization. The Company of New France subcontracted the task to entrepreneurs, known as *seigneurs*, who received extensive grants of land in return for finding prospective settlers and shipping them across the Atlantic. As a result, the population of New France rose from 657 in 1650 to over 3,000 by the early 1660s. By this time, however, the scattered settlements of New Netherlands boasted 8,000 people, while more compact New England had 33,000.[36] So the French Crown took over the colony in 1663, shipping over settlers, soldiers, and servants. To boost the birthrate it even transported girls from a Paris orphanage—nicknamed daughters of the king: *filles du roi*. Even so, the population of New France was only 15,000 in 1700, compared with 234,000 whites in the English colonies of America.[37]

New France clearly faced an uphill struggle. The frigid northern climate was far harsher than in the areas of Dutch and English settlement, and the growing season much shorter. The seigneurial system, though less crushing than back home in France, imposed rents, dues, and other burdens on the settlers that were far more onerous than the largely freehold pattern in British America. In this more hierarchical society there was no elected colonial assembly, while settlers and servants alike were liable for military conscription. Again, all this was in marked contrast to New England.

Nevertheless, the scope of the French empire was impressive. In the late seventeenth century fur traders canoed across the Great Lakes into Illinois country, seeking the headwaters of the Mississippi. Settlements such as Detroit date from this time. At the beginning of 1682 René-Robert Cavelier, Sieur de La Salle—a lapsed Jesuit turned settler and explorer—went down the Mississippi, believing it would carry him to the Pacific and thus open up the route to Asia. It did not, of course, but his expedition still changed the map of America.

With twenty-three Frenchmen and thirty-one Indians, La Salle crossed Lake Michigan and made his way to a river called Checagou by the Indians. This was frozen, and they had to drag their canoes and supplies, but once on the ice-free Mississippi in February 1682 they made rapid progress. Food and supplies were readily obtained from local tribes, most of whom were very friendly. One French priest described a typical encounter: "All those of the village, except the women, who had at first taken flight, came to the bank of the river to receive us. Here they built us cabins, brought us wood to burn and provisions in abundance. For three days they feasted us constantly." The priest noted that the Indians did "not resemble those at the north, who are all sad and severe in their temper; these are far better made, honest, liberal and gay."[38]

Stopping periodically for supplies—which their Indians helped to procure from the locals—La Salle's party pushed south past the abandoned Indian mounds of Cahokia and built a fort where the city of Memphis, Tennessee, now stands. Eventually they reached the ocean on April 9, after a voyage of some eight weeks. On a bare hillock overlooking the Gulf of Mexico La Salle erected a cross and a column, mounted with the arms of France. The territory he claimed as Louisiana, in honor of the Sun King, was far broader than the modern state, stretching all the way to the Great Lakes up the Mississippi (which he called the River Colbert after Louis XIV's finance minister).

La Salle returned the way he came, but in 1684 he set out from France with four ships and 300 men to stake out France's position on the Gulf of Mexico. This expedition was a disaster. Only one of his vessels made it across the Atlantic and this landed too far west, on what is now the coast of Texas. La Salle spent three fruitless years hunting for the mouth of the Mississippi before he was gunned down by his mutinous men in 1687. According to Henri Joutel, his trusted aide, the assassins "barbarously stripped" his corpse, "vented their malice in vile and opprobrious language," and then "dragged it naked along the bushes and left it exposed to the ravenous wild beasts."[39]

A decade later the French tried again. In 1699 and 1702 forts were erected on the Gulf coast east of the Mississippi at Biloxi and Mobile, but these were still only toeholds. It was not until Louisiana was privatized that French colonialism in the South took off.

In 1717 the French Crown, bankrupted by years of war, ceded Louisiana to a joint-stock company run by the Scottish financier John Law. Law was a man way ahead of his time—a pioneer of paper money and speculative stock dealings—who wormed his way into the heart of the French state. Wildly exaggerating the prospects of Louisiana, he talked up his company's shares in 1719–1720 until the boom predictably burst. Although the share value fell by 97 percent, his Company of the Indies still mounted an aggressive campaign of colonization. Between 1717 and 1721 it shipped to Louisiana some 7,000 white settlers (mostly French), but they were soon decimated by disease and crop failure. In 1731, when the bankrupt Company of the Indies was taken over by the French Crown, the colony had only 2,000 white settlers, plus 4,000 black slaves imported from Africa.[40]

By the early eighteenth century French territory stretched from the Gulf of St. Lawrence to the Gulf of Mexico, through the heartland of the American continent and along its greatest waterway. French America thus blocked off British expansion westward from New England and also separated Spain's dominions in Florida from those in Texas and New Mexico. Above all, the port of New Orleans, named for the Prince Regent, was strategically located to command the delta of the Mississippi.

New Orleans took time to get going. In 1722 the French explorer Pierre de Charlevoix found only "a hundred barracks, placed in no very good order," a "large war-house built of timber," and "two or three houses which would be no ornament to a village in France." But he was bullish about the city's prospects: "Rome and Paris had not such considerable beginnings" and "their founders met not with those advantages on the Seine and the Tiber which we have found on the Mississippi, in comparison of which these two rivers are no more than brooks."[41]

Yet New France remained a fragile empire. French settlements were few and far between: La Salle's dream of a network of forts and towns right down the Mississippi was never realized. Population growth depended on continued migration from across the Atlantic, particularly of African slaves but also the castoffs from French prisons, and it did not become self-sustaining. More important, the French colonies were not economically viable: They cost the Crown more to defend and administer than they generated in trade. Truly profitable crops such as sugar and tobacco could not be grown in icy Canada; one could try in Louisiana but the climate there oscillated unpredictably between downpour and drought. In any case, transporting the produce of Canada or Louisiana to Europe took longer and cost more than exports from the Atlantic seaboard controlled by the English. As one governor-general of New France observed ruefully, "We should never delude ourselves that our colonies on the continent . . . could ever rival the neighbouring English colonies in wealth, nor could be very lucrative, for with the exception of the fur trade, the extent of which is limited and the profits continually declining, these colonies can furnish only goods similar to those of Europe at higher prices and of poorer quality."[42]

France's American empire was built on shaky foundations, for which New Orleans served as an apt metaphor. Much of the town was below sea level and in September 1718, within a few months of being founded, it was flattened by a hurricane and ruined by floods. In due course New Orleans would enjoy a glittering and prosperous future but, fundamentally, it rested on mud.

The French did leave their mark on the future United States. They founded what became great cities such as Detroit and St. Louis, and the state of Louisiana's legal code is still based on French Roman law. But France's lasting influence was less profound than Spain's and neither of these European powers capitalized on their head start. As the seventeenth century wore on, the coming power was their despised Protestant enemy across the Channel. The English were more effective imperialists, at least in North America. Their secret was a potent but unstable mixture of liberty and slavery that would define American history.

2

EMPIRE AND LIBERTIES

During the course of the seventeenth century the English established small but viable colonies along the eastern seaboard, governed—unlike their European rivals—by representative assemblies that enjoyed a large measure of self-rule. The liberties that were the source of controversy and conflict for much of the century in England had become norms of colonial life. But although nurtured in English ways, the American colonies grew up very differently. In the South, white liberty came to depend on black servitude. Even in Puritan New England the European identity of state and church soon broke down, while the middle colonies, from New York down to Pennsylvania, attracted a variety of non-English migrants—Dutch and German, Scots and Irish—that helped turn the region into an ethnic melting pot. By the 1760s, when Great Britain resolved its long-standing struggle for North American empire against France, its colonies were prosperous, precocious, and increasingly unstable.*

SOUTHERN PLANTERS AND BLACK SLAVES

The initial English efforts at colonization were not promising. Walter Raleigh's colonists on Roanoke Island in the 1580s disappeared without trace. The Virginia Company's settlement at Jamestown in 1607 was situated on the edge of a malarial swamp: Disease and famine nearly killed off the population in 1609–1610. Captain John Smith, its founder, said the survivors kept going on "roots, herbes, acorns, walnuts, berries, now and then a little fish . . . even the very skins of our horses." So great was the hunger that some of the people cooked dead Indians. According to Smith, one man "did kill his wife, powdered her [with salt], and had eaten part of

---

* Great Britain formally came into existence in 1707, with the Act of Union between the kingdoms of England and Scotland.

her before it was knowne, for which he was executed, as hee well deserved: now, whether shee was better roasted, boyled or carbonado'd [on the grill], I know not; but of such a dish as powdered wife I never heard of."[1]

Cannibalism was only a temporary expedient but the Virginia Company was never a going concern. Hopes of finding gold or a waterway to the Pacific proved as illusory as they did for de Soto or La Salle and eventually in 1624 Virginia was taken over as a Crown colony. But before the Company collapsed, it had set three important precedents that marked this first English settlement out from the French and Spanish experiments.

The first was private ownership of land. To encourage migration to what was fast becoming notorious as a death trap, the Company started a "headright" system. Anyone who paid his own passage across the Atlantic received fifty acres of land in Virginia. Not surprisingly, settlers with private property proved more enterprising than mere company employees.

Equally important was an annual assembly, comprising the governor, his appointed council, and a House of Burgesses elected by local freemen, which the Company established in 1619. The assembly survived the takeover of Virginia by the Crown and increased its powers in the 1630s at a time when, back in England, Charles I was trying to suppress the rights of Parliament. The right to vote was generally restricted to men owning at least fifty acres—not exactly democracy but still a generous franchise by contemporary English standards. Underpinning this was a network of county courts, which were really agents of local government, handling tax-gathering, land deeds, and highways, as well as policing and justice.

Private ownership of land and local self-government were signs that Virginia was putting down English-style roots. Its settlers were developing a stake in their colony, rather than remaining subjects of an artificial and autocratic royal outpost like the inhabitants of New Spain and New France. But the colony would not have survived without an economic rationale. The Virginia variety of tobacco was too bitter for English taste, but John Rolfe (better known as husband of the Indian "princess" Pocahontas) experimented with a milder West Indian strain. His first shipments to London in 1614 showed that it was possible, in the words of one contemporary, "to found an empire upon smoke."[2]

During the 1620s tobacco sold in England for five or ten times what it cost to produce in Virginia. The Crown naturally took its cut through hefty taxation and, eyeing further profits, in 1632 it set aside 12 million acres further north for a new colony. Called Maryland, after the wife of Charles I, this was not directly run by the Crown but was a "proprietary colony" granted to a royal favorite, Lord Baltimore. He hoped that Maryland would become a refuge for Catholics, but most of the colonists were Protestants and many simply moved north from Virginia, attracted by Maryland's especially generous headright of 100 acres. Soon Maryland was caught up in the tobacco boom.

Virginia and Maryland were known as the Chesapeake colonies, after the vast estuary that stretches 450 miles from Norfolk, Virginia, well beyond the modern city of Baltimore. For most of the seventeenth century their inhabitants were predominantly white. The Indians had been ravaged by disease and driven west by land-hungry tobacco planters, so labor was provided by a steady supply of migrants from England. Some were outright landowners under the headright system but most came as indentured servants—in other words, they paid their passage by temporarily contracting themselves to work for a master. He, in turn, had to provide them with food, clothing, and shelter, plus some kind of payoff in money and clothing at the end. Of 120,000 emigrants to the Chesapeake during the seventeenth century, perhaps three-quarters arrived in this manner.[3] Most were poor, unskilled men in their late teens or early twenties.

Indentured servitude—though a form of bondage and often very harsh—was only temporary: The standard term was seven years. Moreover, it did not, in principle, eradicate basic legal rights. Afterward the freedman was free to practice his trade or work for wages on tobacco plantations. Either way, ex-servants could accumulate the means to buy land of their own at a time when such social climbing was rare in England. With his own property, a freedman was then in a position to seek a wife—although that was not easy, given the three-to-one predominance of males in the seventeenth-century Chesapeake.

Indentured servitude got Virginia and Maryland going but, as wages rose in England after the end of the Civil Wars, the supply tailed off. So the planters made a fateful decision, turning from white servitude to black slavery.

The precedent was set by Carolina, a new proprietary colony south of Virginia that was founded in 1670. Whereas Maryland had been modeled on Virginia, Carolina was an offshoot of Barbados—England's boom colony in the Caribbean. The wealth of Barbados derived from the production of sugarcane using slave labor from West Africa—a pattern already established by the Portuguese in Brazil. In 1670 three ships from Barbados founded Charles Town (Charleston), named (like the colony) for King Charles II. Generous headrights and religious toleration attracted settlers—urgently needed as defense against the Spanish from Florida—but, to satisfy its labor needs, the colony also imported slaves. Thereafter, population growth was rapid: In 1712 Carolina was divided into separate colonies, North and South, and by 1740 slaves outnumbered free whites by two to one in South Carolina, making it the only English colony in mainland America with an African majority.[4] As white servant labor became harder to obtain in the Chesapeake, the planters in Virginia and Maryland also turned to slavery on a large scale to sustain their tobacco economy.

Back in the mid-seventeenth century the distinctions between slavery and servitude were still fuzzy: There were cases in which slaves initiated actions in the Virginia courts. Nor was the racial divide clear-cut: Free blacks who fulfilled the property qualification were probably able to vote in elections.[5] But as the number of black people increased, so the divisions became stark. In 1680 the clergyman Morgan Godwyn wrote that "these two words, Negro and Slave, [are] by custom grown Homogeneous and Convertible; even as Negro and Christian, Englishman and Heathen, are by the like Custom and Partiality made Opposites."[6]

From the 1660s, custom was gradually written into law and in 1705 Virginia pulled its various statutes into a formal slave code that stated, among other things:

> All servants imported and brought into this Country by sea or land . . . who were not Christians in their native Country . . . shall be accounted and be slaves, and such be here bought and sold notwithstanding a conversion to christianity afterwards. . . . And be it further enacted, That no minister . . . or person . . . within this colony and dominion, shall hereafter wittingly presume to marry a white man with a negro or mulatto woman; or to marry a white woman with a negro or mulatto man, upon pain of forfeiting and paying, for every such marriage the sum of ten thousand pounds of tobacco. . . . And if any slave resist his master . . . correcting such slave, and shall happen to be killed in such correction . . . the master . . . shall be free and acquit of all punishment . . . as if such accident had never happened.[7]

Thus, according to the Virginia code, the root distinction between slavery and servitude was that slaves were not Christians. You could not reduce a Christian servant to a slave but equally you could not convert a slave into a servant: The code made clear "that baptism of slaves doth not exempt them from bondage." So religion had become the pretext; the real barrier was race—that difference of skin pigment that was the visible badge of the Negro. There were still free Negroes in the eighteenth-century South but color was now becoming the great divide. Increasingly colonists adopted the stark language of black and white; the treatment of slaves was usually harsher than in the Spanish colonies, where they often had the right to marry and even hold property. British America gave more liberty to whites, but less to blacks, than New Spain.[8]

We should not make the mistake of thinking that, because Negro slaves were deemed mere property, they were entirely passive victims of a brutal system. Carolina's money derived from rice, a crop foreign to most Englishmen. Many of the slaves came from the so-called Rice Coast of West Africa, in present-day Ghana, and their skills were probably vital in making rice cultivation a success—adapting traditional African patterns of planting, hoeing, and threshing and maybe also the mortar-and-pestle method of removing rice grains from their husks.[9]

The clearest sign that blacks were not passive is to be found in their periodic revolts. On September 9, 1739, twenty slaves stole guns and powder from a store at Stono Bridge, some twenty miles from Charles Town. Banging two drums and chanting "Liberty," they started marching south toward Spanish Florida, which welcomed runaway slaves. En route they burned seven plantations and killed more than twenty whites, in some cases cutting off their heads. But by midafternoon a posse of planters had caught up with the fugitives, now swollen to around a hundred. Mounted and well armed, they shot and decapitated many of the slaves and hunted down the rest over the next few days. According to an account written soon afterward by an unknown white man, "this is to be said to the honour of the Carolina Planters, that notwithstanding the Provocation they had received from so many Murders, they did not torture one Negroe, but only put them to an easy death."[10]

The Stono rebellion was a relatively minor affair, in all costing about sixty lives, but it cast terror into whites across South Carolina. According to a report written a couple of years later: "Every one that had any Relation, any Tie of Nature; every one that had a Life to lose were in the most sensible Manner shocked at such Danger hanging daily over their Heads."[11] Such insurrections served as a terrible warning of incipient black violence, yet slave labor also seemed essential for the prosperity of the South. As a result, the slave codes were made even tighter.

There was one notable attempt to move in a different direction. In 1732 a group of London merchants and philanthropists known as the Georgia Trustees received a royal charter for a new English colony. Georgia was to be a kind of public-private partnership—run by the Trustees but mostly funded by British taxpayers—and one of its most striking features was a ban on slavery. The Trustees and the colony's first governor, James Oglethorpe, were not against slave-owning in principle; they simply thought it wrong for Georgia. They saw the new colony as a safe haven for persecuted European Protestants and as a fresh start for the "miserable wretches" of England's cities. Georgia's settlers were to be productive small farmers, growing useful crops such as hemp and flax and serving in the militia. In this way they would act as a buffer for South Carolina against the threat from Spanish Florida. Promotional literature talked up the new colony as both a "Garden of Eden" and the "Gibraltar of America."[12] To make Georgia a slave society, the Trustees feared, would undermine those principles by encouraging whites to live lives of "luxury" and "idleness." According to one of the boosters, Benjamin Martyn, "the People being oblig'd to labour themselves for their Support, will be, like the old Romans, more active and useful for Defence of their Government."[13] In this austere social experiment, landholdings were kept deliberately small and other vices were also banned, including liquor and lawyers.

Life in the new colony was hard and many settlers laid the blame on the restrictive policies of the Trustees. A petition signed by more than a hundred citizens of Savannah in 1738 criticized the "want of the use of Negroes . . . which if granted would both induce great numbers of white people to come here and also render us capable to subsist ourselves by raising provisions upon our lands, until we could make some produce fit for export and in some measure balance our importation."[14] The campaigners gradually wore down the Trustees. The bans on lawyers, liquor, and large landholdings were dropped and, after peace with Spain removed the threat of attack from Florida, public funds dried up. In 1751 the defeated Trustees handed Georgia over to the Crown. Within a few years it had become a plantation society like South Carolina, run by a wealthy slave-owning elite.

The pro-slavery lobby's rallying cry in Georgia was "Liberty and Property without restrictions."[15] In other words, the liberty of whites depended on the unfettered ownership of blacks as property. By the mid-eighteenth century that had become unequivocally the southern way. Much of subsequent American history has been an attempt to escape from its consequences.

FAITH AND FREEDOM IN NEW ENGLAND

The New England way was very different but equally important for America's future. Although the *Mayflower* is probably the most famous immigrant ship in American history, the hundred or so Puritans who founded Plymouth in 1620 could easily have gone the way of the isolated outposts of New Spain and New France. Half of them died during the ensuing winter and, even after a decade of further migration, only 1,500 English settlers lived in Plymouth in 1630.

What really got New England going was the Great Migration of the 1630s by settlers who created the Massachusetts Bay colony to the north of Plymouth. During this decade more than 13,000 men, women, and children crossed the Atlantic to settle in Massachusetts. They came overwhelmingly from the eastern counties of England, particularly Essex, Suffolk, Norfolk, and Lincolnshire. They brought with them English ways and English names, founding towns such as Chelmsford, Ipswich, Cambridge, and Boston—the center of the new colony.

These were very different settlers from those who carved Virginia out of the forests and inlets of the Chesapeake. The Virginians were mostly young men of limited means—the sort who contracted to be servants for a period of years to pay their passage. Migrants to Massachusetts, by contrast, were mostly families and often interrelated family groups. They usually brought a servant or two to help with the hard labor, but servants accounted for only a quarter of the total, compared with three-quarters of the immigrants to Virginia. These settlers also paid their own way, even though equipping and moving a family of six across the Atlantic cost the equivalent of a year's income for a yeoman farmer. In other words, these migrants were people of substance—farmers, artisans, and craftsmen who were already successful back home and had much to lose by starting again in an unknown land. Why did they do it?

The pressures on them were partly economic, especially soaring inflation and a severe depression in the wool trade, on which many of them depended, but their principal motive was religious. In the words of their leader, John Winthrop, a member of the Suffolk gentry, they intended to "rayse a bullwarke against the kingdom of Antichrist which the Jesuites labour to reare up in all places of the worlde. All other Churches of Europe are brought to desolation, and it cannot be but the like Judgment is comminge upon us: and who knows but that God hathe provided this place [New England] to be a refuge for manye whom he meanes to save out of the general destruction."[16]

Winthrop and most of these migrant families were fervent Protestants who feared that England was literally going to hell under Charles I. Against the advice of Parliament, the king had married a Catholic, and his hard-nosed archbishop, William Laud, was trying to impose uniformity on the Church of England. Puritans like Winthrop wanted to purify worship of "popish" practices such as bishops, priests, and complex rituals, basing faith and order squarely on the Bible interpreted by a preaching ministry. Instead, it seemed, Charles and Laud were trying to take the country back to Rome at a time when European Protestants and Catholics were locked in the ruinous Thirty Years War. In 1629 Charles dissolved an unruly Parliament, resolving to govern alone, and this he did until 1640. What became known as the "eleven years tyranny" triggered the Great Migration.

Had Charles and his advisers grasped what was happening in Massachusetts, they would have intervened, but the Puritan leaders proceeded by stealth. The king had granted a charter for a joint-stock company to colonize Massachusetts Bay as a commercial venture. Winthrop and the other gentlemen and merchants who invested in the company hijacked it for their own ends, exploiting a loophole in the charter that did not require them, unlike the Virginia Company, to keep the headquarters in London. When they crossed the ocean, the company's General Court, or board of directors, became the colony's government, with Winthrop as governor. In 1634 the General Court was enlarged to include two delegates elected by each town, and it secured the right to elect the governor and his deputy each year.

Winthrop wanted the colony to be self-governing but not to become a full-blown democracy: "[I]f we should change from a mixt Aristocratie to a meere Democratie: first we should have no warrant in scripture for it: there was no such government in Israel." He also claimed that "a Democratie is, amongst most Civill nations, accounted the meanest & worst of all formes of Government," adding that "Historyes doe recorde that it hath been allwayes of least continuance & fullest of troubles."[17] But John Winthrop knew how to play the politics game. He managed to get reelected as governor of Massachusetts most years in the 1630s and 1640s.

Even today the Massachusetts legislature is still known as the General Court, but the Bay colony was hardly democratic by modern standards. The General Court was a mixture of executive, legislature, and judiciary rolled into one. Its electorate—though again broad by English standards—comprised only property-owning males, and its goal in those early years was to establish not democracy but a "Christian commonwealth." In a sermon on brotherly love preached to his fellow emigrants in 1630, Winthrop warned that "when God gives a special commission he looks to have it strictly observed in every article," and "we are entered into Covenant with Him for this work . . . for we must consider that wee shall be as a City upon a Hill."

The eyes of all people are upon us; so that if wee shall deal falsely with our God in this work we have undertaken, and so cause him to withdraw his present help from us, we shall be made a story and a by-word through the world."[18]

Winthrop was simply reiterating biblical commonplaces and his sermon had little contemporary impact.[19] Eventually the "city on the hill" became a central text for those claiming that America was a unique nation with a unique mission but, at the time, the concept of a covenant had much more impact; indeed, it lay at the heart of the Christian commonwealth. According to the Puritans' Calvinist theology, although human beings were naturally depraved, God made a covenant with those he had saved. Similarly, the people of God covenanted together as members of a church and, in a larger sense, they were part of a social covenant that constituted the political fabric. In their relations with God, Puritans believed, men and women were equal, but social relations were firmly based on the principle of patriarchal authority. The father was head of the household, only men could be ordained ministers of the church, and women were excluded from voting or holding office. All this was justified on scriptural grounds, going back to the story of Adam and Eve.[20]

The Christian commonwealth was not a theocracy. New England was to be run by "godly magistrates," rather than by ministers of the church, and clergy were barred from holding civil office. There were no church courts, and marriage was a civil contract, not a religious sacrament, with divorce permitted by law. On the other hand, only males who were church members could vote, every town was required by law to maintain a church, supported by local taxes, and its people were obliged to attend religious worship—including weekday lectures and two lengthy sermons on Sundays. Despite church being distinct from state, Massachusetts was to be a godly society.

Although the Puritans are often depicted as seeking freedom of conscience, that is misleading. They really wanted freedom from error—in other words, liberty from false religion imposed by Charles and his advisers in order to foster true religion according to their Calvinist standards. Not only Catholics but also Anglicans were excluded from the colony: Two of the first settlers, the Browne brothers, were shipped back home because they wanted to worship according to the Book of Common Prayer. Equally abhorrent were the so-called enthusiasts who claimed the right to interpret the Gospel according to the dictates of conscience. Most of the Bay colonists agreed with the sixteenth-century French theologian Theodore Beza that full liberty of religion was "a most diabolical doctrine because it means that every one should be left to go to hell in his own way."[21]

The rulers of Massachusetts fought a running battle to maintain their notions of purity and discipline. In 1636 they banished the minister Roger Williams, who argued that freedom of worship should be extended even to Catholics and Jews because religion was an affair of the heart. He and his followers founded the town of Providence, later part of the colony of Rhode Island, which was committed to the principle of religious toleration. But Winthrop and his allies still had to deal with those they called the "antinomians" and "libertines," who claimed a direct and personal revelation from God unmediated by scripture or the ministry. The most notorious of these was Anne Hutchinson, wife of a substantial Boston merchant, whom Winthrop called "a woman of a haughty and fierce carriage, of a nimble wit and active spirit, and a very voluble tongue, more bold than a man."[22] Yet she also knew her place and did not speak out in public, at least not initially. Instead she spread her opinions in the most private and purely female spheres of seventeenth-century society—the bedroom at childbirth.[23]

Bearing children was a fact of life for New England women. Puritans were not, in fact, as puritanical as later stereotypes suggest. They believed that an active sex life was essential to a good marriage and on scriptural grounds they also considered contraception to be a sin. As a result, many women were with child every year or two; Anne Hutchinson herself produced fifteen children in two decades from 1613. Yet childbirth was a hazardous business: One woman in every five died in the process. In a community obsessed with heaven and hell, the long hours of labor were therefore fraught with spiritual as well as physical anguish.

A midwife helped the expectant mother give birth, but she was attended by an anxious and supportive crowd of female relatives and friends. Anne Hutchinson became renowned for her bedside manner, using the life-or-death situation to encourage the women to reflect on the state of their souls. Then she began to hold twice-weekly meetings in her own house where she would comment on sermons and criticize ministers. Between fifty and eighty women were said to attend, which from a population totaling only 1,000 was a significant number. Finally, she went public: When ministers whose theology she disapproved of were preaching, she and her followers would stand up ostentatiously and walk out of church. Little wonder that Reverend Hugh Peters told her: "[Y]ou have stept out of your place, you have rather bine a Husband than a Wife and a preacher rather than a Hearer; and a Magistrate than a Subject."[24]

Anne Hutchinson was part of a larger movement in Boston claiming that many ministers preached salvation by "works"—in other words, good behavior that could be measured by society—rather than by "grace" based on God's free gift of salvation known in the believer's heart. This seemed to threaten the fabric of church discipline on which Massachusetts was based and the theological debate became tied into a larger power struggle in colonial politics. In 1637 Winthrop was able to have Anne's brother-in-law, one of his leading critics, banished from the colony and he was now free to prosecute Anne. Although she defended herself with skill and resolution, her trials before the General Court and the Boston church were stacked against her. She told her accusers defiantly: "[Y]ou have power over my body but the Lord Jesus hath power over my body and soul."[25]

Anne Hutchinson was excommunicated from the Boston church and banished from Massachusetts—eventually being killed by Indians on land that is now part of the Bronx in New York—but the tide of history was with her. As in other utopias, the founders of Massachusetts could not maintain the colony's original fervor and purity, particularly among a new generation for whom Archbishop Laud was only a name and who had not experienced the traumatic ocean crossing as something like a new birth. In 1647 the General Court abandoned the requirement that voters must be church members. In 1662 the so-called Half-Way Covenant allowed children of church members who could not testify to a conversion experience to be "Half-Way" members—permitted to have their own children baptized though not to partake in the Lord's Supper. Although the colony struggled to repel new apostles of private revelation, even hanging several Quakers who repeatedly tried to proselytize in Massachusetts, in 1691 it was forced to adopt Britain's new Act of Toleration and extend freedom of worship to all Protestants.

What became known as Congregationalism still maintained a special position in New England life. Indeed, the intention behind the Half-Way Covenant was to make the criteria for church membership less exclusive in order to maintain a godly society.[26] But by the middle of the seventeenth century the church had lost its tight control over daily life as the population grew through continued immigration and natural increase.

The demography of New England followed a pattern very different from that of the Chesapeake, owing to the preponderance of families, instead of single men, and of what were called the "middling sort," rather than a mix of big landowners and indentured servants. Instead of large, widely dispersed farms, as in Virginia, settlement was on a township model, with the land for each town allocated by the General Court and then divided up by the "original proprietors" of that town.

Take, for instance, the story of John Moulton, a husbandman or tenant farmer from Ormsby St. Margaret in Norfolk. Aged thirty-eight, he landed in Boston in the middle of June 1637 with his wife, Anne, five children, a manservant, and a maid. They settled in Newbury, twenty-five miles north, but this, like Boston, proved too crowded. Within a year Moulton and sixteen others had successfully petitioned the General Court to found a new township across the Merrimack river—what is now Hampton, New Hampshire. This was a shrewd move because, as an original proprietor, he would have the best cut of the land and a prominent role in town affairs. In 1639 he received 250 acres in the initial allocation and was elected Hampton's first representative to the Massachusetts General Court. By the time John Moulton died a decade later, he had transformed himself from a struggling tenant in the Old World to a prosperous landowner in the New.[27]

The Moulton story was typical of thousands of other New England families as townships spread along the coast and into the interior. But although some people became very rich, particularly merchants trading with England and the West Indies, there was no southern-style landed elite supported by slaves. This was not because Puritans were against slaves on ethical grounds. In 1645 Emmanuel Downing told his brother-in-law John Winthrop, "I do not see how we can thrive until we get a stock of slaves sufficient to do all our business, for our children's children will hardly see this great continent filled with people, so that our servants will still desire freedom to plant for themselves and not stay for very great wages." And, he added, "I suppose you know very well how we shall maintain 20 Moors cheaper than one English servant."[28] The real obstacle to slavery in New England was economic, not ethical. The climate was too harsh for big commercial crops like tobacco and rice; this also meant that New Englanders lacked both the need and the means to invest in slavery on a large scale. Those few slaves to be found in Boston and other towns were usually treated as additional servants.

Without plenty of slaves or indentured servants, New England therefore faced a persistent shortage of labor. In the old country land was scarce and wage labor abundant; in Massachusetts men like John Moulton had land beyond their wildest dreams but not the labor to cultivate it. The answer lay in the family. Sons started helping on the land as early as age five. By the time they were ten they often had independent responsibilities, such as tending livestock. That was also the pattern in England but, instead of then being sent away as servants in their midteens, Massachusetts boys would often continue to work the family farm, albeit on a more cooperative basis, well past the age of majority (twenty-one). In due course the father might identify some section of the land as a wedding portion or inheritance and the son would concentrate on that, but he would not come into his own fully until his father died. Some young men, of course, decided to strike out on their own, but that was risky. Yet staying at home was a form of servitude. In seventeenth-century Massachusetts, "children differed from servants in many respects, but as labour they possessed little liberty."[29]

THE MIDDLE COLONIES AND THE "MELTING POT"

In the first half of the seventeenth century the English concentrated on the extremities of North America—what became New England in the north and the southern colonies running from Maryland down to Georgia. The middle part of the coast had been colonized in a patchy way by Dutch, Swedes, and other European migrants. After the Restoration of the Stuart monarchy in 1660, however, that all changed. Charles II and his brother James, Duke of York, were determined to challenge the Dutch trading empire. They also wanted to impose tighter royal control over the various private English colonies that had grown up higgledy-piggledy while king and Parliament were at odds. On a more personal note, James was heavily in debt: A colony of his own would help with the cash flow.

In 1664 James sent an expedition to seize the Dutch colony of New Netherland, astride the Hudson river and Long Island, commanded by Colonel Richard Nicholls. This was gunboat diplomacy, using three frigates and a freighter, but the Dutch were even less prepared and they surrendered without a fight. The director-general of New Netherland, Peter Stuyvesant, had wanted to resist: He was an ex-soldier who had lost a leg fighting in the Caribbean. But his main town, New Amsterdam on the tip of Manhattan Island, was poorly fortified and had only 150 soldiers to defend it. The English offered generous terms that the citizens were determined to accept, warning Stuyvesant that otherwise "we cannot conscientiously foresee that anything else is to be expected for this fort and city of Manhattans . . . than misery, sorrow, conflagration, the dishonor of women, murdered children in their cradles, and in a word the absolute ruin and destruction of fifteen hundred innocent souls."[30]

Stuyvesant acknowledged defeat and signed the surrender. On August 30, 1664, he and his soldiers marched out of New Amsterdam, flags flying, and most were soon on a boat home. Nicholls renamed the town New York, after his patron. Today the site of the fort is Battery Park, marked by cannons and cannonballs, from where tourists take ferry boats to the Statue of Liberty. New Amsterdam's main thoroughfare, Broad Way, is the most famous street in the modern city; one of its outlying villages, New Haarlem, is known the world over. Nicholls also secured the Dutch villages on nearby Long Island and Fort Orange, far up the Hudson river, which he renamed Albany after another of James's many titles. Although the Dutch briefly regained their territories during the next Anglo-Dutch War, the English took possession for good in the peace settlement of 1674.

The conquest of New Netherland opened a new chapter for North America. For the first time the English were ruling over people whom they regarded as their racial equals, unlike the Indians and the Africans, and who also shared their Protestant religion, in contrast with the Catholic French and Spanish. Nicholls's terms were deliberately generous because he lacked the troops to hold down a resentful Dutch populace. Nor did he want to drive them out, killing off a prosperous commercial center. That is why the Dutch were allowed to retain their language and religion. Stuyvesant himself returned from the Netherlands to retire on his sixty-acre farm on the edge of town. Today his name is preserved in Manhattan's Stuyvesant High School and cherished by its football team, the Peglegs. Another Dutch family who stayed were the descendants of Claus van Roosevelt, the site of whose farm is now under the Empire State Building, and from whose line came two of America's greatest modern presidents, Theodore and Franklin Roosevelt.

So Nicholls's strategy paid off. In 1700 the Dutch constituted more than half of New York's 5,000 whites. The town had also become home not only to several hundred French Huguenots, fleeing from persecution in Louis XIV's France, but also to a small population of Jews. All these groups were allowed freedom of public worship; in fact, New York had a synagogue before it had a purpose-built Anglican church. This diversity was never eradicated even though the English had become the dominant group by the middle of the eighteenth century.[31]

In New York, pluralism was tolerated; further south, in Pennsylvania, it was positively encouraged. William Penn is one of the more unlikely characters in America's often improbable history. He was the son of one of Cromwell's admirals who adroitly switched to the Royalists and was amply rewarded when Charles II regained the throne. Young William therefore grew up as the eldest son of a big landowner. Always something of a dandy, he studied at Oxford and inherited his father's estates and country house in Sussex. Yet he was also deeply religious and, in his early twenties, became a member of the Society of Friends. This sat uneasily with his high social and political position because Quakers, as they were nicknamed, gave priority to the "inner light" in each person. Accordingly, they advocated religious toleration and inclined toward social equality, having no truck with "capping" or "kneeing" to those of higher rank. Quakers also refused on principle to swear oaths, so they were widely regarded, like Catholics, as a political threat because they would not pledge allegiance to church and state. Penn himself spent several spells behind bars.

Penn was therefore a man of paradox—part of the English elite but also a religious outsider—and this paradox was crucial in the making of Pennsylvania. In 1681 Penn, at thirty-six years of age, secured from Charles II a huge grant of land north of Maryland running from the Delaware river across the Appalachian Mountains. This was in payment of a debt owed to Penn's father. The king insisted on calling it "Pennsylvania," Penn's woods, in honor of the admiral; Penn had wanted the title "New Wales." In fact, Pennsylvania was larger than England, Wales, and Scotland combined.

Although William Penn paid only two visits to his colony, in 1682–1684 and 1699–1701, he stamped his mark firmly on its character. He named its capital Philadelphia, the city of brotherly love, and—as a statement of his peaceful aspirations—designed it as a "green country town" without walls or fortifications. He wanted his colony to be a haven for the religiously oppressed so that, as he told Quaker friends in England, "an example may be set up to the nations. There may be room there, though not here, for such a holy experiment. . . . [M]y God that has given it me through many difficulties will I believe bless and make it the seed of a nation."[32] But although Penn gave thanks to God, the gift would not have come without extensive lobbying through his connections at court and the king's need to buy off some of the growing opposition to his rule. And, like other colonial promoters, Penn wanted to make money, selling off thousands of acres of land to absentee landlords in an attempt to cover the debts run up by his comfortable lifestyle.

Penn was therefore no unworldly saint, but his experiment was certainly unusual by the standards of the age. The basic laws he wrote allowed freedom of worship to all "who confess and acknowledge the one almighty and eternal God to be the creator, upholder, and ruler of the world, and that hold themselves in conscience to live peaceably and justly in civil society." The right to vote and to hold office were open to "such as profess faith in Jesus Christ, and that are not convicted of ill fame or unsober and dishonest conversation, and that are of one and twenty years at least."[33] Penn never thought to say here that, of course, he was referring only to men: Female politicians and votes for women were totally outside even his worldview. But complete freedom of worship for non-atheists and political rights for all Christian men were still huge advances on Massachusetts in the 1680s, let alone the England of Charles II.

Religious toleration and generous land grants averaging 250 acres attracted the sort of pious, hardworking farm families that Penn wanted. Twenty-three shiploads arrived in 1682, most of them Quakers from the North Midlands and the Pennines. His grant of land also included the older settlements of Swedes and Finns across the Delaware river. By 1700 the population had grown to 18,000, including many Welsh, Irish, Dutch, and German Quakers, as well as other German Protestants such as Mennonites and Moravians who tended to congregate in and around Germantown, today a suburb of Philadelphia. Even though British Quakers continued to dominate Pennsylvania's politics during the first half of the eighteenth century, the colony was already a rich ethnic and religious mix.[34]

Penn also adopted an unusually open attitude to the Native Americans. He told the Delaware Indians that he wanted to enjoy the land "with your love and consent, that we may always live together as neighbors and friends," adding that he was "very sensible of the unkindness and injustice that has been too much exercised towards you by the people of these parts of the world, who have sought . . . to make great advantages by you, rather than be examples of justice and goodness." Penn did not regard the Indians as an integral part of his Christian community but he did deal with them much more fairly than was the norm, paying money to extinguish their claims over the land and taking an interest in their culture and language.[35] The natives called Penn Brother Onas, from the Indian word for "quill."[36]

Like many visionaries, William Penn left a mixed legacy. To his distress, Quakers proved as quarrelsome as the rest of the world—the city of brotherly love quickly degenerated into factional politics—and his enlightened policy toward the Indians did not outlast his death in 1718. Nor did his colony make the hoped-for profits: Penn spent his last years ruined by debts and paralyzed by a massive stroke. But Pennsylvania did confirm the pattern set by New York and emulated in smaller New Jersey, which lay between them. Compared with New England and the Chesapeake, here was a greater variety of European ethnic groups and much broader religious toleration. The Middle Colonies pioneered the melting pot. In this, as Penn hoped, they were indeed the seed of a nation.

ENGLISH AMERICA IN TRANSITION

By 1700, therefore, the English were firmly established on the North American continent. Being largely ventures of private enterprise, rather than state-directed as with New France and New Spain, their colonies had developed distinctive regional characteristics that were accentuated as the eighteenth century progressed. During the period 1700–1750 the population of the North American colonies grew almost fivefold, from about 250,000 to around 1.2 million.[37] Far more than in other

European empires, this growth was achieved through immigration. Whereas in the seventeenth century thousands had fled England as a land of poverty and persecution, encouraged by the authorities as a social safety-valve, in the eighteenth century the patterns changed. Greater prosperity and religious toleration encouraged more English people to stay at home, and the government needed manpower for manufacturing and the military.

Consequently, only 80,000 English migrants came to America between 1700 and 1775, of whom around 50,000 were convicted criminals shipped across the Atlantic to serve out their sentences. Most ended up in the South: The Virginia planter William Byrd wrote feelingly to an English friend in 1736, "I wish you would be so kind as to hang all your felons at home." German-speakers, mostly from the Rhineland, a prime battleground in continental wars, accounted for another 100,000 immigrants in this period—three-quarters of them funneled through Philadelphia.[38] By 1775 nearly 10 percent of the population of the mainland American colonies was German-speaking (about one-third in the case of Pennsylvania).[39]

The biggest group of immigrants in the years 1700–1775 was of Scottish descent, 145,000 in all, who tended to settle in the backcountry from Pennsylvania southward. These were Ulster Protestants, whom the colonists called Scots-Irish, and Highlanders whose clan system had been smashed after the Jacobite rebellion of 1745. One group from the Inverness area summed up America's attractions: "The price of land is so low . . . that forty or fifty pounds will purchase as much ground as one thousand in this country. . . . There are few or no taxes at present in the colonies. . . . The climate in general is very healthy. . . . Lastly, there are no titled, proud lords to tyrannize over the lower sort of people, men there being upon a level and more valued in proportion to their abilities than they are in Scotland."[40]

In these increasingly non-English colonies, the South was still predominantly rural but the Middle Colonies and New England were organized around towns, some of which grew significantly because of the surge of immigration. In 1743 Boston's population was 16,000 and Philadelphia's 13,000.[41] Although small by European standards, these colonial port-cities became hubs of trade, with links across the Atlantic to Britain and the West Indies, also up and down the coast and into the interior. The colonies manufactured little of their own and imported heavily from Britain—agricultural implements including ploughs, hoes, and iron nails and also consumer goods such as linens, tableware, and clothing, often in the latest London fashions. The colonies were becoming part of an embryonic consumer society, spanning the Atlantic, mostly paid for on extended credit.

Some of these cities were also centers of information. The first colonial newspaper was not established until 1704, but by 1740 there were twelve papers in the mainland colonies—including five in Boston, two in New York, and three in the Philadelphia area.[42] The *Pennsylvania Gazette* and *Poor Richard's Almanack* were part of a printing business that made Benjamin Franklin one of the wealthiest men in North America. Another local paper was the *Pennsylvanische Berichte* (Pennsylvanian Reporter), started by Christopher Saur in 1739 to serve the mushrooming German communities in and around Philadelphia. Saur also printed pamphlets and newssheets that circulated back in the Rhineland to guide would-be migrants.

Some of the Germans had to serve for a period of years to redeem the cost of their passage, but most of these immigrants had crossed the Atlantic of their own volition. Yet this migration from Europe was matched in the period 1700–1775 by the forced transportation of over 250,000 Africans.[43] The Atlantic network of commerce and communication that brought over the Scots and the Germans also made the slave trade an integral part of American development. In fact, during each decade in the middle of the eighteenth century more than a half-million Africans were shipped to all the Americas, the bulk of them to the Caribbean and Brazil. This was not totally a story of whites exploiting blacks: There were probably as many slaves held within Africa as in the Americas—between 3 million and 5 million people. The slave trade was organized at its starting points by Africans, and more slaves probably died in overland transit to the West African coast than in crossing the Atlantic.

That said, the ocean passage was an appalling experience—no fun for anyone in the age of sail, at the mercy of winds, waves, and disease, but for those incarcerated below decks truly a nightmare. The slaves were chained and stacked on wooden shelves about six feet long, sixteen inches wide, and thirty inches high (convicts got about double the space). They slept without bedding, often in their own urine and excrement. Twice a day they were brought above decks for food and exercise. Many died of disease, especially a form of dysentery known as the "bloody flux." Some starved themselves to death out of depression or tried to jump overboard.

Olaudah Equiano, already a slave, was kidnapped at age eleven from a village in the kingdom of Benin and taken to the coast, destined for Virginia. He had never seen the sea or a ship before, let alone a white man. He believed at first that they lived out their lives in this "hollow place" and could not imagine how pieces of cloth on a pole could make it move, unless by magic. Below decks, he wrote later,

> I became so sick and low that I was not able to eat, nor had I the least desire to taste any thing. I now wished for the last friend, death, to relieve me; but soon, to my grief, two of the white men offered me eatables; and, on my refusing to eat, one of them held me fast by the hands, and laid me across I think the windlass, and tied my feet, while the other flogged me severely. . . . The closeness of the place, and the heat of the climate, added to the number in the ship, which was so crowded that each had scarcely room to turn himself, almost suffocated us. This produced copious perspirations, so that the air soon became unfit for respiration, from a variety of loathsome smells, and brought on a sickness among the slaves, of which many died, thus falling victims to the improvident avarice, as I may call it, of their purchasers. This

wretched situation was again aggravated by the galling of the chains, now become insupportable; and the filth of the necessary tubs, into which the children often fell, and were almost suffocated. The shrieks of the women, and
the groans of the dying, rendered the whole a scene of horror almost
inconceivable.[44]

During the course of the eighteenth century conditions on slave ships did im-
prove, with nine out of ten slaves surviving the voyage by the 1780s. But for slave
traders this was a matter of business, not ethics. "Loose packers" simply calculated
that greater space and better food ensured a healthier and therefore more profitable
cargo. Most slavers were "tight packers," reckoning that the excess mortality rate
was offset by the greater numbers transported on these eighteenth-century human
container ships.

So the American colonies were now part of a thriving Atlantic world, with people and goods circulating in an international market. This was true even of religion. The wave of Protestant revivalism around 1740 that has become known as the
Great Awakening was a genuinely transatlantic phenomenon. At its heart was a
cross-eyed, somewhat effeminate young man called George Whitefield, who became transformed in the pulpit into a charismatic preacher, a "divine dramatist."[45]
Yet Whitefield's cult status would not have been possible without the newssheets,
pamphlets, and advertisements that crisscrossed the Atlantic, hyping up expectations in advance of his preaching tours.

On the morning of October 23, 1740, a Connecticut farmer named Nathan Cole
heard that Whitefield would be preaching at nearby Middletown at ten o'clock. Immediately he dropped his tools, told his wife to get ready, and saddled their horse.
"We improved every moment to get along as if we were fleeing for our lives, all the
while fearing we should be too late . . . for we had twelve miles to ride double in little more than an hour."[46] When the horse got out of breath, Cole would jump down
and run behind until *he* was out of breath and then mount again. As they neared
the main road from Hartford into Middletown, he saw what seemed like a dense
fog rising from the Connecticut river but which close up he realized was a massive
dust cloud created by horses' hooves: "I could see men and horses slipping along in
the cloud like shadows, and as I drew nearer it seemed like a steady stream of horses
and their riders, scarcely a horse more than a length behind another, all of a lather
and foam with sweat, their breath rolling out of their nostrils every jump. Every
horse seemed to go with all his might for the saving of souls."

Cole squeezed his horse into a gap and, like a great stream, they flowed into Middletown. No man spoke, so eager were they to arrive in time, but his wife did mut-
ter through the dust cloud: "Law, our cloaths will be all spoiled." Whitefield was
preaching in the open air, outside the meetinghouse in Middletown. To Cole "he
Lookt almost angelical; a young, Slim, slender youth before some thousands of people with a bold undaunted Countenance . . . as if he were Cloathed with authority

from the Great God; and a sweet sollome solemnity sat upon his brow. And my hearing him preach, gave me a heart wound."

The crowd that day was estimated at 3–4,000. In Boston and Philadelphia Whitefield's open-air preaching would frequently draw 7–10,000—more than half the population. Much of this was due to Whitefield's personal magnetism as he conjured up the torments of hell and called on his hearers for a "New Birth" in the Spirit. He acted out his biblical stories with mimicry and pathos, tears often rolling down his cheeks, and could project his beautifully modulated voice over a remarkably large area. But the religious awakening of the early 1740s was not a one-man show. Many other preachers spread the Word in this new style, in different parts of the colonies, particularly Massachusetts, New Jersey, and Pennsylvania. In fact, historians have steered away from the idea of a one-off Great Awakening around 1740 and tend to talk now about a succession of religious revivals across various parts of America at different times during the rest of the eighteenth century and well into the nineteenth.[47]

The hallmark of these revivals was a religion of the heart based on a conversion experience, rather than on loyalty to a particular church or its covenant. New England Puritanism, once a passionate adventure, had now ossified; Anglicanism in the South was also in a rut. The evangelical churches spawned by the revivalists were more informal and less hierarchical, providing strong emotional support for their members and heeding above all the inner light within each man and woman. This was the religion of Anne Hutchinson more than John Winthrop. If one wants to find the distinctive roots of American Christianity, they lie in the evangelicalism that took hold from the mid-eighteenth century rather than in the Puritanism of a century before. George Whitefield was the spiritual ancestor of Billy Graham.

Revivalism spawned new denominations, notably the Baptists and the Methodists, who reenergized American Protestantism after the Revolution. Although not directly political,[48] evangelicals were socially subversive and the potential threat they posed to the social order was evident when the Baptists hit Virginia around 1770. Traditional Anglican services there were largely a recital of the Book of Common Prayer; local parsons operated at the beck and call of the big landowners. A celebrated Baptist preacher in Virginia was John Waller (known before his conversion as "swearing Jack"), who, one Sunday in April 1771, started a service only to see the parson and some other local worthies riding up. As Waller was praying, according to one observer, they pulled him off the stage, "Beat his Head against the ground," and then "Carried him through a Gate that stood some Considerable Distance," where the sheriff gave him twenty lashes with his horsewhip. But when Waller was released, he "Went Back Singing praise to God, Mounted the Stage & preached with a Great Deal of Liberty."[49] Roughing up the preachers had little effect, however. By 1772 maybe 10 percent of Virginia's population was Baptist.[50]

Evangelicalism was already a force to be reckoned with and it would have particular resonance with the slaves.

Africans brought with them their own languages, religions, and customs, including the widespread practice of polygyny. But in America they developed new cultures, drawing on colonial patterns, and one of the most powerful influences was evangelical religion. The Baptist and Methodist message of New Birth and a coming millennium chimed in with African religion. John Wesley, the founder of Methodism, came out vehemently against slavery; George Whitefield, though more circumspect, had no doubt that the Gospel was for blacks as much as whites. Much of the money raised by his preaching went to support an orphanage that he established in Savannah, Georgia.

It was to this orphanage that there came the only black British missionary ever to work in the British colonies. David Margate arrived in January 1775 and his piety initially made a very good impression on the head of the orphanage, Reverend William Piercy. But then Margate took as his wife a woman who was already married to a slave and started claiming that he was a second Moses, called to deliver his people from slavery. Trying to understand such conduct, Piercy concluded that "his pride seems so great, that he can't bear to think of any of his colour being slaves. There was no making him sensible of the state of the blacks in this country." In the end, after Margate had declaimed against "Egyptian bondage" from pulpits in Charleston, a group of whites—fearing another slave insurrection—banded together as a lynch mob. Just in time, Piercy and his friends spirited the black missionary onto a ship back to England. Margate had been in the colonies little more than six months but he left an indelible impression. Even more than for whites, evangelical religion was an awakening for blacks and it would prove an enduring force in the decades to come.[51]

THE BATTLE FOR EMPIRE: BRITAIN VERSUS FRANCE

By the middle of the eighteenth century, Britain's colonies had achieved a precocious maturity. Late starters in the race for North American empire, they had outstripped their French and Spanish rivals in population, wealth, and trade. Yet the battle for empire was not over. Britain and France had fought three great conflicts in sixty years, each of which was partly played out on the North American continent.* The Seven Years War of 1756–1763 was the climax of this cycle: It was in many ways the first "world war" because the fighting took place not only on the

---

* The first of these conflicts was the War of the League of Augsburg in 1689–1697 (also known as King William's War); the second was the War of the Spanish Succession in 1702–1713 (Queen Anne's War); and the third was the War of the Austrian Succession in 1739–1748 (King George's War).

continent of Europe but in India, Cuba, and the Philippines as well. Its outcome also decided whether North America would speak English or French.

The arc of conflict stretched from Nova Scotia (known as Acadia to the French), up the St. Lawrence valley to the Hudson river and the Great Lakes. But the great prize was the Ohio valley, a vast area of wilderness stretching northwest from the Appalachians to the Great Lakes. Would-be settlers from Virginia and Pennsylvania were now moving into this hinterland. Behind them, powerful groups of speculators dreamed of making a killing, notably the Ohio Company, whose members included a young Virginia landowner called George Washington. To defend their claims, the French started to build a chain of forts running down from Presque Isle on what is now Lake Erie to Fort Duquesne on the fork of the Allegheny and Monongahela rivers. By 1754, two years before the Seven Years War began in Europe, Britain and France were already fighting in North America over control of the Ohio Country.

In the United States this conflict is known as the French and Indian Wars, and aptly so. The putative empires of Britain and France existed largely on the map and in the mind. Ohio Country was, however, Indian terrain, and for years a stable confederacy of Iroquois tribes had held sway in alliance with the French, who, unlike the English colonists, were more interested in trade than settlement. It was the break-up of Indian unity as tribes such as the Mohawks swung over to the British that opened up this vast area from the Appalachians to the Mississippi in the battle of empire. The British would never have been able to wage war on the French without Indian help.[52]

Like most of Britain's wars, this one started chaotically. In the summer of 1754 Washington, an officer in the Virginia militia, was sent to eliminate the threat from Fort Duquesne, only to be driven back ignominiously. Fully in control of the Ohio valley, the French were now in a position to raid into Virginia and Pennsylvania. "All North America will be lost if These Practices are tolerated," warned the Duke of Newcastle, one of the king's principal ministers.[53]

The following summer General Edward Braddock, a veteran British officer with a strong force of regulars and militia, marched northwest from Virginia. His charge was to destroy all the French forts and meet up at Niagara with another British army coming down through French Canada. This ambitious plan had little hope of realization because the roads that looked so clear on a map proved in actuality to be mere tracks through the forest. After weeks spent laboriously cutting trees, blasting rocks, and bridging rivers, Braddock decided to leave his heavy baggage train and press ahead with a flying column. On July 9, 1755, he reached the Monongahela River, ten miles short of Fort Duquesne, the most southerly of the French positions. His column was strung out along a mile of forest track when the French and Indians, largely unseen in the trees, poured devastating fire into his men. Some of the colonial troops broke ranks, raced for cover, and shot back. But many became victims of "friendly fire" from the regulars who, adopting normal military practice, tried to form squares in the middle of the road. Their red coats, packed ranks, and mounted officers made easy targets. Braddock made up in courage what he lacked in wisdom; when he was shot, resistance crumbled and retreat soon became a rout.

Among those rallying the troops was Braddock's aide, George Washington, unscathed despite having two horses shot from under him. Years later he could still vividly recall the retreat: "The dead, the dying, the groans, lamentation, and crys along the Road of the wounded for help," he said, "were enough to pierce a heart of adamant, the gloom & horror of which was not a little encreased by the impervious darkness occasioned by the close shade of thick woods."[54] Braddock died of his wounds and was buried in the middle of the road. The soldiers marched across his grave so that his body would not be found and exhumed as a trophy by the enemy.

Other British defeats followed. In July 1758 General James Abercromby (known behind his back as "Granny") botched completely an assault on Fort Ticonderoga, far up the Hudson river in New York. It left a lasting impression on the young colonial militiamen who served with the regulars. They were appalled at the rigid hierarchies and brutal punishments by which the British army operated. The more religious among them were shocked by the profanity, drunkenness, and lechery of the troops. For officers such as George Washington the war provided invaluable training in how to manage and command an army, and disasters like Monongahela and Ticonderoga, in the words of Benjamin Franklin, "gave us Americans the first suspicion that our exalted ideas of the prowess of British regulars had not been well founded."[55]

This was, however, Franklin in 1788, writing with the benefit of hindsight. In 1754 he was still a loyal British imperialist. It was in fact Franklin who outlined one of the earliest plans for a union of the colonies in an effort to galvanize Britain's war effort against French America. "It would be a very strange Thing if six Nations of ignorant Savages should be capable of forming a Scheme," he wrote, referring to the Iroquois confederacy, "and yet a like Union should be impracticable for ten or a Dozen English Colonies, to whom it is more necessary." A political cartoon designed by Franklin, captioned "Join, or Die," showed the colonies as a cut-up snake, running from the head (New England) to the tail (South Carolina). But although representatives from most of the colonies met in Albany, New York, during the summer of 1754 and drew up a plan for a president general and a grand council of representatives from.each colony to conduct war and diplomacy, this fell foul of the colonial assemblies who feared financial demands and excessive dominance by the Crown. Significantly, the Albany plan was also rejected across the Atlantic, amid growing concern that the colonies might become too powerful to be governed from London. The Speaker of the House of Commons warned of "an Independency upon this country to be feared from such an union." Yet Franklin's dictum "Join, or Die" was sage advice, to be revived on various occasions in the ensuing decades.[56]

The tide of war began to turn in Britain's favor in 1757 when William Pitt took command of the war effort in London. Pitt's strategy was to draw on the country's well-funded national debt to subsidize Prussia and its German allies to hold the balance of power on the continent, while concentrating Britain's naval and military effort on the global battle for empire—in India under Robert Clive and, most of all, in North America.

But first the British had to learn to fight very differently from Braddock. Instead of adhering to parade-ground dress and drill, soldiers began adapting to wilderness warfare—travelling light, adopting camouflage, and abandoning parade-ground tactics. Lord George Howe was the pioneer of these "light infantry" units. One officer wrote home: "You would laugh to see the droll figure we all make. Regulars as well as provincials have cut their coats so as scarcely to reach their waists. No officer or private is allowed to carry more than one blanket and bearskin. A small portmanteau is allowed each officer. No women follow the camp to wash our linen. Lord Howe has already shown an example by going to the brook and washing his own."[57]

The British also started cooperating with the colonies. Instead of issuing demands in the name of the royal prerogative, Pitt asked the colonial assemblies for troops and supplies and offered payment in return, but Massachusetts, from where most of the provincial soldiers came, had less than half its war spending reimbursed.[58] The thousands of colonial soldiers who served in the campaigning seasons of 1758, 1759, and 1760 were essential to British victory.

Equally important, the British started to work with the Indians, buying off France's vital allies. In October 1758 a treaty signed at Easton, Pennsylvania, affirmed Iroquois sovereignty over the whole Ohio valley. The following month, with Indian support, General James Forbes was finally able to take Fort Duquesne, after the French had pulled out and blown it up. As they marched into the smoldering ruins, Forbes's men passed a line of stakes each topped with the skull of a Highlander and wrapped with his kilt, a grisly reminder of Braddock's defeat. Vengeance was sweet. The British built a new and bigger fort on the ruins and named it for their war leader—Fort Pitt, later Pittsburgh.

Well supplied and with colonial and Indian support, Britain's armies were able to bear down on the French in 1759. The key to French North America was the fortress of Quebec, towering some 300 feet above the St. Lawrence. Simply to get an invasion force that far up the hazardous river was a triumph—one of the navigators was James Cook, the future explorer of the Pacific. But capturing the citadel seemed impossible, as the French frustrated a series of frontal and flanking attacks. How victory was won on September 13 is a classic of heroic military folklore: James Wolfe, the sickly young general with a receding chin, who looked like a gawky scarecrow. The daring night landing he mounted at an unprotected cove. The troops clambering up a steep path to the Plains of Abraham in front of the city. Wolfe's thin red line destroying the French attackers in ten minutes with two resounding volleys. The general and his opponent, the Marquis de Montcalm, both falling, mortally wounded. Wolfe attaining the immortality he craved among the pantheon of British heroes.

It's a great story but there were, in fact, two battles of Quebec and the fate of French North America was ultimately decided in 1760, not 1759. After Montcalm's defeat and the French surrender, Wolfe's successor, Brigadier James Murray, occupied Quebec with 7,000 troops. The city was in ruins from the long British bombardment. Food, clothing, and fuel were in short supply; only liquor was abundant, which caused its own problems. The troops were soon sick with dysentery and scurvy and the winter became excruciatingly cold. The spring thaw, though welcome, brought new perils. With the St. Lawrence navigable again, the French were able to move an army of 7,000 downriver from Montreal under an able commander, François Gaston de Lévis. On April 28, 1760, they deployed on the Plains of Abraham. Murray now had only 3,000 troops capable of fighting, less than half of Lévis's strength, but he decided it was better to go out and attack the French rather than cower in the ruins of Quebec; as he wrote to Pitt later, "I considered that our little army was in the habit of beating the enemy, and had a very fine train of artillery."[59]

So the two armies faced off—the British along a rocky outcrop, where Montcalm had deployed his troops the previous September, and Lévis's French regulars, Canadian militia, and Indian warriors roughly where Wolfe's line had stood. The second battle of Quebec was not decided, like the first, by disciplined musketry: It was a bloody hand-to-hand struggle in the mud and snowdrifts. But after two hours, more than a quarter of the British were either dead or wounded and they stumbled back into the city, leaving most of Murray's "very fine train of artillery" left stuck in the mud. Desperately the British worked to strengthen the city walls before the final onslaught.

But the issue was not to be settled by the soldiers. As the ice melted on the St. Lawrence on May 9, 1760, both sides could see warships in the distance. Every available spyglass from the French trenches and the British ramparts was trained on the first masthead. Would it bear the lilies of France or the Union Jack? Suddenly a huge cheer went up from the British. The frigate *Lowestoffe* anchored with news that a British fleet was only a few days away. "Both officers and soldiers mounted the parapets in the face of the enemy and huzzaed, with their hats in the air, for almost an hour," recalled one redcoat. "The garrison, the enemy's camp, the bay and . . . country for several miles, resounded with our shouts and the thunder of our artillery; for the gunners were so elated that they did nothing but fire and load for a considerable time."[60]

When the main British fleet arrived, it dealt briskly with the French frigates and sloops. Lévis had to terminate the siege and retreat to Montreal but, with the British controlling the St. Lawrence, his days were numbered. In September the French surrendered Montreal and the redcoats fanned out to capture the remaining French forts. By the end of November 1760 the last of them, Detroit, was in British hands.

The crux of the war for North America was not land power but sea power. France's empire was unsustainable without command of the Atlantic and this had been lost in two great naval battles in 1759. During the summer the French had massed troops to invade Britain, but they could not embark without control of the Channel, which meant concentrating their Atlantic and Mediterranean fleets to support the invasion. In August the Royal Navy caught the Mediterranean fleet off the coast of Portugal, sinking or seizing four warships and blockading the rest in Cadiz. In November France's Atlantic fleet was cornered and destroyed in rocky Quiberon Bay on the coast of Brittany. These encounters not only finished off the invasion threat but inflicted devastating blows to French sea power, which then decided the fate of North America in 1760.

The Seven Years War dragged on another two years, with Spain entering the war on France's side, and peace was eventually signed in Paris in February 1763. With France evicted from North America, the British were now in total control of a great arc from Nova Scotia and the Great Lakes down the Ohio valley to the Florida Keys (surrendered by Spain).

But the French were bitter. British "atrocities," such as the deportation of some 8,000 French-Canadian settlers from Nova Scotia to Louisiana, fed the stereotype of perfidious Albion. "The English lie at the mid-point between men and beasts," wrote Robert-Martin Lesuire. "All the difference I can see between the English and the Savages of Africa is that the latter spare the fair sex." Nor did the French consider their defeat to be final. "I am completely astounded that England, which is a very tiny bit of Europe, is dominant," declared the Duc de Choiseul, Louis XV's foreign minister, in 1767. "One might reply that it is a fact; I must concur; but as it is impossible, I shall continue to hope that what is incomprehensible will not be eternal."[61]

He had reason to hope. Victory in 1760 had turned on control of the Atlantic; if that were lost in another war, British America would be in jeopardy. Britain's success had also entailed cooperating with the colonials and wooing the Indians. The colonists were jealous of their freedoms and reluctant to assume new burdens, even though the costs of defending the new empire were now enormous. For their part, the Native American tribes in the Ohio valley had no intention of allowing France's loose overlordship to be replaced by a tight British empire, yet the colonials saw Indian lands as fair game now that the French were out of contention. It would be hard for Britain to keep the colonists and the Indians happy at the same time.

So, although the world war of 1756 to 1763 had made Britain a global power, Britain's North American empire rested on fragile foundations. That became clear in the decade after 1763.

3

INDEPENDENCE
AND REPUBLICANISM

In 1763 American colonists, jubilant at the demise of New France, erected statutes to George III and William Pitt. Thirteen years later they declared their independence and in 1783 Great Britain acknowledged the United States as a free and equal nation. Why such a dramatic rupture? The simple answer is that Britain had tried to make the vast new empire pay for itself, provoking a backlash to defend popular rights. In 1776 the Declaration of Independence summed up those rights, purporting to show how they had been undermined by the British Crown, and justified the creation of a new government in order to preserve them.

This Manichean clash of empire versus liberty is at the heart of American tradition. Yet the real story is more nuanced. The United States won its independence during a series of world wars between the British and French empires: Without French support, the new nation would probably have been stillborn. And creating the new government raised the old problems of governance faced by the British— local rights versus the common good, liberty versus centralization—evident in the debates over a new constitution, a bill of rights, and a federal capital. From these emerged a distinctive ideology of republicanism—meaning not just a country without a monarch but one whose vitality depended on a committed and virtuous citizenry, in which the national government was a necessary evil to be carefully restrained.

FROM RESISTANCE TO REVOLT

The war against France had doubled Britain's national debt and increased fivefold the cost of defending and running North America. The ministry of George Grenville was determined to make the colonists pay their share. "The word 'colony,'" declared one member of Parliament, "implies subordination. If America looks to

Great Britain for protection, she must enable [us] to protect her. If she expects our fleets, she must assist our revenue."[1] In March 1765 Parliament approved a law extending stamp duty to the colonies. Across the Atlantic, however, the Stamp Act caused an explosion: This was the first "direct" tax, as distinct from duties on trade, which Britain had imposed on the colonies.

What's more, it was ubiquitously intrusive. A special paper embossed with a revenue stamp had to be purchased for a whole range of public documents, from mortgages to contracts, from wills to newspapers. The new law therefore hit hardest the business and professional classes—merchants, lawyers, and editors—who were best able to shout out and hit back, and it was imposed at a time of economic depression after the war boom, when there was a growing gulf between rich and poor. Boston, like most cities, was used to spasms of mob violence, especially every Pope's Day, the 5th of November. In August 1765 the leaders of local opposition to the Stamp Act roused the city mobs, plied them with drink, and directed them against the agents of the British government.

The elegant three-story mansion belonging to Thomas Hutchinson, the lieutenant-governor of Massachusetts, was a prime target. As he later lamented, the mob was "prevented only by the approaching daylight from a total demolition of the building. . . . Besides my Plate and my family Pictures, household furniture of every kind [and] my own children and servants apparel they carried off about £900 sterling in money and emptied the house of every thing whatsoever except a part of the kitchen furniture not leaving a single book or paper in it."[2]

The violence in Boston, Newport, and elsewhere served to intimidate would-be stamp distributors and the colonists started to coordinate their resistance. Groups calling themselves "sons of Liberty" were organized in various cities, and merchants along the eastern seaboard implemented a boycott of goods from Britain.[3] In October 1765 representatives from nine of the thirteen colonies met in New York's City Hall and petitioned the king for repeal of the Stamp Act.

In a declaration of rights drafted by John Dickinson, an intense young lawyer from Pennsylvania, the Stamp Act Congress set out an axiom that would shape all future debate: "That the only Representatives of the People of these colonies are persons chosen therein, by themselves & that no Taxes ever have been, or can be constitutionally imposed on them, but by their respective Legislatures."[4] Here was the colonists' basic principle: No taxation without representation. The petitioners said they were claiming the "rights of Englishmen" as "His Majesty's liege subjects": Theirs was a protest against the actions of British ministers, not a rebellion against the Crown. On the other side of the Atlantic, there were signs of moderation: A new ministry led by the Marquis of Rockingham, pressed hard by British merchants, repealed the Stamp Act. The news was greeted joyously in the colonies and the protests died down. But Rockingham also pushed through a Declaratory Act affirming that the British Parliament had full authority to make laws "to bind the colonies and people of America in all cases whatsoever."[5] So the underlying issue became clear: Britain wanted more revenue from America, whereas the colonists claimed that this could be raised only with the consent of their legislatures.

In June 1767 Charles Townshend, the Chancellor of the Exchequer, tried again by imposing higher duties on items such as glass, paper, and tea imported into the colonies. This was part of a general tightening of customs administration in North America, where evasion and smuggling were rampant. Townshend's justification was that although the colonial assemblies had the right to decide their own "direct" taxes, the British Parliament had unquestioned authority over "external" taxes such as customs. The Townshend Duties revived the Stamp Act resistance movement—local committees and economic boycotts, backed up by rent-a-mobs. Once again Boston was particularly explosive and the government took the unprecedented step of garrisoning troops there to keep order.

As with any such army of occupation, a serious incident was only a matter of time. On the evening of March 5, 1770, with snow packed hard on the streets, Private Hugh White was doing sentry duty at the Custom House on King Street when some apprentices started taunting him. White hit one of them with the butt of his musket and the local mob converged on the scene. Hearing the clamor, Captain Thomas Preston took a corporal and six men to rescue White. They, too, were cornered by the crowd, now several hundred strong. One of the soldiers, knocked to the ground by a missile, fired his musket. More shots followed, despite Preston's remonstrations. Four Bostonians died that night, and another a few days later. One of them was Michael Johnson, or Crispus Attucks, adopted by anti-slavery Bostonians in the mid-nineteenth century as a black American martyr though he was probably of mixed African and Indian descent.

As with many such incidents, the precise narrative is hard to establish; Preston himself was later tried and acquitted. But, of course, the spin mattered more than the facts. Engraver Paul Revere, a patriot with one eye on profit, plagiarized a sketch of the scene and turned it into a best-selling print of "The Bloody Massacre." This showed a line of redcoats firing a volley into defenseless citizens. As the accompanying verse put it:

> *faithless P[resto]n and his savage Bands*
> *With murd'rous rancour stretch their bloody Hands;*
> *Like fierce Barbarians grinning o'er their Prey*
> *Approve the Carnage, and enjoy the Day.*

Once again a change of ministry in London allowed Britain to back off. Lord North had the Townshend Duties repealed, while retaining the duty on tea to serve, in his words, "as a mark of the supremacy of Parliament and an efficient declaration of their right to govern the colonies."[6] Troops were withdrawn from

Boston and tempers cooled on both sides of the Atlantic. But in May 1773 the East India Company was given the monopoly for selling tea in North America. The government's main aim was to bail out a major British corporation now heavily in debt, but, as before, it was also trying to control the rampant smuggling trade. Once more the networks of resistance swung into action, led by local committees of correspondence, and again Boston was in the vanguard.

Among the sales agents for the East India Company were two sons of Thomas Hutchinson, now governor of Massachusetts. When he insisted that tea ships land their cargo in Boston, about sixty men, some thinly disguised as Indians, converged on Griffin's Walk on the night of December 16, 1773. Many were young sailors and apprentices, but the group included merchants and a doctor, as well as Paul Revere. Within three hours the contents of 340 chests of tea had been dumped in the water. Revere then saddled up and took the news to New York, where it was published and sent on south, spawning new "tea parties" in its wake.

London heard the story a month later. King George III confessed himself "much hurt that the instigation of bad men hath again drawn the people of Boston to take such unjustifiable steps." This was the general view in Whitehall—that a few hot-heads were causing all the trouble—and also that London been appeasing the colonists for too long, ever since repealing the Stamp Act. The king told his prime minister that "all men seem now to feel that the fatal compliance in 1766 has encouraged the Americans annually to increase in their pretensions [to] that thorough independency which one state has of another, but which is quite subversive of the obedience which a colony owes to its mother country." And so, in the spring of 1774 the British Parliament passed a bill closing the port of Boston until compensation was paid for the tea. It also replaced Hutchinson with General Thomas Gage as governor of Massachusetts, and placed Boston under martial law. For the first time, soldiers could be quartered in private houses. Gage assured the king that the colonists "will be lions whilst we are lambs, but if we take the resolute part they will undoubtedly be very meek."[7]

This legislation, dubbed the Intolerable Acts, united the colonies as never before. Thousands of people, from New England right down to the South, sent donations of cash, food, and fuel to the Bostonians. A Continental Congress was summoned to meet in Philadelphia. George Washington, no radical, told a relative in Yorkshire: "The cause of Boston—the despotick Measures in respect to it, I mean—now is and ever will be consider'd as the cause of America (not that we approve their cond[uc]t in destroying the Tea)." To his brother-in-law in Virginia he wrote that "the Crisis is arriv'd when we must assert our Rights, or Submit to every Imposition that can be heap'd upon us till custom and use will make us as tame & abject Slaves as the Blacks we Rule over with such arbitrary Sway."[8] Today it is hard to read that last sentence without raising an eyebrow, but Washington didn't do irony. His words are a telling reminder of the paradoxes of American liberty.

DECLARING INDEPENDENCE

The intellectual leader of the Boston protest was a bustling little lawyer called John Adams. Though delighted at the surge of support from other colonies, he experienced moments of profound doubt as events spiraled, confiding to his diary: "The Objects before me are too grand and multifarious for my Comprehension. We have not Men fit for the Times. We are deficient in Genius, in Education, in Travel, in Fortune—in every Thing. I feel unutterable Anxiety."[9]

But Adams also sensed the portentousness of the Continental Congress: "It is to be a School of Political Prophets I suppose—a Nursery of American Statesmen.... [F]rom this Fountain may there issue Streams which shall gladden all the Cities and Towns in North America, forever."[10]

Adams's hopes proved more justified than his fears. The generation whom he feared to be deficient in everything became the Founding Fathers, whose names and deeds are now part of American mythology. The weeks that these fifty-odd delegates representing the thirteen colonies spent together in Philadelphia—engaged in passionate debate, haggling in committees, or relaxing in taverns—did indeed school them in statecraft. The interaction also helped make them Americans, forging a sense of unity among men from Massachusetts and Virginia, from New York and South Carolina, many of whom had never set foot in each other's homeland.

Yet education is a slow process. In the autumn of 1774 the Continental Congress drew back from radical measures. It agreed to stop imports from Britain but held in reserve a ban on exports there, which would have ruined the economy of the South, until London had responded to its protests. Most delegates still hoped for reconciliation. So did some politicians in London. Edmund Burke urged his fellow MPs to think big and act generously: "[A] great empire and little minds go ill together." In North America, he argued, "our ancestors have turned a savage wilderness into a glorious empire ... not by destroying but by promoting the wealth, the number, the happiness of the human race. Let us get an American revenue as we have got an American empire. English privileges have made it all that it is; English privileges alone will make it all it can be."[11] Burke wanted Parliament to repeal the objectionable legislation and allow the colonials to be represented in the House of Commons, but his motion was rejected by a majority of four to one: Most MPs wanted to teach the Americans a lesson.

Around dawn on April 19, 1775, a force of British soldiers from Boston marched into the village of Lexington, in search of illegal arms and ammunition. Facing them on the green was a company of local militiamen some seventy strong. Major John Pitcairn ordered his column into battle formation—a line of three ranks. With their red coats, white breeches, and Brown Bess muskets, the British infantry were a frightening sight in the cold dawn. Pitcairn, with a few officers, rode to within a hundred feet and shouted: "Lay down your arms, you damned rebels, and disperse."

The militiamen began to leave the green, carrying their muskets. That wasn't enough for Pitcairn: "Damn you! Why don't you lay down your arms?" Another officer cried: "Damn them! We will have them!" What happened next is unclear. American eye-witnesses said a British officer fired; the British denied this. But a shot did ring out. Then a British officer shouted, "Fire, by God! Fire!" One of the British platoons fired a volley. Pitcairn shouted to stop but, before he could make himself heard, a second volley cut into the militiamen. A few of them shot back and then the redcoats charged. Within a minute or so, eight of the Americans were dead and ten wounded.

The British pressed on to nearby Concord, their main target, but failed to find the hoard of arms. Part of the town was set ablaze. Throughout the sixteen-mile journey back to Boston they were harried by militiamen from all around, firing from behind trees or walls and sometimes fighting hand to hand—hatchet or club against bayonet. When the exhausted redcoats struggled into Boston that evening, 70 had been killed and 200 wounded.[12]

Lexington and Concord transformed the political debate. When the Continental Congress met again in May 1775, the issue was not taxation or representation but whether, depending on one's point of view, unprovoked British aggression should be condoned or shooting the king's soldiers approved of. In many colonies, radicals took over the assembly or created their own alternative provincial congress. And in June there was a full-scale battle when British troops attacked patriots fortifying Bunker Hill north of Boston. The British cleared the hill, but lost 250 men. General Gage, the British commander, previously confident that a firm hand would crush the revolt, now advised London that "the rebels are not the despicable rabble too many have supposed them to be. The conquest of this country is not easy."[13]

For its part, the Congress dispatched militia companies from Pennsylvania, Maryland, and Virginia to reinforce what it called the "American army" encircling Boston. It also sent George Washington to act as overall commander. Twenty years earlier Washington and Gage had fought as fellow officers in Braddock's disastrous battle against the French and the Indians. Now they were on opposite sides, with Washington besieging Gage.

Although Boston remained the epicenter of the political earthquake, the fault lines ran far and wide. The Quebec Act of June 1774 allowed freedom of worship for Catholics and the use of Roman law in this largely French Catholic province. To cut through the land claims of various colonies, the Act also gave the governor of Quebec control over the Indian lands of the Ohio valley. At a stroke this legislation therefore antagonized a whole range of interests, from militant Protestants to would-be settlers and greedy speculators. And in November 1775, when Governor Dunmore was trying to control the mounting insurrection in Virginia, he offered to free those slaves who joined his troops and fought against their masters. In a colony where 40 percent of the population was black, nothing could have alienated the whites more.

To American patriots these actions all seemed part of a long-running and systematic assault on colonial liberties. But who was behind the plot? John Dickinson
from Pennsylvania insisted that "every thing may yet be attributed to the misrep-
resentations and mistakes of ministers"—those he called "half a dozen fools or
knaves."[14] With John Wilkes and others in Britain campaigning against a corrupt
Parliament, moderates like Dickinson pinned their hopes not on an American revolution but on a British one that would rebuild Britain's government on the foundation of basic rights. That was why patriots had repeatedly petitioned King George
III for redress against the actions of his ministers. But radicals blamed the king
himself. He had signed the Intolerable Acts, imposing military rule on Boston, and
had approved the Quebec Act: "A prince who can give the royal assent to any bill
which should establish popery, slavery and arbitrary power either in England or
any of its dominions must be guilty of perjury; for it is, in express terms, contrary
to his coronation oath."[15] Now his royal regiments were firing on innocent colonials.

For many colonists, however, such talk was treasonous. The debate was particularly fierce in New York and Pennsylvania—two populous, powerful states in the
middle of the seaboard, separating the radicals of Virginia and Massachusetts. Many
moderates also worried that war with Britain could be won only with aid from
France, the old enemy who had been evicted from North America little more than
a decade before. This was like jumping from the frying pan into the fire. Frustrated,
John Adams wrote home to his wife, Abigail, that America was "a great, unwieldy
Body. Its Progress must be slow. It is like a large Fleet sailing under Convoy. The
fleetest Sailors must wait for the dullest and slowest. Like a Coach and six, the
swiftest Horses must be slackened, and the slowest quickened, that all may keep an
even Pace."[16]

To crack the whip, local radicals sent resolutions in favor of independence to
Philadelphia. At least ninety such messages arrived during the spring of 1776, from
Topsfield, Massachusetts, to the Cheraws District of South Carolina, expressing the
mounting grassroots pressure for radical change in society as well as politics. A decade of protest against British measures, much of it coordinated not by the colonial
assemblies but by ad hoc committees in which ordinary farmers, artisans, and seamen played a major role, had politicized the lower orders and weakened the social
hierarchy. The class struggle was particularly intense in Pennsylvania, where radical artisans running the committee to enforce a ban on trade with Britain demanded that the colonial assembly mandate its delegates to the Congress to vote for
independence. James Allen, a wealthy Philadelphian, was one of many patriots having second thoughts about "the mobility" and its new power. "I love the cause of liberty," he wrote, yet "the madness of the multitude is but one degree better than
submission to the Tea Act." The advocates of independence in the Congress knew
they had let the genie out of the bottle. "The decree is gone forth, and it cannot be
recalled," wrote John Adams on June 3, 1776, "that a more equal liberty than has
prevailed in other parts of the earth must be established in America." Here were

early intimations of America's double revolution: a political break with Britain *and* a social upheaval at home.[17]

On June 7 Adams and Richard Henry Lee of Virginia, judging the moment right, proposed a resolution in the Congress: "That these United Colonies are, and of right ought to be, free and independent States, that they are absolved from all allegiance to the British Crown, and that all political connection between them and the State of Great Britain is, and ought to be, totally dissolved."[18] The Continental Congress approved the motion and established a committee to draft a formal declaration of independence. Adams was one of its members but the principal author was Thomas Jefferson of Virginia, apparently because Adams felt it politically prudent to let a Virginian, rather than the notorious hotheads of Massachusetts, take the lead. It was the beginning of a personal relationship that would shape American history for the next quarter-century—one that oscillated from friendship to enmity and back to friendship again.

The two men made an unlikely pair. Jefferson was thirty-three, seven years younger than Adams. A lanky six foot two, he was also a head taller and a good deal less portly. And as a spendthrift southern planter, with thousands of acres and dozens of slaves, he offended some of Adams's rooted puritan principles. Their personalities were also very different. Adams was fascinated by people—he loved debate and was a forceful orator—but his blunt manner frequently caused offense. Jefferson, personally charming but somewhat remote, was much more interested in humanity in the abstract. He shunned disputation and was a poor speaker. What made him ideal for the task of drafting the Declaration of Independence were his polymathic knowledge and the fluency of his pen.

Philadelphia in summer was hot and smelly, plagued with mosquitoes and horseflies. Jefferson worked in his lodgings, with windows open, on his lap a small folding desk—one of his many ingenious designs. Intellectually he began his Declaration from the familiar premise of radicals in Britain and America that all governments were based on an implied contract between the governors and the governed. But his elegant preamble, scarcely amended by the Congress, developed these ideas in words that have echoed down the centuries.

> We hold these truths to be self-evident; that all men are created equal; that they are endowed by their Creator with certain inalienable rights; that among these are life, liberty and the pursuit of happiness; that to secure these rights, governments are instituted among men, deriving their just powers from the consent of the governed; that whenever any form of government becomes destructive of these ends, it is the right of the people to alter or to abolish it, and to institute new government.[19]

From these first principles, the Declaration then turned to the American case, seeking to show that "the history of the present king of Great Britain is a history of repeated injuries and usurpations, all having in direct object the establishment of an absolute tyranny over these states."[20] Jefferson itemized twenty-one examples of such tyrannical behavior. Like much propaganda, some of the charges were vague or arguable, but the heart of his case were the familiar stories of taxation without representation, the imposition of military rule, and, most recently, the use of brute force.

Jefferson's list of charges built up to an angry peroration about the slave trade. George III, he claimed, had "waged cruel war against human nature itself, violating its most sacred right of life & liberty in the persons of a distant people who never offended him, captivating & carrying them into slavery in another hemisphere, or to incur miserable death in their transportation thither."

This was strange stuff, coming from a Virginian slave owner. The contradiction was heightened a few sentences down when Jefferson complained that the king was "now exciting those very people [the slaves] to rise in arms against us, and to purchase that liberty of which he has deprived them, by murdering the people upon whom he also obtruded them."[21]

The idea that George III had forced the slave trade on Virginians was, of course, preposterous; Jefferson, like most slave owners, was tying himself in knots trying to justify slavery in a declaration about the inalienable right of all men to "life, liberty and the pursuit of happiness." Prudently, the Continental Congress cut the whole tortuous passage. But Jefferson's dilemma—how to throw off British "slavery" while perpetuating slaveholding at home—would be a cancer at the heart of the new nation.

The Declaration of Independence did not carry all before it. John Dickinson, the leading moderate, made a final eloquent plea against war. Gaunt, pale, transparently sincere, he warned against a "premature" break with Britain; taking up the Declaration, he said, would be to "brave the storm in a skiff made of paper." Outside, as if to echo his words, thunder rolled and rain pelted the windows. There was a long silence, then Adams stood up. It was perhaps the most important speech of his life yet no record survives. Although lacking elegance and even fluency, he spoke, recalled Jefferson, "with a power of thought and expression that moved us from our seats." Adams's rhetoric regained the initiative. After a tense night of debate in taverns and coffeehouses, the skeptics from Pennsylvania and New York backed off—Dickinson and others absenting themselves from the proceedings to avoid casting a negative vote.[22]

On July 4, 1776, the Continental Congress formally approved the amended Declaration of Independence. Twelve colonies voted in favor; New York abstained. The Declaration was printed in newspapers throughout the colonies and read out to citizens and soldiers, often accompanied by thirteen musket or cannon shots to symbolize the thirteen new states. Statues of the king were pulled down, pictures of him smashed or burned.

Writing home to his wife, Abigail, Adams predicted that the day of independence would be "the most memorable Epocha in the History of America. I am apt

to believe that it will be celebrated by succeeding Generations as the great anniversary Festival." Then he added a sobering note: "You will think me transported
with Enthusiasm but I am not. I am well aware of the Toil and Blood and Treasure
that it will cost Us to maintain this Declaration, and support and defend these
States. Yet through all the Gloom I can see the Rays of ravishing Light and Glory."
Adams ended, tortuously: "Posterity will tryumph in that Day's Transaction, even
although We should rue it, which I trust in God We shall not."[23]

WINNING INDEPENDENCE (WITH FRENCH HELP)

The war for independence began disastrously for the Americans. The British abandoned Boston to concentrate on New York—the hinge between New England and
the rest of the colonies. Washington's troops were rolled off Long Island in a single
day. Angry and humiliated, the general abandoned New York and explained his
new strategy to the Continental Congress: "[O]n our Side the War should be defensive" and "we should on all Occasions avoid a general Action, or put anything
to the Risque, unless compelled by a necessity, into which we ought never to be
drawn." Washington added that "being fully persuaded that it would be presumption to draw out our Young Troops into open ground, against their Superiors both
in number and Discipline, I have never spared the Spade and Pick Ax."[24]

The spade not the sword: Hardly the stuff of epics, but Washington's strategy
made sense. He was fighting a trained army of British redcoats and German mercenaries, many of them battle-hardened. Most of his troops enlisted for one season
at a time and then went back to their farms. So Washington restrained his instincts
and refused to fight. Avoiding full-scale battles as far as possible, he harried the
British in guerrilla actions and big skirmishes. Some of these he won; more of them
he lost. Like people in most countries, Americans celebrate past victories and dis-
creetly forget the defeats.

The British, too, could not risk all-out war because this was a battle not for territory but for hearts and minds. They were trying to persuade the colonists to end
their rebellion, so putting American homes to fire and sword would be counterproductive. Most of Britain's soldiers and supplies had to be transported 3,000 miles
across the Atlantic and they were fighting in a large, decentralized country. Even
taking a major city like New York would not be decisive. Far more important was
to destroy Congress's main army, which might shatter American morale.

In the first year of the war the British strategy seemed to be paying off. After
two bad defeats and the loss of Philadelphia in the autumn of 1777, Washington
took his men into winter quarters around Valley Forge in Pennsylvania. The troops
lived a dozen to a wood cabin, fourteen feet by sixteen. Their staple food was "fire
cake"—flour mixed with water and baked in coals or on a stick. Many lacked over-
coats; some had no shoes because, as usual, the Continental Congress was delin-
quent about pay and supplies. On December 23, Washington told the president of

the Congress: "I am now convinced beyond a doubt that unless some great and capital change suddenly takes place . . . this Army must inevitably be reduced to one or other of three things. Starve, dissolve, or disperse, in order to obtain subsistence in the best manner they can."[25]

Washington was exaggerating a little, but that winter was a close-run thing. One boost to morale was provided by a severe dose of training administered by Friedrich von Steuben—billed as a baron and general, though the noble title was fake and he had left the Prussian army as a captain. Steuben endeared himself to the men, drilling them in full dress uniform and swearing in colorful German and French. He taught them to speed up their musketry, use a bayonet, and hold formation in attack or retreat. Equally important, he laid down proper sanitation procedures, with kitchens and latrines on opposite sides of the camp—previously men had often relieved themselves wherever they felt the need. But Steuben did not try to introduce "the entire system of drill, evolutions, maneuvers, discipline, tactics and Prussian formation into our army. I should have been pelted had I attempted it, and should inevitably have failed." He told a Prussian officer: "The genius of this nation is not in the least to be compared with that of the Prussians, Austrians, or French. *You* say to your soldier, 'Do this' and he doeth it; but I am obliged to say 'This is the reason why you ought to do that,' and then he does it."[26]

The Valley Forge winter was also important for a different reason. America was in the grip of a smallpox epidemic. Washington had started inoculating his troops back in 1777, but this was done piecemeal and in various locations. In March 1778 he decided to have inoculation done only at Valley Forge, in strict quarantine. To tend his men, he ordered officers to recruit "as many Women of the Army as can be prevailed on to serve as Nurses."[27] Inoculation entailed making an incision in the arm and inserting some pustules from an earlier victim, so it was effectively a mild dose of the disease. Things could go badly wrong, both for the victim and for those in contact. Yet Washington saw no choice. Smallpox was decimating the army, and his troops were spreading it among the civilian population. The redcoats, by contrast, were largely immune, coming from a country where the disease was endemic.[28]

As Washington struggled to keep his army operational, the first of two military turning points in the war occurred at Saratoga in upstate New York. In October 1777 the Americans surrounded some 6,000 British and German troops under General John Burgoyne and forced them to surrender. Rather like Braddock in 1755, Burgoyne had tried to move an army with a huge baggage train through the American wilderness and he paid the price—though not, like Braddock, with his life. Ironically the victors were mostly state militia units from New England, despised by Washington as "a broken staff" and his arch-rival, General Horatio Gates, was credited with having "Burgoyned" the British.

Victory at Saratoga was a big morale boost, yet its real importance was not military but diplomatic. Ever since the loss of Quebec in 1759–1760, the French had been thirsting for revenge. Although no longer hopeful of recovering their North

American colonies, they were determined to deny them to the hated British and 1776 was their chance. "The 'Great' will soon be gone from Britain," the Foreign Ministry in Paris predicted; "in a few years she will fall to the second or third rank of European powers without hope of ever rising again."[29] In 1778, emboldened by Saratoga, France signed a full-scale treaty with the United States, recognizing their independence, and declared war on Britain. Unlike most eighteenth-century wars, this time there was no conflict in Europe, so the French could concentrate on the North American campaign. Sensing their opportunity, Spain and the Dutch joined in, leaving Britain bereft of allies.

Yet the war dragged on and Washington's battles with Congress over money and supplies grew fiercer. The winter of 1779–1780 was harsher than Valley Forge and several units mutinied. In January 1781 a delegation of 1,000 troops from Pennsylvania marched on the Congress in Philadelphia to protest: They hadn't been paid in a year and had no winter clothes. Other units mutinied during 1781. One of those involved, Joseph Martin from Connecticut, explained their grievances: "For several days . . . we got a little musty bread, and a little beef about every other day, but this lasted only a short time and then we got nothing at all. The men were now exasperated beyond endurance . . . they saw no other alternative but to starve to death, or break up the army, give all up and go home."[30] They did not go home but, for a few days, they refused to obey orders. In the short term the mutiny had some effect and Martin's unit got some provisions, but the basic problems of bad food and intermittent pay were never solved. To veterans like Martin the treatment of the army was rank betrayal for loyal service; to Washington and his lieutenants— men such as Alexander Hamilton—it proved that the new nation needed a stronger central government.

Meanwhile, the British had shifted their main campaign to Virginia and the Carolinas. Having failed to knock New England out of the war in 1777, they now hoped to rally southern loyalists. In May 1780 Lord Cornwallis's troops captured Charleston after a three-month siege and won a series of victories against American troops, yet he could not swing southerners back to Britain. Then came the second decisive engagement of the war. Washington finally abandoned a futile attempt to capture New York and, with dramatic surprise, marched his own troops and the French army down to Virginia to trap Cornwallis on the York peninsula. The crucial factor was the French fleet, which blockaded Cornwallis from the sea. Denied reinforcements or the hope of evacuation, the British surrendered in October 1781.

Joseph Martin was among the troops who witnessed the British laying down their arms. American units were on one side of the road, and the French on the other, so Cornwallis's men had to run the gauntlet of humiliation. The general himself did not appear, leaving that embarrassment to his deputy. After long delays, Martin saw the British finally marched out of their camp, "all armed, with bayonets fixed, drums beating and faces lengthening. . . . The British paid the Americans, seemingly, but little attention as they passed them, but they eyed the French with considerable malice." Martin also saw in the woods what he called "herds of Ne-groes which lord Cornwallis (after he had inveigled them from their proprietors) in love and pity to them had turned adrift, with no other recompense for their confidence in his humanity than the small pox for their bounty and death for their wages. They might be seen scattered about in every direction, dead and dying, with pieces of ears of burnt Indian corn in the hands and mouths."[31]

Saratoga turned the war; Yorktown decided it. Without American courage and stamina, the struggle could easily have been lost, yet without French support, outright victory would have been difficult to attain. The conflict could have dragged on for years, with the British controlling some parts of the seaboard and the Americans others. But after Yorktown, Americans knew that a victorious peace was only a matter of time. After a lengthy diplomatic finale, in September 1783 the British signed the Treaty of Paris, acknowledging full independence for the United States.

Eight and a half years had elapsed since Lexington and Concord. Some areas of America had been little touched by the war—Massachusetts, the initial battlefield, after 1776; Virginia until the Yorktown campaign of 1781. Other states had been fought over extensively, particularly the Carolinas and Georgia. Some 25,000 American soldiers died in the battle for independence—a third in combat, two-thirds from disease. But for Washington's farsighted policy of smallpox inoculation, the death toll could have been much higher.

Yet this was not simply a struggle of Americans against British and Germans; it was also a civil war. About a fifth of white Americans remained loyal to the Crown, including many of the colonial elite, and thousands fought with the British army. After the peace treaty they settled in Canada or in sad exile in Britain. Blacks fought on both sides: Some slaves won their freedom fighting with the British against the soldiers of American liberty. The war even split families. Benjamin Franklin was a fervent patriot who had helped Jefferson draft the Declaration of Independence. His son, William, the royal governor of New Jersey, remained an ardent loyalist during the war. Theirs was a genuine clash of principles, but Ben took their breach very personally: "[N]othing has ever hurt me so much and affected me with such keen Sensations, as to find my self deserted in my old Age by my only Son; and not only deserted, but to find him taking up Arms against me, in a Cause wherein my good Fame, fortune and Life were all at stake."[32] The two Franklins met but once after the war, and then only so Ben could secure payment for debts owed to him. They never communicated again.

But on the political level, parent and child—Britain and America—had to get along in the world of nations. On June 1, 1785, John Adams presented his credentials at St. James's Palace as the first U.S. ambassador to Britain. Bowing three times to the king against whom he had rebelled, he declared in a voice quavering with emotion: "I shall esteem my self the happiest of men if I can be instrumental in recommending my country more and more to your Majesty's royal benevolence." His aim, he said, was to restore "the old good nature and the old good humor between people who, though separated by an ocean and under different governments, have the same language, a similar religion, and kindred blood." Even allowing for his notorious stutter, George III seemed yet more moved than his former subject: "I will be very frank with you, I was the last to consent to separation; but the separation having been made, and having become inevitable, I have always said, as I say now, that I would be the first to meet the friendship of the United States as an independent power."[33]

Fine words from both sides; living up to them would prove much harder.

COMPROMISING ON A CONSTITUTION

Breaking from Britain was difficult enough but the United States now had to invent a new government. By the mid-1780s the nation was facing a twofold political crisis.

In 1776 and 1777 each of the former colonies had rewritten their constitutions as independent states. The main agents of British power had been the colonial governors, so most states cut back the powers of their governors and enlarged the authority of the elected assemblies. Pennsylvania went so far as to abolish the governorship entirely, running the state through a single-chamber assembly and an executive council, the presidency of which rotated among its members. Many states reduced the property qualifications required for voters, instituted annual elections, and gave more seats in their assemblies to the western backcountry. In New Hampshire, for instance, the colonial assembly had only thirty-four members in 1765, generally wealthy gentlemen from around the seaport of Portsmouth; in 1786 the new House of Representatives had eighty-eight members, mostly farmers, lawyers, or small merchants, and the state capital had relocated from Portsmouth to Concord in the interior. In Massachusetts the new state constitution was even ratified by the voters, on the grounds that the "people" were "sovereign."

By the 1780s, however, many observers felt that the pendulum had swung too far. State assemblymen, often from low down the social ladder, passed a series of laws to satisfy various interest groups such as farmers, merchants, debtors, and speculators. They also assumed many of the functions of the executive and the judiciary and often recklessly printed paper money to pay the bills. In Virginia, complained Thomas Jefferson, "all the powers of government, legislative, executive, and judiciary, result to the legislative body. The concentrating [of] these in the same hands is precisely the definition of despotic government. It will be no alleviation that these powers will be exercised by a plurality of hands, and not by a single one. 173 despots would surely be as oppressive as one." Jefferson insisted that "an elective despotism was not the government we fought for."[34]

The democratic despotism of the state assemblies was one major problem for the new nation. Equally pressing were the deficiencies of the Articles of Confederation, under which the war for independence had been fought. The Confederation was really a loose league of independent and sovereign states rather than a proper national government. Its controlling principle was one state, one vote—so tiny Rhode Island carried as much weight as its much larger and more populous neighbor Massachusetts. The Confederation had no strong executive but, rather like the state of Pennsylvania, only a rotating presidency. It lacked even the authority to levy taxes: Funds were voted by the states and they proved notoriously reluctant to pay for the war—hence the army mutinies of 1780 and 1781. Since the Congress did have the power to print and borrow money, the result, predictably, was soaring inflation and a massive war debt. America got through the war thanks to a small network of wealthy merchants and financiers who used their personal credit to raise money and manage supplies, notably Robert Morris from Philadelphia. But their corruption and self-aggrandizement caused a backlash after the war among the rural interests that still dominated Congress.

As the 1780s progressed, the crisis of governance became acute. American credit was exhausted: The Dutch and the French kept lending only at extortionate levels of interest. Trade could help balance the books, but power to negotiate trade agreements remained with the states and they were now waging a commercial war among themselves. Connecticut was levying higher tariffs on goods from neighboring Massachusetts than on imports from Britain.[35]

Eventually all but one of the states agreed to send delegates to a Constitutional Convention in Philadelphia in May 1787, presided over by George Washington. Rhode Island, acutely sensitive about its autonomy, refused to have anything to do with the whole business. The fifty-five delegates were largely men of substance— gentry and lawyers; most had already served in the Continental Congress and a third in Washington's army. So they tended to be conservative in social attitudes and nation-minded in political perspective. But this shared outlook, at odds with that of most Americans, did not guarantee consensus: The convention argued and bargained over four long, hot months.

The result, inevitably, was a compromise between many divergent views, but the man who contributed most to the outcome was James Madison from Virginia. He had his chance because the giants of 1776—Thomas Jefferson and John Adams— were representing their country as ambassadors in Europe. Madison was not an obvious leader. Five foot six and sickly, usually dressed in black and often cripplingly shy, he looked like a diffident schoolmaster. But on the debating floor "little Jimmy Madison" was a match for anyone—crisp, fluent, yet disarmingly diffident—and he also had a plan. Madison did not want to tinker with the existing Confederation: A few extra teeth would do little for a body that lacked brawn or brain. He wanted to turn this inefficient alliance into a true national government— one that could check the excesses of the states and their overly democratic assemblies.

As soon as the Convention began, the Virginians mounted a preemptive strike, submitting a full-scale plan based on Madison's ideas. It took those states who opposed it a couple of weeks to get their act together and then, in the person of William Paterson of New Jersey, they offered only a strengthened version of the Articles, with additional powers such as taxation. Paterson argued that "if the confederacy was radically wrong, let us return to our States, and obtain larger powers, not assume them of ourselves. I came here not to speak my own sentiments, but the sentiments of those who sent me."[36] Few delegates wanted to go back to their states for further authority—that would waste the summer—but many were wary of Madison's vision for a national government. The biggest stumbling block, as Paterson noted, was the equality of all the states. This had hamstrung the Congress in wartime and infuriated big states such as Virginia and Pennsylvania, yet smaller states feared that their interests would be overruled without guaranteed equality. "I do not, gentlemen, trust you," thundered Gunning Bedford—a fiery representative from Delaware—to the big states. "If you possess the power, the abuse of it could not be checked; and what then would prevent you from exercising it to our destruction? . . . The small states never can agree to the Virginia Plan. . . . Is it come to this, then, that *the sword* must decide this controversy, and that the horrors of war must be added to the rest of our misfortunes?"[37]

The great compromise made by the delegates at Philadelphia was a split deal. In the lower house of the legislature, representation would be determined by the state's population. So Virginia would have ten seats, Rhode Island one. But in the upper house or Senate, each state regardless of size would have two seats. This ensured a degree of balance.

Madison believed that an even greater danger than the friction between small and large states was "the great southern and northern interests of the continent being opposed to each other."[38] This was code for the institution of slavery, which could not be touched if the Constitution were to gain southern approval. In fact, the South was allowed to use slaves for political advantage, counting them as three-fifths of a person when allocating the number of seats each state held in the House of Representatives, even though slaves were not part of the electorate. A few northerners denounced this as a sordid deal—Gouverneur Morris of New York asking "[U]pon what principle is it that the slaves shall be computed in the representation? Are they men? Then make them Citizens & let them vote. Are they property? Why then is no other property included?" Allowing the South to count slaves to increase its seats in the Congress meant, he said, that someone from Georgia or South Carolina "who goes to the Coast of Africa and in defiance of the most sacred laws of humanity tears away his fellow creatures from their dearest connections & damns them to the most cruel bondages shall have more votes in a Government instituted for protection of the rights of mankind than the Citizen of Pennsylvania or New Jersey who views with a laudable horror so nefarious a practice."[39]

But most Northerners in the Constitutional Convention accepted that slavery was the price of unity. Some hoped at least to stop the import of more slaves from Africa, yet South Carolina and Georgia held out against that—eventually agreeing that the question of banning the international slave trade could be reopened twenty years hence in 1808. This was a fateful decision because over those intervening two decades slavery became entrenched in the South.

Apart from the rights of states and the persistence of slavery, the third big issue was the balance within the new federal government. Madison had wanted the national government to have a veto power over state laws deemed harmful to the country and the right to legislate in areas where the states were incompetent. Again this was too much for many of the delegates at Philadelphia, so another deal was eventually struck. The Constitution listed the responsibilities granted exclusively to the new federal government, including diplomacy, war, taxation, borrowing, and coining money and the regulation of trade. These were all areas where the states had abused their position in the 1780s. On the face of it, all other powers were reserved to the states but, as with so many legal documents, there was a loophole. Congress was granted the authority to "make all Laws which shall be necessary and proper for carrying into Execution the foregoing Powers, and all other Powers vested by this Constitution in the Government of the United States."[40] This "necessary and proper clause"—the so-called implied powers of the federal government—proved to be a loophole through which, over subsequent decades, the national government would repeatedly extend its authority at the expense of the states.

In structuring the federal government, the Convention again compromised—trying to avoid either a tyrannical executive (a new George III) or an all-powerful legislature (Jefferson's "elective despotism"). Delegates wanted the functions of government to balance each other, with a separate executive, legislature, and judiciary. Neither the president nor his departmental heads would sit in the legislature, avoiding a British-style system of a prime minister in control of the Commons, and the Supreme Court would be entirely separate from the legislature, unlike the British House of Lords. To offset the dangers of excessive democracy, in the upper house senators would be chosen by the legislature of their state whereas members of the House of Representatives would be chosen by the people of each state on the basis of the franchise used to elect their lower house. This, it was hoped, would insulate the Senate from the turmoil of popular politics, ensuring that the best men, the aristocracy, would prevail. Senators served for six years, not two as in the House, further enabling them to take the long, enlightened view.

This underlying concept of checks and balances was rooted in a hardheaded view of human nature. "Ambition must be made to counteract ambition," declared Madison. "If men were angels, no government would be necessary. . . . In framing a government which is to be administered by men over men . . . [y]ou must first enable the government to controul the governed; and in the next place, oblige it to controul itself."[41]

The Constitution of 1787 was therefore a bundle of compromises—between big states and small states, between North and South, between the federal government and the states, between the executive and the legislature, between the principles of democracy and aristocracy. But Madison and his colleagues had secured the essence of what they wanted: a national government (though they preferred to call themselves "federalists" rather than the more emotive term "nationalists").

To circumvent both the state governments and the existing Congress, the federalists rested the Constitution on the foundation of popular sovereignty. The preamble proclaimed that "We the People of the United States, in Order to form a more perfect Union . . . do ordain and establish this Constitution."

When the Founders spoke of "the People" they did not entertain notions of democracy—indeed they abhorred the idea. In their republic they assumed that only whites, males, and property owners would vote but, compared with the rest of the world, the franchise was already very broad. As Charles Pinckney of South Carolina remarked,

> The people of the U[nited] States are perhaps the most singular of any we are acquainted with. Among them are fewer distinctions of fortune & less of rank than among the inhabitants of any other nation. . . . I say this equality is likely to continue because in a new Country, possessing immense tracts of uncultivated lands . . . there will be few poor and few dependent—Every member of the Society almost, will enjoy an equal power of arriving at the supreme offices & consequently of directing the strength & sentiments of the whole Community.[42]

"Every member of the Society almost." It would be many decades before women and non-whites gained the vote, but even in the 1780s "the People" had more say in governing America than they did anywhere in Europe and it was to the people that the Constitution was submitted for ratification. Rather than allowing a vote in the state legislatures, the federalists ensured that the Constitution would be approved by specially elected conventions in each state and that the approval of nine of the thirteen states would be sufficient to establish the new government.

Once again the federalists were quick starters. By the New Year of 1788 five states had ratified the Constitution, among them one of the biggest, Pennsylvania. By May another three had followed suit, including Massachusetts, and the "more perfect Union" was close to reaching critical mass. The decisive vote came in New York, where the anti-federalist opposition was particularly well organized. So the federalists mounted an intense propaganda campaign, spearheaded by a series of seventy-seven articles in New York newspapers, mostly written by Madison and the leading New York federalist, Alexander Hamilton.

Hamilton favored a much stronger national government even than Madison, and he continued to say so in these articles. But Madison's political touch was surer, seeking to reassure his readers by showing the compromises on which the Constitution was based. Whereas Hamilton argued that the role of the federal government was to "suppress" factions, Madison argued that it would harness these feuding interest groups within a larger whole. "The latent causes of faction are . . . sown in the nature of man" and these causes "cannot be removed. . . . [R]elief is only to be sought in the means of controlling its effects." Madison felt that the danger was particularly acute in a small country, where a faction could easily become a despotic majority. But "[e]xtend the sphere, and you take in a greater variety of parties and interests; you make it less probable that a majority of the whole will have a common motive to invade the rights of other citizens; or if such a common motive exists . . . to act in unison with each other."[43]

Employing this argument, Madison turned the tables on those who argued that republics could flourish only in small city-states, animated by the "virtue" or civic sense of its populace. The last few years had shown that virtue could not be presumed—the fervent patriotism of 1775–1776 was a peak, not the norm—so realistic politics had to be predicated on "faction" as much as on "virtue." And, in what he called "an extended republic," factions could be managed and tamed.[44]

New York ratified the Constitution, narrowly, in July 1788. How far Hamilton and Madison's rhetoric turned the tide is impossible to say, but their journalism—soon pulled together as a book entitled *The Federalist*—became a classic of American political thought, especially Madison's discussion of faction, what we now call interest-group politics.

Madison and his colleagues at Philadelphia hoped that they had accomplished the necessary balancing act, creating a stronger central government that still reflected the uniquely democratic character of America. Despite its flaws their work endures—still serving as the framework for a country that has changed beyond all recognition in the intervening two centuries. This formal written Constitution marks the United States out from Britain; again and again U.S. political debate has revolved around interpretations of the text. The document itself became a sacred text; together with the Declaration of Independence it is displayed today at the National Archives in Washington, in what can only be described as a shrine. Many Americans revere their Founding Fathers as almost patron saints.

In some ways the United States is a monument to the ideals of the Enlightenment, to the conviction that it is possible to establish politics and society on the basis of human reason. Both the Declaration of Independence and the U.S. Constitution exemplify that belief in rationality. Yet both these documents stemmed from English political practices, from ideas about liberty, representation, and power rooted in the colonial past but radically pruned by the experience of revolution. These great texts were also, as we have seen, intensely political documents—compromises among various views, rather than abstract blueprints. Although some American jurists over the centuries have treated the Constitution as if set in stone, like the tablets brought down from Mount Sinai, it has proved to be a living document—applied elastically by political leaders, interpreted creatively by the Supreme Court, and rewritten on many occasions by formal amendments. This process was essential to make the republic work in practice. And it started with the Founders themselves.

MAKING THE REPUBLIC WORK

A fifty-foot barge manned by thirteen oarsmen clad in white rowed him across the Hudson river. A flotilla of specially decorated ships escorted him into New York Harbor. Cannons fired a thirteen-gun salute and the band played "God Save the King." For all the world it looked like a coronation. But the words sung by the chorus were very different from Britain's national anthem:

> *Thrice welcome to this shore,*
> *Our Leader now no more,*
> *But Ruler thou.*

And the man being honored was not George III but George Washington. He came to New York on April 30, 1789, to be inaugurated as America's first president.

Although intensely ambitious, Washington was genuinely reluctant to become America's political leader. Now feeling his rheumatism and his age—fifty-seven—he yearned to stay at Mount Vernon, his plantation above the Potomac river in Virginia. After leading his country to victory and independence on the battlefield, what could he possibly do as an encore? Any return to public life would surely be an anti-climax, or even a humiliation. He assured a wartime colleague that "my movement to the chair of Government will be accompanied with feelings not unlike those of a culprit who is going to the place of his execution: so unwilling am I, in the evening of a life nearly consumed in public cares, to quit a peaceful abode for an Ocean of difficulties, without that competency of political skill, abilities and inclinations which is necessary to manage the helm."[45]

But Washington accepted the unanimous sentence of the electors—at this stage not the mass of the people but a group of wise men appointed by the states—because he was convinced that America desperately needed a stronger national government if independence and liberty were to survive. In fact, he was the one and only nominee for the post and most of those at the Constitutional Convention in Philadelphia had him firmly in mind when they wrote the Constitution. Otherwise they would have balked at the idea of a chief executive and commander-in-chief with almost regal powers, including the right to veto laws passed by Congress.

One of the Washington administration's earliest tasks was to flesh out the Constitution's vague outline of the judicial branch of the federal government. The president himself considered this department "the Key-Stone of our political fabric." But the states were very sensitive on the issue, partly to protect lawyers' business but also out of jealousy for local autonomy. The judiciary, wrote Edmund Pendleton, a leading Virginian lawyer, "is the Sore part of the Constitution & requires the lenient touch of Congress." Anti-federalists hoped to limit the federal judiciary to a few areas, such as disputes among the states or between the United States and foreign governments. A congressional committee haggled over the issue for months but federalists eventually ensured that a truly national system was established to enforce federal law. The Judiciary Act of September 1789 set up thirteen district courts, largely coterminous with the thirteen states, divided into local circuits and capped by a Supreme Court. The Constitution had already specified that justices of the Court would be appointed by the president with the consent of the Senate, but the scope of their authority remained to be defined. This, as we shall see, would be an abiding source of controversy.[46]

President Washington was one reason the new government got off to a good start in 1789, but equally important was the Bill of Rights. The Founders had considered including such a list of guaranteed rights in the Constitution in 1787 but it was omitted for fear of lengthy debate and also because, as Charles Pinckney remarked to fellow slave owners back home in South Carolina, "[s]uch bills generally begin with declaring that all men are by nature born free. Now, we should make that declaration with a very bad grace when a large part of our property consists in men who are actually born slaves."[47] But in many of the states opponents of the Constitution had demanded a bill of rights, so Madison drafted a set of twelve amendments intended to "extinguish from the bosom of every member of the community any apprehensions that there are those among his countrymen who wish to deprive them of the liberty for which they valiantly fought and honorably bled."[48] After four months of argument, Congress approved a revised version of Madison's amendments to the Constitution—ten of which were ratified by the states. Known as the Bill of Rights, they have been as central to subsequent American history as the Constitution itself.

The most celebrated example is probably the Second Amendment, which reads, in full: "A well-regulated Militia being necessary to the security of a free State, the right of the people to bear Arms shall not be infringed." In other words, because of the need for each state to have its militia, citizens should possess weapons and know how to use them. This was a reasonable principle in the late eighteenth century but it is arguable whether a state militia is so essential today, in the era of a professional army, modern police forces, and the FBI. In June 2008 a conservative majority of the U.S. Supreme Court upheld an unconditional right for individuals to bear arms, but the acrimonious debate about gun control will rumble on. The Second Amendment is a classic example of how, in a manner distinctively American, political debate easily slides into constitutional argument.

Equally important has been the Tenth Amendment, which sought to circumscribe the authority of the federal government: "The powers not delegated to the United States by the Constitution, nor prohibited by it to the States, are reserved to the States respectively, or to the people." Madison had preferred a clear statement, echoing the Declaration of Independence, that "all power is originally vested in, and consequently derived from, the people."[49] Instead, under pressure from anti-federalist supporters of states' rights, the Tenth Amendment equivocated about the source of ultimate power—the states or the people. Here was another battle-ground for the future.

The First Amendment affirmed basic freedoms of speech, assembly, and the press. It also declared that "Congress shall make no law respecting an establishment of religion, or prohibiting the free exercise thereof." So there was to be no state church, no religious tests for people who held office, and freedom of religion for all faiths and for none. During the Revolution, the Anglican Church was disestablished throughout America. Thomas Jefferson, architect of Virginia's far-reaching Statute of Religious Freedom, insisted that the "legitimate powers of government extend to such acts only as are injurious to others." By contrast, said Jefferson, "it does me no injury for my neighbor to say there are twenty gods, or no God. It neither picks my pocket nor breaks my leg." He was sure that "reason and free enquiry are the only effectual agents against error. Give loose to them, they will support the true reli-gion by bringing every false one to their tribunal."[50] Only in New England did Con-gregationalism retain a special position, with local churches supported by tax revenues; elsewhere they had to rely on voluntary contributions.

It is easy from this to conclude that the new United States was a secular society, with no special place for Christianity. But the First Amendment stated only that religion was no concern of the federal government. Most Americans still saw their country as a Protestant nation: It was just that Protestantism would not be enforced and financed by government. Jefferson, a deist, was unusual; for the bulk of his compatriots, faith mattered as much as liberty.

Although the Bill of Rights would be a battleground in the future, its ratification in 1791 helped quell the doubts aroused by the Constitution. Like the person of Washington, it was essential to make the new republic work. Even so, the new gov-ernment nearly fell apart in the president's first term because of the conflict be-tween two of the most senior members of Washington's cabinet—Alexander Hamilton and Thomas Jefferson.

HAMILTON, CAPITALISM, AND THE CAPITAL

These two men came to loathe each other. Jefferson claimed that Hamilton's life, "from the moment at which history can stoop to notice him, is a tissue of machi-nations against the liberty of the country which has not only received and given him bread, but heaped its honors on his head."[51] Personal antipathy aside, however, their root differences were ones of principle. In fact, the clash between Hamilton and Jefferson turned on rival visions of America's future. To understand that, we have to take account of the country's economic situation at the end of the eigh-teenth century.

The United States had continued to grow prodigiously—its population reach-ing 3.9 million by 1790 (including 700,000 slaves)—but in character the country remained overwhelmingly agricultural and rural, unlike Britain, which was now in the throes of rapid industrialization. Around 90 percent of the population was engaged in farming (more than double the proportion in Britain) and most people produced for their own needs rather than for the market. In 1790 there were but five "cities" with more than 10,000 people—they were more like English provincial towns—and even the largest, Philadelphia, did not exceed 50,000 inhabitants. (London by this time had nearly a million.) Industrial activity was mostly small scale and household based, concentrating on basic needs such as textiles and shoes. The economy as a whole remained heavily reliant on manufactured imports from Europe, especially Britain. Yet America's capacity to import depended on its ability to export primary products across the Atlantic. Lumber, fish, and salted meat remained profitable northern exports, but the key commodities were tobacco, rice, and, increasingly, cotton from the South—cultivated by slave labor. This Atlantic trade, and the credit nexus on which it rested, had been seriously disrupted by the war with Britain, leading to a fall in Americans' living standards.

Hamilton and Jefferson adopted very different perspectives on this economic situation—reflecting their own personal background. Hamilton, the illegitimate son of a Scottish merchant in the West Indies, moved to New York at the age of seventeen and trained for the law. His life was therefore bound up with the transatlantic web of trade and finance that connected the east coast of the United States with the Caribbean, Africa, and Britain. For him, these were the arteries of America's wealth; they should not be severed just because the country had broken with Britain. His awareness of the need for efficient finance was strengthened by his years as one of Washington's aides in the Continental Army, haggling with Congress for funds and supplies.

So Hamilton saw America's future as a mercantile, capitalist nation. As America's first secretary of the Treasury, he set out to make that vision a reality. In a series of reports that had a lasting impact, he proposed a national bank to manage government funds, excise duties to raise revenue, protective tariffs to restrict imports and foster American industries, and the promotion of roads and canals to develop internal trade. "Not only the wealth but the independence and security of a country appear to be materially connected with the prosperity of manufactures," Hamilton argued. "The extreme embarrassments of the United States during the late War, from an incapacity of supplying themselves, are still [a] matter of keen recollection: A future war might be expected again to exemplify the mischiefs and dangers of a situation to which that incapacity is still, in too great a degree, applicable, unless changed by timely and vigorous exertion."[52]

But Hamilton's vision of America as a great manufacturing nation appalled Jefferson—a gentleman farmer from Virginia. "In Europe the lands are either cultivated, or locked up against the cultivator," he stated. "Manufacture must therefore be resorted to of necessity not of choice, to support the surplus of their people. But we have an immensity of land courting the industry of the husbandman." In his

most lyrical vein, Jefferson asserted that "those who labor in the earth are the chosen people of God" and claimed that America's greatest asset was its free farmers—
tilling the soil and holding a stake in society by owning land—whereas those who
made money through speculation or wage-labor were parasites on the body politic:
"Dependence begets subservience and venality, suffocates the germ of virtue, and
prepares fit tools for the designs of ambition. . . . While we have land to labor then,
let us never wish to see our citizens occupied at a work-bench, or twirling a distaff."
Big cities, by contrast, were dens of corruption whose unemployed mobs "add just
so much to the support of pure government, as sores do to the strength of the
human body."[53]

Jefferson's image of the industrious self-sufficient husbandmen was a highly romanticized portrait of Virginia, given the state's reliance on crops for the European
market, cultivated by African slaves and funded by British credit. Jefferson's own affluent cosmopolitan lifestyle depended on this system. But his own personal debts
strengthened Jefferson's ideological antipathy toward speculators; deeply distrust-
ful of Britain, unlike Hamilton, he believed that the country's burgeoning industry
and national debt were signs of corruption, not progress. For Jefferson dependence
on others—financial, legal, or political—was the absolute antithesis of liberty.

The two men looked at America in fundamentally different ways. Hamilton had
no native country apart from the United States. An interloper from the Caribbean,
he had gambled on the Revolution and won. His adopted city was the capitalist
hub, New York, and he could not conceive of the intricate bonds of land and people that formed Virginian society. For Jefferson, by contrast, New York, like most
cities, represented an alien world. When speaking of his "country," he really meant
Virginia. His backcountry estate at Monticello near Charlottesville faced toward
the Appalachians and into the heartland of the continent. That, for him, was where
America's future lay. Each man had no doubt that the new republic was destined for
greatness, both speaking of it as a coming "empire," but they looked quite literally
in opposite directions—Hamilton to the east and Jefferson to the west. The issue
was not resolved in their lifetimes—in fact, it became one of the most enduring
debates in American history—and, in the end, both men were proved right.

But that is to look far ahead. In 1790 Hamilton's plan for funding America's
wartime debts generated a political crisis for the new nation. As Treasury secretary he
was trying to sort out the financial mess left over from massive and chaotic wartime
borrowing. Hamilton estimated the country's total obligations at $77 million—
equivalent to perhaps $5 trillion today—some of it owed to foreign governments but
most to Americans. He believed that a sound national debt was one of Britain's great
assets, enabling it to wage war without financial bankruptcy (as happened in France),
and he was sure that America needed to emulate the British example: "To be able to
borrow upon good terms, it is essential that the credit of a nation should be well established. . . . States, like individuals, who observe their engagements, are respected and
trusted: while the reverse is the fate of those, who pursue an opposite conduct." Hamil-

ton believed that this reflection derived "additional strength from the nature of the debt of the United States. It was the price of liberty. The faith of America has been repeatedly pledged for it."[54]

Hamilton therefore proposed that the federal government take over $40 million of debts owed to individual lenders by the Continental Congress and to do so at par—meaning paying the face value on the notes and securities. Madison objected that many patriots who had originally lent money to the cause, including soldiers who had been given the securities in lieu of pay, had since sold the notes at a fraction of their original value. Redeeming them at par would benefit the speculators who had bought them up, mostly men from the North. Hamilton, in good capitalist fashion, contended that each speculator had "paid what the commodity was worth in the market, and took the risks of reimbursement upon himself." So he "ought to reap the benefit of his hazard" because a "discrimination between the different classes of creditors of the United States cannot with propriety be made."[55]

Hamilton's proposals provoked a general outcry. Benjamin Rush, one of the firebrands of 1776, told Madison: "Never have I heard more rage expressed against the Oppressors of our Country during the late War than I daily hear against the men who . . . are to reap all the benefits of the revolution, at the expence of the greatest part of the Virtue & property that purchased it." In his opinion, "many of them are not worthy of the priviledges of Citizenship in the United States."[56]

In February 1790, however, the House of Representatives voted by a majority of two to one to approve Hamilton's proposals for funding the debt. So a furious Madison was all the more determined to block Hamilton's other big idea, that the federal government assume the debts that individual states had run up in order to finance their share of the war. Amounting to about $25 million, these outstanding obligations were largely the preserve of northern states. Virginia and most of the South had virtually paid off their war debts. Hamilton's proposal was therefore unjust to southerners, said Madison, by "compelling them, after having done their duty, to contribute to those states who have not equally done their duty."[57]

Madison managed the opposition with great skill and by June 1790 Hamilton was in despair about the keystone of his plans to rebuild the nation's credit. Given their mutual antipathy, Jefferson might have been expected to plunge in the knife, but he was also a practical politician who did not stand on principle when opportunity knocked. What interested him was not capitalism but the debate about where to situate America's capital.

This question had become almost a joke. Since independence the Congress had moved from town to town like a travelling circus. By 1790 no fewer than sixteen sites had been proposed, from New York to the Potomac. The front-runner seemed to be Philadelphia, America's largest city located in the middle of the eastern seaboard, but no group was willing to give way. Local pride was a big factor but so was the economic benefit from new industries and services, by now estimated at half a million dollars a year. A newspaper editor from the state of Maine deplored all the wrangling: "We should remember the question is not what will be most convenient or best suit the interest of New England. But what does the interest of the Union require? . . . But that last I suppose would be an odd question in Congress. There it is the *Southern* interest, or the *Northern*; and every man of them ranges himself upon one side or the other and contends with as much earnestness and warmth as if at an Olympic Game."[58]

The Virginians were particularly fierce competitors: Convinced that the Potomac river led deep into America's interior, they believed it could be a gateway to the riches of the West. Jefferson, though despising commerce in principle, had no intention of missing such a chance. In a typical piece of casuistry he told George Washington: "All the world is becoming commercial. Was it practicable to keep our new empire separated from them we might indulge ourselves in speculating whether commerce contributes to the happiness of mankind." But, insisted Jefferson, "we cannot separate ourselves from them. Our citizens have had too full a taste of the comforts furnished by the arts and manufactures to be debarred the use of them. We must then in our own defense endeavor to share as large a portion as we can of this modern source of wealth and power. . . . Nature . . . has declared in favour of the Patowmac, and through that channel offers to pour into our lap the whole commerce of the Western world." Washington replied: "My opinion coincides perfectly with yours."[59]

The deadlock between Hamilton and Madison over the debt gave Jefferson his chance. He invited the two men to dinner at his house in New York—57 Maiden Lane, a few blocks from present-day Wall Street. He was living there in 1790 because the federal circus was then encamped in New York. During the evening, a deal was reached. Madison would withdraw his opposition to assuming the state debts but since, in Jefferson's words, "the pill would be a bitter one to the Southern states, something should be done to soothe them." It was agreed that the decision to build the new seat of government on the Potomac "would probably be a popular one with them, and would be a proper one to follow the assumption."[60]

There was, of course, more to the deal than Jefferson's laconic letter—the dinner was actually the centerpiece of a complex set of meetings among politicians—but essentially Hamilton got his financial plan through Congress, while Madison and Jefferson brought the federal capital to the Potomac.[61] As Jefferson grasped the full scope of Hamilton's financial system, he felt that he had been "duped," later telling George Washington that "of all the errors of my political life, this has occasioned me the deepest regret."[62] But the deal he brokered in 1790 held the infant United States together, when it seemed in danger of breaking up just months after the new Constitution had been ratified. This was the first of three great compromises thirty years apart—in 1790, 1820, and 1850—that kept North and South in the Union despite growing sectional strains.

In 1791 a diamond of land ten miles by ten was carved out of Virginia and Maryland. Known as the District of Columbia, it belonged to no state and even today remains under the overall control of the federal government. As president, Washington devoted an enormous amount of time and energy to designing the new capital, which Congress decreed would bear his name. The plans drawn up by his chosen architect, Pierre L'Enfant, situated the "President's Palace" on one small hill and the "Congress House" on another to the east, linked together by a spacious avenue 160 feet wide. But L'Enfant's designs were deemed too grandiose, funds were cut, and little was built.[63] Worse still, it seemed that nobody wanted to live in Washington. Land auctions attracted virtually no takers, merchants did not want to relocate, and trade along the Potomac was pathetic; Philadelphia, New York, and Boston remained America's great ports. In 1800 the new capital had fewer than 400 "habitable" dwellings, most of which were described as "small miserable huts."[64]

When President John Adams, George Washington's successor, was finally able to move down to the city at the end of that year, the presidential mansion stood in a weed-ridden field full of stones and rubble and the building itself reeked of wet paint and new plaster. "The house is made habitable, but there is not a single apartment finished," complained Adams's wife, Abigail. "We have not the least fence, yard, or other convenience, without, and the great unfinished audience-room I make a drying-room of, to hang up the clothes in."[65] So Mrs. Adams pegged out her laundry in the unplastered East Room—venue today for the grandest of state occasions. Despite their grumbles, however, John and Abigail Adams sensed the potential of this raw building. The morning after moving in, the president sat down at his desk, took out a sheet of paper, and wrote: "President's House, Washington City, Nov. 2, 1800. I pray heaven to bestow the best of blessings on this house and all that shall hereafter inhabit. May none but honest and wise men ever rule under this roof."[66]

For decades the great capital on the Potomac remained a mess; with boardwalks through the mud linking isolated, often unfinished, classical buildings, the effect was rather like wandering through Roman ruins. Diplomats in full regalia paying their respects at the White House would often alight from their carriages only to sink ankle deep into red mud. European visitors, accustomed to London or Paris, scoffed at the squalor of America's invented capital. It seemed to sum up the bombastic pretensions of the upstart new republic. The grandeur of modern Washington, D.C., like Hamilton's economic empire, lay far in the future.

Yet the desolation that was Washington testified to a deeper truth about U.S. politics. The president disappeared for at least three months of the year; Congress was usually in session only from November to March, between harvest and spring planting; and the Supreme Court needed just a couple of months to transact its annual business. The federal government had been created, reluctantly, for specific purposes such as defense (which accounted for 70 percent of the 9,000 federal employees in 1802) or collection of customs and distribution of the mail (another 25 percent).[67] The real locus of governmental power lay in the states and especially the towns or counties. That's what the Founders meant by federalism—not centralization but its very opposite, devolution. Washington, D.C., looked marginal because it *was* marginal to the lives of most Americans, and so it remained for much of the nineteenth century.

Here was the essence of American republicanism. The Founders, borrowing from classical and English political thought, believed in "a civic and patriot ideal in which the personality was founded in property, perfected in citizenship but perpetually threatened by corruption."[68] The classical republican ideal was expressed in the public architecture of the time, from Jefferson's Palladian mansion at Monticello to L'Enfant's designs for the new capital. "I think it of very great importance to fix the taste of our country properly," wrote Gouverneur Morris to George Washington in 1790, "and I think that your example will go very far in that respect," adding that "everything about you should be *substantially good and majestically plain*."[69] Such majestic plainness was also expressed in the new nation's historic portraiture, pioneered by Benjamin West, the self-taught son of a Philadelphia tavern-keeper, and continued by John Trumbull of Boston, who immortalized the men of 1776. Here were depicted America's modern Romans—the intellectual descendants of Cato and Cicero—garbed in eighteenth-century dress but embodying the same noble republican virtues.

Yet the new government that the Founders celebrated was, according to their classical values, also the principal source of corruption, operating through such means as political patronage, factions, established churches, and standing armies (as opposed to local militias). Many of the Founders, like Jefferson, also believed that a moneyed interest, founded in a national debt, was a particularly corrupting force, but Hamilton, for one, did not agree and the debate over the capital showed that for Jefferson pragmatism often outweighed principle. This, too, was a sign of things to come. As America's independence remained under threat in the 1790s and 1800s, more compromises would be made with the hallowed ideals of republican liberty in order to protect national security.

4

LIBERTY AND SECURITY

The United States was the child of world wars. In the conflict of 1756–1763 the British drove the French from North America; in the next round, French support for the American rebels helped ensure their independence in 1783. Yet that conflict bankrupted the French monarchy—opening the floodgates to revolution, dictatorship, and another two decades of global conflict.

The infant American republic took its first shaky steps amid this third world war, as France and Britain battled for hegemony. In foreign policy the United States experimented with neutrality and belligerency, even suffering the humiliation of British redcoats burning Washington. Internally, the country was torn apart by partisans of Britain and France, each offering a very different model for America's future development and polarizing the country at times between North and South. This atmosphere of intense insecurity prompted a conservative backlash and the Founders did not follow through on the full implications of 1776. They baulked at allowing equal freedom for women, and even the most assertive libertarians, such as Thomas Jefferson, could not break their bondage to slavery.

In this dangerous world of predatory empires, the Founders had little doubt that the United States needed to become an empire of its own in order to survive. Jefferson was both the architect and builder, but westward expansion came at a price—driving the Native American tribes off their lands and using slave labor to help cultivate the new territories. Jefferson envisaged the United States as the great "empire of liberty," closing his eyes to the paradoxes entailed by this felicitous phrase. His founding generation defined the scope of empire and the limits of liberty in ways that would shape the rest of American history.

WAR AND TERROR

The Bastille fell on July 14, 1789, three months after George Washington's inauguration as president. Before the end of his first term, Louis XVI had been guillotined and Paris radicals were waging total war on the rest of France and Europe, coining our modern terms "terror" and "terrorist." By the time Washington died in 1799, France had a dictator with megalomaniac ambition. "I wanted to rule the world," Napoleon admitted in 1815. "[W]ho wouldn't in my place?"[1]

Washington offered clear guidance about what should be America's place in this world at war, namely to stay out and stay united. In 1793 he issued a proclamation of American neutrality in the European conflict and he stuck to that policy through the rest of his presidency. In what became known as his Farewell Address of 1796, he told his compatriots: "The great rule of conduct for us in regard to foreign nations is, in extending our commercial relations to have with them as little political connection as possible." Europe, said Washington, "has a set of primary interests which to us have none or a very remote relation. Hence she must be engaged in frequent controversies, the causes of which are essentially foreign to our concerns. . . . Our detached and distant situation invites and enables us to pursue a different course."[2]

Washington believed America could get through the world crisis if it managed to "remain one people under an efficient government."[3] But that was a big "if." Most of his Farewell Address was an impassioned plea for unity. Washington urged his countrymen not to put sectional allegiance before national loyalty, not to let partisanship for the North, South, East, or West outweigh their sense of being American. Even more, he warned in true republican vein against "the baneful effects of the spirit of party," particularly parties polarized by the war between Britain and France: "[A] passionate attachment of one nation for another," he said, "gives to ambitious, corrupted, or deluded citizens (who devote themselves to the favorite nation) facility to betray or sacrifice the interests of their own country without odium, sometimes even with popularity."[4]

In Washington's second term as president (1793–1797) the political elite and much of the country became polarized between partisans of Jefferson and Hamilton, known respectively as the Republicans and the Federalists. In part, this was a continuation of the arguments over ratification of the Constitution, with the Republicans taking up the anti-federalist suspicion of a strong national government. Mutual animosity was intensified by the French Revolution, about which the two parties held fiercely contrasting views, especially on its implications for America. The Republicans were strongest in the South and the Federalists in the North. This was exactly the scenario Washington feared.

Jefferson, who loved France and all things French, believed that the Revolution of 1789 was carrying on the cause that Americans had begun a decade earlier. "The liberty of the whole earth was depending on the issue of the contest," he declared in 1793. "My own affections have been deeply wounded by some of the martyrs to this cause, but rather than it should have failed, I would have seen half the earth desolated. Were there but an Adam and Eve left in every country, and left free, it would be better than as it now is."[5] Even after the Terror broke in full frenzy, Jefferson turned a blind, or at least indulgent, eye. He was much more worried that Hamiltonians would play up events in France to justify a pro-British foreign policy and the repression of liberty at home. He also feared that Washington and Vice-President John Adams were becoming Hamilton's tools, writing to an Italian friend that "in place of that noble love of liberty and republican government which carried us triumphantly thro' the war, an Anglican, monarchical and aristocratical party has sprung up, whose avowed object is to draw over us the substance, as they have already done the forms of the British government." He added cryptically that "it would give you a fever were I to name to you the apostates who have gone over to these heresies, men who were Samsons in the field & Solomons in the council, but who have had their heads shorn by the harlot England."[6] When this letter was leaked to the press, it was widely taken as an attack on Washington and Adams.

Washington, for all his limitations, had been a unifying force but he retired after two four-year terms—setting a firm precedent for his successors—and the political battle intensified when Adams won the election of 1796. Hoping for unity, he retained most of Washington's cabinet, but this was unwise as its members proved passionate Federalists, tied to Hamilton and determined to maintain social order through a strong national government. Relations with Jefferson, an old friend and officially Adams's vice-president, soured into suspicious silence.

By 1798, however, the Jeffersonians were in full retreat as U.S. relations with France teetered on the edge of war. French warships were seizing American merchant ships and, when Adams sought a diplomatic solution, French agents brazenly demanded a loan to the government and a sweetener for the foreign minister, Talleyrand, before talks could even commence. Adams refused to negotiate under such humiliating circumstances and, when he published the French correspondence in the summer of 1798, there was a nationwide outcry. The wife of the British minister wrote jubilantly that the "tide is turned and now flows with violence against the French party."[7] The "Marseillaise," formerly all the rage, was dropped for American patriotic songs such as "Hail, Columbia"—more or less adopted as the national anthem. "Millions for defense but not a cent for tribute" became the slogan of the day and thousands flocked to join the local militias. Hamilton and the Federalists—as paranoid about the French revolutionary threat to America as the Jeffersonians were obsessed about Anglophile "monocrats"—saw their chance. Hamilton got himself made inspector general of the army, effectively its head, and talked of joining forces with Britain to evict France and Spain from the Americas and win a vast American empire. He even proposed borrowing British warships for the infant U.S. navy—an early version in reverse of World War II Lend-Lease.[8]

In the panic the Federalists pushed through Congress four draconian laws known collectively as the Alien and Sedition Acts, under which the president could deport any alien considered "dangerous to the peace and safety of the United States." Adams did not have to use these powers—there was a mass exodus of foreigners, especially French, long before the legislation was passed. And, under the Sedition Act, those found guilty of "any false, scandalous and malicious writing" against the U.S. government, the Congress, or the president, intended to bring them into "contempt or disrepute . . . or to stir up sedition within the United States," could be fined up to $2,000 or imprisoned for a maximum of two years.[9] To critics, this seemed like a blatant attempt to stifle free speech and political debate.

At the end of 1798 Jefferson and Madison prepared special resolutions against the Alien and Sedition Acts, which were passed by the states of Kentucky and Virginia. Their main objection was not the threat to civil liberties but, as they saw it, the unconstitutional abuse of power by the central government. The "several States composing the United States of America are not united on the principle of unlimited submission to their General Government," insisted the Kentucky Resolution drafted by Jefferson. Instead, they had "constituted a General Government for special purposes, delegated to that government certain definite powers, reserving, each State to itself, the residuary mass of right to their own self-government; and that whensoever the General Government assumes undelegated powers, its acts are unauthoritative, void, and of no force." Here was a classic statement of states' rights—a doctrine that would bedevil the Union for the next sixty years and eventually fracture it in civil war.[10]

Initially Virginia and Kentucky could get little support for their arguments in other states. They saw their chance, however, in the election of November 1800, a replay of Adams versus Jefferson in 1796, but this time for much higher stakes and with no holds barred. There was heady talk of rebellion in the manner of 1776 if the other side won.

Adams was pilloried by Republicans as a closet monarchist who wanted to impose a British-style centralized government. They mocked his vanity and love of titles: Whereas Washington was addressed with natural respect as "His Excellency," Adams was lampooned as "His Rotundity." On the other side, Federalists warned that Jefferson wanted a French-style revolution to subvert the Constitution and undermine Christianity. Reverend Timothy Dwight, the president of Yale University, predicted all manner of abominations if the Republicans won: "[W]e may behold a strumpet personating a Goddess on the altar of JEHOVAH," while the Bible would be "cast into a bonfire, the vessels of the sacramental supper borne by an ass in public procession, and our children, either wheedled or terrified, uniting in chanting mockeries against God." Dwight even predicted that "we may see our wives and daughters the victims of legal prostitution."[11]

The 1800 election was a real mess. Each state could select its election day, so the voting spread out from April to October—further increasing the tension. Six states chose their presidential electors by popular vote; the other ten left the choice to the state legislature. Although Jefferson beat Adams, he amassed the same number of electoral college votes as Aaron Burr from New York. Officially Burr was Jefferson's vice-presidential running mate but in 1800 that was not specified on the voting papers. In the event of a tie between two candidates, the issue had to be decided in the U.S. House of Representatives and Federalists saw this as their last chance to stop Jefferson, by throwing their weight behind Burr.

Over ten days in February 1801 the House voted thirty-five times. On each occasion Jefferson fell one short of the absolute majority he needed. In the end the deadlock was broken by James Bayard, a Federalist and the sole congressman from Delaware. He now switched to Jefferson, convinced that "we must risk the Constitution and civil war or take Mr. Jefferson."[12]

John Adams left Washington early on the morning of the inauguration. Humiliated by the Republican press, he could not bear to be present at the handover of power. But Adams left office with a great achievement—a peace treaty with France. Though it came too late to win him reelection, it saved America from being dragged into the world war. Contrary to all the propaganda and paranoia, there was no attempt at an armed uprising; Jefferson's inaugural address was a model of conciliation. He had always believed that extreme Hamiltonians were a tiny, perverted minority in an essentially united nation. Few in the Senate chamber at noon on March 4, 1801, actually heard what Jefferson said. No orator, he mumbled into his script. But his words were printed and read around the nation. "We have called by different names brethren of the same principle. We are all Republicans, we are all Federalists. . . . Let us then with courage and confidence pursue our Federal and Republican principles, our attachment to union and representative government."[13]

Jefferson's irenic message was partly propaganda but it expressed a real truth: The Republican devotion to local liberties and the Federalist commitment to a union of states were both becoming entrenched. On the other hand his administration waged a determined war on the Federalists who, bereft of their leader after Hamilton's death in 1804, gradually withered away outside New England. But Federalist thinking did hang on in the judiciary, despite Jefferson's purge of both judges and their powers. When Supreme Court Justice Samuel Chase stated publicly in 1803 that Jefferson's purge amounted to "mobocracy" and threatened to destroy "peace and order, freedom and prosperity," the president urged his party leaders in Congress to have Chase impeached—in other words, tried before the Senate. The intemperate Chase was unpopular and the Republicans had a large majority in the Senate, so the cards seemed stacked against him. But in 1805 the Senate acquitted him on every charge, judging that his indiscretions did not amount to "treason, bribery, or other high crimes and misdemeanors"—the criteria the Constitution listed as the sole grounds for conviction in a case of impeachment. Here was a fundamental affirmation of the independence of the Supreme Court and the federal judiciary.[14]

Even more important, the Supreme Court carved out for itself a breathtaking claim of judicial supremacy. This was the achievement of John Marshall, who, as the Court's longest-serving chief justice (1801–1835), exerted more influence on U.S. history than many presidents. A Virginian gentleman and lawyer, Marshall was appointed as head of the Supreme Court in the dying days of the Adams administration. Although he and Jefferson were cousins, they were personal and political foes—Marshall being a Federalist imbued with the need for an effective national government. Under him the justices no longer wrote separate opinions; instead the Court delivered a single verdict, usually written by Marshall, and his judgment in *Marbury v. Madison* (February 1803) was a landmark decision in the Court's evolution.

This case was brought by William Marbury, one of Adams's last-minute Federalist appointees (the so-called midnight judges) who had been denied his commission by the Republicans. Marshall's opinion went out of its way to strike down part of the Judiciary Act of 1789 as unconstitutional, thereby arrogating to the Supreme Court the position of final arbiter of the meaning of the Constitution. Written constitutions, he stated, form "the fundamental and paramount law of the nation, and consequently the theory of every such government must be that an act of the legislature repugnant to the constitution is void." Since, Marshall argued, "it is emphatically the province and duty of the judicial department to say what the law is," the highest level of the judiciary—the Supreme Court—had the right to review the constitutionality of legislation. Here in embryo was the doctrine of "judicial review," which gave the Court a role far beyond that specified by the Founders. Yet, equally important, Marshall's verdict demolished Marbury's suit. This followed from his interpretation of the law and the Constitution, but it was also politically adroit because it made the verdict difficult for the Jefferson administration to denounce. Here was an early sign that Supreme Court opinions would be political acts as much as legal judgments.[15]

The doctrine of judicial review would be enlarged over subsequent decades; in the *Marbury* judgment it existed only in outline. But the case established the Supreme Court as an institution of nationwide competence, at odds with a narrow anti-federalist approach to the Constitution. Jefferson certainly regarded the Supreme Court under Marshall as inimical to his conception of America, later describing the U.S. judiciary as "the subtle corps of sappers and miners constantly working underground to undermine the foundations of our confederated fabric." To understand what Jefferson meant by this "confederated fabric" we must look more closely at his understanding of the Union, its liberty, and its future.[16]

JEFFERSON'S WESTERN EMPIRE

One of the biggest challenges for the new nation was what to do about the West. In 1783, at the end of the War of Independence, the British ceded the area north of the

Ohio river and west of the Appalachian Mountains—more than 230 million acres. Americans, from George Washington downward, had been chafing to get into it for years and British attempts at restraint had been a major grievance in the prelude to 1776. But the Ohio territory was still the preserve of Indian tribes and the focus of conflicting land claims by Virginia, New York, and other states. Jefferson was the man who, more than anyone, established a policy for the West; indeed, this was one of his greatest contributions to U.S. history.

Jefferson's approach was summed up in the apparently paradoxical concept of an "empire of liberty."[17] For him, as for many Americans, "empire" did not have to be imperialistic or oppressive; that, he argued in the Declaration of Independence, was the British perversion. His concept of empire was more like a free association of like-minded communities. This was an association constructed horizontally, as it were, through a union of states spreading out across America and also vertically, in layers of self-governing but interdependent republics. He identified "1, the general federal republic, for all concerns foreign and federal; 2, that of the State, for what relates to our own citizens exclusively; 3, the county republics, for the duties and concerns of the county; and 4, the ward republics, for the small, and yet numerous and interesting concerns of the neighborhood."[18] For Jefferson, the republics were bound together in a federal union; hence his declaration in 1801: "[W]e are all republicans, we are all federalists."

This was all at the level of rhetoric, however. Jefferson also made two huge practical contributions to opening the West. The first was in 1784—after peace with Britain, when would-be settlers were pouring across the Appalachians into Indian territory. Congress appointed Jefferson chairman of two committees to deal with the West, and their reports—largely his work—proved of lasting importance. The first set out a general framework for the overall government of the western lands, until the population was sufficient for new states to be formed and admitted into the Union. The second proposed a grid for dividing up this vast area into townships of manageable size. Although Jefferson's proposals were not adopted completely or immediately, they formed the basis of two major laws: the Land Ordinance of 1785 and the Northwest Ordinance of 1787.

Jefferson was a devotee of the decimal system (he also designed America's new currency of dollars and cents) and he advocated a grid of ten-mile squares. Congress thought that too large and, following the New England pattern, its Land Ordinance opted for squares six miles by six, dividing up the terrain into thirty-six subunits each a mile square, or 640 acres. Most of these subunits would then be divided again for sale as smaller lots but, like Jefferson, Congress held back some of the land—reserving four of the thirty-six squares for federal use, such as supporting veterans, and one more—section sixteen—for public education.

Surveying began that summer but it took decades to complete. The work had to be done with compass, theodolite, and, above all, a metal chain of twenty-two yards—the last of which was pegged out again and again. Ten chains made a furlong,

80 chains a mile, and 480 chains constituted one side of a new township. Even on flat land, this would have been demanding work but swamps and forests, rivers and mountains were hard to accommodate in tidy squares and the mapmakers resorted to discreet little zigzags every so often in order to make ends meet. Yet, in modified form, Jefferson's squares are what you can still see today if you fly over the Midwest and the Plains, etched out for mile upon mile in rectilinear fields and straight roads. This was the grid that made the West.

Jefferson's other report, on western government, served as the basis of the Northwest Ordinance of 1787. Again there were modifications. Jefferson had come up with a scheme for the whole of the West, including lands not yet a part of the United States. He mapped fourteen states and even named ten of them—two of which, Michigania and Illinoia, have passed into history. Jefferson, it has to be said, was a bit obsessive. Congress concentrated on those areas recently acquired from Britain and it did not presume to tell the locals what to call themselves. But it did adopt Jefferson's staged progression toward statehood, starting with a territorial governor appointed by Congress, electing an assembly once the population reached 5,000, and applying to join the Union as a state after a territory had 60,000 inhabitants. Despite fierce opposition from the South, Congress also prohibited slavery in any of these Northwest Territories, at a time when it was still legal in some northern states such as New York and New Jersey. The ban on slavery had also been in the Jefferson committee's original report.

The Northwest Ordinance, like the Land Ordinance, provided a template for the future. This step-by-step progression of moving from territory to statehood was adopted right across the United States in the decades that followed. Many in the American West denounced it as colonialism by another name. In 1884, a century after Jefferson had reported, Martin Maginnis of Montana told Congress that territories "are the colonies of your Republic, situated three thousand miles away from Washington by land, as the thirteen colonies were situated three thousand miles away from London by water. And it is a strange thing that the fathers of our Republic . . . established a colonial government as much worse than that which they revolted against as one form of government can be worse than another."[19]

Stripped of its hyperbole, Maginnis's point was valid. Territories were often pawns of Washington, their people denied the basic political rights enjoyed by Americans elsewhere in the Union—as many migrants from the East discovered to their dismay when they lost the right to vote in U.S. elections. And, in some cases, territorial subordination could last a lifetime—more than sixty years for New Mexico and Arizona.

But the vital difference between the United States and the European empires is that the Northwest Ordinance established a clear procedure for moving beyond the colonial stage into equal membership of the Union. Britain usually conceded independence under duress; most of Spain's South American colonies had to fight bitter wars for independence. Of course, far-flung seaborne empires were hard to hold together by consent but the other great continental empire of the nineteenth century, that of tsarist Russia, which was expanding prodigiously at just this time across Asia, also had no such mechanisms. By comparison, what Jefferson had sketched out was indeed an empire of liberty and that empire became massively bigger in 1803, twenty years after victory over Britain. Again Jefferson played a leading role in events, this time as president.

At the end of the eighteenth century the European empires—Britain, France, and Spain—still owned large tracts of North America. Spain was a particular headache for the new republic, since it controlled much of the Mississippi (then the western border of the United States)—including the port of New Orleans, through which the West's vital exports such as flour, meat, and tobacco passed. Under a treaty signed in 1800 in the latest round of horse-trading in the Napoleonic Wars, New Orleans and the whole Spanish territory of Louisiana reverted to France.

Desperate to safeguard America's position, Jefferson, newly inaugurated as president, opened talks in Paris to purchase New Orleans. After they made little progress, he struck a threatening note, strikingly at odds with his reputation as an ardent Francophile, warning the French: "There is on the globe one single spot, the possessor of which is our natural and habitual enemy. It is New Orleans, through which the produce of three-eights of our territory must pass." If France took possession of New Orleans, he thundered, "from that moment we must marry ourselves to the British fleet and nation." French diplomats knew this was bluster and the tangled negotiations dragged on. In the end it was Napoleon who cut the knot. By the spring of 1803, set on invading England and needing ready cash, he exclaimed: "Irresolution and deliberation are no longer in season. I renounce Louisiana."[20]

The U.S. negotiators, Robert Livingston and James Monroe, were supposed to be bargaining simply about New Orleans and had only $10 million to play with. But this offer was clearly too good to refuse and they settled on a price of $15 million for the whole of the vast Louisiana Territory. When the treaty was signed on April 30, 1803, Livingston, who in 1776 had helped Jefferson draft the Declaration of Independence, declared: "We have lived long but this is the noblest work of our whole lives. . . . From this day the United States take their place among the powers of first rank."[21]

Livingston and Monroe had negotiated on their own initiative. It took months for the news to reach Jefferson; he announced it to the American people on the Fourth of July 1803. Republicans hailed the symbolism of a new Declaration of Independence; Federalists asked how a president so ardent for limited government could accept this act of executive power. This was a fair question: If John Adams, let alone Alexander Hamilton, had arranged such a deal, Jefferson would have screamed to the heavens. But, like most politicians, he had no doubts about his own rectitude and was sure that the deal was a godsend for America: "The world will here see such an extent of country under a free and moderate government as it has never yet seen. . . . By enlarging the empire of liberty we . . . provide new sources of renovation should its principles at any time degenerate in those portions of our country which gave them birth."[22]

Under Jefferson's management, the treaty was duly ratified by the U.S. Senate. No one knew the precise dimensions of Louisiana—Jefferson sent an expedition to survey it—but its vastness was clear to all. In fact, Livingston and Monroe had added 530 million acres to the national domain (double the area ceded by Britain in 1783). This pushed America's western border from the Mississippi to the Rockies in an enormous wedge spreading out from a point at New Orleans. Even allowing for interest payments, it was one of the best bargains in history, at roughly four cents an acre.[23]

VICTIMS OF LIBERTY: INDIANS AND BLACKS

For the Indians, however, the Revolution was but another round in a dogged rearguard effort to retain their lands and safeguard their way of life. In 1783 the British government negotiated away the western lands without consulting their inhabitants. A few people in Parliament had qualms—Lord Walsingham asked, "[W]hy not stipulate for their return and peaceful possession of their native lands? . . . Humanity, interest, policy require it." He reminded fellow peers that "the most solemn assurances had been given to these unhappy people from the Crown that they should be for ever protected" and argued that these treaties "ought to have been binding on our honour."[24]

But Lord Shelburne—the shifty prime minister whose government had negotiated the treaty of 1783—ridiculed the idea of "everlasting protection" as "one of those assertions which always sounds well and is calculated to amuse the uninformed mind." What, he asked, "is the meaning of in perpetuo in all treaties? That they shall endure as long as the parties are able to perform the conditions. This is the meaning of all perpetual alliances; and in the present treaty with America, the Indian nations were not abandoned to their enemies; they were remitted to the care of neighbours."[25]

Indian support for Britain against U.S. independence gave the victorious Americans justification for treating them as conquered enemies who, like the Loyalists, had forfeited the rights to their lands. The 1780s saw a succession of frontier skirmishes and crop burnings that gradually chipped away at Indian territory. Fighting subsided for a while in the mid-1790s: The Indians were exhausted and the U.S. government tried to bring some order to frontier affairs through federal purchases of Indian land and the development of trade. Instead of conquered peoples, the policy was now that the tribes were foreign nations, with whom agreements should be negotiated by the U.S. government.

Unlike many frontiersmen who believed that the "savages" were incorrigible, Jefferson hoped they could be "civilized" and brought into the American way of life.

He cherished the Enlightenment ideal of the "noble" savage, believing the Indian "to be, in body and mind, equal to the white man" and judging that "the proofs of genius given by the Indians of North America place them on a level with Whites in the same uncultivated state."[26] Cultivation, in fact, was the name of the game. Jefferson wanted to convert the Indian warriors from nomadic hunters into industrious farmers, thereby freeing their womenfolk for spinning and weaving instead of work in the fields. When, he predicted, they started to tend "a small piece of land, they will perceive how useless to them are their extensive forests, and will be willing to pare them off from time to time in exchange for necessaries for their farms and families. To promote this disposition to exchange lands, which they have to spare and we want, for necessaries, which we have and they want, we shall push our trading uses." In this way, Jefferson was confident, "our settlements will gradually circumscribe and approach the Indians, and they will in time either incorporate with us as citizens of the United States, or remove beyond the Mississippi. The former is certainly the termination of their history most happy for themselves."[27]

This, then, was Jefferson's benevolent solution of the Indian question—to civilize them into U.S. citizens. Some Indian tribes were ready to follow his lead but many were determined to keep their ancestral lands and safeguard their way of life—so the frontier in the great Ohio valley became a war zone. Settler stories about Indian scalpings and massacres, though exaggerated for propaganda purposes, were rooted in fact; cornered and vengeful, many Indian warriors showed no mercy. But the Americans committed atrocities of their own. In eastern Ohio in 1782 men from the Pennsylvania militia butchered nearly a hundred Indian men, women, and children—even though they were converts to Christianity and had already surrendered—systematically crushing their skulls with mallets. One of the militiamen bludgeoned fourteen Indians to death before finally handing his mallet to a comrade: "My arm fails me. Go on with the work. I have done pretty well."[28]

Indian resistance became much more formidable with the advent of a remarkable new leader in 1809. Tecumseh was a Shawnee chief who formed a potent partnership with his brother, a one-eyed religious leader known as The Prophet. Together they played on tribal tradition and nostalgia. Tall, eloquent, and charismatic, Tecumseh forged a coalition of Indian tribes against further cessions of territory, both in his native Ohio country and further south among the Creeks. Even his arch-enemy, William Henry Harrison, the governor of Indiana Territory, who had crafted many of the unequal treaties, described Tecumseh as "one of those uncommon geniuses which spring up occasionally to produce revolutions and overturn the established order of things. If it were not for the vicinity of the United States, he would, perhaps, be the founder of an empire that would rival in glory that of Mexico or Peru."[29]

But, of course, the United States was in the vicinity and its power was too much for Tecumseh. Late in 1811 Harrison defeated some of Tecumseh's followers at

Tippecanoe—a small skirmish but embellished by time and propaganda to win Harrison the presidency three decades later. In 1813 Tecumseh himself was killed by Harrison's troops in a battle in Upper Canada. His confederacy was broken and westward expansion resumed. In the long term, as we shall see, the only option for those who resisted assimilation on American terms was Jefferson's alternative solution of the Indian question—removal and segregation far beyond the Mississippi.

For America's blacks, the Revolutionary era seemed to promise more. Protests against enslavement by Britain made it harder to justify slavery at home and, although the Constitutional Convention of 1787 steered clear of the issue, individual states did not. When Vermont drew up its new constitution in 1777, it affirmed that slavery was a violation of "natural, inherent, and inalienable rights." When a master suing for the return of one of his runaway slaves produced proof of ownership, he was told by a Vermont judge that this wasn't good enough: He would need nothing less than a bill of sale from "God Almighty."[30]

Other states followed suit, but this did not mean black freedom overnight. Because slaves had been economic assets, their owners were given time to adjust. Pennsylvania, which in 1780 became the very first state to abolish slavery, made March 1 the cut-off. No slave born before that date was freed and those children of slaves born after March 1, 1780, would not be freed until the age of twenty-eight—after their owners had extracted some useful work from them. In other words, under the 1780 law no slave would have liberty until at least 1808. Hardly the floodgates of freedom, more a dripping tap.

For those who benefited, however, this was a revolution. Mum Bett was a female slave in western Massachusetts. Her husband fought and died early in the war for America's freedom; eventually she could endure mistreatment no longer and ran away. When her owner sued for return, Mum Bett became a test case in the Massachusetts legal battle against slavery. An all-white jury upheld the plea of her lawyer that she was as free as anyone else. As with all ex-slaves, her first act of independence was the selection of her own name, becoming Elizabeth Freeman. (Many slaves took symbolic surnames such as Freeman, Newman, or Liberty.) Elizabeth was a woman of natural dignity, who became a respected local midwife and nurse and lived until 1829. But she insisted passionately: "Any time while I was a slave, if one minute's freedom had been offered to me, and I had been told I must die at the end of that minute, I would have taken it—just to stand for one minute on God's airth a free woman—I would."[31]

By 1804 all the northern states had laws or constitutions that would gradually kill off slavery. The Northwest Ordinance of 1787 had already banned slavery around the Great Lakes—what became the tier of six states from Ohio to Minnesota—and in 1808 the U.S. Congress voted to end American participation in the African slave trade within two years. Although in the years 1801 to 1810 over 150,000 slaves were shipped across the Atlantic into the United States—the highest figure for any decade in American history[32]—it now seemed that the end of slavery was only a matter of time. As slaves died off, slavery would die out.

That was not what happened, however. Ending the international slave trade enhanced the importance of the internal slave trade. Many slave owners concentrated on breeding new slaves for sale, like prize animals; home-produced slaves replaced African imports. This proved profitable because of the massive demand for slaves as southerners spread west to the Mississippi and beyond. In America's new Southwest, unlike the old Northwest, there was no ban on slave-owning. As New England abolitionists feared, the Louisiana Purchase gave slavery a new lease of life.

Technological change helped sustain the old order. In the eighteenth century cotton had been a minor crop in the South, compared with tobacco and rice. Long-staple cotton could easily be separated from its seed by using a roller contraption rather like a clothes wringer, but this kind of cotton grew only along the coast of South Carolina and Georgia. Inland, short-staple varieties held sway and rollers did not work; the cotton could be separated from the sticky green seeds only by hand and very laboriously.

In heroic narratives of America's development, credit for solving this problem was accorded to one person: Eli Whitney, a young man from Massachusetts living on a plantation in Georgia. According to tradition he came up with an answer in ten days in 1793 using nothing more than Yankee ingenuity. In fact, Whitney was one of several inventors who refined the process. His big contribution was to abandon rollers and use wire teeth and brushes mounted on revolving cylinders to remove the sticky seeds. Even with Whitney's rudimentary gin (short for "engine") fifty pounds of cotton could be extracted per day, compared with one pound by manual methods. But at the same time in South Carolina, Ogden Holmes developed a different method using a series of small circular saws mounted on a single shaft. This proved more successful and is closer to the technology used today.[33]

Whoever invented it, the cotton gin transformed production, making it possible to grow short-staple cotton for the world market. The new Southwest from South Carolina and Georgia across the Mississippi to what became Louisiana was ideal climatically, with at least twenty-three inches of rain a year and 200 frost-free days. During the harvest season from late August to early January, as the bolls of cotton burst on the plants, the cotton fields looked like a white carpet. For the cotton planters, slaves seemed the only possible workforce because paying wages for free labor, assuming whites were available, would have raised production costs and slashed profits. Instead planters and farmers could net big profits selling to the factories of England. So Jefferson's empire of liberty became the cotton kingdom.

For black Americans the Revolutionary era was therefore double-edged. In the North, slaves were gradually able to realize its promise of freedom, but in the South the institution of slavery was confirmed and strengthened. The war that made a nation also deepened its divisions.

The Founders knew they were passing on a poisoned chalice to the next generation. In New England John Adams likened the slavery issue to a "black cloud"
hanging over the country. Telling Jefferson "I know it is high treason to express a
doubt of the perpetual duration of our vast American Empire," Adams nonetheless
warned that a struggle over slavery might fragment the country and "produce as
many Nations in North America as there are in Europe."[34]

Jefferson recognized the danger but had no solution. He agreed in principle that
hanging on to slavery was both indefensible and dangerous: "The love of justice
and the love of country pled equally the cause of these people, and it is a moral re-
proach to us that they should have pleaded it so long in vain."[35]

But his elegant lifestyle at Monticello depended on the labors of 200 Negro
slaves, whom he could not afford to set free. In any case, he did not think a biracial
society could work, both sides being too locked in the master-slave relationship.
So, whereas Jefferson believed that Indians could grow into Americans, he considered that impossible for blacks. All he could hope was that a future generation
would free the slaves and help them establish their own nations "back" in Africa—
a continent, of course, that most of them had never seen. But the coming generation of southerners was reworking the language of 1776 to justify black bondage.
If all men were created equal and some men were slaves, so this argument ran, then
perhaps those who remained in the debased condition of slaves were not fully
men.[36]

In 1820 Congress—after months of wrangling between North and South—drew
an east-west line through the Louisiana Purchase, decreeing that, apart from Missouri, all new states north of 36 degrees 30 minutes (36°30') should be barred to
slavery. Jefferson was utterly appalled: "[T]his momentous question, like a fire bell
in the night, awakened and filled me with terror. I considered it at once as the knell
of the Union." He judged the Missouri Compromise (which admitted Missouri as
a slave state and Maine as a free state, thereby maintaining a sectional balance) to
be "a reprieve only, not a final sentence. A geographical line, coinciding with a
marked principle, moral and political, once conceived and held up to the angry
passions of men, will never be obliterated."[37] The Missouri Compromise of 1820
was another North-South bargain, like that over the federal capital in 1790. For the
moment sectional feeling abated but Jefferson's warning proved prophetic.

IGNORING THE LADIES

Indians and blacks were two groups who ended up being short-changed by the
Revolution's new coinage of liberty. The other group, even larger, was American
women.

In March 1776, when the Continental Congress was preparing to break with
Britain, Abigail Adams wrote to her husband, John, in Philadelphia: "I long to hear
that you have declared an independancy—and by the way in the new Code of Laws

which I suppose it will be necessary for you to make I desire you would Remember the Ladies, and be more generous and favourable to them than your ancestors. Do not put such unlimited power into the hands of the Husbands. Remember all Men would be tyrants if they could."[38]

Mrs. Adams had a point. In colonial America wives remained dependants of their husbands: barred from holding their own property and rarely able to obtain a divorce. No woman could vote, females being regarded as "idiots" in the classical Greek sense of the word—people who were outside the political system. But in July 1776 America proclaimed itself independent in the name of liberty against tyranny. So why not a Declaration of Independence for women? Abigail warned John, only slightly tongue in cheek: "If perticuliar care and attention is not paid to the Laidies we are determined to foment a Rebelion, and will not hold ourselves bound by any Laws in which we have no voice, or Representation."[39]

The war for independence mobilized women as well as men. With their husbands away, many had to work doubly hard to keep home and family together, often without much money since soldiers were rarely paid. Some served as nurses or cooks with the army; others marched with their husbands or were drawn into prostitution. A few even saw combat. Private Joseph Martin recalled that during the battle of Monmouth, New Jersey, in June 1778, a woman worked with her husband at the guns the whole time. "While in the act of reaching a cartridge and having one of her feet as far before the other as she could step, a cannon shot from the enemy passed directly through her legs without doing any other damage than carrying away the lower part of her petticoat. Looking at it with apparent unconcern, she observed that it was lucky it did not pass a little higher, for in that case it might have carried away something else."[40] From this story emerged the legendary figure of "Molly Pitcher"—a woman who carried water among the troops, quenching their thirst or cooling the guns.

Most daughters of liberty did not fight but they certainly became politicized by the protests against Britain. In wartime South Carolina, recalled Eliza Wilkinson, the daughter of a local planter, "none were greater politicians than the several knots of ladies who met together. All trifling discourse of fashions and such low chat were thrown by, and we commenced perfect statesmen." The men, she noted, "say we have no business with political matters . . . it's not in our sphere!" But "I won't have it thought that because we are the weaker Sex (as to bodily strength . . .) we are Capable of nothing more than minding the Dairy, visiting the Poultry house, and all such domestic concerns." No, said Eliza, the women "have as just a sense of honor, glory and great actions as those 'Lords of the Creation.'"[41]

Thanks to the upheavals of the Revolution, some American women even got the vote. In July 1776, as the Declaration of Independence was promulgated, the Provincial Congress of New Jersey adopted a new constitution for that state, giving the franchise to all "free inhabitants" who were of full age, worth at least fifty pounds, and resident in the state for at least twelve months. Fifty pounds was not a large sum for the time and most white males probably qualified. Although wives could not meet the property qualification since everything they owned belonged legally to their husbands, spinsters and widows might well be eligible—and the war made widows of many wives.

So women played a significant role in New Jersey politics, particularly in the turbulent 1790s when there was intense competition for every vote. In 1797 in the town of Elizabeth, seventy-five female Federalists turned out en masse to vote against the Democratic-Republican candidate. In those days, there was no secret ballot: Voting was a public act and easily susceptible to intimidation, so the women showed considerable courage. Although the Republican won, this display of women's activism was picked up by sympathetic newspapers. A poem in the Newark *Centinel of Freedom* proclaimed:

> *Let Democrats with senseless prate,*
> *maintain the softer Sex, Sir,*
> *Should ne'er with politics of State*
> *their gentle minds perplex, Sir:*
> *Such vulgar prejudice we scorn;*
> *their sex is no objection. . . .*
> *While woman's bound, man can't be free,*
> *nor have a fair election.*[42]

But many New Jersey men were appalled at this petticoat revolution. Political commentator William Griffith considered the spectacle of women voting to be "perfectly disgusting. . . . It is evident that women, generally, are neither by nature, nor habit, nor education, nor by their necessary condition in society, fitted to perform this duty with credit to themselves, or advantage to the public."[43] There were fears that the disease of equality would infect more than politics. Another versifier imagined a mother of twins addressing her husband:

> *Henceforth, John, she cried, Our employments are common,*
> *Be women like man, and be man like to women!*
> *Here, take this child, John, and I'll keep his brother;*
> *While I WETNURSE the one, you shall DRY NURSE the other.*[44]

Eventually conservative males got their revenge. In 1807 a referendum on where to site a local courthouse produced a turnout three times the previous norm: Clearly many citizens had voted early and often. After a backroom deal between the parties, the New Jersey legislature disenfranchised women and blacks, so as to restore "the safety, quiet, good order and dignity of the state."[45]

The New Jersey constitution of 1776 was an aberration. It was unique in allowing votes for some women and it lasted only three decades. No state changed the law whereby a wife's property was absorbed into that of her husband, denying her financial independence. In a few places—Massachusetts, Connecticut, and Pennsylvania—it became possible to sue for divorce in civil courts. But much more normal was the fate of Nancy Shippen, teenage daughter of a rich Philadelphia family.

During the war Nancy fell in love with Louis Otto, a young attaché at the French legation. But in 1781 her father married her off to Colonel Henry Livingston, almost twice her age and son of a prominent New York family. The marriage was a disaster from the start. Even before her first and only child was born, Nancy had returned to her parents' home. Then she lost custody of her daughter, Peggy, to the Livingstons. She sought a divorce but in New York, as in most states, this could be obtained only if some obliging man agreed to shepherd a private bill through the state legislature. No such knight in shining armor came forward; eventually it was the philandering Livingston who divorced her. When Peggy came of age, she moved back to Philadelphia to support her mother, now clinically depressed and estranged from her own parents. Both women died as lonely, reclusive old maids.[46]

In 1798 Judith Sargent Murray, a leading American writer on the role of women, predicted "a new era of female history . . . the revolution of events is advancing in that half of the human species, which hath hitherto been involved in the night of darkness, toward the irradiating sun of science." Murray was wrong: The American Revolution was not that revolutionary. The Founders themselves, radicals about liberty in politics, remained strict patriarchs in the home. Women were supposed to contribute to the new republic indirectly, by breeding and raising good citizens. In 1796 John Adams told his daughter Nabby that there was "a young generation coming up in America. . . . You my dear daughter will be responsible for a great share of the duty and opportunity of educating a rising family, from whom much will be expected."[47] As for equality, that was also taken care of within marriage. "Every man, by the Constitution, is born with an equal right to be elected to the highest office," noted Reverend John Ogden in *The Female Guide.* "And every woman is born with an equal right to be the wife of the most eminent man."[48]

When Jefferson declared back in 1776 that all "men" were created equal, he used that word in the literal sense. Jefferson never believed that women had a role to play in politics and his experience in France, on the eve of its Revolution, confirmed these feelings. He wrote home in 1788: "The gay and thoughtless Paris is now become a furnace of Politics. All the world is now politically mad. Men, women, children talk nothing else." But, added Jefferson, "our good ladies, I trust, have been too wise to wrinkle their foreheads with politics. They are contented to soothe & calm the minds of their husbands returning ruffled from political debate. They have the good sense to value domestic happiness before all other." And in 1807, as president, he wrote sternly: "The appointment of a woman to office is an innovation for which the public is not prepared, nor am I."[49]

In fact, presidents and public were not prepared to countenance such an innovation throughout the nineteenth century. The first female member of Congress,

Jeanette Rankin of Montana, was elected in 1916—four years before women throughout the United States got the vote—and it was not until 1933 that Jefferson's taboo was broken and President Franklin Roosevelt appointed a woman, Frances Perkins, to his cabinet.

None of this is particularly remarkable, of course, given the mentality of the age; in Europe attitudes toward women were little different. What does merit comment is that some Americans clearly did sense the radical implications of the nation's revolutionary rhetoric—that is evident from the correspondence between John and Abigail Adams and from the New Jersey constitution enfranchising some women and blacks. The war did shake up many conventions but the 1790s and 1800s saw a general conservative backlash, not least because of the insecurities of global war. Yet the rhetoric of 1776 would serve as a benchmark for future radicals. "The American war is over, but this is far from the case with the American Revolution," wrote Benjamin Rush of Philadelphia in 1787. "On the contrary, nothing but the first act of the great drama is closed."[50]

THE SECOND WAR OF INDEPENDENCE

The Napoleonic Wars were a great opportunity for the U.S. economy. With most of the major European powers entangled, their lucrative colonial trade became the spoils of war, vulnerable to raiders from the other side. The best way to ship consumer goods such as coffee and sugar and vital naval stores into Europe was by using a neutral country with a large merchant navy, and the United States was more than happy to oblige. As Thomas Jefferson put it, the New World would "fatten on the follies of the Old."[51]

This was, however, a dangerous game. Both Britain and France routinely intercepted American ships they believed to be trading with the enemy. The British also seized deserters from the Royal Navy, even if they had become U.S. citizens. President Jefferson, like his predecessors, Washington and Adams, wanted to keep out of the European war but he was also determined to assert U.S. rights. Convinced that America's new economic muscle would bring the British to heel, in 1807 he instituted an almost total embargo on trade. This *did* damage Britain, but it hurt America more—like trying to "cure the corns by cutting off the toes," complained John Randolph of Virginia.[52] Merchants were ruined and seamen thrown out of work; the collapse of trade decimated local business and employment. Newburyport in Massachusetts was typical of most northeastern ports. According to a local newspaper: "Our wharves now have the stillness of the grave. Nothing flourishes on them but vegetation."[53]

The embargo lasted fifteen months before Congress lifted it in March 1809, days before the end of Jefferson's presidency. His successor, James Madison, another Virginian, imposed more selective bans on trade with Britain and France but the British tightened their own economic warfare. With Napoleon in control of most of the continent, blockade had become one of Britain's most important weapons of war and its ships enforced it right up to the American coast.

On June 1, 1812, after months of debate, President Madison sent a message to Congress condemning British depredations on the high seas. Their cruisers, he said, "hover over and harass our entering and departing Commerce" and "have wantonly spilt American blood within the sanctuary of our territorial jurisdiction." He also blamed the British for stirring up "the warfare just renewed by the Savages on one of our extensive frontiers; a warfare which is known to spare neither age nor sex, and to be distinguished by features peculiarly shocking to humanity." Madison summed up that there was "on the side of Great Britain a state of war against the United States; and on the side of the United States a state of peace towards Great Britain."[54]

Congress agreed with the president that the situation was intolerable. On June 18, 1812, the United States declared war on Great Britain. Madison had argued that this was a defensive war against British imperialism, but many Americans had imperial motives of their own. The so-called War Hawks—congressmen such as Henry Clay of Kentucky and John C. Calhoun of South Carolina—saw the war as a way to expand west into Indian territory and north into Canada. Jefferson even predicted that "the acquisition of Canada . . . as far as the neighborhood of Quebec will be a mere matter of marching."[55]

But the British and their Indian allies resisted fiercely and, for all the war talk, the U.S. army proved woefully unprepared. Fighting ebbed to and fro indecisively along the long Canadian border. But then in 1814, with Napoleon apparently defeated for good, the British were able to concentrate ships and men against America's heartland, the Chesapeake Bay, and Admiral George Cockburn prepared a daring plan to attack Washington itself.

The capital was almost defenseless. On the morning of August 24, 1814, President Madison, as commander-in-chief, rode out to rally his troops, but he was nearly caught in the crossfire as British troops rolled them aside. Back at the President's Mansion his wife, Dolley, was overseeing arrangements for dinner—scheduled as usual for three in the afternoon. Every so often she stopped to add a few more lines to a letter intended for her sister Lucy. Then Mrs. Madison heard the rumble of artillery. Her servants found a wagon and hastily loaded four cases of state papers and a trunk of clothes. She threw in some silver, books, a clock, and her beloved crimson velvet curtains from the sitting room. "Three o'clock—Will you believe it, my sister? We have had a battle or skirmish near Bladensburg, and I am still here within sound of the cannon! Mr. Madison comes not; may God protect him. Two messengers covered with dust come to bid me to fly, but I wait for him."[56]

Dolley Madison was determined to save Gilbert Stuart's portrait of George Washington—already an iconic image of the Father of the Nation—but it was a full-size canvas with its frame screwed to the wall. Slaves tried hacking at the wood with an axe. Eventually her French servant used his penknife to cut out the canvas—which she had no choice but to entrust to two unknown though apparently respectable gentlemen who had called by to see if they could help. As her carriage was made ready, Dolley hastily finished her letter: "It is done," she scribbled, "the precious portrait placed in the hands of the gentlemen. . . . And now, my dear sister, I must leave this house. . . . When I shall again write to you, or where I shall be tomorrow, I cannot tell."[57] After she drove off, her steward carefully locked the doors and took the Madisons' pet parrot three blocks to the French mission—to secure for it diplomatic immunity.

That evening the British advance guard reached a deserted Capitol Hill. In the deepening gloom the chambers of the Senate and the House stood grand and imposing, though linked only by a rough wooden walkway where the great dome would eventually be raised. Admiral Cockburn did not intend to sack the city; but he did plan to destroy its public buildings as retaliation for the American burning of the Parliament in the Canadian city of York (present-day Toronto). In the House chamber, completed only a year before, soldiers piled up the mahogany desks and chairs and started a massive bonfire. Soon the intense heat melted glass, cracked sculptures, and brought down the roof. The redcoats then torched the Senate building, one of whose rooms housed the Library of Congress. Heavily paneled and full of books, it was utterly destroyed.

Having dealt with the legislature, the British turned to the executive branch of government. A mile up Pennsylvania Avenue they found the president's table set for forty people, with wine in the coolers. After a long day of marching and fighting, recalled Lieutenant James Scott, Cockburn's aide-de-camp, "Never was nectar more grateful to the palates of the gods than the crystal goblet of Madeira and water I quaffed off at Mr. Madison's expense."[58] After refreshment and many sarcastic toasts, the British helped themselves to souvenirs. Cockburn took one of the president's hats, another officer one of his best shirts, while a cushion from Mrs. Madison's chair occasioned "pleasantries too vulgar to repeat."[59] Then the soldiers and sailors set to work, upstairs and downstairs, setting fire to beds, curtains, and furnishings. Although the great sandstone walls survived, when the inferno finally died down the President's Mansion was a shell.

As promised, Cockburn burned only public buildings. Private houses were spared, unless used by snipers; likewise the French mission (and the presidential parrot). Defiantly the Congress voted to stay in Washington while the city was rebuilt and Jefferson offered his own personal book collection, accumulated over a half-century, as nucleus of the new Library of Congress—an act of great generosity (though it also helped pay off some of his hefty debts). But there was no doubting the humiliation inflicted on the new nation.

Or the sectional strains. In New England, the disasters of 1814 capped years of anger. The region had been marginalized in Congress as bigger states in the South and new West eclipsed it in population and wealth. Apart from one term of John Adams, the presidency had been held continuously for a quarter-century by what New Englanders dubbed the "Virginia Dynasty." Jefferson's trade embargo and now

"Mr. Madison's War" had devastated the Atlantic commerce on which New England's prosperity depended and by the summer of 1814 it seemed that the Republicans could not even defend the country from invasion. Their Federalist opponents, still strong in New England, capitalized on the mounting anger: "Our common interests, liberties, and safety are now more injured . . . by the doings of our own National Government than they were when in 1775 we took arms to protect and defend them against the measures of the government of Great Britain."[60] Hotheads even talked of seceding from a Union that, like the British empire in the 1770s, now seemed inimical to New England's interests.

In December 1814 the legislatures of Massachusetts, Connecticut, and Rhode Island sent delegates to a New England convention, held in the Connecticut town of Hartford. After three weeks of secret and heated debate, they issued a report setting out their grievances and affirming that in cases of "deliberate, dangerous, and palpable infractions of the constitution, affecting the sovereignty of a state and liberties of the people; it is not only the right but the duty of such a state to interpose its authority for their protection."[61] This was almost a mirror image of the claims made by Jefferson and Madison in the Kentucky and Virginia Resolutions of 1798 when the Federalists imposed the Alien and Sedition Acts. In extremis, each section was asserting the right of the states to nullify actions of the federal government.

The Hartford Convention called for seven constitutional amendments to offset the growing power of the South and the West. The most important was repealing the clause that allowed slave states to claim extra seats in Congress by counting slaves as three-fifths of a person (which had probably lost Adams the election of 1800). The Convention also demanded one-term presidencies and a ban on the same state from holding the presidency for successive terms—transparently a strike against the Virginia dynasty.

In February 1815 a delegation of Massachusetts Federalists left Boston to take their complaints to Washington. But by the time they arrived there ten days later, the ground had been cut from under their feet. News came through from Europe that British and American commissioners had finally negotiated a peace treaty. There were also reports from New Orleans of a great British defeat.

After the raids around the Chesapeake, the British had pushed south for the winter, targeting the port of New Orleans. Their real aim was to relieve the pressure on Canada but many Americans feared a concerted campaign to rouse the Indians of the South and take over the Spanish colonies of west and east Florida. The British commander at New Orleans was General Edward Pakenham, Wellington's brother-in-law. Unlike the Iron Duke, however, Pakenham was rash and none too clever. He mounted a frontal attack on the American earthworks outside the city, but neglected to bring up the scaling ladders. Those soldiers who were not mown down in the open by American artillery were picked off as they clambered ineffectually on the shoulders of comrades. The Americans repulsed the assault at the cost of only 13 dead; nearly 300 British soldiers were killed, including Pakenham and two other generals. New Orleans was sweet revenge for the burning of Washington; it ended the war on a triumphant note, confirming American independence and quelling any talk of northern secession.

The U.S. commander at New Orleans was Andrew Jackson. Emboldened by his celebrity status, he used a punitive raid against Seminole Indians in 1818 as an excuse to seize east Florida from the Spanish. The following year Spain signed a treaty conceding all of Florida to the United States. By now the Spanish empire in South America was on its last legs. Chile, Peru, Colombia, and finally Mexico had become independent republics and Spain itself was falling under French control. Anxious to ensure that France did not try to gain Spain's American empire, the British foreign secretary, George Canning, proposed a joint Anglo-American warning. James Monroe, now president, sought the advice of his predecessors and both Madison and Jefferson, despite their past Anglophobia, urged him to work with Britain. But Secretary of State John Quincy Adams—articulating the real lesson of the previous half-century—argued that it would be more appropriate for America to make its own independent declaration than "to come in as a cockboat in the wake of a British man-of-war."[62]

Adams carried the day, though the eventual declaration immortalized the president's name, not his own. In December 1823 Monroe stated that "the American continents, by the free and independent condition which they have assumed and maintain, are henceforth not to be considered as subjects for future colonization by any European powers." He also warned the Europeans to keep their hands off the new republics:

> With the existing colonies or dependencies of any European power we have not interfered and shall not interfere, but with the Governments who have declared their independence and maintained it, and whose independence we have, on great consideration and on just principles, acknowledged, we could not view any interposition for the purpose of oppressing them, or controlling in any other manner their destiny, by any European power in any other light than as the manifestation of an unfriendly disposition toward the United States.[63]

The Monroe Doctrine, as it came to be called, extended the ideology of 1776, affirming the independence not just of the United States but of all the American republics. It also defined a great divide between the values of the Old World and the New. But Monroe and Adams were living in an era when the United States embraced only half the continent, with much of the Louisiana Purchase still unsettled wilderness. In the quarter-century after the Monroe Doctrine, the political geography of America and the ambitions of its leaders enlarged dramatically—as the Indians and Mexicans would learn to their cost.

5

EAST AND WEST

During the first half of the nineteenth century America's center of gravity lurched dramatically westward. In 1815 its border was effectively the Appalachians—the mountain chain that runs diagonally northeast to southwest some 500 miles inland from the Atlantic. Only one in seven people and four of the eighteen states were west of the mountains. By 1850, however, half of America's 23 million people and half of its thirty states lay beyond the Appalachians.[1]

This was one of the biggest migrations in history. People were on the move in massive numbers—from the older eastern states and from economically depressed areas of Europe—and as they surged west the Native Americans were evicted, often brutally, into tribal homelands on the margins. Early settlers traveled by foot and wagon; from the 1830s, however, canal boats and then railroads conquered distance in amazing ways. The new West also started to assert itself in national politics, most notably through the protean figure of Andrew Jackson, president from 1829 to 1837.

These vast movements shook the foundations of the country created by the generation of 1776; by the 1830s the United States had become a democracy for white males, based on a new style of mass politics. But older elites viewed democratization as a threat to the social order and they were also alarmed at the dilution of Protestant America by Catholic immigrants from Ireland and Germany. Part cause, part consequence of this panic was the wave of evangelical revivals in the 1820s and 1830s, which spawned controversial new sects such as the Mormons and also crusades for temperance, Sabbath observance, and, above all, the abolition of slavery.

JACKSON AND DEMOCRACY

Andrew Jackson was utterly different from all six presidents who had served before him. Men of learning, Thomas Jefferson and John Adams were two of the leading

95

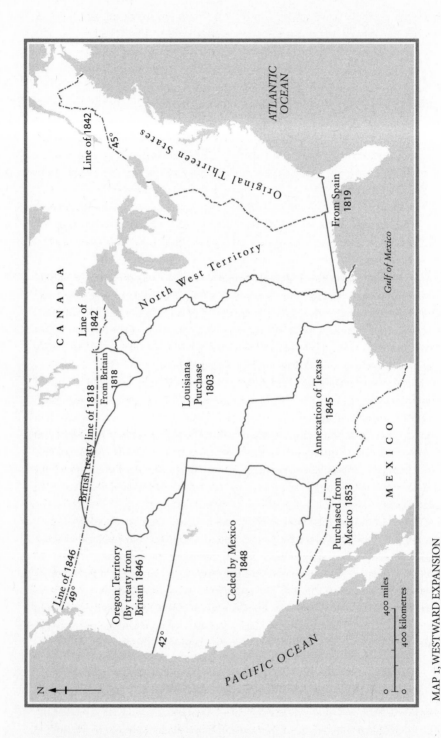

MAP 1, WESTWARD EXPANSION

intellectuals of the age. They were also from the eastern seaboard, familiar with Europe and imbued with its culture. Four of these early presidents hailed from Virginia (Washington, Jefferson, Madison, and Monroe), the other two from Massachusetts: John Adams and John Quincy Adams—the only father and son to hold the U.S. presidency until the Bush dynasty.

But Jackson, born in 1767, grew up in poverty in the backcountry of the Carolinas, the son of poor immigrants from Ulster. As a teenager he lost his brother and mother in the Revolutionary War and was himself wounded and scarred on the face, leaving him with an enduring hatred of the British and of Anglophile Americans. Jackson—lean and mean, with a shock of red hair—made a new life for himself in the state of Tennessee, where his lack of formal education was less of an impediment to making his way as a frontier lawyer. A man of fiery temper, ever ready to take offense, he fought at least a dozen duels—killing one opponent and ending up with many pieces of lead shot inside him. His endless intestinal problems may have been the result of lead poisoning.

Above all, Andrew Jackson had charisma. Annie Jarret, a North Carolina woman who knew him as a young man, recalled later that "he was by no means good-looking. His face was long and narrow, his features sharp and angular and his complexion yellow and freckled." But, she said, "his eyes *were* handsome. They were very large, a kind of steel-blue, and when he talked to you he always looked straight into your own eyes . . . as much as to say 'I have nothing to be ashamed of and I hope you haven't.'" Whether Jackson was "calm or animated," Jarret felt "there was always something about him I cannot describe except to say that it was a *presence,* or kind of majesty I never saw in any other young man."[2]

Jackson, nicknamed "Old Hickory" on account of his toughness, won national fame as a general in the War of 1812. After his victory over the hated British at New Orleans he was talked of as a second Washington, but initially did not fancy the presidency: His health was not up to it and his wife, Rachel, dreaded the prospect of being first lady. Jackson did let his name go forward in 1824; in a four-horse race between essentially regional candidates (so-called favorite sons) he won the highest number of votes in the electoral college but not a majority. Under the Constitution this left the decision to the House of Representatives and gave the presidency to John Quincy Adams (second by some way on the electoral vote) after a backroom deal with Henry Clay of Kentucky, the Speaker of the House. Clay considered Jackson a "military chieftain," a budding Bonaparte who could easily take America down "the fatal road which has conducted every other republic to ruin."[3] Jackson was furious at what he called the "corrupt bargain" between Adams and Clay. Getting into the White House now became a search for vindication.

The election of 1828 between Jackson and Adams was the nastiest presidential contest so far. Adams's supporters harped on Jackson's dueling, slave-trading past, and even insinuated that Rachel was a whore. Jacksonians played up the general's war record and presented him as a man of the West, battling for the people against the eastern aristocracy. This time Jackson was clear victor, but the cost was high. A few weeks later Rachel collapsed and died of a massive heart attack—Jackson blamed the Adams men for hounding her to death. Her body had to be pried from his arms to prepare it for burial and he wrote with anguish: "O, how fluctuating are all earthly things. At the time I least expected it, and could least spare her, she was snatched from me, and I left here a solitary monument of grief, without the least hope of happiness here below, surrounded with all the turmoil of public life."[4]

On March 4, 1829, Jackson was sworn in at the east portico of the Capitol. Afterward an immense crowd rushed up the steps to shake hands with their hero. Jackson eventually escaped on horseback up Pennsylvania Avenue but hundreds of his pursuers crashed the reception in the White House. Margaret Bayard Smith, a horrified observer, saw "a rabble, a mob, of boys, negros, women, children, scrambling, fighting, romping. . . . Cut glass and china to the amount of several thousand dollars had been broken in the struggle to get to the refreshments. . . . Ladies fainted, men were seen with bloody noses, and such a scene of confusion as is impossible to describe. Those who got in could not get out by the door again, but had to scramble out of windows."[5] Jackson's inauguration, declared censorious critics, gave a new meaning to the concept of the "sovereignty of the people."

Jackson was a prosperous cotton planter, owning 100 slaves, who farmed over 1,000 acres near Nashville, Tennessee. But he believed passionately in his image as tribune of the new democratic West against the elitist East and was determined to use the presidency vigorously in this cause. In eight years as president he vetoed twelve bills passed by Congress—more than all his predecessors combined over the previous three decades.

The most important battle, both symbolically and in substance, was against the Bank of the United States. The bank, a private corporation located in Philadelphia, had been founded 1791 at the urging of Alexander Hamilton, who saw it as an American version of the Bank of England, acting as a repository for federal tax revenues and providing a stable source of credit. After its charter expired, President Madison decided that the government could not do without it and chartered the Second Bank of the United States in 1816. The bank's president, Nicholas Biddle, was an urbane Philadelphian who epitomized everything Jackson hated about the eastern establishment. Biddle also made generous loans to some of Jackson's political enemies, including Henry Clay who ran against Jackson in 1832. The bank's charter would expire in 1836; whether it should be renewed became a major political controversy.

Biddle's supporters argued that the Bank of the United States was actually the people's champion. In a country that still had no nationwide paper currency, its promissory notes served as a surrogate and helped offset the unbacked notes and easy credit offered by many state and local banks. But Jacksonians took a different line. Senator Thomas Hart Benton of Missouri charged that Biddle's bank was flooding the country with its notes and then sucking back, vampire-like, all the "hard money"—gold and silver coin—from the dynamic South and West to its shady backers in the Northeast and in Britain. Since the notes carried interest, hardworking westerners would fall irrevocably into debt and their properties would be auctioned off. Benton argued that "in these mock sales of towns and cities may be laid the foundation for the titles and estates of our future nobility—Duke of Cincinnati! Earl of Lexington! Marquis of Nashville! Count of St. Louis! Prince of New Orleans!" So, thundered Benton, a vote for rechartering the Bank would be a vote for "the establishment of lords and commons in this America, and for the eventual establishment of a King, for when the lords and commons are established, the King will come of himself!"[6]

Jackson's rhetoric was not quite so extravagant but he viewed the bank as a "hydra-headed monster" whose tentacles "threatened our liberty."[7] When Congress voted to renew its charter, Jackson issued a presidential veto on July 10, 1832. In his message he played the democratic card: "Of the twenty-five directors of this bank, five are chosen by the Government and twenty by the citizen stockholders. . . . It is easy to conceive that great evils to our country and its institutions might flow from such a concentration of power in the hands of a few men irresponsible to the people." Jackson also used the states' rights argument: "Nor is our Government to be maintained or our Union preserved by invasions of the rights and powers of the several States." Its "true strength," according to him, "consists in leaving individuals and States as much as possible to themselves."[8]

Above all, the president declared the Bank unconstitutional, going beyond what was "necessary and proper" for the federal government to do. This opinion stood in flat contradiction to the judgment of the Supreme Court, which, under Chief Justice John Marshall, had set itself as the final arbiter of what was or was not constitutional. But Jackson argued that the Supreme Court was abusing its proper function: "The Congress, the Executive, and the Court must each for itself be guided by its own opinion of the Constitution. . . . The opinion of the judges has no more authority over Congress than the opinion of the Congress has over the judges, and on that point the President is independent of both."[9]

This was powerful stuff: Jackson's supporters called it a "second Declaration of Independence" and lauded him as "the man of the People." But Nicholas Biddle called Jackson's veto message "a manifesto of anarchy, such as Marat or Robespierre might have issued to the mobs."[10] The president's interpretation of the Constitution laid him open to the charge of setting himself up as supreme autocrat—"King Andrew the First" in a celebrated cartoon of the time, which depicted him crowned and robed, holding his veto message with his foot on the Constitution.

Henry Clay made the bank veto the central issue of the 1832 presidential election, with thousands of dollars pumped into his campaign by Nicholas Biddle. Jacksonians used the state and local banks for equally partisan purposes—it was a dirty business on both sides—but the upshot was a massive victory for the president. To his supporters "Jackson" and "democracy" had become synonymous;

his party became known simply as the Democrats. In 1836 Jackson's vice-president and anointed successor, Martin van Buren, won another landslide.

To a considerable extent, politics in the 1830s were about Jackson. By personalizing political problems and exploiting the powers of the presidency as never before, he made himself the big issue. But the political ferment also reflected more profound changes in America, summed up in that slippery but potent word "democracy."

Back in the 1780s the Founders had not intended to establish a democracy. In the strict sense of the word that meant government by all the people, as supposedly in the city-states of ancient Greece. No, they were founding a "representative democracy" in which politicians were chosen to act for the people. But the preamble to the Constitution affirmed that the people were ultimately sovereign and in the early nineteenth century the barriers to popular participation in politics were falling fast. Although some states still retained a property or tax qualification, there was no longer a significant hurdle given rising wealth and incomes. In most states by 1832 all white adult males were able to vote.

Equally important, they were now voting directly for the president in a way the Founders had not envisaged. Article 2 of the Constitution left it up to each state legislature to decide how to select its presidential electors (the quota being equal to its total number of senators and representatives), and in the early days of the republic the legislatures generally made the choice themselves. By 1832, however, all states except South Carolina chose their presidential electors by popular vote, and the electors were usually committed to a particular candidate. Although American states had moved over to ballots, rather than voting by voice and show of hands, they had not yet adopted the secret ballot (pioneered in Australia in the 1850s). Voters usually chose a printed slip or "ticket" from one party or another that listed its "slate" of candidates for office from U.S. president down to the proverbial local dog-catcher—hence the expression "voting the ticket." This meant that elections were still a very public display of allegiance.

So, by the 1830s the presidency had been tossed into the popular arena and Jackson's autocratic, dogmatic style made the struggle to control it matter as never before. A transsectional coalition of interest groups helped get him to the White House. That forced Jackson's opponents, usually the local elites, to combine their forces under the name of "Whigs"—evoking the patriots of the 1770s who had rallied against an earlier despot, George III. By 1840 the Whigs had developed an effective organization and their candidate William Henry Harrison won the White House. Nearly fourth-fifths of the electorate voted, compared with little more than a quarter in 1824.[11]

Conventionally the Democrats have been seen as an agrarian party and the Whigs as the representatives of commerce and industry (with Jackson's Bank War as a litmus test). Yet such a distinction is very crude, not least because the United States was still overwhelmingly an agrarian society. Democrats did tend to have strong support among small farmers and in frontier areas while bigger planters in the South and the rich of the Northeastern cities were predominantly Whig, but a more significant marker than class was ethnic and religious background: As we shall see, Catholics were overwhelmingly Democrat and militant Protestants strongly Whig. The most important point about American political parties, both in the 1830s and ever since, was their heterogeneous character. Each was an uneasy nationwide coalition always in danger of falling apart. Tidy-minded political scientists like to delineate different phases of the American "party system," but the political configurations were hardly systematic: The "system" characterized by competition between Whigs and Democrats had fallen apart by the early 1850s.

More durable than precise party divisions was the notion of party itself. The Founders, true to the classical republican tradition, had viewed party as a threat to liberty, or at best a temporary necessity to root out an evil faction (as Jefferson claimed in 1800), but parties were now becoming accepted as a fact of political life in such a diverse and fractious nation. Martin van Buren claimed that they "rouse the sluggish to exertion, give increased energy to the most active intellect, excite a salutary vigilance over our public functionaries, and prevent that apathy which has proved the ruin of Republics."[12]

By 1840 the United States therefore had two political parties, built around nationwide organizations. Candidates were chosen by a nominating convention of the whole party, backed by party newspapers, and the electorate was mobilized to vote through food, drink, and mass rallies. During the 1832 campaign Michel Chevalier, a French visitor, watched a parade through New York nearly a mile long: "The Democrats marched in good order, to the glare of torches. The banners were more numerous than I had seen them in any religious festival." Chevalier noted that on some were inscribed the names of the Democratic societies or sections; "others bore imprecations against the Bank of the United States; Nick Biddle and Old Nick figured largely."[13]

In Chevalier's view, democracy had become America's civic religion. For Alexis de Tocqueville, a more famous French observer, it was almost the American way of life, expressing the dynamic, egalitarian, anti-aristocratic ethos of the country. But Tocqueville also noted that equality did not transcend "natural" as opposed to social divisions: "In America, more than anywhere else in the world," he wrote in his 1830s classic *Democracy in America*, "care has been taken constantly to trace clearly distinct spheres of action for the two sexes. . . . Nor have Americans ever supposed that democratic principles should undermine the husband's authority and make it doubtful who is in charge of the family." Yet Tocqueville also believed that Americans showed a much greater respect for women and their judgment than any other nation—"nowhere does she enjoy a higher station." He offered the striking conclusion that, "if anyone asks me what I think the chief cause of the extraordinary prosperity and growing power of this nation, I should answer that it is due to the superiority of their women."[14]

Tocqueville's judgment was relative, comparing the United States with Europe, whereas many American women compared themselves against the country's own elevated standards of democratic liberty. In society as a whole there were also still huge extremes of riches and poverty: In Boston, for instance, the richest 1 percent of the population owned a third of the wealth, while the economy of Jackson's fabled democratic Southwest depended overwhelmingly on the labor of slaves.[15] But Tocqueville's broad contrast between American democracy and Old World Europe was true as far as white males were concerned.

Pride in the country's distinctive democratic ethos also animated American intellectuals. "Our days of dependence, our long apprenticeship to the learning of other lands, is drawing to a close," the writer Ralph Waldo Emerson told students at Harvard in 1837. "We have listened too long to the courtly muses of Europe. The spirit of the American freeman is already suspected to be timid, imitative, tame." Emerson's address, entitled "The American Scholar," became known as America's "intellectual declaration of independence."[16]

Emerson was a lapsed Unitarian preacher. Unitarianism—a watered-down version of Christianity that denies the Trinity and the Calvinist doctrine of human sinfulness—had wide appeal among New England intellectuals in the early nineteenth century, becoming dominant at Harvard (though not Yale). It helped undermine the hold of the Congregational Church on society, and its confident faith in human capacities accorded with the new democratic ethos of Jacksonian America. But Unitarianism was a dry rationalism, lacking a mystical spark, and this Emerson eventually found in the ideas of Kant and German Romanticism, as interpreted by English writers such as Coleridge and Carlyle. Against formal religion, Emerson preached the supremacy of the individual Soul, in communion with the underlying harmonies of nature. Man, rational and moral, was the measure of all things. These ideas, known as Transcendentalism, were promoted by Emerson and like-minded intellectuals based particularly in the Massachusetts towns of Cambridge and Concord.

Although Transcendentalism, seen in retrospect, was the "final phase" of European Romanticism,[17] at the time it seemed the base for that distinctively American culture championed by Emerson. Out of it grew several major writings of the 1850s that have become classics of American literature. In 1854 Henry David Thoreau, a protégé of Emerson, published *Walden, or Life in the Woods*—a literary rendition of two years he spent in a cabin on Walden Pond, near Concord. In this book he celebrated Transcendentalist values such as self-reliance, reflection, and closeness to nature.

Nathaniel Hawthorne was also an associate of Emerson, but his version of Romanticism was bleaker and blacker. Hawthorne, who grew up in the coastal town of Salem—one of the first settlements in Massachusetts—was preoccupied by Puritan New England. His vivid evocations of sin and guilt in novels such as *The Scarlet Letter* (1850) did much to establish a negative "puritanical" image of the Puritans in American culture. Even darker was the vision of Herman Melville, whose epic *Moby-Dick, or The Whale* (1851) was dedicated to Hawthorne. Although a failure in his lifetime, this highly symbolic allegory about obsession, revenge, and the cosmic struggle between good and evil is now seen as one of America's greatest novels.

Neither Hawthorne nor Melville articulated Emerson's optimism about man but they did produce the kind of authentically American writing that he had advocated. And in Walt Whitman there emerged a distinctively American poetic voice. His collection *Leaves of Grass* (1855), with its free verse, earthy sexuality, and characters from ordinary life, was lauded by Emerson. Here was the common man using common speech—a far cry from the "courtly muses" of Europe, a poetry that in Whitman's words was "transcendent and new."[18]

A CHRISTIAN REPUBLIC?

Yet Transcendentalism, for all its influence over intellectuals, was the worldview of a minority. Most Americans still cleaved to the doctrines of biblical Protestantism, but these, too, were being shaken up by the democratization of American life. New evangelical revivals surged across the country, especially the West, in waves from the 1790s to the 1830s.

Although often led by charismatic autocrats like the Mormon Joseph Smith or Alexander Campbell, principal founder of the Disciples of Christ, the faith these men preached was populist and egalitarian. Believers, both male and female, were encouraged to express their emotions and trust their own experience. In the words of one anonymous homespun evangelist:

> What I insist upon, my brethren and sisters, is this: larnin isn't religion, and eddication don't give a man the power of the Spirit. It is grace and gifts that furnish the real live coals from off the altar. St Peter was a fisherman—do you think he ever went to Yale College? When the Lord . . . wants to blow down the walls of the spiritual Jericho, my beloved brethren and sisters, he don't take one of your smooth, polite college larnt gentlemen, but a plain, natural ram's-horn sort of man like me.[19]

Another of those "ram's-horn sort" was Lorenzo Dow, who, with his disheveled clothes and long mane of hair parted down the middle, looked like a modern John the Baptist. Dow was a spellbinding preacher, who spoke all over the United States. His sermons ran the gamut of moods from humor to brimstone and were famed for provoking displays of religious ecstasy known as the "jerking exercise." Dow's specialty was camp meetings—folk festivals of preaching, praying, singing, and weeping—but, like other evangelists, he hammered home his message through pamphlets and tracts, which became best-sellers among an increasingly literate population. Even more powerful were new hymns, often local folk-tunes set to words that had a simple, strong message about Christ and Redemption.

This was religion forged in "the fiery furnace of democracy,"[20] and the heat was too intense for some of the older, hierarchical churches. In the early nineteenth century the Congregationalists in New England and the Episcopal Church in Virginia lost their hold on local society. On the other hand, the more populist denominations really took off, particularly the Methodists with their network of itinerant preachers. By 1860 there were almost as many Methodist churches in the United States as there were post offices, about 20,000, having started from none at the time of the Revolution. Baptist congregations numbered over 12,000 and the Disciples of Christ had more than 2,000—about the same as both the Congregationalists and the Episcopalians.[21]

The democratization of religion seemed to European observers one of the most striking features of Jacksonian America. "In France I had seen the spirits of religion and of freedom almost always marching in opposite directions," Alexis de Tocqueville reflected. "In America I found them intimately linked in joint reign over the same land."[22]

There had been revivals before, of course. But, in what historians call the First Great Awakening of the 1740s, charismatic preachers like George Whitefield tried to bring sinners back to the established churches. Revivalists of this Second Awakening, convinced that the old denominations had fallen from grace, created their own churches. Their aim was not just to convert individuals but to build movements and to reform society.

This zeal for reform was also evident in the older churches, not all of them as moribund as critics claimed. Lyman Beecher was a graduate of Yale and a respected revivalist pastor in the Presbyterian Church in Connecticut. He believed that society as well as individuals needed a conversion experience to check American decadence. Beecher was a central figure in new national organizations such as the American Bible Society, the Sunday School Union, and the Board of Foreign Missions, intended to proselytize and educate at home and abroad. "A Bible for every family, a school for every district, and a pastor for every thousand souls must be the motto," he exhorted. "Our religious institutions must be invigorated or we are undone. They must move onward with our flowing emigration to the Mississippi—must pass the Rocky Mountains; and pour their waters of life into the ocean beyond; and from the north to the south they must bear salvation on their waves."[23]

Institutions like the Sunday School Union reflected what Tocqueville considered an even more basic feature of Jacksonian America—its passion for "associations." He noted that "Americans of all ages, all stations in life, and all types of dispositions, are forever forming associations" and that they "combine to give fêtes, found seminaries, build churches, distribute books, and send missionaries to the antipodes. Hospitals, prisons, and schools take place in that way." In every case, said

Tocqueville, "at the head of any new undertaking, where in France you would find the government or in England some territorial magnate, in the United States you are sure to find an association."[24]

Saving society as well as souls required an assault on the national vices of the day. Lyman Beecher was one of the founders of the American Temperance Society in 1826; within a decade it boasted 8,000 local chapters and 1.5 million members who had voluntarily "taken the pledge" against demon drink. Women were usually prime victims of male alcoholism—beaten, abused, and left to run the home—so, not surprisingly, they played a major role in temperance agitation. In Greenfield, Ohio, a saloon brawl ended in gunshots that killed a passerby. He was, according to a witness called Mother Stewart, "the son and only support of an aged and feeble widow. There was no law to reach the case, but a large number of respectable ladies of the town, after some secret counsels, accompanied by the bereaved mother, proceeded to the saloon and with axes and some other weapons knocked in the heads of barrels and casks, and demolished bottles and fixtures."[25]

For many evangelicals, their campaign against social decadence was defined by the case of Hugh Wylie of Washington, Pennsylvania. He was an elder in the Presbyterian Church and also the local postmaster with a nice salary of $1,000 a year—three times what a laborer might earn. Under instructions from the Postmaster General's Office to sort any mail on the day it arrived, including Sunday, Wylie went one better, opening his post office on Sunday mornings so that people could combine worshipping at church and collecting their mail on the same trip into town. But this efficient way of serving God and Mammon upset his local church and Wylie was expelled, despite appealing all the way to the Presbyterian General Assembly.

In 1810 Congress passed a law requiring all postmasters to open on any day when the mail arrived. This sparked a long campaign by Protestant churches, with women again in the vanguard because the post office was now becoming the respectable equivalent of the saloon—an excuse for men to evade their domestic duties. In 1828, several pressure groups combined in the General Union for the Promotion of the Christian Sabbath. Members signed a pledge card (like that for the Temperance Society) promising to boycott stagecoach and steamboat companies that operated on the Sabbath and they deluged Congress and local postmasters with petitions. Opponents also mobilized and Sabbath observance became a litmus test of how far you wanted government to go in regulating private behavior.[26]

This issue often served as a dividing line between the two main parties. The Whigs were initially a nationwide alliance of politicians and groups that opposed Jackson and the Democrats—often simply political "outs" who wanted to get "in"—and the "issues" on which they campaigned could vary markedly from one part of the country to another. But those who felt strongly about the need to take a firm line against alcohol, gambling, and commercialization tended to vote for

Whig candidates. Those who believed that these were essentially private matters inclined toward the Democrats. Jackson became an emblematic figure—loathed by Whigs as the embodiment of crude frontier values and lauded by Democrats as the champion of states' rights and individual freedom.

At stake here were different concepts of liberty: negative versus positive. Democrats wanted to minimize government interference, particularly by the federal government; many Whigs espoused the idea of "Christian liberty"—freedom informed by obedience to God's law. One of them, Benjamin Franklin Tefft, declared: "A republic is the body. Christianity is the soul." In a country where perhaps 40 percent of the population were members or worshippers at Protestant churches, this was a politically potent idea.[27] On the other hand, Catholic immigrants from non-British stock, particularly the Irish and Germans, voted overwhelmingly Democrat because evangelicalism stigmatized their values and threatened to make them second-class citizens.

Religion also shaped higher education. The older universities had a strong denominational bias—Yale being Congregational, Princeton Presbyterian—and they founded many small liberal arts colleges in the first half of the nineteenth century. These were usually little more than gentlemanly finishing schools, where students studied classics, mathematics, and some traditional science in an atmosphere of confined religiosity punctuated by binge drinking and evangelical revivals. Many were located in small country towns, such as Amherst College in western Massachusetts or Dartmouth in remote New Hampshire. But, in another vein, a few states founded their own secular universities on the model of Jefferson's University of Virginia (1819), whose spacious classical campus at Charlottesville was deliberately built around a library rather than a chapel. Frontier states like Michigan and Wisconsin followed suit, endowing their universities with proceeds from the land reserves set aside by Congress to support education. Technical training was, however, minimal. The U.S. Military Academy at West Point on the Hudson river north of New York was established by Jefferson in 1802; its curriculum centered on civil engineering and its graduating officers went on to build many of America's bridges, harbors, and roads in the first half of the nineteenth century. West Point was, however, a government foundation. Very few secular universities, among them Virginia, established engineering departments before the Civil War. On the whole, American higher education remained dominated by the liberal arts curriculum and by religious orthodoxies.

In New England and the Midwest, the biggest social issue for Christian evangelicals from the 1830s was black slavery. William Lloyd Garrison, a Baptist printer who had campaigned for temperance and peace, decided to start his own abolitionist newspaper, the *Liberator*, in Boston. In the inaugural issue, on New Year's Day 1831, Garrison affirmed the words of the Declaration of Independence that all men were created equal, and demanded the immediate emancipation of slaves. His famous clarion call deserves extended quotation:

I am aware that many object to the severity of my language; but is there not cause for severity? I will be as harsh as truth, and as uncompromising as justice. On this subject, I do not wish to think, or to speak, or write, with moderation. No! no! Tell a man whose house is on fire to give a moderate alarm; tell him to moderately rescue his wife from the hands of the ravisher; tell the mother to gradually extricate her babe from the fire into which it has fallen;—but urge me not to use moderation in a cause like the present. I am in earnest—I will not equivocate—I will not excuse—I will not retreat a single inch—AND I WILL BE HEARD.[28]

In the South, however, the story was different. Back in the 1780s the new Methodist and Baptist churches had condemned slavery as contrary to God's law but then they had to pull back or be drummed out of the South. In 1822 Reverend Richard Furman, a substantial slave owner, defended slavery on behalf of South Carolina Baptists not simply because it was accepted in the Bible but as a positive social benefit borne by the owner. Furman argued that slaves "become a part of his family (the whole forming under him a little community) and the care of ordering it, and providing for its welfare, devolves on him. The children, the aged, the sick, the disabled, and the unruly, as well as those who are capable of service and orderly, are the objects of his care." So, claimed Furman, "what is effected, and often at a great public expense, in a free community by taxes, benevolent institutions, bettering houses, and penitentiaries, lies here on the master, to be performed by him."[29]

Southern evangelicals such as Furman, while endorsing the bondage of black bodies by the chains of slavery, worked to free their souls from the shackles of sin.[30] Southern Methodist and Baptist congregations were largely of mixed race. Black and white deacons served alongside each other; some churches even had ordained black ministers. Yet they were run on a strict hierarchy of race and class, and all matters of church discipline were handled by whites. Little wonder that blacks, especially in the more liberal cities, set up their own congregations as a statement of resistance and independence.

In Charleston, South Carolina, one of these breakaway Methodist churches was led by a fiery black carpenter called Denmark Vesey, who had bought his freedom after winning $1,500 on the lottery. Vesey used the Bible very differently from Richard Furman—claiming that just as the Jews had had to fight for their freedom so now must black slaves in America. He painted a lurid picture of all-out war, as in one of his favorite texts from the book of Zechariah: "Behold the day of the Lord cometh, and thy spoil shall be divided in the midst of thee. For I will gather all nations against Jerusalem to battle; and the city shall be taken, and the houses rifled, and women ravished, and half the city shall go forth into captivity."[31]

In 1822 Vesey was convicted of plotting a slave revolt; he and thirty others were hanged. Details of the plot are shadowy, and were probably exaggerated by white leaders as a warning of what would happen if blacks were let off the leash. But Vesey the black carpenter was as much a man of faith as the white slave owner Richard Furman and the northern abolitionist William Lloyd Garrison—they all envisaged America as a Christian republic. These men were testimony to the power of evangelical Protestantism in the early nineteenth century as it tore through America like a whirlwind.

Women as well as men were drawn into the slavery debate. In Massachusetts in February 1838 an abolitionist petition signed by 20,000 women was presented to the state legislature in Boston by Angelina Grimké, who with her sister Sarah had left their native Charleston in South Carolina because of antipathy to slavery. Small and plainly dressed in Quaker grey, Angelina nevertheless spoke words that were deeply provocative. Because slavery was "a political subject," she observed, "it has often been said that women had nothing to do with it. Are we aliens because we are women? Are we bereft of citizenship because we are mothers, wives and daughters of a mighty people? Have women *no* country," she asked, "no partnership in a nation's guilt and shame?" Grimké demanded that the current "dominion of women should be resigned—the sooner the better; in the age which is approaching she should be something more—she should be a citizen."[32] The anti-slavery movement of the 1830s—with its meetings and petitions—inducted hundreds of northern women in the arts of political organization—and, like Angelina Grimké, many used the opportunity to demand rights of their own. During the 1830s and 1840s New York and some other states passed laws allowing married women to own property; women workers in the textile mills of Lowell, Massachusetts, went on strike to protest wage cuts; and America's first co-educational institution, Oberlin College in Ohio, was opened. "I ask no favors for my sex," declared Sarah Grimké. "All I ask our brethren is that they will take their feet from off our necks and permit us to stand upright on that ground which God designed us to occupy."[33]

This agitation came to a head in a meeting in the Methodist chapel at Seneca Falls, New York, in July 1848. Sixty-eight women and thirty-two men led by Elizabeth Cady Stanton signed a Declaration of Rights and Sentiments, which adapted the Declaration of Independence in 1776. "We hold these truths to be self-evident: that all men and women are created equal," the Seneca Falls document began. "The history of mankind is a history of repeated injuries and usurpations on the part of man toward woman, having in direct object the establishment of an absolute tyranny over her." It went on, like Jefferson, to list examples of man's tyrannical acts. "He has made her, if married, in the eye of the law, civilly dead. He has taken from her all rights in property, even to the wages she earns. . . . He has denied her the facilities for obtaining a thorough education, all colleges being closed against her." Above all, "he has never permitted her to exercise her inalienable right to the elective franchise."[34]

It would be another seventy years before women throughout the United States were granted the vote, but the Seneca Falls declaration signaled the emergence of women's rights on the political stage. Like the agitation against slavery that had helped give it birth, this reform movement was inspired by evangelical Protestantism and its vision of a Christian republic.

THE INDIAN "TRAIL OF TEARS"

Amid these debates about slavery and the rights of women, another problematic minority group, Native Americans, was being pushed off the map. The root issue, as in the days of John Winthrop, remained the Indians' failure to conform to white notions of productive agriculture. Accepting their obduracy, declared John Quincy Adams, would "doom an immense region of the globe to perpetual desolation" and condemn to "everlasting barrenness" the "fields and the vallies which a beneficent God has framed to teem with the life of innumerable multitudes."[35]

In the Northeast, Indians were no longer a big political issue. By the 1820s the remnants of once-great nations like the Iroquois or the Mohicans were confined to remote reservations. In the Southeast, however, numbers were much larger—probably close to 100,000—and the tribes were complex political organizations, centered on large towns that were heirs to the sophisticated Mississippi civilization of the eleventh century. What is more, they were sitting on prime real estate. The Seminoles, for instance, occupied the center of Florida; the Creeks had 5 million acres of potential cotton land in Alabama.

In the 1800s President Jefferson had held out two alternative scenarios for the Indians—civilization or removal; in other words, adopt the lifestyle of American whites or be evicted west of the Mississippi. The Southeastern Indians had made a big effort to assimilate—in fact, they were known as the Five Civilized Tribes. Led by strong chiefs, often of mixed Indian and American ancestry, they had established schools, accepted Protestant missionaries, and developed agriculture and craft industries. The half-breed elite took on the marks of southern gentility, including the ownership of slaves.

John Ross, principal chief of the Cherokees, was a typical member of this elite. The son of a Scottish trader and a part-Indian mother, he became a substantial merchant and slave owner. His settlement in Tennessee, Ross's Landing, later grew into the city of Chattanooga. Fluent in English and also competent in the Cherokee language, Ross became a natural negotiator for his people in Washington, encouraging them to stand up for their rights while assimilating to American ways. The Cherokees adopted many features of American politics, including a two-house legislature and a judicial system. And on the Fourth of July 1827 they formally declared their independence from the United States, adopting a constitution modeled on that of the Founding Fathers.

Here was a dramatic reminder that 1776 and 1787 were not unique events: Indians could play the liberty card against the Americans, too. They were saying, in effect, that an Indian nation could be independent, sovereign yet Americanized.

Had the Cherokees succeeded, the consequences could have been momentous. The United States might have developed into a much looser structure, almost a confederation, with a clear message that Union did not mean uniformity. But that did not happen: The fate of the Indians in the 1830s prefigured that of the Southern Confederacy three decades later.

To the people of Georgia, the idea of Cherokee independence was outrageous. The Indians would constitute a state within their state, *imperium in imperio*, a little empire within the greater American one. To make matters worse, in 1828 gold was discovered on Cherokee land. That December Georgia's state legislature passed a law affirming that all the Cherokees came under its jurisdiction. Since the Indians claimed their sovereignty under treaties negotiated with the federal government, this clash of state versus nation had to be decided in Washington. And the incoming president was Andrew Jackson.

On a personal level, Jackson was capable of great kindness to Indians. After war against the Creeks in 1814 he adopted a young Indian child whose parents had been killed by his soldiers. He brought up the boy, named Lincoyer, in his home and referred to him as his son.[36] Yet, viewing the Indians as a group, Jackson had no doubt that they were savages, obstructing American progress, and he had waged brutal war against them in the 1810s. He also shared the hunger for Indian land, using well-placed relatives and contacts to buy up several thousand acres in Alabama and Mississippi.

The Cherokee assertion of independence stirred Jackson to act. In his first State of the Union message in December 1829, the president asked Congress to set aside "an ample district west of the Mississippi" for the Indian tribes where they could live under their own governments with minimal control from Washington. Jackson justified his policy partly on legal grounds: "The Constitution declares that 'no new State shall be formed or erected within the jurisdiction of any other State' without the consent of its legislature. . . . A State cannot be dismembered by Congress or restricted in the exercise of her constitutional power." In other words, the rights of Georgia as a state took precedence over the treaties signed between the Indians and the federal government.[37]

But Jackson also portrayed Indian removal as an act of benevolence, given the sad condition to which these once proud peoples had been reduced: "Surrounded by the whites with their arts of civilization, which by destroying the resources of the savage doom him to weakness and decay, the fate of the Mohegan, the Narragansett, and the Delaware is fast over-taking the Choctaw, the Cherokee, and the Creek." Jackson asserted that "humanity and national honor demand that every effort should be made to avert so great a calamity." The president was at pains to say that the migration "should be voluntary, for it would be as cruel as unjust to compel the aborigines to abandon the graves of their fathers and seek a home in a distant land." But he said that the Indians "should be distinctly informed that if they remain within the limits of the States they must be subject to their laws."[38]

Jackson had chosen his words carefully but, despite the humanitarian gloss, this plan to move the Indians west of the Mississippi caused an outcry. Political opponents depicted it as another act of executive "despotism" by the "military chieftain."[39] There was also a marked sectional division between the frontier states of the South and West, where Indian warfare had been a fact of life since the 1750s, and the North and East, where the Indian was a remote, even pathetic figure—familiar only in romanticized form via novels such as James Fenimore Cooper's 1826 best-seller, *The Last of the Mohicans*. So Indian removal provoked moral outrage among evangelical Protestants in the North. The religious revivals of the 1820s inspired a crusade to bring Christ to the heathen, not only in far-flung parts of the world but also among the American Indians. Northern Protestants supported missionaries and schools in Indian territories—they favored civilization over removal—and there was genuine horror at driving these people from their ancestral lands into the western "desert."

In Congress, the leading spokesman for these moral reformers was Senator Theodore Frelinghuysen of New Jersey, whose credentials as a "Christian statesman" were unmatched—president at various times of the American Bible Society, the Sunday School Union, and the new American Temperance Union. Why the need for land? Frelinghuysen asked his fellow senators. There were millions of acres still unsettled in the East. Why the agitation for removal? Many of the Indians had assimilated to American ways. What about the sanctity of treaties? And what, above all, about basic American principles? "Our ancestors found these people, far removed from the commotions of Europe, exercising all the rights, and enjoying all the privileges, of free and independent sovereigns of this new world. . . . We successfully and triumphantly contended for the very rights and privileges that our Indian neighbors now implore us to protect and preserve to them."[40]

Many others added their voices to Freylinghuysen's appeal but Jacksonians argued back with equal fervor about states' rights, accusing their opponents of hypocrisy. The struggle was fierce—in the House of Representatives the bill passed only by five votes—but on May 28, 1830, Jackson signed into law the "Act to Provide for an Exchange of Lands with the Indians Residing in Any of the States or Territories, and for Their Removal West of the River Mississippi." Put that way, in anodyne legal language, the whole process sounded very reasonable. The exchange was to be voluntary. It was to be based on a fair appraisal of the Indians' existing lands. "Aid and assistance" should be "furnished to the emigrants" and a sum of half a million dollars was set aside to implement the legislation. Above all, it was "lawful for the President solemnly to assure the tribe or nation with which the exchange is made, that the United States will forever secure and guaranty to them, and their heirs or successors, the country so exchanged with them."[41]

The Chickasaw nation was the first of the Five Civilized Tribes to play ball. A personal audience with Jackson, speaking as their "Great Father," plus covert bribes to the key chiefs, induced them to sign a treaty exchanging their territory in northern Mississippi for land farther west. Over the next couple of years the Choctaws and the Creeks followed suit, though only after bitter internal arguments. At the other extreme, the Seminoles in Florida resorted to arms. It took the U.S. army six years, 1,500 American dead, and $20 million to break their resistance.

John Ross and his Cherokees watched these events with mounting anger. Ever since the white men had arrived in America, Ross fumed, "we have been made to drink of the bitter cup of humiliation; treated like dogs; our lives, our liberties, the sport of the whitemen; our country and the graves of our Fathers torn from us." In the future, he predicted, "our descendants will perhaps be totally extinguished by wars, driven at the point of the bayonet into the Western Ocean, or reduced to a State more deploreable and horrid—the condition of slaves."[42]

Once again Ross and the Cherokees were the most adept at combating the Americans with their own weapons, by filing suit in the U.S. Supreme Court. The case became another legal landmark, confirming how, under Chief Justice John Marshall, the Court was becoming a factor in American politics. On behalf of the Indians, William Wirt—a former U.S. attorney general—argued that the Cherokees were a sovereign foreign nation whose treaties with the United States were being breached by the state of Georgia. Two justices agreed completely; had they been in a majority, the implications for future American history would have been profound, requiring the United States to deal with the Indians in the same way as it dealt with Britain or France—imagine a U.S. ambassador to the Cherokees in Atlanta or to the Seminole capital in Orlando, Florida! But the other five justices denied that the Cherokees were a sovereign foreign nation and refused their request to nullify the Georgia laws.

Yet Marshall explained this in March 1831 on grounds that gave some comfort to the Cherokees, arguing that they were a "domestic dependent nation" whose "relation to the United States resembles that of a ward to his guardian."[43] The following year the Supreme Court went on to rule that Georgia law had no validity in Cherokee territory: Jurisdiction lay solely with the federal government. But Georgia politicians ignored the ruling, Marshall had no power to compel them, and Jackson had no intention of intervening. He commented gleefully that "the decision of the Supreme Court has fell still born, and they find they cannot coerce Georgia to yield to its mandate."[44]

Eventually the Cherokees went the same way as the other Indian tribes. Factional splits gave the federal government the chance to bribe and cajole. In October 1835 the pro-removal group signed a sham treaty that, despite an outcry in the North from notables such as Ralph Waldo Emerson, passed the U.S. Senate by one vote. Ross kept lobbying Congress but, when the deadline for voluntary emigration passed, the U.S. army moved in. Under Winfield Scott, yet another general who was to use his exploits in the West to bid for the White House, U.S. soldiers drove the Cherokees out of their homes at bayonet point, often with only the clothes they wore, and herded them into stockades. The army had difficulty arranging transport to move them west of the Mississippi and in the summer of 1838 hundreds died in the stockades from malnutrition, dysentery, and disease. Eventually the remnant was marched west under military escort.

One traveler from Maine saw them en route:

> The sick and feeble were carried in waggons—about as comfortable for traveling as a New England ox cart with a covering over it—a great many ride on horseback and multitudes go on foot—even aged females, apparently nearly ready to drop into the grave, were traveling with heavy burdens attached to the back—on the sometimes frozen ground . . . with no covering for the feet except what nature had given them. . . . We learned from inhabitants on the road where the Indians passed that they buried fourteen or fifteen at every stopping place.

The man from Maine was particularly struck by one lady who passed with "as much refinement" as "any of the mothers of New England; and she was a mother too" with her youngest child, about three years old, sick in her arms. Soon, he knew, "she must stop in a stranger-land and consign her much loved babe to the cold ground, and that too without pomp or ceremony, and pass on with the multitude."[45] Their journey to the new Indian territory west of the Mississippi took nearly six months. About 13,000 Cherokees set out and probably a quarter died on the way, among them Ross's wife.[46] The Cherokees called it the "Trail of Tears."

In 1820 about 125,000 Indians had lived east of the Mississippi. By the mid-1840s there were only 30,000—mostly in remote reservations around the Great Lakes.[47] The once powerful tribes of the Southeast, sitting on prime land, had been evicted and the way was clear to develop America's cotton kingdom. The Indians' new territories were guaranteed to them in perpetuity by the U.S. government. So, too, of course, had been the lands they had lost.

FRONTIER VALUES

Clearing out the natives was essential to make the West free for white Americans. Morris Birkbeck, an English traveler in Pennsylvania in 1816, witnessed people at the start of their great trek: "Old America seems to be breaking up, and moving westward. We are seldom out of sight, as we travel on this grand track towards the Ohio, of family groups behind and before us." These migrants did not carry much heavy baggage. "A small waggon (so light that you might almost carry it, yet strong enough to bear a good load of bedding, utensils and provisions, and a swarm of young citizens—and to sustain marvellous shocks in its passage over these rocky heights) with two small horses; sometimes a cow or two, comprises their all; excepting a little store of hard-earned cash for the land office of the district."[48]

West of Pennsylvania and Virginia lie, in succession, the states of Ohio, Indiana, and Illinois, most of them divided up on the surveyor's grid devised by Thomas Jefferson. Many of the early settlers came from the South, particularly Virginia, and they settled in the southern parts of Indiana and Illinois, where the forested river valleys offered abundant timber for houses, barns, and fencing.

Taming the wilderness has been a recurrent theme of America's national mythology—technology applied to nature in the name of progress. The first and perhaps most potent technological symbol was the axe, which cut down the forest and built the log cabins from which a succession of nineteenth-century U.S. presidents claimed to have originated. The poet Walt Whitman held up the axe as a symbol that divided the Old World and the New. In Europe, he claimed, the axe was an instrument of autocratic destruction, symbolized by the masked executioner, the "sunsets of the martyrs," and the ghosts of "dead lords, uncrown'd ladies, impeach'd ministers, rejected kings." But in the New World, said Whitman, the axe serves a very different function:

> I see the mighty and friendly emblem of the power of my own race,
> the newest, largest race. . . .
> The axe leaps!
> The solid forest gives fluid utterances,
> They tumble forth, they rise and form,
> Hut, tent, landing, survey,
> Flail, plough, pick, crowbar, spade,
> Shingle, rail, prop, wainscot, jamb, lath, panel, gable.

In Whitman's expanding, exploding imagination,

> The shapes arise!
> Shapes of factories, arsenals, foundries, markets . . .
> Shapes of Democracy total, result of centuries . . .
> Shapes bracing the earth and braced with the whole earth.[49]

For Whitman, the axe had become the instrument and herald of a democracy that would girdle the globe.

By the 1830s the big migration into the Midwest emanated not from the South but from New England, where some areas had been exhausted by a couple of centuries of cultivation. Farms, even whole towns, were simply abandoned and fields turned over to sheep. The New Englanders settled farther north on the undulating prairies of central Indiana and Illinois, and across the Mississippi in Iowa. This was more daunting terrain because of the lack of trees for building materials and also the tough surface soil whose thick grass, several feet high in summer, developed a matted, intertwined root system. Traditional cast-iron ploughs, which worked well in the light soils of New England, were unsuited to breaking up the prairie sod; they also became clogged by the heavy clay soil underneath and had to be cleaned by hand every few yards. Another new technology—more complex than the axe—was needed to transform nature.

John Deere was a blacksmith from Vermont who had joined the trek west because of lack of work in New England. In 1837, soon after arriving in Illinois, he decided to experiment with a highly polished steel blade for a plough. This proved superior both in cutting the sod and in scouring itself of clay. Initially John Deere made only a few ploughs a year but, by the end of the 1840s, he had moved his base to Moline, Illinois, where the neighboring Mississippi provided water power and easy transportation. Today John Deere tractors are a household name in America, but the founder of the company made his reputation with the plough that tamed the prairies.

The settler with axe and plough became part of American mythology, but that image was truly rooted in history. Consider the story of Abraham Lincoln, born in Kentucky in 1809 in a one-room log cabin measuring sixteen feet by eighteen. In 1816 his parents, Thomas and Nancy, took their family north across the Ohio river, partly to get secure title to land but also to escape from a slave society—Thomas belonging to a strict Baptist sect that abhorred slavery. The land that Thomas acquired in Indiana was virgin forest. That winter Abe, aged seven, spent most of the time, axe in hand, helping clear the trees so they could plant corn the following spring.

Just as they were getting established, the neighborhood was decimated by the "milk sickness," caused by local dairy cows grazing on white snakeroot, a plant highly toxic to humans, and thereby contaminating the community's milk supply. Friends and relatives succumbed; finally Lincoln's mother, Nancy, was taken sick. Her tongue turned white, then brown; her innards burned; her feet and hands grew colder and colder. A week later the wood was being cut and sawn again, this time for her coffin.

Thomas Lincoln knew that he and his children could not survive physically or psychologically without a woman in the house. Returning to his hometown in Kentucky, he married a widow called Sarah with three small children of her own and brought them back to Indiana. Thomas wanted a wife, Sarah needed a husband—it started off almost as a business contract—but the relationship blossomed. Sarah managed to fuse the five disparate offspring into a new and happy family. Although Abe received only about twelve months of formal schooling—actually odd weeks scattered over several winters—he was able to read and write. The earliest document of his that has survived runs as follows:

> *Abraham Lincoln*
> *his hand and pen*
> *he will be good but*
> *god knows When.*[50]

In his late teens, Abe began to distance himself from his father. He preferred to lounge around reading, particularly biography, history, and poetry, whereas his father wanted him to work. In those days a strong son was a man's pension—guarantor of some kind of security in old age—and Thomas Lincoln, worn out by years of backbreaking toil, was now ailing. Legally Abe was obliged to do his father's bidding until the age of twenty-one. In fact, he stayed an extra year, helping Thomas move one last time, into more fertile land in Illinois. It was a two-week journey on roads that froze hard by night and thawed into clotted mud each day. During the summer of 1830 Abe helped break fifteen acres of hard prairie sod on the north bank of the Sangamon river. Then the following year he struck out on his own, piloting flatboats and their cargoes down the Mississippi. From there he moved into law and politics—but his frontier years as a man of the axe and the plough were never forgotten.

In the 1890s, Frederick Jackson Turner, a young Wisconsin historian, became famous by arguing that it was this constant confrontation with nature in the West that had made America fundamentally different from Europe: "American social development has been continually beginning over again on the frontier. This perennial rebirth, this fluidity of American life, this expansion westward with its new opportunities, its continuous touch with the simplicity of primitive society, furnish the points dominating American character." For Turner "the true point of view in the history of this nation is not the Atlantic coast, it is the Great West."[51]

Turner celebrated the settler, taming the land by the sweat of his brow, but in fact the speculator was just as important. The federal government was anxious to raise money, so vast tracts of land were sold off to men who had it. After 1820 the minimum price was reduced to $1.25 per acre but at the peak of speculative booms such as 1836 or 1856, the real figure could be $10, $20, or even $60. In the 1840s, the U.S. Congress allowed a legal right of preemption: Squatters who had worked some land could buy it at the minimum price. But they still had to raise the money—loan sharks circled eagerly, ready to offer cash at extortionate rates of interest—and there was always the threat of rival claim-jumpers. Many pioneers, like Thomas Lincoln, worked an acreage for a while, sold at a profit, and then moved on. Land was always as much a speculative investment as a place to settle.

Ad-men also made the West. Newspapers across America were full of notices singing the praises of this or that matchless city of the future. Some places did take off—such as Chicago, incorporated in 1833 with a mere 350 people—but many were just promotional hype. This became something of a joke. One spoof ad lauded the city of Skunksburgh, superbly situated on a river called the Slough, which ran in the rainy season:

> This noble stream, by the use of proper and sufficient means, may be made navigable to the sea. . . . A noble bluff of 18 inches commands the harbour, and . . . will give a sufficient elevation for the principal public edifices. Com-

modious and picturesque positions will be therefore reserved for the Exchange and City Hall, a church, one Gymnastic and one Polytechnic foundation, one Olympic and two Dramatic theatres, an Equestrian circus, an observatory, two marine and two Foundling Hospitals, and in the most commercial part of the city will be a reservation for seventeen banks, to each of which may be attached a lunatic Hospital.[52]

So the West was opened up by the con man and the loan shark as much as by the sturdy settler, but in the end technology proved even more decisive.

"LET US CONQUER SPACE"

After the War of 1812, nationally minded members of Congress demanded a massive program of domestic improvements to strengthen the expanding country's internal ties. In Europe distance reinforced divisions and some politicians feared the same fate for the United States. John C. Calhoun of South Carolina told Congress that whatever "impedes the intercourse of the extremes with this, the centre of the Republic, weakens the Union. The more enlarged the sphere of commercial circulation, the more extended that of social intercourse; the more strongly are we bound together[,] the more inseparable are our destinies." Calhoun urged Congress to "bind the Republic together with a perfect system of roads and canals. Let us conquer space."[53]

Calhoun wanted the U.S. government to finance this program, using the bonus and dividends paid to it by the Bank of the United States, but on March 3, 1817, his last day in office, President Madison vetoed Calhoun's bill, arguing that it would be an abuse of federal power under the Constitution. Six weeks later the New York legislature agreed to construct a canal across the whole state, linking the Hudson river with Lake Erie.

The Erie Canal's leading sponsor was DeWitt Clinton, a tall, imposing, ambitious politician dubbed Magnus Apollo by his foes. His career seemed on the skids—having been defeated by Madison for the presidency in 1812 and then losing his post as mayor of New York City. Clinton believed passionately that a transstate canal would be of huge economic benefit to New York, but he also saw it in personal terms as a political lifebelt.

Thus far, the canal mania that convulsed Britain in the late eighteenth century had passed America by. The country had in all only about a hundred miles of canals, none of them longer than twenty-seven miles. Clinton was proposing a canal double the length of anything in Europe, which posed formidable engineering problems. The federal government had washed its hands of the idea and, with the American economy in its infancy, there were no venture capitalists ready to rush forward. As for the state of New York, it had only a million people, most of them living in and around Manhattan. So it was a huge gamble for the state legislature to approve $7 million in bonds in the hope that they would be taken up by investors. Here was an entrepreneurial act of faith, undertaken by a state government that was determined to outdo rivals such as Pennsylvania in the rush to open up links with the West.[54] Critics called the canal "Clinton's Ditch," but it actually proved his high road back into politics, helping him win election as governor of New York in 1817.

Ground was broken on the Fourth of July 1817, with Clinton presiding. The state allocated construction mile by mile to contractors who hired their own laborers, many of them Irish or Welsh. The middle section of the canal, on almost level ground and with few locks, opened only two years later and the toll revenue came rushing in. Seeing the canal's success, wealthy investors such as John Jacob Astor now joined in, followed by European banks such as Barings in London and Rothschilds in Paris.

The whole canal was formally opened in October 1825 by a chain of cannon salutes booming from Buffalo on Lake Erie east to Albany (the state capital) on the upper reaches of the Hudson, then downriver to Manhattan, and finally all the way back to Buffalo in three hours (killing two gunners in the process). Governor Clinton, the canal commissioners, and other VIPs followed in a ten-day grand progress, stopping for speeches and festivities all along the way. When they arrived off Manhattan, Clinton "poured a libation of the fresh water brought from Lake Erie into the salt water of the Atlantic Ocean—and so typified the joining together of the inland and the outland seas."[55] This became known as the "Wedding of the Waters."

According to Cadwallader Colden, a New York politician, the ceremonies were intended as a message to foreign nations: "They have told us that our government was unstable, that it was too weak to unite so large a territory—that our Republic was incapable of works of great magnitude," but "we say to them, see this great link in the chain of our union—it has been devised, planned and executed by the free citizens of this Republican state."[56]

Colden, Clinton, and fellow New Yorkers had reason to be proud. The Erie Canal was 363 miles in length—roughly the distance from London to Edinburgh. It climbed 600 feet from the Hudson river through eighty-three locks and across eighteen stone aqueducts. Apart from being a marvel of engineering, it generated new towns such as Buffalo, Rochester, and Syracuse, and revolutionized trade. Before, transporting a ton of grain by wagon had cost between fifteen and twenty-five cents a mile, but now the price was two cents or less by boat. Journey times were cut by half.

The Erie Canal confirmed New York's position as America's premier Atlantic port. Boston had faded long before; now Philadelphia's business was squeezed as the produce of the West flowed through the canal and down the Hudson. So Pennsylvania, Ohio, and other states rushed to catch up with New York. By 1840 the United States had over 3,300 miles of canals.

The canals also moved people, using brightly painted packet boats. The journey was much quicker than by stagecoach, but not exactly pleasant with dozens of travelers cooped up in a low cabin that served as lounge, dining room, or sleeping accommodation depending on the time of day. In 1842 Charles Dickens, on a tour of America, sampled a canal boat in Pennsylvania. Around ten o'clock in the evening, going below after a much-needed breath of air, "I found suspended, on either side of the cabin, three long tiers of hanging bookshelves, designed apparently for volumes of the small octavo size. Looking with greater attention at these contrivances (wondering to find such literary preparations in such a place), I descried on each shelf a sort of microscopic sheet and blanket; then I began dimly to comprehend that the passengers were the library, and that they were to be arranged edge-wise on these shelves till morning." As for the ladies, wrote Dickens decorously, "they were already abed, behind the red curtain, which was carefully drawn and pinned up the centre; though, as every cough, or sneeze, or whisper, behind this curtain was perfectly audible before it, we had still a lively consciousness of their society."[57]

The Erie Canal was a unique success story: No other project really made money and canal mania left Pennsylvania and Indiana almost bankrupt. New York had a special advantage for canal building—the Mohawk valley, a natural notch through the Appalachian chain. Elsewhere canals had to cut through the mountains or climb over them, which was either impossible or ruinously expensive.

But another technology was already, literally, steaming into view. In 1825, the year of New York's "Wedding of the Waters," the Stockton to Darlington railway opened in England, earning immortality for George Stephenson. Three years later, ground was broken in America for the Baltimore and Ohio Railroad. The day chosen, inevitably, was the Fourth of July and, as an added attraction, the first earth was turned by Charles Carroll, sole survivor of that now legendary band of brothers who had signed America's founding document in 1776. He considered this "among the most important acts of my life, second only to my signing the Declaration of Independence, if even it be second to that."[58]

Here was Baltimore's answer to New York—a railroad projected right across the Appalachians. Starting, like the canals, with horses, it soon switched to the newfangled steam engines. During the 1830s the Baltimore and Ohio spread its tentacles south to Washington, D.C., and west to the National Road, one of America's first improved highways, at Cumberland in Maryland. Meanwhile Massachusetts, another state that had avoided canal mania, also decided to gamble on the iron horse. The Boston and Maine Railroad helped rejuvenate the region's economy, in decay since the Revolutionary Wars. Although Britain had pioneered steam railways, America soon led the world: By 1840 it already had 3,300 miles of track—the same figure as for canals—and this track mileage was nearly double the figure for the whole of Europe.[59]

Alongside the tracks stood the ubiquitous poles carrying wires for the telegraph—another technological marvel of the age, pioneered in America by Samuel Morse in the 1830s. The New York expansionist John L. O'Sullivan predicted grandly that "the magnetic telegraph will enable the editors of the 'San Francisco

Union,' the 'Astoria Evening Post,' or the 'Nootka Morning News,' to set up in type the first half of the President's Inaugural before the echoes of the latter half shall have died away beneath the lofty porch of the Capitol, as spoken from his lips."[60] In combination, the railroad and the telegraph did indeed conquer existing perceptions of geographical limitation.

New technology was no panacea, of course. Different railroad companies used different gauges—ranging from the British-style four feet eight and a half favored in New England to six feet on a few lines in New York and New Jersey—so there was no such thing as a national network. Nor did the railroads suddenly supplant canals and riverboats, especially for heavy freight like coal: The peak year for tonnage on the Erie Canal was not until 1872. But transport by rail was faster than by canal and also, with branch lines easily built, far more flexible. During the 1840s railroad building eclipsed canal construction; by 1860 the United States had over 30,000 miles of track, compared with roughly 4,000 miles of canals. Once again small investors and state subsidies played a huge part in their development, but now Uncle Sam, who had refused to get his feet wet during the canal-building boom, was also stepping in.[61]

The 1850s equivalent of the Erie Canal was the Illinois Central Railroad, which ran 700 miles north from the southern tip of the state at Cairo, on the junction of the Mississippi and Ohio rivers, and included a branch line into Chicago. Built between 1852 and 1856 at a cost of nearly $27 million, it was dubbed the longest railway in the world. Just as the Erie Canal had confirmed the commercial dominance of New York, so the Illinois Central and the railroads from the east made Chicago into the great transport hub of the Midwest. And, like DeWitt Clinton in New York, there was an ambitious politician behind the project—Stephen Douglas, Illinois's leading Democrat and a senator in Washington.

Douglas was only five foot four—less than the width of some of America's railroads—but his strong voice, massive head, and formidable energy won him the nickname of "Little Giant." Like Clinton, he saw the communications revolution as a double opportunity to transform his state and make his name. He asserted that "no man can keep up with the spirit of this age who travels on anything slower than a locomotive, and fails to receive intelligence by lightning. We must therefore have Rail Roads and Telegraphs from the Atlantic to the Pacific, through our own territory."[62] For years Douglas lobbied relentlessly in Washington for a federal land grant to back a railroad through Illinois. In 1850 Congress gave his state 2.5 million acres—a 200-foot right of way plus alternating sections of land on either side to a depth of six miles.

This was an immense government subsidy. Against the security of the land, the railroad company was easily able to float bonds to finance the construction. It then sold off the land piecemeal to settlers and speculators, spawning new towns along the track whose needs created further business for the railroad: The economic multiplier effect was enormous. The federal land grant for the Illinois Central also set a precedent for the future. During the 1850s railroads spread out from New England and New York across the Appalachians to crisscross the states of Ohio, Indiana, and Illinois.

In March 1849 it took Congressman Abraham Lincoln twelve days to travel back from Washington to his home in Springfield, Illinois—using a mix of train, stagecoach, and steamboat. Twelve years later, President-elect Lincoln could do the whole journey by rail.[63] He was very struck by that contrast. At Lafayette, Indiana— some 200 miles from Springfield—he told the crowd:

> We have seen great changes within the recollection of some of us who are the older. When I first came to the west, some 44 or 45 years ago, at sundown you had completed a journey of some 30 miles which you had commenced at sunrise, and thought you had done well. Now only six hours have elapsed since I left my home in Illinois where I was surrounded by a large concourse of my fellow citizens, almost all of whom I could recognize, and I find myself far from home surrounded by the thousands I now see before me, who are strangers to me.[64]

Lincoln could have done the whole journey from Springfield to Washington in two days—it actually took him twelve because, as president-elect, he took a circuitous route to show himself to as many Americans as possible. As he told the folks in Indiana, although they were strangers to him, "still we are bound together, I trust in Christianity, civilization and patriotism, and are attached to our country and our whole country. While some of us may differ in political opinions, still we are all united in one feeling for the Union."

Lincoln was whistling in the dark; in February 1861 the United States were about to break up. The railroads had given many Americans new prosperity, new freedoms—in that sense, the iron rails had indeed helped bind the country together. Yet opening up the West also aggravated the nation's divisions as North and South, free states and slave states, vied for control of these vast and profitable new territories. Americans could not truly "conquer space" until they faced up to their past. Westward expansion had forced slavery back onto the political agenda and by the 1850s the issue could no longer be fudged.

6

SLAVE OR FREE?

Most northerners were not passionate to abolish slavery itself, but there was widespread opposition to slavery's extension into the western lands because this would undercut free labor and increase the South's influence in Washington. In 1820 the Missouri Compromise had drawn an east-west line through America's expanding domain. North of 36°30' all-new states would be free; to the south slavery was permitted. In the 1830s only two new states entered the Union, Arkansas in the South and Michigan in the North, thereby maintaining the sectional balance. By the end of the 1840s, however, slavery was back on the national agenda with a vengeance— thanks to the vast expansion of America's continental empire through war with Mexico and near-war with Britain, which carried the country right across to the gold coast of California. What northerners called "the slave power" was not the only issue inflaming politics—in the early 1850s faith issues came to the fore in a Protestant backlash against the massive wave of Catholic immigrants—but the place of slavery in the land of liberty eventually swept all else aside, including the Union itself.

THE "ARSENIC" OF MEXICO

Settlers and speculators, canals and railroads—all played a part in westward expansion. But ultimately the West was won by war and the principal victim was the other United States on the American continent, the United States of Mexico.

Both America and Mexico were independent republics, forged in war against a European colonial power—Britain in the 1770s and Spain in the 1810s. Both had federal systems, with separate state governments capped by a president, a two-house legislature, and a Supreme Court, and they were roughly the same size: around 1.75 million square miles. Mexico's vast domain, inherited from the Spanish empire, stretched up from the Gulf of Mexico to the Arkansas river and the Great Salt Lake, then west to reach the Pacific several hundred miles north of the mission town of San Francisco.

With so much in common, the two United States might have chosen to cooperate as fellow New World republics. But ultimately the differences between them were more important than the similarities. The United States of America had a booming economy, knitted together by canals and railroads, whereas the United States of Mexico was still largely agrarian. America's population nearly doubled between 1820 and 1840, to over 17 million, while Mexico's grew only slightly to 7 million. American settlers were pressing into the Mexican states of Texas and California. And although America was strained by sectional tensions among North, South, and West, Mexico's union was near to collapse. Its northern states wanted greater autonomy, but this was resisted by centralizers in Mexico City. Frequent coups and rampant corruption added to the country's malaise.

In Texas the American settlers had no intention of becoming Catholics or accepting Mexico's ban on slavery, so in 1835 they declared independence. Initially the struggle did not go well. Two hundred settlers were overwhelmed in the Alamo Fort in San Antonio in March 1836—including the Indian fighter Davy Crockett, who became one of America's great folk heroes. But the following month the Americans under Sam Houston surprised the main Mexican army during siesta time. Shouting "Remember the Alamo," they vanquished the enemy in less than twenty minutes. Among the prisoners from the Battle of San Jacinto was the Mexican commander-in-chief and president, Antonio de Santa Anna, who, in return for his freedom, conceded independence to the new Republic of Texas.

This did not, however, mean that Texas would become part of the United States of America. It might have remained an independent state, setting a pattern for other breakaways from Mexico. This was certainly the hope in London, where the building that housed the Republic of Texas's legation can still be seen today off St. James Street. The British Foreign Office believed that an independent Texas would act as a buffer to American westward expansion and serve as an alternative to the Deep South as a supplier of cotton. Nor was the U.S. Congress in any hurry to bring Texas into the Union because this would reopen the old question of whether new states should be slave or free, thereby upsetting the delicate balance between North and South in the Senate.

So Texas remained in limbo for nearly a decade until, in the mid-1840s, it was caught up in a larger public debate about America's destiny. Most Americans at the beginning of the century had envisaged the Rockies as a natural boundary, beyond which sister republics—American in ethos but separate politically—would flourish. "Along the back of this ridge," insisted Senator Thomas Hart Benton of Missouri in 1825, "a Western limit of the republic should be drawn, and the statue of the fabled god, Terminus, should be raised upon its highest peak, never to be thrown down."[1] But that was before the railroad and the telegraph. Now a single polity spanning the whole continent from the Atlantic to the Pacific seemed conceivable—indeed, to many, almost inevitable.

In 1845 John L. O'Sullivan, a New York editor, predicted that California would soon follow Texas: "Imbecile and distracted, Mexico can never exert any real governmental authority over such a country. . . . Already the advance guard of the irresistible army of Anglo-Saxon emigration has begun to pour down upon it, armed with the plough and the rifle, and marking its trail with schools and colleges, courts and representative halls, mills and meeting houses." Even if California started out as a separate country, O'Sullivan was confident that a transcontinental railroad would soon draw what he called "the Empires of the Pacific and the Atlantic" together. He looked forward a century to "the two hundred and fifty or three hundred millions—and American millions—destined to gather beneath the fluttering stripes and stars in the fast hastening year of the Lord 1945!" And he denounced the "insolent and hostile interference" of Britain in America's relations with Mexico, "for the avowed object of thwarting our policy and hampering our power, limiting our greatness and checking the fulfilment of our manifest destiny to overspread the continent allotted by Providence for the free development of our yearly multiplying millions."[2]

"Manifest destiny" was a slogan that captured the public imagination, signifying America's God-given right as the instrument of liberty and progress to occupy all the land from the Atlantic to the Pacific. By the 1840s settlers were moving into California and, further north, blazing the trail into Oregon country, an area shared in an uneasy condominium by America and Britain. In 1844 the Democrats decided that the time was politically ripe. Their campaign platform called for "the re-occupation of Oregon and the re-annexation of Texas"—the "re-" in both cases a nice piece of spin, to suggest that American rights had been given away earlier by their political opponents.

The Democrats chose a candidate quietly committed to these goals. James K. Polk, a longtime congressman from Tennessee, emerged as a compromise after the convention became deadlocked between rival big names. Whigs derided him as a political unknown: "Who is James K. Polk?" But after the election the Democrats had the last laugh, answering: "The President of the United States." Aged fifty, Polk was the youngest incumbent of the White House to date. He was a protégé of Andrew Jackson—indeed, with his gaunt face, high forehead, and swept-back hair, he looked very similar—and his loyal support of Jacksonian policies won him the ultimate accolade, "*Young* Hickory." Unlike Jackson, however, Polk was an austere loner, who worked around the clock, shunned social events, and devoted what little leisure time he had to reading the Bible. This was a man with a mission—and with the skill and determination to accomplish it.

Polk's victory spurred lame-duck president John Tyler into pushing through the annexation of Texas. Unable to get the Senate to approve a treaty, which needed a two-thirds majority, Tyler secured a joint resolution, which required only a simple majority of each House. He signed the bill into law just three days before Polk's inauguration on March 4, 1845.

Despite the steady rain on that day and the sea of umbrellas he faced, the new president was upbeat, asserting his confidence that "our system may be safely extended to the utmost bounds of our territorial limits and that, as it shall be extended, the bonds of our Union, so far from being weakened, will become stronger."[3] From the start Polk played it tough with Mexico. He sent U.S. troops into Texas to head off Mexican resistance and possible British intervention. He backed the flimsy Texan claim to a border on the Rio Grande, which would give it a massive additional chunk of Mexican territory. And he dispatched an envoy to Mexico City with instructions to pay up to $40 million for the provinces of New Mexico and California. American settlers were already moving into the area north of San Francisco, threatening a Texas-style uprising against the rickety Mexican state government of California.

Polk's bid for a new version of Jefferson's Louisiana Purchase came to nothing. The Mexicans were not interested in a deal with people whom they despised. "Who," asked Manuel Eduardo de Gorostiza, a former ambassador in Washington, "is not familiar with that race of migratory adventurers that exist in the United States, composed of the most restless, profligate and robust of its sons, who always live in the unpopulated regions, taking land away from the Indians and then assassinating them? Far removed from civilization, as they condescendingly call it, they are precursors of immorality and pillage." At stake, in Gorostiza's view, were no longer just slices of territory. Mexico was engaged in a "war of race, of religion, of language, and of customs," a struggle for its very identity as a nation.[4]

So the U.S. envoy returned empty-handed from Mexico City, and now the president's patience was at an end. He had not wanted war but was confident that, if it came, victory would be gained within three or four months. On May 9, 1846, news arrived that a detachment of Mexican troops had crossed the Rio Grande, leaving sixteen Americans killed or wounded. This was the pretext that Polk needed and he presented Congress with a fait accompli: "[N]ow, after reiterated menaces, Mexico . . . has invaded our territory and shed American blood upon the American soil. . . . As war exists, and, notwithstanding all our efforts to avoid it, exists by the act of Mexico herself, we are called upon by every consideration of duty and patriotism to vindicate with decision the honor, the rights, and the interests of our country."[5] A declaration of war was railroaded through Congress, the House being allowed only two hours for debate.

The big imponderable was Britain's reaction, given its preference for an independent Texas and its interest in the potential of the California ports for Pacific trade. With Oregon also in dispute, Polk believed that the whole West Coast was at stake and he reiterated the Monroe Doctrine of 1823, warning European powers to keep out of the Americas. He felt that "the only way to treat John Bull was to look him straight in the eye" and considered "a bold & firm course on our part the pacific one," believing that "if Congress faultered in their course, John Bull would immediately become arrogant and more grasping in his demands; & that such had been the history of the Brittish [*sic*] nation in all their contests with other Powers for the last two hundred years."[6]

Publicly the Democrats' slogan about Oregon was "fifty-four forty or fight"—which would have placed the border with Canada so far up the Pacific coast as to deny Britain all the ice-free harbors. In private, however, Polk was willing to draw the line at the forty-ninth parallel, giving both America and Britain access to the Juan de Fuca Strait, entryway to what became the great ports of Vancouver and Seattle. By May 1846 the president knew that the British were ready to accept this compromise, aware that in the Pacific Northwest their settlers were far outnumbered by American migrants. As Lord Castlereagh had reportedly told a U.S. diplomat years earlier, "You will conquer Oregon in your bedchambers."[7]

So Polk read the British correctly, and initially he seemed to be right about the Mexicans as well. The war began with American victories in major battles across the Rio Grande and around Santa Fe; U.S. forces also helped the settlers in California to form their own "Bear State Republic" on the Texas model. These campaigns bloodied American officers who later became household names in the 1860s, such as Ulysses S. Grant and Robert E. Lee. The latter made clear the contempt they all felt for the Mexicans as corrupt, incompetent, Catholic half-breeds: "It is a miserable population. Always feared & truckled to by their own government, idle worthless & vicious. . . . [W]ithout an army, without money & revenue, these people are unable to prosecute war & have not power to make peace. They will oblige us in spite of ourselves to overrun the country & drive them into the sea."[8]

But Lee, like Polk, failed to understand the vehement anti-American nationalism that inspired Mexican will to keep fighting. So the conflict dragged on and, as it did so, opposition mounted in the United States. There were questions (not for the last time in American history) about army incompetence, the lack of realistic peace aims, and whether the government had hyped up the case for war. Lincoln, now a Whig congressman from Illinois, argued that Polk's justifications were "from beginning to end, the sheerest deception." Lincoln suspected that "originally having some strong motive . . . to involve the two countries in a war, and trusting to escape scrutiny, by fixing the public gaze upon the exceeding brightness of military glory," Polk simply plunged into it and then "swept, *on* and *on*, till, disappointed in his calculation of the ease with which Mexico might be subdued, he now finds himself . . . a bewildered, confounded, and miserably perplexed man."[9]

A good deal of this was rank political opportunism: Lincoln, like many Whigs, had backed the war at the start when it was popular. Polk kept his nerve and eventually U.S. troops took Mexico City. The Treaty of Guadalupe Hidalgo, signed in February 1848, gave the United States all of New Mexico and California in return for $15 million. Some Democrats had demanded the whole of Mexico, some Whigs wanted none of its lands apart from Texas, and the vote was close, but in the end the president pushed his treaty through the Senate.

Polk had always intended to serve only one term. He retired, exhausted, in March 1849 and died within three months. But this once-derided president left a valuable legacy. Through war and diplomacy he had acquired more land than Jefferson's Louisiana Purchase, roughly a quarter of the present-day United States. America's borders now stretched from coast to coast, fulfilling that "manifest destiny" that expansionists had proclaimed. Yet Polk's clear but blinkered vision of American greatness also created huge problems. Mexico had been brutally stripped of half its territory, engendering lasting enmity against America, and the vast new conquests of Polk's war reopened the debate between North and South about how to govern the West. The author Ralph Waldo Emerson prophesied: "The United States will conquer Mexico, but it will be as the man swallows the arsenic, which brings him down in turn. Mexico will poison us."[10]

GOD, GOLD, AND THE COMPROMISE OF 1850

One problem in the new West was the itinerant Mormons—the most troublesome of the sects created by the evangelical revivals. Wherever their leader, Joseph Smith, and his followers had settled, they stirred up animosity—moving from western New York to Ohio, then Missouri, and finally Carthage, Illinois, on the banks of the Mississippi, where Smith was gunned down by an angry mob in 1844. Smith was an autocrat: The final confrontation exploded when he tried to suppress a local newspaper that criticized him. And he claimed to be the translator of a divinely inspired account of the risen Christ's visit to the Americas, where he founded a society of peace and love. The text was the Book of Mormon; Smith's mission was to rekindle those values in nineteenth-century America.

After his death, the Mormons followed a new leader, Brigham Young, across the Plains and over the Rockies, where in 1847 they found a remote, self-sufficient valley. For one of them, William Clayton, this was a far cry from the moors of his native Lancashire but, looking down from a mountain ridge, it seemed like the promised land: "There is an extensive, beautiful, level looking valley from here to the lake which I should judge from the numerous deep green patches must be fertile and rich. The valley extends to the south probably fifty miles." Apart from a discernible lack of timber, Clayton deemed this "one of the most beautiful valleys and pleasant places for a home for the Saints which could be found."[11]

What William Clayton took from afar to be a fertile valley was actually an arid plateau, rainless for half the year; the water at its center was the Great Salt Lake. But under Brigham Young's stern discipline the Mormons worked together to make the desert bloom and to build their "New Zion," Salt Lake City. When they trekked down into the valley it was still nominally under Mexican control, but within months the area was surrendered to the United States under the Treaty of Guadalupe Hidalgo. In March 1849 Brigham Young applied to join the Union as the state of Deseret (the word for "honeybee" in the Book of Mormon). This posed a tricky problem for the federal government because he was claiming a vast area, what eventually became the states of Utah, Nevada, and Arizona; there was a moral dilemma as well, because the Mormons were widely detested for their practice of polygamy.

California posed an even bigger problem. Here, too, there had been a sudden influx of settlers, but the numbers were far greater than the Mormons, and their motive very different.

John Sutter was a migrant from Switzerland who had settled in northern California. On a rainy afternoon in January 1848 James Marshall, who was building a sawmill for Sutter, called by. As Sutter recalled later: "He told me then that he had some important and interesting news which he wished to communicate secretly to me, and wished me to go with him to a place where we should not be disturbed. . . . I went with him to my private rooms; he requested me to lock the door." Then Marshall pulled a rag from his pocket and showed Sutter some bits of yellow ore he had found in the mill race. "After having proved the metal with aqua fortis, which I found in my apothecary shop, likewise with other experiments, and read the long article 'gold' in the Encyclopedia Americana, I declared this to be gold of the finest quality, of at least 23 carats."[12]

A reference book and a solution of nitric acid were hardly rigorous tests, but Marshall had indeed found gold. Sutter was desperate to keep the news a secret, so he could finish his building projects, but within weeks his property and the whole of northern California were overrun by would-be prospectors. Walter Colton witnessed at firsthand the dramatic effects of gold fever in the coastal town of Monterey, where he was the new American mayor. "My messenger, sent to the mines, has returned with specimens of the gold; he dismounted in a sea of upturned faces. As he drew forth the yellow lumps from his pockets, and passed them around among the eager crowd, the doubts, which had lingered till now, fled." Gripped by frenzied excitement, "all were now off for the mines, some on horses, some on carts, and some on crutches, and one went in a litter. An American woman, who had recently established a boarding-house here, pulled up stakes and was off before her lodgers had time even to pay their bills."[13]

Soon the news got back to the East and from there around the world. The California gold rush began in earnest in 1849. By the end of that year there were 80,000 people in California, whereas in 1846 the population had been only about 10,000. Few of the Forty-Niners got rich but they left their mark on American history. With so many people suddenly living in California, decisions had to be made about whether to admit it into the United States as a state. The same problem had to be faced in Utah and New Mexico—all these new domains needed some form of government to maintain law and order—and that meant grappling anew with the old question of whether the West should be open to slavery.

Since 1846 David Wilmot, a Democratic congressman from Pennsylvania, had been demanding a ban on slavery from all the lands acquired from Mexico. Other northerners proposed that the Missouri Compromise line of 1820 should be extended all the way to the Pacific—in other words, barring slavery north of 36°30'. Neither this motion nor the Wilmot proviso was ever passed, but both aroused deep resentment in the South. So the omens did not look good when the new Congress convened in December 1849 with California topping the agenda. "We are on the very verge of bloodshed in the capital," one journalist warned. "There is no telling when its crimson streaks may deluge the halls of Congress. . . . The Southern members are excited to the highest pitch. Men go armed. . . . We are in the crisis so long and so justly dreaded."[14]

The next few months inspired some of the greatest speeches in American political history. First from Senator John C. Calhoun of South Carolina—a formidable intellect devoid of humor, whose mane of hair, flashing eyes, and fluent tongue had made him one of the great orators of the age. But now, aged sixty-seven, he was ravaged by tuberculosis and his speech had to be read for him by a colleague.

Calhoun believed that this was, in essence, a matter of numbers. In the North and Midwest the population had grown much faster than in the South. Consequently, "the equilibrium between the two sections in the Government, as it stood when the Constitution was ratified and the Government put in action, has been destroyed." The result, he said, "is to give the Northern section a predominance in every part of the Government." Except, that is, in the Senate, where the formula of two senators per state, regardless of population, helped maintain a North-South balance. But if the new West was barred to slavery, then, within a decade or so, even that equilibrium would be upset and the South itself would be in danger. Calhoun cited "the long-continued agitation of the slave question on the part of the North, and the many aggressions which they have made on the rights of the South." What, he asked, "is to stop this agitation before the great and final object at which it aims—the abolition of slavery in the States—is consummated? Is it, then, not certain that if something is not done to arrest it, the South will be forced to choose between abolition and secession?"[15]

As his words were read out, Calhoun sat huddled and motionless, but occasionally his eyes flashed around the chamber, like the last embers of a once-great furnace. The impact of his speech was immense. It sounded like the obituary of the Union, delivered as his own final testament. In fact, Calhoun was dead within the month.

Three days after Calhoun's speech, another titan of the Senate rose to address his colleagues and the nation. Daniel Webster was as striking as Calhoun, with his lion-like head, broad chest, and operatic voice. Whereas Calhoun was the apostle of southern sectionalism, Webster stood for the Union: "Mr. President, I wish to speak to-day, not as a Massachusetts man, nor as a northern man, but as an American." Attempting to reassure New Englanders, Webster claimed that there was no need for Congress to legislate about slavery in the arid Far West because it was excluded from there by the law of nature. "Who expects to see a hundred black men cultivating tobacco, corn, cotton, rice, or anything else, on lands in New Mexico, made fertile only by irrigation?"

To appease the South, for whom the North's assistance to fugitive slaves was another symbolic issue, Webster noted in the same speech that the Constitution obliged northerners "to the return of persons bound to service who have escaped into the free States. In that respect, it is my judgment that the South is right, and the North is wrong." Above all, Webster warned against easy illusions that the South could secede from the Union peacefully. "Sir, your eyes and mine are never destined to see that miracle. The dismemberment of this vast country . . . must produce such a war as I will not describe."[16]

Webster considered himself the voice of reasonable compromise but, to many New Englanders, his was the language of betrayal. Four days later William H. Seward of New York spoke out for northern radicals. Twenty years younger than the old giants Calhoun and Webster, he was actually giving his maiden speech in the Senate. Unlike them, Seward was no great presence, with his birdlike face and husky, monotonous voice. His words had far more impact when read rather than heard—but read they were in newspapers and pamphlets right across the country because what he said was clear, learned, and, above all, utterly intransigent.

Seward insisted that California should be welcomed as a free state, without any equivocations or trade-offs. "Yes, let California come in. Every new state . . . is always welcomed," but "California, the youthful Queen of the Pacific, in her robes of freedom gorgeously inlaid with gold, is doubly welcome." Seward damned the idea of a law to return fugitive slaves as "unjust, unconstitutional and immoral," claiming that "we cannot, in our judgment, be either true Christians or real freemen if we impose on another a chain that we defy all human power to fasten on ourselves." He derided Webster's contention that slavery had reached its natural limits: "Sir, there is no climate uncongenial to slavery. . . . Slave labor is cheaper than free labor . . . it is the indolence of mankind, in any climate, and not the natural necessity, that introduces slavery." As for Calhoun and Webster's talk about what the Constitution required, Seward insisted that "there is a higher law than the Constitution" because California was part of "the common heritage of mankind, bestowed on them by the Creator of the universe. We are his stewards."[17]

Seward's appeal to a Higher Law rang alarm bells throughout the South. But in 1850, after ten months of bitter argument, the advocates of compromise carried the day. An intricate package of measures was designed by Henry Clay—with Calhoun and Webster the third member of the venerable Great Triumvirate that had dominated the Senate for years—but it was steered through Congress by Stephen Douglas of Illinois, at thirty-six one of the youngest senators.

With energy and persistence, Douglas crafted majorities for five separate bills. His core support came from fellow northern Democrats plus southern Whigs— together the moderates favoring compromise. Then, on each individual measure, Douglas won sufficient backing from radicals on one side or the other. In the end, the North could glory in the admission of California as a free state, but the Fugitive Slave Law gave the South some assurance that its interests would be respected in the Union. The rest of the West was shelved for the moment: In fact, nearly fifty years would pass before Utah became a state and then on a far smaller scale than Brigham Young had envisioned.

Douglas insisted that this was an honorable compromise: "The South has not triumphed over the North, nor has the North achieved a victory over the South. Neither party has made any humiliating concessions to the other. Each has preserved its honor." He asserted that "the measures composing the scheme of adjustment are believed to be in harmony with the principles of justice and the Constitution."[18]

The Compromise of 1850 was greeted with bonfires, cannonades, and wild parties in Washington. In Georgia and other states in the Deep South, pro-Union Whigs cooled hothead talk about secession. Webster expressed his relief to a friend: "I can now sleep anights. We have gone thro' the most important crisis which has occurred since the foundation of the Government; and what ever party may prevail, hereafter the Union stands firm."[19] Webster was expressing the hopes of the nation. The Compromise of 1850 seemed to prove the resilience of America's democratic political system.

THE CATHOLIC THREAT TO PROTESTANT VALUES

That system was under strain in other ways, however. Migration westward was not the only mass movement in the mid-nineteenth century; even bigger was the surge of European immigrants across the Atlantic into the Northeast and the Midwest. During the decade from 1845 the United States opened its doors to 3 million people, proportionately the biggest influx in U.S. history. The majority came from Ireland and southwest Germany, victims of economic depression. Although many Germans settled in rural areas, the Irish flocked overwhelmingly to America's burgeoning cities where they took on essential but menial jobs, working as porters or as laborers building the railroads.

Most of the immigrants came in through New York, the third-largest city in the Western world after London and Paris. Often they were enticed by rags-to-riches stories of the sort printed by newspaper editor Moses Beach in his almanac titled *The Wealth and Biography of the Wealthy Citizens of the City of New York*. His aim, said Beach, had been "to hold up to view some of the brightest examples of prosperity in this touch-stone land as beacons for those ambitious of fortune's favors."[20]

Pride of place in Beach's almanac was given to Mr. John Jacob Astor, worth an estimated $25 million: "Landing on our shores as a common steerage passenger—

a poor uneducated boy—a stranger to the language and the people—he has by the sole aid of his industry, accumulated a fortune scarcely second to that of any individual in the globe." Astor, who made his money in the fur trade and then invested it in Manhattan real estate, came originally from Heidelberg, and most of the 600 superrich on Moses Beach's list hailed from Britain or Germany. But near the end was this cryptic entry: "Smith, Peter. $200,000. Came to this country from Ireland. He was a paver, and afterwards a contractor, and thus made his money. Said to have made large sums on the election of 1844."[21]

For most Irish immigrants, however, the reality was very different from the myth. Their ship anchored offshore in the "quarantine ground" to await inspection by a doctor. Those suspected of having cholera, typhus, or other diseases were incarcerated in the marine hospital on Staten Island. Those judged fit were turned over to the tender mercies of "runners" who arranged their passage into Manhattan, fleecing them handsomely in the process. Once ashore, many wandered around aimlessly—dodging the pigs and rabid dogs that roamed the streets—until they ended up, penniless, in the city almshouse. Or in the Five Points area, the prime site for murder, robbery, and prostitution in New York. Typical of the neighborhood was a basement lodging house at 35 Orange Street, described by one *New York Times* reporter as a "damp and filthy cellar" with "a number of wretched bunks, similar to those on shipboard, only not half as convenient, ranged around an apartment about ten feet square. Nearly every one of the half-dozen beds was occupied by one or more persons. No regard was paid to age or sex; but man, woman, and child were huddled up in one undistinguishable mass. . . . The most fetid odors were emitted, and the floor and the walls were damp with pestiferous exhalations."[22]

Yet even this was probably an improvement on the squalor these people had fled in Ireland. Wood floors rather than dirt; a plaster ceiling instead of insect-ridden thatch; and an iron stove, not an open fire in a smoke-filled room. In fact, many Irish immigrants, even in Five Points, managed to better themselves. Dick and Nelly Holland and their three sons arrived from County Kerry in 1851, driven out by the appalling potato blight. Dick became a laborer and Nelly a washerwoman, while the boys, like most of their age, earned money shining shoes, selling newspapers, or setting up the pins in local bowling alleys. Nelly soon lost her husband and eldest son but by 1860, nine years after arriving destitute in Manhattan, she had a balance in the local Emigrants Saving Bank of $200 (equivalent to over $4,000 today). Not exactly rags to riches in the style of John Jacob Astor or even fellow countryman Peter Smith, but still real prosperity compared to her predicament a decade before. Nelly Holland's story shows why, despite all their misery, immigrants believed in the American Dream.[23]

For many established Americans, however, mass immigration was turning the dream into a nightmare. To date, the country had been settled by people largely of British stock and Protestant religion, for whom the newcomers posed a threat. By 1850 immigrants made up half the population of New York and Chicago; two-thirds in the case of St. Louis. Soon they translated this into votes and influence. Many middle-class Americans also regarded the newcomers as riff-raff, teetering on the edge of poverty, alcoholism, and crime. In the words of Reverend Horace Bushnell, a leading Connecticut minister: "If you will glance over the catalogues of our colleges and universities, the advertisements of our merchants and mechanics, you will almost never find an Irish name among them, which shows that they do not rise to any rank among us. At the same time, if you will search the catalogue of almshouses and prisons," he added triumphantly, "there you will find their names in thick order."[24]

The most sensitive issue was religion. Most Irish and many Germans were Roman Catholics; their lifestyle threatened the widespread sense of America as a Protestant nation. A daily flashpoint was the schools. By 1850 most states had made primary education freely available to all children, at taxpayers' expense—a novelty compared with Europe. But the school day began with readings from the King James Bible and with Protestant hymns and prayers. Catholics demanded the right to use their Douai Bible, full of papal annotations, or else sent their children to church schools. To militant Protestants, the drive for Catholic education showed that these immigrants were not ready to become true Americans.

In May 1844 religion sparked a full-scale riot in Philadelphia, where nativist Protestants mounted a campaign to "save the Bible in the Schools." One of their rallies in Kensington, a largely Catholic ward, was broken up by Irish agitators. Fisticuffs turned into a firefight, leaving several Protestants killed. Next morning the *Native American* newspaper proclaimed, "Another St. Bartholomew's Day has begun in the streets of Philadelphia. The bloody hand of the Pope has stretched forth to our destruction. Now we call on our fellow-citizens, who regard free institutions, whether they be native or adopted, to arm. Our liberties are now to be fought for."[25] Several hundred Protestants marched into Kensington. Again the local Irish had the advantage, firing from inside their houses and shops, but their opponents resorted to arson. Two Catholic churches and a convent were set on fire and the city had to impose martial law for a week to cool things down.

The Bible in schools was not the only issue. Many evangelical Protestants were offended by the more relaxed Catholic attitude toward the Sabbath. Temperance enthusiasts disliked Irish saloons and German beer halls, seeing them as dens of vice and corruption. Yet beer halls were community houses, especially on Sundays when whole families whiled away the time, but this in itself caused offense to strict Protestant sabbatarians. At root, here was an age-old clash, pitting longtime residents keen to preserve their way of life against newcomers, defiantly asserting their own. There was also a political dimension. The saloon or beer hall became the local headquarters of the Democratic Party, to which immigrant Catholics largely gravitated. These people were seen as a credulous mass of foot soldiers, doing the sinister bidding of the pope, his priestly officers, and their corrupt political lieutenants.

"If they mingled in our schools, the republican atmosphere would impregnate their minds," lamented Reverend Lyman Beecher. "If they could read the Bible, and might and did, their darkened intellect would brighten, and their bowed down mind would rise. If they dared to think for themselves, the contrast of Protestant independence with their thraldom would awaken the desire of equal privileges, and put an end to an arbitrary clerical dominion over trembling superstitious minds."[26]

The Protestant backlash became serious politics in the 1850s. For years evangelicals had campaigned against demon drink, urging people to take the pledge of temperance. Now they went one step further, inspired by Neal Dow, the mayor of Portland, Maine. Dow was a successful local businessman of Quaker stock who believed that drink and its attendant vices constituted the greatest single barrier to American prosperity. Small, grim, and fanatical, Dow pushed a law banning the sale of alcohol through the Maine legislature, earning himself the nickname "the Napoleon of Temperance." By 1855 twelve other states or territories had followed suit, mostly in the Northeast.

The so-called Maine Laws were not simply an anti-immigrant measure, but Irish and German Catholics, whose economic and social lives were often built around the saloon and the beer hall, were leading opponents. Many advocates of Prohibition saw the liquor-trading immigrant as their prime target. The editor of the *Maine Temperance Watchman* complained that the Irish "come here with all their vicious habits and grovelling tastes uncontrolled, and they think they can make money at this thing, and set to work. They have no previous training in habits of temperance, and they die out before they are reclaimed."[27]

The 1850s also saw the spectacular rise of an explicitly anti-immigrant political movement. The Order of the Star Spangled Banner started out in 1850 as a secret society with Masonic-style lodges. How it acquired the popular name "Know Nothings" is not certain, but was probably because members tended to say "I know nothing" when asked about their organization. Supposedly one of its secret signs was to close one eye and then place thumb and forefinger, formed into an O, around the nose: Eye, Nose, Nothing. This may all sound a bit of a joke, and in fact Know Nothingism was a fringe movement for several years, but during 1854, as the backlash against the new immigrants gained strength, its membership surged from 50,000 to over 1 million. In the elections that autumn Know Nothing candidates swept to power in Massachusetts and the state legislatures of most of New England. They also became the main opposition to the Democratic Party in the rest of the country, including the South, displacing the Whigs.

The following year the Know Nothings went public, reconstituting themselves as the American Party—a title that gave truer indication of their aims. Each member had to be "a native born citizen, a Protestant, born of Protestant parents, reared under Protestant influence, and not united in marriage with a Roman Catholic." They pledged themselves to resist "the insidious policy of the Church of Rome, and all other foreign influences against the institutions of our country, by placing in all offices in the gift of the people, whether by election or appointment, none but native-born Protestant citizens."[28]

Keep America Protestant—that was essentially the Know Nothings' motto. They did not demand an end to immigration, but wanted to control its political consequences by increasing the period that immigrants were required to wait before becoming citizens to twenty-one years (from five) and by barring Catholics from ever holding office.

"The European who would drink from the fountain of liberty," asserted Thomas Whitney, a leading New York nativist, should "leave American politics to Americans. . . . The people of the United States, although they have thrown open their doors in the spirit of generous hospitality to the foot-sore traveller, are not yet willing to admit that . . . those who feast upon their generosity are better able to arrange and manage their household than themselves."[29]

At a deeper level, Know Nothings also capitalized on growing disenchantment among the middle-class and skilled workers with mass politics in general. "I take direct issue with democracy," declared Whitney. "If democracy implies universal suffrage, or the right of all men to take part in the control of the State without regard to the intelligence, the morals, or the principles of the man, I am no democrat. . . . As soon would I place my person and property at the mercy of an infuriated mob . . . as place the liberties of my country in the hands of an ignorant, superstitious, and vacillating populace."[30]

By the 1850s, American democratic politics, born in the days of Andrew Jackson, had fully come of age, but many Americans, not just Know Nothings, doubted that the old political parties, the Democrats and the Whigs, could cope with the immense challenges now facing the nation. Mass immigration and the rise of Catholicism constituted one threat, jeopardizing the hegemony of Protestants from British stock, but as the decade went on "Rum and Romanism" was eclipsed by the issue of slavery, because the Compromise of 1850 fell apart.

SLAVES, MASTERS, AND THE "SLAVE POWER"

The term "slavery" actually covered a multitude of sins. In some places it *did* mean a grand classical mansion, large estates, and gangs of cotton-picking slaves—the stereotype immortalized in the movie *Gone with the Wind*. But in Maryland and other parts of the Upper South, slaves amounted to only about a tenth of the population; in the Deep South—states such as South Carolina and Mississippi—the proportion was over half. Most slave owners, perhaps as many as three-quarters of them, possessed fewer than ten slaves; only an elite were tycoons. At the very top Nathaniel Heyward, a rice planter in South Carolina, owned more than 2,000 slaves, worth at least $1 million, when he died in 1851.[31]

The life of slaves therefore varied greatly. On small farms they often had a close relationship with the owner, working beside him in the fields. On big plantations, by contrast, he was usually a remote figure: Slaves labored in gangs cultivating cotton or rice under the often brutal rule of a black overseer. In general, the experience of house slaves was better than that of field hands. They were part of the family—serving meals, doing household chores, and raising the children. Often a real emotional bond developed.

For instance, John Manning, a South Carolina planter, was genuinely moved to hear of the death of a long-serving slave. He was "pained" to tell his wife that "poor Lelia died of inflammation of the stomach after five days illness. I felt as if one of the family were dead, so greatly did I regard her. Her family . . . have exhibited all the sensibility of refined & educated minds, much more, indeed, than is found in what is called the world."[32] All depended, however, on the character of the master. Harriet Jacobs was a teenage slave girl in North Carolina whose owner, Dr. James Norcom, made repeated sexual advances. "I turned from him with disgust and hatred. But he was my master, I was compelled to live under the same roof with him—where I saw a man forty years my senior daily violating the most sacred commandments of nature. He told me I was his property; that I must be subject to his will in all things. My soul revolted against the mean tyranny. But where could I turn for protection?"[33]

The story of Josiah Henson showed the essential arbitrariness of slavery. Born in Maryland in 1789, he was owned first by a master who was "far kinder to his slaves than the planters generally were, never suffering them to be struck by any one. He was a man of good, kind impulses, liberal, jovial, hearty." A "bright spot in my childhood," recalled Henson, "was my residence with him—bright, but, alas! fleeting." When the kind master died, Henson was sold to a much more brutal owner and, like many slaves, he was sucked into the system in order to survive. "At fifteen years of age there were few who could compete with me in work or sport. . . . I could run faster, wrestle better, and jump higher than anybody about me. . . . All this caused my master and my fellow slaves to look upon me as a wonderfully smart fellow, and prophecy the great things I should do when I became a man. My vanity became vastly inflamed, and I fully coincided in their opinion. . . . One word of commendation from the petty despot who ruled over us would set me up for a month."[34]

Soon Henson was practically the overseer of the plantation. Marriage and conversion to Christianity tempered his zeal to serve and he tried to buy his freedom, but his owners kept raising the price. Now out in Kentucky, he was told to accompany his master's son to New Orleans where, it became clear, he would be sold to a new owner in the Deep South. Henson was desperate. "With tears and groans I besought him not to sell me away from my wife and children. I dwelt on my past services to his father. . . . I fell down and clung to his knees in entreaties. Sometimes when too closely pressed, he would curse and strike me."[35]

Finally, they reached New Orleans but, the night before the sale, the master's son was struck down by the dreaded river fever. "The tables were now turned. I was no longer property, no longer a brute beast to be bought and sold, but his only friend in the midst of strangers. Oh, how different was his tone from what it had been the day before! He was now the supplicant. A poor, terrified object, afraid of death, and writhing with pain, there lay the late arbiter of my destiny. How he besought me to forgive him." Abandoning the sale, they set out for home. "I watched and nursed him like a mother; for all remembrance of personal wrong was obliterated at sight of his peril." Back home the young man said simply: "If I had sold him I should have died."[36]

Such gratitude was fleeting, however. Seeing that he would soon be put up for sale again, in 1830 Henson managed to escape with his wife and children, up the Ohio river following the so-called Underground Railroad of safe houses for fugitive slaves. When Henson set foot on the Canada shore, "I threw myself on the ground, rolled in the sand, seized handfuls of it and kissed them, and danced round till, in the eyes of several who were present, I passed for a madman."[37]

Henson's story was probably the foundation of *Uncle Tom's Cabin*—the bestselling novel by Harriet Beecher Stowe, daughter of Reverend Lyman Beecher. Published in 1852, it sold a staggering 300,000 copies in the first year alone. At the end, the author asserted that the "separate incidents that compose the narrative are, to a very great extent, authentic, occurring, many of them, either under her own observation or that of her personal friends." But, Stowe said, she had "given only a faint shadow, a dim picture, of the anguish and despair that are, at this very moment . . . shattering thousands of families. . . . Nothing of tragedy can be written, can be spoken, can be conceived, that equals the frightful reality of scenes daily and hourly acting on our shores, beneath the shadow of American law, and the shadow of the cross of Christ."[38]

Uncle Tom's Cabin became a sacred text for the growing abolitionist movement in the North, appalled by the law enacted in the Compromise of 1850 that required fugitive slaves to be returned to their owners in the South. One of the movement's most famous orators was the freed slave Frederick Douglass. In an Independence Day oration in 1852 he asked, "What to the American slave is your Fourth of July? I answer; a day that reveals to him, more than all other days in the year, the gross injustice and cruelty to which he is the constant victim. To him, your celebration is a sham; your boasted liberty, an unholy license; your national greatness, swelling vanity . . . your denunciations of tyrants, brass-fronted impudence." There was not, declaimed Douglass, "a nation on the earth guilty of practices more shocking and bloody, than are the people of these United States, at this very hour."[39]

Such fiery rhetoric provoked a backlash in the South. Arguing that all societies were based on an underclass, southern apologists claimed that black field slaves in the South were better treated than white wage slaves in the North. According to Senator James Hammond of South Carolina, the

> difference between us is that our slaves are hired for life and well compensated; there is no starvation, no begging, no want of employment among our people, and not too much employment either. Yours are hired by the day, not cared for, and scantily compensated, which may be proved in the most painful manner, at any hour in any street in any of your large towns. Why you meet more beggars in one day, on any single street of the city of New York, than you would meet in a lifetime in the whole South.[40]

Northerners, naturally, did not see this as a debate between two forms of slavery. For them the issue was slavery versus freedom. What aroused them most was not the fate of slaves but the ambition of slave owners, what was known in the North as the "slave power."

Northerners believed fervently in the dignity of "free labor"—the independent farmer or small shopkeeper—contrasting it with the degradation of the slave South. William Seward of New York was appalled when he traveled through Virginia for the first time in the 1830s: "An exhausted soil, old and decaying towns, wretchedly-neglected roads and, in every respect, an absence of enterprise and improvement distinguish the region through which we have come, in contrast with that in which we live. Such has been the effect of slavery."[41]

On a larger canvas, this was depicted as a battle between "Northern progress" and "Southern decadence." Carl Schurz, another northern apologist, asked America's slaveholders almost incredulously, "Are you really in earnest when you speak of perpetuating slavery? Shall it never cease? Never? Stop and consider where you are and in what day you live. . . . This is the world of the nineteenth century. . . . You stand against a hopeful world, alone against a great century, fighting your hopeless fight . . . against the onward march of civilization."[42]

What northerners meant by the "onward march of civilization" was graphically depicted in "Westward the Course of Empire Takes Its Way" by the German-American artist Emanuel Leutze. Best known for his iconic canvas of "Washington Crossing the Delaware" (1851), Leutze was later commissioned to decorate a staircase in the Capitol. He produced a vivid, sprawling mural of a settler wagon train struggling to the top of the Rockies and glimpsing the golden sunset over the promised land. One of the settlers is a young black: Leutze was a fervent abolitionist. The land is, of course, empty: Indians appear only in the margins of the mural, in Leutze's words "sneeking away from the light of knowledge."[43]

Northerners blamed the persistence of slavery and the backwardness of the South on an aristocratic class that kept the region in thrall for its own benefit. They were increasingly convinced that this "slave power" posed a threat to the whole country. If slavery were allowed in the West, the whole reactionary, elitist southern way of life would come with it and, since slave labor was cheaper than free labor, it would squeeze out the free farmer. The political threat was equally menacing. More slave states would mean more pro-slavery members of Congress; this would perpetuate the South's influence over the nation's policies.

These anxieties had been simmering for years, but hitherto they had been contained within the party system. Both Whigs and Democrats had northern and southern wings, covering the whole spectrum of views on slavery, but the Whigs were undermined in the South by hostility to the Compromise of 1850 and in the North by the Know Nothing crusade against the immigrant. And 1854 saw the birth of a northern party dedicated explicitly to stopping the slave power. The catalyst for this new crisis was Kansas.

"A HOUSE DIVIDED"

Although California had been brought rapidly into the Union after the 1849 gold rush, the Plains were still largely unsettled. But Stephen Douglas, the powerful Democratic senator and architect of the 1850 Compromise, was determined to build a transcontinental railroad across to the West Coast and that meant organizing the Plains into territories. Douglas, being from Illinois, wanted the route to run from Chicago; southerners favored St. Louis, Missouri, as the starting point. So Douglas tried to buy southern support by organizing the Plains into two big territories—Kansas to the south and Nebraska to the north—and by proposing that each territory should decide for itself whether to sanction slavery.

Douglas had long believed that "popular sovereignty" was the truly democratic way. If Congress tried to legislate about slavery in the territories, that would violate "the great and fundamental principle of free government, which asserts that each community shall settle this and all other questions affecting their domestic institutions by themselves, and in their own way; and for the Congress of the United States to intervene and do it for them when they were unrepresented here was a violation of their rights."[44]

Douglas was no advocate of slavery and he did not expect white slave owners and black slaves to flood into Kansas and Nebraska. So, for him, popular sovereignty was an easy way to propitiate southerners, who hated the principle of territorial limits to slavery, in order to get his railroad bill through Congress. But, perhaps too cocky after his triumph in 1850, he fatally miscalculated the reaction across the North. The Kansas-Nebraska Act of May 1854 breached the Missouri Compromise of 1820, a sacred principle for many northerners that slavery would be banned north of latitude 36°30'. To men and women increasingly paranoid about the machinations of the "slave power," the new Act suggested that the West would now be lost to free labor and free men.

Across the North, Douglas became a hate figure. His name was denounced in speeches; his image burned in the streets. He joked ruefully, "I could travel from Boston to Chicago by the light of my own effigy."[45] The Kansas-Nebraska Act also undermined the credibility of Douglas's Democratic Party in the North and impelled opponents to form a new party, dedicated to stopping slavery's further expansion. Known as the Republicans—to emphasize fidelity to basic American values—it campaigned on the slogan "Free Soil, Free Labor, Free Speech, Free Men." The Republicans were an entirely northern party, inimical to southern values. "We require for our country a government of the people, instead of a government by an oligarchy; a government maintaining before the world the rights of man rather than the privilege of masters. . . . We insist that there shall be no Slavery outside the Slave States, and no domination over the action of the National Government by the Slave Power."[46]

The Republican Party drew in many former Whigs such as Lincoln and Seward. "Come on, then, gentlemen of the slave States," Seward exclaimed in the Senate. "Since there be no escaping your challenge, I accept it in behalf of the cause of freedom. We will engage in competition for the virgin soil of Kansas, and God give the victory to the side which is the stronger in numbers, as it is in right."[47]

And so the race was on. Pro-slavery enthusiasts from neighboring Missouri got into Kansas first. Heavily armed, they took over polling places and cast hundreds of fraudulent ballots to elect a pro-slavery legislature. Free-soilers, many of them shipped in from New England by anti-slavery societies, responded by creating a rival anti-slavery assembly. Kansas descended into anarchy—as Edward Bridgman, a new settler, recorded in a letter scribbled to a relative in Massachusetts in May 1856: "In some small towns the men are called up nearly every night to hold themselves in readiness to meet the worst as scouting parties of Alabamians, Georgians and Missourians are around continually, plundering clothes yards, horses and cattle, and everything they can lay hold of." The thuggery was not confined to one side. Bridgman added that "we heard that 5 men had been killed by Free State men. The men were butchered—ears cut off and the bodies thrown into the river. The murdered men (Proslavery) had thrown out threats and insults, yet the act was barbarous and inhuman whoever committed by." Bridgman said he had learned that the murders were committed by a family named Brown. "One of them was formerly in the wool business in Springfield [Massachusetts], John Brown."[48]

Senator Charles Sumner of Massachusetts denounced "The Crime against Kansas" in such vitriolic terms that he was physically attacked on the Senate floor by Congressman Preston Brooks of South Carolina. Brooks said exultantly, "I . . . gave him about thirty first rate stripes. Towards the last he bellowed like a calf. I wore my cane completely out but saved the Head which is gold."[49] Brooks received dozens of replacement canes from all over the South. One, from merchants in Charleston, South Carolina, was inscribed "Hit him again." Across the North, by contrast, a succession of public meetings denounced "Bully Brooks." Sumner was so badly beaten that he could not attend the Senate for a couple of years but, for foes of slavery, his empty chair was more eloquent than a million words.

The stories of "Bleeding Kansas" and "Bleeding Sumner" made superb political propaganda for the Republican Party. They helped to persuade many northerners, recently so alarmed about the influx of Catholics from Ireland and Germany, that the slave power was a far more serious threat to American values. As the Know Nothing party fizzled out, northerners rallied to the Republicans, who won eleven states in the 1856 elections. Yet the Democrats were still a truly nationwide party and they won the presidency again in 1856. Supporters of the Union hoped to defuse the crisis, but they were soon disappointed by a decisive intervention from the U.S. Supreme Court.

As we saw in Chapter 4, Chief Justice Marshall had established the Court as a force in American politics. His successor, Roger Taney—another long-serving head of the Court (1836–1864)—had been appointed by Andrew Jackson and saw himself as a defender of slavery. In March 1857 the Supreme Court delivered its verdict in the case of Dred Scott—a slave suing for freedom on the grounds that his owner had taken him to live in free states. Taney, now nearly eighty, went out of his way to state the Court's decision in the broadest terms. First he declared that no Negroes who were slaves or the descendants of slaves could become citizens because, on his reading, "they are not included, and were not intended to be included, under the word 'citizens' in the Constitution." Taney adopted a fundamentalist view of the Constitution, treating it as almost holy writ, implying that the worldview of the 1780s—with blacks, as he put it, "regarded as beings of an inferior order, and altogether unfit to associate with the white race either in social or political relations, and so far inferior that they had no rights which the white man was bound to respect"— was still binding on nineteenth-century Americans. Taney also ruled that Congress had no constitutional authority to exclude slavery from federal territories because slaves, in his view, were property and the Constitution guaranteed that no man's property could be taken from him without due process of law.[50]

Taney's lengthy opinion was "weak in its law, logic, history, and factual accuracy,"[51] but he had spoken for a majority of the nine-man Court. Although purporting simply to reflect, like a mirror, the ideas of the Founders, he had in fact changed the meaning of the Constitution. Nowhere did that document define U.S. citizenship but Taney had now done so in explicitly racial terms. And the statement that slave owners could not be prevented from taking their human property across state lines had implications far beyond the West. As John McLean of Ohio, one of the two dissenting justices, put it, "The principle laid down will enable the people of a slave state to introduce slavery into a free state."[52]

Dred Scott, like the Marbury decision of 1803, was a dramatic example of judicial activism. Taney was delivering a political statement dressed up in constitutional trappings but it was now the law of the land. For northern radicals, the verdict proved that, as Seward had argued back in 1850, they must appeal to a higher law than the U.S. Constitution. If the Constitution did not accord with modern American values, then it should be overridden. Such talk was anathema in the South.

Meanwhile, in Kansas Territory, the pro-slavery forces, backed again by the strong-arm tactics of Border Ruffians, pushed through an application to join the Union. The bill to admit Kansas as a slave state, supported by the new president, James Buchanan, was eventually stopped in the House, but these new crises in 1857 added to northern paranoia. The *Dred Scott* case suggested that the slave power controlled the Supreme Court; the Kansas constitution indicated that its tentacles had also reached the White House.

The anarchy in Kansas also made nonsense of the doctrine of popular sovereignty. Its architect, Stephen Douglas, came out openly against his own Democratic president in a desperate effort to salvage his reputation in the North. In 1858 Douglas was running for another term as a U.S. senator for Illinois, and his Republican challenger was Abraham Lincoln. Although Douglas eventually won, this campaign, including seven face-to-face debates, made Lincoln into a national figure—not least for his stark reiteration of the biblical warning: "A house divided against itself cannot stand." Lincoln said bluntly:

> I believe this government cannot endure, permanently, half slave and half free. I do not expect the Union to be dissolved—I do not expect the house to fall—but I do expect it will cease to be divided. It will become all one thing, or all the other. Either the opponents of slavery will arrest the further spread of it and place it where the public mind shall rest in the belief that it is in the course of ultimate extinction, or its advocates will push it forward till it shall become alike lawful in all the states, old as well as new—North as well as South.[53]

Throughout the 1850s dramatic new events kept the political temperature near the boiling point. These dramas were what moved people, what made abstract issues of principle real and vital. "Bleeding Kansas" and "Bleeding Sumner" had such an effect in the North; what aroused southerners to similar fury was John Brown.

To his supporters, Brown was a vengeful Old Testament prophet; to his critics, a homicidal maniac. Already an obsessive abolitionist from his days in Kansas, in October 1859 Brown and a score of supporters, five of them black, seized the federal armory at Harper's Ferry, on the edge of Virginia—expecting to trigger a slave revolt across the South. The raid was a fiasco. Within thirty-six hours most of his band had been killed or captured. Brown was tried and sentenced to death by hanging. One celebrated story claimed that, as he walked to the gallows, he leaned down to kiss a black child. This was factually wrong yet poetically true—Brown, unlike many northerners, genuinely loved blacks. But his final note on December 2 is authentic, and sadly prescient: "I John Brown am now quite certain that the crimes of this guilty land will never be purged away but with Blood." When Brown's body stopped quivering on the gallows, Colonel John Preston shouted: "So perish all such enemies of Virginia! All such enemies of the Union! All such foes of the human race." Among those watching in the crowd was a young actor, John Wilkes Booth.[54]

Many moderate northerners had been appalled at the crazy futility of this raid on Harper's Ferry, so damaging to the Republican image, but Brown's eloquence at his trial turned a fanatic into a martyr. Even before his death Ralph Waldo Emerson, America's most famous public intellectual, called Brown "that new saint" who would "make the gallows glorious like the cross."[55] This image of Brown as a Christ-like figure provoked an equal and opposite reaction in the South, where he was widely reviled as an agent of Satan. Andrew Johnson of Tennessee, a southern moderate, told the Senate that "this old man Brown was nothing more than a murderer, a robber, a thief, and a traitor . . . hell entered his heart . . . he shrank from the dimensions of a human being into those of a reptile."[56]

Under the pressure of events like Bleeding Kansas and Harper's Ferry, the Democratic Party—that last political bridge spanning the Union—split into northern and southern wings. This was enough to give victory in the 1860 election to the Republicans, now led by Lincoln, who won virtually no votes in the South. In other words, there were no longer any parties that constituted nationwide coalitions. Southern extremists presented Lincoln's victory as the triumph of abolitionists—intent, like John Brown, on freeing the slaves. South Carolina seceded from the Union before Christmas, the rest of the Deep South soon after. In February 1861 the Confederate States of America was born.

As many historians have argued, this was in many ways an irrepressible conflict, stemming from the failure of the Founders to confront the question of slavery. They ignored it in order to bring the South into the Union but the persistence of slavery in the empire of liberty created a fault line that would eventually break the Union apart. Some southern revisionist historians in the 1930s blamed inept political leaders for what they claimed was a needless conflict but, although mistakes *were* made—such as Douglas's handling of the Kansas question or Taney's provocative verdict in the *Dred Scott* case—it is hard to imagine the rift being healed by abler leaders or wiser policies.

Sectional crises in the early republic—such as that of 1790 over the debt and the capital—had been resolved through haggling among a small political elite, but this kind of brokerage was no longer possible in a volatile mass democracy. The Compromise of 1850 had shown how difficult it was to manage the diversity of interests now represented in Congress; by the mid-1850s the "party system" of the 1830s—Democrats and Whigs—had fractured into increasingly sectional politics. The Constitution had done a remarkable job in creating a flexible federal system for a country that now spanned a continent, but ultimately its operation required an underlying social consensus and, on the meaning of liberty, this no longer existed after the Republican victory in 1860.

So the house finally divided. As Lincoln prophesied, liberty and slavery, like oil and water, could not coexist. The South wanted to establish its own house, founded on slavery—citing the precedent of the American colonies breaking away from Britain in 1776—but the North would not let it go—determined that the Union, the empire of liberty, should remain whole and united. For these principles blood would be spilled on an unimagined scale.

PART II

POWER AND PROGRESS

Thirty years from now America will be a rival for
Europe who vies with her in everything.
> —MICHEL CHEVALIER, 1866

Give me your tired, your poor,
Your huddled masses yearning to breathe free.
> —EMMA LAZARUS, "THE NEW COLOSSUS," 1883

The world must be made safe for democracy.
> —WOODROW WILSON, 1917

7

NORTH AND SOUTH

The Civil War of 1861–1865 proved the most destructive conflict in the history of the United States. In those four years, more Americans died in combat than in both world wars of the twentieth century. After months of muddle, the North eventually mobilized its resources and crushed the South by ruthless firepower fueled by industrial might—here was a foretaste of the American way of war in the century ahead. During the course of the conflict, the North's aims changed. It went to war in 1861 to preserve the Union, but in 1863 Lincoln took the revolutionary step of emancipating the slaves, giving the country what he called "a new birth of freedom." American power had proved an instrument of progress—albeit at terrible cost; that, too, would be a theme of decades to come.

THE NINETY-DAY WAR

Saturday, February 23, 1861. It was the most humiliating entry into Washington ever made by a new president. The Pinkerton Detective Agency had warned of an assassination plot, so Abraham Lincoln slipped through Philadelphia and Baltimore disguised as an invalid passenger on a special train, arriving in America's capital unannounced and before dawn. North and South were not yet at war but the country teetered on the brink. Seven states in the Deep South had declared independence from the Union by February 1861, convinced that Lincoln and his victorious Republican Party were bent on freeing all their slaves.

In fact, at this stage Lincoln was no abolitionist. He had two basic aims: no further expansion of slavery into the West and the preservation of the United States. The new president still hoped that Southern supporters of the Union would restrain their hotheads and it was to these moderates that he reached out at the end of his inaugural address on March 4, 1861. "I have no purpose, directly or indirectly, to interfere with the institution of slavery in the States where it exists," he

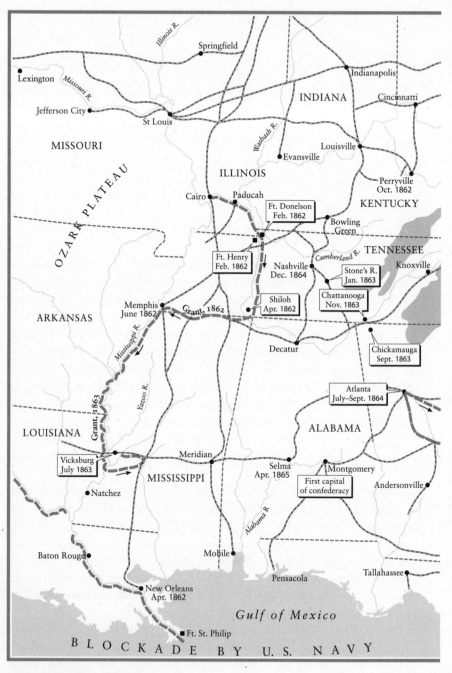

MAP 2, THE CIVIL WAR, 1861–1865

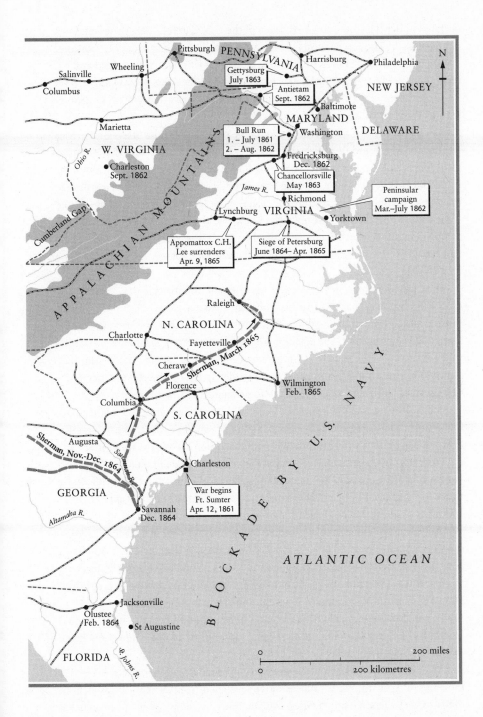

N

Salinville
Columbus
Wheeling
Pittsburgh
PENNSYLVANIA
Harrisburg
Philadelphia
NEW JERSEY

Gettysburg
July 1863

Antietam
Sept. 1862
Baltimore
MARYLAND
DELAWARE

Marietta

W. VIRGINIA
Ohio R.

Charleston
Sept. 1862

Bull Run
1. – July 1861
2. – Aug. 1862
Washington

Fredericksburg
Dec. 1862

Chancellorsville
May 1863

James R.
Richmond
VIRGINIA
Yorktown

Peninsular
campaign
Mar.–July 1862

Cumberland Gap
APPALACHIAN MOUNTAINS

Lynchburg

Appomattox C.H.
Lee surrenders
Apr. 9, 1865

Siege of Petersburg
June 1864– Apr. 1865

Raleigh

N. CAROLINA

Charlotte

Fayetteville

Sherman, March 1865

Cheraw

Florence

Wilmington
Feb. 1865

Columbia

S. CAROLINA

BLOCKADE BY U.S. NAVY

Augusta

Sherman, Nov.-Dec. 1864

Savannah R.

Charleston

War begins
Ft. Sumter
Apr. 12, 1861

GEORGIA

Altamaha R.

Savannah
Dec. 1864

ATLANTIC OCEAN

Jacksonville
Olustee
Feb. 1864
St Augustine

FLORIDA
St. Johns R.

200 miles

200 kilometres

declared under the still unfinished dome of the U.S. Capitol. "We are not enemies, but friends. . . . Though passion may have strained, it must not break our bonds of affection. The mystic chords of memory, stretching from every battlefield and pa- triot grave to every living heart and hearthstone all over this broad land will yet swell the chorus of the Union when again touched, as surely they will be, by the bet- ter angels of our nature."[1]

Moving words, but they came too late. The new Confederate States of America was created in the middle of February. Its Constitutional Convention chose as pres- ident Jefferson Davis—a former senator from Mississippi. His wife never forgot the moment when news of his appointment arrived. He was "in our garden assisting to make rose-cuttings; when reading the telegram he looked so grieved that I feared some evil had befallen our family. After a few minutes' painful silence he told me, as a man might speak of a sentence of death."[2] Davis was a West Point graduate who had served as U.S. secretary of war. He knew how ill prepared the South was for a long conflict.

The Confederacy's only chance was to enlist into the struggle the Upper South, especially Virginia. That was the most populous state in the whole South, with al- most as much industrial capacity as all seven original Confederate states of the Deep South put together. The flashpoint became Fort Sumter in Charleston harbor, in the South Carolina heartland of the new Confederacy. Lincoln made clear that, although averse to war, he would not surrender federal property. Southern fire- brands saw a battle for the fort as a way to persuade the Upper South to fight.

The commander at Fort Sumter, Major Robert Anderson, was a former slave owner from Kentucky who sympathized with the Southern cause. But, as a regular army officer, his loyalties lay ultimately with the Union. Across the water in the city of Charleston, his opponent was General Pierre Beauregard of Louisiana. Years ear- lier Beauregard had made his name at West Point as a superb artillery officer; his instructor had been Robert Anderson. Here was a foretaste of the ruptures, ironic and often tragic, that accompanied civil war.

"Anderson will not capitulate," noted Mary Chesnut, wife of a leading Charles- ton Confederate, in her diary. "Yesterday's was the merriest, maddest dinner we have yet had. Men were audaciously wise and witty. We had an unspoken forebod- ing that it was to be our last pleasant meeting. . . . I did not pretend to go to sleep. How can I? If Anderson does not accept terms at four, the orders are he shall be fired upon. I count four, St Michael's bells chime out and I begin to hope. At half- past four the heavy booming of a cannon. I sprang out of bed, and on my knees prostrate I prayed as I never prayed before."[3]

Under orders from the Confederate government, Beauregard opened fire on the morning of April 12, 1861. Charlestonians watched from their rooftops as hun- dreds of shells flamed and crashed over the Fort. Yet daily life went on as usual. Mary Chesnut noted: "Not by one word or look can we detect any change in the demeanour of these negro servants. . . . You could not tell that they even heard the awful roar going on in the bay. . . . People talk before them as if they were chairs and tables. They make no sign. Are they stolidly stupid? Or wiser than we are; silent and strong, biding their time?"[4]

Anderson, short of supplies and shells, held out for a day and a half and then surrendered. Soon the Confederate Stars and Bars fluttered over the battered fort. Beauregard allowed his old teacher to take the Stars and Stripes with him. Displayed a week later in New York, the flag from Fort Sumter became a rallying point for Northerners, thousands of whom answered Lincoln's call for troops to suppress what he called illegal "combinations" in the South. But Sumter also was the tipping point for the Upper South. Five days later Virginia voted for secession. And so did Robert E. Lee.

In 1861 the U.S. army boasted only two generals who had commanded armies in the field and both were in their seventies. By common consent, the most promising senior officer was Lee, aged fifty-four, a West Pointer who had served in the Mexican War. So, after Sumter surrendered, Lincoln offered him field command of the Union army. But Lee was a Virginian; his hilltop mansion at Arlington looked out across the Potomac to the city of Washington. After Virginia voted to secede, Lee spent an anguished night in his study but, in the end, he put state before country, informing his sister in Baltimore: "The whole South is in a state of revolution, into which Virginia, after a long struggle, has been drawn. . . . With all my devotion to the Union and the feeling of loyalty and duty of an American citizen, I have not been able to make up my mind to raise my hand against my relatives, my children, my home. I have therefore resigned my commission in the Army."[5] Next day, Lee rode south to Richmond, the new Confederate capital, where he was offered command of the Army of Virginia. He never visited his home again. In fact, there was no point. Vengeful Northerners turned his front lawn into Arlington National Cemetery—hallowed ground for the Union dead.

Three other states followed Virginia into the Confederacy, making a total of eleven. Only after desperate effort was Maryland held for the Union—otherwise, Washington would have been encircled by enemy states. On both sides men now flocked to enlist. Lincoln called up the troops for ninety days. This was actually for legal reasons but it seemed to sum up the expectation on both sides of a quick war. Southerners believed that the "Yankees" were too soft to fight; Northerners were sure that the rebels ("Rebs") would fold up as soon as force was applied. Most great wars begin with the illusion that they will be short.

Elisha Rhodes, a nineteen-year-old clerk in Providence, Rhode Island, was desperate to enlist but his widowed mother insisted that he was her only means of support. Such was Rhodes's disappointment that "Sunday night after I had retired, my mother came to my room and, with a spirit worthy of a Spartan mother of old, said: 'My son, other mothers must make sacrifices and why should not I?

If you feel it is your duty to enlist, I will give my consent.'" With many of his friends, Rhodes joined the Second Rhode Island Volunteers. Two months later he got his first sight of the nation's capital: "Hurrah we are in Washington and what a city! Mud, pigs, geese, Negroes, palaces, shanties everywhere. . . . As we passed the White House I had my first view of Abraham Lincoln. He looks like a good honest man, and I trust that with God's help he can bring our country safely out of its peril."[6]

Down South, the mood was very similar. Sam Watkins was twenty-one when he joined the First Tennessee Regiment. After some basic training, his unit was loaded into boxcars in this, the first railway war. "Leaving Nashville, we went bowling twenty or thirty miles an hour, as fast as steam could carry us. At every town and station citizens and ladies were waving their handkerchiefs and hurrahing for . . . the Southern Confederacy. Magnificent banquets were prepared for us all along the entire route."[7]

These boys from Tennessee were being rushed northeast to Virginia. The rival capitals were little more than a hundred miles apart and in mid-July 1861 the Union army marched out of Washington en route to Richmond. Its mood was cheerful and progress was slow. Weighed down with ridiculously heavy packs, the troops kept breaking ranks to pick blackberries or get water. Forewarned, the Confederate forces moved north to meet them and the two armies faced off along Bull Run creek. This was only twenty-five miles from Washington and hundreds of civilians came out from the capital, equipped with binoculars and picnic baskets, to watch the entertainment.

Most of the soldiers had never fought before. Their aim was poor, their morale shaky; and as they were wearing a variety of uniforms, it was often hard to distinguish friend and foe. The Union forces gradually lost cohesion, while Southern reinforcements poured in from the nearby railroad junction at Manassas. Eventually the Confederates surged forward, unleashing a chilling half-shout, half-yelp that became known as the rebel yell. The exhausted Northerners, many of them ninety-day men whose term was almost up, decided they had had enough. Retreat soon turned into a rout. Abandoned civilian carriages clogged the roads and bridges; many soldiers were drowned trying to cross the Bull Run. One of the crowd was Elisha Rhodes: "Of the horrors of that night, I can give you no adequate idea. I suffered untold horrors from thirst and fatigue but struggled on, clinging to my gun and cartridge box. Many times I sat down in the mud determined to go no further, and willing to die to end my misery. But soon a friend would pass and urge me to make another effort, and I would stagger on a mile further. At daylight we could see the spires of Washington, and what a welcome sight it was."[8]

William Howard Russell, a British war correspondent for *The Times*, asleep in his Washington hotel, was awakened by the noise. He saw "a steady stream of men covered in mud, soaked through with rain, who were pouring irregularly, without any semblance of order, up Pennsylvania Avenue towards the Capitol. A dense stream of vapour rose from the multitude. . . . Many of them were without knapsacks, crossbelts and firelocks. Some had neither greatcoats nor shoes, others were covered in blankets." A pale, exhausted young officer told Russell they had been "pretty well whipped" in Virginia. What, asked Russell incredulously, the whole army? "That's more than I know," was the reply. "I know I'm going home. I've had enough of fighting to last my lifetime."[9]

On the Confederate side, Sam Watkins and his trainload of buddies from Tennessee reached Manassas a few hours after the battle had finished and could not believe their bad luck. "We felt that the war was over, and we would have to return home without even seeing a Yankee soldier. Ah, how we envied those who were wounded. We thought at the time we would have given a thousand dollars to have been in that battle, and to have had our arm shot off, so we could have returned home with an empty sleeve."[10]

Sam Watkins need not have worried. The war was not over; in fact, it had hardly begun. After the battle of Manassas (or Bull Run as Northerners called it) Southerners crowed that, with their martial spirit, they could easily whip the spineless Yankees. This proved dangerous complacency because the humiliating defeat forced the North to take the war seriously.

THE KILLERS TAKE COMMAND

Shocked by the shambles, Lincoln called for another 100,000 troops—this time for three years, not three months—and appointed a new commander to whip the army into shape. George B. McClellan was only thirty-four, but he had catapulted to fame with victories in western Virginia, winning the epithet "the young Napoleon." Russell watched McClellan take charge: "He is a very squarely-built, thick-throated, broad-chested man, under the middle height. . . . A short, thick, reddish moustache conceals his mouth. . . . He looks like a stout little captain of dragoons." But, said Russell, "McClellan is nevertheless 'the man on horseback' just now, and the Americans must ride in his saddle, or in anything he likes."[11]

McClellan rooted out the dud officers and drilled the troops, to whom he became a hero, but he got carried away by the adulation of politicians and soldiers, as letters to his wife show: "I find myself in a strange position here: President, Cabinet . . . & all deferring to me. . . . [I] have conversation after conversation calling on me to save the nation. . . . God has placed a great work in my hands." But although a great trainer of men, McClellan shrank from battle—naturally cautious but also intimidated by the Confederate success at Bull Run. Instead, he kept asking for more troops, more supplies, and more time. "I can't tell you how disgusted I am becoming with these wretched politicians—they are a most despicable set of men," he moaned defensively. "The President is nothing more than a well meaning baboon. . . .

It begins to look as if we are condemned to a winter of inactivity. If it is so the fault will not be mine."[12]

By the spring of 1862 Lincoln was impatient for action. He told his advisers: "If General McClellan does not want to use the Army, I would like to borrow it for a time, provided I could see how it could be made to do something."[13] Anxious to make himself into a real commander-in-chief, he even obtained some military textbooks from the Library of Congress.

McClellan kept insisting there was a huge Confederate army waiting for him in northern Virginia if he tried to march south against Richmond. So he decided to move his army by boat down to the York peninsula and approach the Confederate capital from the east. Alerted by spies in Washington, the Southern troops retreated to defend Richmond, revealing to McClellan's embarrassment that some of their imposing gun emplacements were only painted logs.

Once established on the peninsula, McClellan inched his way toward Richmond, earning the derisive nickname "the Virginia creeper." He was one of those generals who, in the last analysis, would not gamble or go for the jugular. More charitably, one could also say that he shrank from the butchery of total war. He told Lincoln that the conflict against the Confederacy must be fought with due respect for property and the Constitution. It "should be conducted upon the highest principles known to Christian Civilization. It should not be at all a war against population, but against armed forces and political organizations. Neither confiscation of property [nor] abolition of slavery should be contemplated for a moment. In prosecuting the war all private property and unarmed persons should be strictly protected, subject only to the necessity of military operations [and] pillage and waste should be treated as high crimes."[14] But Lincoln, now growing into the job, could see that it was no longer possible to fight a gentlemanly war, and other generals had no compunction about taking the gloves off.

Ulysses S. Grant had been a failure most of his life. After serving in the Mexican War, he left the U.S. army—kicked out for boozing, said his detractors, driven to drink by depression, according to those more sympathetic. Grant then tried a succession of jobs, ending up in his late thirties selling saddles and leather goods in his father's store in Galena, Illinois. People noted the vacant expression on his face as he came and went to work each day. In fact, Grant might have spent the rest of his days comatose in the small-town Midwest, but 1861 brought him to life. He understood that war was very simple—what mattered was the body count—and though normally a gentle man, he could be a killer on the battlefield.

Back in uniform, Grant made his name in February 1862 when besieging Fort Donelson in Tennessee. The Confederate commander, Simon Bolivar Buckner, had served with Grant at West Point and in the Mexican War; he expected that membership of the same club would ensure gentlemanly terms. But Grant's reply was terse, courteous, and utterly brutal:

SIR: *Yours of this date, proposing armistice and appointment of Commissioners to settle terms of capitulation, is just received. No terms except an unconditional and immediate surrender can be accepted. I propose to move immediately on your works.*

I am, sir, very respectfully,

Your ob[edien]t se[r]v[an]t.

U. S. GRANT.

Brig[adier] Gen[eral][15]

Buckner protested at Grant's "ungenerous and unchivalrous terms," but he had no choice. Northerners, starving for victories, were jubilant at the surrender of Fort Donelson, newspapers claiming that Grant's initials stood for "Unconditional Surrender." Reports of the general calmly puffing away under fire brought him cigars from all over the country. Free smokes for the rest of his life were, however, a mixed blessing: Grant would eventually die, excruciatingly, from cancer of the throat.

Fort Donelson was an easy victory but Grant's mettle was proved two months later, in April 1862, at a little wooden Methodist church called Shiloh—Hebrew for place of peace. A by-product of Grant's aggressive spirit was periodic overconfidence. That Sunday morning the Confederates surprised his troops finishing breakfast and drove them back in disarray. The Unionists rallied and there was bitter fighting in a peach orchard, with pink blossoms raining down in the hail of bullets. Sam Watkins of Tennessee was one of the follow-up troops. "We had to pass over the ground where troops had been fighting all day. . . . I never realized the 'pomp and circumstance' of the thing called glorious war until I saw this. Men were lying in every conceivable position; the dead lying with their eyes wide open, the wounded begging piteously for help." For Watkins it "all seemed to me a dream; I seemed to be in a sort of haze . . . but when the order to charge was given, I got happy. I felt happier than a fellow does when he professes religion at a big Methodist camp-meeting. I shouted. It was fun then. Everybody looked happy. . . . One more charge, then their lines waver and break. They retreat in wild confusion. We were jubilant."[16]

For the North, that day at Shiloh was a disaster but, crucially, Grant kept his nerve. Overnight, thousands of reinforcements arrived, many of them by boat at a landing on the nearby Tennessee river. In the morning, these fresh troops ploughed into the weary Confederates, driving them from the field. The carnage was immense. More Americans were killed in two days at Shiloh in April 1862 than in all the country's previous wars combined.

Grant's was the new way of war and on the Confederate side, another warrior got the message. When Sam Watkins first saw Robert E. Lee, the general "looked like some good boy's grandpa. I felt like going up to him and saying, good evening, Uncle Bob! . . . His whole make-up of form and person, looks and manner had a kind of gentle and soothing magnetism about it that drew every one to him and made them love, respect and honor him. I fell in love with the old gentleman and felt like going home with him."[17] But Bobby Lee was a different man in the heat of battle; then, like Grant, he became a killer.

When Lee took command in Virginia, McClellan was delighted, claiming that he "is *too* cautious and weak under grave responsibility . . . wanting in moral firmness when pressed by heavy responsibility & is likely to be timid & irresolute in action." He was sure Lee would "never venture upon a bold movement on a large scale."[18] In reality, McClellan was describing himself. Lee, like Napoleon, believed that audacity and aggression were the most important attributes of a general. His cavalry literally ran rings around McClellan. Taking terrible risks, he divided his meager forces and launched them in surprise attacks. His June 1862 campaign was named, aptly, the Seven Days battles. All but one was a Union victory, with Southern losses double those of the enemy, but Lee won the campaign. McClellan's unnerved army was evacuated back to Washington.

The dreadful losses on both sides in these battles were due most of all to rifles. Using a rifled barrel and a cone-shaped bullet, instead of a smooth-bore musket and a round ball, was a military revolution. Spinning a rifled bullet through the air increased its range fourfold and enhanced its accuracy to lethal effect: This gave defenders a massive advantage. Yet West Point tactics still gave pride of place to the offense and Lee proved himself a master of that game. He, not McClellan, was the true Napoleon of the 1860s.

By mid-1862, more than a year into the war, things looked promising for the South. It could not hope to defeat the North, which had double the population and most of America's industry. But all it needed to do was avoid defeat until Northerners lost the will to fight, whereas the North could end the war only by invading and occupying Southern territory, particularly the heartland of Virginia.

A critical factor was the attitude of Great Britain, whose textile industry relied on cotton from the South. British opinion was not pro-slavery, but slavery did not seem to be the issue because Lincoln said the fight was to preserve the Union, not to free the slaves. In which case, many in Britain felt that the South was simply fighting for freedom from an overmighty empire, as the Italians had against the Hapsburgs a few years before. *The Times* declared: "[W]e are but uttering the thoughts of nine Englishmen out of ten when we say that should it appear that the army of M'Clellan has been so totally defeated as to be incapable of resuming offensive operations, then the propriety of treating the Confederates as an independent people may be justly discussed by the British Cabinet."[19]

Lee decided to give history a nudge, hoping that an invasion of the North would prompt European mediation. This in turn would put political pressure on Lincoln because, said Lee, a proposal of peace "would enable the people of the United States to determine at their coming elections whether they will support those who favor a prolongation of the war, or those who wish to bring it to a termination."[20] The midterm congressional elections in November 1862, he hoped, might be decisive in undermining the Northern will to fight.

But Lee overreached himself when he marched into Maryland. The Union army was not as demoralized as Confederates believed and McClellan brought massive superiority of numbers to bear. This time even he knew his advantage, thanks to a careless Confederate officer who left a copy of Lee's orders wrapped around some cigars dropped in a field. Over two days in September 1862 Lee and McClellan slugged it out around the little town of Sharpsburg, Maryland—in rolling farmland, along a sunken road, and across Antietam creek. Total casualties were four times those inflicted on the U.S. army in Normandy on the morning of D-Day. Lee suffered less than McClellan but his small, shattered army had no choice but to leave enemy territory and turn back to Virginia.

A general with more nerve than McClellan would have finished off Lee in retreat. Lincoln was furious that he did not and sacked McClellan for good. But the failure of the South's invasion turned British opinion against the idea of recognizing the Confederacy. Prime Minister Lord Palmerston noted, "I am very much come back to our original view of the matter, that we must continue to be lookers-on till the war shall have taken a more decided turn."[21] The South's defeat at Antietam also gave Lincoln the political leeway to issue a statement drafted months before but kept in his desk drawer for a propitious moment. What he said transformed the whole meaning of the conflict.

"A NEW BIRTH OF FREEDOM"

Lincoln had gone to war to preserve the Union, not to free the slaves. Although personally detesting the institution of slavery, he aimed as president to end the rebellion as quickly and peacefully as possible. This meant trying to conciliate Southerners and also pro-Union, slave-owning border states such as his birthplace, Kentucky. At the end of 1861, eight months into the conflict, Lincoln told Congress: "In considering the policy to be adopted for suppressing the insurrection I have been anxious and careful that the inevitable conflict for this purpose shall not degenerate into a violent and remorseless revolutionary struggle." He even suggested that those slaves freed as a consequence of the fighting might be resettled abroad, "at some place or places in a climate congenial to them. It might be well to consider, too, whether the free colored people already in the United States could not, so far as individuals may desire, be included in such colonization." He asked Congress to appropriate money for this settlement project, as Jefferson had done for the Louisiana Purchase, arguing that it was a matter of "absolute necessity" without which "the Government itself can not be perpetuated."[22]

For Lincoln, like Jefferson before him, the ideal solution was to end slavery but keep America white, yet events were slipping out of his hands. As Southern men marched off to war, the slave system crumbled behind them. With "massa" gone, wives found it hard to keep blacks in their place. One woman wrote to her army husband, "We are doing as best we know, or as good as we can get the Servants to do; they learn to feel very independent." Even male overseers were losing their clout. When one of them told a slave he was going to be whipped, the black man simply walked away. The overseer wrote to his master, "I wish you would . . . come down and let the matter be settled, as I do not feel wiling [sic] to be run over by him."[23] Even where there was not outright resistance, slaves indulged in "go-slows" or quietly sabotaged equipment.

Slave labor was essential to the Southern economy yet, quite literally, slavery was no longer working. In fact, many blacks took advantage of the chaos in battle areas and fled to Union lines. Under the Supreme Court's interpretation of the U.S. Constitution, slaves were regarded as property, but the Confederacy was no longer part of the United States. Initially these refugee slaves were treated as "contraband of war," but by 1862 more and more Northerners shared the opinion of black abolitionist Frederick Douglass that to "fight against slaveholders while not fighting against slavery is but a half-hearted business, and paralyzes the hand engaged in it. . . . Fire must be met with water. . . . War for the destruction of liberty must be met with war for the destruction of slavery."[24]

The failure to win a quick victory strengthened the case for more radical policies. Reconciliation no longer seemed possible—most Northerners accepted that they could win only by conquering the South—and the 4 million slaves could be of decisive importance. Encouraging them to escape would sap the Southern war effort. Going a step further and enlisting freed blacks as soldiers would strengthen the Northern armies.

Lincoln could see that, despite his intentions, the war had turned revolutionary but as long as Union forces were losing, any change of policy would be criticized as an act of desperation. The bloody victory at Antietam in September 1862 gave him the pretext he needed. Five days later he announced that "on the 1st day of January, A.D. 1863, all persons held as slaves within any State or designated part of a State the people whereof shall then be in rebellion against the United States shall be then, thenceforward, and forever free." When that fateful New Year's Day arrived, he also declared "that such persons of suitable condition will be received into the armed service of the United States to garrison forts, positions, stations, and other places and to man vessels of all sorts in said service." Here was a fundamental break with Lincoln's previous ideal of the United States as a free, *white* society. He was allowing free blacks a place; their ideal home was not Africa.[25]

Down in Richmond, President Jefferson Davis cited the Emancipation Proclamation as proof that the South was right to secede. He even claimed that, because blacks were incapable of surviving on their own, it was a crime against them. The Proclamation, he asserted, was "a measure by which several millions of human brings of an inferior race, peaceful and contented laborers in their sphere, are doomed to extermination, while at the same time they are encouraged to a general assassination of their masters. . . . Our own detestation of those who have attempted the most execrable measure recorded in the history of guilty men is tempered by profound contempt for the impotent rage which it discloses." Henceforth, he stated, captured Union officers, white or black, should be dealt with under state laws for the punishment of criminals engaged in inciting slave revolts—the kind of treatment meted out to John Brown, hanged in 1859.[26]

Davis's angry response was predictable. More disconcerting for Lincoln was the ferocious Northern backlash against the Emancipation Proclamation, particularly in the Midwest and in vital border states. Hundreds of soldiers deserted and in the 1862 elections, pro-peace Democrats won thirty-two seats in the House and took control of several state legislatures. The lawmakers of Illinois—the president's home state—called the Proclamation

> a gigantic usurpation at once converting the war professedly commenced by the Administration for the vindication of the authority of the Constitution into the crusade for the sudden, unconditional and violent liberation of 3 million negro slaves; a result which would not only be a total subversion of the Federal Union but a revolution in the social organization of the Southern States . . . the present and far-reaching consequences of which to both races cannot be contemplated without the most dismal foreboding of horror and dismay.[27]

Despite such apocalyptic rhetoric in South and North, Lincoln's Emancipation Proclamation was not a total break with the past. It applied only to areas that were in rebellion and it did not affect slaves in states like Missouri that had remained loyal to the Union. But black leaders not surprisingly saw the Proclamation as a turning point. Frederick Douglass observed: "Once let the black man get upon his person the brass letters, US; let him get an eagle on his button, and a musket on his shoulder and bullets in his pocket, and there is no power on earth which can deny that he has earned the right to citizenship."[28] Blacks flocked to enlist—amounting to nearly a tenth of the Union soldiery by the end of the war.

Two of Douglass's sons joined the 54th Massachusetts Regiment—an all-black unit, though nearly all the officers were white. That summer the Regiment won national renown for its courageous assault on Fort Wagner, part of the defenses of Charleston. Douglass's boys survived, but nearly half of their comrades did not. The white commander of the 54th, Colonel Robert Gould Shaw, was among the dead. Confederates stripped his corpse and threw it into a ditch with his men but Shaw's father told the press: "The poor benighted wretches thought they were heaping indignities upon his dead body, but the act recoils upon them. . . . They buried him with his brave, devoted followers who fell dead over him and around him. . . . We can imagine no holier place than that in which he is."[29]

Equal in death they may have been, but not in life. White soldiers received thirteen dollars a month, blacks only ten. After Fort Wagner James Gooding, a corporal in the 54th but previously a newspaperman in Massachusetts, wrote a letter of complaint to the president on behalf of his less literate fellow-soldiers: "Your Excellency will pardon the presumption of an humble individual like myself in addressing you, but the earnest Solicitation of my comrades in Arms besides the genuine interest felt by myself in the matter is my excuse." Corporal Gooding respectfully told his commander-in-chief that "the main question is, Are we Soldiers, or are we Labourers? . . . Let the rich mould around Wagner's parapets be upturned and there will be found an Eloquent answer. Obedient and patient and Solid as a wall they are. All we lack is a paler hue and a better acquaintance with the Alphabet. Now your Excellency, we have done a Soldier's Duty. Why can't we have a Soldier's pay?"[30] The U.S. Congress did eventually pass a bill for pay equality, although blacks remained the butt of abuse and discrimination and they fought mostly in segregated units.

Fort Wagner was a symbolic moment for civil rights, but it was not a major engagement in the Civil War. Two other battles counted far more in 1863—in fact, together, they decisively tipped the struggle in favor of the North.

Vicksburg, some 200 miles north of New Orleans, was strategically situated on bluffs above the Mississippi river, and in May 1863 Grant's advancing armies laid siege to the city. What followed foreshadowed Europe during the Great War. Soldiers in trenches sometimes only yards apart traded shots, grenades, and sometimes friendly banter. Union guns from land and riverboats pulverized the town into ruins. Citizens burrowed deep into the clay for shelter. As one of them, Dora Miller, recorded:

> Cave-digging has become a regular business; prices range from twenty to fifty dollars, according to the size of cave. Two diggers worked at ours for a week and charged thirty dollars. It is well made in the hill that slopes just in the rear of the house, and well propped with thick posts. . . . It has a shelf, also, for holding light or water. When we went in this evening and sat down, the earthy suffocating feeling, as of a living tomb, was dreadful to me. I fear I shall risk death outside than melt in the dark furnace. The hills are so honeycombed with caves that the streets look like avenues in a cemetery.[31]

Grant directed the strangulation of Vicksburg with cold calculation, cigar in mouth—though there were times when he got blind drunk, such was the strain. But eventually, after forty-seven days, the Confederate soldiers were literally starved into submission. Some of them sent their commander, General John Pemberton, an anonymous note stating that "[o]ur rations have been cut down to one biscuit and a small bit of bacon per day, not enough scarcely to keep soul and body together. . . . If you can't feed us, you had better surrender us, horrible as the idea is, than suffer this noble army to disgrace themselves by desertion. . . . The army is now ripe for mutiny, unless it can be fed. . . . From—MANY SOLDIERS."[32]

Vicksburg capitulated on the Fourth of July 1863—Pemberton reckoned he could obtain more generous terms that day. But for many Southerners, surrendering on Independence Day added insult to injury and the Fourth of July was not celebrated again in the city until the end of World War II. Union troops, however, were jubilant. Captain Ira Miltmore wrote home to Illinois: "We are going to celebrate this Fourth of July in spirit and in truth. . . . The backbone of the Rebellion is this day broken. The Confederacy is divided. . . . The Mississippi River is opened, and Gen[eral] Grant is to be our next President."[33] That last sentence was a touch premature—Grant didn't move into the White House until 1869—but Vicksburg turned him into a true celebrity. Vices like tobacco and drink made him more, not less, appealing to the man in the street.

In the East, that Fourth of July brought news of an even bigger battle. In the spring of 1863 Robert E. Lee had run rings around the Union army again in Virginia. Emboldened, he persuaded the Confederate leadership to authorize another invasion of the North, threatening Washington and Philadelphia. Lee led 70,000 men into hitherto peaceful areas of Pennsylvania, stripping the countryside of supplies and sending free blacks south into slavery. But he ran, almost by accident, into the North's Army of the Potomac under General George Meade, a commander who may have lacked Lee's brilliance and charisma—looking like a doleful turtle—but who was nevertheless a capable defensive tactician with steely nerves.

After initial confusion, Meade gradually curled the Union line like a hook along some low ridges south of the little town of Gettysburg. It was a strong position— too strong in the judgment of Lee's senior corps commander, James Longstreet. But Lee was fired up by the victories in Virginia; he had supreme confidence in his men and profound contempt for the Northerners they had beaten so frequently. After two days of fierce but episodic fighting, he was sure the Union army would crack under a coordinated blow. And so, on July 3, he ordered Longstreet to attack the center of the enemy line on Cemetery Ridge. That meant advancing nearly a mile, uphill and across open farmland, against an enemy dug in or sheltering behind stone walls and backed by strong artillery. Longstreet protested, arguing that they should move east toward Washington: This would force the Union army to follow and attack the Confederates on *their* chosen ground. But Lee was adamant: "[T]he enemy is there, and I am going to strike him there."[34]

Longstreet tried again later, warning Lee: "I have been in pretty much all kinds of skirmishes, from those of two or three soldiers to those of an army corps, and I think I can safely say there never was a body of fifteen thousand men who could make that attack successfully."[35] But Lee's blood was now up, so Longstreet grimly set about arranging his troops.

The lead division was commanded by General George Pickett, a dashing Virginian who looked like a Cavalier with his long hair worn in ringlets. For two hours

Confederate guns blasted the enemy line. The Unionists fired back, turning the air into a deafening inferno, but then they fell silent. Lee took this as a favorable sign; in fact, they were conserving ammunition for the attack that was clearly imminent. Pickett asked whether his men should now advance. Choked with emotion and unable to speak, Longstreet simply nodded. Around three in the afternoon, the Confederates moved out of the woods, fanned out into line, and marched forward, briskly and in silence.

To all who watched, it was a scene of terrible beauty. Frank Haskell, from Wisconsin, was one of the Unionists waiting on the opposite side of the field:

> More than half a mile their front extends; more than a thousand yards the dull gray masses deploy, man touching man, rank pressing rank, and line supporting line. The red flags wave, their horsemen gallop up and down . . . barrel and bayonet gleam in the sun, a sloping forest of flashing steel. Right on they move, as with one soul, in perfect order, without impediment of ditch, or wall or stream, over ridge and slope, through orchard and meadow, and cornfield, magnificent, grim, irresistible.
>
> All was orderly and still upon our crest; no noise and no confusion. The men had little need of commands, for the survivors of a dozen battles knew well enough what this array in front portended, and, already in their places, they would be prepared to act when the right time should come. The click of the locks as each man raised the hammer to feel with his fingers that the cap was on the nipple; the sharp jar as a musket touched a stone upon the wall when thrust in aiming over it, and the clicking of the iron axles as the guns were rolled up by hand a little further to the front, were quite all the sounds that could be heard.[36]

Suddenly the Union artillery opened up, to deadly effect. The Confederates closed ranks and marched on. The Union infantry held fire until the men in grey were within a couple of hundred yards. Then 1,700 muskets and 11 cannons went off at once. The Confederates were literally blown apart—limbs, heads, knapsacks flying into the air. Other Northern soldiers poured withering fire into the flanks. At only one point did the Southerners even reach the Union line.

Longstreet had been proved dreadfully right. Only half of the 15,000 made it back to their lines. Tearfully, Lee rode out to meet them: "It was all my fault; get together, and let us do the best we can toward saving that which is left us."[37] Next day, the Fourth of July, in pouring rain, Lee started the retreat to Virginia. His wagon train, full of wounded, stretched back seventeen miles.

Gettysburg was the high-water mark of the Confederate advance. Never again did Lee invade the North. After this massive defeat and the loss of Vicksburg, the South was on the defensive. The Northern press was ecstatic: "WATERLOO

ECLIPSED!" proclaimed one headline. Lee was indeed the Napoleon of the Civil War, but his belief that victory could be won mostly by audacity and courage failed to take account of the brutality of modern firepower. With hindsight, the third day of Gettysburg seems terribly similar to the carnage seen in World War I.

It took months to clear up the battlefield. Contractors tendered for the grisly work of burying the bodies. The winning bid was $1.59 per corpse—limbs, torsos, and heads pro rata—and a special cemetery was officially opened four months later. The featured speaker at its dedication was Edward Everett, one of the most famous orators of the day. The president was asked to add only "a few appropriate remarks." In fact, Lincoln nearly did not make it at all. On the morning of his departure from the White House, Tad, his little boy, was too sick to eat breakfast. Lincoln and his wife, Mary, had already lost two sons, one of them to typhoid fever only eighteen months before. Convinced that Tad was about to die, Mary became hysterical, begging her husband not to desert her at such a terrible moment. He had literally to pull himself away in order to get to the train.

On November 19, 1863, Everett spoke for nearly two hours. When he finished, people went off to relieve themselves or to buy refreshments from enterprising stallholders. Many missed Lincoln's speech, a mere 272 words. But the president made each one count:

> Four score and seven years ago our fathers brought forth on this continent a new nation, conceived in liberty and dedicated to the proposition that all men are created equal.
>
> Now we are engaged in a great civil war, testing whether that nation or any nation so conceived and so dedicated can long endure. We are met on a great battlefield of that war. We have come to dedicate a portion of that field as a final resting-place for those who here gave their lives that that nation might live. It is altogether fitting and proper that we should do this.
>
> But in a larger sense, we cannot dedicate, we cannot consecrate, we cannot hallow this ground. The brave men, living and dead, who struggled here have consecrated it far above our poor power to add or detract. The world will little note nor long remember what we say here, but it can never forget what they did here.
>
> It is for us the living rather to be dedicated here to the unfinished work which they who fought here have thus far so nobly advanced. It is rather for us to be here dedicated to the great task remaining before us—that from these honored dead we take increased devotion to that cause for which they gave the last full measure of devotion—that we here highly resolve that these dead shall not have died in vain, that this nation under God shall have a new birth of freedom, and that government of the people, by the people, for the people shall not perish from the earth.[38]

Everett had described the battle—vividly—but Lincoln redefined the whole war. Instead of uttering the usual constitutional jargon about the Union versus the states, he talked about the values of America as a single democratic nation. In fact, he used the word "nation" five times at Gettysburg and made no reference to "the Union." Before the Civil War, people usually referred to their country as a plural noun—"the United States are a republic." Afterward, thanks in large part to Lincoln, they tended to say "The United States is. . . ."[39]

Lincoln anchored his arguments in the American Revolution, avoiding the controversies of recent years, but he put his own spin on what the Founders had done. In fact, they had ducked the issue of slavery in a land of liberty—for which the country was now paying an appalling price in blood. But the Emancipation Proclamation had begun to redress that wrong and then at Gettysburg Lincoln rewrote America's past to give meaning to the terrible chaos of the present and to offer hope for an uncertain future. In 1863 reactions to the speech divided along essentially partisan lines. The Republican *Chicago Tribune* predicted it would "live among the annals of man"; its rival paper, the Democrat *Chicago Times*, damned it as "a perversion of history."[40] In time those ten sentences, delivered in a couple of minutes, would become one of the great texts of American and world history, but only after the war was won and Lincoln had become its martyr.

TIGHTENING THE SINEWS OF WAR

At Gettysburg Lincoln had proclaimed a "new birth of freedom" yet the old freedoms for which both sides had taken up arms in the first place were some of the biggest casualties of the war. Both North and South breached traditional liberties on a revolutionary scale. They suspended habeas corpus, allowing arrest without trial; they imposed martial law on civilians in war areas; and they enacted the first conscription laws in American history. The draft, as it was called, aroused particular resentment because rich people could find loopholes, such as paying for exemption or hiring a substitute.

Private Sam Watkins of Tennessee had volunteered at the start of the war; he was furious when he heard of the South's conscription act. "From this time till the end of the war, a soldier was simply a machine. . . . All our pride and valor had gone, and we were sick of war and the Southern Confederacy." Even more infuriating was the law exempting from the draft men who owned more than twenty slaves. Ostensibly this was to prevent anarchy on plantations with large numbers of blacks, but it enabled rich Southern boys to avoid military service. "It gave us the blues; we wanted twenty negroes," complained Watkins. "Negro property suddenly became very valuable, and there was raised the howl of 'rich man's war, poor man's fight.'"[41]

In the North, Lincoln's conscription law, enacted in March 1863, also had its loopholes. J. P. Morgan, Andrew Carnegie, and John D. Rockefeller were among those who bought themselves out of military service for $300 and used the war to build their fortunes. Rockefeller, aged twenty-one when the fighting started, made big profits selling grain to the Union armies and then used the money to move into the oil business. The Civil War began his rise to become the richest man in America.

The inequities of the Draft Law produced a fierce backlash across the North. Protestors sang this parody of a popular recruiting song:

> *We are coming Father Abraham, three hundred thousand more.*
> *We leave our homes and firesides with bleeding hearts and sore,*
> *Since poverty has been our crime, we bow to the decree,*
> *We are the poor who have no wealth to purchase liberty.*[42]

New York's Irish community had provided much of the cannon fodder for the gruesome battles of 1862–1863, and after Gettysburg the city exploded. Mobs burned draft offices, beat up anyone well dressed who looked like a "three-hundred-dollar man," and sacked the homes of well-known abolitionists. Above all, they turned their rage against the blacks, for whom, it seemed, the war was now being fought. The writer Anna Dickinson watched in horror as a crowd converged on the city's Orphan Asylum for Colored Children on Fifth Avenue, near where the New York Public Library now stands: "The few officers who stood guard over the doors and manfully faced these demoniac legions were beaten down and flung to one side, helpless and stunned, whilst the vast crowd rushed in. All the articles upon which they could seize—beds, bedding, carpets, furniture, the very garments of the fleeing inmates, some of these torn from their persons as they sped by—were carried off." All those inside, orphans and caretakers, were "exposed to every indignity and every danger." When they had been driven on to the street, the building was set on fire.[43]

Over a hundred people died in the New York draft riots of July 1863; there were disturbances on a smaller scale from urban Chicago to rural Vermont. It all served to remind Lincoln—if reminder were needed—of the mounting war weariness. During 1864, the North's armies could not finish off the enemy even though the two great killer commanders were now face-to-face. Grant, promoted to head the Union armies, had moved to Virginia, trying to destroy Lee's forces but unable to get in the death blow.

Grant believed that the Confederates were near collapse and would succumb to a final push. As with Lee at Gettysburg, his confidence was hubris and his men paid a high price. Near a little crossroads called Cold Harbor, Grant threw his troops across open ground against the Confederate trenches. Unlike their commander, the soldiers could see what was coming. General Horace Porter, one of Grant's aides, noticed that "many of the soldiers had taken off their coats, and seemed to be engaged in sewing up rents in them. This exhibition of tailoring seemed rather peculiar at such a moment, but upon closer examination it was found that the men were calmly writing their names and home addresses on slips of paper, and pinning them on the backs of their coats, so that their dead bodies might be recognized upon the field, and their fate made known to their families at home."[44] Seven thousand Union soldiers fell at Cold Harbor, mostly in the first few minutes. Grant admitted in his memoirs: "I have always regretted that the last assault at Cold Harbor was ever made . . . no advantage whatever was gained to compensate for the heavy loss we sustained."[45]

In 1864, amid the bloodbath, Lincoln was running for reelection. His opponent was General George B. McClellan, who had earlier urged the president to fight a conservative war, respecting constitutional rights and retaining slavery. Anti-war Democrats even managed to insert a peace plank in their party platform, damning "four years of failure to restore the Union by the experiment of war, during which, under the pretense of military necessity of a war power higher than the Constitution, the Constitution itself has been disregarded in every part, and public liberty and private right alike trodden down, and the material prosperity of the country essentially impaired." Therefore, declared the Democrats, "justice, humanity, liberty, and the public welfare demand that immediate efforts be made for a cessation of hostilities."[46]

The Democratic platform did not advocate total surrender. It insisted that the United States must be reunited as part of the final settlement, ruling out Southern independence, and McClellan himself disavowed the peace plank entirely. But these were signs of mounting Northern disenchantment at what seemed like a war without end. In August 1864 Lincoln told a friend bleakly: "You think I don't know I am going to be beaten, but *I do* and unless some great change takes place *badly beaten*."[47]

Although Lincoln did not realize it, however, the South was now on its last legs. The North had more than double the population—22 million to 9 million—and it was home to four-fifths of America's industry. Its war effort was almost self-sustaining, whereas the South relied heavily on imports from Europe and the Northern blockade had begun to bite. The South paid for the war by printing money, which fueled roaring inflation, whereas the North, with its more developed fiscal and banking systems, imposed the first income tax in U.S. history, issued the first paper currency (known as Greenbacks), and created what became a Board of Internal Revenue. These innovations, implemented in the first eighteen months of the war, enabled the North to endure the conflict with only 80 percent inflation— comparable to the levels for World Wars I and II.

In the South, however, the Confederate government never established that kind of control. President Davis was no great administrator or politician and could not get the Southern states to pull together in a common war effort. Probably no one could have done so: After all, Southerners were fighting against just that kind of centralized control. Joseph Brown, the Confederate governor of Georgia, complained: "It seems military men are assuming the whole powers of government to themselves and setting at defiance constitutions, laws, state rights, state sovereignty, and every other principle of civil liberty. . . . I fear we have much more to apprehend from military despotism than from subjugation by the enemy."[48]

And so, in the South, economy and finance fell apart. By early 1863 it required seven dollars to purchase what a single dollar would have bought two years before— if the goods were available. In the case of salt, essential for preserving meat, the price in some places had risen thirtyfold. Growing shortages of food sapped morale among civilians and at the front. George Eggleston, a Virginian who fought in the Cold Harbor campaign, subsisted like the rest of his unit on a cracker a day and a slice of pork—which they nibbled raw because cooking would have involved some wastage. Twenty years later he had not forgotten:

> Hunger to starving men is wholly unrelated to the desire for food as that is commonly understood and felt. It is a great agony of the whole body and of the soul as well. It is unimaginable, all-pervading pain inflicted when the strength to endure pain is utterly gone. . . . It is a horror which, once suffered, leaves an impression that is never erased from the memory, and to this day the old agony of that campaign comes back upon me at the mere thought of any living creature's lacking the food it desires.[49]

By 1864 Northern generals of skill and ruthlessness, unlike the men of 1861–1862, were now in charge. They were waging all-out war, designed to smash both the Confederate armies and their home front. In Georgia General William Tecumseh Sherman besieged Atlanta for months, gradually severing all road and rail links. At the beginning of September 1864 Sherman instructed the City Council to evacuate Atlanta because it was going to be totally destroyed to prevent it from continuing to supply the Confederacy: "The use of Atlanta for warlike purposes is inconsistent with its character as a home for families. There will be no manufactures, commerce, or agriculture here." Sherman was unapologetic: "War is cruelty, and you cannot refine it. . . . You might as well appeal against the thunder-storm as against these terrible hardships of war. They are inevitable, and the only way the people of Atlanta can hope once more to live in peace and quiet at home is to stop the war." But he assured the citizens of Atlanta, "my dear sirs, when peace does come, you may call on me for anything. Then I will share with you the last cracker."[50]

After burning Atlanta, Sherman marched east across Georgia to the sea, his soldiers carving a swathe of systematic devastation twenty or thirty miles wide that Southerners never forgot or forgave. A local woman, Eliza Andrews, recorded her horror a little while afterward when

> we struck the "Burnt Country," as it is well named by the natives, and then I could better understand the wrath and desperation of these poor people. I almost felt as if I should like to hang a Yankee myself. . . . [The fields] were trampled down and the road was lined with carcasses of horses, hogs, and

cattle that the invaders, unable either to consume or to carry away with them, had wantonly shot down to starve out the people and prevent them from making their crops. The stench in some places was unbearable; every few hundred yards we had to hold our noses or stop them with . . . cologne . . . and it proved a great boon. All the dwellings still standing showed signs of pillage. Here and there lone chimney-stacks, nicknamed "Sherman's Sentinels," told of homes reduced to ashes.[51]

Sherman's victory at Atlanta electrified Northerners. It transformed the election campaign and helped Lincoln, though still controversial in the North, to win a landslide victory. In the South, by contrast, the mood was grim. Mary Chesnut, who had watched the first shots of the war from her rooftop in Charleston, South Carolina, confided to her diary: "Since Atlanta fell I have felt as if all were dead within me forever. . . . We have but two armies, and Sherman is between them now. . . . The reserves, as somebody said, have been secured only by robbing the cradle and the grave—the men too old, the boys too young. . . . The end has come. No doubt of the fact," she wrote grimly. "We are going to be wiped off the face of the earth."[52]

By the beginning of 1865, with the Confederate armies ravaged by death and desertion, Southerners now had to think the unthinkable—filling up the ranks with slaves in return for an offer of freedom after the war. Confederate soldiers were bitterly divided on the issue. "To think that we have been fighting four years to prevent the slaves from being freed, now to turn round and free them to enable us to carry on the war. The thing is outrageous," fumed Grant Taylor in a letter to his wife in Alabama. "I say if the worst comes to the worst let it come and stop the war at once and let us come home for if we are to depend on the slaves for our freedom it is gone anyway."[53] But a sergeant from Louisiana thought the idea made sense: "If we continue to lose ground as we have for the last 12 months, we will soon be defeated, and then slavery will be done any way. . . . I think we should give up slavery and gain our independence."[54]

At the top, Lee wrestled with both sides of the argument: "Considering the relation of master and slave, controlled by humane laws and influenced by Christianity and an enlightened public sentiment, as the best that can exist between the white and black races while intermingled as at present in the country, I would deprecate any sudden disturbance of that relation unless it be necessary to avert a greater calamity to both." But, Lee went on, in the present dire crisis, "I think . . . we must decide whether slavery shall be extinguished by our enemies and the slaves be used against us, or use them ourselves at the risk of the effects that may be produced upon our social institutions. My own opinion is that we should employ them without delay" and the "best means of securing the efficiency and fidelity of this auxiliary force would be to accompany the measure with a well-digested plan of gradual and general emancipation."[55]

This letter from Lee, by now a Southern saint, carried the day (narrowly) in the Confederate Congress. It was an immense symbolic act because, throughout U.S. history, military service had been a mark of full citizenship. Yet the racial code on which Southern slavery was based assumed that most blacks were not capable of being free men and citizens, so allowing them to bear arms in defense of the Confederacy was a radical step. General Howell Cobb, from Georgia, recognized this clearly: "I think that the proposition to make soldiers of the slaves is the most pernicious idea that has been suggested since the war began. You cannot make soldiers of slaves, nor slaves of soldiers," he spluttered. "The day you make soldiers of them is the beginning of the end of the revolution. If slaves will make good soldiers, our whole theory of slavery is wrong."[56]

Diehards like Cobb were finally getting the message: Two hundred thousand black soldiers and sailors in the North had shown that the South's theory of slavery was indeed fallacious, and by March 1865, when the Confederacy accepted blacks into the army, the South's revolutionary bid for independence *was* at an end. But its last rites were dramatic.

"THE PASSING OF THE DEAD"

On March 4, 1865, Abraham Lincoln stood on the east steps of the U.S. Capitol to take the oath of office for his second term as president. His address avoided any hint of triumphalism: "With malice toward none, with charity for all, with firmness in the fight as God gives us to see the right, let us strive on to finish the work we are in, to bind up the nation's wounds, to care for him who shall have borne the battle and for his widow and his orphan, to do all which may achieve and cherish a just and lasting peace among ourselves and with all nations."[57]

At the start of his presidency, in 1861, Lincoln talked very little about God: He had never been one for conventional piety. But his mind and heart had been seared by the war; he sat for hours in the telegraph room during battles or anguished, sleepless, over the young men he had sent to their deaths and the families he had thereby bereaved. Here is one of the letters he wrote, to a girl called Fanny McCullough:

> *Dear Fanny*
>
> *It is with deep grief that I learn of the death of your kind and brave Father; and, especially, that it is affecting your young heart beyond what is common in such cases. In this sad world of ours, sorrow comes to all; and, to the young, it comes with bitterest agony, because it takes them unawares. The older have learned to ever expect it. . . . Perfect relief is not possible, except with time. You can not now realize that you will ever feel better. Is not this so? And yet it is a mistake. You are sure to be happy again. . . . I have had experience enough to know what I say. . . . The memory of your dear Father, instead of an agony, will*

yet be a sad sweet feeling in your heart, of a purer, and holier sort than you
have known before. . . .
    Your sincere friend
    A. LINCOLN.[58]

By the spring of 1865 the president's great frame was stooped, his eyes cavernous. He complained that nothing could soothe the tired spot deep within. One relief from the burdens of office was his sense of humor. When a senator rebuked him for some ridiculous story, he protested: "I say to you now that were it not for this occasional vent, I should die."[59] Lincoln also read and reread the Shakespeare classics—particularly *Hamlet*, *Macbeth*, and *King Lear*—fascinated by great men destroyed by fatal flaws or crushed under moral burdens. Just occasionally he allowed himself the luxury of an evening at the theater.

But in March 1865 there was little time for entertainment. The U.S. Congress had recently passed the Thirteenth Amendment to the Constitution—the first constitutional amendment for more than sixty years. This stated: "Neither slavery nor involuntary servitude, except as a punishment for crime where of the party shall have been duly convicted, shall exist within the United States, or any place subject to their jurisdiction. Congress shall have the power to enforce this article by appropriate legislation." Southerners had defended slavery as part of their constitutional rights, so now the Constitution had been rewritten. The Thirteenth Amendment made stark and irrevocable the liberation of the slaves, accomplished piecemeal by presidential proclamations during the war. It was approved, of course, by a Congress made up of Northerners and ratified only by Northern states, but the defeated South would have to accept it in order to return to the Union.

The end was in sight. For nine months Lee's fading but still valiant army had kept Grant at bay around Petersburg, Virginia, in trench warfare that again prefigured the Western Front in World War I. By early April, however, Lee could hold the line no longer and his retreat made the capital, Richmond, untenable. The city became an inferno as the Confederate government burned its papers and ignited the supply depots. Frances Hunt, a fourteen-year-old girl, recorded these last days in her diary:

> April 3rd 1865. This morning I was awakened from my restless slumber by a loud explosion. . . . [O]ur troops were blowing up the magazine to keep the Yankees from getting it. . . . Richmond evacuated, I cannot realize it. . . . All Cory St. is burnt and Maine is on fire, it is spreading rapidly: almost every minute Flory & I are running out to see if the Yankees are coming and if we see them we run as fast as our feet can carry us.

> April 4th. All is very quiet today. The Yankees are behaving very well considering it is them. . . . The Negroes of Richmond are delighted. We have no

school now and don't know when we will have any. . . . Old Abe has just gotten into the city, & they are firing salutes in honor of his arrival. . . .[60]

Lincoln's arrival in the Confederate capital was an unforgettable moment. He
was mobbed by a crowd of black people, praising God and even calling him the
Messiah. Several freed slaves touched Lincoln, to find out whether he was real. "I
know I am free, for I have seen Father Abraham and felt him." Lincoln was overcome
with emotion. "Don't kneel to me," he told one black man. "That is not right. You
must kneel to God only, and thank him for the liberty you will enjoy hereafter."[61]

The bedraggled remnants of the Confederate army were cornered near the village of Appomattox Court House. Lee dismissed the idea of a breakout as a futile
waste of life; as for fighting a guerrilla war, that would devastate most of Virginia.
So, with deep, deep sadness, he decided "there is nothing left for me to do but to go
and see General Grant, and I would rather die a thousand deaths."[62] They met in the
largest house in the village, which belonged to Wilmer McLean. Back in 1861 the
Confederates had commandeered McLean's home in Manassas, Virginia, as their
headquarters for the opening battle of the Civil War; a Yankee shell even landed in
his dining room. So McLean retreated to this remote village in the south of Virginia,
only to watch the denouement of the conflict played out in his living room.

The two commanders sat a few feet apart—Grant looking like a mud-stained
private, Lee in his best dress uniform. (Actually it was the only one he had left after
he was forced to abandon his baggage train a few days before.) To break the ice,
there was a little chitchat about the Mexican War, in which both men had served,
before they got down to business. Terms had been broadly agreed in advance and
Grant was particularly keen that all weapons should be surrendered. But, as a con-
cession, he said he would allow Southern officers to keep their swords and horses.
Lee replied, "This will have a very happy effect on my army" and then added, "The
cavalrymen and artillerists own their own horses in our army. Its organization in
this respect differs from the United States." Northern officers were brought up
short by those last words, which showed that Lee was still thinking of two distinct
countries.[63]

Grant started to insist that only officers could take their horses with them but
then he reflected: "I take it that most of the men in the ranks are small farmers,
and as the country has been so raided by the two armies, it is doubtful whether
they will be able to put in a crop to carry themselves and their families through the
next winter without the aid of the horses they are now riding." So on this, too, he
relented. Again Lee showed his appreciation: "It will be very gratifying and do much
toward conciliating our people." And when Lee later remarked that his men had
been "living for the last few days principally upon parched corn, and we are badly
in need of both rations and forage," Grant replied, "Suppose I sent over 25,000 rations, do you think that will be a sufficient supply?" Said Lee, "I think it will be
ample and it will be a great relief, I assure you."

This meeting was a dignified end to a barbarous conflict. Dignified, that is, until the generals had left and the souvenir hunters rushed in while Wilmer McLean hysterically tried to protect his property. According to Horace Porter, one of Grant's aides, "Bargains were at once struck for all the articles in the room, and it is even said that some mementos were carried off for which no coin of the realm was ever exchanged." The table at which Lee had sat went for $20 to a Union officer called George Custer.

But dignity was restored on April 12, a chill grey morning, when the Southern regiments paraded for the last time to lay down their weapons and their battle-flags. As they marched down the main street of Appomattox—lined on either side by Northern units that had fought them at Antietam, Gettysburg, and dozens of other places from hell—Colonel Joshua Chamberlain ordered the Union troops to present arms: "Before us in proud humiliation stood the embodiment of manhood: men whom neither toils and sufferings, nor the fact of death, nor disaster, nor hopelessness could bend from their resolve; standing before us now, thin, worn, and famished, but erect, and with eyes looking level into ours, waking memories that bound us together as no other bond;—was not such manhood to be welcomed back into a Union so tested and assured?" In response, recalled Chamberlain, the Confederates "pass us with the same position of the [drill] manual,—honor answering honor. On our part not a sound of trumpet more, nor roll of drum; not a cheer, nor word nor whisper of vain-glorying . . . but an awed stillness rather, and breath-holding, as if it were the passing of the dead!"[64]

Northerners went wild at the news of Lee's surrender. In New York and other cities, cannons fired salutes and people cheered and partied, singing "John Brown's Body" and other favorites. On April 14 Lincoln welcomed Grant to the White House, to hear firsthand about Appomattox. The president seemed like a different man. His wife exclaimed, "Dear Husband, you almost startle me by your great cheerfulness," to which he replied, "And well I may feel so, Mary. I consider *this day* the war has come to a close."[65]

That evening the Lincolns went to Ford's Theatre, a few blocks from the White House, to see an English comedy, *Our American Cousin*. To warm applause they settled down in the presidential box, on the right of the stage. The president laughed heartily at the play; his wife sat close, delighting in his pleasure. Suddenly there was a sharp crack. A man jumped down from the box to the stage. He landed heavily on one foot but hobbled off the stage shouting, "Sic semper tyrannis!"—the motto of Virginia—meaning "So is it always for tyrants." Some of the audience thought this was all part of the entertainment. But then, as a curl of white smoke drifted up from the box, Mary Lincoln screamed: "They have shot the president! They have shot the president!"

The assassin was John Wilkes Booth, a noted actor and also a passionate secessionist who had gloated at the hanging of John Brown back in 1859. His deed was part of a plot to kill the leaders of the Union and give the Confederacy one last chance. The coup fizzled out and Booth was cornered and killed two weeks later, but he had taken the president with him.

Lincoln had been shot in the back of the head at point-blank range. It was Good Friday evening. Unconscious, he was carried to a house on the other side of Tenth Street. Gideon Welles, secretary of the navy, found him there in a small, crowded room. "The giant sufferer lay extended diagonally across the bed, which was not long enough for him. . . . His slow, full respiration lifted the [bed] clothes with every breath he took. His features were calm and striking. . . . About once an hour Mrs. Lincoln would repair to the bedside of her dying husband and with lamentation and tears remain until overcome by emotion."[66]

Lincoln fought hopelessly for life all night. In the cold dawn, it started to rain. The death struggle had begun. Lincoln's breathing became erratic and then finally ceased at twenty-two minutes past seven. Edwin Stanton, another member of Lincoln's cabinet, watched from the foot of the bed, his face streaked with tears. He picked up his hat, raised it respectfully to his head, and then removed it, saying, "Now, he belongs to the ages."[67]

Right up to his death Lincoln remained a divisive figure, even in the North. Democrats still blamed him for an unnecessary war, Republican warhawks had not forgiven the shambolic muddles of 1861–1862, and radicals were unhappy about his plans, outlined in the second inaugural address, to welcome the South back quickly into the Union. But his assassination at the moment of victory changed the whole perspective, and this reminds of a deeper truth. Presidents are both political leaders and heads of state: Their place in public esteem can often shift suddenly and dramatically during their tenure of office depending on which hat they seem to be wearing. And that is what happened to Abraham Lincoln in April 1865.

Easter Sunday saw an outpouring of anger in churches across the North; two days later, on April 19, churches opened again from coast to coast for a national day of mourning to mark his funeral in Washington. Afterward Lincoln's coffin was placed on a train en route to his home in Springfield, Illinois, retracing the long meandering journey he had made to Washington for his inauguration four years earlier. Alerted by newspapers and word of mouth, Northerners turned out in droves. The open coffin lay in state in cities along the way so people could see the dead president and pay their respects. In small towns crowds lined the tracks as the train passed slowly by. The throng in Philadelphia was estimated at half a million; even more turned out in New York City, where voters had rejected Lincoln by a margin of two to one in the election six months earlier. On went the train, up to Albany and Buffalo, across to Cleveland and Columbus, Indianapolis and Chicago, before the entombment in Springfield on May 4. This remarkable display of public emotion was double edged. "We regret that man," remarked the *New York World*, "but we feel the country is eternal."[68] Lincoln the politician, warts and all, had been transmuted into the icon of the reborn nation.

8

WHITE AND BLACK

During the Civil War, slavery was finally abolished in the land of liberty; after the conflict was over, no one talked again about secession from the Union. Yet, despite its magnitude and impact, the Civil War was an unfinished conflict. The slaves were freed but they did not become equal citizens. The twelve-year northern occupation of the South from 1865 to 1877, known as Reconstruction, was too short and not radical enough to reconstruct southern ways; in fact, the South defiantly romanticized the prewar order as part of its separate identity. From the perspective of civil rights, Reconstruction was therefore a tragic missed opportunity—not rectified until the so-called Second Reconstruction of the 1960s, which depended on an assertion of federal power inconceivable to the still essentially states'-rights mentality of the 1860s. In any case, most northerners of the late nineteenth century were just as racist as their southern counterparts; they had little inclination to force on the South racial policies they rejected for themselves. So, instead of slave and free, the great divide in American society became the one between white and black.

DEAD STATES, NEW BIRTH

After the Confederacy surrendered, Lieutenant John Wise returned home to Richmond, Virginia, and removed his uniform. "When I looked in the glass, instead of confronting a striking young officer, I beheld a mere insignificant bit of an eighteen-year-old boy. I had received a great set back in manhood." Next morning, before starting his new postwar life, Wise wrote his last will and testament as a rebel officer: "[B]eing of unsound mind and bitter memory . . . I give, device, and bequeath all my slaves to Harriet Beecher Stowe. . . . My interest in the civil government of the Confederacy I bequeath to any freak museum that may hereafter be established. My sword, my veneration for General Robert E. Lee . . . and my undying love for my old comrades, living or dead, I set apart as the best I have or shall ever have to bequeath to my heirs forever." And so, wrote Wise, "having experienced a death to Confederate ideas and a new birth unto allegiance to the Union, I depart, with a vague but not definite hope of joyful resurrection and of a new life upon lines somewhat different from those of the last eighteen years. I see what has been pulled down very clearly. What is to be built up in its place I know not. It is a mystery; but death is always mysterious. AMEN."[1]

As John Wise said, anyone looking at the South in 1865 could see what had been pulled down. Nearly one-fifth of white southern males aged thirteen to forty-three died in the war and many of the survivors were severely disabled: In Mississippi one-fifth of the state's revenue in 1865 was spent on artificial limbs.[2] Cities like Atlanta and Richmond were in ruins, and in the countryside two-fifths of the livestock had been destroyed. Whites at all levels of society had to start anew. Colonel John Cary, a staff officer during the war and before it principal of the prestigious Hampton Military Academy, returned home to find the school burnt and his family destitute. Having walked around what was left of his estate, he told his wife, "My dear, I have taken stock of our assets. You pride yourself on your apple pies. We have an apple tree, and a cow. I will gather the apples and milk the cow, and you will make the pies and I will go around and sell them."[3]

Yet the extent and durability of destruction have been exaggerated by southern mythology. Only a third of the Confederacy's territory had direct experience of war; Virginia was the single state where war was virtually all-pervasive. The ruined cities were quickly rebuilt and most of the South's railroads back in operation by the beginning of 1866. The biggest disruption to the southern economy came from the abolition of slavery. Slaves had been one of the South's principal assets; now the southern economy would have to reinvent itself.[4]

The ex-slaves, meanwhile, were savoring their first taste of freedom. Many asserted it in the most literal way, by walking off the plantations to which they had been bound—delighted that no one could stop them. One ex-slave, recognizing his former owner among a group of military prisoners, shouted, "Hello massa; bottom rail top dis time!"[5] Freedom is heady stuff but it does not fill stomachs. Frederick Douglass, the northern black leader, noted that many a freed slave, after a lifetime of dependence, lacked the means or training to set up on his own. Now "he must make his own way in the world, or as the slang phrase has it, 'Root, pig, or die'; yet he had none of the conditions of self-preservation or self-protection. He was free from the individual master but the slave of society. He had neither money, property, nor friends. He was free from the old plantation," but was turned loose "naked, hungry and destitute to the open sky."[6] And there were 4 million freed slaves across the South in 1865.

Most southern whites, though defeated, were defiant. Mary Chesnut, grand dame of Charleston, South Carolina, poured out her bitterness and loathing in her diary: "They are everywhere, these Yankees . . . like the locusts and frogs which were the plagues of Egypt. . . . The death of Lincoln I call a warning to tyrants. He will

not be the last President to be put to death in the capital, though he is the first. . . .
I shut my eyes and made a vow that if we were a crushed people . . . I would never
be a whimpering, pining slave."[7] And, when her husband discovered that all his
blacks now had rifles: "The next move will be on pretense of hunting public arms
to disarm all white men. Then we shall have the long desired Negro insurrection."[8]

The challenge of Reconstruction therefore broke down into two main issues.
How extensively were the southern states to be punished or purged before being
readmitted into the Union? And what would be the place of blacks in the New
South—equals of the whites or still their inferiors?

After Lincoln's assassination, the burden of Reconstruction devolved on his vice-
president, Andrew Johnson—now suddenly catapulted into the White House. Johnson was a former Democrat from Tennessee, a self-made man who in the 1850s
had stood up for small farmers against the slave-owning elite. During the war he
sided with the Union and was chosen as Lincoln's running mate in 1864 to appeal
to voters in the border states. But, as so often occurs in American politics, the qual-
ities that looked good in an election campaign did not make for a great president.
According to Richard Taylor, a leading southern Democrat, Johnson, although honest and industrious, "was of an obstinate, suspicious temper. Like a badger, one had
to dig him out of his hole; and he was ever in one except when on the hustings, addressing the crowd."[9]

Johnson, like Lincoln, was determined to bring the South back into the Union
as quickly as possible. Convinced that this was a matter for the president alone, he
stuck to that view with all his badger-like obstinacy, taking advantage of the fact that
Congress was not due to convene again until December 1865. During the summer
the president set out his program. There were to be no trials or witch hunts, provided that ex-Confederates swore allegiance to the Union. States could be readmitted once they repudiated secession and accepted the abolition of slavery.
Johnson left the vital question of whether blacks could vote up to the individual
states, but had no doubt that "it would not do to let the negro have universal suffrage now; it would breed a war of races."[10]

In December 1865 the president gave an upbeat progress report to the Senate:
"The people throughout the entire South evince a laudable desire to renew their allegiance to the Government and to repair the devastations of war by a prompt and
cheerful return to peaceful pursuits." He admitted that "perplexing questions are
naturally to be expected from the great and sudden change in the relations between
the two races; but systems are gradually developing themselves under which the
freedman will receive the protection to which he is justly entitled and, by means of
his labor, make himself a useful and independent member in the community in
which he has a home."[11]

Most Republicans, however, thought Johnson was talking dangerous nonsense.
During 1865 southern states had passed legal codes to keep blacks in subordination—
denied the right to vote or serve on juries, prohibited from bearing arms or testifying

in court against whites. Unemployed blacks could be prosecuted for vagrancy and then hired out to planters as virtual slaves and many of the resurrected states elected leaders who had been high-ranking rebels a few months before. There was particular anger to see the Confederacy's former vice-president, Alexander Stephens, chosen as U.S. senator from Georgia. He did not take up his seat, since Georgia had not been readmitted to the Union, but the message was clear.

The majority of Republicans were moderates, but such blatant southern intransigence drove them into the radical camp when Congress finally convened in December 1865. One of the radical leaders, Thaddeus Stevens of Pennsylvania, argued, "Dead men cannot raise themselves. Dead States cannot restore their existence 'as it was.'" He stated flatly that "the future condition of the conquered power depends on the will of the conqueror. They must come in as new states or remain as conquered provinces." In Stevens's view, creating a New South also meant actively helping free blacks. "This Congress is bound to provide for them until they can take care of themselves. If we do not furnish them with homesteads, and hedge them around with protective laws; if we leave them to the legislation of their late masters, we had better have left them in bondage."[12]

Stevens also wanted to confiscate the property of leading Confederates and put the former master class to work: "Strip a proud nobility of their bloated estates; reduce them to a level with plain republicans; send them forth to labor, and teach their children to enter the workshops or handle the plow, and you will thus humble the proud traitors. . . . Conspirators are bred among the rich and the vain, the ambitious aristocrats." Above all, he insisted, give the blacks the vote: "Have not loyal blacks quite as good a right to choose rulers and make laws as rebel whites?" Stevens believed votes for blacks were "a necessity to protect loyal white men in the seceded States" who otherwise were "in a great minority." They would also "ensure the ascendancy of the Union party"—the Republicans—on whose "continued ascendancy," he said, "depends the safety of this great nation."[13]

Not all Republicans were ready to go as far as Stevens in enfranchising blacks, but they were sure that the president's attempt at reconstruction had failed. So Congress set to work on its own plans, passing a Civil Rights Act to override the Black Codes passed by southern states to limit the freedom of ex-slaves. This set it on a collision course with Johnson, who, as an ex-Democrat from the border states, had little in common with Republicans from the Northeast and Midwest. He continued to insist that Reconstruction was a matter for the White House, not the Congress, and tried to veto key items of radical legislation including the Civil Rights Act giving full citizenship to blacks, which, he said, sought to "establish for the security of the colored race safeguards which go infinitely beyond any that the General Government has ever provided for the white race." It was, argued Johnson, "another step, or rather stride, toward centralization and the concentration of all legislative powers in the National Government."[14]

But radicals argued that this was a case in which the rights of recalcitrant states had to be overridden by the federal government to guarantee the freedom of southern blacks and the stability of the Union. They passed the Civil Rights Act over Johnson's veto in April 1866 and went on in June to enshrine its provisions in the Constitution as the Fourteenth Amendment, to ensure that they could not be reversed by a bare majority of a future Congress. The amendment was ratified in July 1868 by a Union of states that was still overwhelmingly northern, but its acceptance became a precondition for southern acceptance back into the United States.

In numerous ways the Fourteenth Amendment was a turning point in American law. Its affirmation that "all persons born or naturalized in the United States, and subject to the jurisdiction thereof, are citizens of the United States and of the State wherein they reside" reversed the Supreme Court's decision in the *Dred Scott* case of 1857 that blacks were not and could not become U.S. citizens. Yet the amendment also introduced for the first time into the Constitution the word "male," specifically by affirming the voting rights of "male citizens." Nineteenth-century feminists such as the Grimké sisters, as we saw in Chapter 5, believed that the abolition of slavery for blacks would pave the way for women to attain full citizenship as well. The radicals' conservatism on gender in the Fourteenth Amendment therefore left a deep sense of betrayal among feminist leaders: It showed, said one of them, Elizabeth Cady Stanton, that woman "must not put her trust in man" when seeking her own rights.[15]

The Fourteenth Amendment had other implications. It stipulated that no state shall "deprive any person of life, liberty, or property, without due process of law; nor deny to any person within its jurisdiction the equal protection of the laws." The initial set of amendments to the Constitution back in 1791, the Bill of Rights, had protected the rights of the individual only against violation by the federal government, but now some rights were being protected against violation by the states as well. What exactly the "due process" and "equal protection" clauses covered has been a highly contested legal terrain. Initially the Supreme Court interpreted their scope very narrowly but since the 1960s, as we shall see, more liberally minded justices have spun out of "due process" a law of privacy to legitimize abortion and homosexuality, while "equal protection" has served to justify affirmative action programs for all sorts of disadvantaged groups.

All this, however, was long in the future. In 1866 the Civil Rights Act and the Fourteenth Amendment were widely supported in the North, and the congressional elections of November resulted in a resounding victory for the Republicans, giving them far more than a two-thirds majority in both Houses. This was enough to pass even more radical Reconstruction Acts over the president's veto, including legislation to put the South under peacetime military rule until it changed its ways.

Passions reached such a pitch that, in the spring of 1868, the Republicans impeached the president for "high crimes and misdemeanors." Impeachment, an old

English procedure, involved the House bringing a case against a federal official before the Senate. Senator Charles Sumner called the trial "one of the last battles with slavery. Driven from these legislative chambers, driven from the field of war, this monstrous power has found a refuge in the Executive Mansion." Sumner claimed that Johnson was "the impersonation of the tyrannical slave power. In him it lives again."[16] Determined to get Johnson out of the White House, the Republicans had resorted to actions of dubious constitutional validity. The articles of impeachment largely revolved around the authority of the president to choose and remove his own cabinet, on which his constitutional position was strong.

Andrew Johnson was the first president in U.S. history to be impeached, Bill Clinton becoming the second in 1999. In Johnson's case the outcome was much closer—after a three-month trial the radicals fell just one vote short of the two-thirds majority in the Senate they needed to remove him from office. But Johnson's presidency now had only a few months to run. His successor was Ulysses S. Grant, the northern war hero and now a darling of the radicals because he had defied the president over army appointments. Grant won the White House in a landslide in November 1868, becoming at forty-six the youngest U.S. president to that date. But he had virtually no political experience and the political initiative lay with Congress. The Fourteenth Amendment and the Reconstruction Acts had cleared the way for military rule to try to remake the South along radical lines.

REUNION BUT NOT RECONSTRUCTION

For a flavor of what changed, consider this description of the South Carolina House of Representatives in 1873: "The Speaker is black, the Clerk is black, the door-keepers are black, the little pages are black, the chairman of the Ways and Means is black, and the chaplain is coal-black . . . the body is almost literally a Black Parliament, and it is the only one on the face of the earth which is the representative of a white constituency."[17] These were the words of James Pike of Maine, one of America's best-known political journalists. Pike was often patronizing about Negro politicians, but here he accurately captured the drama of the South's revolution under radical Reconstruction.

In 1873 South Carolina's House of Representatives had 123 members. Only 23 of them were white. "They sit, grim and silent," said Pike. "Grouped in a corner of the commodious and well-furnished chamber, they stolidly survey the noisy riot that goes on in the great black Left and Center." Loftily he described the "intellectual level" as that of "a bevy of fresh converts at a Negro camp meeting . . . endless chatter . . . interruptions from all quarters. . . . The Speaker's hammer plays a perpetual tattoo . . . the peanuts are cracked and munched faster than ever. . . . [T]he sable crowd . . . laugh as hens cackle—one begins and all follow." But, Pike admitted, "underneath all this shocking burlesque upon legislative proceedings, we must not forget that there is something very real to this uncouth and untutored multitude" because "they have a genuine interest and a genuine earnestness in the business of the assembly which we are bound to recognize and respect." Seven years ago, he noted, "these men were raising corn and cotton under the whip of the overseer. Today they are raising points of order and privilege. They find they can raise one as well as the other. They prefer the latter. It is easier and better paid. . . . It means escape and defense from old oppressors. It means liberty."[18]

South Carolina was an extreme case—in no other southern state in the 1870s were blacks in a majority in a legislature—but in all of them blacks played an active part in politics, thanks to the imposition of northern military rule. Any person who had broken an oath of allegiance to the Union by supporting the Confederacy was denied the vote—thus disfranchising thousands of whites—while, at the same time, blacks were given the vote. Many blacks held office in tandem with white supporters of the Union. The new state governments endorsed the end of slavery and full citizenship for blacks. They also imposed property taxes at a much higher level than before the Civil War and used these to vote large appropriations to rebuild roads, bridges, and especially railroads.

But the biggest spending program in many states was to fund, for the first time in the South, a system of free public education. This received substantial help from the North. "In the very act of emancipation there is the sacred promise *to educate*," declared the president of the National Teachers' Association. "We can now, for the first time, meet the demands of humanity, civilization, and freedom. We can not only teach the negroes, but we can emancipate the 'poor whites' whom ignorance has kept so long in bondage. The old slave states are to be new missionary ground for the national schoolmaster."[19]

Both races benefited, but blacks were particularly keen. In one school in North Carolina, "side by side sat representatives of four generations in a direct line, viz.: a child six years old, her mother, grandmother, and great-grandmother, the latter over 75 years of age. All commenced their alphabet together, and each one can read the Bible fluently." Apart from benefiting from formal schooling, many blacks simply helped educate each other: "Some young man, some woman, or old preacher, in cellar or shed, or corner of a negro meeting house, with the alphabet in hand, or a torn spelling-book, is their teacher. All are full of enthusiasm with the new knowledge the book is imparting to them."[20]

Radical Reconstruction was therefore a massive attempt at social engineering but, like many such grand projects, it expected too much of human nature. Although many northerners who came South to teach or govern were genuinely altruistic, others had an eye toward self-advantage. Henry Warmoth was a native of Illinois but, after the war, he made his name (and his fortune) down South. According to an investigation by the U.S. Congress, Warmoth "retired from the army in 1865; went to Texas; was indicted there for embezzlement and appropriating Government cotton." He moved to Louisiana and got himself elected governor. His annual salary was $8,000 but he told congressional investigators he made far more than $100,000 in the first year, and by the 1870s was estimated to be worth anything up to $1 million.[21]

Southern critics of Reconstruction labeled this type of northerner a "carpet-bagger"—meaning someone who lived out of a suitcase and stayed around only long enough to rip off what he could. They were even more incensed about southern fellow-travelers who worked with the northerners and the blacks, dubbing them "scalawags." Again this was a caricature—many white politicians during Reconstruction were poor farmers from the backcountry who had long opposed the slave-owning elite—but there were also men like Frank Moses of South Carolina, whose life was described in 1878 by the New York Times as "a romance of rascality." During his thirty-eight years, said the paper, he "has been a rebel, a Radical, and a robber, a Governor, a millionaire, and a beggar."[22]

A dashing member of Charleston high society, in April 1861 Moses claimed the honor of lowering the Union flag over Fort Sumter after the first battle of the Civil War. But, despite his bravado, he avoided active service, instead spending the war hunting down draft dodgers. Down and out in 1865, he cozied up to South Carolina's military governors and wormed his way into the state's new Republican Party. Once elected to the House, he got himself made Speaker and then, in the words of the New York Times, "commenced in earnest a career of corruption, 'fee-taking,' bribery and robbery, which, for extent and audacity, is without a parallel in the history of any English-speaking people." Moses had no shame. He told one man who wanted a bond issue passed: "I want a pair of horses—good horses, you understand. See that I get them; give me $1,000 to-day and I'll pass the bill." The lobbyist spluttered but coughed up. The bill got through a third reading and then stalled. When the lobbyist asked why, Moses coolly told him he would have to "oil the machine" a bit more. "Just agree to give me $10,000 of the bonds after the bill becomes a law, and I will put it through at once." When Moses moved on to become governor, he developed a new and lucrative line in the sale of pardons to convicted criminals. On the proceeds he purchased one of the best mansions in the South, furnished it at the state's expense, and laid out the gardens in the style of Versailles.[23]

With crooks like Moses in charge, opposition to Republican rule mounted across the South, often in violent form. A secret society called the Ku Klux Klan (from "kuklos"—the Greek for "circle"), which was started by Confederate veterans in Tennessee in 1866, spread rapidly across neighboring states. Clad in white robes and hoods, brandishing fiery crosses, the KKK sought to terrorize black and white supporters of the Republican Party, thereby helping the Democrats gain power. The Klan also took it upon themselves to police what was called racial etiquette. "I never will forget when they hung Cy Guy," recalled Ben Johnson, an ex-slave from South Carolina, years later:

> They hung him for a scandalous insult to a white woman, and they comed after him a hundred strong. They tries him there in the woods, and they

scratches Cy's arm to git some blood, and with that blood they writes that he shall hang 'tween the heavens and earth till he am dead, dead, dead, and that any nigger what takes down the body shall be hunged too. Well, sir, the next morning there he hung, right over the road, and the sentence hanging over his head. Nobody'd bother with that body for four days, and there it hung, swinging in the wind, but the fourth day the sheriff comes and takes it down.[24]

In 1871 the federal government cracked down on Klan violence and outlawed the organization, so southern conservatives changed tack and now targeted the cost and corruption of Reconstruction. Switching from race to high taxes enabled them to pick up support from moderate Republicans, poor farmers, and even some blacks. These conservatives, known as Redeemers, were learning to play the new politics game as adroitly as their opponents.

Meanwhile, the North's enthusiasm for Reconstruction began to wane. The wartime radicals had died or retired, and northerners were more concerned with their own economic problems, especially after a bank crisis in 1873 triggered a long recession for which the ruling Republicans got the blame. Grant was the first president since Andrew Jackson (1829–1837) to serve a full two terms but he was out of his depth in an economic crisis, unable to coordinate policies or reassure the public. His administration stumbled to its end reeking of corruption, most notoriously the Whiskey Ring scandal of 1875 in which senior Republicans, some of them close to the president, were exposed for having defrauded the government out of some $3 million in tax revenues. By 1876 Democrats were confident of winning the White House for the first time in two decades.

The election turned on the three southern states that were still under Republican rule—Louisiana, Florida, and South Carolina. The Democrats intimidated voters with displays of armed force that brought back memories of the Ku Klux Klan. But the Republicans controlled the governmental machinery and were therefore able to disqualify votes from counties where there had been notable intimidation. So the Democrats set up rival state legislatures and the situation descended into farce.

In South Carolina the newly elected Republican House of Representatives convened in the State House but the rival Democratic House was determined to do the same. The story was colorfully told by chronicler Myrta Avary:

"Come, men, let's get at it!" cried Colonel Alex. Haskell, seizing the doorkeeper in front of him. Each man followed his example; a struggle began . . . the door, lifted off its hinges, fell with a crash. The full Democratic House marched in, headed by Speaker Wallace, who took possession of the Speaker's chair. Members of his House took seats on the right of the aisle, negroes giving way and taking seats on the left.

Speaker Wallace raised the gavel and called the House to order. Speaker Mackey entered, marched up and ordered Speaker Wallace to vacate the chair. Speaker Wallace directed his sergeant-at-arms to escort Mr Mackey to the floor where he belonged. Speaker Mackey directed his sergeant-at-arms to perform that office for General Wallace. . . . There was bedlam, with two Speakers, two clerks, two legislative bodies, trying to conduct business simultaneously![25]

The stand-off lasted four days and four nights—with food and blankets passed in through the windows—before federal troops compelled the Democrats to withdraw, but they simply resumed business in nearby South Carolina Hall.

The deadlock in these three states left the national result in limbo; 1876 was America's first disputed election since Jefferson versus Burr in 1800. Eventually Congress established a bipartisan commission to decide the issue. This voted on essentially party lines, giving victory to the Republican candidate, Rutherford B. Hayes of Ohio, by one electoral vote, just days before the new president was to be inaugurated. But, in a murky backroom deal, the Republicans agreed to stop using federal troops to guarantee black rights. Bereft of federal support, the three disputed southern legislatures were soon in Democrat hands. Or, as one black from Louisiana lamented, "the hands of the very men that held us as slaves."[26]

Radical Reconstruction had been a bold experiment, seeking to make former slaves into full and equal citizens, but it became too radical for most northerners. They did not want to see federal power used aggressively to overrule states' rights. Nor were they in favor of forcibly giving blacks their own land as a platform for economic and political independence. Most Americans believed that liberty meant freedom from government intervention, not the use of government power to help minority groups.

By 1877 the South had rejoined the Union and slavery was firmly abolished. These changes were enough for most northern whites. One journalist predicted that "the negro will disappear from the field of national politics. Henceforth, the nation, as a nation, will have no more to do with him."[27] This was a bleak prediction but a shrewd one. It would take a second era of Reconstruction in the 1960s—more radical on the issues of federal power and black rights—to complete the task left unfinished in 1877.

"NEW SOUTH," OLD WAYS

Henry W. Grady, like many children in Georgia, had lost his father during the Civil War. But Henry wasn't the sort to moan about the past. An enterprising young journalist, he turned the *Atlanta Constitution* into one of the South's great newspapers and worked tirelessly to sell the South to the nation. In 1886 he was addressing a VIP banquet in New York, whose guests included General William Tecumseh Sherman, who had burned Atlanta to the ground two decades before. Grady's speech went down in southern folklore.

"I want to say to General Sherman, who is considered an able man in our parts, though some people think he is a kind of careless man about fire, that from the ashes he left us in 1864 we have raised a brave and beautiful city." When the laughter died down, Grady declared boldly: "There was a South of slavery and secession—that South is dead. There is now a South of union and freedom—that South, thank God, is living, breathing, growing every hour." The Old South, said Grady, "rested everything on slavery and agriculture, unconscious that these could neither give nor maintain healthy growth," whereas the New South "presents a perfect democracy." There were, he enthused, "a hundred farms for every plantation, fifty homes for every palace, and a diversified industry that meets the complex needs of this complex age."[28]

On the face of it, the New South was there for all to see by the end of the nineteenth century. During the 1880s the region more than doubled its railroad mileage, opening up areas like West Virginia to profitable coal mining and creating hundreds of small towns whose needs stimulated economic growth. In 1900 Birmingham, Alabama, was the eleventh-biggest city in the South, yet it had started from nothing in a cornfield thirty years before. Some enterprising local real-estate men saw that the local deposits of iron, coal, and limestone were ideal for steelmaking. They deliberately adopted the name of the great English industrial metropolis to signal its potential.

An icon of the industrial New South was James Buchanan Duke of North Carolina—known as "Buck." This tall, rugged red-head turned his father's little tobacco company into an international giant. He invested in machines that fed in tobacco and paper at one end and churned out rolled cigarettes at the other. Previously this had been done by hand: A skilled worker might manage 2,000 cigarettes in a day but a machine could produce 100,000. Duke also developed the cigarette box in place of flimsy paper packaging and inserted photos of celebrities and sportsmen as a sales gimmick.[29] Shrewd advertising, sharp practice, and ruthless mergers created the American Tobacco Company, which then divided up the world with its British rivals. At the end of his life, "Buck" left half his massive wealth to endow Duke University in Durham, North Carolina, intended as a Gothic-cum-Georgian imitation of Oxford and Harvard.

Like most industrial tycoons, Duke presented his success as a classic rags-to-riches American story: "I have succeeded in business not because I have more natural ability than those who have not succeeded, but because I have applied myself harder and stuck to it longer." Duke said he always had confidence in himself: "I resolved from the time I was a mere boy to do a big business. I loved business better than anything else. I worked from early morning until late at night." He insisted that "any young man can succeed if he is willing to apply himself. Superior brains are not necessary."[30]

But despite the real changes in the late nineteenth century, much of the South remained set in old ways. The region was still overwhelmingly agricultural, with cotton even more predominant than before. And although the old slave plantations had gone, the planters had bounced back, often joined as major landowners by the owners of local general stores. These men had a monopoly of business on their patch and grew rich by charging extortionate interest on unpaid bills. The new agrarian system was known as sharecropping. Most blacks and many poor whites lacked the means to farm on their own, so they received land and rudimentary housing from a landowner, in return for his getting a half-share of the crop. And because they could not afford to buy their own seed and equipment, these were advanced on credit—driving them further into debt. They ended up bound to the landowner almost as tightly as if they had been slaves.

One black farm laborer in Georgia recorded what happened when he came, as he thought, to the end of his contract. His employer, a state senator, "said to some of us with a smile (and I never will forget that smile—I can see it now): 'Boys, I'm sorry you're going to leave me. I hope you will do well in your new place—so well that you will be able to pay me the little balances which most of you owe me.'" According to the account books from the employer's store, this laborer's "little balance" amounted to $165; most of his friends owed between $100 and $200. They were told that, after signing an account of their debts, they could go and seek new employment.[31]

The blacks were, of course, illiterate but, the laborer said, "we would have signed anything, just to get away. So we stepped up, we did, and made our marks." That night they were thrown into the stockade, together with convicts whom the senator, like many well-connected whites, had leased (no questions asked) from the local prison. "The next morning it was explained to us by the two guards appointed to watch us that, in the papers we had signed the day before, we had not only made acknowledgment of our indebtedness, but that we had also agreed to work for the Senator until the debts were paid by hard labor. . . . Really we had made ourselves lifetime slaves, or peons, as the laws called us." It took the man three years in this squalid stockade to pay off his debts. He ended up in Birmingham, Alabama. "I reckon I'll die either in a coal mine or an iron furnace. It don't make much difference which. Either is better than a Georgia peon camp," which, he said feelingly, "is hell itself."[32]

So, for many black laborers and sharecroppers, the New South was little better than the Old. Now that the North had lost interest in Reconstruction, the blacks had to make the best they could of the situation. That, at least, was the view of Booker T. Washington, a former slave from Virginia who became head of the Tuskegee Institute in Alabama. His goal was to produce a network of teachers and schools that would provide basic education for blacks. Washington's philosophy of self-help and hard work attracted the financial support of many white businessmen and politicians and he became the first African-American to be invited to the White House as a guest (rather than a servant).

Washington urged his people to focus for the moment on economic advancement, not political rights. "The wisest among my race understand that the agitation of questions of social equality is the extremest folly," he asserted. "No race that has anything to contribute to the markets of the world is long in any degree ostracized. It is important and right that all privileges of the law be ours, but it is vastly more important that we be prepared for the exercise of these privileges. The opportunity to earn a dollar in a factory just now is worth infinitely more than the opportunity to spend a dollar in an opera-house."[33]

Just as Henry Grady presented a South to suit the North, so Booker T. Washington presented blacks who would appeal to whites. Behind the scenes he was more assertive—for instance, funding court cases in support of black rights—but his public stance was regarded by many blacks as obsequious and misguided. The most tenacious critic was W.E.B. Du Bois, a free black from Massachusetts who had earned a PhD from Harvard. Du Bois insisted that black people could progress only if the "talented tenth" of "exceptional men" were educated for leadership and an active struggle for civil rights. He called Washington "The Great Accommodator."

"Mr. Washington," said Du Bois, "distinctly asks that black people . . . concentrate all their energies on industrial education, the accumulation of wealth, and the conciliation of the South." But, complained Du Bois, the return had been "1: The disfranchisement of the Negro. 2: The legal creation of a distinct status of civil inferiority for the Negro. 3: The steady withdrawal of aid from institutions for the higher training of the Negro."

He admitted that these developments were not "direct results of Mr. Washington's teachings" but claimed that "his propaganda has, without a shadow of doubt, helped their speedier accomplishment." How, asked Du Bois indignantly, could black southerners "make effective progress in economic lines if they are deprived of political rights, made a servile caste, and allowed only the most meagre chance for developing their exceptional men?"[34]

Washington and Du Bois offered different strategies for dealing with white supremacy in the New South—incremental economic progress within the system or active political opposition against it. Both were particularly appealing to the black middle class that was emerging in the new southern towns and cities—teachers, lawyers, ministers, and bankers catering for black needs in an increasingly segregated urban society. Among them was "Mike" King. Born in 1899, he started out as a sharecropper in rural Georgia, spending day after day plowing behind a mule. Defiantly he shouted, "I may *smell* like a mule, but I don't *think* like a mule."

Mike made it to Atlanta, working days as a mechanic or a railroad fireman and nights gaining his education. Eventually he completed a bachelor's degree in divinity and became a Baptist pastor. He also renamed himself after the founding father of Protestantism—Martin Luther King.[35]

In the Old South, the place of blacks had been clearly defined—most were slaves—but in the New South all people were free, so conservatives drew a new dividing line: white or black. This seemed particularly important in the growing southern cities, where the races mingled all the time. Under what were known as the "Jim Crow" laws, black and white were separated in public places—schools, restaurants, housing, even cemeteries. Transport was a particularly sensitive arena, as Du Bois discovered after riding on a southern train: "The 'Jim-Crow' car is up next the baggage car and engine. It stops out beyond the covering in the rain or sun or dust. Usually there is no step to help you climb on." As for your compartment, this "is a half or a quarter or an eighth of the oldest car in service on the [rail]road. Unless it happens to be a through express, the plush is caked with dirt, the floor is grimy, and the windows dirty." It was, said Du Bois, "difficult to get lunch or clean water. Lunch rooms either don't serve niggers or serve them at some dirty and ill-attended hole in the wall. As for toilet rooms—don't!"[36]

Not all blacks were willing to accept such discrimination. In Louisiana Homer Plessy, a light-skinned black, deliberately sat in a whites-only part of a train. After refusing to budge, he was arrested and jailed. Plessy and his supporters took the case all the way to the U.S. Supreme Court but it was rejected in January 1896 with only one dissenting vote. Plessy had based his argument on the Fourteenth Amendment of 1868 affirming the equal rights of all citizens. But, according to the Court, the Amendment "could not have been intended to abolish distinctions based upon color, or to enforce social, as distinguished from political, equality." The Court judged that any state was "at liberty to act with reference to the established usages, customs, and traditions of the people, and with a view to the promotion of their comfort and the preservation of the public peace and good order."[37]

Plessy v. Ferguson was a landmark decision, restricting the Fourteenth Amendment's scope to political equality rather than social relationships. The Supreme Court went on to affirm that segregation was constitutional as long as the separate facilities were equal in quality. That, of course, was rarely the case but the Court judged that, in these and most other issues, it was up to the states, not the federal government, to maintain standards—leaving policing to be handled by judges in local federal districts who were acutely vulnerable to state pressure. The Court also addressed another assumption of Plessy's case, "that social prejudices may be overcome by legislation, and that equal rights cannot be secured to the negro except by an enforced commingling of the two races." The Court said it could not accept this proposition. "If the two races are to meet upon terms of social equality, it must be the result of natural affinities, a mutual appreciation of each other's merits, and a voluntary consent of individuals."[38]

It would be a half-century before the Supreme Court changed its mind about the enforced mixing of races. When it finally overturned the *Plessy* "separate-but-equal" verdict in 1954, this opened the floodgates to affirmative action on behalf of black rights. Mike King's son—Martin Luther King, Jr.—would be on the crest of that wave.

In the meantime, however, the line between white and black was etched more harshly into American life by Darwinism—or at least the bowdlerized social Darwinism that became fashionable in the late nineteenth century. This encouraged the idea that there were scientifically separate "races," each with distinct characteristics, that were competing to survive. White supremacists had no doubt that the "Caucasians"—variously known as the "Teutonic" or "Anglo-Saxon" race—were inherently superior to other races, be they Slavs, Negroes, or Asiatics. This pseudo-scientific racism gave spurious legitimacy to racial discrimination and, as we shall see, also helped to justify the movement to restrict immigration. For best-selling Congregationalist minister Josiah Strong of Ohio, in fact, "Anglo-Saxonism" became nothing less than a global mission statement.

Strong was confident that "God, with infinite wisdom and skill, is training the Anglo-Saxon race for an hour sure to come in the world's future," when the pressure of population on resources would drive the world into "a new stage of history—the final competition of races, for which the Anglo-Saxon is being schooled." Then, he predicted, "this race of equalled energy," which had been "strengthened in the United States," would "move down upon Mexico, down upon Central and South America, out upon the islands of the sea, over upon Africa and beyond." Could anyone doubt, asked Strong, that "the result of this competition of races will be the 'survival of the fittest'"?[39]

Social Darwinism helped reinforce the new dividing line between white and black. With Negroes no longer legally inferior, as most had been in the era of slavery, the dogma of racial hierarchy provided a new way to justify their subordination. The rituals and rules of "racial etiquette" allowed southerners to "maintain both white privilege at home and a sense of Southern distinctiveness within the nation."[40] Race and southernness went together; only when barriers against blacks were finally broken down in the 1960s did the South really start to become Americanized.

WAR AND MEMORY

As the New (or not so New) South took shape, the visible scars of war disappeared, but at the same time the war became ingrained in American memory, though very differently in North and South.

Oliver Wendell Holmes became one of the most celebrated justices of the U.S. Supreme Court in the twentieth century, but in his youth he had been a Civil War soldier. Holmes went off to fight as a young Harvard graduate, fired up with the abolitionist cause; yet, as with so many, the reality of war soon appalled him. He described one battle as "an infamous butchery in a ridiculous attempt" and, after the war was over, he refused to read about it or to observe its anniversaries. Holmes recognized that the details of battle "rapidly escape the memory in the mist which settles over a fought field." He was happy for the mist to come down, shrouding the bloody horrors of war.[41]

Holmes was typical of many Civil War veterans. Robert E. Lee, the South's greatest general, declined all the lucrative offers to write his memoirs and shunned reunions and anniversary events. "I think it wisest," he wrote, "not to keep open the sores of war, but to follow the example of those nations who endeavored to obliterate the marks of civil strife, and to commit to oblivion the feelings it engendered."[42] In North and South, soldiers mostly got on with new lives. Relatively few of them participated in veterans' associations, nor was there much public appetite for books or magazine articles about the war. The Civil War, it seemed, was dead and buried.

Time is a great healer; gradually perspectives change. As the young warriors turned grizzled and rheumatic, they began to look back with nostalgia. Again, Oliver Wendell Holmes was typical. At the end of the war he had put his uniforms in a back closet. In the 1880s, however, he grew again the curled military moustache of his youth. He brought out his sword and regimental flag, placing them on display above his mantelpiece. In an age of comfort and commercialism, he preached the heroic virtues of fighting for a cause.

The annual Maytime ritual of Memorial Day, he told fellow veterans in words that would be echoed in John F. Kennedy's inaugural address, was the moment "to recall what our country has done for each one of us, and to ask ourselves what we can do for our country in return. . . . It embodies in the most impressive form our belief that to act with enthusiasm and faith is the condition of acting greatly." On this day, said Holmes, "when we decorate their graves, the dead come back and live with us" and "it is not of the dead alone that we think" but also of "those lovely, lonely women, around whom the wand of sorrow has traced its excluding circle." Holmes believed that "the generation that carried on the war has been set apart by its experience. Through our great fortune, in our youth, our hearts were touched with fire. It was given to us to learn at the outset that life is a profound and passionate thing."[43]

During the 1880s, commemoration of the war really took off. The principal northern veterans' association was the Grand Army of the Republic (GAR). In 1878 it had only 30,000 members. At its peak in 1890, the figure was 428,000.[44] Veterans did not just visit graves and attend reunions; the GAR's local posts became a focus of community life in small towns across the North. And, because of their size and organization, veterans also became a powerful lobby group. Early in the war Congress had passed a law giving pensions to disabled soldiers and to the widows of soldiers who had been killed. In 1890 veterans persuaded Congress to extend pension rights to anyone who had served in the Union army for at least ninety days and had subsequently become disabled for any cause. In the 1890s nearly a million veterans and their dependants were receiving government pensions, amounting to over 40 percent of the federal budget. And this in a country where any form of socialism was anathema. Here was an early intimation of the power of the veterans' lobby in American life.[45]

There were other ways for veterans to make money from war service. One publication in Georgia included a picture of John Conway, a northern soldier from Ohio, sitting on the ground with his knee bandaged. The text read: "I was wounded in the leg at the battle of Stone River, December 31st, 1862. My blood was poisoned from the effects of the wound, and the leg swelled to double its natural size, and remained so for many years. The poison extended to my whole system, and I suffered a thousand deaths. Nothing did me any good til I took SWIFT's SPECIFIC, which took the poison out of my blood, and enabled me to feel myself a man again."[46]

War was now becoming memory and money. In 1913 the decision was made to mark the fiftieth anniversary of the battle of Gettysburg with a weeklong reunion of veterans from North and South. This calculated attempt at bridge-building was meticulously planned. A huge tented city was erected across the battlefield—together with bakeries, kitchens, dining tents, washing facilities, water fountains, and other conveniences of civilized life that had not been on offer during the soldiers' first visit to Gettysburg in 1863. There was even a discreet stockpile of coffins in case some of the old men did not survive the excitement or the summer heat. Actually only nine veterans died, out of an encampment of over 50,000. The youngest to attend was sixty-one; the oldest claimed to be a hundred and twelve.

The reunion attracted swarms of souvenir-sellers and photographers, keen to make a killing, at least commercially. Philip Myers, an eighteen-year-old photographic assistant, recalled one Yankee veteran who wanted to be pictured in the Devil's Den, where a southerner had shot him for real fifty years before. The Yankee stood puffing on his cigar, with one hand holding his cheek. When Myers protested that this spoiled the picture, the veteran explained, "I'm a-fightin' and a-yellin' at the top of my lungs, when his bullet come along an' catches me right in my mouth. But what with yellin' my mouth is wide open, so it misses my teeth an' comes outta my cheek. An' when it heals, it don't close up tight. There is still a little hole there. If I don't plug it with my finger I don't get no draft on my smoke." He inhaled deeply and, with lips pursed tight, blew the smoke out of his cheek.[47]

Relations between the two sides were remarkably cordial although, at lunch one day, a southerner and a Yankee did go for each other with forks. The climax of the reunion was a reenactment of Pickett's Charge—that unforgettable Confederate assault across open fields into withering Northern fire. Myers was among the thousands watching as the Southerners emerged from the woods, just as they had done fifty years before. Except that it was not quite the same. "We could see, not rifles and bayonets, but canes and crutches," Myers noted. "We soon could distinguish the more agile ones aiding those less able to maintain their places in the ranks." Nearer they came, toward the stone wall where the Union guns had waited and where so many of their comrades had fallen. "As the Rebel yell broke out after a half century of silence, a moan, a gigantic sigh, a gasp of unbelief, rose from the onlookers. It was then that the Yankees, unable to restrain themselves longer, burst from behind the stone wall, and flung themselves upon their former enemies," said Myers, "not in mortal combat, but re-united in brotherly love and affection."[48]

Veterans and nation reunited: That was the official message from Gettysburg in 1913. In the North, certainly, this was the predominant mood because the Civil War was no longer a live issue. But it is easy for victors to be magnanimous; in the South an undercurrent of real bitterness remained. Many there lamented what was known as the "Lost Cause." This took the line, "We wus' robbed; they didn't play fair." In other words, the South went to war to defend states' rights against centralizing government, the issue of slavery being quietly airbrushed out of the picture. The South, it was claimed, had braver soldiers and better generals, notably Lee (now almost a deity), but the North had more men and greater resources. Lee and his fellow officers were the epitome of nobility, whereas northerners were immoral brutes, notably Sherman, the fire-raiser of Georgia. This was a struggle between Southern Cavaliers and Yankee Roundheads, backed by the clunking fist of industrial power, and Reconstruction was depicted as a continuation of the war by political means, as northern carpetbaggers descended like locusts, picking the South bare with the help of "uppity" blacks and a few local traitors.

More insidiously the war and its aftermath became memorialized in literature, most famously in the novels of William Faulkner. On one level Faulkner has been seen as a leading practitioner of modernism—defying the canons of traditional story-telling through multiple narrators, abrupt shifts of time, and stream-of-consciousness writing. But Faulkner also was an author rooted in time and space, insisting: "No man is himself. He is the sum of his past."[49] Faulkner's most celebrated novels from the 1920s and 1930s (such as *The Sound and the Fury* and *Absalom, Absalom!*) imaginatively explore the mentality of his home region of northern Mississippi, rather as Thomas Hardy did with his fictional Wessex. Faulkner's Yoknapatawpha County (from an Indian word meaning "split land") is the setting for universal dramas—of love and sex, of anger and guilt—but his protagonists are rooted in the by-then-stereotypical southern images: toppled aristocrats, carpetbaggers and sharecroppers, the cults of martial masculinity and feminine refinement, the unhealed scars of slavery and the Civil War. As Faulkner's South moves into the machine age, which he deplored, it remained haunted by a past that also seemed in some ways like a lost Eden.

Lingering, too, is the belief that it might all have turned out differently. In *Intruder in the Dust* (1948) Faulkner conjures up a mystical moment in history, suspended in time just before Pickett's Charge:

> For every Southern boy fourteen years old, not once but whenever he wants
> it, there is the instant when it's still not yet two o'clock on that July after-
> noon in 1863, the brigades are in position behind the rail fence . . . and it's
> all in the balance, it hasn't happened yet, it hasn't even begun yet, it not only
> hasn't begun yet but there is still time for it not to begin against that position

and those circumstances. . . . This time. Maybe this time with all this much
to lose and all this much to gain: Pennsylvania, Maryland, the world, the
golden dome of Washington itself to crown with desperate and unbelievable victory the desperate gamble, the cast made two years ago.[50]

Faulkner's South was complex and subtle, but Hollywood offered an un-
abashedly romanticized version. In 1915, two years after the Gettysburg fiftieth reunion, D. W. Griffith's *Birth of a Nation* hit the box offices. The film, based on a
novel called *The Clansman*, celebrated the Confederate soldier and the Ku Klux
Klan as defenders of southern values and southern woman against the barbarians
from the North. Then in 1939 *Gone with the Wind* took the whole world by storm.
The movie was based on a novel by Margaret Mitchell that drew on stories she had
been told when growing up in Georgia. The film's opening scenes depict a land of
colonnaded mansions and rolling acres, of cotton fields and magnolia blossoms.
The white women are elegant, their menfolk noble or at least dashing. And, in the
background, the black slaves are mostly dutiful and content, clearly incapable of
an independent existence. This idyllic world is swept away by the Civil War. Some
of the film's most dramatic scenes take place amid the burning of Atlanta by
Sherman—the "Great Invader." Then his Yankee "Juggernaut" moves on through
Georgia, bringing "desolation" to what once had been "a land of grace and plenty."
The plantations are looted and devastated, southern men spared by the war are
mostly broken reeds, and the northerners who flit in and out of the film are rob-
bers or crooks.

Gone with the Wind won ten Oscars, one of them awarded to Hattie McDaniell
for her portrayal of the stereotypical black Mammy. When the film had its gala pre-
miere in Atlanta in 1939, McDaniell did not attend—to avoid having to sit in the
"colored" section of the cinema. Her fellow black actress, Butterfly McQueen,
played another stereotype—the childish black slave. Malcolm X, the 1960s black
radical, recalled seeing *Gone with the Wind* as a boy in Michigan. "I was the only
Negro in the theater, and when Butterfly McQueen went into her act, I felt like
crawling under the rug."[51]

Audiences across America and all over the world flocked to see *Gone with the
Wind*, which is reckoned to have sold more tickets than any other movie in history.
Much of its appeal, of course, was attributed to the screenplay and the acting, the
sets and the music, but its depiction of the Old South—white and black—had a
profound subliminal effect. The film was suffused by the ideology of the Lost Cause.
It liberated its viewers from the burden of the South's real past, allowing an escape
into flights of romantic nostalgia. They are told at the start of the movie, written in
antique script against a rose-tinted skyscape:

> *There was a land of Cavaliers and Cotton Fields called the Old South. . . .*
> *Here in this pretty world Gallantry took its last bow.*

Here was the last ever to be seen of Knights and their Ladies Fair,
of Master and of Slave. . . .
Look for it only in books, for it is no more than a dream remembered.
A Civilization gone with the wind.

For the first seventy-two years of the United States, from 1789 to 1861, the South had dominated national politics, or at least acted as arbiter. For two-thirds of that time the president had been a slave-owning southerner; likewise twenty-three of the thirty-six Speakers of the House of Representatives. But the Civil War ended the South's "peculiar institution"—slavery—and the region's peculiar hold on national politics. It would be a half-century before the House had another southern Speaker and a century before a resident of an ex-Confederate state (Lyndon Johnson of Texas) was elected president.[52] Yet as the South became marginalized in national life, it romanticized its past.

9

CAPITAL AND LABOR

Lee's surrender at Appomattox in 1865 was a landmark not only for America but for the world. Instead of two rival feuding nations, the United States would reign supreme across North America. This portended a future great power: In 1866 the French commentator Michel Chevalier urged the nations of Europe to unite in the face of the "political colossus that has been created on the other side of the Atlantic." He even foresaw war between the two continents.[1] Appomattox also meant that Americans could exploit the continent's vast resources without sectional friction. The last third of the nineteenth century saw America's industrial revolution— eclipsing in speed, intensity, and impact that of Britain, the world's first industrial nation over the preceding hundred years. The rapid growth of industrial capitalism created fierce social tensions and sharp class divisions, with radicals applying the old language of master and slave to industrial relations. But the United States did not end up emulating the political conflicts of Europe: Marxian socialism, the dynamite of old Europe in the early twentieth century, failed to explode in the United States.

BIG BUSINESS

From the outside, the building might have been taken for a big, domed theater but inside it seemed like something out of Dante's *Inferno* with "three giant cauldrons, big enough for all the devils of hell to brew their broth in, full of something white and blinding, bubbling and splashing, roaring as if volcanoes were blowing through it—one had to shout to be heard in the place." Suddenly, without warning, one of the cauldrons began to tilt, pouring out "a cascade of living, leaping fire, white with a whiteness not of earth, scorching the eyeballs."[2]

This is an extract from a novel, *The Jungle* (1906) by Upton Sinclair, but its vivid depiction of a Chicago steel mill in the 1900s was true to life. Or certainly to the way steelmaking would have seemed to Jurgis Rudkis, an immigrant from Lithuania and the novel's hero. He watched in appalled fascination as a red-hot ingot, the size of a man's body, was squeezed through huge rollers and flattened again and again. "Like a great red snake escaped from purgatory," it "writhed and squirmed." Violent shudders passed through its tail. "There was no rest for it until it was cold and black—and then it needed only to be cut and straightened to be ready for a railroad."[3]

Steel and rails: These were the fundaments of America's industrial revolution. After the Civil War the construction of transcontinental railroads, previously dead-locked by the rivalry between North and South, proceeded apace. The first one was completed in May 1869 in a symbolic meeting of the rails in the salt flats of Utah. Other east-west links followed, many of them funded as before with generous fed-eral land grants. Steel, from which the rails, coaches, and bridges were all made, was an alloy tougher and more durable than iron. Those giant cauldrons that terri-fied Jurgis Rudkis were steel converters. The technology had been pioneered in Sheffield by a British inventor called Henry Bessemer, but it was in the United States that the Bessemer process really took off. America's Mr. Steel was an immigrant from Scotland called Andrew Carnegie.

Andy was born in Dunfermline—Scotland's ancient capital, across the Forth es-tuary from Edinburgh. His father was a skilled weaver who had fallen on hard times in the "Hungry Forties," so the family sold up and moved to Pittsburgh in western Pennsylvania. The city had a substantial Scots community, whose motto was "wor-ship on Sunday and whiskey on Monday, thus blending the spirits."[4] Andy—a sparky little lad, charming and full of energy—began work at thirteen in a bobbin factory, earning $1.20 a day, but he moved on to become a telegram delivery boy and then a telegraph operator. By the age of twenty-five he was running the whole Western Division of the Pennsylvania Railroad Company. Carnegie was called up during the Civil War but, like many of America's future titans of industry, he paid for an Irish immigrant to act as substitute and after the war he invested his grow-ing wealth in coal and railroads, being one of the first to recognize the superior po-tential of steel rails.

Pittsburgh was ideal for steel production, at the intersection of major rivers and railroads and close to coal and iron fields. Carnegie and his brother identified a prime site near the city but, with his sense of history, he was also struck that this was where General Edward Braddock and his troops had been overwhelmed in 1755 by the French and the Indians. In excavating for the plant they found bayonets, swords, and many other relics of the battle. The Braddock plant started operations in 1872 and over the next quarter-century Andrew Carnegie made himself the dominant figure in the American steel industry.

His axioms on how to succeed in business became legendary, advising juniors to aim high: "I would not give a fig for the young man who does not already see himself the partner or the head of an important firm." He proposed that the "rising man must do something exceptional, and beyond the range of his special department. HE MUST ATTRACT ATTENTION." Carnegie had no time for misplaced deference: "Boss your boss just as soon as you can; try it on early. There is nothing he will like so well if he is the right kind of boss; if he is not, he is not the man for you to remain with—leave him whenever you can, even at a present sacrifice, and find one capable of discerning genius." As for the proverb "Don't put all your eggs in one basket," that, in Carnegie's opinion, was nonsense. His advice was to "put all your eggs in one basket, and then watch that basket."[5]

Carnegie, of course, was preaching what he practiced, for these were the methods he had used to get to the top (although, to give a rounded picture, he should also have mentioned the benefits of insider trading, crony capitalism, and screwing down wages). His generation of industrial titans—men like John D. Rockefeller in oil and Cornelius Vanderbilt in railroads—became known as the Robber Barons. Ruthless when making their money, they were, however, munificent philanthropists in later life—perhaps to expiate their guilt.

Again Carnegie stood out. In 1901 he sold his steel business to the banker J. P. Morgan. The new conglomerate, U.S. Steel, was the first company ever to be capitalized at over $1 billion. For the rest of his life, Carnegie applied his still considerable energies to giving away the fortune he had accumulated so ferociously. A self-made man, he believed passionately in education, supporting some 3,000 public libraries in America and overseas—the first in his birthplace, Dunfermline. He also funded technological institutes, concert halls, the Peace Palace in The Hague, and some 7,000 church organs.

Carnegie's philosophy was summed up in a celebrated essay that became known as "The Gospel of Wealth." In the Old World, he noted, monarchs and aristocrats handed down their fortunes to the next generation of their family. In the proposed communist utopia, millionaires would be forcibly stripped of their wealth. But, he argued, American capitalists should voluntarily treat their fortunes as a trust for society as a whole. He advised the "Man of Wealth," "[f]irst, to set an example of modest, unostentatious living, shunning display or extravagance; to provide moderately for the legitimate wants of those dependent upon him; and after doing so to consider all surplus revenues which come to him simply as trust funds." These, said Carnegie, he should administer in what he judged was likely "to produce the most beneficial results for the community—the man of wealth thus becoming the mere agent and trustee for his poorer brethren."[6] According to Carnegie, the capitalist should aim to give away his fortune during his lifetime. He did not quite succeed—$30 million still remained when he died in 1919—but he had already given away a staggering third of a billion dollars.

Other tycoons followed suit, with American higher education a notable beneficiary of their philanthropy. In Pittsburgh Carnegie established what became known as the Carnegie Institute of Technology, Vanderbilt founded a university bearing his name in Nashville, Tennessee, and Rockefeller endowed the University of Chicago so munificently in the 1890s that it immediately became a major research and teaching institution. Out in California at the same time Leland Stanford, the railroad magnate, created Stanford University in memory of his teenage son who died of typhoid; one of its first students was the future president Herbert Hoover.

These were all private universities but state universities were also booming, thanks to a farsighted piece of legislation—the Morrill Land Grant Act of 1862, which gave each state federal land (30,000 acres per member of Congress) to endow institutions of higher education. Many of America's state universities have their roots in this legislation, and also some private ones such as the college established in upstate New York by Ezra Cornell, one of the founders of the Western Union telegraph company. Under ambitious and long-serving university presidents such as Andrew D. White at Cornell and Charles W. Eliot at Harvard, America's leading universities moved into the industrial age with graduate and research programs to match those of the great universities of Germany. The late nineteenth-century university boom was therefore an interesting symbiosis of the public and the private. Creative use of federal land laid a basic platform, but private capital was essential to push some universities up to world rank.

Carnegie and his rival tycoons were vivid, dramatic figures who aroused fervent admiration and also vehement hatred. But, good or bad, they came and went like meteors, flashing across the sky. The lasting legacy of America's industrial revolution was not big businessmen but big business. Again the Carnegie story is typical. He gradually bought out the rival steel plants—what was known as horizontal integration—and he also gained control of all the stages of the production process, from acquiring the necessary coal and iron fields to owning steamships and railroads to transport the finished products—vertical integration. James Buchanan Duke did the same for tobacco and there was an explosion of similar mergers around the turn of the century. Many of America's great corporations were forged at this time, including General Electric, Du Pont, and Eastman Kodak. But no one man, or even a family, could run these industrial giants. Day-to-day operations were handed over to professional managers and an increasingly large staff. This was corporate managerial capitalism. By 1900 half the U.S. working population was employed for salaries or wages, rather than working for themselves.[7]

Behind them stood in-house research laboratories, developing and refining new technologies. Here the pioneering figure was Thomas Edison—like Carnegie a product of the telegraph business with little formal education but also a man of energy and ingenuity. The "invention factory" he established in Menlo Park, New Jersey, in 1876 generated major innovations such as the phonograph, the X-ray machine, and the movie projector. But Edison's most important achievement was the first viable electric lightbulb, using a carbon filament, from which he moved rapidly into electric power generation; his first power station started up in Lower Manhattan in 1882. Edison did not get it all right—his business used direct current (DC) against the more easily transmitted alternating current (AC) championed by his rival George Westinghouse, who eventually won their "war of the currents." But, by the end of the 1880s, the electrical revolution was well and truly launched, with the first electric streetcars and the electric elevator without which skyscrapers would have been impossible.

Many Americans considered the development of big business an alarming erosion of the independent middle class cherished by Thomas Jefferson as the backbone of the republic. One New York magazine imagined the corporations saying dismissively, "Independent business enterprises conducted by individuals are not up to date. Those of you who are wasting your lives as our competitors may sell out to us if you like. We will pay your salaries to work for us if we find you worthwhile. Or you can go through bankruptcy if that suits you better. As for you professional gentlemen," the imaginary corporation went on, "you speak your mind too freely. If you want to make a living from now on, you will have to preach, or practice law, or lecture, or conduct your newspapers to suit us."[8]

So big business became a big issue for Americans around 1900. Was it a benefit or a curse? A sign of progress or a betrayal of the country's values? Was it corrupting politics? Destroying the workers? Ruining the cities? America answered those questions over the next two decades by both design and default, as we shall see, and its answers would shape the rest of the twentieth century.

"MADE IN AMERICA"

On February 7, 1890, Andrew Carnegie addressed a letter to William Ewart Gladstone, formerly Britain's prime minister:

> I am traveling homeward from Pittsburgh to New York at rate of forty miles an hour upon the Pennsylvania Limited. . . . The cars are connected by a covered passage-way, so that we can pass from end to end of the train. The train has a Dining car, its tables beautifully ornamented with flowers, excellent meals provided, fresh cooked on the train, a Ladies' Maid . . . men servants, all the latest daily and weekly papers, bath rooms for ladies and gentlemen, a barber shop, an excellent library, special telegrams of public interest are received as we proceed.

The latest novelty, Carnegie told Gladstone proudly, "is the Official Stenographer to whom I am now dictating," which meant that "passengers can thus write home and business men can clear up their correspondence. We happen to have on board to-day a Clergyman who has dictated the heads of his Sunday sermon." Gladstone had no doubt received thousands of letters over the years, Carnegie concluded, "but none written, I venture to say, under such circumstances."[9]

A "Pullman Palace Car" does not seem so remarkable in the modern era of business-class air travel, nor an official stenographer in the age of BlackBerrys and cellphones. But for its time, 1890, Carnegie's account of rail travel American-style sounded very impressive and he enjoyed rubbing in U.S. superiority even to admirers like Gladstone, the Grand Old Man of British politics.

Pullmans were only the icing on the cake, however. What really mattered, in economic terms, was that the railroad boom after the Civil War had connected the United States together into a single market for both people and goods. The merger movement produced a handful of big railroad companies, such as the Pennsylvania and the New York Central, and imposed a nationwide uniform gauge of four feet eight and a half inches. Even more striking, the railroads standardized time.

In Civil War America, time was local. A jeweler or amateur astronomer would set the town clock to noon when the sun passed directly overhead, so there were literally thousands of time conventions being observed all across America. To avoid chaos individual railroads tried setting timetables by reference to their headquarters city, but this could still prove very confusing. For instance, a traveler from Portland, Maine, who arrived in Buffalo, New York, had to choose among four different times. The New York Central Railroad clock might indicate noon (the time in New York City) but the Lake Shore & Southern Michigan clock would show 11.40 A.M. (which was Columbus time), while the Buffalo city clock registered 11.25. Nor could our traveler resolve the confusion by checking his own pocket watch: That was still set on Maine time at 12.15.[10]

The idea of standard time zones had been debated for years but it was the railroads that pushed it through. The man in charge of the project was William Frederick Allen, who held the nightmare post of managing editor of the *Official Railway Guide* for all the United States. After eighteen months of study and consultation he presented his plan for four time zones, roughly straight lines north-south across the country. At a special meeting of railroad executives Allen held out two maps—one color-coded to show local times, the other indicating his four standard zones. Contrasting the two maps, he asked them which system appeared more desirable—"the one, as variegated as Joseph's coat of many colors, or the other, with its solid masses of uniform tints; the one representing the barbarism of the past, the other the enlightenment which we hope for the future."[11]

The railroads opted for enlightenment and so did most of America's cities and towns. D-Day, Sunday, November 18, 1883, became known as "The Day of Two Noons" because towns in the eastern half of a zone observed midday as usual by the sun and then put their clocks back, maybe as much as three-quarters of an hour, and celebrated noon again on standard time. Although most people welcomed the change, a few critics saw it as evidence of the overweening power of the railroads. "The Sun is no longer to boss the job. People—55,000,000 of them—must eat, sleep and work as well as travel by railroad time," the *Indianapolis Sentinel* complained. "Ministers will be required to preach by railroad time, banks will open and close by railroad time. . . . We presume the sun, moon and stars will make an attempt to ignore the orders of the Railroad Convention, but they, too, will have to give in at last."[12] The heavens held out but Americans did not. Standard Time became federal law a quarter of a century later, during World War I.

Also revolutionized by the railroad age was America's diet. In the 1860s most people subsisted on bread, potatoes, root vegetables, dried fruit, and meat—usually heavily salted. Fresh fruit and vegetables were available briefly during the ripening season—once harvested they soon went bad—and cucumbers and pickles were the only salad in winter. So the average diet was not very nutritious or appetizing, though homemade sauces and "relishes" added a bit more taste. From the 1870s, however, special freight cars—insulated and packed with ice—enabled meat, fruit, and vegetables to be moved from the warm farmlands of the West and South to the North and Midwest.

Even more important, Americans started eating out of tin cans. The master of the can was a German-American called Henry John Heinz. A chipper little man with blue eyes and reddish mutton-chop whiskers, Heinz grew up, like Andrew Carnegie, in Pittsburgh. His genius was to bring the benefits of the railroad into the American kitchen. Starting out with horseradish, pickles, and mustard, in 1876 Heinz's Pittsburgh factory branched out into tomato ketchup. Previously ketchup had been watery and thin, being made from unripe tomatoes, but Heinz used ripe ones, plus vinegar and tomato solids—all of which gave his ketchup body and taste. Since then it has helped cover a multitude of culinary sins, serving in the words of one Heinz advert as "Blessed relief for Mother."

H. J. Heinz also had a genius for advertising. There was the trademark green pickle pin stamped with the name "HEINZ," handed out to all and sundry, and the famous "57 Varieties" slogan that echoed around the world. According to Heinz, when sitting on a train in Manhattan he noticed a shoe ad headed "21 Styles." He said to himself, "we do not have styles of products, but we do have varieties of products." Counting up, he went well beyond fifty-seven, but that was the number that kept coming back into his mind. "Seven, seven," he said, "there are so many illustrations of the psychological influence of that figure and of its alluring significance to people of all ages and races that '58 Varieties' or '59 Varieties' did not appeal at all to me as equally strong." He got off the train immediately, went into a lithographer's, and designed a streetcar card that he had distributed throughout the United States. "I myself did not realize how highly successful a slogan it was going to be."[13]

Entrepreneurs like Heinz seized on the potential of railroads to create a single market across a country the size of a continent. So did the new mail-order companies such as Montgomery Ward and Sears Roebuck, which offered thousands of items—from Baldwin pianos to Stetson hats—to customers all over America. In Europe, by contrast, there was a plethora of nation-states, each with their own tariffs and standards, and many of these countries would go to war against each other in 1914. So America's single market and its political unity after 1865 were huge economic bonuses, enabling the country to capitalize on its vast population and its abundant natural resources—wood, coal, iron, and, increasingly, oil.

Here the titanic figure was John D. Rockefeller, whose Standard Oil Company relentlessly bought up all major rivals to dominate both extraction and refining. Like Carnegie, Rockefeller—raised a Baptist in the evangelical revivals of the mid-nineteenth century—amassed great wealth by cutthroat ruthlessness and gave much of it away in systematic philanthropy, outdoing the steel magnate at both ends. Biographer Ron Chernow called him "an amalgam of godliness and greed, compassion and fiendish cunning." But while the Standard Oil Trust was a passing phase—broken up by the Supreme Court under antitrust legislation into more than thirty companies in 1911—the industry endured. In the 1870s and 1880s much of its production had been kerosene for lamps, both in America and globally, but after the Edison revolution oil production was geared more toward cooking and heating before finding its real raison d'être in the new century in the "horseless carriage."[14]

Rockefeller was another example of the economies of scale possible in a vast continental market, but new technologies were also important in boosting productivity. In the United States, labor was less plentiful and more expensive than in Europe and this provided greater incentive to develop labor-saving devices. In the mid-nineteenth century, British observers had started taking note of what they called "the American system of manufactures." A specially appointed committee of military experts had toured U.S. munitions factories in 1854 and then reported to the House of Commons with near incredulity on the way muskets were made—not individually by skilled craftsmen but by an unskilled laborer assembling, with the help of only a thumbscrew, interchangeable parts that had been produced by machines. "With regard to the fitting of these muskets when thus interchanged, the Committee are of opinion that all the parts were as close, and the muskets as efficient, as they were before the interchange took place."[15]

Mass production became a priority after the Civil War and American industrialists were also encouraged by the cost of labor to develop bulk handling. A Swedish immigrant, Gustaf Unonius, marveled at the grain elevators in Chicago—stone buildings right at the river's edge, with water on three sides. Along one wall of an elevator ran two railroad tracks, spurs from a main line that, branching out in all directions, connected Chicago with the grain regions in Illinois and the Mississippi valley. On each spur, six freight cars could be hauled into the elevator for unloading at one time. And so, enthused Unonius, "in ten minutes, the grain from a train loaded with about 3,000 bushels is raised by 12 elevators, weighed and transferred to the bins." If a vessel on the river needed loading, it "is brought to the side of the elevator, a lid in the bottom of the bin is opened, and the grain runs into the elevator to be hoisted up and weighed . . . whereupon it is run through a spout into the hold of the vessel. . . . Thus in less than an hour two ships are loaded with 12,000 bushels apiece."[16]

Using their superior manpower, resources, and technology, Americans had leapfrogged the British to produce a third of the globe's manufactured goods by the eve of the Great War. In 1913 America's population of 97 million was double Britain's; its annual per capita income of $377 eclipsed the British figure of $244; and total U.S. iron and steel production of 32 million tons was not much less than that of Britain, Germany, France, and Russia combined.[17]

American entrepreneurs were now penetrating Britain itself, even burrowing into the foundations of its great metropolis. London had built the world's first underground railways back in 1863, but at the turn of the century there were only a few lines, run by rival companies, and most of them used steam trains—that is, until the arrival of Charles Tyson Yerkes. A shady tycoon from Chicago, he had built up an empire of tramways and electric railways known as the "Chicago Traction Tangle." One of his maxims for success was to "buy up old junk, fix it up a little and unload it upon other fellows." Eventually Yerkes was drummed out of Chicago, so he tried his luck in London. Dame Henrietta Barnett, one of the founders of Hampstead Garden Suburb, noted with pained concern that Yerkes was "typical of what a Yankee is thought to be." She was appalled at his plan to "carry all London about in tunnels" but her protests were vain. In just five years from 1900 Yerkes and his American financial backers consolidated the London underground into something like a single network. He also moved from steam to electrification, using rolling stock made in America.[18]

Yerkes was just one of many American business predators loose in Britain in the first decade of the twentieth century. "Buck" Duke was trying to buy up British tobacco, J. P. Morgan was bidding for the Cunard shipping line, H. J. Heinz started a factory in Peckham in southeast London, and Frank Woolworth opened his first British store in Liverpool. The British press raised a storm about this "American invasion." One journalist, Frederick Mackenzie of the *Daily Mail*, warned: "In the domestic life we have almost got to this. The average citizen wakes in the morning at the sound of an American alarum clock; rises from his New England sheets, and shaves with his New York soap, and a Yankee safety razor. He pulls on a pair of Boston boots . . . fastens his Connecticut braces, slips his Waterbury watch into his pocket and sits down to breakfast . . . at which he eats bread made from prairie flour . . . and a little Kansas City bacon. . . . The children are given Quaker oats." Rising from table, Mackenzie went on, "the citizen rushes out, catches an electric tram made in New York, to Shepherds Bush, where he gets into a Yankee elevator, which takes him on to the American-fitted railway into the city. At his office of course everything is American."[19]

Journalistic hyperbole, but Mackenzie's satire rang painfully true to many in Britain in the 1900s. America had once been Britain's colony but now, it seemed, the economic roles were reversed: The New World was buying up the Old. "The advent of the United States of America as the greatest of world-Powers is the greatest political, social, and commercial phenomenon of our times," declared British journalist W. T. Stead, describing this as "the salient fact which will dictate the trend of events in the Twentieth Century." The "only consolation" Stead offered to "the susceptible Briton" was that "the American Constitution, like American people, owes its origins to the island which was the cradle of the race." So, Stead argued, the impending "Americanisation of the world" could be seen as "the spirit of Old England reincarnate in the body of Uncle Sam." Here, in embryo, was the cultural conceit that lay behind the British idea of a "special relationship."[20]

Another sign of the times was the rash of marriages between British aristocrats and the daughters of American plutocrats. Between 1870 and 1914 no fewer than 134 peers of the realm secured American wives (the peerage was 700 strong in 1914). Love may have played a part but these were mostly business transactions—cash for coronets—bailing out struggling British lords by offering an alluring title. Consuelo Vanderbilt, daughter of the railroad tycoon, became Duchess of Marlborough in return for a dowry reputed to be $2.5 million. Miss Jennie Jerome, daughter of a New York financier, came more cheaply at a tenth of the price. But her marriage to the duke's uncle proved of far greater significance for Anglo-American relations: They were the parents of Winston Churchill.[21]

The emotional and financial entanglements of the Old World and the New were immortalized in the literature of the prolific Henry James. In early novels such as *The Portrait of a Lady* (1881) and again in late masterpieces like *The Ambassadors* (1903), James—a New Yorker who spent much of his life in England—explored the interactions between Europeans who were cultured, enticing, but often corrupt and Americans characterized by innocence and often ignorance but also by keener moral sensitivities. Here was the proverbial clash between democratic values and Old World hierarchies, usually centered on the experiences of young, intelligent American women. James was a novelist, not a social commentator, but the overriding impression from his writings, as critic Leon Edel has noted, is that it was "bad business to mix America and Europe" because their values were ultimately "irreconcilable." In the end James made his own choice: In 1915, the year before his death, he became a British citizen in protest against America's assertion of innocent neutrality in Europe's Great War.[22]

THE CITIES: PRIDE AND SHAME

Industrial America was an urbanized society. In 1860 one-sixth of the population lived in urban areas—defined as towns with a population of more than 2,500 people—and by 1900 the proportion was one-third. No fewer than forty cities had over 100,000 people and in the biggest of them the whole skyline was being transformed.

"Skyscraper" once meant a triangular sail on the top of a ship's yardarm but in the 1890s the term began to be applied to buildings. In the center of cities like Chicago and New York, where land was scarce and costly, businesses were keen to add as many stories as possible and now, in the age of steel, they could—it almost seemed that the sky was the limit.

One of the leading architects of the era was Louis Sullivan. He grew up on a farm in Massachusetts and studied in Paris, but made his career in Chicago. For Sullivan the skyscraper was a new art form, something almost spiritual. "It must be tall, every inch of it tall. The force and power of altitude must be in it, the glory and pride of exaltation must be in it." Designers, he said, should realize that "the problem of the tall office building is one of the most stupendous, one of the most magnificent opportunities that the Lord of Nature in His beneficence has ever offered to the proud spirit of man."[23]

In the years around 1900 Sullivan and other architects such as Daniel Burnham redesigned the center of Chicago with soaring new buildings and a series of parks along the shore of Lake Michigan. But although the new "commercial style" of architecture had its roots in the Midwest, it blossomed in New York. Unlike Chicago, Manhattan did not impose any height restrictions until 1916 and so, in America's corporate capital, the country's biggest businessmen vied to produce the world's tallest building. In late 1902 no fewer than sixty-six skyscrapers were under construction in Lower Manhattan, some of them rising to twenty-five stories. The Flatiron Building, shaped like an iron to fit its narrow triangular site, particularly impressed photographer Alfred Stieglitz: "It appeared to be moving toward me like the bow of a monster ocean steamer—a picture of new America still in the making." His father asked how he could be interested in such a "hideous" building. "Why, Pa," he replied, "it is not hideous, but the new America. The Flat Iron is to the United States what the Parthenon was to Greece."[24]

The grandest of these prewar New York skyscrapers was the Woolworth Building, located on Broadway opposite City Hall. When the plans were unveiled, there were many critics, even within the building profession. "Just why such a tall structure is considered desirable is something of a mystery," one engineering journal complained—finding no excuse for "the rearing of this great pile, shutting off the light of its neighbors, darkening the streets, and containing a population of several thousand people whose concentration on a little piece of ground will add another heavy burden to the transportation facilities in the vicinity."[25] What explained the "mystery" was quite simply the ego of Frank Woolworth, whose original five- and ten-cents stores had mushroomed into a retail empire of 600 outlets. As the building went up, Woolworth kept increasing the number of stories to ensure that it ended up higher than the tower of the Metropolitan Insurance Building. The result was indeed the world's tallest building—for seventeen years.

These early skyscrapers were a far cry from the smooth, unadorned modernist concrete and glass towers of the late twentieth century. Instead they were festooned with piers, bays, and moldings, their façades covered with ornamental panels in wrought iron or terra-cotta. The Woolworth Building took all this to an extreme—being designed in a flamboyant late-Gothic style and capped with a spire that earned it the apt nickname "Cathedral of Commerce." Inside, the vaulted lobbies, mosaic ceilings, and marble walls, all trimmed in bronze, continued the theme. Yet the Cathedral of Commerce was also totally up-to-date—with a basement swimming pool, high-speed elevators, and superb electric lighting that was shown off spectacularly during the opening ceremony on April 24, 1913. At 7:29 in the evening, when Mr. Woolworth's 900 guests were seated at dinner tables on the twenty-seventh floor, a telegrapher of the Western Union, stationed there, notified the operator in the White House that all was ready. A minute later, at exactly 7:30, President Wilson pressed a button, closing the circuit and causing a bell to ring. Suddenly, said the *New York Times*, "lights flashed from every floor of the fifty-five stories, from the sub-basement 37 feet below the street level, to the top of the tower, 792 feet above the street."[26]

During the quarter-century before World War I, the New York skyline—indeed the whole city—had been transformed. Sailing into the bay again in 1904, after a long absence, the Boston intellectual Henry Adams found the view "more striking than ever—wonderful—unlike anything man had ever seen," yet also, said Adams,

> like nothing he had ever much cared to see. Power seemed to have outgrown its servitude and to have asserted its freedom. The cylinder had exploded, and thrown great masses of stone and steam against the sky. The city had the air and movement of hysteria, and the citizens were crying, in every accent of anger and alarm, that the new forces must at any cost be brought under control. Prosperity never before imagined, power never yet wielded by man, speed never reached by anything but a meteor, had made the world irritable, nervous, querulous, unreasonable and afraid.[27]

Henry Adams was a morose conservative from patrician stock—two of his forebears, John and John Quincy Adams, had served as president—but people at all levels of society were terrified by the new megalopolis. Across America the spectacular new downtowns were offset by some of the world's most appalling slums. Take Chicago, for instance. A few miles from the City Beautiful of Sullivan and Burnham were the Union Stockyards, vividly evoked by novelist Upton Sinclair with his gritty, almost photographic realism. Taking a streetcar out there, one passed endless rows of dirty wooden houses, punctuated periodically by filthy streams, grim factories, and railroad crossings.

> Every minute . . . the colors of things became dingier; the fields were grown parched and yellow, the landscape hideous and bare. And along with the thickening smoke they began to notice . . . a strange, pungent odor. . . . It was now no longer something far off and faint, that you caught in whiffs; you could literally taste it, as well as smell it . . . an elemental odor . . . rich, almost rancid, sensual, and strong. There were some who drank it in as if it were an

intoxicant; there were others who put their handkerchiefs to their faces . . . when suddenly the car came to a halt, and the door was flung open, and a voice shouted—"Stockyards!"[28]

The skyscraping wealth of downtown Chicago was indeed founded on bodies—of cattle and also, let it be acknowledged, of men and women. By the 1900s the Union Stockyards on the southwest side of Chicago covered almost a square mile and produced 80 percent of America's meat. So appalling was the pollution spewing into the Chicago river that the city, with a massive series of canals and locks, reversed its flow: Instead of running into Lake Michigan, the river now defies nature and flows out of the lake in the opposite direction.

Yet farm-families from America and immigrants from Europe kept flocking into the cities for work. The biggest by far was New York, which grew from 1 million inhabitants to 3.5 million between 1860 and 1910. Decent, affordable housing became almost impossible to find; in his book *How the Other Half Lives* the journalist Jacob Riis described life in a typical Manhattan tenement block: "[F]our families occupy each floor, and a set of rooms consists of one or two dark closets, used as bedrooms, with a living room twelve feet by ten. The staircase is too often a dark well in the center of the house, and no direct through ventilation is possible, each family being separated from the other by partitions." Riis said it no longer excited "even passing attention" when the sanitary police reported nearly 200 adults and children in a single house or found 150 "lodgers" sleeping on filthy floors in two buildings. Despite the "brown-stone trimmings, plate-glass and mosaic vestibule floors, the water does not rise in summer to the second story, while the beer flows unchecked to the all-night picnics on the roof." The saloon on the ground floor and the landlord divide the income between them while, said Riis, "the tenant, in sullen submission, foots the bills."[29]

A survey of workers in Pittsburgh, hometown of H. J. Heinz and Andrew Carnegie, found a similar story: "An altogether incredible amount of overwork by everybody, reaching its extreme in the twelve hour shift for seven days in the week in the steel mills and the railway switchyards. Low wages for the great majority of laborers employed by the mills, not lower than in other large cities, but low compared with prices—so low as to be inadequate to the maintenance of a normal American standard of living" and "still lower wages for women." Family life was being destroyed by the demands of daily work, not to mention widespread typhoid fever and industrial accidents. The Pittsburgh survey lamented "the contrast between the prosperity on the one hand of the most prosperous of all the communities of our western civilization, with its vast natural resources . . . technical development, the gigantic tonnage of the mines and mills, the enormous capital of which the bank balances afford an indication; and, on the other hand, the neglect of life, of health, of physical vigour, even of the industrial efficiency of the individual."

Unquestionably, it stated, "no community before in America or Europe has ever had such a surplus, and never before has a great community applied what it has so meagerly to the rational purposes of human life."[30]

Pittsburgh, Chicago, and New York—each displayed these two faces. The cities were America's pride and shame: monuments to capital and capitalism, yet also graveyards of labor. But now the workers were ready to fight back.

THE FARMERS AND THE WORKERS REVOLT

The Chicago World's Fair of 1893 was intended to celebrate four centuries of American achievement since Christopher Columbus. Its "white city" of gleaming stucco and electric lights was a wonder of modernity and during the six months the fair was open 27 million people—equivalent to two-fifths of the U.S. population—came to marvel. But by the time it closed in the autumn of 1893, the United States was in the grip of the worst depression it had yet experienced.

Like most economic crises, the depression started with a stock market collapse and a rash of bank failures, but confidence did not recover. For five consecutive years unemployment soared above 10 percent. Those workers who kept their jobs faced savage wage cuts, while farmers watched the value of their crops fall precipitously. The depression of the 1890s brought to a head the mounting antagonism between the beneficiaries and the victims of America's frenzied industrial revolution.

America's farmers lurched from one side of this divide to the other. The opening up of the Great Plains after the Civil War produced a new wheat and cattle frontier, in the cities there were now millions of people who could not feed themselves, and the railroad revolution made it possible to move food quickly to satisfy urban demand. The result was massive growth in American agriculture—between 1870 and 1900 the number of farms doubled to 5.7 million, wheat production more than doubled to 600 million bushels, and the number of cattle virtually tripled to 68 million. Yet America's farmers were now even more dependent on the vicissitudes of the market—not just in the nearby town or city but across the country and on the other side of the world. They were also at the mercy of middlemen, having to accept whatever the cotton trader or grain-elevator manager offered and being obliged to pay the rates the railroad charged. And they were chronically in debt—long-term to buy land and short-term to survive from planting to harvest—at a time when America's money supply did not keep pace with growth. Moreover, banking remained localized—unlike commerce—without an effective nationwide system to move funds around easily to where they were needed. The result was crippling interest rates—often 10 percent, sometimes up to 40.[31]

So in good years, farm income soared; in depressions like that of the 1890s the situation was grim. By 1900 a third of America's farmers were working as tenants—hardly Jefferson's vision of liberty. The farmers formed sales cooperatives in an effort to cut out middlemen and boost their profits. These local Farmers' Alliances were not just marketing organizations: Masonic-like, their lodges provided fraternal support and regular mass picnics drew hundreds of families into something like revivalist meetings. Above all, through their newspapers and lecturers, the Alliances became instruments of political education in the backwaters of rural America: "People commenced to think who had never thought before, and people talked who had seldom spoken," noted the writer Elizabeth Higgins. "On mild days they gathered on the street corners, on cold days they congregated in shops and offices. Everyone was talking and everyone was thinking." Thoughts and theories sprouted, she said, "like weeds after a May shower."[32]

By 1890 the National Farmers' Alliance had more than a million members. Despairing of Republicans and Democrats alike, it went political—creating the People's Party, commonly known as the Populists. This was a genuinely radical movement that reached out to black sharecroppers in the South and also gave a prominent role to women. A leading Kansas Populist was Mary Elizabeth Lease—variously known as "Queen Mary" and the "Pythoness of the Plains"—a tall, spare farm mother of four but also a lawyer with a hot Irish tongue: "What you farmers need to do is raise less corn and more Hell," she chastised them. "Wall Street owns the country. It is no longer a government of the people, by the people, and for the people, but a government of Wall Street, by Wall Street, and for Wall Street. The great common people of this country are slaves, and monopoly is the master. The West and South are bound and prostrate before the manufacturing East. Money rules."[33]

The Populists came up with various far-reaching demands, including a graduated income tax and government ownership of the railroads, but by 1896 one issue predominated: the gold standard. This, above all, critics claimed, had constricted the money supply; in its place they advocated a bimetallic currency with silver coins as readily available as gold. (It was no coincidence that America's silver was mined in Rocky Mountain states that were Populist strongholds.)

In 1896 the silver lobby seized control of the Democratic Party from the bosses, nominating as candidate for the presidency William Jennings Bryan, a thirty-six-year-old lawyer from Nebraska. Bryan was a devout evangelical who believed liquor and gambling were sins; like many Populists, he treated silver as a mixture of political campaign and religious crusade: "It is the issue of 1776 over again. Our ancestors, when but three million, had the courage to declare their political independence of every other nation upon earth. Shall we, their descendants, when we have grown to seventy million, declare that we are less independent than our forefathers? No, my friends, it will never be the judgment of this people." Bryan challenged the "gold bugs": "If they dare to come out in the open field and defend the gold standard as a good thing, we shall fight them to the uttermost, having behind us the producing masses of the nation and the world." The Democrats would, he said, "answer their demands for a gold standard by saying to them, you shall not press down upon the brow of labor this crown of thorns. You shall not crucify mankind upon a cross of gold."[34]

Bryan's "cross of gold" speech was one of the classics of American political oratory, but his silver crusade and evangelical style played into the hands of the Republicans. Fanning business fears, they accumulated an unprecedented campaign chest in 1896, enabling them to outspend the Democrats by ten to one and ensuring a landslide for the Republican candidate, William McKinley. The 1896 election proved a landmark in American politics. Not only did it bury the Populists as a radical third-party alternative, it tarnished the Democrats as economically unsound and established the Republicans as the dominant party for a generation. Apart from Woodrow Wilson's presidency (1913–1921)—made possible by a split within the Republican Party in 1912—the Republicans dominated both the White House and Congress from 1897 to 1933.

The Republicans' success in 1896 was also attributable to the turmoil in America's cities, particularly Chicago. On July 6, 1894, the special correspondent for the *Washington Post* could hardly contain his righteous excitement: "War of the bloodiest kind in Chicago is imminent, and before tomorrow goes by the railroad lines and yards may be turned into battle fields strewn with hundreds of dead and wounded." Chicago, he claimed, "was never before the scene of such wild and desperate acts," asserting that "furious mobs have for hours at a time been in complete control of certain sections of the city."[35] One of the casualties was the "White City" of the 1893 World's Fair, which went up in flames—probably the work of arsonists.

What seemed like mob rule was a strike at the Pullman plant that had escalated. The workers there manufactured not only the plush Pullman sleepers but ordinary railroad coaches and city streetcars, so the strike had a nationwide effect. The workers had been provoked by massive wage cuts and by the refusal of George Pullman to make a parallel reduction of rents in the company town, which he ran like a feudal despot. Their cause was taken up by the new American Railway Union, headed by Eugene Debs, who told them, "The paternalism of Pullman is the same as the self-interest of a slave holder in his human chattels. You are striking to avert slavery and degradation."[36] The strike soon spread beyond Chicago as railroad workers across the West came out in sympathy and union membership soared.

In panic, the Democratic administration of President Grover Cleveland obtained court injunctions against the strikers for impeding the delivery of U.S. mail. It resorted to the Sherman Act of 1890—ironically passed by Congress to prevent big-business cartels "in restraint of trade or commerce" between the states—turning it into an instrument against the unions. There was an outcry in the press, even in papers that condemned the strike. "So outrageous a stretch of federal power was not attempted during the Civil War, when amid the tumult of arms laws were silent," commented the *New York World*. "It is infinitely more harmful and dangerous than the stupid strike against which it is directed."[37]

With government and the courts stacked against them, however, the strikers had little chance, and public opinion turned sour following the riots caused by fringe hoodlums. Cleveland sent in the U.S. army to supplement the state militia and local police, which enabled Pullman to bring in new workers, desperate for jobs, who signed no-union pledges. The strike was broken and so was the American Railway Union. Yet 1894 also destroyed the good name of George Pullman. When he died three years later he was buried at dead of night in a lead-lined coffin within a reinforced concrete vault covered with tons of cement, so fearful was his family that the grave would be desecrated by labor activists.

For his pains Eugene Debs spent six months in jail, but during that time he read Karl Marx, which helped convert him to socialism. Debs—with his bald, domed head and burning eyes—was a charismatic orator who ran five times as Socialist Party candidate for the presidency. Yet even at his peak, in the election of 1912, he won only 6 percent of the popular vote. These were the years when socialism swept across Germany and France and the Labor Party was becoming established in Britain. So why did socialism never catch on in the United States?

Part of the answer is that Debs was, by European standards, an odd kind of socialist. Although employing the rhetoric of class struggle, he never advocated a "labor party" along British lines and adapted socialist discourse to the American political tradition. He believed that the real revolution needed in the United States was a return to the spirit of 1776, which had been perverted by the corporations and the millionaires who had bought up the judges and politicians. American workingmen, he declared, were not "hereditary bondsmen" but the sons of "free-born" fathers who, for all their suffering, still had the ballot. Debs argued that there was nothing in America's government that use of the ballot could not remove or amend. It could "make and unmake presidents and congresses and courts" and could "sweep away trusts, syndicates, corporations, monopolies, and every other abnormal development of the money power designed to abridge the liberties of workingmen and enslave them . . . as cyclones scatter the leaves of the forest."[38]

Debs had a point. In Britain and Germany at the beginning of the twentieth century, the struggle for the vote was a prime goal for workers, but in the United States white adult males had been voters since the 1830s. So most workers felt an underlying faith in the existing political system; they saw no need for a new class party to advance their goals, particularly after, as we shall see, both the main parties started to adopt progressive reforms.

Moreover, America's major unions worked within the system. The most significant by far was the American Federation of Labor, or AFL, founded in 1886 and dominated for forty years by Samuel Gompers. The son of Dutch Jews, he was born in the East End of London but the family migrated to New York when Sam was thirteen. He was trained as a cigar maker—in those premechanized days a craft. Workers rolled their cigars in a large room, often employing one of their number to relieve the monotony by reading aloud from newspapers or literary classics and engendering lively debate. This fraternal, almost intellectual ethos left a durable impact on young Sam and it underpinned his approach to trade unionism. He believed that workers should be organized along craft lines—in other words, separate unions for the cigar makers, the garment workers, the granite cutters, and so on— and opposed the idea of a single union for all the workers in a plant. Nor did the AFL do much to organize unskilled workers in heavy industry, concentrating instead on the skilled trades and on winning incremental gains in wages, benefits, and conditions. Gompers had no time for socialists, convinced that they cared only for their own party and aimed to "rule or ruin" the unions. In his view, unions were an integral part of American business, like management, rather than a subversive force. "We American trade unionists want to work out our problems in the spirit of true Americanism," he declared, "a spirit that embodies our broadest and our highest ideals."[39]

So Debs managed to Americanize socialism, while Gompers made unions part of the economic mainstream. But there were other reasons why socialism did not catch on in America. The German socialist Werner Sombart noted the high standard of living relative to Europe: "[T]he American worker lives in comfortable circumstances" and "this prosperity was not in spite of capitalism but because of it." That, he felt, cooled worker radicalism: "All Socialist utopias came to nothing on roast beef and apple pie."[40] Sombart was painting too rosy a picture—millions of American workers lived in grinding poverty and few enjoyed the rags-to-riches trajectory of an Andrew Carnegie—but many did eventually rise into the middle class, or watched their children do so. Even more important, hundreds of thousands of workers simply moved to better jobs in another city or in the ever-widening suburbs. The United States had an unusually high degree of geographical mobility compared with Europe and this helped to undermine the sense of local working-class community that formed the bedrock of socialism in urban Britain and Germany.

So living standards and geographical mobility were barriers to strong class consciousness. But there was another powerful force at work: America, more than ever around 1900, was a nation of immigrants.

HUDDLED MASSES OR SAVAGE HORDES?

"We landed in New York after twenty-two days at sea. . . . Gus ask me, 'What's the statue?' And then we're looking at the statue, and his father say, 'That's Christopher Columbus.' And I put my two cents out. I say, 'Listen, this don't look like Christopher Columbus. That's a lady there.'"[41]

Theodore Spako, from a small fishing village in Greece, came to New York in 1911, aged sixteen, with his father. Like millions of immigrants, his first sight of

America was the Statue of Liberty, a gift from France to mark the centenary of the American Revolution. On its base was written a poem by Emma Lazarus about this "New Colossus," which was

> *Not like the brazen giant of Greek fame,*
> *With conquering limbs astride from land to land;*
> *Here at our sea-washed, sunset gates shall stand*
> *A mighty woman with a torch, whose flame*
> *Is the imprisoned lightning, and her name*
> *Mother of Exiles. . . .*
> *"Keep, ancient lands, your storied pomp!" cries she*
> *With silent lips. "Give me your tired, your poor,*
> *Your huddled masses yearning to breathe free,*
> *The wretched refuse of your teeming shore.*
> *Send these, the homeless, tempest-tost to me."*

Lofty, heartwarming words but the huddled masses' first real experience of America was much more chilling—the Ellis Island Immigration Station, opened in 1892. Theodore Spako never forgot Ellis Island. After the interrogation and the inspections, people ended up with chalk marks on their backs. Spako asked if he had one. Gus looked and said "no" but Spako could see that both Gus and his father had gotten one. "And I'm thinking, either they go back to Greece or I go back to Greece." Chalk marks were made by the doctors to indicate medical or psychological problems, some of which were serious enough to preclude entry into the United States, and it turned out that Gus and his father had received in effect the black spot. Eighty years later, Theodore Spako said, "To this day, I . . . thank God, that I was admitted to the United States, that they didn't put a chalk mark on my back."[42]

Transatlantic migrants who could afford first- or second-class tickets were allowed into America automatically; Ellis Island was for the steerage passengers. Paulina Caramando arrived there from Sicily with her parents. "I remember going into this great big hall, and they took all our clothes off. The men and women separate. They give us a blanket. It was the first time I ever saw a naked woman. It was quite an experience; my mother was holding me. We took showers, and then wrapped ourselves up in the blanket. . . . They took our clothes to fumigate them, delouse them. When we got our clothes back . . . [they] were all wrinkled." Paulina and her parents traveled on to Boston, where her aunt's family was already established. Like Theodore Spako, she felt the move was providential: "I always say thank God my father decided to come here because during the Second World War our house in Sicily was bombed. One of my cousins and three children were killed . . . found in pieces."[43]

Theodore Spako and Paulina Caramando were just two of the so-called new immigrants who flooded across the Atlantic in the years around 1900. For most of the nineteenth century, immigrants had emanated mainly from northern and western Europe—from Britain, Ireland, Germany, and Scandinavia. The Germans still kept coming but by the turn of the century the bulk of the immigrants were from southern and eastern Europe—Italy, the Austro-Hungarian empire, the Balkans, and Russia. The numbers were unprecedented, even by American standards—15 million during the quarter-century from 1890 to 1914. In the peak year of 1907, nearly 1.3 million people gained admittance to the United States, 80 percent of them from southern or eastern Europe.[44] Some of these new immigrants became household names. The bodybuilder Charles Atlas and the film star Rudolph Valentino arrived from Italy in these years. Irving Berlin and Sam Goldwyn were both Jews from the Russian empire.

Some of these newcomers were temporary migrant workers, Italians being particularly likely to come for short periods to earn money. Between 1907 and 1911, for every four Italians arriving in the United States, there were three other Italians returning home.[45] But the majority of immigrants did settle, making city centers like Lower Manhattan even more cosmopolitan. In its alleys and courtyards, wrote reporter Jacob Riis, "one may find for the asking an Italian, a German, a French, African, Spanish, Bohemian, Russian, Scandinavian, Jewish, and Chinese colony. Even the Arab, who peddles 'holy earth' from the Battery [on the waterfront] as a direct importation from Jerusalem, has his exclusive preserves at the lower end of Washington Street. The one thing you shall vainly ask for in the chief city of America is a distinctively American community." Instead, he commented, "has come this queer conglomerate mass of heterogeneous elements, ever striving and working like whiskey and water in one glass, and with the like result: final union and a prevailing taint of whiskey."[46]

Yet the union was only skin-deep. Although these recent immigrants constituted America's new working class and some, such as Jewish garment workers in New York, became ardent socialists, most had little sense of class consciousness— divided as they were from their fellows by language, religion, and lifestyle and living in their own little ethnic communities. They thought of themselves as Italian-speaking Catholics, Greek Orthodox, or Russian Jews, rather than as members of a unified working class. After five years they were eligible to become naturalized U.S. citizens and therefore voters, so they were much keener to keep their jobs and avoid a police record than to agitate for a left-wing utopia. Mass immigration was a major reason for socialism's failure to take root in America at a time when it was flourishing in Europe.

These new immigrants had a visibly different culture from that of northern and western Europeans, evident in their dress, food, language, and religion. And the depression of the 1890s helped revive the nativist passions of the 1850s about immigrants as an alien threat to American values—Italians being stereotyped as criminals, Jews as crooks. "The flood gates are open. The bars are down. The sally-ports unguarded. The dam is washed away. The sewer is choked," railed one New York newspaper. "The scum of immigration is viscerating upon our shores. The horde of $9.60 steerage slime is being siphoned upon us from Continental mud tanks."[47]

Heading the rush to close the open door were the elite families of New England, who grandly claimed descent back to the Pilgrim Fathers. In the words of a celebrated verse:

> *And this is good old Boston,*
> *The home of the bean and the cod,*
> *Where the Lowells talk only to Cabots*
> *And the Cabots talk only to God.*

The leaders of the Immigration Restriction League included Senator Henry Cabot Lodge and A. Lawrence Lowell, president of Harvard. The League's avowed object was to "work for the further judicious restriction or stricter regulation of immigration . . . and to arouse public opinion to the necessity of a further exclusion of elements unsuitable for citizenship or injurious to national character."[48] Its chosen instrument was a literacy test and in 1897 it got a bill through Congress requiring future immigrants to read the U.S. Constitution and then write down twenty words from it, in any language. But President Grover Cleveland vetoed the test as inimical to American traditions: "A century's stupendous growth, largely due to the assimilation and thrift of millions of sturdy and patriotic adopted citizens, attests the success of this generous and free-handed policy which, while guarding the people's interests, exacts from our immigrants only physical and moral soundness and a willingness and ability to work."[49]

Underlying the campaign to restrict immigration was the racist ideology that also served to justify Jim Crow laws in the American South. This racism was quite overt toward the so-called Yellow Peril—Chinese immigration was banned from 1882 and Japanese entry severely restricted after 1908—but comparable levels of animosity were often evinced toward Europeans as well. Boston economist Francis A. Walker warned that fifty years earlier the would-be immigrant from Britain or Germany required thrift and enterprise to get across the Atlantic, but now railways and steamships had created what he termed "Pipe Line Immigration": "So broad and smooth is the channel, that there is no reason why every foul and stagnant pool of population in Europe, which no breath of intellectual or industrial life has stirred for ages should not be decanted upon our soil." Walker called the immigrants from southern and eastern Europe "beaten men from beaten races; representing the worst failures in the struggle for existence."[50]

This Darwinian language became a motif of the immigration debate. It expressed the growing fear that world history would turn on the survival of the fittest race; America must therefore keep itself pure and strong. Madison Grant, another leader of the Immigration Restriction League, celebrated what he called "the Nordics" as the global elite: "The Nordics are, all over the world, a race of soldiers, sailors, adventurers, and explorers, but above all, of rulers, organizers, and aristocrats in sharp contrast to the essentially peasant character of the Alpines. Chivalry and knighthood, and their still surviving but greatly impaired counterparts, are peculiarly Nordic traits, and feudalism, class distinctions, and race pride among Europeans are traceable for the most part to the north." Grant advocated the sterilization of "worthless race types." His best-seller, *The Passing of the Great Race*, was—not surprisingly—a favorite of Adolf Hitler.[51]

Patricians of British descent such as Lodge, Walker, and Grant took the lead in advocating immigration restriction, but many Irish-Americans were also vocal supporters. The journalist Finley Peter Dunne satirized their attitude through the mouth of his stereotypical Irish-American bartender, Mr. Dooley:

> As a pilgrim father that missed th' first boats, I must raise me claryon voice again' th' invasion iv this fair land be th' paupers an' arnychists iv effete Europe. Ye bet I must—because I'm here first. 'Twas diff'rent whin I was dashed high on th' stern an' rockbound coast. In thim days America was th' refuge iv th' oppressed iv all th' wurruld. . . . As I told ye I come a little late. Th' Rosenfelts an' th' Lodges bate me be at laste a boat lenth, an' be th' time I got here they was stern an' rockbound thimsilves. So I got a gloryous rayciption as soon as I was towed off th' rocks. Th' stars an' sthripes whispered a welcome in th' breeze . . . an' I was pushed into a sthreet excyvatin' as though I'd been born here.

Mr. Dooley admitted to being

> afraid I wasn't goin' to assimilate with th' airlyer pilgrim fathers an' th' instichoochions iv th' counthry, but I soon found that a long swing iv th' pick made me as good as another man an' it didn't require a gr-reat intellect, or sometimes anny at all, to vote th' dimmycrat ticket, an' before I was here a month, I felt enough like a native born American to burn a witch.

Now, as an established American, Mr. Dooley had no doubt it was "time we put our back again' th' open dure an' keep out th' savage horde."[52]

And so, as Jacob Riis noted, the "once unwelcome Irishman has been followed in his turn by the Italian, the Russian Jew, and the Chinaman, and has himself taken a hand at opposition, quite as bitter and quite as ineffectual, against these later hordes." But the Irishman got his revenge, seizing control of inner-city politics from the old elite in places like Boston and New York, while ripping off the new immigrants as their landlord and saloon keeper.[53]

To many old-stock Americans the corruption of urban politics was the prime evil of the day. Reforming the cities—in fact, redeeming them from poverty, vice, and corruption—became the mission of so-called progressives, whose reforms would inject a new dynamism into American politics.

10

REFORM AND EXPANSION

America's industrial revolution took only about thirty years—powered by railroads and mass production, leveraged by business mergers, and lubricated by the sweat and blood of the new immigrants. Economy and society had changed faster than ever before in U.S. history—in world history even—but the country's institutions had failed to adapt and this was the deficiency that progressive reform tried to address. Progressivism was not a coherent movement—more a variety of campaigns at different levels of the federal structure in the first two decades of the twentieth century—but a common factor was an attempt to update America's political system, economic regulation, and social practices for this new era. These intense spasms of reform coincided with a new era of territorial expansion, both within the United States as the West was populated and domesticated and also abroad. In Cuba and the Philippines Americans got their first taste of the foreign wars and imperial responsibilities that would prove a recurrent theme of the ensuing century.

POLITICS AND PROGRESS

The British author H. G. Wells, writing in 1906, claimed that "the typical American" had no "sense of the state." Wells was not questioning America's vigorous sense of patriotism; rather, he meant that the average citizen "has no perception that his business activities, his private employments, are constituents in a large collective process."[1]

Wells had a point. In continental Europe, even in liberal Britain, the state—meaning a strong national government—had promoted industrialization and then gradually conceded democracy to its increasingly restless proletariat. In the United States, by contrast, democracy came first—in the 1830s for most white adult males. And because the Founding Fathers were afraid of repeating what they saw as British tyranny, they kept the national government very weak; even state and local

governments had limited power. But by 1900 the industrial revolution had generated huge economic and social forces that government simply could not control—
tycoons like Carnegie and Rockefeller, nationwide businesses such as U.S. Steel and
J. P. Morgan's, mass problems like urban slums and labor conflict. America's essentially eighteenth-century institutions needed revision to face the challenges of the
twentieth century.

The prime target of progressive reformers was the corruption of big-city governments and the failure of those governments to deal with the evils of urban life.
The most notorious inner-city political machine was Tammany Hall in Manhattan,
whose philosophy was expounded bluntly by George Washington Plunkitt—an
Irish-American who rose from butcher's boy to ward boss and eventually New York
senator: "There's only one way to hold a district: you must study human nature and
act accordin.'" For instance, said Plunkitt, "if there's a fire in Ninth, Tenth, or
Eleventh Avenue . . . any hour of the day or night, I'm usually there . . . as soon as
the fire engines. If a family is burned out I don't ask whether they are Republicans
or Democrats, and I don't refer them to the Charity Organization Society, which
would investigate their case in a month or two and decide they were worthy of help
about the time they are dead from starvation. I just get quarters for them, buy
clothes for them . . . and fix them up till they get things runnin' again." Said Plunkitt,
"It's philanthropy, but it's politics, too—mighty good politics."[2]

Plunkitt's motto was "I seen my opportunities and I took 'em." In his view, politics had nothing to do with grand ideas: It was "as much a regular business as the
grocery or dry-goods."[3] So-called "muck-raking" journalists like Lincoln Steffens
agreed with Plunkitt that, in America, politics was business. But for Steffens, "that's
what's the matter with it. . . . The commercial spirit is the spirit of profit, not patriotism; of credit, not honor; of individual gain, not national prosperity; of trade and
dickering, not principle." Yet, Steffens went on, "there is hope, not alone despair, in
the commercialism of our politics. If our political leaders are to be always a lot of
political merchants, they will supply any demand we may create. All we have to do
is to establish a steady demand for good government."[4]

And that was what progressives tried to do, mobilizing grassroots campaigns
to clean up city corruption. The political machines were often in league with the
utility companies, which provided gas, light, and streetcars at high prices and low
standards. So, reformers fought to establish regulatory commissions to police the
operations of the utilities. In some smaller cities they also reconstructed America's
antiquated system of urban government, built around a mayor and an elected
council. After Galveston in Texas was overwhelmed by a tidal wave in 1901, government was placed in the hands of elected commissioners. More than 400 other
cities followed suit and some went even further, following Dayton, Ohio—also
after a great flood—by handing over day-to-day running to a professional city
manager.

Reforming the cities was not enough, however, because many of industrial America's problems ran far wider. The power of the railroads was a case in point. In *The Octopus*, a celebrated novel about the clash between the Southern Pacific (SP) and the wheat farmers of California, author Frank Norris used a railway map of the state as a metaphor for its politics: "The whole map was gridironed by a vast, complicated network of red lines," which "centralized at San Francisco and thence ramified and spread north, east, and south, to every quarter of the State . . . laying hold upon some forgotten village or town, involving it in one of a myriad branching coils, one of a hundred tentacles, drawing it, as it were, toward that centre from which all this system sprang." The map, noted Norris, was white. "It was as though the State had been sucked white and colourless, and against this pallid background the red arteries of the monster stood out . . . gorged to bursting; an excrescence, a gigantic parasite fattening upon the life-blood of an entire commonwealth."[5]

The California railroad tycoons established themselves on Nob Hill—the fashionable center of San Francisco—men such as Leland Stanford and Charles Crocker. Crocker's mansion had a tower on the top, with a superb view over the bay. To spite his neighbor—an undertaker who refused to sell up—Crocker had a forty-foot-high fence built around three sides of the man's property. This "spite fence" became a symbol of all that was hated about California's rail magnates.

Eventually the octopus met its match, however, or at least lost some of its grip. A coalition of liberal Republicans led by Hiram Johnson, a fiery lawyer, campaigned in 1910 on an anti-corruption ticket. Johnson kept blasting the alliance of business and crime—"your big banker, your big merchant—sinning respectability joining hands with the criminal and the thug." And when the powerful *Los Angeles Times* attacked his campaign, Johnson turned his vitriol on the owner, Harrison Gray Otis: "Here he sits in senile dementia, with gangrened heart and rotting brain, grimacing at every reform and chattering in impotent rage against decency and morality, while he is going down to his grave in snarling infamy."[6] After Johnson and his reformers won the control of the California statehouse in 1910, they passed the first serious law to regulate the Southern Pacific and then went on to strip away the right of the state legislature to choose California's two U.S. senators in Washington—men who were staunch supporters of Southern Pacific interests because the SP funded most of the politicians' campaigns.

Here was a major change in American politics. Leaving the choice of U.S. senators to each state legislature had been a feature of the Constitution of 1789, because the Founders wanted to guard against too much democracy, but it seemed like a dangerous anachronism in the industrial age when the Senate was apparently in the pay of big business, the "interests." Direct election of senators by the people was one of the great campaigns of the progressive era. It swept across the states, starting in the West, and was eventually adopted in 1913 as the Seventeenth Amendment to the Constitution. More democracy seemed to be the remedy for the corrupt interest-group politics of states like California and it was in the same spirit that progressives also initiated primary elections—to prevent candidates being nominated by the party bosses and their financial backers and give the choice to the party rank and file.

Yet it would be wrong to depict progressivism as simply a battle of the idealists against big business. One of the watchwords of the times was "efficiency"—to us a rather grey concept but in the 1900s a battle cry. The nineteenth century had seen the application of science to the natural order—harnessing coal, steam, and oil for industrial development. Now, in the twentieth century, reformers argued, science should be applied to human affairs to put society and politics on a rational footing: That would be real progress.

Major businesses were in the vanguard of this kind of reform. Metropolitan Life—the giant of the insurance industry with an appropriately gigantic skyscraper in Lower Manhattan—pioneered insurance schemes at a nickel or dime a week for workers and their families. Young policyholders aged six to eighteen were encouraged to join Metropolitan's Health and Happiness League, and as bait for essay prizes, field trips, and other outings the children had to sign a pledge: "I will wash my hands and face before every meal, and my mouth and teeth each morning and evening. . . . As spitting is unclean and helps spread consumption and other diseases, I will not spit upon the public streets or in public places. . . . I will not use a public drinking cup. I will use only paper ones, or carry my own cup. . . . I will destroy every house-fly I possibly can."[7]

And so on. All very progressive, but also good business because healthy policyholders would keep on paying their nickels and dimes for longer and would need fewer dollars in return from Metropolitan Insurance. So business supported some progressive reforms but opposed or ignored others, such as direct election of senators or social welfare legislation. Yet in the confused patchwork of reforms that was progressivism, these measures were backed by the urban political machines, often regarded by middle-class progressives as their main opponents.

Here is one appalling example. The Triangle Shirtwaist Factory was just a few blocks from Metropolitan Life's skyscraper, but the two businesses could not have been more different. The factory occupied the top three floors of a ten-story building where young immigrants, mostly women, worked up to seventy-two hours a week for six or seven dollars. The rooms were full of flammable materials, lighting was by gas lamps, and cigarette smoking was permitted. No one knows how the fire started on Saturday, March 25, 1911, but one exit door had been locked by the bosses to prevent theft and the rickety fire escape soon collapsed.

"The building was fireproof," the *New York Times* observed sardonically. "In fact, after the flames had done their worst last night, the building hardly showed a sign. Only the stock within it and the girl employees were burned." Some of them tried to escape down the stairs but this exit was soon engulfed by flames. The girls rushed to the windows and looked down at Greene Street, 100 feet below. "The crowd yelled 'Don't jump!' but it was jump or be burned," said the *New York Times* reporter, "the proof of which is found in the fact that fifty burned bodies were taken from the ninth floor alone. They jumped, they crashed through broken glass, they crushed themselves to death on the sidewalk." Those who remained inside the building ended up like charred trunks. Surveying a body laid out later on the side-walk, a reporter asked if it was male or female. "It's human, that's all you can tell," a policeman replied. The corpse was "just a mass of ashes, with blood congealed on what had probably been the neck."[8]

The Triangle Shirtwaist inferno was Manhattan's worst fire until 9/11, with a death toll of 148. But some good did come out of the tragedy. Under pressure from the International Ladies Garment Workers Union, the state of New York set up an investigatory commission, whose recommendations resulted in fifty-six new wel-fare laws. Interestingly these major reforms were shepherded through the state leg-islature by Al Smith and other Tammany Hall leaders—successors to George Washington Plunkitt. Although the politicos opposed some progressive causes, such as city managers and commissions that undercut their power, several politi-cal machines were in the vanguard of legislation to promote health, safety, and workers' insurance.

In other words, progressivism was a broad church. The demand for reform ran the gamut from middle-class Yankees to immigrant workers, from utopian ideal-ists to pragmatic businessmen—each group having a specific agenda that reflected its interests. Much of their rhetoric reflected the traditional American discourse of republican virtues under threat from various forms of corruption, but there was also a growing awareness that the old laissez-faire libertarianism was no longer sufficient in the industrial age. America's unusual combination of "highly devel-oped democratic politics without a concentrated governmental capacity" made the country "the great anomaly" among Western nations.[9] Progressives generally agreed that government had to take a more proactive role in American life. That did not mean just the cities and the states: The really big problems, such as railroads or banking, were national in scope and required action by the federal government—by Congress and, above all, by the president.

ROOSEVELT, WILSON, AND REFORM

Since the era of Abraham Lincoln, the White House had been home to mediocrities. Most of his successors are barely remembered—men such as Rutherford Hayes or Chester Arthur. The British scholar James Bryce, writing in 1888, blamed this malaise on the pressures of democratic politics and the mass media: "Fiercer far than the light which beats upon a throne is the light which beats upon a presiden-tial candidate, searching out all the recesses of his past life. Hence, when the choice lies between a brilliant man and a safe man, the safe man is preferred." In any case, remarked Bryce, "a president need not be a man of brilliant intellectual gifts" because "four-fifths of his work is the same in kind as that which devolves on the chairman of a commercial company or the manager of a railway, the work of choosing good subordinates, seeing that they attend to their business, and taking a sound practical view of such administrative questions as require his decision."[10]

On these criteria, Theodore Roosevelt would probably never have been elected president. All his life, T.R. (he hated the popular nickname "Teddy") had been hyperactive. A sickly, asthmatic child, he had built himself up through sports and exercise. After his first wife and his mother died on the same day, he decamped out West for a few years, becoming a rancher and sheriff in the badlands of Dakota yet also having what it took to write a four-volume history of the American frontier. Above all, he relished politics—not boring management but the dramas of good versus evil. As police commissioner in New York City, he had walked the beat with local cops. When the United States went to war with Spain in 1898, he led a volunteer cavalry regiment into battle in Cuba. And when President William McKinley needed a vice-presidential running mate in 1900, T.R. seemed an asset to the ticket. Roosevelt got into the White House only by stepping into a dead man's shoes when an anarchist shot McKinley in September 1901. Initially the new president (America's youngest-ever at the age of forty-two) was careful not to antagonize the Republican party bosses, retaining McKinley's cabinet and declaring fidelity to his policies; but after being elected in his own right in 1904, he was able to let rip.

Roosevelt loved being in the White House. He was, in fact, the first president to call it officially by that name rather than the "Executive Mansion." He carried on wrestling and boxing—losing the sight in his left eye after suffering a detached retina—and he ordered construction of the West Wing as offices for the presidential staff evicted from the White House to make room for the six Roosevelt children. According to Ike Hoover, the White House usher, "the children left no nook or corner unexplored. From the basement to the flagpole on the roof, every channel and cubbyhole was thoroughly investigated. . . . Nothing was too sacred to be used for their amusement, and no place too good for a playroom." Hoover recalled that "one of the favorite stunts of the children was to crawl through the space between ceilings and floors where no living being but rats and ferrets had been for years. They took delight also in roller-skating and bicycle-riding all over the house, especially on the smooth hardwood floors" and loved giving their pet pony rides in the elevator. "This little fellow, spotted and handsome, had free access to any of the children's bedrooms."[11]

In all their high jinks, the Roosevelt children were eagerly abetted by their father. As Cecil Spring Rice, an old British friend, observed, "You must always remember that the President is about six."[12]

Roosevelt loved the White House above all because he saw it as a powerhouse. America's malaise, on his diagnosis, was an overdose of Jeffersonian individualism. During the century that had elapsed since Jefferson's presidency, he asserted, "there had been in our country a riot of individualistic materialism, under which complete freedom for the individual . . . turned out in practice to mean perfect freedom for the strong to wrong the weak." In T.R.'s assessment "the power of the mighty industrial overlords of the country had increased with giant strides, while the methods of controlling them, or checking abuses by them, on the part of the people, through the Government, remained archaic and therefore practically impotent."[13]

What should be done? Roosevelt used the Justice Department to prosecute the most notorious monopolies for attempts to rig the market, but he dismissed the radical libertarian answer of breaking up all the corporations, reckoning that the clock could not be turned back to the preindustrial era. In any case, big business had brought undreamt-of prosperity to millions. He certainly had no time for the socialist remedy of outright government ownership; instead T.R. wanted tighter regulation of big business—above all, railroads—to set fairer rules of the game. This was not a novel idea: Back in 1887 President Cleveland had created the Interstate Commerce Commission to try to regulate railroad rates, but it lacked real teeth. Roosevelt wanted the Commission to have "the power to decide, upon the case being brought before it, whether a given rate prescribed by a railroad is reasonable and just," and if it was found not to be so, then "to prescribe the limit of rate beyond which it shall not be lawful to go—the maximum reasonable rate, as it is commonly called—this decision to go into effect within a reasonable time."[14]

It took the president two years to get such a law passed by Congress. Along the way he cajoled and bargained, shifting his weight between progressive Republicans, conservatives, and even opposition Democrats in an effort to find a workable compromise. The Hepburn Act in June 1906 was the first serious attempt by the federal government to regulate the railroads and their charges; the president saw it as central to his larger goal to "assert the sovereignty of the National Government."[15] The Act was the precursor of dozens more regulatory commissions in the decades that followed. Here was a distinctively American way to manage big business. The intensity of Roosevelt's engagement with Capitol Hill also represented a novel approach to presidential power, again setting precedents for the future. The president was emerging as a real political manager.

Roosevelt left the White House in 1909, respecting George Washington's tradition of two terms even though his first term had not been elected. He went off on safari around Africa for a year but then turned against his handpicked successor, William Howard Taft. In fact, Taft authorized more anti-monopoly cases than his predecessor, including one that led to the break-up of Rockefeller's giant Standard Oil, but T.R. decided he was not progressive enough. In all probability, Roosevelt would have disapproved of any successor, because he could not stand retirement. In 1912, determined to win another term in the White House, he turned a game of dirty politics with Taft for the Republican nomination into an apocalyptic moral battle. "We are warring against bossism, against privilege social and industrial; we are warring for the elemental virtues of honesty and decency," he proclaimed. "We fight in honorable fashion for the good of mankind; fearless of the future;

unheeding of our individual fates; with unflinching hearts and undimmed eyes. We stand at Armageddon, and we battle for the Lord."[16]

When the Republican convention nominated Taft, Roosevelt started his own Progressive Party with a fervently revivalist convention in Chicago. The party adopted the bull moose as its symbol, in contrast with the Democratic donkey and the Republican elephant. Roosevelt survived an assassination attempt while campaigning in Milwaukee in October 1912. His courage captured the national imagination but it did not change the election: By splitting the Republican vote between himself and Taft, T.R. let the Democrats into the White House.

The new president was Woodrow Wilson, a Princeton academic who had made his name as a progressive governor of New Jersey. Wilson was severe, intense, and private—a big contrast with Roosevelt. During the campaign the two men had offered competing slogans: T.R.'s "New Nationalism" called for stricter regulation of business monopolies while Wilson's "New Freedom" advocated their break-up in a more competitive marketplace. In fact, the differences were largely rhetorical: In office Wilson continued the mix of anti-trust actions and regulatory bodies used by Roosevelt and Taft to rein in big business. He established the Federal Trade Commission to protect the consumer against anti-competitive business practices and pushed through the Federal Reserve Act to make the rickety American banking system more stable.

Creating "the Fed" was perhaps the biggest reform of the progressive era. Unlike Britain, the United States did not have a central bank to manage the financial system—as we saw in Chapter 5, Andrew Jackson had abolished the Bank of the United States in 1832. Yet the frequent business panics, most recently in 1907, showed the need for a lender of last resort when individual banks got into difficulties. The bankers wanted to provide this through a new central bank, run by themselves, with twelve regional branches, but that was anathema to the Democrats, who believed banks were too important to be left to the bankers. So the eventual act, pushed through Congress by Wilson during 1913, placed the whole system under a seven-man independent agency of the government—the Federal Reserve Board, chosen by the president but then left to its own devices.

As with Roosevelt and the railroads, this banking legislation was the result of energetic and skilled presidential leadership. Wilson had, in fact, an even more elevated conception of his constitutional role than T.R., arguing that, to cope with the modern industrial age, America needed a much stronger president akin to a British prime minister leading the legislature—not a presidency fettered by eighteenth-century checks and balances. He considered it "manifestly a radical defect in our federal system that it parcels out power and confuses responsibility as it does. The main purpose of the [Constitutional] Convention of 1787 seems to have been to accomplish this grievous mistake." Wilson had no doubt that "were it possible to call together the members of that wonderful Convention to view the work of their hands in the light of the century that has tested it, they would be the first to admit that the only fruit of dividing power had been to make it irresponsible," and he had long held the view that "the Constitution is not honored by blind worship. The more open-eyed we become, as a nation, to its defects, and the prompter we grow . . . to make self-government among us a straightforward thing of simple method, single unstinted power, and clear responsibility, the nearer will we approach to the sound sense and practical genius of the great and honorable statesmen of 1787."[17] This was a powerful statement—at odds with the fundamentalist veneration of the Constitution as sacred writ that often prevailed among constitutional lawyers.

Progressivism was much more than Roosevelt and Wilson, but these two presidents symbolized the impulses for reform in the years before World War I. They also greatly expanded the powers of the presidency—setting a pattern for the rest of the twentieth century.

GOD AND MAMMON

The progressive era was not simply an epoch of earnest reform. America's expanding economy, its booming cities and suburbs, created wealthier consumers who sought new opportunities to enjoy themselves. But this new hedonism alarmed Christians who sought to apply the Gospel to challenges of contemporary living. The years before 1914 pitted God against Mammon with an intensity that had not been seen since the 1830s.

One of the great pleasures of the age was baseball: Although regarded as America's "national game" since the 1880s, it really came of age in the 1900s. Attendance at major-league games doubled during the decade to 7 million a year and the World Series was inaugurated between the winners of the two rival leagues, the National and the American. Minor-league baseball was yet more popular; even small cities had their own team. Baseball, it was claimed, built civic pride; the sport was often lauded as "the greatest single force working for Americanization. No other game appeals so much to the foreign-born youngsters and nothing, not even the schools, teaches American spirit so quickly, or inculcates the idea of sportsmanship or fair play as thoroughly."[18] Baseball was not, however, a force for racial integration. Black Americans had to play in their own separate and badly funded Negro leagues.

During this booming prewar era, owners pulled down the wooden ballparks, seedy fire traps, and replaced them with fireproof structures—steel-framed and cased in concrete—one of which, Fenway Park, is still used by the Boston Red Sox to this day. These imposing new stadiums helped reposition baseball as a family game for the respectable middle class. The Brooklyn Dodgers, for instance, opened their new ballpark, Ebbets Field, in 1913 on the site of a garbage dump known as Pigstown. The ticket office was a huge marble-floored rotunda graced with a chandelier; the seats were no longer narrow and straight-backed but curved with armrests. There were places to check your coat and also women's "comfort rooms"—all reminiscent of a theater or opera house. "The inside of the park was a picture," a

New York Times reporter rhapsodized. "The great stand of steel and concrete loomed high in the air, holding its admiring thousands. The upper and lower tiers of boxes held the galaxy of Brooklyn's youth embellished and intensified by a glorious display of Spring finery and gaudy color. The girls of Brooklyn never turned out to a ball game like this before . . . from now on they will always be considered a big feature of a ball game at the new park."[19]

Ebbets Field even had a purpose-built parking lot—another sign of the times because America was now entering the automobile age. Cars were still only for a minority: In 1908, the U.S. population was nearly 90 million, but car output was only 63,000 a year and the big firms—Buick, Cadillac, and Oldsmobile—concentrated on expensive cars for the elite. Henry Ford, however, followed a different route. A farm boy from Michigan with a talent for mechanics, he had worked as an engineer for others before setting up on his own. After some false starts, Ford decided to aim for the bottom end of the market: "I will build a motor car for the great multitude. It will be large enough for the family but small enough for the individual to run and care for. It will be constructed of the best materials, by the best men to be hired, after the simplest designs that modern engineering can devise." But, pledged Ford, "it will be so low in price that no man making a good salary will be unable to own one—and enjoy with his family the blessing of hours of pleasure in God's great open spaces."[20]

Ford's Model T went on sale in October 1908. By today's standards it was a strange car. There was no ignition switch: You started it with a hand crank. The throttle, or accelerator, was controlled by a lever on the side of the steering wheel. The right foot pedal operated the brake, the middle one put the car into reverse, while the left was used to engage the two forward gears. And there were no frills on a Model T, Henry Ford famously decreeing that "any customer can have a car painted any colour that he wants as long as it is black."[21]

The so-called Tin Lizzie was the butt of many jokes. For instance: "It's easy to gauge your speed in a Model T. When you go ten miles an hour, your lamps rattle; when you get up to twenty miles an hour, the fenders rattle; at twenty-five miles, the windshield begins to rattle; and when you go faster than that, your bones rattle." But Ford fans could laugh back with anecdotes like this: "Two brothers each received a legacy of $2,000. Frank, the haughty one, bought a large six-cylinder luxury car. On the way home, he was passed by his brother Ed, driving a Model T. In the driveway, Frank looked down on his brother's Ford, and said, 'Good Lord, Ed, what makes that rattling noise I heard coming out of that thing?' 'That's the $1,500 rolling around in my pocket,' said the proud Ford owner."[22]

Price was indeed the Model T's trump card. By 1914 the car cost less than $500 and production exceeded half a million a year. Henry Ford's ability to respond to soaring demand reflected his revolutionary assembly-line methods; no longer were his workers building each car by hand in a separate area of the factory. Ford claimed the idea came to him from the stockyards, where hogs were hung by the hind legs on an overhead conveyor and each worker hacked off a specific part as a carcass went by. In fact, the process was worked out by his staff through trial and error over five years. As explained by Charlie Sorensen, Ford's Danish-born factory superintendent, the operative principle was that "assembly would be easier, simpler, and faster if we moved the chassis along, beginning at one end of the plant with a frame and adding the axles and the wheels; then moving it past the stockroom, instead of moving the stockroom to the chassis."[23]

The first car was assembled this way experimentally one Sunday morning in July 1908, with Sorensen and a foreman pulling the chassis through the factory on a tow rope. The system was then refined in Ford's new plant in Highland Park, a suburb of Detroit. It was a complex business because some parts took longer to attach than others. "This called for patient timing and rearrangement until the flow of parts and the speed and intervals along the assembly line meshed into a perfectly synchronized operation throughout all stages of production."[24] But by the end of 1913 Highland Park had moved over to assembly-line production, reducing the time required to make each car from almost twelve and a half hours to just over ninety minutes.[25] In January 1914, having transformed production, Ford changed the face of labor relations by announcing "the greatest revolution in the matter of rewards for its workers ever known to the industrial world." He said he would "reduce the hours of labor from nine to eight, and add to every man's pay a share of the profits of the house. The smallest to be received by a man 22 years old and upwards will be $5 a day."[26]

The five-dollar day—nearly double the average earnings in the automobile industry—hit all the headlines. Pragmatically, it stemmed from the company's need to retain trained workers in what was now a monotonous production process but it also reflected the sense of Christian responsibility shared by Ford and his senior managers in an era of poverty and class tension. Like many big tycoons, Ford left most of his vast wealth to establish a charitable foundation.

Yet critics alleged that Ford, Carnegie, and Rockefeller were simply trying to assuage their guilt. Many Christian intellectuals of the progressive era demanded a radical change in America's overall social philosophy, one of the most influential being Jane Addams, daughter of a prosperous Illinois business family, who threw herself into philanthropy in the slums of Chicago. Addams helped set up Hull House, which offered food, shelter, and education for the urban poor on the model of Toynbee Hall in London's East End. The "settlement house" movement she pioneered spread widely through America's cities in the early twentieth century. Addams believed that "Christianity has to be revealed and embodied in the line of social progress." The early Christians, she said, "were eager to sacrifice themselves for the weak, for children, and for the aged; they identified themselves with slaves." Addams believed that "there is a distinct turning among many young men and women toward this simple acceptance of Christ's message. They resent the assumption that Christianity is a set of ideas which belong to the religious consciousness" and "insist that it cannot be proclaimed and instituted apart from the social life of the community."[27]

The most influential philosopher of this "social gospel" movement was Walter Rauschenbusch, a Baptist minister and theologian. His sermons and books called for a fundamental shift away from the values of competitive capitalism: "For a century the doctrine of salvation by competition was the fundamental article in the working creed of the capitalistic nations." Rauschenbusch asserted that Christianity should help end competition because it was "immoral," being "a denial of fraternity. . . . [I]t establishes the law of tooth and nail, and brings back the age of savage warfare where every man's hand is against every man." Competition, he insisted, "dechristianizes the social order."[28]

For proponents of the social gospel such as Addams and Rauschenbusch, Christianity was not simply a matter of individual salvation—it had to permeate the whole of society—but many evangelical Protestants of the day took a very different view. They believed that this kind of religious liberalism was undermining the Church's essential message. Funded by Lyman and Milton Stewart, two wealthy Christian oil magnates, they published a series of volumes entitled *The Fundamentals: A Testimony to the Truth*. This influential set of ninety essays, brought out just before World War I, had many targets—from atheism to socialism, from the theory of evolution to the techniques of biblical criticism—but all the authors believed that what really mattered was a faith rooted in the divine inspiration of the Bible and that on this issue no "middle ground" was tenable.[29]

From these "widely known, if little studied, volumes," twentieth-century American "fundamentalism" took its name and inspiration. The term itself dates from 1920.[30] Likewise, the social gospel movement deeply influenced later Christian reformers, among them Martin Luther King, Jr. All this reminds us of the many crosscurrents of the progressive era. Spectacular new baseball stadiums and Henry Ford's amazing assembly line were undoubted landmarks, vindicating Americans' faith in progress, but *Christian* faith was still a powerful influence on American society—even though it was, as ever, interpreted in disparate ways.

THE "WILD" WEST

In 1890 the superintendent of the U.S. Census announced that for the first time in American history there could "hardly be said to be a frontier line." Picked up and popularized by the historian Frederick Jackson Turner, as we have seen, the "closing" of the frontier became a national event.[31] As historians have subsequently pointed out, this was a misleading, almost meaningless, statement because vast areas of the United States were still to be settled, but at the time its psychological impact was considerable because the frontier had become part of the American mentality.

One of the most lastingly popular evocations of frontier values is *The Adventures of Huckleberry Finn* (1884) by Mark Twain (the pen name for Samuel Longhorn Clemens). This novel was rooted in his youth in the 1840s in Hannibal, Missouri, a small town on the Mississippi. Missouri was a slave state and the plot revolves around the relationship between Huck and Jim, a fugitive slave, as they escape down the river on a raft, so modern critics have focused on issues of race, seeing this as essentially a novel about the prewar South. But for most readers, then and since, *The Adventures of Huckleberry Finn* is a rollicking yarn written in homespun speech that evokes the tangled innocence of youth and the freshness of frontier society— "a fundamental myth of self-creating American freedom" won on the open river despite the enslaving pressures of society. In other words, a novel that brought back to life America's lost Eden in the West.[32]

The frontier's last dramatic fling occurred in the spring of 1889, in what a correspondent for the *New York Times* called "the biggest race ever run in the United States." At noon on April 22 the territory of Oklahoma was being opened up for settlement by the U.S. government and the land boomers were ready and waiting. They got up with the sun, having probably not slept at all the previous night. Later in the morning the newsman watched them move out of their camps to where a wide stretch of sand, with no more than an eighth of a mile of water, constituted the only barrier to Oklahoma. "Here they formed a line, and patiently waited for the signal to break for the promised land."[33]

The race was to be started by Lieutenant Samuel Adair of the Fifth U.S. Cavalry. For days he and his men had been trying ineffectually to prevent interlopers from jumping the gun. Now as the clock neared noon, all eyes were upon him. Suddenly he nodded to a nearby soldier and the strains of a bugle rang out. As the *New York Times* man reported vividly, "There is a mighty shout, and the advance guard of the invading army is racing like mad across the sands toward the narrow expanse of water. . . . In they go, helter-skelter, every rider intent on reaching the bank first. There goes a horse into a deep hole and his rider falls headlong out of the saddle. Before he can arise he is apparently crushed by another animal, which has stumbled and fallen in." By this time the swiftest riders are through the water and speeding up the slope of the nearest ridge, but a telescope detects dozens of men miles beyond the river. These are the "boomers" who crossed early and have been hiding. A white flag is raised over what appears to be a wagon two miles away. "That's Dr. Johnson's claim," says an anxious watcher, "and the doctor is riding for it for all he's worth. I reckon he will lose it though." From another direction, about a mile away, six shots ring out in rapid succession. "They're settling one dispute already," remarks a man who has pioneered all through the West.[34]

Such scenes were repeated all across the Oklahoma Territory. Another observer, William Howard, wrote, "Unlike Rome, the city of Guthrie was built in a day. To be strictly accurate in the matter, it might be said that it was built in an afternoon. At twelve o'clock on Monday, April 22d, the resident population of Guthrie was nothing; before sundown it was at least 10,000. In that time streets had been laid out, town lots staked off, and steps taken toward the formation of a municipal government. At twilight the camp-fires of ten thousand people gleamed on the grassy slopes," reflected Howard, "where, the night before, the coyote, the gray wolf, and the deer had roamed undisturbed."[35]

On April 22, 1889, an estimated 50,000 people flooded out across 2 million acres of free land. Except that Oklahoma was not truly free. Its name comes from two Indian words meaning "red people" because, back in the 1830s, the area had been set aside as reservations for Indian tribes evicted from their lands east of the Mississippi. But the inexorable march of America's empire of liberty could not be stopped. With settlers, ranchers, and railroad tycoons all eyeing these "unassigned lands," the federal government evicted the Indians yet again, setting up the land rush of 1889.

Further north on the Great Plains the Sioux and Apaches—formidable horsemen—put up serious resistance, most famously in June 1876, when they destroyed the Seventh U.S. Cavalry commanded by a flamboyant Civil War veteran called George Custer. Exactly what happened on the Little Bighorn River in Montana will never be known—none of Custer's contingent survived—but it seems that he unwisely divided his regiment and was caught in the open by superior Indian forces, armed with rifles as well as bows. Probably Custer's line of dismounted men was broken by the first charge. Some of the soldiers panicked and tried to flee, while others, including Custer, fought to the death in small, isolated groups scattered across the battlefield. It was a sorry, unnecessary mess but the debacle went down in heroic American mythology as "The Massacre of Little Bighorn" and "Custer's Last Stand"—depicted in numerous prints and, later, in movies and earning immortality for the reckless colonel. The outrage back east intensified the drive to corral the remaining Indians on reservations: In 1890, as Oklahoma was being settled, the final flames of Indian resistance were snuffed out at Wounded Knee, South Dakota, when a botched surrender ended with 200 Indians dead as the Seventh Cavalry exacted its revenge.

Once the West was conquered, it was ripe for commercialization and no one did more to sell the West to America and the world than William F. Cody. Cody was a genuine frontiersman—at various times army scout, buffalo hunter, and Indian fighter—but it was "Buffalo Bill's Wild West" that really made his name. Modeled on travelling circuses like Barnum's, the show toured America and Europe for more than thirty years. Packed with exciting acts and shrewdly marketed, it was seen by a million people during the winter of 1886–1887 in Madison Square Garden in New York. The following summer it took Britain by storm. Queen Victoria attended a special performance at Earls Court in London, writing in her diary afterward:

> All the different people, wild painted Red Indians from America, on their wild bare backed horses . . . cow boys, Mexicans &c., all came tearing around at full speed, shrieking and screaming, which had the weirdest effect. An at-

tack on a coach & on a ranch, with an immense deal of firing, was most exciting, so was the buffalo hunt, & the bucking ponies, that were almost impossible to sit. [The Indian war dance,] to a wild drum & pipe, was quite fearful, with all their contorsions [*sic*] & shrieks, & they came so close.[36]

One of the stars was a tiny young woman called Miss Annie Oakley. Demure and domestic, she would come out waving sweetly to the audience, but her whole act was built around shooting at her husband. She could hit a dime held between his thumb and forefinger; she could blow the ash off a cigarette between his lips. She could even do her tricks with the rifle reversed over her shoulder, aiming through a mirror. After the performance, Queen Victoria told her, "You are a very, very clever little girl."[37]

Staged in huge arenas, with panoramic backdrops evoking the endless Plains, "Buffalo Bill's Wild West" was gripping entertainment but it also confirmed the romanticized image of the West through episodes such as "Pony Express" and "Attack on a Settler's Cabin," in which Buffalo Bill and his cowboys swooped down on the marauding Indians in the nick of time. Cody even staged a fanciful version of "Custer's Last Rally," with himself in the starring role. A somewhat skeptical *New York Times* reporter described its climax:

> The sound of a bugle is heard. The Indians instantly prepare an ambush. Custer and his men dash into the open space from the Madison Avenue end of the Garden. The bugler sounds the charge. Custer waves his sword, puts spurs to his charger, and, followed by his men, rides down upon the Indian village like a cyclone. Instantly the troops are surrounded by whooping Indians, and a "terrific hand-to-hand combat" ensues. In an extremely short space of time the Indians gain a complete victory. Custer is the last man killed, and he dies after performing prodigies of valor. Then the surviving red men indulge in a war hop and a shrieking match and the curtain falls to slow music.[38]

The public lapped it up and Custer's devoted widow thanked Cody "from my heart for all that you have done to keep my husband's memory green. You have done so much to make him an idol among the children and young people."[39]

Ironically, the Sioux Indians, Custer's mortal foes, were now a feature of Cody's show. He had considerable sympathy for why they had fought, explaining, "Their lands were invaded by the gold seekers, and when the US government failed to protect them they thought it was time to do so themselves . . . but the white men wouldn't be held back. No one can blame the Indians for defending their homes." But, said Cody in 1885, "that is all passed."[40] In other words, "On with the show."

Artists also helped to define the image of the West. In the 1860s and 1870s Albert Bierstadt, a German immigrant who grew up in Massachusetts, produced epic panoramas of the Rockies and the Plains, often dramatically lit at sunrise or sunset. By the turn of the century the public had developed an insatiable appetite for cowboy and Indian stories in magazines and dime novels, and the top illustrator was Frederic Remington—an easterner, educated at Yale, who specialized in Custer-like "Last Stand" pictures. According to critic Robert Hughes, Remington romanticized the Old West as "an Arcadia of noble violence," a red-versus-white world of frontier conflict that had now gone for ever. "I shall never come to the West again—it is all brick buildings," Remington wrote his wife in 1900. "It spoils my earlier illusions."[41]

Aside from cowboys and Indians, a completely different, though equally wild, image of the West was emerging at the same time. In 1872 the U.S. Congress created America's first national park at Yellowstone in the Rockies, declaring that it was "hereby reserved and withdrawn from settlement, occupancy or sale . . . and set apart as a public park or pleasuring-ground for the benefit and enjoyment of the people."[42] Twenty years later, alarm at the relentless logging of the West led to the Forest Reserves Act, under which millions of acres of federal timberland were protected from sale or settlement. Until now Uncle Sam had doled out land in the West to railroads and settlers, loggers and miners, with little care for the ecological consequences, but by the 1890s reformers were arguing that the government must limit short-term private liberty for the longer-term public good.

It was President Theodore Roosevelt who put this issue firmly on the national agenda. In 1906 he signed an Antiquities Act, allowing presidents to declare as national monuments "historic landmarks, historic and prehistoric structures, and other objects of historic or scientific interest that are situated upon the lands owned or controlled by the Government of the United States."[43] The Act was originally intended to protect prehistoric Indian remains, but Roosevelt interpreted it broadly to save many sites of natural beauty such as the Grand Canyon. He also created millions of acres of new national forest, despite the efforts of conservatives in Congress to block him.

In a quite unheard-of way T.R. devoted large parts of his State of the Union messages in the 1900s to what was being called "conservation"—articulating a mood of deep disquiet in America's progressive middle class. He insisted, for instance, in 1907, "The conservation of our natural resources and their proper use constitute the fundamental problem which underlies almost every other problem of our National life. . . . We are prone to speak of the resources of this country as inexhaustible; this is not so. The mineral wealth of the country, the coal, iron, oil, gas, and the like, does not reproduce itself, and therefore is certain to be exhausted ultimately."[44]

It all sounds very familiar to modern ears, as does the dilemma that conservationists were already having to face. All of them opposed the thoughtless despoiling of America's forests, lakes, and mountains for private gain but some wished to preserve the "wilderness" in its raw, pristine beauty whereas others—preaching the contemporary gospel of "efficiency"—wanted to manage nature for current use and future benefit.

This clash of views was dramatically exposed in the controversy over whether to flood the Hetch Hetchy valley—part of the Yosemite National Park—as a reservoir to supply San Francisco. John Muir, a bearded Californian romantic of Scottish extraction, believed this would be a crime against the natural order, arguing that the "devotees of ravaging commercialism, seem to have a perfect contempt for Nature, and instead of lifting their eyes to the God of the Mountain, lift them to the Almighty Dollar." Yet his opponents included not just plutocrats but men such as Gifford Pinchot—head of the Bureau of Forestry and a pioneer of scientific woodland management—who was convinced that "the injury by substituting a lake for the present swampy floor of the valley" was "altogether unimportant compared to the benefits to be gained from its use as a reservoir."[45] Eventually the reservoir won out. In 1913 Congress voted to flood the Hetch Hetchy valley, but only after a national political dispute that showed how far America had moved from the old slogans of free land and unlimited resources.

The Wild West myth celebrated a heroic past that never really existed. The wilderness movement fought to preserve the present against a rapacious future. As far as most Americans were concerned, the Indian problem had finally been "solved," but managing America's natural resources would be a challenge throughout the twentieth century and beyond.

"THE TASTE OF EMPIRE"

The night of February 16, 1898, was a quiet one in the newsroom. The first edition of the New York *World* had appeared but its front-page stories were a bit of a yawn: railroad corruption in Kansas, the Dreyfus trial in France, and a three-column spread headlined "Shot Himself Facing His Actress Lover." Then early in the morning a cable from Cuba shocked the sleepy newsmen into life—and into a new edition:

> HAVANA. Feb. 15—At a quarter of 10 o'clock this evening a terrible explosion took place on board the United States battleship Maine in Havana harbor.
> Many were killed and wounded. . . .
> As yet the cause of the explosion is not apparent. . . .
> The explosion shook the whole city.[46]

The New York *World* was owned by Joseph Pulitzer. Across town his great rival in sensational journalism—William Randolph Hearst, owner of the New York *Journal*—was phoned at home with the news. Hearst asked his night editor what had been done with the story.

"We have put it on the front page, of course," was the reply.

"Have you put anything else on the front page?" asked Hearst.

"Only the other big news."

"There is no other big news. Please spread the story all over the front page. This means war."[47]

For years before 1898 Americans had seethed about the situation in Cuba, an island only ninety miles off the Florida coast and a remnant of Spain's once mighty empire in the Americas. Cuban rebels had waged periodic wars for independence and the latest, starting in 1895, had caused huge damage to the extensive sugar and tobacco plantations owned by Americans on the island. The growing success of the rebels prompted the Spanish to crack down with a brutal policy of "reconcentration"—herding the Cubans into towns and cities and then stripping the countryside to deny food and shelter to the insurgents. An official U.S. observer, William J. Calhoun, reported to Washington in 1897 that the country outside the Spanish military posts was "practically depopulated. Every house had been burned, banana trees cut down, cane fields swept with fire, and everything in the shape of food destroyed." Calhoun said he "did not see a house, man, woman or child, a horse, mule, or cow, nor even a dog. I did not see a sign of life, except an occasional vulture or buzzard sailing through the air. The country was wrapped in the stillness of death and the silence of desolation."[48]

In the cities, diseased and starving Cuban victims of reconcentration turned to violence. That was why the *Maine* and its contingent of Marines were sent to Havana: to protect U.S. citizens and property amid the riots. Even today we still do not know why the *Maine* blew up. The immediate cause was an explosion in the powder magazine, but whether that was triggered by hostile action or, more probably, by a fire in the coal bunker remains in dispute. What mattered in 1898, however, was what people believed had happened. Six weeks after the explosion, a U.S. naval court of inquiry concluded that "the *Maine* was destroyed by the explosion of a submarine mine, which caused the partial explosion of two or more of her forward magazines."[49]

The court of inquiry said it could not establish who had planted this mine, yet the press and much of the country were convinced from the start that this was another atrocity perpetrated by the dastardly Spanish. War fever mounted, but President William McKinley could see many reasons to hold back. The United States was just pulling out of a deep economic depression; the army, mostly used for Indian fighting, was totally unready for a real war; and McKinley was both a sincere Methodist and a Civil War veteran, who told one warhawk, "I shall not get into a war until I am sure that God and man approve. I have been through one war; I have seen the dead pile up; and I do not want to see another."[50]

To many Americans, however, his restraint seemed like cowardice. Economic interests and moral outrage alike seemed to demand war. Theodore Roosevelt was sure "the *Maine* was sunk by an act of dirty treachery on the part of the Spaniards" and he fumed that McKinley had "no more backbone than a chocolate éclair."[51]

The president was burned in effigy; crowds chanted, "Remember the *Maine*! To Hell with Spain!" Politically, McKinley felt he could hold the line no longer. On

April 11, 1898, he sent a message to Congress setting out the crisis in Cuba and stating that "the destruction of the *Maine*, by whatever exterior cause, is a patent and impressive proof of a state of things in Cuba that is intolerable." The "only hope of relief," declared the president, "is the enforced pacification of Cuba. In the name of humanity, in the name of civilization, in behalf of endangered American interests . . . I ask the Congress to authorize and empower the President to take measures to secure a full and final termination of hostilities between the government of Spain and the people of Cuba . . . to secure in the island the establishment of a stable government . . . and to use the military and naval forces of the United States as may be necessary for these purposes."[52]

Congress readily obliged and the war in Cuba proved immensely popular. Theodore Roosevelt was among many who rushed to the fight, even though his wife was just recovering from grave abdominal surgery, raising a volunteer unit known as the Rough Riders (a name taken from the full title of Buffalo Bill's Wild West show). Chafing for action and glory, Roosevelt personally led a charge up the San Juan Heights, mounted on his horse, Little Texas, and frenziedly waving his hat.

For Roosevelt, the war was great sport, like a race or a hunting trip, and it made him a national celebrity. Even more popular was Commodore George Dewey—a beak-nosed little sailor who commanded the U.S. navy's Asiatic Squadron. The Spanish empire included the Philippine Islands and Dewey surprised Spain's Pacific flotilla early on May 1, 1898, in Manila Bay. This time it was the *Chicago Tribune* that scooped the story in exultant headlines:

DIRECT NEWS FROM DEWEY! . . .

THE ENTIRE SPANISH FLEET OF ELEVEN
VESSELS WAS DESTROYED.

THREE HUNDRED SPANIARDS WERE KILLED AND
FOUR HUNDRED WOUNDED.

OUR LOSS WAS NONE KILLED AND
BUT SIX SLIGHTLY WOUNDED.

NOT ONE OF THE AMERICAN SHIPS WAS INJURED.[53]

(Actually there was one American fatality, from heat stroke.)

The *Maine* had been avenged and George Dewey, rapidly promoted to admiral, became the pride of America—celebrated in songs such as "How Did Dewey Do It?" and toasted in potions such as "Dewey's Cocktail," a blend of whisky, brandy, and Benedictine. According to a journalist, "One of them will make you feel like a true American; two will cause you to wonder why you are not fighting for your country; and five or six will make you believe yourself to be as big a man as Dewey."[54]

For nationalist Americans, the whole war was intoxicating. In less than four months Spain's crumbling empire from Cuba to the Philippines had fallen into U.S. hands. "The policy of isolation is dead," the *Washington Post* editorialized. "A new consciousness seems to have come upon us—the consciousness of strength, and with it a new appetite, a yearning to show our strength. . . . The taste of empire is in the mouth of the people, even as the taste of blood in the jungle."[55]

There was, however, also a strong anti-imperialist lobby. The Cuban rebels were fighting for independence and many in Congress saw that as entirely consistent with America's own traditions. Ben Tillman, a populist senator from South Carolina, repudiated any proposal "to take Spain's place and become the policeman of the Western Continent and keep in order on that Island the Latin races that have settled there." Tillman wished there to be no attempt to "interfere with their own affairs, other than to expel Spain and enable the Cuban patriots to inaugurate, under their own auspices and under their own machinery, a government of the people, by the people, and for the people." As a condition of going to war, anti-imperialist senators pushed through an amendment sponsored by Henry Teller of Colorado disclaiming "any disposition or intention to exercise sovereignty, jurisdiction, or control over said island except for the pacification thereof," and asserting America's determination, "when that is accomplished, to leave the government and control of the island to its people."[56]

The Teller Amendment, it seemed, was a firm bar against American imperialism, but McKinley and his colleagues never believed that the Cubans were capable of stable self-government and they were determined to protect U.S. interests in an island right on America's doorstep. So, when U.S. forces withdrew from Cuba in 1901, it was on terms that made the island effectively an American protectorate, banning the Cuban government from signing a treaty or agreement with any foreign power that would "impair or tend to impair the independence of Cuba" and conceding America's "right to intervene for the preservation of Cuban independence [and] the maintenance of a government adequate for the protection of life, property, and individual liberty." The Cuban government also promised to "sell or lease to the United States lands necessary for coaling or naval stations at certain specified points to be agreed upon."[57] One such "naval station," located on the southeast of the island, has been under American jurisdiction ever since. Its name is Guantánamo Bay.

In the Philippines, as in Cuba, there was a nationalist movement that had been fighting for independence from Spain for several years and this, too, was shunted aside, even though the rebels had established an independent republic in the wake of the Spanish defeat. Again there were vehement protests in America that this was a betrayal of the principles of 1776. Carl Schurz, the Republican elder statesman, believed that, like America's Founding Fathers, the Cubans should be allowed to experiment with self-government. "The conduct of no people is perfect, not even our own," Schurz remarked wryly. "They may have bloody civil broil. But we, too, have had our Civil War which cost hundreds of thousands of lives. . . . They may have troubles with their wild tribes. So had we, and we treated our wild tribes in a manner not to be proud of. They may have corruption and rapacity in their government, but Havana . . . may get municipal government almost as good as New York has under Tammany rule; and Manila may secure a city council not much less virtuous than that of Chicago."[58]

The U.S. government had not originally intended to take over the Philippines, but all the alternatives seemed much worse. President McKinley reportedly told fellow Methodists that he finally concluded

> (1) That we could not give them back to Spain—that would be cowardly and dishonourable; (2) that we could not turn them over to France and Germany—our commercial rivals in the Orient—that would be bad business and discreditable; (3) that we could not leave them to themselves—they were unfit for self-government and they would soon have anarchy and misrule there worse than Spain's was; and (4) that there were nothing left for us to do but to take them all, and educate the Filipinos, and uplift and civilize and Christianize them.[59]

McKinley may not have used those exact words but they encapsulate his thinking. The problem was that taking control of the country was no easy task. The Philippines is a collection of 7,000 islands—some tiny and unsettled but others large and well populated. The nationalists, in reality a mix of rival ethnic groups, took to the hills in a brutal guerrilla war and as atrocities mounted on both sides the Americans resorted to repression and torture, such as the so-called water cure whereby water was forced down a man's throat and then his stomach and abdomen were repeatedly kicked.

The island of Samar became notorious. After insurgents had mutilated the bodies of U.S. troops, General Jacob H. Smith, known as "Hell Roaring Jake," reportedly instructed Major Littleton Waller, "I want no prisoners. I wish you to kill and burn, the more you kill and burn the better you will please me. I want all persons killed who are capable of bearing arms in actual hostilities against the United States." In answer to Waller's question, Smith said this treatment should be administered to anyone over the age of ten.[60] For what he did on Samar, Major Waller was eventually court-martialed, only to be acquitted when Smith's order came to light. On the positive side U.S. troops in the Philippines also built schools and roads and established systems of sanitation and health care, but it took them two years and 4,000 dead to defeat the insurgents. Estimates of the number of Filipinos who died from war and starvation range up to a quarter of a million. The Philippines remained an American protectorate until 1946 and an economic annex for years thereafter—1898 was an early lesson for America that it is easier to start a war than to secure a peace.

The conflict of 1898 is conventionally known as the Spanish-American War, which gives the impression that the United States intervened to evict a crumbling Old World empire from the New World on the pattern of 1776. But it is more accurate to describe 1898 as two triangular wars—Spanish-Cuban-American and Spanish-Filipino-American—in which the United States asserted its own interests against both the Spanish empire and the (admittedly fragmented) independence movements in Cuba and the Philippines.[61] Although the acquisition of overseas colonies seemed a new departure for the United States, it could be seen as an extension of the process by which the nation had spread across the continent in the nineteenth century, engrossing new lands such as Louisiana or Oregon and weak states like the Indian nations or Mexico. Not leaving Cuba to the flaky Cubans seemed to some the logical next step in that process. According to A. Lawrence Lowell of Harvard, "The question is not whether we shall enter upon a career of colonization or not, but whether we shall shift into other channels the colonization which has lasted as long as our national existence."[62]

This theme of continuity was particularly evident in Theodore Roosevelt's approach to Central America. In both Venezuela and the Dominican Republic corrupt governments were in hock to European creditors—the German and British navies had even bombarded Venezuelan forts and imposed a blockade in order to secure payment. Roosevelt accepted that small unruly states needed to be policed (a favorite term of his) by big stable ones but he, like the American public, was concerned about the challenge to the Monroe Doctrine of 1823, warning European powers to keep out of the Americas. So in December 1904 the president articulated what became known as the Roosevelt Corollary to the Doctrine:

> Chronic wrongdoing, or an impotence which results in a general loosening of the ties of civilized society, may in America, as elsewhere, ultimately require intervention by some civilized nation, and in the Western Hemisphere the adherence of the United States to the Monroe Doctrine may force the United States, however reluctantly, in flagrant cases of such wrongdoing or impotence, to the exercise of an international police power.

Roosevelt promised that America would intervene "only in the last resort," and his statement applied simply to the western hemisphere, but this idea of the United States as an international policeman would grow in scope as the twentieth century went on.[63]

Probably the most significant foreign policy development of Roosevelt's presidency was the construction of the Panama Canal. The idea of a shortcut between the Atlantic and the Pacific had been debated since the sixteenth century; the

French, after building the Suez Canal, began a serious project in the 1880s. But their company went bankrupt and then the United States became intensely interested after the war against Spain showed the desirability of being able to move warships quickly from one ocean to the other. After the *Maine* had been destroyed, it took more than nine weeks to send a replacement battleship from San Francisco around Cape Horn to Cuba—a voyage of only three weeks if there had been a canal through the isthmus of Panama.

As president, Roosevelt took a keen interest in the project, buying out the bankrupt French and negotiating with the Colombian government, which controlled Panama, for the necessary rights. But when the Colombian Senate refused to ratify this treaty Roosevelt secretly encouraged Panamanian separatists in their plans to revolt and sent a U.S. gunboat to deter Colombian intervention. The revolt went ahead in November 1903; the U.S. government recognized the new government of Panama within forty-eight hours and signed a new Canal Treaty with it less than two weeks later. In return for a flat sum of $10 million and a payment of a $250,000 a year, the United States was given the right in perpetuity to build and operate a canal through the isthmus of Panama.

In fairness to Roosevelt, Panama had been struggling for years to achieve independence from Colombia, so the president could (and did) wrap himself in the mantle of 1776.[64] But even jingoist newspapers such as Hearst's Chicago *American* blasted the president for "a rough-riding assault upon another republic over the shattered wreckage of international law and diplomatic usage," and Roosevelt's own colleagues thought he protested far too much in his own defense. "Have I answered the charges?" asked the president after giving a lengthy self-justification to his cabinet. "You certainly have, Mr. President," replied Elihu Root, the secretary of war. "You have shown that you were accused of seduction and you have conclusively proved that you were guilty of rape."[65]

But, as with Jefferson's acquisition of Louisiana exactly a century before, Roosevelt's Panamanian coup was too good a deal for critics to question and the treaty was approved by the U.S. Senate. The canal became the greatest engineering project of its day—slicing some fifty miles across the isthmus, much of it through solid rock, and creating two artificial lakes and three sets of locks. The price was 5,600 lives (mostly black employees) and $350 million—nearly five times the cost of all the land acquired by the U.S. government to date, including Louisiana, California, and the Philippines. As construction neared completion, preparations began for a spectacular opening in January 1915. The plan envisaged a 100-warship armada progressing from Hampton Roads, Virginia, to San Francisco in a modern version of the "Wedding of the Waters" when the Erie Canal was opened nearly ninety years before. The first oceangoing ship to traverse the canal was a cement boat called the *Cristóbal* on August 3, 1914, but the grand opening was overtaken by events. That same day Germany declared war on France.[66]

11

WAR AND PEACE

In America, as in most of Europe, it was assumed that the conflict would be over in a matter of months, but the short war became the Great War—one in which the United States' new wealth and power eventually became central to the outcome. Animated by a providentialist sense of America's special role in global affairs, President Woodrow Wilson took his country into the war in 1917 to create a new world order "safe for democracy." His bid was a dramatic demonstration of America's new influence on the world stage; his failure served as an abiding lesson for his successors about the perils of presidential leadership. The war also stirred up debate about the parameters of liberty and democracy within America itself. Among its various by-products were votes for women, controls on immigration, a ban on the sale of alcohol, and a dramatic crusade against the "menace" of Darwinism.

"TOO PROUD TO FIGHT"

At the outset of the European war in August 1914, Wilson did his best to keep America neutral. That was, after all, the tradition set out by the Founders, Washington and Jefferson. Not isolation in the strict sense because the United States had never been isolated from the global ebb and flow of trade, ideas, and migration, but the Founders had established a durable tradition of nonentanglement in the political affairs of Europe. Wilson believed that this was particularly applicable to the melting-pot nation over which he presided. More than 8 million of the country's 105 million people had been born in Germany or had at least one German parent. The Irish-American population, some 4.5 million strong, included many who believed that Britain's defeat would aid the cause of Irish independence; conversely, many Czechs and Serbs felt that the defeat of Austria-Hungary, Germany's main ally, would promote the freedom of their home nations from the Hapsburg empire. Little wonder that Wilson feared that entering a world war abroad could trigger a civil war at home. "The people of the United States are drawn from many nations, and chiefly from the nations now at war," he reflected. "Some will wish one nation, others another, to succeed in the momentous struggle." That was why he believed the United States should be "neutral in fact as well as name during these days that are to try men's souls."[1]

This was not, however, to be a timid neutrality, for Wilson also believed that the United States had a unique moral role to play, as "the one great nation at peace, the one people holding itself ready to play a part of impartial mediation and to speak the counsels of peace and accommodation."[2] Here in August 1914, at the very start of the conflict, the president had set out his abiding goal—to stand above the war so that America could shape the peace. Wilson was instinctively an Anglophile— loving England's countryside and literature and steeped in the tradition of English liberalism, with Gladstone his great hero. But he did not believe that either side in this conflict had a monopoly of right. In his view, the arms race and the scramble for empire had been driven by Britain and France as much as by Germany and the other Central Powers. Militarism and imperialism throughout Europe had to be curbed in the interests of a better world.

So prudence and principle dictated U.S. neutrality, but that did not mean curbing America's right, as a neutral nation, to trade freely with the belligerents. This had been traditional American policy in times of war, dating back to the 1790s, and Jefferson's attempts to impose a trade embargo in 1807 had proved economically and politically disastrous. But during the Great War the Allies benefited more than the Central Powers from this policy, thanks to Britain's large merchant fleet, strong navy, and vast financial reserves. U.S. exports to Britain and France soared from $750 million in 1914 to $2.75 billion in 1916, while exports to Germany slumped during the same period from $345 million to a derisory $2 million.[3] The war boom helped pull the United States out of recession and opened up new markets around the world that the belligerents were abandoning. "Europe's tragic extremity," gloated the New York American, "becomes . . . America's golden opportunity—the opportunity not of a lifetime, but of a century of national life."[4]

Yet all opportunities entail costs. America's exports—grain and textiles, machine tools and munitions—had to be shipped across the Atlantic and, as a neutral, the United States claimed the right to do so without interference. But for the belligerents, Britain as well as Germany, the war at sea was becoming a decisive battleground as the war on land became bogged down in the trenches. Each side declared the waters around the other's coast to be a war zone. Under international law belligerents could search neutral ships and seize their cargoes if these were destined for the enemy's war effort. The British navy, with its superiority on the surface, could easily stop ships, board them, and inspect the contents. The Germans relied on a new weapon, the submarine, which was extremely vulnerable if it came to the surface, so—as the British blockade tightened—the German High Command abandoned the legal niceties of stop and search and struck from underwater.

That is what happened to the British Cunard liner *Lusitania* on May 7, 1915, off the southern coast of Ireland on the last stage of its voyage from New York to Liverpool. The Henderson family, picnicking on the Old Head of Kinsale, saw it happen. One moment the huge four-funneled liner was steaming majestically eastward. Then suddenly a plume of water and smoke burst skyward; the liner's bow started to sink, its stern reared up into the air, and in less than twenty minutes it had disappeared beneath the waves. Seventy years later George Henderson still had not forgotten: "As a six year old boy it is something which has stuck in my mind for the rest of my life. Although time fades and grey cells wear out, I can still sit here now and see that great liner just sliding below the waves."[5]

There was never any question about who was responsible. The German press made the captain of the U-boat into a national hero and justified the attack on the grounds that the liner was secretly shipping arms and ammunition to Britain. Although this was true, the liner's main cargo was ordinary passengers and nearly 1,200 of them had died in the tragedy. Newsmen sent back gruesome reports of the makeshift morgue in the market hall at Queenstown (Cobh) in southern Ireland, where most of the bodies were laid. A correspondent for *The Times* described a young mother, with her baby "folded in her protective arms," and a sailor who was found with a body of a little child strapped to his shoulders. "Some of the dead wore expressions of terror," wrote the reporter; "others were calm and beautiful." Queenstown, he said, was "seething with the fury of men who ask themselves what they can do to make the Germans answerable for this appalling crime."[6]

There was fury not just in Queenstown and London but in the United States, too, because 128 Americans had gone down with the *Lusitania*. This seems an almost trivial death toll today, after the century of Hitler, Stalin, and Mao, but in 1915 the sinking seemed an act of utter barbarity and millions of Americans always remembered exactly where they were on hearing the news. Wilson was deeply shaken—after hearing the first reports that Friday evening, he walked the streets of Washington for several hours—but the attack on the *Lusitania* did not change his fundamental policy that America should avoid being drawn into the conflict. In any case, the president had other things on his mind in May 1915: Although nearly sixty years old he was head over heels in love.

Wilson's first wife had died at the start of the war, leaving him distraught with grief. He was by nature a loner—an intense former academic with a keen Presbyterian sense of his own rectitude—who relied on female company to unwind. Introduced in the spring of 1915 to Edith Galt—an attractive and vivacious widow in her forties—he was absolutely entranced and within six weeks had proposed. Mrs. Galt was taken aback. As she recalled later, "I said the first thing that came to my mind, without thinking it would hurt him. 'Oh, you can't love me, for you don't really know me; and it is less than a year since your wife died.'"[7] But she did not rebuff him completely. This was on May 4, three days before the *Lusitania* went down. On the 9th he had another more encouraging tête-à-tête with Edith. So both Wilson's mind and heart were in turmoil when he went to speak in Philadelphia on May 10. In his speech to newly naturalized citizens—immigrants from all over Europe who had just taken the oath of allegiance—the president celebrated the uniqueness of America:

> This is the only country in the world which experiences this constant and repeated rebirth. Other countries depend upon the multiplication of their own native peoples. This country is constantly drawing strength out of new sources. . . . Americans must have a consciousness different from the consciousness of every other nation in the world. . . . The example of America must be a special example. The example of America must be the example, not merely of peace because it will not fight, but of peace because peace is the healing and elevating influence of the world, and strife is not. There is such a thing as a man being too proud to fight. There is such a thing as a nation being so right that it does not need to convince others by force that it is right.[8]

As usual Wilson spoke off the cuff, using only brief notes. Naively he had not realized that the line about being too proud to fight—the sort of advice his mother gave him about dealing with schoolyard bullies—would be taken as a statement about the *Lusitania*. But he was not thinking straight—as he wrote to Edith afterward, "I do not know just what I said in Philadelphia (as I rode along the streets in the dusk I found myself a little confused as to whether I was in Philadelphia or New York!) because my heart was in such a whirl from that wonderful interview of yesterday and the poignant appeal and sweetness of the little note you left with me. . . . I am waiting and am already your own."[9]

The ill-judged phrase about being too proud to fight did enormous damage. In London people joked that Wilson was too *scared* to fight; on the Western Front shells that failed to explode were nicknamed "Wilsons." At home, opponents seized on the remark. Ex-president Theodore Roosevelt—who saw the war as an apocalyptic battle of good against evil in which America should ally itself with Britain and France against German militarism—thundered, "Every soft creature, every coward and weakling, every man who can't look more than six inches ahead, every man whose god is money, or pleasure, or ease, and every man who has not got in him both the sterner virtues and the power of seeking after an ideal, is enthusiastically in favour of Wilson." The president and his colleagues, Roosevelt fumed, were "abject creatures and they won't go to war unless they are kicked into it."[10]

Wilson backed away from his remarks at Philadelphia but the speech actually expressed his deepest sentiments—that America should set a special example, an example of peace in a warring world, showing a transcendent concern for the interests of humanity as a whole. Despite the *Lusitania*, he was still determined to avoid being sucked into the cauldron of war, but that meant stopping Germany's U-boat campaign; otherwise more incidents on the high seas would make neutrality untenable. So, sitting at his typewriter, Wilson drafted a note holding Germany to a "strict accountability" for any loss of American ships or lives within the war zone, and calling on it in the name of "the sacred principles of justice and humanity" to abandon its indiscriminate U-boat campaign.[11]

Secretary of State William Jennings Bryan was deeply unhappy. Bryan, the anti-gold crusader of 1896, had moved on to other causes, of which peace was now first on his list. Fearful that the country would be sucked into the conflict, he urged the president to forbid Americans from entering the war zones and to ban them from sailing on passenger vessels such as Cunard liners that belonged to belligerent countries. Bryan, a lawyer by training, wanted the United States to curtail its neutral rights in order to safeguard its neutrality. That might have been a prudent policy but Wilson refused and Bryan resigned. The public demanded a tough line and Bryan's advice seemed inconsistent with America's honor. What is more, Wilson believed he was standing up for the honor and the rights of all peace-loving nations. But in taking the position he did over the *Lusitania*, the president had made a fateful decision: If Germany did not back down on U-boat warfare, the United States might eventually have to choose between peace and honor.

So Wilson began a war of words with Berlin, tapping out diplomatic notes of protest on his own typewriter. It took a year of diplomacy and more American deaths but eventually—in May 1916, after Wilson had threatened to break off diplomatic relations—the Germans gave the pledge Wilson wanted. They agreed that in the future U-boats would not attack any noncombatant passenger or cargo vessels without warning. It was a major victory for Wilson: The typewriter, it seemed, was mightier than the sword. In domestic affairs, too, the president's notes bore fruit: Edith Galt became Mrs. Wilson.

But the United States was not as neutral as Wilson claimed. Its economy was now closely entangled with that of Britain, which, unlike Germany, had both the financial reserves and the merchant shipping to exploit America's industry and agriculture for the Allied war effort. As the war progressed, J. P. Morgan's and other U.S. banks also started raising massive loans for the Allies. As a result, the U.S. economy had become heavily tilted against Germany. Here was the tension Bryan had anticipated between neutrality and neutral rights and there was little Wilson could do about it, especially since the war boom helped him win reelection in November 1916.

By this time both sides were deadlocked on the battlefield, so economic warfare seemed the main hope of victory. That was why the Germans had resorted to unrestricted U-boat warfare until Wilson reined them in, but he was equally angry about Britain ratcheting up its naval blockade of Germany—blacklisting companies suspected of trading with the enemy and even opening American mail sent to and from Europe. These were humiliating infringements of U.S. rights. "I am, I must admit, about at the end of my patience with Great Britain and the Allies. This black list business is the last straw," Wilson told his closest confidant, Colonel Edward

House, in July 1916. "I am seriously considering asking Congress to authorize me to prohibit loans and restrict exportations to the Allies."[12]

The president reckoned that Britain was now so economically dependent on America that it would have to come to heel—and that was certainly the fear in London. The British government was spending the equivalent of $25 million a day on the war, of which $10 million had to be raised in loans from Americans. The Chancellor of the Exchequer warned the cabinet in October 1916, "If things go on as at present, I venture to say with certainty that by next June or earlier the president of the American Republic will be in a position, if he wishes, to dictate his own terms to us."[13] Just before Christmas Wilson dispatched identical notes to the belligerent governments, asking them to state their peace terms clearly and fully, so he could try to discern any common ground. For, he noted, "the objects which the statesmen of the belligerents on both sides have in mind in this war are virtually the same, as stated in general terms."[14] The insinuation that the Allies were on the same moral level as Germany aroused deep anger in London—reportedly the king wept when he read the note.

Then suddenly the whole international situation was transformed. Early in 1917 Germany decided to resume all-out submarine warfare, shooting on sight all ships—belligerent or neutral, warship or merchantmen—bound for Britain and France. This was a direct breach of the May 1916 pledge; the German High Command knew it was risking American entry into the war but reckoned that an all-out U-boat campaign could cut the Allies' Atlantic lifeline before the United States could mobilize its vast economic power. Ironically, if Germany had done nothing, Britain might have succumbed from financial exhaustion within months.

Unlimited U-boat warfare drove Wilson into a corner. He still tried to avoid all-out war, adopting a policy of arming U.S. merchant vessels to protect American neutral rights, but the public mood hardened as German U-boats started to sink U.S. vessels. There was also public outrage in early March when the press printed the so-called Zimmermann Telegram—a message from the German foreign minister to the government of Mexico suggesting an alliance against the United States through which Mexico could recover the territory it had lost in the war of 1846–1848. The message had been intercepted by British intelligence and passed on to the U.S. ambassador in London.

Eventually Wilson stopped wriggling and stood firm. On April 2, 1917, he asked a special session of Congress to approve a formal declaration of war against Germany. In words that brought sighs of relief in London, he promised "the utmost practicable cooperation in counsel and action with the governments now at war with Germany" and "the extension to those governments of the most liberal financial credits." But Wilson also made clear that the United States still had its own special agenda, on a moral plane more elevated than that of Britain and France: "We have no selfish ends to serve. We desire no conquest, no dominion. We seek . . . no material compensation for the sacrifices we shall freely make." And, in a phrase that echoed around the globe and down the twentieth century, "The world must be made safe for democracy."[15]

Edith Wilson accompanied her husband to Capitol Hill. Afterward she wrote in her diary, "Through cheering multitudes we drove home in silence. The step had been taken. We were both overwhelmed."[16] Congress quickly approved the war message and on Good Friday, April 6, 1917, Woodrow Wilson signed the declaration of war. No longer too proud to fight, he was now ready to go to war for America's pride but, more than that, for a new and better world.

A WORLD SAFE FOR DEMOCRACY

Fighting Germany did not mean becoming a formal ally of Britain and France. Wilson insisted that the United States would be an "associate power," working with the Allies for the defeat of German militarism but able to make peace on its own terms when it chose. Still convinced of his mission to eliminate the imperialism and armaments that had helped to cause the war, he was sure this meant reforming the Allies as well. He told Colonel House in July 1917, "England and France have not the same views with regard to the peace that we have by any means. When the war is over we can force them to our way of thinking, because by that time they will, among other things, be financially in our hands."[17]

Waging war in 1917, as in 1861, meant abridging traditional liberties. After months of chaos on the railroads—individual companies even refused to let their locomotives be used on the track of rivals—Wilson took the unprecedented step of bringing the whole network under federal control as of January 1, 1918. Radicals were delighted; if this experiment worked, declared Hiram Johnson of California, "a tremendous impetus will be given to government ownership."[18] But it was not to be: The railroad companies successfully lobbied Congress for a law to make absolutely clear that government control would be only a wartime experiment. Nationalization, European-style, would not be the American way.

In another erosion of traditional liberties, Wilson's war message announced that young men would be conscripted into military service. Having opposed the idea while America was neutral, the president changed his tune because conscription would establish a rational manpower policy and avoid a chaos of volunteers denuding industry of vital skills. Some members of his administration also believed conscription offered real social benefits. In the view of George Creel, head of U.S. war propaganda, "Universal training will jumble the boys of America all together, shoulder to shoulder, smashing all the petty class distinctions that now divide, and promoting a brand of real democracy."[19] Those concerned about the ethnic diversity of the United States argued that conscription would "yank the hyphen" out of German-Americans, Polish-Americans, and others with supposedly dual allegiances. One congressman called conscription "a melting pot which will . . . mold us into a new nation and bring forth the new Americans."[20]

Training soldiers took months and there was also an acute shortage of ships to get them across the Atlantic, so it was not until the summer of 1918 that U.S. troops started arriving in France in earnest. By then the British and French were reeling under a series of massive German offensives, mounted as a last bid for victory. But General John J. Pershing—the tough, no-nonsense U.S. commander—would not be rushed. Rather than fritter away his troops by plugging gaps in the Allied line, he intended to use them as a new American army that would go on the offensive when *he* was ready. Field Marshal Douglas Haig, the British commander in France, fumed that Pershing did "not seem to realize the urgency of the situation," hankering after a "great self-contained American Army." Haig considered it "ridiculous to think that such an Army could function unaided in less than two years' time."[21] But Pershing's obduracy was a sign of what Wilson meant by America being an "associate" power, using its might when it chose and for its own ends.

As for the American soldiers, known as doughboys, William Langer, later an eminent Harvard historian, recalled: "One would think that, after almost four years of war, after the most detailed and realistic accounts of murderous fighting on the Somme and around Verdun . . . it would have been all but impossible to get anyone to serve without duress." But, said Langer, "We men, most of us young, were simply fascinated by the prospect of adventure and heroism. . . . Here was our one great chance for excitement and risk. We could not afford to pass it up."[22]

But turning Americans into soldiers was hard work. One of those who had to do so was a fresh artillery captain from Missouri called Harry Truman. In July 1918 he was sent to command Battery D of the 2nd Battalion of the 129th Field Artillery—the notorious "Dizzy D" full of wild young Irish Catholics from Kansas City. Truman, aged thirty-four, was a straightlaced Freemason who loved history books and wore owlish spectacles—few thought he would last a week. At the first parade, one of the men recalled "a stirring among the fellows. . . . Although they were standing at attention, you could feel the Irish blood boiling—as much as to say, why, if this guy thinks he's going to take us over, he's mistaken."[23]

Truman stared back at 200 pairs of hostile eyes: "I could just see my hide on the fence. . . . Never on the front or anywhere else have I been so nervous." Unable to say much, he eventually told the men they were dismissed. They let out a Bronx cheer—an enormous raspberry of derision—and staged a big brawl in the evening but next morning Captain Truman posted a list of all the noncommissioned officers he had "busted"—reduced to the ranks—for leading the trouble. He told the remainder, "I didn't come over here to get along with you. You've got to get along with me. And if there are any of you who can't, speak up right now and I'll bust you right back now." But he ended with a promise: "You soldier for me, and I'll soldier for you."[24] Truman was as good as his word, becoming a respected and effective officer who whipped Dizzy D Battery into shape for the battle to come.

Meanwhile, another war for democracy was being fought back in America. Most American women still did not have the vote and they demanded that democracy, like charity, must begin at home. Women workers were playing an important part in the war effort—taking the place of men in factories and offices as well as serving as nurses at the front. Some states in the West including Colorado and California had already conceded women's suffrage, and campaigners wanted to enact this nationwide through an amendment to the U.S. Constitution.

Yet there was intense opposition from big-business interests—particularly the liquor trade, which feared that women voters would campaign for temperance reform—and from southerners who saw this as the thin end of the wedge for black rights. Many men, and some women, also believed that female suffrage would undermine the American home; one propaganda leaflet entitled "Household Hints" announced, "*Housewives!* You do not need a ballot to clean out your sink spout. A handful of potash and some boiling water is quicker and cheaper. . . . Good cooking lessens alcoholic craving quicker than a vote on [a] local [prohibition] option. . . . Clean houses and good homes, which cannot be provided by legislation, keep children happier and healthier than any number of laws."[25]

Some women concentrated on behind-the-scenes lobbying of the president and Congress. This was the policy of Mrs. Carrie Chapman Catt—the energetic head of the National American Woman Suffrage Association—but the militants favored marches and protests along the lines adopted by the suffragettes in Britain. Their leader, Alice Paul, in her thirties with a PhD, organized a picket of the White House. Her so-called Silent Sentinels stood outside the gates bearing placards demanding votes for women—often quoting back to the president his own rhetoric about how the world needed democracy, liberty, and self-government.

- Democracy should begin at Home.
- We demand justice and self-government in our own land.
- Russia and England are enfranchising their women in war-time. How long must American women wait for their liberty?
- Mr. President, How long must women be denied a voice in a government which is conscripting their sons?

When the president demanded that Kaiser Wilhelm allow full democracy in Germany, the Sentinels retorted with banners telling "Kaiser Wilson" to "Take the Beam Out of Your Own Eye."[26]

At the start of the protests the president had been studiously polite—raising his hat to the ladies as he drove past—but after a few months their endless vigil began to get under his skin. What is more, Alice Paul and many radicals were Quakers and pacifists who also opposed the war as unjust and imperialist. At the end of June 1917 the administration decided to crack down and local police suddenly started to arrest the Sentinels for "obstructing the traffic." Undeterred, the women kept on picketing, so eventually some were brought to trial—not only earnest young college graduates but also silver-haired grandmas, some of them women from distinguished families.

Mrs. Florence Hilles, the daughter of a former U.S. ambassador to Britain, told her fellow protestors in the dock, "Well, girls, I've never seen but one other court in my life and that was the Court of St. James. But I must say they are not very much alike."[27]

The judge fined the women twenty-five dollars. On refusing to pay they were given sixty days in the local workhouse. One of the prisoners, Doris Stevens, recalled its horrors: "An assistant matron, attended by negress prisoners, relieves us of our clothes. Each prisoner is obliged to strip naked without even the protection of a sheet, and proceed across what seems endless space, to a shower bath. A large tin bucket stands on the floor and in this is a minute piece of dirty soap, which is offered to us and rejected. We dare not risk the soap used by so many prisoners. Naked, we return from the bath to receive our allotment of coarse, hideous prison clothes."[28]

All this was, of course, standard treatment for any woman sent to the workhouse. But these were not standard workhouse inmates and some had very well-connected husbands; one man, called Hopkins, went in person to the White House and asked the president, "How would you like to have your wife sleep in a dirty workhouse next to prostitutes?" Wilson professed to be "shocked"—and well he might be, for, as Doris Stevens noted, "Mr. and Mrs. Hopkins had been the president's dinner guests not very long before, celebrating his return to power. They had supported him politically and financially in New Jersey. Now Mrs. Hopkins had been arrested at his gate and thrown into prison."[29]

Although conservative advocates of women's suffrage were furious with the radicals, there is little doubt that the prison sentences and the outrage they provoked made a huge impact on political leaders, not least Wilson himself. In January 1918 the president finally came out publicly for a constitutional amendment enshrining votes for women and started to put pressure on his fellow Democrats in Congress. But he chose his words carefully, avoiding the language of equal rights, of finally giving women what the Declaration of Independence had promised men back in 1776. Instead he argued mainly from expediency, later justifying women's suffrage as essential to help win the war: "The tasks of women lie at the very heart of the war and I know how much stronger that heart will beat if you do this just thing and show our women that you trust them as much as you in fact and of necessity depend upon them." Wilson also warned that otherwise America might forfeit its moral leadership of other nations in the crusade for democracy: "They are looking to the great, powerful, famous democracy of the West to lead them to the new day for which they have so long waited; and they think, in their logical simplicity, that democracy means that women shall play their part in affairs alongside men and upon an equal footing with them. If we reject measures like this, in ignorant defiance of what a new age has brought forth," asserted Wilson, "they will cease to follow or to trust us."[30]

Despite the president's appeal, the Senate remained obdurate and it was not until June 1919 that the opposition was worn down. The Nineteenth Amendment giving women the vote came into effect in August 1920. Alice Paul argued that this was not enough, pressing for another amendment stating that "equality of rights under the law shall not be denied or abridged by the United States or by any State on account of sex." (The Equal Rights Amendment was first introduced in Congress in 1923 and reappeared every session thereafter, though it got nowhere until 1971 when the whole debate had been transformed by the civil rights movement.) But as Wilson's speech indicated, the Nineteenth Amendment had been passed in Congress as a war measure, not a rights issue, and by the 1920s the Great War and the idealism it had engendered were long gone.

THE LOST PEACE

The war ended abruptly. Many had expected the fighting to drag on into 1919, but suddenly in the autumn of 1918 Germany and its allies crumbled—squeezed by economic blockade and steamrollered by massive autumn offensives. Much of the punch came from Britain's sixty-division army, but reports of hundreds of thousands of strong, well-fed Americans flooding into France and into battle also had a devastating effect on German morale. By now 4 million Americans were serving in the armed forces—half of them in France.

Among the doughboys in at the kill was Captain Harry Truman's Battery D—part of the huge American offensive in the Argonne Forest that began at the end of September 1918. In the first three hours U.S. artillery fired more ammunition than during the whole of the Civil War of 1861–1865, at an estimated cost of $1 million a minute. After a week or so of fighting, the exhausted artillerymen were pulled back for a rest—Truman had lost twenty pounds—but they returned to the front for the grand finale. Early on November 11, 1918, Truman got word that an armistice would take effect at 11 o'clock: "When the firing ceased all along the line it was so quiet it made me feel as if I'd been suddenly deprived of my ability to hear. The men at the guns, the Captain, the Lieutenants, the sergeants and corporals looked at each other for some time and then a cheer arose all along the line. . . . The French battery behind were dancing, shouting and waving bottles of wine. . . . Celebration at the front went on the rest of the day and far into the night."[31]

The war was over, but now Wilson had to win the peace. On the face of it, the president seemed well placed to achieve his aims. As he had predicted, by 1918 the British and French war effort was dependent on American finance and the U.S. army was the main source of fresh new troops. What is more, when the Germans negotiated the armistice they did so with Wilson and not his European allies. This was to be based on the president's Fourteen Points of January 1918, his blueprint for a new world order.

In this speech Wilson had called for "open covenants of peace, openly arrived at"—not the kind of secret treaties that Britain and France had used to stitch up the Middle East. He demanded "absolute freedom of navigation upon the seas"—not Britannia's navy ruling the waves—and "adequate guarantees" that national armaments would be "reduced to the lowest point consistent with domestic safety," to stop the arms races that had helped to make the world war possible. He also wanted a "free, open-minded, and absolutely impartial adjustment of all colonial claims, based upon a strict observance of the principle that in determining all such questions of sovereignty the interests of the populations concerned must have equal weight with the equitable claims of the government whose title is to be determined." This sounded like a threat to the British empire. The new world order was to be based, according to Wilson, on a "general association of nations" formed "for the purpose of affording mutual guarantees of political independence and territorial integrity to great and small states alike."[32]

It was to create this new League of Nations that Wilson decided to come to Paris for the peace conference. In Europe the president was treated as a hero. At Dover schoolgirls strewed rose petals in his path; in London he stood on the balcony of Buckingham Palace, acknowledging the crowds chanting "We Want Wilson." At the great state banquet in Buckingham Palace to celebrate the end of the war, Wilson arrived in an ordinary black suit—an almost Puritan figure amid all the dress uniforms loaded down with medals and braid. His message to the king was positively chilling: "You must not speak of us who come over here as cousins, still less as brothers; we are neither. Neither must you think of us as Anglo-Saxons, for that term can no longer be rightly applied to the people of the United States. Nor must too much importance in this connection be attached to the fact that English is our common language." No, declared Wilson, "there are only two things which can establish and maintain closer relations between your country and mine: they are community of ideals and of interests."[33] Wilson seemed to be announcing that America's ideals and national interests had little in common with those of the British empire. He had come to teach the Old World new ways.

Wilson's power was on the wane, however. Once the fighting ended, Britain and France became much less dependent on American finance and manpower, particularly as the Kaiser's Germany and its armed forces disintegrated in revolution. At home Wilson's position was undercut by the Republican victory in the November 1918 congressional elections. This meant that the peace treaty would have to be approved by a Senate in which his opponents constituted a majority and held the chairmanship of the crucial Foreign Relations Committee. Yet Wilson did not trim his sails in any way, refusing to include any prominent Republicans on the U.S. delegation to the peace conference in Paris. Some of Wilson's advisers also felt that he was weakening his leverage by attending the conference in person. Newspaper editor Frank Cobb warned, "The moment President Wilson sits at the council table with these Prime Ministers and Foreign Secretaries he has lost all the power that comes from distance and detachment. Instead of remaining the great arbiter of human freedom he becomes merely a negotiator dealing with other negotiators."[34]

Wilson, however, was sure of his mission and confident about his own powers. "I really think that no personal prestige is worth anything that cannot be exposed to the experience of the worka'day world," he wrote. "If it is so sensitive a plant that it cannot be exhibited in public, it will wither anyhow, and the sooner the better."[35] But Frank Cobb was right. Instead of a short conference to fix the outlines of a treaty and the new League of Nations, Wilson got dragged into months of detailed haggling with Allied leaders. On one occasion Mrs. Wilson found them on their hands and knees in some grand Paris salon, poring over maps of Europe to determine the new frontiers. "You look like a lot of little boys playing a game," she declared. Her husband replied, "Alas, it is the most serious game ever undertaken, for on the result of it hangs, in my estimation, the future peace of the world."[36]

Playing the great game with Wilson were men like David Lloyd George of Britain and Georges Clemenceau of France—both wily negotiators, schooled in the cut and thrust of parliamentary politics. They were not against some kind of League of Nations but believed that Wilson's new world order was rigid and utopian. "God gave us the Ten Commandments, and we broke them," remarked Clemenceau wryly. "Wilson gives us the Fourteen Points. We shall see."[37]

No previous U.S. president had ever left the western hemisphere while in office; Wilson was away in Europe for most of six months and in the process he lost touch with domestic political realities. His main aim was to bind the League of Nations into the peace treaty with Germany, hoping this would deter American opponents of the League from wrecking everything. But the three weeks he spent back home in March demonstrated the strength of feeling on Capitol Hill, and on his return to Paris he had to request some concessions from the Allies. These included clauses to ensure that the League would not meddle in U.S. domestic politics or in the affairs of the western hemisphere—classified as America's preserve by the Monroe Doctrine and the Roosevelt Corollary. Wilson also needed to make clear that any obligations to collective security—the duty of all members of the League to come to the aid of countries under attack—would not override the right of Congress to declare war.

Lloyd George and Clemenceau were willing to make the changes Wilson needed but they naturally demanded concessions in return, including financial reparations from Germany and a fifteen-year occupation of the Ruhr. Wilson was now tired and ill—even bedridden for a while by the great influenza epidemic—and there was a growing sense in Paris that, while the peacemakers fiddled, Europe was burning in the fires of revolution. At the end of March 1919 Colonel House noted in his diary, "The President looked worn and tired. . . . I am discouraged at the outlook. . . . Bolshevism is gaining ground everywhere. Hungary has just succumbed. We are sitting on an open powder magazine and some day a spark may ignite."[38]

The pressure was now intense to finalize the peace treaty before Europe followed Russia down the road to revolution, and that meant compromise. So Wilson got his League of Nations, but the harsh peace in which it was embedded—requiring heavy reparations from Germany and a massive loss of territory—seemed a far cry from the new world order outlined in his Fourteen Points. Liberal opinion in America and Europe felt outraged. The economist John Maynard Keynes resigned in protest from the British delegation to the peace conference, writing home, "I've never been so miserable as in the last two or three weeks; the Peace is outrageous and impossible and can bring nothing but misfortune behind it. . . . Certainly, if I was in the Germans' place I'd die rather than sign such a peace."[39]

Six months after being welcomed to Europe as a New World Messiah, Wilson had become almost a Judas figure among liberals—betraying the cause he had championed. He returned home exhausted, facing an uphill fight to get the League and the treaty through the U.S. Senate. Irish-Americans, for instance, had assumed—after all Wilson's talk of self-determination for subject nations—that Ireland's independence would be first on the list. Yet Wilson had enough problems with Britain at Paris without adding the Irish question, so Irish-Americans—traditionally leading supporters of Wilson's Democratic Party—became ardent campaigners against his League. One Irish-American paper in Philadelphia even claimed, "If the League of Nations goes into effect as now presented, Americans will be found to assist England in crushing any insurrection that might occur in Ireland."[40] Although preposterous, this charge was symptomatic of the fog of rumor and suspicion that now swirled around Wilson's League.

The president had hoped to blast away the opposition with a barrage of high principles, but his critics were not cowed. The crux of the debate was article 10 of the League's Covenant, which would commit all signatories "to respect and preserve as against external aggression the territorial integrity and existing political independence of all Members of the League." This violated one of the most hallowed principles of U.S. foreign policy—no entangling alliances—and threatened to commit America automatically to peacekeeping anywhere in the world. "Are you willing to enter into a covenant of death secretly arrived at . . . to become the policeman of the world?" asked Senator Thomas Hardwick of Georgia, a radical Democrat. This, he said, would "plunge our people forever into the maelstrom of European and Asiatic slaughter."[41]

Although a few senators rejected the League in any form—so-called irreconcilables—most opponents rallied around Henry Cabot Lodge, the Republican chairman of the Senate Foreign Relations Committee. Lodge hated Wilson but he kept his personal feelings in check, shrewdly crafting a position that would draw in most Republicans and many Democrats. Lodge was not against specific commitments in Europe—he favored the United States joining Britain in a guarantee of security for France against future German aggression—but declared, "I object in the strongest possible way to having the United States agree, directly or indirectly, to be controlled by a league which may at any time . . . be drawn in to deal with internal conflicts in other countries, no matter what those conflicts may be." Lodge wanted it "made perfectly clear that no American soldiers . . . can ever be engaged in war or ordered anywhere except by the constitutional authorities of the United States."[42]

Constitutionally any treaty necessitated a two-thirds majority of the Senate to be ratified, so one did not need higher mathematics to see that Wilson required a lot of Republican votes. But the exhausted president did little to satisfy doubters, telling the Foreign Relations Committee that article 10 constituted "a moral, not a legal obligation," which "leaves our Congress absolutely free to put its own interpretation upon it in all cases that call for action," yet going on to assert that "a moral obligation is of course superior to a legal obligation, and, if I may say so, has a greater binding force."[43] Such casuistry was hardly persuasive. But the president was in no mood to compromise—poisoned by his loathing of Lodge and powered by an almost messianic sense of mission. His line was that rejection of article 10 meant no League and no peace treaty; he would accept no modifications.

Deadlocked on Capitol Hill, Wilson took his case to the people through a whirlwind speaking tour. Twenty years later a president could have stayed in the White House and addressed the nation by radio—as Franklin Roosevelt did during the Depression. In our own era he might have used television or shuttled from city to city by plane. In September 1919, however, the only way to reach the people—as in the days of Abraham Lincoln—was by rail. So Wilson set out from Washington on September 3 aboard a special train with his wife, staff, and anxious doctor. The South was safely Democrat and the East firmly Republican, so he concentrated on the swing states of the Midwest and Far West, hoping to put pressure on their senators. As the train rattled along, the president sat hunched over his portable typewriter, tapping out his next speech, but wherever he went the arguments were essentially the same—about power, principle, and the impossibility of compromise:

> *St Louis, Missouri:* [L]et me predict that we will be the senior partner. The financial leadership will be ours. The industrial primacy will be ours. The commercial advantage will be ours. The other countries of the world are looking to us for leadership and direction.

> *Sioux Falls, South Dakota:* America is the only idealistic nation in the world. . . . If America goes back upon mankind, mankind has no other place to turn.

> *Portland, Oregon:* If we want a League of Nations we must take this League of Nations. We must leave it or take it.[44]

In three weeks Wilson covered 8,000 miles, giving thirty-six set speeches, innumerable conferences, and many impromptu talks from the back of the train.[45]

Although now suffering from excruciating headaches, he was buoyed up by the people's enthusiasm. In Billings, Montana, he recalled later, the train was pursued by boys cheering for "Woody" and waving flags. "One youngster in his enthusiasm insisted I should take his flag and handed it up to me. The boy next to him did not have a flag and he looked a good deal disgruntled for a moment, and then he put his hand in his pocket and said: 'Here, I will give you a dime.' I would like to believe that that dime has some relation to the widow's mite—others gave something; he gave all he had." When Wilson died five years later, his wife found, in a little change purse he always carried, a dime wrapped in a piece of paper. "I am convinced," she wrote, "that it was the dime that the little boy gave him on that September day in 1919."[46]

Despite such uplifting moments, the strain became intolerable. Almost blinded by the pain in his head, Wilson agreed to cancel the rest of the tour; back in the White House, on October 2, he suffered a massive stroke, paralyzing his whole left side. "He lived on; but oh, what a wreck of his former self!" lamented Ike Hoover, one of his staff. "He did grow better, but that is not saying much" since he was reduced "from a giant into a pygmy." He was physically almost incapacitated and, though able to speak, could form only indistinct words. "It was so sad that those of us about him, who almost without exception admired him, would turn our heads away when he came along or we went near him."[47]

The public was told only that the president was suffering from "nervous exhaustion." In a manner unimaginable today, the whole thing was hushed up, with his wife becoming almost acting president—filtering the information coming to Wilson and relaying his wishes. The stroke hardened the president's intransigence about the League. In November 1919 Senator Lodge had sufficient votes to reject Wilson's League but Wilson still commanded enough support among loyal Senate Democrats to block Lodge's League with reservations. Neither side was able to secure the necessary two-thirds majority; there was paralysis on Capitol Hill as well as in the White House.

So the United States failed to join the League of Nations that its president had designed. More than that, the country's mood had changed. After the crusade came the backlash.

"100 PERCENT AMERICANISM"

The man's only mistake was not to stand up for the national anthem, but that was enough. Such apparent lack of patriotism enraged a sailor at a victory pageant in Washington in May 1919. When the band finished playing "The Star Spangled Banner," the sailor fired three revolver shots into the back of the seated spectator. As the man crumpled, the audience clapped and cheered.[48]

A minor incident, perhaps, but symptomatic of the mood of ultrapatriotism in America engendered by the Great War. The targets varied—first Germans and pacifists, then radicals, finally all who were not of Aryan descent—but these campaigns to ensure "100 percent Americanism" had lasting effects: closing the open door to immigrants from Europe and even, for a decade, closing America's saloons and breweries.

German-Americans were the first group to experience the heat of this new nationalism, even before the United States entered the war in 1917. Supporters of Britain such as ex-president Theodore Roosevelt thundered against what were called hyphenate Americans, groups with supposedly a divided loyalty. Roosevelt insisted in the winter of 1915–1916, "The overwhelming issue at this moment is whether or not we are a real nation, able to command unfaltering loyalty from all our citizens. . . . If the German-American vote is solid against me, because of the position I have taken, then, in my judgment, it shows that the German-Americans are solidly against this country." Roosevelt insisted he was not against "decent Americans who are of German descent. . . . But the professional hyphenated German-Americans I shall smite with the sword of the Lord."[49]

Once Germany and America were at war, anti-German feeling became almost a crusade. In scores of cities and several states the German language was removed from the school curriculum. German music was ostracized—Wagner, Brahms, even Beethoven. Hamburgers were renamed "liberty steaks," sauerkraut "liberty cabbage," and many people of German stock decided to Americanize their names. Encouraged by President Wilson, Congress passed tough wartime Espionage and Sedition Acts—the latter targeting anyone who spoke or wrote any "disloyal, profane, scurrilous, or abusive language" against the government, flag, or uniform of the United States. Nothing of the sort had been seen since the notorious Alien and Sedition Acts of the 1790s during the panic caused by the French Revolution.

One of those who fell foul of the new legislation was Eugene Debs, the veteran socialist leader, when he linked the "plutocracy" in Germany with that of the United States. "I hate, I loathe, I despise Junkers and junkerdom. I have no earthly use for the Junkers of Germany, and not one particle more use for the Junkers in the United States. They tell us that we live in a great free republic; that our institutions are democratic; that we are a free and self-governing people. This is too much, even for a joke."[50] Debs was sentenced to ten years under the Espionage Act and served a quarter of that time. He ran for the presidency yet again in 1920 while in the Atlanta Penitentiary.

The crusade for "100 percent Americanism" did not abate after the war; instead it turned on those like Debs whose political views seemed a threat. These were the years when Bolshevism had surged from Russia into central Europe and many Americans feared it would engulf them as well. The communist movement in the United States was minuscule—some 70,000 people in 1919, less than 0.1 percent of the population.[51] But when a rash of strikes broke out after victory was won, reflecting the pent-up reaction of workers against wartime wage restraint, many Americans feared this was the thin end of the Bolshevik wedge. The result was the Red Scare of 1919–1920.

Coal, steel, and textiles—basic industries reliant on immigrant labor—were at the heart of the strikes in 1919 and vigilante groups sprang up in retaliation. A member of the so-called Loyal Legion in the steel town of Gary, Indiana, recalled how they kept "law and order" with blackjacks—lumps of lead wrapped up in leather and swung like clubs: "A bunch of these foreigners, six or eight times the number of our posse, met us this side of the tracks, and we went into them. . . . Our method of work was to grab a man's right arm with the operator's left hand, then bring down the blackjack across the hand bone or wrist of the man thus caught. One rap was enough, and . . . we could go on to the next man. . . . We have a nice hospital in Gary. There were some thirty-five people in there next day with broken wrists and hands."[52]

There was also a small anarchist movement in America who made no secret of their aims. One circular that appeared in New England declared, "The senile fossils ruling the United States see red! . . . We, the American Anarchists, do not protest, for it is futile to waste any time on feeble minded creatures led by His Majesty Phonograph Wilson. Do not think that only foreigners are anarchists, we are a great number right here at home. . . . The storm is within and very soon will leap and crash and annihilate you in blood and fire. You have shown no pity to us! We will do likewise. . . . *We will dynamite you!*"[53]

And they nearly did. Just before May Day 1919—the international holiday for workers—postal office staff in New York found a set of homemade parcel bombs addressed to members of Congress and officials who were noted opponents of immigration and radicalism as well as business tycoons like John D. Rockefeller and J. P. Morgan. Most of the packages had been put to one side because of insufficient postage but a couple did get through and one—addressed to a former U.S. senator—blew off the hands of the maid who opened it. The perpetrators were never found but that only added to the fears of an all-embracing plot, and the press had no doubts with headlines like "REDS PLANNED MAY DAY MURDERS."[54]

Having botched the mail bombs, the plotters opted for special delivery. Around midnight on June 2, explosions occurred at the homes of prominent figures in seven cities from Boston to Pittsburgh. The most sensational was at the Washington residence of the U.S. attorney general, A. Mitchell Palmer. The whole front of his house was blown in and windows were shattered along the street—Palmer himself being showered with glass. Police quickly discovered that the bomber had gone up with his bomb; according to the officer in charge, "We could not take a step without seeing or feeling the grinding of a piece of flesh. The house across the street was plastered with pieces."[55]

Putting together the remains, forensic experts decided the bomber was of Italian descent—actually he was a twenty-four-year-old called Carlo Valdinoci, part of a cell of Italian anarchists. The threat was real but tiny, yet neither the country nor the government knew that and, in the fevered atmosphere, they acted on their fears. Attorney General Palmer, smarting from his brush with death, shook up the

Justice Department, creating a new Bureau of Investigation—forebear of the FBI—and a General Intelligence Division to track radicals. Its first boss was a young, ambitious clerk called J. Edgar Hoover; in 1924 Hoover took over the Bureau of Investigation and went on to run it for nearly a half-century until his death in 1972.

In November 1919 Palmer's revamped Justice Department mounted a series of raids all over the country, rounding up several thousand alien radicals. Arrests were made without warrants, and men were beaten without provocation, then held for weeks or months in crowded, unsanitary jails; about 800 were eventually deported.[56] There was widespread support for the "Palmer Raids" and the deportations, with one patriotic speaker in California declaring, "These murderous wild beasts of our otherwise blessed republic should be given a bottle of water and a pint of meal and shoved out into the ocean on a raft, when the wind is blowing seaward."[57] But others protested at the ruthless violation of civil liberties. A group of distinguished lawyers, including Felix Frankfurter of Harvard and Ernst Freund of Chicago, condemned "the utterly illegal acts which have been committed by those charged with the highest duty of enforcing the laws—acts which have caused widespread suffering and unrest, have struck at the foundation of American free institutions, and have brought the name of our country into disrepute."[58]

Eventually Palmer overreached himself. With one eye on the Democratic presidential nomination, he whipped up a public panic in advance of May Day 1920, abetted by the dutiful Hoover with a series of bulletins predicting a new wave of strikes, bombings, and assassinations. But nothing happened—not even some stormy rallies—and Palmer was transformed almost overnight from one of the most respected men in America into a figure of fun. With strikes abating, the country pulling out of its postwar slump, and the Bolshevist tide receding in Europe, the Red Scare was over.

But the tide of "100 percent Americanism" surged into new channels or, rather, back into older ones. The movement to restrict immigration gained new life at the end of the war when the Atlantic was reopened to immigrants at a time when the United States was suffering from a short but sharp postwar recession. So, in addition to the patrician Americans of British stock who had been the vanguard of immigration restriction, union leaders joined the cause. Sam Gompers, influential head of the American Federation of Labor, warned of the threat posed by cheap foreign labor to American workers' jobs, adopting the language of the 100-percenters: "America has not yet become a nation. It is still a conglomerated mass of various and diverse ethnic groups . . . honeycombed with 'foreign groups' living a foreign life."[59]

Succumbing to these pressures, in 1921 and 1924 Congress passed acts that finally closed the open door. The legislation did not affect migrants from Latin America because of the need for Mexican farm labor, nor did it alter the near total ban on immigration from China and Japan. But it slashed migration from Europe to a mere 150,000 a year and imposed quotas based on the proportion of nationalities in the census of 1890, thereby penalizing later immigrant groups from Italy, Russia, and the Balkans who were considered to be racially different from Americans of Nordic stock. A few members of Congress made the case for legislation in explicitly racist terms, among them Senator Ellison Smith of South Carolina. "I think we now have sufficient population in our country for us to shut the door and to breed up a pure, unadulterated American citizenship. . . . Who is an American?" he asked. "Would it be the son of an Italian immigrant, the son of a German immigrant, the son of any of the breeds from the Orient, the son of the denizens of Africa?" No, insisted Smith. "Thank God we have in America perhaps the largest percentage of any country in the world of the pure, unadulterated Anglo-Saxon stock; certainly the greatest of any nation in the Nordic breed. . . . I would make this not an asylum for the oppressed of all countries, but a country to assimilate and perfect that splendid type of manhood that has made America the foremost Nation in her progress and in her power."[60]

The crusade for social conformity had one other triumph. For decades evangelical Protestants, mostly from British and Scandinavian stock, had campaigned against demon drink. In the 1900s their efforts were given new momentum by the Anti-Saloon League—a dynamic pressure group funded mostly by subscribers in local churches. Preacher Billy Sunday spoke for many of them: "The saloon is an infidel. It has no faith in God; has no religion. . . . It respects the thief and it esteems the blasphemer; it fills the prisons and the penitentiaries. It cocks the highwayman's pistol. It puts the rope in the hands of the mob. It is the anarchist of the world."[61]

This struggle to close the saloons and ban the sale of liquor had an ethnic dimension, since the main opponents were Catholics of German and Irish descent. The anti-German mood of the war strengthened the Prohibitionist case by silencing the powerful German brewing industry—companies like Pabst and Schlitz— and by adding the telling argument of helping the war effort. Closing down the breweries, it was claimed, would keep soldiers sober and ensure that grain was used for food. "German brewers in this country have rendered thousands of men inefficient and are thus crippling the Republic in its war on Prussian militarism," asserted the Anti-Saloon League.[62]

So in December 1917 Congress approved an amendment to the Constitution that banned the manufacture, import, and sale of "intoxicating liquors." After being ratified by the states—in some cases very reluctantly—the Eighteenth Amendment came into force on January 17, 1920. The Anti-Saloon League was exultant: "At one minute past twelve to-morrow morning a new nation will be born. . . . To-night John Barleycorn makes his last will and testament. Now for an era of clear thinking and clean living! The Anti-Saloon League wishes every man, woman and child a happy Dry Year."[63]

As with many crusades, the campaign for Americanization was fired by anxiety. Although the United States had become immensely powerful, many Americans feared enemies within: a German fifth-column, Red agitators, the threat to racial purity, even the danger that national values would be poisoned by alcohol. Some of the Americanization laws passed during the fevered war years proved enduring—immigration quotas survived until the 1960s—but the dry utopia of clear thinking and clean living was a fantasy. Almost immediately the backlash against Prohibition began—the centerpiece of a decade that celebrated life, liberty, and the pursuit of happiness as never before.

THE JAZZ AGE HITS MAIN STREET

Clara Bow was one of the icons of the New. An unwanted child of two drunken, violent parents who slid in and out of mental illness, she was raised in a Brooklyn tenement but found her escape in watching movies and dreaming of a career on the screen. Eventually she talked her father into giving her a dollar so she could have some photo portraits taken. These helped get her a screen test; her cute looks and acting talent did the rest. Above all, Bow had "It"—the title of her most famous film and a word that became the 1920s synonym for sex appeal. She was the proverbial "It girl" whose screen romances and off-screen affairs became the subject of endless press gossip. Bow and other stars of the 1920s such as Louise Brooks were the quintessential "flappers"—new women flouting old values with their heavy makeup, boyish haircuts, straight loose dresses and high heels, who smoked in public and drove automobiles. They symbolized the collision between the new social freedoms of the Jazz Age and the traditional values of small-town Protestant America.

The cinema was probably the most important mechanism for spreading new values and new fashions across the nation. In an attempt to defuse criticism by traditionalists, the movie industry developed its censorship guidelines, regulating the portrayal of sex, violence, and irreligion. It also upgraded sleazy nickelodeons in dubious parts of town into new "theater palaces"—luxurious halls that were classical in design but egalitarian in ethos. William Fox, one of the most successful cinema owners in New York, claimed, "Movies breathe the spirit in which the country was founded, freedom and equality. In the motion pictures there are no separations of classes. Everyone enters the same way. There is no side door thrust upon those who sit in the less expensive seats." Fox called the movies "a distinctly American institution."[64]

By 1928 there were 28,000 movie theaters in America and 65 million tickets were sold on average every week.[65] The business, now just entering the talkies era, was controlled by eight major companies led by Warner Brothers and Paramount, which, as in other industries before them, had integrated vertically to control every part of the process from production through distribution and the cinemas themselves. Film-making had also migrated from its early center, New York, to the environs of Los Angeles—Hollywood was already a byword for movies—and its highest level was now dominated by Jewish immigrants from eastern Europe. Men such as Samuel Goldwyn and Adolph Zukor had started in the garments business and, as social outsiders, had a keen eye for new niches and consumer demand. Goldwyn used to sit in front of the audience with his back to the screen in order to gauge viewers' reactions. He explained, "If the audience don't like a picture, they have a good reason. The public is never wrong. I don't go for all this thing that when I have a failure, it is because the audience doesn't have the taste or education, or isn't sensitive enough. The public pays the money," declared Goldwyn. "It wants to be entertained. That's all I know."[66]

The movies had cleaned up their act enough to fend off the moral reformers. The saloons did not, but Prohibition simply drove alcohol underground. Right from the start in 1920 the law was widely flouted as winemaking, brewing, and distilling moved into the home. In the words of one verse:

> Mother's in the kitchen
> Washing out the jugs;
> Sister's in the pantry
> Bottling the suds;
> Father's in the cellar
> Mixing up the hops;
> Johnny's on the front porch
> Watching for the cops.[67]

These home-brew family industries were outposts of large business empires—initially run by the big brewers who were trying to maintain their operations by underground means but increasingly by organized crime. Gangsters like Al Capone in Chicago or Maxie Hoff in Philadelphia used the profits from illicit liquor to dominate their own territories, settling turf wars through dramatic shootouts. But Capone, the son of Italian immigrants whose face was scarred from a vicious knife attack, was at pains to represent himself as a businessman: "I make my money by supplying a public demand. If I break the law, my customers, who number hundreds of the best people in Chicago, are as guilty as I am." The only difference, said Capone, is that "I sell and they buy. . . . When I sell liquor, it's bootlegging. When my patrons serve it on a silver tray on Lake Shore Drive, it's hospitality."[68] And it was for business misdemeanors—tax evasion—that Capone was eventually put behind bars, not for setting up some 300 deaths including the notorious St. Valentine's Day Massacre in 1929 when a rival gang was gunned down in a Chicago garage.

As the gangsters replaced the brewers, so the saloon gave way to clubs and speakeasies, where you could buy alcohol if you spoke softly and paid the right price. As cover many of these places offered dance music and one of those who made his name in the nightclubs of Chicago was trumpeter Louis Armstrong. Like Clara Bow, Armstrong was a high achiever from a broken home—but he was black and had grown up in New Orleans, learning his musicianship during spells in the city's Home for Colored Waifs. Armstrong started on the cornet before moving on to the trumpet, earning the nickname Satchmo for his "satchel mouth." New Orleans was the cradle of American jazz—building on older traditions such as slave work-songs, black "cakewalk" dances, and ragtime piano music—but the style matured when its great exponents went north. These were players like Sidney Bechet, Joe "King" Oliver (Armstrong's mentor), and Satchmo himself, who developed the new jazz tradition of a charismatic, improvising soloist. As he recalled later, "[U]s kids who turned out to be good musicians migrated from New Orleans to Chicago when times were real good. There were plenty of work, lots of Dough flying around, all kinds of beautiful women at your service. A musician in Chicago in the early twenties were treated and respected just like—some kind of a God."[69]

Armstrong and his fellow jazzmen from New Orleans were part of a larger so-cial trend—the mass movement of half a million blacks out of the South during the 1910s and three-quarters of a million in the course of the 1920s. In the main they were fleeing racial discrimination and economic depression but the pull of moder-nity was also strong. One girl who left the Sea Islands of South Carolina explained, "Got tired of living on Island. Too lonesome. Go to bed at six o'clock. Everything dead. No dances. No moving picture show, nothing to go to. . . . That's why people move more than anything else."[70]

In contrast to Louis Armstrong, however, most black migrants were not treated in the North like a God but instead found themselves corralled in ghettos and made the butt of discrimination and violence. Chicago, where the black population more than doubled to 110,000 during the 1910s, was the scene of a serious race riot in July 1919 that left thirty-eight people dead. "The 'German Hun' is beaten but the world is made no safer for Democracy," exploded a black magazine commentator. "I hate every Hun, and the worst I know are the ones that thrive under the free in-stitutions of America."[71]

Blacks who stayed in the South were often victims of lynchings and burnings by the Ku Klux Klan. This white supremacist movement, moribund since the 1870s but resurrected in World War I, boasted 4–5 million members in the early 1920s. Al-though blacks were the main target of the KKK, it also went for Asians, Catholics, Jews, and all the foreign born. This new Klan aimed at "uniting native-born white Christians for concerted action in the preservation of American institutions and the supremacy of the white race,"[72] and its supporters campaigned actively in support of Prohibition and reading the Bible in schools. So, rather than being a thuggish one-off, the Klan was really an extreme manifestation of the continuing backlash by conservative white Anglo-Saxon Protestants against a country that seemed to be losing these characteristics. And although the new Klan had support in northern and Midwestern cities, especially Chicago, its roots were essentially in rural small-town America.

The 1920 census was a defining moment in American history: For the first time more than half the population lived in urban areas. Actually "urban" merely meant towns of more than 2,500 inhabitants—hardly megalopolis—and only New York and Chicago had more than 2 million people, but the 1920 census, like the sup-posed end of the frontier in 1890, was a psychological landmark.[73]

Cultural and political debate became preoccupied by the supposed clash of rural and urban values. The runaway best-seller of the early 1920s was *Main Street* by Sinclair Lewis, which sold nearly 300,000 copies in its first year and went on to earn him what today would be about $3 million.[74] His fictional small town of Gopher Prairie was modeled on the remote village in Minnesota where he had grown up before going to Yale and settling in the East. Lewis's rural-urban odyssey mirrored that of millions of Americans and this was part of the book's appeal, but *Main Street* was also notable for having a strong female heroine—Carol, a vibrant college grad-uate who ended up marrying the dull local doctor—and for its satirical depiction of the rooted provincialism that she tried and failed to dispel.

According to Carol, the problem in Main Streets all over America was "an unimaginatively standardized background, a sluggishness of speech and manners, a rigid ruling of the spirit by the desire to appear respectable." People achieved con-tentment but it was "the contentment of the quiet dead, who are scornful of the liv-ing for their restless walking. It is negation canonized as the one positive virtue. It is the prohibition of happiness. It is slavery self-sought and self-defended. It is dull-ness made God."[75] Although Lewis always had a soft spot for small-town America, at root he saw it as blocking the twentieth-century realization of Jefferson's vision of life, liberty, and the pursuit of happiness.

Prohibition—the battle between dries and wets—was part of this rural-urban cultural war, but its most dramatic clash occurred over religion. In the early 1920s the fiery old populist William Jennings Bryan—three times Democratic candidate for the presidency—mounted a crusade against "The Menace of Darwinism." Bryan saw Darwinian evolution as the thin end of a secularist wedge; he also believed that Darwinist ideas about the survival of the fittest had animated the Great War. "To destroy the faith of Christians and lay the foundations of the bloodiest war in history would seem enough to condemn Darwinism," he declared. Bryan also ar-gued his case on democratic grounds. "Teachers in public schools must teach what the taxpayers desire taught," he told West Virginia legislators. "The hand that writes the pay check rules the school." And he had no time for expert opinion: "A scien-tific soviet is attempting to dictate what is taught in our schools." Here was a pow-erful cocktail of religion and democracy; Bryan's campaign drew fundamentalists out of their hitherto narrow theological debate into a battle against the cultural mainstream.[76]

Bryan's opponents claimed that his campaign threatened free speech and sci-entific inquiry. When in 1925 the state of Tennessee passed a law banning any teaching that denied "the story of the Divine Creation of man as taught in the Bible" and stated instead that "man has descended from a lower order of animals," the American Civil Liberties Union offered to fund a test case. A young teacher called John Scopes came forward and the case was tried in his town, Dayton—an East

Tennessee version of Main Street—over a sweltering week in July 1925. (Actually the civic leaders of Dayton had contrived the whole case, seeing it as a great way to boost interest and investment in their flagging town.) Two hundred reporters covered the so-called trial of the century, which was also carried live by a radio station in Chicago. What drew them was the presence of Bryan as one of the prosecution team and, appearing for the defense, Clarence Darrow—one of the great criminal lawyers of the age and a militant atheist.

The high point came when Darrow, in a brilliant coup, persuaded Bryan to take the stand as an expert witness on the Bible. For two hours he grilled the old campaigner on his literalist interpretation of Scripture.

> DARROW: Mr. Bryan, do you believe that the first woman was Eve?
> BRYAN: Yes.
> DARROW: Do you believe that she was literally made out of Adam's rib?
> BRYAN: I do. . . .
> DARROW: You don't care how old the earth is, how old man is, or how long the animals have been here?
> BRYAN: I am not so much interested in that.
> DARROW: You have never made any investigation to find out?
> BRYAN: No, sir, I have never. . . . Your Honor . . . [t]he only purpose Mr. Darrow has is to slur at the Bible, but I will answer his questions. . . . I want the world to know that this man, who does not believe in a God, is trying to use a court in Tennessee . . . to slur at it. . . .
> DARROW: I object to your statement. I am examining you on your fool ideas that no intelligent Christian on earth believes!

And when Bryan tried to evade Darrow's efforts to pin him down on the date of Noah and the Flood:

> DARROW: What do you think?
> BRYAN: I do not think about things I don't think about.
> DARROW: Do you think about things you do think about?
> BRYAN: Well, sometimes.[77]

That set off ripples of laughter around the courtroom. Darrow's cross-examination exposed Bryan's ignorance, even indifference, about science, geology, history, languages, and other religions. Modernists held up the Dayton "Monkey Trial" as the end of an era—lampooning into oblivion the provincial values of Main Street America—and it was certainly the end of the evangelicals' big public campaign. Bryan himself died a few days later from the stress of the trial. Behind the scenes, however, fundamentalists imposed anti-evolution laws in many parts of the South, and over the next few decades they created their own subculture of Bible colleges, camps, conferences, and radio stations. Fundamentalism was not dead but dormant—a veritable sleeping giant, as would be clear at the end of the twentieth century.

America's two presidents of the early 1920s seemed to sum up the culture clash of the age. Warren Gamaliel Harding was a small-town newspaper editor from Ohio. Handsome, sociable, and unintellectual, he made his way up Republican politics and in 1920—much to everyone's surprise, not least his own—he emerged as a compromise candidate for the presidency from a "smoke-filled" room of party bosses. The Republican campaign slogan "Back to Normalcy" caught the national mood after the strenuous novelties of the Wilson years and Harding won by a landslide. But he was out of his depth in the White House, admitting to one visitor, "I knew that this job would be too much for me."[78] He could not control the "Ohio Gang" that came with him—enmeshed in bribes, sex scandals, and illicit liquor—whose exploits became notorious after Harding's sudden death from a heart attack in August 1923. Reports also surfaced of the president's long-standing affairs and an illegitimate child.

If Harding embodied the temptations of the Jazz Age, his vice-president and successor, Calvin Coolidge, seemed like Mr. Main Street. The son of a Vermont store-owner, Coolidge was honest, low key, and hardworking—exactly the Yankee virtues needed to restore public trust in the presidency. He believed that the federal government should play a minimal role in national affairs, being best known for his dictum that "the chief business of the American people is business." Coolidge did add that "the chief ideal of the American people is idealism"[79] but also claimed that "economy is idealism in its most practical form."[80] Under his aegis, Treasury Secretary Andrew Mellon cut back the tax burden dramatically. The 1926 Revenue Act abolished the gift tax, halved the estate tax, and reduced the top rate of the surtax to 25 percent—all hugely beneficial to the rich. But by raising the threshold at the bottom to $4,000, Mellon also exempted most Americans from paying federal income tax—the centerpiece of Woodrow Wilson's progressive taxation policies. "The income tax in this country," announced Mellon proudly, "has become a class rather than a national tax."[81]

In 1928 the presidential election itself became the main arena for America's culture wars. The Democratic candidate was Al Smith of New York, who had made his name as a spokesman for Irish-Americans, championing the cause of downtrodden workers and maintaining a reputation for probity despite being part of the Tammany Hall political machine. With the Republicans campaigning on their record of peace and prosperity—"A Car in Every Garage and a Chicken in Every Pot"—any Democratic candidate would have found 1928 hard going. But Smith's Catholic faith and his antagonism toward Prohibition lost him votes in much of rural Protestant America. (Choosing as his campaign song "The Sidewalks of New York" did not help, given the city's notoriety across much of the country.) The propaganda against Smith was ferocious. It was said that his thick, gravelly voice was "whiskey breath"; the Ku Klux Klan burned a fiery cross as his train passed into Oklahoma. In Daytona Beach, Florida, the school board gave each child a card to take home stating, "If he is chosen President, you will not be allowed to have or read a Bible." Even the Kansas editor William Allen White—one of the most respected voices in 1920s America and a barometer of heartland values—claimed that Smith was "a representative of the saloon, prostitution and gambling" and warned that "the whole Puritan civilization which has built up a sturdy, orderly nation is threatened."[82]

Al Smith was the first Catholic presidential candidate for a mainstream party— hence the vitriol and bigotry. On the other hand, being both Catholic and "wet" won him the support of millions of urban, ethnic workers who had never voted Democrat before. With hindsight it is evident that, although Smith lost, the 1928 election signaled the start of a fundamental shift in U.S. politics; the days of Republican hegemony and boom-time prosperity were now numbered.

12

FROM BOOM TO BOMB

Inauguration Day, March 4, 1929. Despite pouring rain, the mood was sunny as incoming president Herbert Hoover painted a glowing portrait of American life: "[W]e have reached a higher degree of comfort and security than ever existed before in the history of the world. Through liberation from widespread poverty we have reached a higher degree of individual freedom than ever before. . . . In no nation is the government more worthy of respect," Hoover declared. "I have no fears for the future of our country. It is bright with hope."[1]

Hoover seemed like the perfect leader for progressive America—a Quaker farm boy from Iowa who trained as an engineer and made his name organizing food relief in Europe during the Great War, in other words an attractive blend of traditional values and modern managerialism. For years the "Great Engineer" had seemed a towering figure, wooed by both parties. Back in 1920 the Democrat Franklin D. Roosevelt had remarked, "He is certainly a wonder and I wish we could make him President of the United States. There could not be a better one."[2]

A decade later Roosevelt had changed his mind, partly because Hoover chose to run as a Republican, but mostly because the presidency that started so promisingly ended up as a disaster. This is the story of how the 1920s boom turned to bust with a speed and completeness that undermined not only America's prosperity but also the country's belief in itself. And of how Roosevelt, Hoover's successful rival for the presidency in 1932, led America through the twin crises of depression and a second world war to even greater prosperity, renewed self-confidence, and unprecedented global power symbolized by the atomic bomb. Thanks to Roosevelt's New Deal and war spending the federal government became, for the first time, a dominant force in the lives of ordinary people.

BOOM AND BUST

Although the United States did not join the League of Nations, its position in the world had been changed irrevocably by the world war. "By the sheer genius of this people and the growth of our power we have become a determining factor in the history of mankind," Woodrow Wilson declared in 1919, "and after you have become a determining factor you cannot remain isolated, whether you want to or not."[3] Wilson was right: In the 1920s the U.S. navy was nearly as large as Britain's and America had the second-biggest merchant fleet in the world. Above all, it was now the decisive force in international finance.

In 1913 the United States had been a net debtor to the tune of $3.7 billion; by 1919 it was a net creditor at exactly the same level.[4] This dramatic transformation reflected two related trends in war finance—Britain sold off its still substantial U.S. investments while America became the Allies' main banker. America's financial system had been geared largely toward internal investment, but from 1915 the wartime loans to Britain and France turned New York into a major world money market as finance houses like J. P. Morgan's and National City Bank mobilized American funds for investment abroad. In finance, unlike diplomacy, the United States did not turn in on itself after the war. Great Britain still held a larger portfolio of foreign assets but the United States was now the prime source of *new* investment, lending $6.4 billion overseas in the period 1924 to 1929—nearly double Britain's contribution. About half America's new investment was in Europe, particularly Germany, where it helped fund reparation payments and the Weimar Republic's welfare state.[5] Here were the seeds of future problems, but in the mid-1920s it seemed that America's new financial power had helped restore the world economy after the trauma of war.

In trade the story was similar. The United States had become the world's leading exporter—with nearly one-sixth of global exports in 1929—and, after Britain, the second-largest importer as well, sucking in raw materials for its booming economy.[6] The lead sector for exports was automobiles and ancillary industries such as rubber and petroleum; U.S. companies were also building their own plants abroad during the 1920s, including Britain. The most striking sign of the contemporary passion for Fordism and U.S. business methods was in the new Soviet Union. "The combination of Russian revolutionary sweep and American efficiency is the essence of Leninism," Josef Stalin told party workers in 1924, at the height of the *Fordizatsia* craze.[7] His Five-Year Plans were a frenzied effort to forge a mass-production economy along American lines before the capitalist countries tried to crush Soviet communism.

But Americans gave little thought to Russia in the 1920s; their main preoccupation seemed to be getting rich. Businessman George F. Babbitt—the satirical creation of novelist Sinclair Lewis—became the emblem of the age:

As he approached the office he walked faster and faster, muttering, "Guess better hustle." All about him the city was hustling, for hustling's sake. Men in motors were hustling to pass one another in the hustling traffic. Men were hustling to catch trolleys, with another trolley a minute behind, and to leap from the trolleys, to gallop across the sidewalk, to hurl themselves into buildings, into hustling express elevators. . . . Men who had made five thousand, year before last, and ten thousand last year, were urging on nerve-yelping bodies and parched brains so that they might make twenty thousand this year; and the men who had broken down immediately after making their twenty thousand dollars were hustling to catch trains, to hustle through the vacations which the hustling doctors had ordered.[8]

An even more powerful cultural critic was novelist F. Scott Fitzgerald—like Lewis a native of Minnesota who came east but a writer who looked more penetratingly and poignantly into the Jazz Age. Fitzgerald's most celebrated novel, *The Great Gatsby*, published in 1925 at the height of the boom, is almost prophetic about what was to come. Shifting between the grand estates of Long Island and the squalor of New York City and its suburbs (*Among Ash-Heaps and Millionaires* was an early title), Fitzgerald traces the doomed love affair between Jay Gatsby, a shadowy plutocrat, and Daisy Buchanan against the backdrop of those whose lives were ruined in the process. These gilded rich were "careless people . . . they smashed up things and creatures and then retreated back into their money or their vast carelessness." At the end of the book Fitzgerald famously evokes the original Long Island that, he imagined, Dutch sailors had espied—"a fresh, green breast of the new world" glimpsed in "a transitory enchanted moment" when "man must have held his breath in the presence of this new continent." Here again, as in many other works of literature from the period, is that sense of a lost Eden of American innocence. Yet Fitzgerald knows this is as much of a dream as the idealized American future, for individuals and countries can never fully escape their past.

Gatsby believed in the green light, the orgastic future that year by year recedes before us. It eluded us then, but that's no matter—to-morrow we will run faster, stretch our arms further. . . . And one fine morning—

So we beat on, boats against the current, borne back ceaselessly into the past.[9]

All through the 1920s the green-light sector was consumer goods—fridges, radios, above all cars. Automobile output more than doubled during the decade; by 1929 there was one car for almost every household. Whereas, two decades before, Henry Ford's democratic Model T had opted for black standardization, new-era companies like General Motors were building their marketing strategy on planned obsolescence. "Our chief job in research," said one GM executive, "is to keep the customer reasonably dissatisfied with what he has."[10] Many of these consumer goods were being bought on credit—"buy now, pay later"—with easy installment plans at high rates of interest. Debt was nearly 10 percent of household income in 1929, more than double the percentage in 1900.[11] And seductive advertising spread the message that every self-respecting American needed the very latest design. "Automobiles change with the calendar," said banker Paul Mazur. "Last year's offerings are made social pariahs, only this year's model is desirable until it, in turn, is made out of fashion by next year's style."[12] In the 1920s consumer boom the luxuries of yesterday became the norms of today: As one commentator put it, "every free-born American has the right to name his necessities."[13]

In mid-decade the U.S. economy was growing at around 7 percent a year; unemployment dropped below 2 percent in 1926. The most striking indicator of the boom was the New York Stock Exchange, where share values increased fifteenfold between 1923 and 1929.[14] By the time Hoover took office some commentators were warning that the market had become overheated, fueled by the easy-credit policies of the Federal Reserve banks, but few investors took note and the speculation reached fever pitch. At the end of October 1929 the inevitable happened and the bubble burst; a week of panic selling cut the value of the market by one-third. On Black Tuesday October 29 alone, over 16 million shares changed hands—a record that stood for nearly forty years.[15]

In a broker's office that was typical of hundreds across America you saw "men looking defeat in the face. One was slowly walking up and down, mechanically tearing a piece of paper into tiny and still tinier fragments. Another was grinning shamefacedly, as a small boy giggles at a funeral. Another was abjectly beseeching a clerk for the last news of American & Foreign Power. And still another was sitting motionless, as if stunned, his eyes fixed upon the moving figures on the screen, those innocent-looking figures that meant the smash-up of the hopes of years."[16]

In itself the stock market crash of October 1929 was not decisive. Share prices had become vastly inflated and were ripe for correction; in any case, only about 1 percent of the population owned securities in 1929.[17] But millions of Americans had come to see the stock market as a barometer for the economy as a whole; with the future economic climate uncertain, they cut back on more spending and new debts. The result was a massive contraction of the whole economy, but particularly affected were the boom industries such as cars and electrical goods and in turn the rubber and steel manufacturers that supplied them. In 1930 spending on consumer durables fell by a catastrophic 20 percent.[18] As factories closed and workers were laid off, the ripples were felt in mill towns and mining communities, in Main Street's shops and eateries.

The collapse of demand was also the last straw for millions of America's farmers. They, too, had boosted production all through the 1920s, for the country's voracious cities and for export to the wider world. But farm prices were already falling because of competition from Australia, Asia, and Latin America; once the U.S. economy spiraled down in 1930, farmers were getting far less for their wheat, corn, or meat than it cost to produce.

Workers without jobs, farmers on slashed incomes—these people could no longer keep up on their interest payments for goods or mortgages and that in turn undermined America's rickety banking system. Such was the ingrained suspicion of the "money power" since the days of Andrew Jackson in the 1830s that there was no central bank—only the loose Federal Reserve system. Nor had local banks been consolidated as in Britain to become branches of a few nationwide giants. In America most banks were local, one-off operations—prevented by law from forming chains and allowed to keep only small reserves against their outgoings. So, if there was a run on a specific bank, it had scant defenses of its own and no one to bail it out.

At the end of 1930 the economic pressures became overwhelming: Banks started closing not only in small towns but even in big cities. During Hoover's presidency, 20 percent of America's banks closed their doors.[19] Millions of Americans lost most of their savings and parts of America almost literally ran out of money. Notes and coins were scarce because banks had closed; in any case, many people had no income so they resorted to barter. In Salt Lake City, for instance, barbers cut hair in return for onions or potatoes. In nearby Ogden, Utah, one local banker tried to keep going by sheer bluff. He told his staff, "If you want to keep this bank open, you must do your part. Go about your business as though nothing unusual was happening. Smile, be pleasant, talk about the weather, show no signs of panic. . . . Pay out in fives and singles, and count slowly."[20]

America's liquidity crisis had an impact worldwide as U.S. banks cut back on lending overseas. In the middle of 1931 there was a run on the Austrian and German banks that British finance alone could not staunch and in September Britain was forced off the gold standard. Congress insisted on repayment of war debts, despite the burden this imposed on Europe's already precarious balance of payments, and in 1930 it raised U.S. tariffs on foreign imports to new heights—shutting out foreign goods and raw materials from the vast American market and thereby deepening the world depression. Congress was taking a narrow view of U.S. interests rather than adopting countercyclical policies that might have helped international recovery. In the words of economic historian Charles Kindleberger, "The world economic system was unstable unless some country stabilized it, as Britain had done in the nineteenth century and up to 1913. In 1929, the British couldn't and the United States wouldn't. When every country turned to protect its national interest the world public interest went down the drain, and with it the private interests of all."[21]

And so the Depression deepened during 1931 and 1932. Millions of respectable citizens now found themselves jobless and homeless—because when they failed to keep up their mortgage payments the bank repossessed their houses. One reporter in Massachusetts noted this cross section of comment:

- [M]y husband can't find work—he's out every day looking—and I get afraid about him: he gets so black.
- If anyone had told us a year ago we'd come to this I'd have said he was a liar; and what can we do.
- It's a terrible thing when decent people have to beg.
- What's the use of looking for work any more; there isn't any. And look at the children. How would you feel if you saw your own kids like that: half naked and sick.
- We can't go crazy; we've got the kids to think about.
- I don't want to ask for nothing. I hate this charity. But we haven't got any shoes; do you think you could get us something to put on our feet?[22]

These were the voices not just of hardship but of hopelessness. The Depression became a psychological as well as economic crisis—almost a loss of faith in the American Dream. A "dreadful apathy, unsureness and discouragement seem to have fallen upon our life," wrote the critic Edmund Wilson in 1931. "What we have lost is, it may be, not merely our way in the economic labyrinth but our conviction of the value of what we are doing."[23]

Inevitably the president got the blame. According to a parody of the 23rd Psalm:

> Hoover is my shepherd, I am in want,
> He maketh me to lie down on park benches,
> He leadeth me by still factories,
> He restoreth my doubt in the
> Republican Party. . . .
> Yea, though I walk through the alley
> of soup kitchens,
> I am hungry. . . .
> Surely poverty and hard times will follow me
> All the days of the Republican administration.
> And I shall dwell in a rented house forever.[24]

Hoover was not completely bereft of ideas. Sharing the progressives' belief in a greater role for government in the economy, he persuaded Congress to allocate federal funds to underwrite the banks and finance work relief projects. But this was all too little, too late. The president was immortalized in the Hoovervilles, the shanty towns for the homeless that grew up around major cities. When a leader's name becomes a synonym for a slum, his political credibility has hit rock bottom with no hope of resurrection.

The most notorious Hooverville grew up on the very edge of America's capital. In the summer of 1932 unemployed veterans converged on Washington demanding that the government pay them now a bonus promised for 1945. Twenty thousand strong, the so-called Bonus Marchers lobbied Congress and settled in with their families in a shanty town on mudflats just across the Anacostia river. Some had small tents, but many lived in shacks made out of scrap lumber, packing boxes, and bits of tin. Sanitation was rudimentary and disease spread in the summer heat. So, too, did fears in official Washington. Although most of the men were genuine veterans, some had turned communist and agitators had infiltrated their ranks. When marchers clashed with police near Capitol Hill on July 28, 1932, Hoover had an excuse to send in the U.S. army. Cavalry with drawn sabers, infantry with fixed bayonets, and six tanks moved in—under the command of General Douglas MacArthur, the army chief of staff.

MacArthur's orders were simply to clear the city but the general and his gung-ho deputy, Major George Patton, marched on to the camp, giving the occupants an hour to leave. Then they set fire to the shacks, tossing tear-gas bombs at stragglers and even bayoneting one seven-year-old boy in the leg when he came back for his pet rabbit. Two veterans were shot and killed; two infants died from the gas. A defiant MacArthur told reporters, "That mob down there was a bad-looking mob. It was animated by the essence of revolution. . . . It is my opinion that had the President not acted today, he would have been faced with a grave situation which would have caused a real battle. Had he let it go on another week, I believe that the institutions of our government would have been very severely threatened."[25] But there was widespread outrage. "What a pitiful spectacle is that of the great American Government, mightiest in the world, chasing unarmed men, women and children with Army tanks," declared the Washington *News*. "If the Army must be called out to make war on unarmed citizens, this is no longer America."[26]

The brutal treatment of the Bonus Marchers was a typical example of Hoover's ineptitude at public relations and, at a deeper level, his inability—as an intensely private, highly organized technocrat—to empathize with the lives and passions of ordinary people. Journalist Walter Lippmann noted that Hoover had "the peculiarly modern, in fact the contemporary American, faith in the power of the human mind and will, acting through organization, to accomplish results." He was "a devotee of the religion of progress," and the acclaim that greeted the arrival of an "engineer" in the White House was a recognition that America at last had a president who "believed that politics could be conducted by the kind of intelligence which has produced such excellent motor cars, airplanes, and refrigerators." But, argued Lippmann, Hoover was "paralyzed by his own inexperience in the very special business of democracy. . . . He has never before been elected to any office. He has never

been a legislator, a mayor, a governor. . . . The political art deals with matters peculiar to politics, with a complex of material circumstances, of historic deposit, of
human passion, for which the problems of business or engineering as such do not
provide an analogy."[27]

By contrast, Hoover's Democratic opponent in the election of 1932—his former
admirer Franklin Roosevelt, now governor of New York—was a consummate
politician, but Lippmann believed he lacked the character and intellect to be president, calling him "a highly impressionable person, without a firm grasp of public affairs and without any very strong convictions. . . . He has been Governor for
three years, and I doubt whether anyone can point to a single act of his which involved any political risk. . . . For Franklin D. Roosevelt is no crusader. He is no
tribune of the people. He is no enemy of entrenched privilege. He is a pleasant
man who, without any important qualifications for the office, would very much
like to be President."[28]

On Hoover, Lippmann was shrewdly accurate. On Roosevelt he could not have
been more wrong.

NEW DEAL

Early 1933 was the nadir of America's Depression. In March at least a quarter of the
workforce was unemployed; so grave was the financial crisis that all but ten of the
forty-eight states had been forced to close their banks. The only country that
matched America's economic slump was Germany, where Adolf Hitler had been
appointed chancellor on January 30, 1933, and he exploited the crisis to establish
a brutal dictatorship. Five weeks later, on March 4, Roosevelt took the oath as president of the United States, promising a New Deal for the American people.

This was a very different inauguration from four years before, when Hoover discerned a future bright with hope. Now Roosevelt faced the worst economic crisis in
America's history. But his message, though grim, was resolute: "This great Nation
will endure as it has endured, will revive and will prosper. So, first of all, let me assert my firm belief that the only thing we have to fear is fear itself—nameless, un-
reasoning, unjustified terror which paralyzes needed efforts to convert retreat into
advance."[29]

That line about fear paralyzing action came from the heart. At the end of the
Great War, FDR, a distant cousin of Theodore Roosevelt, had been assistant secretary of the navy in the Wilson administration. In 1920 he was the Democratic candidate for the vice-presidency. But in 1921, at age thirty-nine, he was stricken by
polio and never recovered the use of his lower body. The waspish general "Vinegar"
Joe Stilwell called him "Rubberlegs"—a nickname that was mean but apt. After
years of exercising his torso, Roosevelt did manage to move again but only by leaning on somebody's arm and with heavy metal braces holding his legs rigid so that
he walked like a man on stilts. One journalist remembered how difficult it was for

FDR even to get up from a chair: "He was smiling as he talked. His face and hand muscles were totally relaxed. But then, when he had to stand up, his jaws went absolutely rigid. The effort of getting what was left of his body up was so great his face changed dramatically. It was as if he braced his body for a bullet."[30]

Remarkably, press and cameramen kept the truth under wraps so most Americans believed FDR was lame rather than crippled.[31] Yet in reality this was a wheelchair president, who needed help to dress and undress, even to go to the toilet. Each day could have been a succession of humiliations; instead Roosevelt managed to retain his ebullient good humor. Whatever the difficulties, he seemed calm and in control, commenting, "If you had spent two years in bed trying to wiggle your big toe, after that anything else would seem easy."[32] The long battle to rebuild his career deepened his empathy with human suffering.

So America's new president understood the power of confidence to vanquish fear and that became the watchword of his presidency. It was needed in his very first crisis: how to get the banking system going again. Using the dubious pretext of the wartime Trading with the Enemy Act, the president declared a three-day Bank Holiday during which Treasury officials worked around the clock to draw up a list of which banks could open for business again and which were so rickety that they should be shut down for good. To cover the expected dash for cash when the banks reopened, the Federal Reserve was authorized to issue additional notes. These emergency measures were passed by the House of Representatives in less than forty minutes, sight unseen—the Speaker read out the bill from the one available draft.[33]

The Banking Act was not radical and no one knew if it would reassure the public. But that was where Roosevelt came into his own as a leader. He started holding regular press conferences without written questions—just an informal exchange as reporters crowded around his desk, with some material labeled "off the record" or "background information." One pressman said afterward that in the first press conference "the new president gave the correspondents more sensational news than some of his predecessors had handed out in four years."[34]

Another notable innovation was the broadcasting of periodic "Fireside Chats," as they became known, beamed by radio directly into the living rooms of the American people. FDR was the first president of the radio age and no one used the new medium more effectively. His initial talk, less than a week into his presidency, reached an estimated audience of 60 million.[35] He dealt in simple language with the recent run on the banks and with the administration's plan for a phased reopening. He promised that "the phantom of fear will soon be laid" and ended with an assurance that "it is safer to keep your money in a reopened bank than under the mattress."[36]

When the banks reopened, to general amazement deposits far exceeded withdrawals. Roosevelt, the political artist, had pulled off the trick in a way Hoover, the dour technocrat, never could have. In legislation passed during a congressional session lasting from March 9 to June 16, 1933, which was dubbed the "Hundred Days,"

FDR went on to honor the Democrats' election pledge to end Prohibition and its sordid underworld of bootleg liquor and violent crime. Congress and the states quickly amended the Constitution and beer became legal again within a month of Roosevelt's inauguration. By April the national mood had turned upbeat and positive—testament that the Depression was in part a psychological malaise.

By summer Congress had addressed the fundamentals of the banking system, at the heart of the nation's crisis of confidence. The Glass-Steagall Act of June 1933 established a system of federal insurance for bank deposits, initially set at $2,500 per account but raised over the years. The Act also separated investment banks (engaged in the capital markets) from commercial banks (handling loans and deposits) because a blurring of the line, it was believed, had contributed to the Crash and Depression. This legal demarcation remained in place until 1999; its removal, as we shall see in Chapter 18, led in part to the financial crisis of 2008.

Federal deposit insurance proved extremely popular, and FDR was later happy to take the credit, but in 1933 he had been deeply skeptical about the idea. His economic instincts were in fact conservative: He hoped to balance the budget, avoid a big bureaucracy, and solve the nation's problems mainly by manipulating the currency. In reforming the banks, Roosevelt and the Congress failed to take the opportunity to create a system of branch banking of the sort that protected both neighboring Canada and Britain from an American-style banking crisis. And the new deposit insurance system helped keep in business many small banks that should have been rationalized. One of the president's biggest steps toward recovery in 1933 was not domestic at all. He took America off the gold standard, which effectively devalued the dollar and pushed up the price of grain, cotton, and other U.S. exports on the world market.

Yet Roosevelt, despite his conservative instincts, was no rigid ideologue. During the election campaign of 1932 he had declared, "The country needs and, unless I mistake its temper, the country demands bold, persistent experimentation. It is common sense to take a method and try it. If it fails, admit it frankly and try another. But above all, try something. The millions who are in want will not stand by silently forever while the things to satisfy their needs are within easy reach."[37] When the measures taken during the Hundred Days in 1933 did not cut unemployment and boost investment, FDR was pushed deeper into improvisation.

Yet the president, however important, was not the only player. Such had been the backlash against Hoover that the 1932 election also brought to Washington an overwhelmingly Democratic Congress for the first time in nearly two decades. Although the party's southern leadership was conservative, many Democrats from the West and the northern cities wanted to force the pace of reform. In the country at large there were demagogues preaching overt class warfare—most notoriously Senator Huey Long of Louisiana, who, despite his clownish manner, had a stranglehold on his home state. Long's "Share Our Wealth" campaign—promising to soak the rich and give every family enough to buy a home, a car, and a radio—captured the imagination of millions. In the utopian chorus of his campaign song:

> *Ev'ry man a king, ev'ry man a king,*
> *For you can be a millionaire. . . .*
> *There'll be peace without end*
> *Ev'ry neighbor a friend,*
> *With ev'ry man a king.*[38]

So in 1935 the president shifted leftward to reflect the mounting pressures in Congress and the country. Instead of doling out money to the unemployed, the federal government embarked on a massive program of work relief, headed by the Works Progress Administration, which by the end of 1938 had signed up 5 million people, an eighth of the workforce. Most were employed on construction projects— roads, hospitals, and airports—but many professionals were paid to overhaul public libraries, teach in schools, or run theater programs. Critics said that the initials WPA meant "We Piddle Around," claiming that the agency was a sewer of political patronage, but in the 1980s President Ronald Reagan—a trenchant critic of big government—had different memories of the New Deal from his youth in rural Illinois: "Now a lot of people remember it as boondoggles and . . . raking leaves. Maybe in some places it was. Maybe in the city machines or something. But I can take you to our town and show you things, like a river front that I used to hike through once that was swamp and is now a beautiful park-like place built by WPA."[39]

In 1935 Congress also started to create a welfare state. The United States— thanks to its federal system and libertarian tradition—had lagged far behind European countries such as Germany, Sweden, and Britain in government support for the needy. But the Social Security Act of 1935 established unemployment compensation and old-age pensions for the whole nation—a major innovation. Yet these schemes were to be financed not by the federal government but by contributions from employers and employees, extracted as payroll taxes. The taxes reduced purchasing power at a time when the economy was crying out for consumer spending; what is more, many of the neediest were excluded from pensions, notably domestic servants and farm laborers. These two groups were largely female or black.

Even Roosevelt's controlled version of social security was a very sensitive issue, however. To quote one southern newspaper, "The average Mississippian can't imagine himself chipping in to pay pensions for able-bodied Negroes to sit around in idleness on front galleries, supporting all their kinsfolk on pensions, while cotton and corn crops are crying out for workers to get them out of the grass." Many Americans felt that the whole principle of social security breached the traditional American belief in self-help. "It would take all the romance out of life," protested

Senator Harry Moore of New Jersey. "We might as well take a child from the nursery, give him a nurse, and protect him from every experience that life affords."[40]

This kind of opposition explains why FDR was sure the program had to be based on employee contributions: "[T]hose taxes were never a problem of economics. They are politics all the way through. We put those payroll contributions there so as to give the contributors a legal, moral, and political right to collect their pensions and their unemployment benefits. With those taxes in there, no damn politician can ever scrap my social security program."[41] He was right: Social security has remained largely off-limits for even the most vehement Republican critics of welfare.

Despite its deficiencies, the New Deal represented a marked break in American attitudes toward poverty. During the 1930s over a third of the population received public aid or social insurance at one time or other. Public funds for such programs scarcely existed in 1929; ten years later they accounted for more than a quarter of all government spending. Although the figures were cut back in the 1940s, both the programs and the constituencies for them endured.[42]

Another major piece of legislation in 1935 was the National Labor Relations Act. For the first time this threw the weight of the federal government firmly behind the right of American workers to organize unions and engage in collective bargaining. Roosevelt was not personally keen but eventually gave the bill his support to head off radical pressures. The Act's sponsor was Senator Robert Wagner, son of a German immigrant who had started out as a janitor in the tenements of New York. Wagner worked his way up the Tammany Hall political machine—among other things crafting the health and safety reforms that followed the notorious Triangle factory fire of 1911—and became a long-serving member of the U.S. Senate, where his potent mixture of diligence and charm earned him immense success as a lawmaker. "Whether you like his laws or deplore them," one journalist wrote, "he has placed on the books legislation more important and far-reaching than any American in history, since the days of the Founding Fathers."[43] That was only a touch hyperbolic because Wagner was largely responsible for the 1935 Social Security and Labor Relations laws, the latter being generally known as the Wagner Act.

The president himself was passionate about setting up the Rural Electrification Administration (REA). Behind this prosaic title lies one of the most fundamental transformations of American life because, when Roosevelt entered the White House, only one farm in ten had electricity. This not only ruled out a fridge, an iron, or a vacuum cleaner—highlights of the 1920s boom in consumer durables—but also meant that farm families spent an average of ten hours each week pumping and carrying water by hand. The problem was that the big utility companies could not see any profit in running miles of cable to isolated farmsteads. So, when the market failed to deliver, Uncle Sam stepped in by making low-interest loans to local nonprofit cooperatives. The program was democratic, cost-effective, and life-changing: The REA motto was, "If you put a light on every farm, you put a light in every heart." By 1939 a quarter of farm families had electricity, by 1950 nearly all.[44]

The New Deal addressed the challenge of generating as well as distributing electricity. The Tennessee Valley Authority (TVA), established with Roosevelt's enthusiastic backing in 1933, challenged the stranglehold of privately owned power companies. Covering much of Tennessee and also reaching into neighboring states, the TVA was not only a provider of electricity but also a regional planning agency—eradicating malaria, improving crop yields, and building model towns in one of the poorest parts of the country. Constructing its network of dams also provided work for thousands of those previously unemployed.

The TVA proved a one-off; plans to create similar regional authorities under federal aegis, "little TVAs," in other parts of the country fell foul of business and states' rights opposition. But in the Far West the New Deal spent millions on more hydroelectric projects: the Boulder Dam on the Colorado river in Nevada, Fort Peck Dam on the Missouri river in Montana, and, most famous of all, the mile-long, 550-foot-high Grand Coulee Dam on the Columbia river in Washington state. Boulder was planned by Hoover—and today bears his name—but it and the other dams were constructed in the Roosevelt years, mostly by the army's Corps of Engineers and the New Deal's Public Works Administration. These vast projects had two primary objectives—providing water and generating electricity—but there were also huge economic spin-offs. The need, for instance, to house and entertain thousands of workers building the Boulder Dam turned a small mining and railroad town into the modern city of Las Vegas.

FDR's critics damned all this federal spending as revolutionary socialism compared with America's free-market past, but one Democratic senator retorted:

> Don't let anyone tell you that government bounties were not being given in those days. The difference was that the real pioneers who grubbed and slaved and really developed the country got none of them. The railroads got their sections in each township. . . . Vast tracts of timber were available for . . . the timber operators. . . . A protective tariff by which hidden taxes were removed from the pockets of everyone who labored in industry and agriculture [was established]. . . . There were bounties galore. But the people who worked and who bought and consumed our products never got in on them.[45]

Now, in a piecemeal way, the Democrats and the New Deal were reallocating federal largesse to those groups who had missed out before in U.S. history—small farmers, urban workers, and ethnic minorities.

During his first term, Roosevelt's New Deal programs consolidated the new Democratic coalition prefigured in Al Smith's campaign of 1928, drawing the urban

North in with the rural South. By the 1936 election even America's blacks—traditional Republican voters dating back to the days of Lincoln the "Great Emancipator"—were coming on board. Although New Deal agricultural policies, the aim of which was to raise prices by taking inefficient land out of production, had hit hardest the black tenant farmers of the South, millions of blacks, especially in the northern cities, benefited from New Deal welfare programs run with a sense of racial justice by administrators such as Harold Ickes and Harry Hopkins. And although the president was personally cautious on racial issues—commenting that "if I antagonize the Southerners who dominate Congressional committees through seniority, I'd never get any bills passed"[46]—he did create an informal "Black Cabinet" that at least made good public relations. His wife, Eleanor, publicly championed black causes through her newspaper columns and privately prodded FDR and his cabinet about institutional discrimination. Eleanor was carving out a role very different from the traditional first lady's, not least by indefatigably travelling all over the country as the crippled president's "eyes and ears." In June 1935 the Washington *Star* ran a headline on its society page: "MRS. ROOSEVELT SPENDS NIGHT AT WHITE HOUSE."[47]

In November 1936 Roosevelt was reelected by a landslide, winning all but two states. The "New Deal coalition" he had put together would remain the basis of Democratic dominance in Congress for more than thirty years.

"FOR THE SURVIVAL OF DEMOCRACY"

By the time Roosevelt began his second term in January 1937, the political battle lines were sharply drawn.* His supporters viewed the New Deal as the country's salvation; for opponents it was a socialist-style threat to basic American liberties. Roosevelt also saw this fight in a global context at a time when Mussolini and Hitler were on the march in Europe, telling an election rally in 1936 that "here in America we are waging a great and successful war. It is not alone a war against want and destitution and economic demoralization. It is more than that; it is a war for the survival of democracy. We are fighting to save a great and precious form of government for ourselves and for the world."[48] His second term would become a war on both fronts.

In 1937 the president decided to take on one of the country's most revered institutions, the Supreme Court, which, two years before, had moved out of the Senate building into a new classically designed temple of justice built in white marble. This physical declaration of independence from the other two branches of the federal

---

* In 1937 the date of the inauguration was changed from March 4 to January 20 to avoid any repeat of the debilitating four-month power vacuum that had occurred during the banking crisis of 1932–1933 (and the secession crisis of 1860–1861).

government was encapsulated in the legend above the east entrance: "Justice the Guardian of Liberty." Since the 1800s, as we have seen, the Court had asserted a right of judicial review—using its verdicts on specific cases to adjudicate whether the actions of the executive and the legislature were constitutional. All but two of the nine members of the Supreme Court in 1933 had been appointed by Republican presidents and they were generally hostile to the expansion of federal power during FDR's first term, in 1935–1936 unanimously striking down as unconstitutional the centerpieces of the early New Deal—the National Industrial Recovery Act and the Agricultural Adjustment Act. New Dealers feared it was only a matter of time before social security and the Wagner Act went the same way. Once appointed, Supreme Court justices served for life or until they chose to retire and Roosevelt's leading opponents on the Court seemed determined to slug it out to the bitter end. James McReynolds—actually a Wilson appointee—reportedly exclaimed, "I'll never resign as long as that crippled son-of-a-bitch is in the White House."[49]

FDR considered trying to amend the Constitution but that would have been too time-consuming and uncertain, so he took up an idea that had been around for a while and proposed that if justices did not retire at seventy the president could appoint additional members of the Court. "Modern complexities," said Roosevelt, "call for a constant infusion of new blood in the courts, just as it is needed in executive functions of the Government and in private business."[50] The president presented his Court packing plan to Congress as an efficiency measure, but few were fooled about its essentially political purpose. His own party leaders in Congress thought it unwise and many commentators were appalled. William Allen White, the celebrated sage of Kansas, warned that if, in time, America had "a reactionary president, as charming, as eloquent and as irresistible as Roosevelt, with a power to change the court," then "we should be in the devil's own fix if he decided to abridge the bill of rights by legislation which he could easily call emergency legislation."[51]

In fact, key members of the Court were starting to modify their opinions in deference to FDR's landslide election victory. In the spring of 1937 a majority of the justices upheld his collective bargaining, unemployment insurance, and old-age pension legislation. Chief Justice Charles Evans Hughes, delivering judgment against opponents of the Wagner Act, said they were asking him and his fellow justices to "shut our eyes to the plainest facts of our national life" and to deal with legal issues in "an intellectual vacuum."[52] In other words, the Court was starting to interpret an eighteenth-century Constitution in the light of twentieth-century attitudes—a process that will be central to the chapters that follow.

So Roosevelt had achieved what he wanted and he should have pulled back gracefully in the spring of 1937, but his blood was up and he stubbornly persisted with his plan into the summer before acknowledging defeat. For a skillful political leader, Court packing was a bizarre error of judgment and also immensely damaging because it played into the hands of those who accused him of being hell-bent to undermine the Constitution.

In 1937 the president's labor reforms also alarmed conservatives. Exploiting the provisions of the Wagner Act, union leaders mounted a massive drive to organize workers in the manufacturing industry—still largely untouched by unionization (another big contrast between the United States and western Europe). In key industries such as steel, textiles, rubber, and automobiles, they made enormous strides, so that total union membership tripled to nearly 9 million between 1933 and 1939.[53] It wasn't just this surge in numbers that alarmed conservatives but also the means used—sit-down strikes in some of America's largest factories that forced industrial giants like General Motors and U.S. Steel to accept unions and collective bargaining. Genora Johnson was a union organizer in GM's grim company town of Flint, Michigan. After the successful United Auto Workers strike, she recalled, "these men were not afraid of the boss anymore. They got a raise in their wages, and they weren't always followed to the can where somebody would step in to check how many cigarette butts were in the toilet. They became human beings to a degree."[54]

The Court-packing plan and the sit-down strikes convinced many Americans that Roosevelt was dangerously radical. Then in the autumn of 1937 the bottom dropped out of the economy, with a surprise recession that pushed unemployment back up to nearly 20 percent. The administration, believing that the Depression was ending and that the main danger was now inflation, had cut back too quickly on spending and credit—in other words it had not been radical enough—but most Americans were less concerned with cause than effect. FDR and the Democrats had prospered all through the 1930s by blaming the Depression on the Republicans, but that line did not work in what became known as the "Roosevelt Recession" of 1937–1938. Not surprisingly the Republicans made big gains in the November 1938 congressional elections. Allying with conservative Democrats now alienated from Roosevelt, they effectively brought the New Deal to an end. In January 1940, with just a year left of his second term, Roosevelt signed a contract to write fortnightly articles for *Collier's* magazine after he left the White House. The salary was to be $75,000; *Collier's* would have gone higher but FDR felt it would not be proper to earn more as a columnist than he did as president.[55]

Had Roosevelt served only two terms, to January 1941, he would have been regarded as a president who started well but then lost his way. What changed everything were events not in America but in Europe.

Back in 1936 FDR had spoken, rather like Wilson in 1917, of waging a global war for the survival of democracy, but during his first term most Americans were preoccupied by the Depression at home. There was also widespread disenchantment at the failure of the Great War to bring European peace. "Of the hell broth that is brewing in Europe we have no need to drink," wrote Ernest Hemingway. "We were fools to be sucked in once in a European war, and we should never be sucked in again."[56] With Wall Street and big business already scapegoated for the Depression, attention now turned to their role in foreign policy. The 1934–1936 Senate inquiry into the munitions industry encouraged the belief that bankers and arms manufacturers (the so-called merchants of death) had inveigled America into the war for their own financial gain.

Lobbied energetically by various peace groups, Congress passed a series of Neutrality Acts in 1935–1937. These banned Americans in any future war from selling arms or making loans to belligerent countries; U.S. citizens would also be prohibited from travelling on belligerent passenger vessels. All this was an attempt to prevent the economic and emotional entanglements that, it was believed, had dragged the United States into the Great War. America's commercial and financial reach that in the mid-1920s seemed a mark of international power was now viewed as a source of vulnerability. So the Neutrality Acts were a sign of how nervous and introverted Depression America had become—a far cry from Wilson's determination to impose himself on the world in 1917. The mid-1930s marked the apogee of American isolationism.

During that period the president shared the national mood and went along with the Neutrality Acts, insisting, "If we face the choice of profits or peace, the Nation will answer—must answer—'We choose peace.'"[57] Although he detested Nazism, the president believed that the primary responsibility for dealing with Hitler lay with France and Britain, but the Munich agreement of September 1938 dramatized their reluctance to act resolutely. "What the British need today is a good, stiff grog," Roosevelt wrote, "inducing the desire not only to save civilization but the continued belief that they can do it. In such an event they will have a lot more support from their American cousins."[58]

In January 1939 the president told senators that America could no longer feel safe behind the Atlantic and Pacific oceans, as it had in the era of sea power. In the looming age of air power the country's first line of defense lay far away in western Europe and the Pacific islands. He also warned publicly, "We have learned that God-fearing democracies of the world which observe the sanctity of treaties and good faith in their dealings with other nations cannot safely be indifferent to international lawlessness anywhere. They cannot forever let pass, without effective protest, acts of aggression against sister nations—acts which automatically undermine all of us."[59] Here in embryo was a new foreign policy that challenged the hallowed tradition of nonentanglement in the affairs of Europe: Roosevelt was saying that, on grounds of both security and ideology, the country could not ignore events thousands of miles away.

When Britain and France finally did draw a line over Poland and war broke out in Europe in September 1939, FDR promptly proclaimed U.S. neutrality. But he did not ask Americans to remain impartial as President Wilson had in 1914: "This nation will remain a neutral nation, but I cannot ask that every American remain neutral in thought as well. Even a neutral has a right to take account of facts. Even a neutral cannot be asked to close his mind or his conscience."[60]

After a hard fight, Roosevelt persuaded Congress to amend the Neutrality Acts onto what was called a "cash-and-carry" basis. This meant that Americans could now trade with belligerent countries provided that no credits were offered and no U.S. vessels were involved. The president's aim was to provide covert aid to Britain, which, unlike Germany and Japan, had the foreign exchange and the merchant shipping to import American goods, yet he continued to talk the language of peace and noninvolvement. Arthur Vandenberg, a leading Senate Republican, was unhappy, writing in his diary, "I hate Hitler and Nazism and Communism as completely as any person living. But I decline to embrace the opportunist idea—so convenient and so popular at the moment—that *we* can stop these things in *Europe* without entering the conflict with everything at our command, including men and money. There is no middle ground. We are either *all the way in* or *all the way out*."[61] Vandenberg's comment would prove shrewd, but in 1939 Roosevelt still hoped that Britain and France, with some American economic muscle behind them, would fulfill their roles as defenders of America's front line.

This hope went up in smoke with the Nazi blitzkrieg of May 1940. In four weeks Hitler, the ex-corporal, did what the Kaiser's best generals had failed to do in four years of war, forcing France to surrender. Germany now dominated most of Europe and Roosevelt faced really tough decisions in diplomacy and in politics. Would he commit America to supporting Britain, apparently on the edge of invasion? And would he use the crisis to justify running again for the presidency?

On aid to Britain, Roosevelt moved cautiously. The new prime minister, Winston Churchill, was an improvement over Neville Chamberlain, who had appeased Hitler and signed the Munich agreement surrendering Czechoslovakia. But New Dealers viewed Churchill as a reactionary old stager with a dubious reputation, Roosevelt saying privately that he "supposed Churchill was the best man that England had, even if he was drunk half of his time." In any case, Britain had its back to the wall after the fall of France: In early July FDR privately rated British chances of survival at one in three.[62]

Churchill was pressing for fifty old U.S. destroyers to help protect his country's vital supply lines and, after weeks of debate, Roosevelt decided this was worth the risk. But he avoided going to Congress—instead signing an executive agreement on his authority as commander-in-chief—and he gave the destroyers in return for the right to build U.S. bases on eight British possessions in the western Atlantic from Newfoundland to Trinidad. That way he could present the transaction not as an unneutral gift but as a hardheaded deal benefiting the United States—"an epochal and far-reaching act of preparation for continental defense in the face of grave danger."[63]

Roosevelt got away with the Destroyers Deal but no rhetoric flourish could conceal his frontal assault on the practice of no third term, which had been established by America's founding president, George Washington. All through 1939 and 1940 Roosevelt refused to rule out running again—otherwise he would become a complete lame duck—but it was not until the crisis caused by the fall of France that he had a credible reason for seeking a third term. Even then he told the Democratic convention he had no desire to be a candidate, whereupon his aides whipped up the delegates with chants of "We Want Roosevelt." This seedy charade of presidential reluctance gave more ammunition to those who claimed that FDR was not a tribune of democracy but a budding dictator.

Roosevelt was, however, both honest and bold in his decision to endorse the Selective Service Act in September 1940. As with the Destroyers Deal, the initiative came from pressure groups, but FDR could have deflected demands until after the election. This was the first time that America had imposed conscription in peacetime and critics damned it as a bellicose act and even a social revolution. Senator Burton Wheeler of Montana called draft "the greatest step toward regimentation and militarism" that Congress had ever undertaken and warned it would "slit the throat of the last Democracy still living." But Congress approved the legislation by two-to-one majorities, though with the proviso that no troops would serve outside the western hemisphere unless on U.S. territory. Roosevelt carefully avoided the words "draft" and "conscription"—calling it instead "a muster," which evoked memories of Lexington and Concord—and he drew the first numbers for the draft lottery on October 29, just a week before the election.[64]

The campaign had started quietly; Wendell Willkie, the Republican candidate, was a former Democrat who also supported aid to Britain. But as he sagged in the opinion polls, Willkie took off the gloves and attacked Roosevelt at his most vulnerable point for many Americans—on the question of whether, after all FDR's twists and turns, he could be trusted. "I have given you my pledge many times over: I will work for peace," thundered Willkie. "On the basis of his past performances with pledges to the people, if you re-elect him you may expect war in April 1941."[65] (This was an attempt to impute guilt by association: Woodrow Wilson had campaigned on "Peace and Prosperity" in November 1916 and then taken the country into war the following April.) Messages flooding into the White House showed that Willkie had touched a raw nerve, so in his final campaign speech in Boston FDR declared, "And while I am talking to you mothers and fathers, I give you one more assurance. I have said this before, but I shall say it again and again and again: Your boys are not going to be sent into any foreign wars. They are going into training to form a force so strong that, by its very existence, it will keep the threat of war far away from our shores."[66]

In November 1940 Roosevelt won the election by almost as big a margin as in 1936, carrying all but ten of the forty-eight states. This victory gave him more freedom of maneuver to help Britain fight on as America's front line against Hitler, but his pledge of no foreign wars would tie his hands in the months to come.

FLOUNDERING INTO WAR

In his State of the Union message in January 1941 the president set out a remarkable vision of the postwar world centered on what he called "four essential human freedoms":

- Freedom of speech
- Freedom of worship
- Freedom from want
- Freedom from fear

This, he insisted, was "no vision of a distant millennium" but "a definite basis for a kind of world attainable in our own time and generation."[67]

The United States was still a neutral nation and the war was far from finished, so the president was really sticking his neck out in what became known as the Four Freedoms speech. But, as he had said back in 1936, Roosevelt saw the issues at stake in the war as a continuation of New Deal battles and, like Wilson in 1917–1918, he was determined to impose an American peace on a warring world.

First, however, Hitler and Nazism had to be overthrown, and this seemed a remote possibility at the turn of 1940–1941. The British government was running out of gold and foreign exchange to purchase munitions from the United States. Yet it was politically impossible for Roosevelt to offer anything as a free gift and he did not want to repeat the tangle of debts that had ensnared Anglo-American relations after the Great War. So, in a press conference just before Christmas 1940 he came up with the idea of lending Britain the supplies and munitions it needed. "Suppose my neighbor's home catches fire, and I have a length of garden hose four or five hundred feet away. If he can take my garden hose and connect it up with his hydrant, I may help him to put out his fire." In such an emergency, Roosevelt went on, there was no point in haggling about payment before handing over the hose. You just lend the hose on the expectation of getting it back afterward. If it got damaged, the neighbor would simply replace it with a new one.[68]

Lending the garden hose was an inspired homely analogy—Roosevelt at his most effective as a leader—but his Lend-Lease bill still had an uphill fight in Congress. The main opposition group was America First—a grassroots lobbying organization that at its peak had over 800,000 members in 450 local chapters.[69] These critics of Lend-Lease claimed that Roosevelt was being disingenuous in talking of aid to Britain short of war. According to Senator Robert Taft of Ohio, the bill gave the president "power to carry on a kind of undeclared war all over the world, in which America would do everything except actually put soldiers in the front-line trenches where the fighting is." Taft did not see "how we can long conduct such a war without actually being in the shooting end of the war as well as in the service-of-supply end which this bill justifies."[70]

Many supporters of America First were not literally "isolationists"; they recognized that Nazism posed a potential threat but believed, unlike FDR, that the United States could and should concentrate on defending North and South America. "We are strong enough in this Nation and in this hemisphere to maintain our own way of life regardless of what the attitude is on the other sides," argued the aviator Charles Lindbergh, a leading America First spokesman. "I do not believe we are strong enough to impose our way of life on Europe and on Asia. Therefore, my belief is that the only success for our way of life and our system of government is to defend it here at home and not attempt to enter a war abroad."[71]

In mid-March 1941, after two months of debate, Congress passed the Lend-Lease Act on largely partisan lines with most Democrats in favor and most Republicans against. It also voted an initial appropriation of $7 billion; included on the first list of goods to be transferred to Britain was, appropriately, nearly a million feet of fire hose. During the whole war Lend-Lease would cover over half Britain's balance of payments deficit. Winston Churchill called it "the most unsordid act in the history of any nation," but Roosevelt continued to present his foreign policy as a matter of prudent self-interest, and deliberately labeled Lend-Lease "An Act to Promote the Defense of the United States."[72]

Even members of Roosevelt's own cabinet wished he would be more candid with the American people but, as speechwriter Robert Sherwood observed, "the tragedy of Wilson was always somewhere within the rim of his consciousness"[73]—meaning that FDR could never forget what happened to a president who got too far ahead of Congress and public opinion. For the rest of 1941 he was content to proceed slowly and stealthily, incrementally extending U.S. naval patrols in the Atlantic to protect the aid that was being sent to Britain. He did this in his capacity as commander-in-chief rather than risk another bruising fight on Capitol Hill. The pressure on Britain eased a little in June when Hitler invaded Russia but, given the speed of the Nazi advance toward Moscow, no one knew if this was more than a temporary respite.

Roosevelt and Churchill met off Newfoundland in August 1941. Afterward the prime minister told his cabinet that Roosevelt had said, "If he were to put the issue of peace and war to Congress, they would debate it for three months. The president had said he would wage war, but not declare it, and that he would become more and more provocative. If the Germans did not like it, they could attack American forces."[74] During the autumn of 1941 there were several incidents between German U-boats and U.S. vessels and it seemed that the United States was sliding into the "undeclared war" that Senator Taft had predicted. But in fact the catalyst came not in the Atlantic but the Pacific.

Since 1937 the Japanese had been waging a brutal war in China but, despite substantial gains, they could not land the killer blow. Then in the summer of 1941,
with Britain at bay and the Russians now fighting for their lives against Hitler, they
seized the opportunity to expand into Southeast Asia. Conscious that only the
United States remained as a significant Pacific power, Roosevelt sent heavy bombers
to the Philippines and kept the main U.S. fleet at Pearl Harbor in the Hawaiian
Islands—2,000 miles from its usual base at San Diego—hoping that these actions
would deter the Japanese. In fact, they had the opposite effect: Taking the Philippines and destroying Pearl Harbor now became the first steps in Japan's bid for domination of the Pacific. The United States had not developed an Asian empire to the
same degree as the British, the French, or the Dutch, but the islands acquired during that imperialist spasm in the 1890s—the Philippines and Hawaii—now became
hostages to fortune.

The 7th of December 1941 was a normal Sunday afternoon across America.
People were reading the football scores, dozing on the porch, going out for a walk,
or perhaps listening to the New York Philharmonic's Sunday concert. As British
journalist Alistair Cooke recalled, "The Philharmonic was tuning up for the
Shostakovich First Symphony when a flash was handed to a bewildered announcer.
He read it, and at twenty-six minutes after two, a lot of people were left sitting in
their homes . . . fuzzily wondering where Pearl Harbor was."[75]

The attack had come out of the blue. The administration knew that the Japanese were preparing for war against Britain and America but expected the assault to
come in Southeast Asia—against Malaya and the Philippines. At Pearl Harbor the
main concern was not air raids but sabotage by local Japanese. Undetected, a Japanese carrier task force had made its way across a vast expanse of the western Pacific
before launching two devastating waves of dive bombers and torpedo planes
against the unsuspecting U.S. base. Ed Sheehan, an iron-fitter from Massachusetts,
never forgot the sight: "It was like looking into Hell on a sunshiny day. Each of the
great battleships . . . was in agony. Only the cage-top sections of the masts on the
West Virginia and *Tennessee* were visible through the roiling filth. The *California*
looked half-sunk, listing on one side in snapping fires. The *Arizona* . . . tilted at a
crazy angle amid oily clouds rising like thick black cauliflowers."[76]

In a couple of hours 2,400 Americans were dead and eight battleships had been
sunk or badly damaged. Fortuitously the aircraft carriers were out at sea. If they
had been at anchor or if the planes had destroyed Pearl Harbor's massive fuel depot,
then the U.S. navy would probably have been forced to retire to California, leaving
Japan as master of the Pacific. Instead, though crippled, the fleet lived to fight another day.

Roosevelt drove to Capitol Hill to address Congress. As senators and representatives rose to their feet, Alistair Cooke watched the disabled president move down
the aisle. "With infinite slowness, limping from side to side, Roosevelt came up the

ramp to the dais, one arm locked in his son's, the other hand feeling every inch of the long sloping rail." Suddenly the atmosphere in the great chamber turned somber, "touched with something very like humility." Cooke had seen this mood swing before when the president spoke at university commencements or party conventions, but on this particular morning "the tabloid cliché that he was a symbol of his country was a visible fact." Once at the dais, said Cooke, Roosevelt "expanded again" into his familiar newsreel image—"the big-headed man, the enormous shoulders, the tolerant paternal smile, the confident hands grasping the lectern, the uninhibited laugh or grimace." But for a moment "we had seen him as the hurt psyche of the nation . . . we saw him walk and thought of the wounded battleships slumped over in Pearl Harbor."[77]

Grimly the president told Congress, "Yesterday, December 7, 1941—a date which will live in infamy—the United States of America was suddenly and deliberately attacked by naval and air forces of the Empire of Japan."[78] There was only one dissenter from a formal declaration of war—Jeanette Rankin, the veteran pacifist from Montana, who had also voted against war in 1917. Three days later Hitler declared war on the United States, probably calculating that hostilities were coming anyway, given the ongoing skirmishes in the Atlantic, and confident in his warped mind that America's mongrel people and crippled president would not be formidable foes.

Hitler's declaration of war was the only silver lining for Roosevelt; otherwise he would have faced all-out war against Japan when he was sure that Germany was the real enemy. But Pearl Harbor was a massive disaster; the intelligence failure and the disorganized defenses even led some Roosevelt-haters to suspect that he had let the attack happen to get America into war by the back door. In fact, the evidence points not to conspiracy but to muddle, symptomatic of the general chaos in the winter of 1941–1942 as America floundered into war.[79]

In the days after the shock of Pearl Harbor there were air-raid panics up and down America's west coast. All of them, we now know, amounted to nothing even though General John DeWitt, the local army commander, told San Franciscans, "Death and destruction are likely to come to this city any moment. These planes were over our community for a definite period. They were enemy planes. I mean Japanese planes. They were tracked out to sea. Why bombs were not dropped I do not know. It might have been better if some bombs had been dropped to awaken this city."[80]

This fevered atmosphere fed suspicions that Americans of Japanese descent constituted a fifth column, plotting sabotage or even conniving at invasion. After talking with DeWitt the pundit Walter Lippmann, normally a staunch supporter of civil liberties, warned breathlessly in his newspaper column that "the Pacific Coast is in imminent danger of a combined attack from within and without. . . . It is a fact that the Japanese navy has been reconnoitering the coast more or less continuously. . . .

The Pacific Coast is officially a combat zone. Some part of it may at any moment be a battlefield. And nobody ought to be on a battlefield who has no good reason for being there."[81]

Roosevelt and the War Department took a similar view. On February 19, 1942, the president signed an executive order highlighting the dangers of sabotage and authorizing the creation of "military areas" from which "any or all persons may be excluded." Over the next few months nearly 120,000 Japanese-Americans were moved from their homes on the west coast to prison camps in Arizona, Utah, and other remote parts of the interior. Ironically in Hawaii, where nearly a third of the population was of Japanese ancestry and the war danger was much greater, fewer than 2,000 were interned. Conditions in the U.S. camps were rudimentary. One Japanese-American woman wrote, "The toilets are one big row of seats, that is, one straight board with holes about a foot apart with no partitions at all and all the toilets flush together . . . about every five minutes. The younger girls couldn't go to them at first until they couldn't stand it any longer, which is bad for them."[82]

The executive order was never used against those of German or Italian descent, only Japanese-Americans, and this reflected a deeper history of racial discrimination. The 1924 Immigration Act had virtually stopped immigration from Asia, although children of Japanese immigrants—the Nisei—automatically became U.S. citizens if born in America. But this was no defense against the war panic: Nearly two-thirds of the Japanese-Americans who were interned in 1942 were American citizens. Supreme Court justice Frank Murphy went as far as to say, "Today is the first time, so far as I am aware, that we have sustained a substantial restriction of the personal liberty of citizens of the United States based on the accident of race or ancestry. . . . It bears a melancholy resemblance to the treatment accorded to members of the Jewish race in Germany and other parts of Europe."[83]

On the east coast, the big danger was not panic but complacency. It took months for the U.S. navy to institute a proper system of convoys and escorts for vessels travelling along the coast; seaboard towns and cities were equally slow to impose a blackout, so German U-boats had no difficulty picking off conveniently silhouetted targets, many of them vital oil tankers. They sank 3 million tons of Allied shipping in the first seven months of 1942. "Losses by submarines off our Atlantic coast and in the Caribbean now threaten our entire war effort," warned General George Marshall, the army chief of staff. "I am fearful that another month or two of this will so cripple our means of transport that we will be unable to bring sufficient men and planes to bear against the enemy in critical theatres to exercise a determining influence on the war."[84]

America's economy was also ill prepared for war. It took months to impose a proper system of rationing to ensure that iron, steel, rubber, and other vital materials were used for the war effort rather than to make consumer goods. Despite the rearmament drive generated by Lend-Lease, nearly a million more cars rolled out of Detroit in 1941 than in 1939. The government decided that industry had to be paid to cooperate. "If you are going to try to go to war, or to prepare for war, in a capitalist country," said Secretary of War Henry Stimson, "you have got to let business make money out of the process or business won't work."[85] In an ironic reversal of the New Deal era, big business was now the government's favored partner. Of the $240 billion of government war contracts, two-thirds went to just 100 corporations; the top 10 companies received nearly one-third.[86]

At the grassroots, too, Uncle Sam was throwing money at every problem. Alistair Cooke recorded this conversation in rural Georgia:

> "These few acres of yours are going to be mighty useful to the government," says an agent to the poor Negro.
>
> "Mr McDowell," the Negro replies, his thumbs locked in his suspenders, "the go'ment can have 'em. This ain't nothin' but bad old cotton land." He is informed that the government will give him a loan if he'll put his land into peanuts.
>
> "Peanuts!" he howls. "The go'ment must sho' nuff be in te'ble shape."
>
> "Yes, we want peanuts for the fats and oils. And we need eggs, millions of 'em, to dry for the Army, and to send overseas. Can you raise some hens here, you think?"
>
> The Negro looks aghast. "Mr McDowell, ef the go'ment wanna pay me for raisin' elephants, ah'll sho' make a powerful try!"[87]

In the Pacific, the war went disastrously for the first half of 1942. The Japanese attack on Pearl Harbor was the prelude to a series of dramatic campaigns that drove the Americans from the Philippines, the British from Malaya and Burma, and the Dutch from the East Indies. In the spring it looked as if India and Australia might also succumb. But the American aircraft carriers that survived Pearl Harbor became the nucleus of a new fleet fighting a new kind of seaborne air warfare that made the battleship era obsolete. In June 1942, alerted by U.S. intelligence, their dive bombers surprised the Japanese carriers near the island of Midway. The Japanese lost four carriers and—equally important—many of their crack pilots, veterans of Pearl Harbor.

Midway marked the limit of Japan's advance across the Pacific; it also showed that, despite being thrown into war, the United States was no longer floundering. When Winston Churchill heard the news of Pearl Harbor he recalled a comment made to him a few years before the Great War that the United States was like "a gigantic boiler. Once the fire is lighted under it there is no limit to the power it can generate."[88] By the summer of 1942 the fire was well and truly lit.

"A HELL OF A WAR"

During World War II, Europe was occupied, Russia invaded, and Britain was bombed but, despite the panics of early 1942, the nearest that the war got to the continental United States were some submarine shells and a few incendiary bombs along the west coast. For those who fought, this war—like all others—was hell, but most Americans never experienced it at firsthand and for millions on the booming home front, World War II proved "a hell of a war."[89]

The conflict finally pulled the country out of the Depression. In 1940 unemployment was still running at nearly 15 percent; by 1944 it was a little over 1 percent.[90] Much of the recovery was due to conscription into the armed forces—for many young soldiers the army was their first proper job—but war production also had a massive effect on the economy. One of the boom towns was Mobile, Alabama—suddenly a major shipyard. According to the writer John Dos Passos:

> The mouldering old Gulf seaport with its ancient dusty elegance of tall shut-tered windows under mansard roofs and iron lace overgrown with vines . . . looks trampled and battered like a city that's been taken by storm. Sidewalks are crowded. . . . Garbage cans are overflowing. Frame houses on tree-shaded streets bulge with men in shirtsleeves who spill out onto the porches and trample grassplots and stand in knots at the street corners. . . . The trailer army has filled all the open lots with its regular tanks. In cluttered backyards people camp out in tents and chickenhouses and shelters packed together out of packingcases.[91]

These scenes were repeated in cities across the South and the west coast—from Charleston, South Carolina, across to San Diego, California, and up the coast to Seattle. The trailer parks and shanty towns that sprang up around the shipyards and aircraft factories were nicknamed "New Hoovervilles"—an ironic reference to the slums of jobless during the Depression. Some people likened them to the mining camps of 1849—except this time the rush was for real wages, not fool's gold.

So the war got America moving again, both economically and geographically. The United States was the only belligerent country to have both guns and butter—a boom in arms production and also greater output of civilian goods. As a result of war work in industry or service in the armed forces, almost one in ten of the American population ended up settling permanently in a different state.[92] One of the biggest migrations was of black Americans from the rural South into northern cities, resuming a flow that had surged in the 1910s and 1920s but then dried up during the Depression. Employers still discriminated on racial grounds but the demand for labor forced them to accept African-Americans at least for basic factory jobs—a real gain for those used to the grinding poverty of tenant farming. One Mecca for blacks was the massive Willow Run factory, Ford's "Bomber City," just outside Detroit. But the resultant housing crisis, typical of most boom towns during the war, became racially polarized and in the hot summer of 1943 Detroit eventually exploded in three days of riots that left thirty-four people dead (mostly black) and $2 million of damage.[93]

Racial discrimination was rife in the armed forces as well. Blacks served in segregated units and in noncombatant roles, such as construction and trucking. They had inferior facilities and were commanded by low-quality white officers, usually racist southerners. As head of the army, General Marshall ruled out the idea of integration. That, he said, "would be tantamount to solving a social problem which has perplexed the American people throughout the history of this nation. The army cannot accomplish such a solution, and should not be charged with the undertaking. The settlement of vexing racial problems cannot be permitted to complicate the tremendous task of the War Department."[94]

In Marshall's judgment his job was to win the war, not engage in social engineering, but critics insisted that the two were inseparable because racial integration and better training would boost the morale and efficiency of black GIs. Their slogan was the Double V: victory against fascism abroad and racism at home. According to black leaders, "Though thirteen million American Negroes have more often than not been denied democracy, they are American citizens and will as in every war give unqualified support to the protection of their country. At the same time we will not abate one iota our struggle for full citizenship rights here in the United States. We will fight but we demand the right to fight as equals."[95]

Yet segregation had become almost an American way of life. The American Red Cross even segregated the plasma of white and black blood donors. For one black soldier, Lloyd Brown, the ultimate moment was his reception at a lunchroom in Salina, Kansas:

> As we entered, the counterman hurried to the rear to get the owner, who hurried out front to tell us with urgent politeness: "You boys know we don't serve colored here."
>
> Of course we knew it. They didn't serve "colored" anywhere in town. . . . There was no room at the inn for any black visitor. . . . "You know we don't serve colored here," the man repeated. . . .
>
> We ignored him, and just stood there inside the door, staring at what we had come to see—the German prisoners of war who were having lunch at the counter. . . .
>
> This was really happening. It was no jive talk. The people of Salina would serve these enemy soldiers and turn away black American G.I.'s.[96]

Meanwhile Marshall's army was going to war. Not where he had wanted, in France, but in North Africa because the British feared that an early cross-Channel attack would be suicidal. At this stage, in 1942, the British were still the senior partner in the alliance: Britain and its empire provided more of the combat troops in Europe and its military planners were better organized. "We came, we saw and we were conquered," one senior U.S. army planner reported home after the Anglo-American conference at Casablanca in January 1943. "We were confronted with generations and generations of experience in committee work, in diplomacy, and in rationalizing points of view. They had us on the defensive practically all the time."[97]

The initial American landings in Morocco and Algeria in November 1942 were successful and there were hopes of clearing the Germans and Italians out of North Africa by Christmas, but then Hitler reinforced Tunisia and resistance stiffened. The U.S. army learned a rude lesson at Kasserine Pass, when whole battalions panicked and fled after a surprise German attack. Harry Butcher, press aide to the U.S. commander General Dwight Eisenhower, wrote in his diary, "The outstanding fact to me is that the proud and cocky Americans today stand humiliated by one of the greatest defeats in our history." Butcher admitted "there is a definite hangheadedness. . . . [F]rom top rank to the G.I., all those concerned have learned now that this is not a child's game."[98] Britons contemptuous of the cocky Yanks put new lines to the World War I song "Over There"—not "The Yanks are coming" but "The Yanks are running."

It took the Americans and the British until May 1943 to conquer Tunisia. This made it impossible to build up sufficient manpower and supplies in Britain to mount an invasion of France in 1943. So the Allies invaded Italy, hoping to knock it quickly out of the war and gain air bases from which to bomb southern Germany, but again Hitler decided to fight and the Italian campaign bogged down in mud and ice. Italy had been Churchill's hobby horse and by late 1943 Roosevelt and his advisers were losing patience with their ally. "We cannot now rationally hope to be able to cross the Channel and come to grips with our German enemy under a British commander," Stimson told Roosevelt bluntly. "The shadows of Passchendaele and Dunkerque still hang too heavily over the imagination of these leaders." The British, he said, believe that "Germany can be beaten by a series of attritions in northern Italy, in the eastern Mediterranean . . . and other satellite countries." Stimson advised the president that "the time has come for you to decide that your government must assume the responsibility of leadership in this great final movement of the European war."[99]

During 1944 the United States did become the senior partner in the Anglo-American alliance—in manpower, supplies, and command. The Allied landings in Normandy in June 1944 were headed by Eisenhower, and the "broad front" strategy he adopted for the final advance into the Reich overruled the British preference for a narrow, British-led thrust into northern Germany. There were setbacks—notably the German counteroffensive in December known as the Battle of the Bulge, which initially routed some ill-trained U.S. troops—but American dominance was now clear. Just before Christmas Churchill wearily told those who wanted him to take a tougher line with Washington to remember that "our armies are only about one-half the size of the American and will soon be little more than one-third . . . it is not so easy as it used to be for me to get things done."[100]

Millions of Americans served overseas during the war—3 million passing through Britain alone—and some commentators hoped this would make them more internationally minded. It did for a few service personnel but probably not for the majority. GIs (sardonic soldier slang for "Government Issue") were better paid and better supplied than the armies of their allies, let alone the enemy—"over-sexed, over-paid and over here," to quote the British wisecrack. (The American response was that the British were "under-sexed, under-paid and under Eisenhower.") GIs lived on bases that were little Americas, which the Pentagon, anxious to boost troop morale, supplied in abundance with the familiar material comforts of home such as magazines, gum, cigarettes, and Pepsi, even though all this used up vital shipping capacity. Most GIs probably went home with a new sense of American superiority compared with the rest of the world.

And also, quite probably, with a keener sense of being American. The initial effect of military service was an enhanced awareness of regional and ethnic difference: Most of the training camps were in the South, which was terra incognita for millions of young men from the North and Midwest. In their units, immortalized in movies and novels, diversity was rough-edged at first: The platoon on the South Pacific island of "Anopopei" in Norman Mailer's *The Naked and the Dead* included a Pole, a Mexican migrant, a Brooklyn Jew, a South Boston Irish, and a brutalized Texan sergeant. But when serving overseas the ethnic and sectional diversity was gradually subsumed into a larger sense of being American. Similarities seemed more significant than differences when compared with the alien values of Europe or Asia.

The sharpest contrasts were experienced by black personnel. In Europe, unlike the American South, there was no formal color bar and they were free to go into pubs, bars, and restaurants, even though the U.S. army by decree and white GIs by force often imposed their own patterns of segregation. Serving abroad opened the eyes of many black GIs to what might be possible in the land of liberty. So homecoming was often a bittersweet experience. One African-American, Timuel Black, stayed below as his troopship entered the Hudson river. White GIs were on deck excitedly talking about the Statue of Liberty but Black, who had been deeply impressed by his treatment in Europe, felt churned up and angry. Then suddenly he dissolved into tears. "Glad to be home, proud of my country, as irregular as it was. Determined it could be better . . . I could no longer push my loyalty back, even with all the bitterness I had." But another black soldier felt utterly negative as his ship berthed in New York, murmuring, "Now we're niggers again."[101]

At home the United States had truly become the "arsenal of democracy," as Roosevelt promised in 1940. By 1944 it was producing 40 percent of the world's armaments—a tribute to both the country's resources and its greater productivity.[102] A legendary example was Henry J. Kaiser, a construction tycoon who tried his hand at ships with spectacular success, winning the nickname "Sir Launchalot." Instead of building the vessel from the keel upward, one rib at a time, employing a plethora of specialist trades, Kaiser adopted production-line methods using prefabricated parts and semiskilled labor. According to Alistair Cooke, visiting San Francisco, "the Kaiser yards look like something out of Disney. They are absurdly clean and neat. The elements of a ship are divided into separate piles. . . . Innumerable cranes swing through the air and clutch precisely at the piles, deposit them at the plate shop, heave them down to the [ship]ways, where small armies of Disney characters rush forth with welding guns and weld the parts into a ship as innocently as a child fits A into B on the nursery floor and confronts a destroyer made with his very own hands."[103] Henry Kaiser's Liberty ships were to merchant shipping what Henry Ford's Model T had been to car travel.

The most striking testimony to America's industrial might was the atomic bomb. In the early years of the war the British were ahead in the theoretical work but building and testing a bomb in cramped, Luftwaffe-ravaged Britain was impossible. So in 1941 Churchill shared the research with Roosevelt, kick-starting a massive project innocuously codenamed the Manhattan Engineer District. The mastermind of the "Manhattan Project" was a burly army engineer called General Leslie Groves, already the construction genius behind the Pentagon. Groves was described by one subordinate as "the biggest sonovabitch I've ever met in my life, but also one of the most capable individuals. He had an ego second to none, he had tireless energy . . . and he was absolutely ruthless in how he approached a problem to get it done. . . . I hated his guts and so did everybody else."[104]

Uncertain about the best and fastest way to build an atomic bomb, the Americans took what was called the "Napoleonic approach" of trying them all simultaneously.[105] Groves built the plant—commandeering vast tracts of wilderness in the Pacific Northwest to produce plutonium and in the mountains of Tennessee for uranium enrichment. Both of these installations—at Hanford, Washington, and Oak Ridge, Tennessee—depended upon electricity generated by the New Deal power projects of the 1930s. More space was needed to design the weapons and this was found at Los Alamos on a remote desert plateau in northern New Mexico. The first atomic test took place at the White Sands Proving Ground near Alamogordo in the south of the state on July 16, 1945. The total cost of the whole project was nearly $2 billion. No other nation could have found the land and the resources; years later, when Niels Bohr, the Danish physicist, visited Los Alamos, he was astounded: "I told you it couldn't be done without turning the whole country into a factory. You have done just that."[106]

The atomic bomb had been intended for possible use on Germany, but the Nazi regime surrendered in May 1945. By then America had also entered a new era because Roosevelt had collapsed and died from a cerebral hemorrhage on April 12. Elected for a fourth term the previous November, FDR ended up spending more than twelve years in the White House, and they were some of the most anguished years in the country's history, spanning the Depression and World War II. Many young American soldiers and sailors could not remember any other president. The day he was buried was the eightieth anniversary of Abraham Lincoln's assassination and a folk cantata about Lincoln's funeral and his eternal spirit became the most widely played item on America's radio networks:

> *A lonesome train on a lonesome track—*
> *Seven coaches painted black—*
> *They carried Mr. Lincoln down,*
> *The train started—the wheels went round—*
> *You could hear that whistle for miles around*
> *Crying, Freedom! Freedom![107]*

Roosevelt's vice-president was Harry Truman of Missouri, a longtime Democratic politician who had been pulled out of the Senate for the election of 1944 to help balance the ticket. So it was Truman, completely inexperienced in foreign affairs, who had to decide whether to use the atomic bomb on Japan. In the final hours of World War I, Captain Truman had been happily firing off artillery shells at the Germans. In 1945 both his job and the weaponry were substantially more powerful, but President Truman saw no reason to hesitate. Since the battle of Midway in 1942, the U.S. army and navy had gradually hopped across the Pacific, island to island, but the losses had been high and an invasion of the Japanese home islands would face savage resistance. So using the atomic bomb to end the war would save American lives. In any case, the Japanese had never been forgiven for Pearl Harbor and the U.S. Army Air Force was already indiscriminately firebombing their wooden cities. The Pacific War had a frankly racist element that was lacking in America's war in Europe.

The only two operational atomic bombs were dropped, on Hiroshima and Nagasaki, on August 6 and 9, 1945. On the 9th the Soviet Union entered the Pacific War and a few days later Japan surrendered.

Watching the first atomic test a few weeks earlier, scientist Robert Oppenheimer thought of the legend of Prometheus, "of that deep sense of guilt in man's new power, that reflects his recognition of evil, and his long knowledge of it. We knew it was a new world, but even more we knew that novelty itself was a very old thing in human life, that all our ways are rooted in it."[108] Oppenheimer's words prefigured the anxieties of the nuclear age, but that was not the dominant mood in the United States at the war's end. According to the *New York Herald Tribune*, "Every American faces himself and his countrymen with a new confidence, a new sense of power. . . . We cannot, if we would, shut our eyes to the fact that ours is the supreme position. The Great Republic has come into its own; it stands first among the peoples of the earth."[109]

In the jargon of the time, the United States was not just a great power, like the now creaky British empire, but a "superpower." The nation that had lost its way in the Depression had now been reborn: Postwar America was "conceived in victory," to quote one baby boomer.[110] So August 1945 was a heady moment but, like all such moments, it proved ephemeral. The war also brought forth another super-power with diametrically opposed values; the new nuclear age would become a worldwide struggle between them.

PART III

EMPIRE AND EVIL

We are the first empire of the world to establish
our sway without legions. Our legions are dollars.
—REINHOLD NIEBUHR, 1930

The Soviet leaders . . . are the focus of evil in the
modern world.
—RONALD REAGAN, 1983

Liberty is both the plan of Heaven for humanity,
and the best hope for progress here on earth . . .
we believe that liberty is the direction of history.
—GEORGE W. BUSH, 2003

13

RED OR DEAD?

In March 1943 *Life* magazine devoted a special issue to the Soviet Union. It told readers, "Today the U.S.S.R. ranks among the top three or four nations in industrial power. She has improved her health, built libraries, raised her literacy to about 80%—and trained one of the most formidable armies on earth. It is safe to say that no nation in history has ever done so much so fast. If Soviet leaders tell us that the control of information was necessary to get the job done, we can afford to take their word for it for the time being." In similarly positive vein, *Life* stated that Lenin was "perhaps the greatest man of modern times," that the Russians were "one hell of a people" who to a "remarkable" degree "look like Americans, dress like Americans and think like Americans," and that the feared People's Commissariat for Internal Affairs (NKVD) was actually "a national police similar to the FBI."[1]

Life was no pinko rag but a cheerleader of U.S. capitalism. Such gush was testimony to American enthusiasm for the Russians at the height of the wartime alliance against Hitler. Four years later, however, in 1947, President Harry Truman identified the Soviet Union as America's greatest foe, declaring that the world had to decide between two ways of life—freedom or totalitarianism. During Truman's presidency (1945–1953) and that of Dwight Eisenhower (1953–1961) the United States became locked in a global Cold War that would define the country for nearly a half-century, not just in flashpoints in Berlin and Korea but in the country's booming suburbs as well. In the process America became more prosperous—yet also more insecure—than at any time in its history.

FROM WORLD WAR TO COLD WAR

The Red Scare of 1919 showed that Americans shared the European panic about the spread of Bolshevism; in fact, the United States extended diplomatic recognition to the USSR only when Roosevelt became president in 1933. During the 1930s,

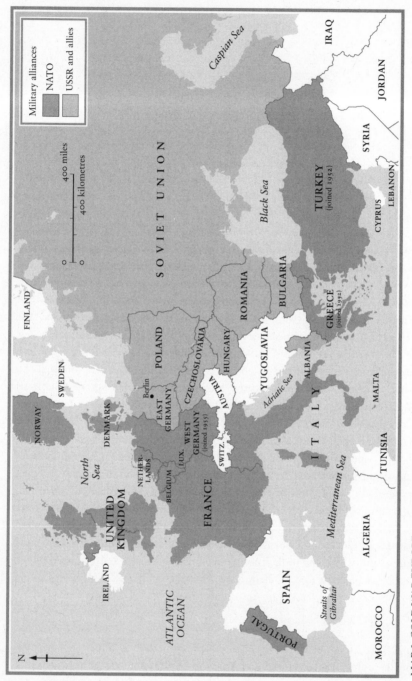

MAP 3, COLD WAR EUROPE, 1949

however, it seemed that the Soviet Union was growing out of its infant revolutionary excesses. New Dealers thought that the country would gradually evolve toward Western social democracy; conservatives, though more wary, saw it largely as a nationalist state preoccupied by security. Roosevelt himself believed that the wartime alliance offered a historic chance to bring Russia in from the cold—from its suspicious, insular past into the new family of nations. He also felt sure that man-to-man he could win over Stalin, telling Churchill in 1942, "I know you will not mind my being brutally frank when I tell you that I think I can personally handle Stalin better than either your Foreign Office or my State Department. Stalin hates the guts of all your top people. He thinks he likes me better, and I hope he will continue to do so."[2]

Not everyone shared the president's breezy self-confidence, but even skeptical right-wingers felt that the Soviet Union was no longer bent on expansion and revolution. In any case, its overriding task would be reconstruction. After visiting the USSR in 1943, the journalist Quentin Reynolds stated confidently, "It will take Stalin at least ten years after the war to clean up his own country: to repair the damaged cities. . . . For a long time Russia is going to be a giant on crutches. . . . [W]hen the war is over Stalin will be very easy for us to do business with."[3]

This was not all pie in the sky. The Soviet leader had no desire to end the alliance at the end of the war. His ravaged country had lost a seventh of its population (28 million people) and a quarter of its assets; he did not need Western hostility and hoped for more loans, like wartime Lend-Lease, to help with reconstruction. Nor was Stalin hell-bent on revolution, warning the French and Italian communist leaders against making a bid for power at the end of the war. Privately he opined that there were now many ways to advance the socialist international, even arguing that the strategy of imposing the Soviet system on Germany is "an incorrect one; an antifascist democratic parliamentary system must be established."[4]

Stalin was, however, determined to ensure Soviet control over key states on Russia's borders, using elected coalitions as a convenient front. During 1945 the Soviets and the Americans haggled over the composition of new governments in Poland, Bulgaria, and Romania—all under Red Army control; in each case Stalin eventually got what he wanted with a few token non-communists. In early 1946 there was a major row about the Soviets' failure to withdraw their troops from northern Iran—another sensitive border region for Stalin. On the other side of the world, in Asia, Soviet troops were now entrenched in northern Korea and communist forces had reignited the civil war for control of China.

Initially the American response to Soviet actions was confused. Dean Acheson, the undersecretary of state, said in November 1945, "I can tell you in three sentences what the 'popular' attitude is toward foreign policy today. 1. Bring the boys home; 2. Don't be a Santa Claus; 3. Don't be pushed around."[5]

In 1945 the first two aspirations dominated public opinion: Most Americans wanted to get out of the armed forces and get on with their lives; they were also tired of helping faraway nations. But as tensions mounted with the Soviets in pressure points all over the world, the third attitude grew in importance—not to be pushed around or to squander the hard-won fruits of victory.

The USSR did not possess the atomic bomb until 1949; even then it lacked long-range aircraft capable of striking the United States. So the Soviets posed no more of a direct threat to America than Hitler had done in 1939. But as a result of the war U.S. policymakers had developed a much more expansive definition of core national interests. In the age of air power, the Atlantic and Pacific no longer seemed meaningful barriers in the long term, so the Pentagon sought air and naval bases far from home to preempt an attack. And according to senior strategic planners in 1947, "two world wars in the past thirty years have demonstrated the interdependence of France, Great Britain and the United States. . . . The maintenance of these two countries in a state of independence, friendly to the United States and with economies able to support the armed forces necessary for the continued maintenance of their independence, is still of first importance to the national security of the United States."[6]

So America's definition of security had expanded from simply defending the western hemisphere to embracing key military-industrial areas in Europe and also Asia—notably Japan—where the United States controlled the postwar occupation. America's ideological reach had also expanded after having, as it was widely felt there, saved the world twice over from the menace of militarism and dictatorship. Harry Hopkins, Roosevelt's closest aide, put the point succinctly in 1945:

> I have often been asked what interests we have in Poland, Greece, Iran, or Korea. Well I think we have the most important business in the world—and indeed, the only business worthy of our traditions. And that is this—to do everything within our diplomatic power to foster and encourage democratic government throughout the world. We should not be timid about blazoning to the world our desire for the right of all people to have a genuine civil liberty. We believe our dynamic democracy is the best in the world.[7]

In the light of this newly expansive sense of security and ideology the Truman administration moved toward a tougher line against Russia during 1946. In early 1947 it was forced to act dramatically when the British government, wracked by economic crisis, told Truman it could no longer provide economic aid to anti-communist forces in the Greek civil war or to the Turkish government, being pressured by Stalin for bases and other concessions. The news from Britain seemed momentous in Washington. *Time* magazine reflected, "Great empires, like old soldiers, never die; they just fade away. Britain's legacy, like Rome's, will cling for centuries to history's pages, shaping men and events. Yet to all empires comes a day of which it can be said: 'At this point the sceptre had passed to other hands.' That day came last week to Britain."[8]

Truman, a history buff, was ready to take up the sceptre but that would not be politically easy. The Republicans, in control on Capitol Hill for the first time in fifteen years, were keen to cut government spending, and the idea of pulling "British chestnuts out of the fire" yet again did not go down well with leading members of Congress. Much more persuasive were administration warnings that Greece was like the proverbial "rotten apple in the barrel" from which the blight of communism, if unchecked, would soon spread throughout southern Europe. So Truman decided to go for the ideological big sell when he presented the case for aiding Greece and Turkey to the Congress in March 1947:

> [T]otalitarian regimes imposed upon free peoples, by direct or indirect aggression, undermine the foundations of international peace and hence the security of the United States. . . . At the present moment in world history nearly every nation must choose between alternative ways of life. The choice is too often not a free one. One way of life is based upon the will of the majority, and is distinguished by free institutions, representative government, free elections, guarantees of individual liberty, freedom of speech and religion, and freedom from political oppression. The second way of life is based upon the will of a minority forcibly imposed upon the majority. It relies upon terror and oppression, a controlled press and radio, fixed elections, and the suppression of personal freedoms. I believe that it must be the policy of the United States to support free peoples who are resisting attempted subjugation by armed minorities or by outside pressures.[9]

Truman carefully used the word "totalitarian" rather than "communist," but everyone knew what he meant; the word also skillfully linked the threat from Stalinism to the recent fight against Hitler. The Truman Doctrine, as the speech quickly became known, depicted a whole world teetering between freedom and totalitarianism. Although more rhetoric than reality, it would define the discourse of U.S. policy; more immediately, it helped get the package of aid for Greece and Turkey through Congress.

At the center of what was now being called the Cold War was the struggle for mastery of Germany. In 1945, after the end of Hitler's Reich, American and Russian forces joined Britain and France in the occupation of Germany. The aim of the Allies was to denazify the country, develop democratic institutions, agree to a peace treaty, and then withdraw: The occupation was intended to be only temporary. But instead the Allies stayed because the stakes were too high. Although now ruined and occupied, Germany was potentially Europe's strongest economy and also the originator of two world wars.

The Russians, backed initially by the French as the two powers that had suffered most from Germany, wanted to keep the country weak. The Americans, together with Britain, wanted to kick-start the German economy—fearful that poverty and depression would foster extremism, as in the 1930s, only this time communism rather than Nazism. The economic crisis would also drag down Germany's neighbors. A fact-finding mission told the president, "We can keep Germany in these economic chains but it will also keep Europe in rags."[10]

Matters came to a head in the spring of 1947, just after the Truman Doctrine speech. Secretary of State George Marshall—America's military mastermind of World War II—spent most of March in Europe. He was shaken by the continent's slow recovery and frustrated by the continuing deadlock over Germany. Two weeks in Moscow and forty-three meetings achieved nothing. "Stalin's seeming indifference to what was happening in Germany made a deep impression on Marshall. He came to the conclusion that Stalin, looking over Europe, saw that the best way to advance Soviet interests was to let matters drift," noted Marshall's aide Charles Bohlen. Europe was struggling to recover from the war. Highways, railroads, and canals were still ruined, unemployment was high, and millions of people were short of food. "This was the kind of crisis that Communism thrived on. All the way back to Washington, Marshall talked of the importance of finding some initiative to prevent the complete breakdown of Western Europe."[11]

Once home the secretary of state warned that "the patient is sinking while the doctors deliberate,"[12] and he set his staff to work on a remedy, which he announced to the world via a speech at Harvard on June 5, 1947. Three years before, U.S. soldiers had been waiting in boats on a storm-tossed Channel to begin the liberation of Europe from Nazism. Now Marshall, the great organizer of victory as Churchill called him, was offering American aid to liberate Europe from depression and communism: "Our policy is directed not against any country or doctrine but against hunger, poverty, despotism, and chaos. Its purpose shall be the revival of a working economy in the world so as to permit the emergence of political and economic conditions in which free institutions can exist. . . . Any country that is willing to assist in the task of recovery will find full cooperation, I am sure, on the part of the United States Government," Marshall declared. But "the initiative, I think, must come from Europe. . . . The program should be a joint one, agreed to by a number of if not all European nations."[13]

On the face of it, Marshall's last words embraced the Soviet Union and the Russians did send a delegation to the conference in Paris at which interested European states, led by Britain and France, tried to formulate a plan. But once it became clear that a recovery program would entail opening up the Soviet economy, and those of its satellites, to Western investment and scrutiny, Stalin pulled out of the discussions and drew the iron curtain more tightly across eastern Europe. It would take Truman months to get what became known as the Marshall Plan through Congress, but in four years from 1948 the United States provided $13 billion of aid to western Europe. During that same period the Soviet Union took out roughly the same amount from eastern Europe. Here was a graphic illustration of the Truman Doctrine in action.[14]

A WORLD HALF-SLAVE, HALF-FREE

On March 5, 1948, Truman scribbled a hasty note to Marshall: "Will Russia move first? Who pulls the trigger? Then where do we go?"[15] That same day the U.S. commander in Germany, General Lucius Clay, warned, "For many months, based on logical analysis, I have felt and held that war was unlikely for at least ten years. Within the last few weeks I have felt a subtle change in [the] Soviet attitude which I cannot define but which now gives me a feeling that it may come with dramatic swiftness."[16]

On March 17 the president delivered a special message to Congress. A year before, in his Truman Doctrine speech, he had talked in abstract terms about a global clash between freedom and totalitarianism, but now he named names: "Since the close of hostilities, the Soviet Union and its agents have destroyed the independence and democratic character of a whole series of nations in Eastern and Central Europe. It is this ruthless course of action, and the clear design to extend it to the remaining free nations of Europe, that have brought about the critical situation in Europe today." Truman asked Congress to introduce a peacetime draft, emphasizing that it was of "vital importance" for America "to keep our occupation forces in Germany until the peace is secure in Europe. . . . We must be prepared to pay the price for peace, or assuredly we shall pay the price of war."[17]

Congress agreed to impose conscription, despite a sobering precedent: The last, and only, time this had been done in peacetime, in September 1940, the United States went to war little more than a year later.

The four wartime allies—America, Britain, France, and Russia—were still unable to agree on whether to rebuild Germany, and its population remained dependent on Allied food and supplies in order to survive. Because wartime inflation had made the old currency worthless, Germany was reduced to a barter economy using American cigarettes as the main medium of exchange—the price of butter or eggs being measured against a packet of Camels or Lucky Strikes. So in June 1948 the Americans, British, and French introduced a new currency, the Deutschmark, into their zones of Germany. Literally overnight, goods started appearing in the shops: People said it was like Christmas in summer. But the Soviets retaliated by blockading Berlin.

Although the old capital was occupied by all four allies, America, Britain, and France had to cross Soviet-controlled territory in order to reach their sectors of the city. During June 1948 Stalin closed off all access to Berlin by rail, road, and river. The Western presence in the city seemed almost untenable, but General Clay emphasized that there were larger issues at stake: "We are convinced that our remaining in Berlin is essential to our prestige in Germany and in Europe. Whether for good or bad, it has become a symbol of the American intent."[18]

Truman agreed and Marshall sent a crisp telegram to London summarizing the new U.S. policy:

We stay in Berlin. . . .

We will supply the city by air as a beleaguered garrison. . . .

[W]e will further increase US air strength in Europe. . . .

[W]e and Brit[ish]—and French if possible—should send [a] note to Sov[iet]s asserting our rights in Berlin and stressing Sov[iet] responsibility for, and callousness to, threatened starvation of civilian population. . . . We see advantage in keeping Berlin situation before world attention by every feasible device. . . . We are hopeful that war can be avoided by these means.[19]

This seemed a very tall order. Many pundits believed it impossible to keep 2 million people supplied by air but the Americans and British mounted "Operation Vittles," as the Americans called it (the RAF codename was "Operation Plain Fare"). Against all odds the airlift continued all through the winter; at its height a plane landed every thirty seconds, carrying essentials such as food, coal, and clothing. But nonessentials mattered, too, for people's morale. Gail Halvorsen, a young U.S. pilot, took a liking to some Berlin kids, "so I told them to be down at the end of the runway next day and I'd drop them some gum and candy. That night I tied up some candy bars and gum in handkerchiefs and had my chief sling them out on a signal from me next day. Day by day the crowd of kids waiting for the drop got bigger, and day by day my supply of handkerchiefs, old shirts, GI sheets, and old shorts, all of which I use for parachutes, gets smaller."[20]

Halvorsen became famous in the German media as the "Chocolate Flyer" and other pilots followed his lead, so what started as a human gesture became brilliant PR. In fact, the whole airlift, or "Airbridge" as Berliners called it, helped transform America from enemy to friend in the minds of millions of Germans. One U.S. air force officer remarked, "Seems to me I've met every German in Berlin. They come down here, clutching extremely valuable heirlooms against their breasts, and they want to make a little ceremony of giving the stuff to the pilots. . . . It's no act either. An old man so thin you could see through him showed up a few days ago with a watch that would have fed him for months on the black market. He insisted on giving it to an American. He called it 'a little token from an old and grateful heart.'"[21]

The Soviets could have shot down the planes at any time but they did not: Stalin's bluff had been called and he had no stomach for war. In May 1949 he backed down and lifted the blockade. In a further blow for the USSR, the Truman administration used the crisis to justify negotiating the North Atlantic Treaty, under which the United States, Canada, and the countries of western Europe pledged to treat an attack on one of them as an attack on them all. The treaty was justified to Congress as providing vital reassurance to western Europe against the Soviet war of nerves. "It is a simple document," Truman remarked at the signing ceremony on April 4, "but if it had existed in 1914 and in 1939, supported by the nations who are represented here today, I believe it would have prevented the acts of aggression which led to two world wars."[22]

Simple or not, the North Atlantic Treaty was a landmark in U.S. foreign policy— the first time the New World had made peacetime military commitments to the Old. It was also a landmark in bipartisanship at home, built on cooperation between the Truman administration and moderate Republicans led by Senator Arthur Vandenberg of Michigan. An ardent isolationist until Pearl Harbor, Vandenberg now worked with the Democrats to craft a bipartisan policy toward Europe, helping steer the Atlantic pact through the Senate. "If Soviet Russia does start to march," he told skeptics, "it would seem completely inevitable that the United States will be the ultimate target and that we shall inevitably be in that war—Pact or no Pact." So he reckoned that America's "best insurance" was to "make our position plain in advance" so that the country spoke "with maximum authority against those who would divide and conquer us and the free world." This, said Vandenberg, was about putting "national security ahead of partisan advantage."[23]

But the Republicans were becoming restless over the political costs of this bipartisan policy. In 1945 Truman had stepped into a dead man's shoes, and many people felt that these had proved to be several sizes too big for him. Behind his tough talk there were frequent fumbles—in the words of one Washington joke, "To err is Truman"—and for a while the president was undecided about whether to run in his own right in 1948. He even thought about backing General Dwight Eisenhower, now a national hero after leading the Allied armies to victory in Europe in 1944–1945. "I told Ike," Truman wrote in his diary, "he should announce for the nomination on the Democratic ticket and that I'd be glad to be in second place, or Vice President. I like the Senate anyway. Ike & I could be elected and my family & myself would be happy outside this great white jail known as the White House."[24]

Eventually Truman did decide to run and he fought a blistering campaign, delighted to get out of jail. He crisscrossed the country on a special train, delivering fiery, populist speeches from the platform of the rear coach. He told an early-morning crowd at the railroad depot in Dodge City, Kansas, "I think you have a right to see your President, and your President has a right to see you." In the last few weeks, said Truman, "I have talked to a great many people, and a great many people have talked to me, and . . . I think I have definitely fixed the issues which are before the country now. It is merely the fact: are the special privilege boys going to run the country, or are the people going to run it? It is up to you to decide."[25]

This image of a little man fighting for America's little men captured the national imagination, and Truman kept blasting the "do-nothing" Republican-controlled Congress as "the worst" in U.S. history. Against all predictions, even within his own party, he ended up winning a famous victory in November 1948. The Democrats also regained control of both houses of Congress.

The election sounded the death knell of bipartisanship, however. Having lost five presidential elections in a row, the Republicans had nothing to lose from playing politics with foreign policy. And during 1949, after the successes of the Berlin airlift and North Atlantic Treaty, Truman's diplomatic record began to look much more vulnerable.

On September 23 the president grimly told the American people, "We have evidence that within recent weeks an atomic explosion occurred in the U.S.S.R. Ever since atomic energy was first released by man, the eventual development of this new force by other nations was to be expected. This probability has always been taken into account by us."[26] Truman was blustering. In private, U.S. policymakers were shaken by the Soviet atomic test, which they had not expected for several more years: The CIA had just told Truman the most probable date was mid-1953.[27]

Although it would still be some time before the Soviets had an operational atomic bomb, their test forced a basic rethink of U.S. strategy, which was based on countering Soviet superiority in conventional forces—troops, tanks, and artillery—by the threat of a nuclear attack on the Soviet homeland delivered by strategic bombers. Some of these aircraft would operate from the United States; most would be based in Britain and Germany. But the Soviets would now be able to deliver or threaten atomic retaliation against western Europe, thereby jeopardizing U.S. strategy and security.

While U.S. policymakers were absorbing the shock of the Soviet test, the long-running Chinese civil war reached its climax. For years the United States had poured vast amounts of aid into the corrupt Nationalist regime, to no avail. On October 1, 1949, Mao Zedong proclaimed the new People's Republic from the Gate of Heavenly Peace in Beijing. The world's most populous nation was now under communist control and, although U.S. planners foresaw possible friction between China and Russia, they had no doubt that Mao's victory was a massive gain for Stalin. "The USSR is now an Asiatic power of the first magnitude with expanding influence and interests extending throughout continental Asia and into the Pacific," the president's National Security Council stated. "The extension of communist authority in China represents a grievous political defeat for us; if southeast Asia is also swept by communism we shall have suffered a major political rout the repercussions of which will be felt throughout the rest of the world, especially in the Middle East and in a then critically exposed Australia."[28]

By the spring of 1950 the world picture therefore seemed much grimmer for American leaders than it had a year earlier. The East was going Red and the West looked fragile. So Truman now gave the go-ahead to develop a hydrogen bomb, known as the "super" because of its vastly enhanced power. Pentagon planners led by Paul Nitze summed up the situation bleakly for the president as nothing less than a worldwide confrontation between America and Russia, the forces of good and evil. The Soviet Union, he warned,

is animated by a new fanatic faith, antithetical to our own, and seeks to impose its absolute authority over the rest of the world. . . . The Kremlin regards
the United States as the only major threat to the achievement of its fundamental design. There is a basic conflict between the idea of freedom under a
government of laws, and the idea of slavery under the grim oligarchy of the
Kremlin. . . . The implacable purpose of the slave state to eliminate the challenge of freedom has placed the two great powers at opposite poles.[29]

This document, known as NSC 68, echoed the words of Abraham Lincoln in
the 1850s when he depicted the United States as a country "half-slave" and "half-
free." Lincoln had also predicted that America could not remain in that half-and-
half state indefinitely: One side would eventually make the other conform to its
values. Lincoln was proved right but at appalling human cost. Now Nitze was in-
scribing Lincoln's bipolar design onto a global plane. The implications, in the nuclear age, were truly chilling. Shaping the world was a much more prodigious task
than redefining a single country, but postwar American policymakers believed they
had both the might and the right to do so.

THE SUBURBAN REPUBLIC

In August 1950 the Association of Women Real Estate Agents in America published
their "creed":

> I believe in my America, the Land of Freedom and the Home of peoples
> from all the earth, who have and seek the comforts derived from the pursuit
> of free enterprise, worship of God in their own way and self-expression of
> their own individual talents. . . . I promise to defend, with all my strength of
> conviction, every movement which will help to maintain the right of indi-
> vidual home ownership. . . . And, I will encourage every mother to instill in
> the minds of her children the joys and privileges of living in their own
> home.[30]

The "right of individual home ownership" was not written into the U.S. Constitution, but for many Americans in the 1940s and 1950s it might as well have been.
Home ownership seemed to sum up everything the free world stood for at the
height of the Cold War.

Back in 1945 the biggest worry for millions of Americans was not the fate of
Germany or the civil war in China but finding somewhere to live. Very few houses
had been built for a decade and a half because of the Depression and then the war
effort. In Omaha, Nebraska, a newspaper ad offered "Big Ice Box, 7 x 17 feet, could
be fixed up to live in." Two newlyweds in New York set up home for a few days in

the window of a department store to publicize their plight.[31] Compounding the problem was the postwar baby boom. Older Americans, their lives disrupted by Depression and war, were making up for lost time, while young people started marrying in their early twenties and then had several kids in quick succession: The year 1946 saw a record 3.4 million births; by the mid-1950s the annual birthrate was running at 4 million.

So, American business turned its energies to the housing crisis, using the mass-production methods that had helped win the war. They were pioneered on some flat potato land on Long Island, New York. In July 1950 *Time* magazine described how

> an army of trucks sped over new-laid roads. Every 100 feet, the trucks stopped and dumped identical bundles of lumber, pipes, bricks, shingles and copper tubing—all as neatly packaged as loaves from a bakery. Near the bundles, giant machines with an endless chain of buckets ate into the earth, taking just 13 minutes to dig a narrow, four-foot trench around a 25-by-32 ft. rectangle. Then came more trucks, loaded with cement, and laid a four-inch foundation for a house in the rectangle. After the machines came the men. On nearby slabs already dry, they worked in crews of two and three, laying bricks, raising studs, nailing lath, painting, sheathing, shingling. Each crew did its special job, then hurried on to the next site.[32]

This was Levittown, a name that became literally a household word. Bill and Alfred Levitt did for housing what Henry Ford's Model T had done for the automobile industry. Their company offered a couple of standard designs—the four-room Cape Cod box and the larger, single-story ranch house—at prices that could be afforded by millions of people. They also threw in a Bendix washing machine as part of the deal and designed the whole area as a garden community with curved streets and no fences. Levittown building methods—concrete slab, prefabricated parts, and power tools—were copied by developers all over America; Cape Cod cottages and easy-living ranch houses became the suburban form from Philadelphia to San Francisco. Bill Levitt discerned larger national benefits as well: "No man who owns his own house and lot can be a Communist. He has too much to do."[33]

The cultural historian Lewis Mumford was scathing about America's new mass-produced suburbs:

> a multitude of uniform, unidentifiable houses, lined up inflexibly, at uniform distances, on uniform roads, in a treeless communal waste, inhabited by people of the same class, the same income, the same age group, watching the same television performances, eating the same tasteless pre-fabricated foods, from the same freezers, conforming in every outward and inward respect to a common mold. . . . Thus the ultimate effect of the suburban escape in our

own time is, ironically, a low-grade uniform environment from which escape is impossible.[34]

But millions of Americans had no time for such cultural snobbery; a suburban home was payback for the Depression and the War.

Suburban living was also automobile living. By the mid-1950s three-quarters of American families owned a car;[35] motels, shopping malls, and drive-in movie theaters all came of age. Los Angeles was the ultimate "centerless city" of the automobile age, with neighboring Orange County a succession of sprawling suburbs. One local resident spoke for many: "I live in Garden Grove, work in Irvine, shop in Santa Ana, go to the dentist in Anaheim, my husband works in Long Beach, and I used to be president of the League of Women Voters in Fullerton."[36]

But as cars and trucks flooded America's roads, they clogged up the traffic. During the 1940s politicians and bureaucrats in Washington debated ideas for a national system of highways; eventually it came to fruition with the Interstate Highway Act of 1956, pushed through by President Dwight Eisenhower. Ike explained that the new network was needed to reduce accidents—more than 36,000 deaths a year—and to develop the great national market: "Our unity as a nation is sustained by free communication of thought and by easy transportation of people and goods," which, he said, "are dynamic elements in the very name we bear—United States. Without them, we would be a mere alliance of many separate parts." The president also identified a Cold War imperative: "In case of an atomic attack on our key cities, the road net must permit quick evacuation of target areas, mobilization of defense forces and maintenance of every essential economic function. But the present system in critical areas would be the breeder of a deadly congestion within hours of an attack."[37]

Ike had seen the need for a nationwide system of highways back in 1919, when as a young soldier he had traveled laboriously from coast to coast in an army convoy. Now, in the nuclear age, speed could be literally a matter of life and death. National defense as much as civilian benefit explains why the federal government decided to cover 90 percent of the cost of more than 40,000 miles of interstate highway. The eventual bill was more than $1 million per mile.[38]

The Interstate Highway Act of 1956 was the latest in a series of massive but selective federal subsidies. In the mid-nineteenth century there had been huge land grants to railroads, which helped open up the West but also enabled thousands of speculators and businessmen to get rich. Now, a century later, Uncle Sam was subsidizing roads—and therefore the private car—rather than public transport such as rail and buses. In other words, benefits for the suburban middle class rather than the urban poor. Despite its Cold War rhetoric about the free market, the U.S. government was engaged in selective socialism on a vast scale.

Not just the interstates but also the postwar housing boom owed a huge amount to federal spending. "If it weren't for the Government," said one San Francisco

builder in June 1950, "the boom would end overnight." Government agencies in-
sured up to 95 percent of the value of a house, making it easy for builders to borrow money with which to build low-cost homes. They also guaranteed mortgages
on terms so liberal that it was almost as easy to buy as to rent. As of 1950 the terms
were 5 percent down (nothing at all for veterans) and thirty years to pay. For an ex-
GI that meant installments of only $56 a month. Said *Time*, "The countless new
housing projects made possible by this financial easy street are changing the way
of life of millions of US citizens, who are realizing for the first time the great American dream of owning their own home."[39]

GIs did particularly well after the war. Around 16 million men and women had
served—an eighth of the U.S. population—and their pressure group, the American
Legion, successfully lobbied for what it cleverly called the "G.I. Bill of Rights" as repayment. The legislation was passed in June 1944; over the next decade 3.7 million
former GIs took out guaranteed home loans and 7.8 million received grants for education and training.[40]

The "G.I. Bill," officially the Serviceman's Readjustment Act, was a remarkably
enlightened measure, intended to help prevent a postwar recession and head off
protests like the Bonus March on Washington in 1932. Millions of soldiers started
a new and better life as a result of the bill but, like subsidized road building, this federal largesse benefited a selected part of the population whereas Roosevelt had
wanted universal benefits. In his State of the Union Address in January 1944, just
days after the American Legion published its "G.I. Bill of Rights," the president
called for nothing less than a "Second Bill of Rights" for the whole nation. The first
Bill of Rights in 1791 had concentrated on political rights, among them free speech,
a free press, and freedom of worship. But now, said Roosevelt, "we have come to a
clear realization . . . that true individual freedom cannot exist without economic
security and independence. . . . People who are hungry, people who are out of a job
are the stuff of which dictatorships are made. In our day these economic truths
have become accepted as self-evident. We have accepted, so to speak, a second Bill
of Rights under which a new basis of security and prosperity can be established
for all—regardless of station, or race or creed."[41]

Roosevelt went on to list these universal rights, among them "a useful and re-
munerative job," a "decent home," "adequate medical care," protection from the
economic fears of sickness, old age and unemployment, and "the right to a good education."[42] But his proposal for a second Bill of Rights—economic rather than
political—fell on deaf ears. Instead, after the war, federal economic benefits were
extended to specific segments of the population, those most likely to enhance economic growth. "Only if we have large demands can we expect large production,"
insisted one leading economist, and this meant that "ever-increasing consumption
on the part of our people" was "one of the prime requisites for prosperity. Mass
consumption is essential to the success of a system of mass production."[43]

Primed by this generous but selective federal spending, the U.S. economy really took off after the war. Unlike the boom of the 1920s, this surge would continue with only a few blips for a quarter-century. In 1950 the United States, with only 7 percent of the world's population, accounted for half of its manufacturing production and 80 percent of its annual output of motor vehicles. Per capita income and levels of home ownership were double the figures for Britain and western Europe.[44] During the 1950s millions of Americans moved into the suburban middle class. A quarter of families still subsisted below the national poverty line (around $3,000 a year) but even America's poor were rich by global standards. The per capita income of Harlem ranked with the top five nations in the world. In Harlan County, Kentucky, one of the country's poorest areas, two-thirds of the homes had a TV and three-fifths had a car.[45]

America's poor were disproportionately non-white and this was no accident. Roosevelt's vision of an economic Bill of Rights foundered on the opposition of leading southern members of Congress, who wanted to keep African-Americans in place as cheap farm labor.[46] And the new suburbs like Levittown remained largely white. Bill Levitt argued:

> The Negroes are trying to do in 400 years what the Jews in the world have not wholly accomplished in 600 years. As a Jew I have no room in my mind or heart for racial prejudice. But . . . I have come to know that if we sell one house to a Negro family, then 90 or 95 percent of our white customers will not buy into the community. That is their attitude, not ours. . . . As a company our position is simply this: we can solve a housing problem, or we can try to solve a racial problem, but we cannot combine the two.[47]

Race remained America's Achilles' heel, the worm in its rosy apple of prosperity. Eventually in the 1960s the federal government would be forced to address the racial problem that economic growth alone could not resolve.

THE COLD WAR TURNS HOT

On Saturday June 24, 1950, Harry Truman was enjoying a quiet weekend at home with his wife and daughter. He had flown back to Independence, Missouri, in America's heartland for a rare break from the cares of the White House. But it didn't work out that way, as Truman later recalled: "It was a little after ten in the evening and we were sitting in the library of our home on North Delaware Street when the telephone rang. It was the Secretary of State calling from his home in Maryland. 'Mr. President . . . I have very serious news. The North Koreans have invaded South Korea.'"[48]

This was about the last thing that Truman had expected. At the end of World War II the Japanese had surrendered to the Soviets in the north of Korea and to the Americans in the south. With neither superpower ready to withdraw, Korea (like Germany) became divided under separate governments, with the border along the 38th parallel. The situation, though not ideal from the American standpoint, seemed to be stabilizing. But each Korean regime was determined to control the whole country and in 1950 the North Koreans got the green light from Stalin for an invasion of the south. The Soviet leader had assumed from recent administration speeches that the Americans did not consider South Korea to be of vital importance. He also noted that Truman had done nothing to stop the communist takeover of China, a far more important country. This was a fateful error by Stalin.

On hearing of the North Korean attack, the president abandoned his vacation and flew back to Washington.

> I had time to think aboard the plane. In my generation, this was not the first occasion when the strong had attacked the weak. . . . I remembered how each time that the democracies failed to act it had encouraged the aggressors to keep going ahead. Communism was acting in Korea just as Hitler, Mussolini, and the Japanese had acted ten, fifteen, and twenty years earlier. I felt certain that if South Korea was allowed to fall Communist leaders would be emboldened to override nations closer to our own. . . . If this was allowed to go unchallenged it would mean a third world war.[49]

The "lessons" of appeasement haunted the generation of leaders who came of age during World War II. So Truman took a tough line on Korea, announcing the commitment of U.S. forces. "The attack upon Korea makes it plain beyond all doubt that communism has passed beyond the use of subversion to conquer independent nations and will now use armed invasion and war."[50]

The president was undoubtedly right that this was a test case: Stalin had expected to get away with the North Korean attack. Fortunately for Truman, the Soviets were boycotting the Security Council in support of communist China's claim for a seat, so the defense of South Korea could be mounted as a United Nations action. But Truman committed U.S. armed forces on his personal say-so as commander-in-chief and critics accused him of usurping Congress's constitutional authority. "His action unquestionably has brought about a de facto war with the government of North Korea," declared Senator Robert Taft, a leading Republican, and had done so "without consulting Congress and without congressional approval." If, warned Taft, "the president can intervene in Korea without congressional approval, he can go to war in Malaya or Indonesia or Iran or South America."[51]

Lamely, Truman argued that Korea was not a war, only a "police action" under the aegis of the UN, but few people believed him as the North Koreans rampaged southward. Gradually the Americans got a grip on the crisis and in September 1950 the U.S. commander, General Douglas MacArthur, turned the tables with a daring amphibious landing behind enemy lines at the western port of Inchon. Soon the Korean capital, Seoul, was back in Allied hands and MacArthur pushed on into North Korea to unify the whole country. This supremely arrogant general was always hard to control but Truman and his advisers did not make much of an effort. Their mood had now shifted from panic to hubris, sensing a dramatic victory that would reverberate at home and abroad. They brushed aside warnings that if U.S. forces marched up to Korea's border with communist China, this would trigger Chinese intervention.

On November 24 the U.S. Eighth Army celebrated Thanksgiving in traditional style—with turkey and trimmings delivered at massive expense by truck and by air. The men talked of being home by Christmas. But next day their camps were overwhelmed by thousands of Chinese troops in a terrifying cacophony of guns, grenades, bugles, and rattles. The U.S. soldiers had not been properly trained, their commanders were paralyzed, and the supply chains broke down. Soon it was every man for himself.

Colonel Paul Freeman told a fellow officer bitterly, "Look around here. This is a sight that hasn't been seen for hundreds of years: the men of a whole United States Army fleeing from the battlefield, abandoning their wounded, running for their lives." Private Jimmy Cardinal wrote to his parents back in the Bronx, "The Chinese are kicking hell out of the US Army, I think we are getting out, at least I hope so . . . as it's impossible to stop these Chinese hordes. . . . The troops over here are mad, mad at America, Americans and America's leaders. We all feel we've been let down by our incompetent blundering leadership, from the White House down. . . . It's about time that all of you back home awakened to the truth of the matter, and let your voices be heard thru letters to your congressmen."[52]

Congress proved very receptive. For months right-wing Republicans had accused the Truman administration of being soft on communism by letting China "fall" and by not purging the "Reds under the bed" at home. In February 1950 Senator Joseph McCarthy—a Republican from Wisconsin—gave a speech in Wheeling, West Virginia, in which he stated, "While I cannot take the time to name all of the men in the State Department who have been named as members of the Communist party and members of a spy ring, I have here in my hand a list of 205 that were known to the Secretary of State as being members of the Communist party and who nevertheless are still working and shaping the policy of the State Department."[53]

The apparent precision of McCarthy's accusation hit the headlines, but in succeeding weeks the press was unable to pin him down. He would not name names and his numbers varied—205, 81, 57 (people wondered whether that last came from Heinz's fifty-seven varieties). Covering one such speech, Edward Olsen of the Associated Press became deeply frustrated: "The man just talked circles. Everything was by inference, allusion, never a concrete statement of fact. Most of it didn't make sense." Afterward journalists pressed for more but "by three or four in the morning we were stony drunk, McCarthy worst of all." At the end "he was screaming at us that one of us had stolen his list of Communists. He'd lost it, and he knew he'd made a fool of himself. . . . He lost his list between his eighth and ninth bourbons."[54]

To millions of well-bred Americans, especially Democrats, McCarthy epitomized the worst in Cold War partisanship and demagoguery. Other Republicans from the Plains and the West followed suit, among them Richard Nixon from California, capitalizing on popular suspicion of the so-called Eastern Establishment. The problem was that although McCarthy was indeed an unsavory rabble-rouser, his sensationalized accusations were not completely unfounded—as the Truman administration knew well.

In 1943 a small group of U.S. army code-breakers had set out to crack intercepted cables between Moscow and the Soviet embassy in Washington. Their aim was to find out if Stalin was planning a negotiated peace with Hitler; on that they drew a blank but their laborious work eventually revealed the shocking news that 349 Americans had been in contact with agents of Soviet intelligence. Some of these Americans were people in high places—including Harry Dexter White of the U.S. Treasury and Alger Hiss in the State Department. The project, code-named Venona, also revealed the nexus of top-level British spies including Guy Burgess and Donald Maclean, and it incriminated the scientist Klaus Fuchs, who had passed on blueprints from the American atomic test in 1945, which formed the basis of the Soviet bomb four years later.

So the new Red Scare had a foundation in fact: no smoke without fire. But the fire had burned itself out by 1950—these Soviet agents were products of the Depression—while the smoke billowed on to suffocate American politics and cultural life.

In 1947, on the strength of information from Venona, Truman imposed a loyalty program on federal employees and gave the FBI its head in investigating their backgrounds. Under its veteran director, J. Edgar Hoover—a skilled bureaucratic infighter who had the dirt on most people in government—the Bureau was almost a law unto itself. Privately, Truman was unhappy: "We want no Gestapo or Secret Police. FBI is tending in that direction. They are dabbling in sex life scandals and plain blackmail when they should be catching criminals. . . . *This must stop.*"[55] But he did little to restrain Hoover and in public the House Committee on Un-American Activities pilloried not merely left-wingers but also Jews, intellectuals, and free spirits in the media. The Truman administration had encouraged Americans to see the Cold War as an either/or struggle between good and evil, a mentality that fostered McCarthyism.

Even a cultural icon like Charlie Chaplin became a victim. Although resident in America for nearly forty years, British-born Chaplin had never taken on U.S. citizenship. In 1952, at Hoover's behest, he was interviewed by investigators from the Immigration Service:

- "You say you've never been a Communist?"
- "You made a speech in which you said 'comrades'—what did you mean by that?"
- "Have you ever committed adultery?"
- "If this country were invaded, would you fight for it?"[56]

After that inquisition, Chaplin didn't return to the United States for twenty years. An estimated 1,500 people in radio and television were blacklisted—many unable to work again. Schools and colleges were cowed as well. "There will be no witch hunt at Yale," announced the University's president, "because there will be no witches. We do not intend to hire Communists."[57]

It was in this fog of suspicion, justified and also imagined, that Truman tried to sort out the mess in Korea. After the Chinese routed U.S. troops at the end of 1950, the president gave a press conference in which he said, "We will take whatever steps are necessary to meet the military situation, just as we always have." "Will that include the atomic bomb?" he was asked. "That includes every weapon that we have." Reporters jumped on this phrase: "Does that mean that there is active consideration of the use of the atomic bomb?" Truman replied testily, "There has always been active consideration of its use." Asked about possible targets, he said this was "a matter that the military people will have to decide. I'm not a military authority that passes on those things. . . . The military commander in the field will have charge of the use of the weapons, as he always has."[58]

Truman's ill-chosen words sent shock waves around the world, particularly since the commander in the field, General MacArthur, was telling journalists that this was no longer a "limited" war and that he should be allowed to bomb industrial targets in China, if necessary with atomic weapons. MacArthur was also openly critical of the priority given by the administration to Europe: "It seems strangely difficult for some to realize that here in Asia is where the Communist conspirators [Russia and China] have elected to make their play for global conquest, and that we have joined the issue thus raised on the battlefield." He went on to say that "if we lose the war to Communism in Asia the fall of Europe is inevitable; win it and Europe most probably would avoid war and yet preserve freedom. . . . [W]e must win. There is no substitute for victory."[59]

When Joe Martin, the House Republican leader, read out this letter in Congress, it became front-page news. Truman, who had hesitated to sack such a revered general, finally acted. But MacArthur came home to a hero's reception; his ticker-tape parade through New York lasted nearly seven hours and generated 2,800 tons of litter.[60] Messages to members of Congress and the White House ran overwhelmingly against the president; many demanded Truman's impeachment. Yet when MacArthur addressed a special session of Congress, he pulled his punches, avoiding any talk about bombing China, and the final words of his melodramatic performance were passive, even bathetic: "The world has turned over many times since I took the oath on the Plain at West Point, and the hopes and dreams have long since vanished. But I still remember the refrain of one of the most popular barrack ballads of that day, which proclaimed, most proudly, that 'Old soldiers never die; they just fade away.' And like the old soldier of that ballad, I now close my military career and just fade away, an old soldier who tried to do his duty as God gave him the light to see that duty. Goodbye."[61]

And that was what happened. MacArthur toured the country blasting the administration, but gradually he became a parody of himself. Most people, whatever they felt about Truman, endorsed the basic constitutional principle that civilians, not soldiers, decided policy: Americans often elevated generals to the presidency but they did so by democratic means—there would be no Caesars or Bonapartes. The Pentagon also mounted a strong defense of the priority that the administration gave to Europe. General Omar Bradley delivered the punch line: "Red China is not the powerful nation seeking to dominate the world. Frankly, in the opinion of the Joint Chiefs of Staff, this strategy would involve us in the wrong war, at the wrong place, at the wrong time, and with the wrong enemy."[62]

This was a repeat of the strategic priorities in World War II. As in 1941–1942 the administration had no doubt that Europe was the vital theater and it was now afraid that the Korean War was prelude to a Soviet attack in Europe. During the winter of 1950–1951 Truman "put the O into NATO," turning the North Atlantic Treaty from a diplomatic pact into a proper military alliance, backed by four new U.S. combat divisions and an American commander—Dwight Eisenhower. This served to institutionalize America's commitment in Europe and the priority it gave to that continent rather than to Asia. NATO also provided Eisenhower, rather than his erstwhile boss MacArthur, with the perfect springboard from which to jump into the White House.

DEFENDED TO DEATH

By the summer of 1952 the United States had been mired for two years in a war in Korea. For can-do Americans, proud of their power, the deadlock was frustrating, even humiliating, and the whole global struggle against communism seemed to be running against them. Eisenhower, now a presidential candidate, laid it on the line in a speech to U.S. veterans using the hallowed language of liberty and slavery: "We are threatened by a great tyranny, a tyranny that is brutal in its primitiveness. It is a tyranny that has brought thousands—millions of people—into slave camps and is attempting to make all human kind its chattel." Ike spelled out the countries of eastern Europe that had fallen under the Soviet yoke, from the

Baltic to the Black Sea, 90 million people in countries like Poland and East Germany, declaring that "all these people are blood kin to us" and that "the American conscience can never know peace until these people are restored again to be masters of their own fate."[63]

In speeches like this, candidate Eisenhower implied that, as president, he would "roll back" the Red tide. Although this was election rhetoric that he later downplayed, Eisenhower spoke for millions of Americans who saw bipolarity not as a steady state but as a zero-sum game that the United States must and would eventually win.

Eisenhower won the 1952 election by a landslide—the Democrats were irreparably tarnished by the mess in Korea, and his military record and cheery manner ("I like Ike") provided the kind of reassurance Americans now craved. His Republican Party also took control of the Senate, though the Democrats still had a majority in the House. The new administration believed in balanced budgets, or at least reduced government spending; it also wanted to avoid getting bogged down in another unwinnable ground war. The answer it proposed was greater reliance on America's nuclear arsenal. "There is no local defense which alone will contain the mighty landpower of the Communist world," explained John Foster Dulles, Eisenhower's secretary of state. "Local defenses must be reinforced by a further deterrent of massive retaliatory power."[64]

In other words, rather than fight land wars that were hard to win, America should prevent aggression in the first place by letting Russia and China know that the result would be a massive nuclear onslaught. So the administration built up Strategic Air Command (SAC) with its network of jet-propelled heavy bombers, airborne refueling tankers, and overseas bases. The scenario for possible war was outlined in 1954 by General Curtis LeMay, architect of the saturation bombing of Japan during World War II. He said that SAC could strike with up to 750 nuclear bombs by approaching Russia from many directions. According to an admiring officer, "this part of the briefing was skillfully done by showing successive charts of Europe based on one-half-hour time intervals after SAC bombers first hit the Russian early warning system." Many heavy lines were shown progressively converging on the heart of Russia with "pretty stars" to indicate the numerous bombs being dropped on what the military called Desired Ground Zeros. The impression given by LeMay, said the officer, "was that virtually all of Russia would be nothing but a smoking, radiating ruin at the end of two hours" and that, although other parts of the communist world would need attention, thirty days would be "long enough to conclude World War III."[65]

The Pentagon was adept at slick, seductive briefings but the promise of massive retaliation by airborne nuclear weapons was undoubtedly the centerpiece of Eisenhower's "New Look" defense policy. At the opposite end of the administration's spectrum of ways to avoid costly ground wars, it advocated "covert operations" to destabilize its enemies. This became a big new enterprise for the Central Intelligence

Agency, now headed by Allen Dulles—a wartime spymaster and brother of the secretary of state. A special report for the president in 1954 justified the new no-holds-barred policy:

> It is now clear that we are facing an implacable enemy whose avowed ob-jective is world domination by whatever means and whatever cost. There are no rules to such a game. Hitherto acceptable norms of human conduct do not apply. If the United States is to survive, long-standing American con-cepts of "fair play" must be reconsidered. We ... must learn to subvert, sab-otage and destroy our enemies by more clever, more sophisticated and more effective methods than those used against us.[66]

In this new Cold War world, those who weren't for you were deemed to be against you. Anti-Western nationalists were lumped in the same category as die-hard communists, or at best not given the benefit of the doubt. The CIA helped topple the Mossadeq government in Iran in August 1953 because of its challenge to Western oil interests; the Agency then turned to the Arbenz government in Guatemala. Jacobo Arbenz was a democratically elected socialist whose land re-form program threatened the interests of the United Fruit Company, an Ameri-can multinational with close ties to the administration. The CIA spent maybe $20 million funding and training a 500-strong "Liberation Army," which toppled Arbenz in June 1954 and established a pro-American military junta under Castillo Armas. Afterward Allen Dulles and his team reported to the White House. The president wanted to know how many men Armas had lost. Only one, he was told, a courier. He shook his head, perhaps thinking of the thousands who died in France in 1944. "Incredible." He turned to the chairman of the joint chiefs of staff. "What about the Russians? Any reaction?" General Matt Ridgway answered, "They don't seem to be up to anything." Eisenhower shook hands all around. "Thanks, Allen, and thanks to all of you. You've averted a Soviet beachhead in our hemisphere."[67]

Successes like Guatemala fed Washington's confidence that covert operations were an easy way to roll back communism and foster regime-change—a belief that would have dangerous consequences. In the mid-1950s, however, things seemed rosy for millions of Americans, both abroad and at home. Between 1952 and 1955 the number of households with TV sets doubled to 32 million—roughly three-quarters of all the homes in America.[68] With the three main networks all funded by commercials, broadcasters concentrated on mass-market programs: westerns, de-tective stories, light comedies, and quiz shows. The effect was increasingly a mass, nationwide culture. News and current affairs were marginal, encouraging a confi-dently American-centered view of the world.

Television began to influence politics as well. Whereas Truman in 1948 had cam-paigned from a train—nineteenth-century style—four years later Eisenhower's strategists concentrated on "spot" commercials on TV to sell the general to the nation. Rosser Reeves, Ike's ad man, explained his target: "I think of a man who hesitates between two levers as if he were pausing between competing tubes of toothpaste in a drug-store. The brand that has made the highest penetration on his brain will win his choice."[69] The idea of the presidential election as a contest between Colgate and Gleem appalled democratic purists, but this was increasingly the name of the game.

Not just television but supermarkets came of age in the 1950s. The word itself dates back to the 1930s, but it was in the Eisenhower years that the supermarket business really took off, accounting for 60 percent of America's retail food trade by 1955. The iconic design features were now in place—huge plate-glass windows to entice you in, wide aisles stacked high with shrewdly placed goods, shopping carts to be maneuvered through the store like the automobile in which you would take your shopping home, and the checkout surrounded by candy, cigarettes, and other essential nonessentials. Not to mention the Hollywood-style openings, like this one reported by *Time* in 1951: "Even blasé New Yorkers gawked at the razzle-dazzle last week when Food Fair Stores Inc. opened two spick & span new supermarkets. Skywriting planes soared overhead. Models paraded by in hats adorned with lobsters and sirloin steaks." One TV star, Dagmar, mobbed by a crowd estimated at 7,000, had her car license plate ripped off as a souvenir.[70]

As in the 1920s, music was central to the consumer boom—spread by the new vinyl-coated records and, even more, by transistor radios. The rage was now for rock and roll, a blend of black blues and white country music. Early exponents were Bill Haley and Chuck Berry, but Haley was too old for megastardom and Berry was black. Sam Phillips of Sun Records in Memphis, Tennessee, lamented: "If I could find a white boy who could sing like a nigger, I could make a million dollars."[71] His prayer was answered by a young, music-mad truck-driver called Elvis Aaron Presley. With his greased hair, curled lip, upturned collar, and gyrating pelvis, Elvis drove teenage girls into hysterics and their elders into apoplexy. The American correspondent for the London *Times* reported snootily: "Mr Presley, now the proud owner of three Cadillacs and hundreds of the violent sports shirts he affects, says: 'I wouldn't want no regular spot on no T.V. programme. I love to act. I don't care nothing whatsoever about singing in no movie.' . . . Mr Presley adds, by way of illustration, that English was what he liked best at school." Despite what Elvis said, a string of movies in the 1960s turned him into a global superstar.[72]

The spread of American popular culture provoked an outcry among European elitists. The French, for instance, anguished over whether the Coca-Cola company should be allowed to set up business, as it had already done in much of postwar western Europe. (One peeved U.S. congressman said that drinking Coke would give the French just what they had needed ever since World War II: "a good belch.")[73] In the 1960s France was flooded by Levi jeans, Marlboro cigarettes, Scotch tape, Tupperware, and Tampax, and there was panic about the purity of the French language itself being perverted into "Franglais."

At the same time, Europe's "high" culture seemed literally to be going west. Wealthy American collectors were buying up European art, as Christie's, the premier London auction house, acknowledged when it opened a New York office in 1963. Manhattan was already home to a diverse group of so-called Abstract Expressionists, including Mark Rothko and Willem de Kooning, prewar immigrants from Europe. Before his death by car crash in 1956, Jackson Pollock from Wyoming had become their best-known representative, because of his technique of dripping paint across a canvas on the floor. Although Pollock was often derided at home as "Jack the Dripper," his works were promoted by the State Department as emblems of American freedom and widely emulated in Europe. According to critic Clement Greenberg, the appeal of Abstract Expressionism showed that "the main premises of Western art have at last migrated to the United States, along with the center of gravity of industrial production and political power."[74]

American cultural values even became a battleground in the Cold War when Richard Nixon, Eisenhower's vice-president, visited Moscow in July 1959. He and the Soviet leader, Nikita Khrushchev, debated the merits of their rival systems in a mock-up of a modern American house at an international exhibition.

> NIXON: I want to show you this kitchen. It is like those of our houses in California.
> KHRUSHCHEV: We have such things.
> NIXON: This [dishwasher] is our newest model. This is the kind which is built in thousands of units for direct installations in the houses. In America, we like to make life easier for women. . . .
> KHRUSHCHEV: Your capitalistic attitude toward women does not occur under Communism.
> NIXON: I think that this attitude towards women is universal. What we want to do is make life more easy for our housewives.

But the Soviet leader gave as good as he got:

> KHRUSHCHEV: This is what America is capable of, and how long has she existed? 300 years? 150 years of independence and this is her level. We haven't quite reached 42 years, and in another 7 years, we'll be at the level of America, and after that we'll go farther. As we pass you by, we'll wave "hi" to you, and then if you want, we'll stop and say, "please come along behind us."[75]

Khrushchev was a feisty little braggart, but in 1959 his confidence did not seem misplaced. He was still pumped up by what had happened two years before when on October 4, 1957, the Soviets had launched the first man-made satellite—silver-colored, beachball-sized, with two whisker-like antennae. The beeps from it were replayed all over the world, haunting the Eisenhower administration. The following month the Soviet Union rubbed in its lead over the supposedly high-tech Americans by sending Sputnik II into orbit, complete with Laika the dog, to mark the fortieth anniversary of the Bolshevik Revolution.

Criticism of Eisenhower had already been mounting: There were reports of heart trouble and he seemed to be spending too much time on the golf course. Now America's leader looked dangerously out of touch. The governor of Michigan, a Democrat, penned this scathing verse:

> *Oh little Sputnik, flying high*
> *With made-in-Moscow beep,*
> *You tell the world it's a Commie sky*
> *and Uncle Sam's asleep.*[76]

Sputnik was a huge shock to America's national pride: Eisenhower immediately established the National Aeronautics and Space Agency (NASA) to coordinate America's space race. But there were deeper issues at stake. Sputnik upset complacent American assumptions about the inherent superiority of a capitalist society over a communist state. "The Soviet Union is like one vast, sprawling college campus on the eve of a football game with its great rival," warned the U.S. commissioner of education. "That rival is the United States. The game is economic and cultural conquest of the world."[77] And the Soviets seemed to be winning. From the panicky inquest that followed Sputnik it emerged that 75 percent of U.S. high-school pupils studied no physics at all. "The nation's stupid children get far better care than the bright," remarked *Life* caustically. Edward Teller, "father" of America's H-bomb, issued a stark warning: "Ten years ago there was no question where the best scientists in the world could be found—here in the U.S. . . . Ten years from now the best scientists in the world will be found in Russia."[78]

So the Sputnik furor prompted a massive program to strengthen science and mathematics education in schools, funded by the federal government. Here was a marked break with tradition—historically, education had been financed largely by states and localities—yet the enhanced role of Uncle Sam was presented not as an erosion of states' rights but as an imperative of national security: The legislation was titled the National Defense Education Act.

Equally important were the massive sums of federal money channeled into key universities. In the 1950s the military bankrolled major science installations such as Berkeley's Lawrence Livermore Laboratory (for nuclear weapons) and the Lincoln Lab (air defense) at Massachusetts Institute of Technology (MIT). Lincoln, on Route 128 outside Boston, became the crucible of advanced technology research in the Northeast; likewise, Stanford University's Electronic Laboratory spawned an industrial park that was the nucleus of Silicon Valley. After the Sputnik crisis, funding surged not just for defense projects but for basic science in general. Between 1957 and 1961 the federal budget for research and development more than doubled, to $9 billion. One of the projects financed, to the tune of over $100 million, was Stanford's linear accelerator—the basis of subsequent research into lasers and missile defense. Major universities became heavily dependent on federal grants and research contracts. Physicist Alvin Weinberg joked that it was hard to tell whether MIT was "a university with many governmental research laboratories appended to it or a cluster of government research laboratories with a very good educational institution attached to it."[79]

The crux of the Sputnik challenge was military. The satellite had been launched by an R-7 rocket, which had sufficient range and power to hit the United States with a nuclear warhead in less than an hour. When Americans absorbed this news, a media panic set in, which the Democrats fanned for partisan advantage. "We meet today in the atmosphere of another Pearl Harbor," Senator Lyndon Johnson told special hearings on Capitol Hill. "We are in a race for survival, and we intend to win that race."[80] That required resources—and not just for building missiles. Land, too, was commandeered for missile testing: The White Sands site in New Mexico, where the first atomic test had taken place in 1945, grew into the largest military installation in the United States, covering 3,200 square miles (double the area of Rhode Island). And, as we shall see in Chapter 17, the Pentagon also bankrolled some of the advanced technologies essential for missile development, playing a decisive role in the development of computers and transistors.

Talk about Sputnik as "the Pearl Harbor of the Cold War" became commonplace; indeed, the situation seemed worse than in 1941. Pearl Harbor was an outlying possession of the United States, 2,000 miles from California. Throughout World War II the continental United States remained virtually untouched; nor was it threatened in the early Cold War because the Soviet Union did not have bombers of sufficient range. But now, in the dawning era of truly intercontinental missiles, Americans felt vulnerable as never before. The Cold War had come home. Until now, "Better dead than Red" had been an easy slogan; soon it might be a real choice.

Eisenhower knew that the situation did not warrant panic. Secret aerial surveillance flights indicated that the United States was ahead in missile technology; the Soviets had improvised frantically to get Sputnik up first. But that was not how it looked to the world when America's Vanguard rocket subsided in flames on the launch pad in December 1957—earning the nickname Flopnik. At the UN Soviet delegates offered America aid from its fund for underdeveloped countries.[81]

In his State of the Union Address in January 1958 Eisenhower tried to sound firm but not alarmist. He said that "what makes the Soviet threat unique in history is its all-inclusiveness. Every human activity is pressed into service as a weapon of expansion"—armaments, trade, education, ideas. "The Soviets are, in short, waging total cold war." Yet he also told Americans that "we could make no more tragic mistake than merely to concentrate on military strength. For if we did only this, the future would hold nothing for the world but an Age of Terror."[82]

It was a prescient warning. Ike was keenly aware that in the struggle against what he had called back in 1952 the "tyranny" and "slavery" of communism, the "free world" might start to become like its enemy. This was the danger of arms races and covert operations, even of "soft" power-plays like the "kitchen debate" between Nixon and Khrushchev. Eisenhower had hoped to make progress in reducing the Cold War tensions but talks about a nuclear test-ban treaty got nowhere and his last summit meeting with Khrushchev in May 1960 fell apart when the Soviet leader revealed clandestine U.S. reconnaissance flights over the USSR and paraded Gary Powers, a U-2 spy-plane pilot who had been shot down and captured.

In one area America did steal a march on the Russians. In 1959 Alaska and Hawaii were admitted as states of the Union, bringing the total neatly to fifty. Hawaii had been a territory of the United States since 1898; Alaska was purchased from Russia in 1867 for $7.2 million. At the time this did not look like much of a bargain—though double the size of Texas, Alaska is predominantly subarctic in climate and in the 1950s attempts to find oil on its frigid north coast proved abortive. Even if it were found, extraction was believed to be too expensive. "It would cost $5 a barrel, and oil will never get to $5 a barrel in our lifetime," snorted one senior executive. But in December 1967 the Atlantic Richfield company struck lucky at Prudhoe Bay. Further drilling showed that this was the largest oil field in North America, eclipsing anything in Texas, and one of the biggest in the world. The challenges of exploitation remained immense: It would take another decade before a pipeline was completed to move the oil 800 miles through the frozen tundra to shipping terminals on Alaska's south coast. But the Prudhoe Bay strike more than vindicated the millions paid to the tsars a century before. At two cents an acre Alaska had come even cheaper than Jefferson's Louisiana Purchase.[83]

Alaska's black gold was all in the future, however, when Ike ended his presidency in 1961. He said farewell with somber words about where the Cold War was taking America:

> [W]e have been compelled to create a permanent armaments industry of vast proportions. Added to this, three and a half million men and women are directly engaged in the defense establishment. We annually spend on military security more than the net income of all United States corporations. This conjunction of an immense military establishment and a large arms industry is new in the American experience. The total influence—economic, political, even spiritual—is felt in every city, every State house, every office of the Federal government. . . . [W]e must guard against the acquisition of unwarranted influence, whether sought or unsought, by the military-industrial

complex. The potential for the disastrous rise of misplaced power exists and will persist.[84]

Eisenhower's Farewell Address echoed and updated the fears of the Founding Fathers about how the values of the republic could be corrupted. An earlier draft had spoken more explicitly of the "military-industrial-congressional complex."[85] In this global struggle against tyranny, would the burdens of America's new empire subvert the country's cherished liberties? Eisenhower had no answer and, as we shall see, his question became ever more pressing.

14

RIGHTS AND RIOTS

What we might call the "long" 1960s—running from Kennedy's inauguration in 1961 to the end of Nixon's presidency in 1974—was a period of enormous importance for the United States both at home and abroad, establishing patterns that would shape the country right up to the present day. That is why I devote two overlapping chapters to the period centering on the two Democratic presidencies of the 1960s, those of John F. Kennedy (1961–1963) and Lyndon Johnson (1963–1969). Chapter 15 will look at how U.S. foreign policy in the 1960s, above all the disastrous war in Vietnam, raised questions about whether the country was an "imperialist" power like any other, with an "imperial presidency" at its very top. This chapter explores the redefinition of American "liberty" through the rights revolution precipitated by black protest.

The great American slogan of the 1940s and 1950s was "freedom." In 1941 President Roosevelt proclaimed his "four freedoms" and spoke of a world war between slavery and freedom. After the defeat of Nazism, Truman and Eisenhower carried over the concepts and the bipolar framework into a new struggle that pitted the "free world" and the "free market" against the repressions of communism. In 1947–1949 the "Freedom Train" carrying the sacred texts of American liberty, from the Declaration of Independence to the Truman Doctrine, toured all forty-eight states; the exhibition was visited by 3.5 million people.

Yet Roosevelt had also used the language of "rights," calling in 1944 for "a second Bill of Rights under which a new basis of security and prosperity can be established for all—regardless of station, or race or creed." And in 1948 the United Nations promulgated a Universal Declaration of Human Rights, intended to apply to anyone "without distinction of any kind," including race or gender.

By the 1960s the language of rights was being used to question the claims of freedom. How, it was asked, could the United States profess to be leader of the free world when millions of its own people were denied basic human rights? African-Americans took the lead here; their civil rights movement in the 1960s achieved bigger gains for blacks than at any time since the end of slavery a century before. Their rhetoric was picked up by other groups, including women and homosexuals, and was vindicated by the Supreme Court. The rights revolution of the 1960s changed the landscape and the language of American politics.

BACK OF THE BUS

The struggle for black rights took place on the streets of America in the early 1960s, through sit-ins and marches that caught the imagination of the world and encouraged emulation by other "rights" movements, including those for women. But what made that struggle feasible was a legal verdict in a quiet courtroom back in May 1954.

Earl Warren seemed friendly but rather dull. He was also a novice, having been appointed chief justice of the United States only six months before, after ten years as governor of California. President Eisenhower was repaying a political debt: Warren had been the Republicans' vice-presidential candidate in 1948 but stood aside in 1952 to expedite Ike's campaign. Eisenhower assumed that Earl Warren would be a reliable conservative; instead the new chief justice orchestrated one of the bombshell legal decisions of the twentieth century.

The case was officially called *Brown et al. v. Board of Education of Topeka et al.* The Supreme Court's decision actually rolled together five cases concerning alleged racial discrimination in schools that had been appealed all the way to the top of the American legal system. This was the result of diligent, undramatic work by the National Association for the Advancement of Colored People (NAACP) spearheaded by Thurgood Marshall, a black lawyer from Baltimore who had an impressive track record in civil rights cases. The NAACP's aim was to reveal the disjunction between current practice and the statements of racial equality written into the U.S. Constitution after the Civil War. Public education in cities like Topeka, Kansas, was segregated, with the separation of pupils into white and black schools justified under the 1896 Supreme Court decision in *Plessy v. Ferguson*, which decreed that segregation was not discriminatory provided the facilities were "separate but equal." After two rounds of legal argument, and a lot of arm-twisting behind the scenes to achieve unanimity among all nine justices, Warren read out the Court's decision on Monday, May 17, 1954.

The chief justice believed that the Constitution had to be interpreted in the light of changing social conditions: Its meaning was not fixed for all time. His argument cited recent works of psychology and sociology to show the effect of discrimination on blacks. Warren argued that education was now central to democratic citizenship in a way that had not been true in the nineteenth century; for this reason the Court could not "turn the clock back" and rest its decision on what may or may not have been intended in 1896. He stated:

> We must consider public education in the light of its full development and its present place in American life throughout the Nation. . . . Does segregation of children in public schools solely on the basis of race, even though the physical facilities and other "tangible" factors may be equal, deprive the children of the minority group of equal educational opportunities? We believe that it does. . . . To separate them from others of similar age and qualifications solely because of their race generates a feeling of inferiority as to their status in the community that may affect their hearts and minds in a way unlikely ever to be undone. . . . We conclude that in the field of public education the doctrine of "separate but equal" has no place. Separate educational facilities are inherently unequal.[1]

The verdict in the Brown case polarized opinion. The *Washington Post*, invoking words from Lincoln's Gettysburg Address of 1863, called the Court's decision "a new birth of freedom" and predicted that it would have "a wonderfully tonic effect" by ridding America of "an incubus which impeded and embarrassed it in all its relations with the world." Abroad and at home, said the *Post*, "this decision will engender a renewal of faith in democratic institutions and ideals."[2]

But southern segregationists used this Cold War rhetoric of freedom to opposite effect. Judge Tom Brady of Mississippi, in a widely disseminated pamphlet, denounced "Black Monday"—May 17, 1954—as a date that would rank with the Fourth of July, except that this was a declaration not of independence but of "socialistic doctrine": "It was on Black Monday that the judicial branch of our government usurped the sacred privilege and right of the respective states of this union to educate their youth." Brady insisted that "the States were not created for the establishment of a paternalistic or totalitarian Government" and even claimed that "the resistance of communism and tyranny, irrespective of whatever guise they may adopt, is not treason. It is the prerequisite of freedom, the very essence of liberty." Brady believed that the term "Black Monday" was aptly symbolic. "Black denoting darkness and terror. Black signifying the absence of light and wisdom. Black embodying grief, destruction and death."[3]

Brady's polemic about freedom and blackness expressed the sentiments of millions of white southerners, as the Supreme Court was well aware. Having decreed that segregated schools were unconstitutional, Warren and his colleagues then decided not to force the pace of change. They did not demand immediate desegregation or even set a timetable for implementation. In a second decision in May 1955 they simply instructed lower-level federal courts to ensure that the schools were desegregated "with all deliberate speed." This left the issue in the hands of the southern political elite: As the attorney general of Texas, John Ben Shepperd, put it, "Texas loves its Negro people and Texas will solve their problems in its own way."[4]

Nor did President Eisenhower intend to use the power of the presidency, or even its moral authority. He kept silent in public on the Brown decision, but his private views were clear: "I don't believe you can change the hearts of men with laws and decisions. . . . I am convinced that the Supreme Court decision set back progress in the South at least fifteen years." Ike went on to say, "[I]t's all very well to talk about school integration—if you remember you may also be talking about social *dis*integration. Feelings are deep on this." He added that "the fellow who tries to tell me that you can do these things by force is just plain nuts."[5]

The Supreme Court had unlocked the door to equal rights but the federal government would not push it open, so black Americans took matters into their own hands. One of the most visible marks of their social inferiority in the South was the practice on buses of requiring black passengers to enter by the rear door and to move to the back or stand when the bus became crowded. On the evening of December 1, 1955, in Montgomery, Alabama, a woman called Rosa Parks decided not to budge. As she recalled later, "When the driver saw that I was still sitting there, he asked if I was going to stand up. I told him, no, I wasn't. He said, 'Well, if you don't stand up, I'm going to have you arrested.' I told him to go on and have me arrested."[6]

Rosa Parks was duly taken to jail. Local black leaders decided to make her a test case: Married, middle-aged, and a steady churchgoer, she would be a perfect symbol. On the day of her trial they arranged a boycott of Montgomery's city buses. A reporter for the local paper described what happened:

> Negroes were on almost every corner in the downtown area, silent, waiting for rides or moving about to keep warm, but few got on buses. Negro cabs were packed tight and it seemed as if they stopped to pick up more passengers at every corner. . . . Scores of Negroes were walking, their lunches in brown paper sacks under their arms. None spoke to white people. They exchanged little talk among themselves. It was an event almost solemn.[7]

The bus boycott had been intended as a one-day event but its success emboldened black leaders. That evening they formed the Montgomery Improvement Association and they elected as leader a new young black minister—a man outside the factions that fractured the black elite. Martin Luther King, Jr., was the son of the famous Baptist minister from Atlanta encountered in Chapter 8. Studious and intellectual, the young King had a PhD in theology from Boston University and would have liked to stay in the North as a professor, but his ties to the South were too strong. When pushed into the breach at short notice that December evening in 1955 he showed a rare talent for leadership.

King often took fifteen hours to prepare a sermon; now he had barely fifteen minutes to scribble a few notes before addressing a mass meeting in a local church, with a battery of TV cameras in the front row. He began slowly, rehearsing the situation on the buses and the case of Rosa Parks, but then soared into a passionate oration about how black people were tired of being kicked around. "We have no alternative but to protest," he declared. "If we are wrong, the Supreme Court of this nation is wrong. If we are wrong, the Constitution of the United States is wrong. If we are wrong, God Almighty is wrong." The crowd was now ecstatic, stamping and cheering, but King tempered crusading zeal with Christian forbearance. Blacks, he insisted, were not to emulate the mob violence of the Ku Klux Klan but must follow the fundamental teaching of Jesus: "Love your enemies, bless them that curse you." King quoted Booker T. Washington. "Let no man pull you so low as to make you hate him."[8]

The speech was both electrifying and judicious, outlining the philosophy of nonviolent protest that was to animate King's whole career. It also made the twenty-six-year-old minister a national figure. His shrewd leadership helped keep the protest alive in the ensuing weeks despite the city government's intransigence and growing violence against blacks. When a bomb shattered the front of his house, King still preached forgiveness and nonviolence; when he and other black leaders were prosecuted, they lined up to be taken to jail—milking the nationwide publicity. The boycott was now beginning to pinch the city, particularly the bus company and downtown businesses. Eventually a case against segregated buses made its way up the federal courts and in November 1956 the Supreme Court declared Montgomery's practices unconstitutional.

King warned against triumphalism: "We must take this not as a victory over the white man but as a victory for justice and democracy." But he treated it as a metaphor for the black condition in American society: "In the past, we have sat in the back of the buses, and this has indicated a basic lack of self-respect." On the other hand, "the white people have sat in the front and have thought of themselves as superior." Both approaches, said King, were wrong. "Our duty in going back on the buses is to destroy this superior-inferior relationship . . . to act in the manner best designed to establish man's oneness."[9]

Despite foot-dragging and obstruction by the city authorities, Montgomery ended segregation on its transport system. Symbolically King rode one of the first integrated buses four days before Christmas 1956 and bus boycotts spread to other cities in the South. King and fellow ministers across the South also formed the Southern Christian Leadership Conference (SCLC) to coordinate further protests.

But change was piecemeal and white resistance deepened: In September 1957 the governor of Arkansas blocked school integration in the name of states' rights, warning that otherwise "blood would run in the streets." Eisenhower was obliged to send in the U.S. army to prevent "mob rule." The sight of paratroopers from the 101st Airborne Division—vanguard of the army that brought freedom to France in 1944—protecting black teenagers going to school in America was richly symbolic.

Daisy Bates, co-editor of the local black newspaper in Little Rock, recalled the soldiers arriving at her home to escort nine black students to the Central High School:

> Paratroops . . . stood across the width of the street at each end of the block. . . .
> An Army station wagon stopped in front of our house. While photographers,
> perched precariously on the tops of cars and rooftops, went into action, the
> paratrooper in charge of the detail started up our driveway. As he approached,
> I heard Minniejean say gleefully, "Oh, look at them, they're so—so soldierly!
> It gives you goose pimples to look at them!" And then she added solemnly,
> "For the first time in my life I feel like an American citizen."[10]

Getting the students through the doors of Central High was only the beginning. All through the school year they were subject to persistent harassment. One of the nine, Ernest Green, recalled a defining moment just before Christmas: "For a couple of weeks there had been a number of white kids following us . . . continuously calling us niggers. 'Nigger, nigger, nigger'—one right after the other. Minniejean Brown was in the lunch line with me, and there was this white kid who was shorter than Minnie . . . he reminded me of a small dog yelping at somebody's leg. Minnie had just picked up her chili. . . . [She] turned around and took that chili and dumped it on the dude's head." For a moment, there was total silence in the cafeteria and then the helpers, all black, broke into applause. "And the white kids there didn't know what to do. It was the first time that anybody had seen somebody black retaliate."[11]

Minniejean Brown was suspended from school and then expelled. Her family moved to New York but the other students struggled through the year and received their graduating diplomas. That was a symbolic victory, but segregationists called graduation day "Liberation Day" and, for the whole of the following year, Little Rock's public schools were closed. They reopened only after another Supreme Court decision.

These dramatic events in Montgomery, Alabama, and Little Rock, Arkansas, were signs that the fabric of segregation was finally beginning to tear across the Deep South in the mid-1950s. Pressures from the Supreme Court, newly attentive to racial issues, and from local black citizens, ready to stand up for their rights, were having an effect. But it was all painfully slow: African-Americans, in Martin Luther King's phrase, were still at the back of the bus. It would take a new generation and new methods to make real breakthroughs.

"AND WE SHALL OVERCOME"

In the South segregation was pervasive but irrational. A department store like Woolworth's would sell socks or toothpaste to blacks and whites indiscriminately, but then designate the lunch counter for "whites only." On February 18, 1960, a group of black students in Nashville, Tennessee, staged a carefully planned protest, sitting down and asking for food. "The first sit-in we had was really funny," Diane Nash recalled. "The waitresses were nervous. They must have dropped $2,000 worth of dishes that day." It was, she said, "almost like a cartoon . . . we were sitting there trying not to laugh" but "at the same time we were scared to death." The black students were not served but they sat tight, and they kept returning day after day. Young whites came to insult them, grinding out cigarette butts on their backs and pulling them off the stools, but it was the black students who were arrested by the Nashville police for "disorderly conduct." "So," recalled Diane Nash, "we all got up and marched to the wagon." But when the police turned and looked at the lunch counter again, a second wave of students had taken their seats; after they had been marched off a third wave took their place. No matter what the police did and how many they arrested, said Nash, "there was still a lunch counter full of students."[12]

The Nashville disturbances were part of a wave of sit-ins across the South in 1960 and 1961. Some were spontaneous but many of the students, black and white, had been trained in techniques of nonviolent action based on the precepts of Mahatma Gandhi. Before going to the lunch counters they had held a role-play workshop to practice what might happen—talking to the manager, coping with abuse, learning not to retaliate when blows were rained down from behind. These workshops were sponsored by mainstream black organizations like the Congress on Racial Equality (CORE) and King's SCLC, but the students were not King clones. They were of a different generation, impatient with the incrementalism and compromise of older blacks. Offspring of the new black middle class, aroused and often radicalized by higher education, they were now ready to take the initiative. In the early 1960s it was often the young who led and the black leaders who followed.

One of the older generation who reached out to the young was Ella Baker, a black activist in her late fifties who worked for the SCLC. Disenchanted herself with the established black organizations, she helped students like Diane Nash set up their own Student Non-Violent Coordinating Committee (SNCC). This, she said, "made it crystal clear that current sit-ins and other demonstrations are concerned with something bigger than a hamburger or even a giant-sized Coke. Whatever may be the difference of approach to their goal, the Negro and white students, North and South, are seeking to rid America of the scourge of racial segregation and discrimination—not only at lunch counters, but in every aspect of life."[13]

Global events also had an impact. In 1960 no fewer than sixteen African countries gained independence from their European colonial masters. "Here were black people, talking of freedom and liberation and independence, thousands of miles away," John Lewis, one of the founders of SNCC, recalled. "We could hardly miss the lesson for ourselves. They were getting their freedom, and we still didn't have ours in what we believed was a free country."[14]

In 1961 it was another group of activists, the "Freedom Riders," who hit the headlines. James Farmer of CORE explained their rationale: "I was impressed by the fact that most of the activity thus far had been of local people working on their own local problems. . . . I thought that this was going to limit the growth of the Movement. . . . We somehow had to cut across state lines and establish the position that we were entitled to act any place in the country, no matter where we hung our hat and called home, because it was our country."[15] The catchy title "Freedom Rides" captured this idea well.

Travel between states was the preserve of federal law and the Supreme Court had ruled in 1960 that segregation on interstate buses and trains was unconstitutional. But the new Kennedy administration, despite its liberal image, was not keen on enforcing the decision for fear of losing the support of racist southern Democrats, who mattered on Capitol Hill. So "what we had to do," said Farmer, "was to make it more dangerous politically for the federal government *not* to enforce federal law than it would be to enforce federal law. . . . We felt we could count on the racists of the South to create a crisis."[16]

In May 1961 the Freedom Rides began. Specially trained pairs of volunteers would board an interstate bus. The white went to the back, where blacks were supposed to sit, while the black sat at the front—refusing to move when ordered. At rest stops, blacks would go into the whites-only waiting rooms and try to use the facilities. Predictably the volunteers were beaten up, several buses were firebombed, and scores of Riders were imprisoned and abused in the South's brutal jails. But students took up the cause—in all, some 430 people participated in the Freedom Rides, 40 percent of them black activists from the South. Not a huge number, but they had an enormous impact.[17]

As Farmer intended, the Riders seriously embarrassed the Kennedy administration during a summer when America was facing off against Russia over the freedom of Germany. "Look, Father," the president told a leading Catholic priest, "I may have to send the Alabama National Guard to Berlin tomorrow and I don't want to have to do it in the middle of a revolution at home." Attorney General Bobby Kennedy, the president's brother, tried to get southern white leaders to stop the violence, while appealing to black activists to cool their protests. But a black minister from Montgomery told him, "Had there not been a cooling-off period following the Civil War, the Negro would be free today. Isn't 99 years long enough to cool off, Mr. Attorney General?" Martin Luther King also rebuked Bobby Kennedy: "It's difficult to understand the position of oppressed people. Ours is a way out—creative, moral and non-violent. It is not tied to black supremacy or Communism, but to the plight of the oppressed. It can save the soul of America."[18]

Eventually white violence did force the Kennedy administration to act. In September 1961 the Interstate Commerce Commission announced that interstate carriers and terminals must display signs that seating was "without regard to race, color, creed or national origin." The success of the Freedom Rides showed that direct action was working.

In 1963 King and black leaders targeted the city of Birmingham, Alabama, using marches and sit-ins to press for an end to all segregation. In his Letter from Birmingham City Jail—written in April on the margins of a newspaper and scraps of toilet paper—King defended himself against those who urged patient negotiation:

> Nonviolent direct action seeks to create such a crisis and foster such creative tension that a community that has constantly refused to negotiate is forced to confront the issue. It seeks so to dramatize the issue that it can no longer be ignored. . . . We have waited for more than 340 years for our constitutional and God-given rights. The nations of Asia and Africa are moving with jetlike speed toward the goal of political independence, and we still creep at horse-and-buggy pace toward the gaining of a cup of coffee at a lunch counter.[19]

The previous year, 1962, King had been outwitted in Albany, Georgia, by a shrewd police chief who avoided violence, at least on camera, and even arranged to have King's fines paid, so he would not languish in jail. But Birmingham was the South's most segregated city, a stronghold of the Ku Klux Klan, and the police chief, Eugene "Bull" Connor, was "a vain, short-tempered, publicity-seeking bully, with a notorious reputation for racial extremism."[20] Connor's vicious tactics played into King's hands: TV pictures flashed around the world showing children being blasted with water from fire hoses and chased by snarling police dogs. Embarrassed by the bad publicity and losing income every day, Birmingham business leaders caved in and conceded to his demands.

King kept up the pressure with a march on Washington on August 28, 1963, attended by around a quarter of a million people. The presence of thousands of whites, including celebrities such as singers Bob Dylan and Joan Baez and Christian and Jewish leaders, testified to the widening appeal of the civil rights movement. On the steps of the Lincoln Memorial, a century after the Emancipation Proclamation, King voiced his hope that one day America would honor its creed of freedom and justice. "I have a dream" was King's most resonant oration, but turning dreams into realities required action by the federal government.

Aware of the changing public mood, President Kennedy proposed a new civil rights bill, but little progress was made in Congress before his assassination that November. It was Kennedy's successor, Lyndon Johnson, who pushed the legislation through on the back of JFK's martyrdom, telling Congress that it would be the most fitting way to honor his memory. Johnson utilized his unrivaled experience on Capitol Hill, doling out pork-barrel projects to win support and finally mustering enough votes to end the longest southern filibuster to date in Senate history (fifty-seven working days). But, less cynically, he also elevated the civil rights bill to the level of a crusade. In the 1860s, he said, Americans had put an end to "the moral evil of slavery" but once again, a century later, "the problem of racial wrongs and racial hatreds is the central moral problem of this Republic." Reminded that, when a senator, he had an indifferent record on civil rights, Johnson replied, "some people get a chance late in life to correct the sins of their youth and very few get a chance as big as the White House."[21]

The Civil Rights Act made illegal all forms of segregation and discrimination, but it did not really grapple with the underlying problem of black disfranchisement in the South. Once again it was black protest in the South that forced action in Washington, and indeed by Martin Luther King himself.

Although King gained the headlines—in December 1964 receiving the Nobel Peace Prize—many black activists had their doubts about him. As Ella Baker explained, "I have always felt it was a handicap for oppressed peoples to depend so largely upon a leader, because unfortunately in our culture, the charismatic leader usually becomes a leader because he has found a spot in the public limelight." Baker believed that a person who is "called upon to give public statements and is acclaimed by the establishment" often "gets to the point of believing that he *is* the movement. Such people get so involved with playing the game of being important that they exhaust themselves and their time, and they don't do the work of actually organizing people."[22]

For activists like Baker, organizing the people was the heart of the matter. In a federal democracy presidents always had to be sensitive to the weight of political opinion and in the early 1960s this was still overwhelmingly white. In Mississippi and Alabama, probably the poorest and most racist states in the Union, fewer than 10 percent of blacks of voting age were registered to vote. Registration in the United States was not a case of simply returning a form in the mail; it was a public act, and in the Deep South this act was made as difficult as possible.

The local registration office usually opened only a few days each month; registrars tended to arrive late, leave early, and have long lunch breaks. So blacks had to take time off work to register and those who did so knew their names would be published in the local press, jeopardizing their jobs and hence their mortgages. Nor was registration itself a formality. In Alabama blacks had to fill in a detailed form, read part of the Constitution, and answer obscure questions including:

- If a person charged with treason denies his guilt, how many persons must testify against him before he can be convicted?
- Name the attorney general of the United States.
- If the president does not wish to sign a bill, how many days is he allowed in which to return it to Congress for reconsideration?[23]

One elderly black man failed this "literacy test" because he wrote in a shaky hand. He told the registrar, "I am 65 years old, I own 100 acres of land that is paid for, I am a taxpayer and I have six children. All of them is teachin', workin'. . . . If what

I done ain't enough to be a registered voter with all the tax I got to pay, then Lord have mercy on America."[24]

So student activists made voter registration their top priority in the Deep South. Volunteers, many of them white and female, targeted Mississippi in "Freedom Summer" before the 1964 election and several were brutally killed. In 1965 King took up the cause by focusing on Selma, Alabama—where, like "Bull" Connor, the local police chief, Sheriff Jim Clark, was both viciously racist and tactically inept. Employing the same methods as in Birmingham, King got himself locked up; so did dozens of teachers and hundreds of their schoolchildren. On Sunday, March 7, the protestors tried to take their case to Alabama's capital, Montgomery, only to find the way barred across the bridge out of Selma. When they refused to turn back, state troopers and Clark's mounted posse attacked with clubs and tear gas. "The horses," Amelia Boynton recalled, "were more humane than the troopers; they stepped over fallen victims."[25]

"Bloody Sunday," as the clash became known, shocked the nation. Two weeks later Martin Luther King led a far bigger crowd on the fifty-mile march from Selma to Montgomery. With Governor George Wallace refusing to provide protection to the "Communist-trained anarchists," President Johnson federalized the Alabama National Guard and sent in the U.S. army. "Bloody Sunday" had outraged Johnson. Barely a week later, moving faster and further than many aides thought wise, the president asked Congress for a voting rights act, which would use the power of the federal government to eliminate all state and local barriers to color-blind democracy in accordance with what he called "The American Promise":

> At times history and fate meet at a single time in a single place to shape a turning point in man's unending search for freedom. So it was at Lexington and Concord. So it was a century ago at Appomattox. So it was last week in Selma, Alabama. . . . Our mission is at once the oldest and the most basic of this country: to right wrong, to do justice, to serve man. . . . And should we defeat every enemy, should we double our wealth and conquer the stars, and still be unequal to this issue, then we will have failed as a people and as a nation. For with a country as with a person, "What is a man profited, if he shall gain the whole world, and lose his own soul?"[26]

Picking up one of the most famous songs of the civil rights movement, Johnson intoned, to prolonged applause, "And we shall overcome." It still took months of arm-twisting by Johnson to get the bill through Congress, but on August 6, 1965, the president signed into law the Voting Rights Act. Watching him in the Rotunda of the U.S. Capitol were many specially invited African-Americans including Rosa Parks and Martin Luther King.

The Act was a landmark for many reasons. Now that federal examiners were policing the process, black registration rose rapidly—reaching 60 percent of potential

voters in Mississippi and Alabama by 1968. And once blacks had unlocked the ballot box, they could elect their own representatives to the state assemblies and
the U.S. Congress. These people would then promote the interests of African-
Americans, just as had happened before for immigrant groups when they became
citizens in large numbers. Equally significant were the methods that brought about
the legislation. As King intended, it was the sit-ins, beatings, and publicity that
forced the White House to act; the direct-action methods of the civil rights movement became a model for other protestors.

The Voting Rights Act also mattered constitutionally. Although equal rights
had been written into the Constitution for nearly a century, enforcement had been
left largely in the hands of the states. Here was an unresolved clash between rival
understandings of American liberty—the federal and the local. Now the 1965 Act
signaled that states' rights were overridden by individual rights, enforced by the
federal government. This, too, set a precedent for the future, accelerating the rights
revolution.

BLACK POWER

When Johnson signed the Voting Rights Act he spoke of how the first Africans arrived in the New World: "They came in darkness and they came in chains. And
today we strike away the last major shackle of those fierce and ancient bonds. Today
the Negro story and the American story fuse and blend."[27] Five days later, on August 11, 1965, Watts, the black section of Los Angeles, went up in flames.

The Watts riots were triggered by a routine incident: White policemen arrested
a black youth for drunk driving, a crowd gathered, and tempers flared in the smog-
laden summer heat. After a night of rioting, the governor of California sent in the
National Guard and then imposed a curfew, but six days of burning and looting left
thirty-four dead and an estimated $200 million of damage over an area of nearly
fifty square miles.

The governor of California appointed a commission of inquiry chaired by John
McCone, formerly director of the CIA. Its report blamed the riots on a small minority of malcontents: "They looted stores, set fires, beat up white passersby whom
they hauled from stopped cars, many of which were turned upside down and burned,
exchanged shots with law enforcement officers, and stoned and shot at firemen. The
rioters seemed to have been caught up in an insensate rage of destruction."[28]

But deeper research by social scientists suggested that 15 percent of the local
black population was actively involved, while another third approved of the rioting. Nor was the looting random or "insensate"—most of it was targeted at white
pawn-shops, supermarkets, and department stores, while black property and most
schools and libraries were spared. There was also widespread satisfaction in having hit back at the L.A. police, reviled as racist and brutal. "The mood in Watts last
week," according to *Newsweek*, "smacked less of defeat than of victory and power."[29]

Martin Luther King was appalled when he flew in: "How can you say you won when thirty-four Negroes are dead, your community is destroyed, and whites are using the riots as an excuse for inaction?" A young jobless black told him bluntly, "We won because we made the whole world pay attention to us."[30]

The Watts riots put into perspective America's mood of self-congratulation a week before. They showed that the country's racial problems could not be solved simply by new laws to guarantee civil and voting rights.

Outside the Jim Crow South, the underlying problems were economic and social. In Chicago, home to more than a million blacks, they found work mostly in low-paying service jobs; the few with skills found little opportunity for promotion. According to the SCLC, in 1960 "Negroes, who represented twenty-three percent of the population, accounted for forty-three percent of the unemployed" and those blacks "fortunate enough to achieve professional and managerial status found themselves victimized in their search for adequate housing."[31] Chicago real estate agents ran two separate, carefully controlled housing markets and blacks found they had to pay 10 to 20 percent more than whites on rentals, house purchases, insurance, and interest rates.

On July 10, 1966, designated as "Freedom Sunday," King drew up a series of demands about Chicago's endemic discrimination in jobs and housing. Flanked by pressmen and TV cameras he stuck the document with adhesive tape to the door of City Hall—deliberately emulating his namesake Martin Luther, who had nailed his ninety-five theses to the church door in Wittenberg nearly 450 years before.

But 1966 did not mark the start of a modern-day Reformation. In Chicago, unlike the South, there were no obvious targets such as white-only drinking fountains, and King's program of marches through leafy white suburbs to dramatize the housing issue provoked unprecedented hatred. Well-dressed men and women waved Nazi flags, threw rocks and bottles, and shouted abuse at the marchers. Al Raby, one of the black leaders in Chicago, recalled that women were often the "most vicious," screaming "young monkeys" at the blacks and "white trash" at their supporters. They told the blacks "to go back to Africa." An elderly white woman stood sobbing, "God, I hate niggers and nigger-lovers." An old man shouted at the marchers, "I worked all my life for a house out here, and no nigger is going to get it."[32]

These middle-class whites were the children of immigrants—Poles, Germans, and Italians who had bought into the American Dream and were not inclined to share it with blacks. King persisted with the marches but he was deeply shaken: "I've never seen anything like it. I've been in demonstrations all across the south, but I can say that I have never seen—even in Mississippi and Alabama—mobs as hostile and hate-filled as I've seen in Chicago."[33] He began to realize the real depths of racism in America—among not just whites but blacks as well. In Chicago many of the slum landlords and ghetto shop-owners were Jewish and King was shocked at the virulence of black anti-Semitism. Although a month of marches did force Chicago leaders to sign an agreement about integrated housing, Mayor Richard Daley, a much savvier politician than "Bull" Connor, quietly wriggled out of its implementation.

Failure in Chicago was a sign of a deeper problem for King: He was losing control of the civil rights movement. Its unity had always been tenuous, with student radicals particularly impatient with his strategy of nonviolence, and in June 1966 there came a symbolic turning point.

Black activists were marching through Mississippi, trying to galvanize the locals to exercise their voting rights. One of the marchers, Stokely Carmichael, a veteran of the Freedom Rides, was thrown into jail for putting up his tent in the grounds of a black high school. On being released that evening, he addressed a large rally, 3,000 strong, standing on the back of a flatbed truck. The crowd roared their greeting and he responded with a raised arm and a clenched fist. Realizing he was in his element, with his people, Carmichael declaimed, "This is the twenty-seventh time I have been arrested—and I ain't going to jail no more!" More cheers and clapping. "The only way we gonna stop them white men from whuppin' us is to take over. We been saying freedom for six years and we ain't got nothin.' What we gonna start saying now is Black Power!" The crowd was totally with him. "BLACK POWER!" they chanted again and again.[34]

The cry was taken up across the country, in hope or fear. Stokely Carmichael did not coin the term "Black Power" but he did make it a phrase on everyone's lips. Here was a frontal assault on the orthodox civil rights movement, with its philosophy of integration and its slogan "Freedom Now." Admittedly in his more sober statements Carmichael talked about empowerment—getting African-Americans to take control of their lives politically, economically, and also culturally through the inculcation of racial pride. But to radicals and most whites "Black Power" sounded like a call for revolution, and increasingly Carmichael's rhetoric pointed in that direction: "When you talk of Black Power, you talk of bringing this country to its knees. When you talk of Black Power, you talk of building a movement that will smash everything that Western civilization has created."[35] Carmichael and his sidekicks never resorted to violence—they just threatened it—but, as the civil rights movement splintered and the slide to extremism gained momentum, there were others who were ready to use guns.

The Black Panther movement was formed in San Francisco in October 1966. Its ten-point program mingled traditional civil rights slogans with the rhetoric of Marxism and anti-imperialism:

- We want freedom. We want power to determine the destiny of our Black Community. . . .
- We want full employment for our people. . . .
- We want an end to the robbery by capitalists of our Black Community. . . .

- We want decent housing, fit for the shelter of human beings. . . .
- And as our major political objective, a United-Nations supervised plebiscite to be held throughout the Black colony in which only Black colonial subjects will be allowed to participate, for the purpose of determining the will of the people as to their national destiny.[36]

This was the language not of racial integration but of black separatism. And the Panthers—in their telegenic black leather jackets, black berets, and dark glasses—backed it all up with the gun. Starting out as a ghetto self-defense force offering free breakfasts and "liberation schools" for local kids, the Panthers soon got into murder and rape, bank robberies, and drug trafficking. By the end of the 1960s they had been crushed by the police and FBI.

Black Power and the Black Panthers, although fringe movements, marked a deeper sea-change in attitudes. Increasingly the word "black" replaced "Negro" or "colored" among African-Americans. This was an attack on the idea, rooted in Western culture and in America since colonial times, that black was a synonym for everything evil and degraded. Now the line was "Black is beautiful"; business and advertisers rushed to pitch their wares accordingly. The publisher of *Ebony* magazine explained that "the Negro market . . . is not a special market *within* the white market—it is, on the contrary, *a general market* defined, precisely, by its exclusion from the white market. . . . Negro consumers tend to think, buy, and act in significantly different ways from white consumers" and "are growing not less self-conscious but more self-conscious."[37]

An internationally celebrated symbol of black pride was the boxer Cassius Clay—born in Louisville, Kentucky, and named for a white anti-slavery campaigner of the nineteenth century. Although a big man, Clay had lightning fists and dancer-like feet; his motto was "Float like a butterfly, sting like a bee." But it was his arrogance as much as his skill that hit the headlines—Clay would taunt his opponents outside and inside the ring. This was also the theme of his poems, like this one published in 1963 and called "I'm the Greatest":

> *This is the story about a man*
> *With iron fists and a beautiful tan.*
> *He talks a lot and he boasts indeed*
> *Of a powerful punch and blinding speed. . . .*
> *This colourful fighter is something to see,*
> *And heavyweight champ he's certain to be.*[38]

This was no idle boast: The following year, 1964, Clay won the World Heavyweight Boxing Championship, remaining undefeated until 1971. Clay was also radicalized during the 1960s, joining a Muslim sect called the Nation of Islam and symbolically changing his name to Muhammad Ali. His transition from white clone into a symbol of black pride and then of radical separatism was a parable of 1960s America.

Sport had long been a way for at least a few African-Americans to get to the very top. And no black athletes in the 1960s got more attention than Tommie Smith and John Carlos, who won gold and bronze in the 200-meter final at the Mexico Olympics in October 1968. When "The Star-Spangled Banner" was played at the medal ceremony, each man raised a black-gloved fist in the Black Power salute. For doing so, they were suspended from the U.S. team and pilloried by mainstream America, receiving many death threats. Some black athletes were also unhappy but Smith was and remained unrepentant: "We are black and proud to be black. White America will say 'an American won,' not 'a black American won.' If it had been something bad, they would have said 'a Negro.'"[39]

WOMEN'S LIBERATION

The civil rights movement and Black Power provoked other groups to demand similar rights. For homosexuals a catalyst was a police raid on the Stonewall Inn—a racially mixed gay bar in Greenwich Village, New York, in June 1969. The patrons fought back, brawling with police, and the bar went up in flames; riots flared in the neighborhood for several days. A month later the Gay Liberation Front was formed, initially with ties to the Black Panthers, and during the next year Gay Lib groups sprang up in many American cities, staging "Gay Pride" marches and parades on the anniversary of the Stonewall riot. As the extremists were purged, a nationwide gay rights movement took root, demanding full civil rights for homosexuals.

Native Americans were also emboldened. Nominally the United States maintained the nineteenth-century fiction that the Indian tribes constituted sovereign nations, but in practice their reservations were regulated by the federal government through the Bureau of Indian Affairs. For much of the twentieth century the Bureau's goal was essentially Jeffersonian, to persuade and prod the Indians into full assimilation in American life. This changed, however, in the late 1960s as Native American radicals emulated blacks in demanding rights and celebrating cultural pride. Best-sellers such as *Bury My Heart at Wounded Knee* by Dee Brown and Ralph Nelson's film *Soldier Blue* presented a new "victims" history of how the West was won, at odds with heroic myths about settlers and cowboys. Like the new black histories, they raised troubling questions about the limits of American liberty.

But the most significant group to take up the banner of "minority rights" was American women. In December 1962 the *Saturday Evening Post*—a popular American weekly magazine—concluded, after an extensive survey, that "the American woman has all the rights she wants and—like American men—doesn't exercise all she has."[40] The following year, however, the writer Betty Friedan blew the lid off such complacency by asserting that American women were living in a "comfortable concentration camp." She claimed that "the women who 'adjust' as housewives, who grow up wanting to be 'just a housewife,' are in as much danger as the millions who walked to their own death in the concentration camps. . . . American women are not, of course, being readied for mass extermination, but they are suffering a slow death of mind and spirit."[41]

Friedan's book *The Feminine Mystique* proved a runaway best-seller. The author offered it as a cri de coeur from one of millions of educated women, imprisoned in suburban domesticity. Her raw material came from questionnaires and interviews with college-educated women from the 1940s. A Nebraska mother of three who had a PhD in anthropology told her:

> A film made of any typical morning in my house would look like an old Marx Brothers' comedy. I wash the dishes, rush the older children off to school, dash out in the yard to cultivate the chrysanthemums, run back in to make a phone call about a committee meeting, help the youngest child build a blockhouse, spend fifteen minutes skimming the newspapers so I can be well informed, then scamper down to the washing machine where my thrice-weekly laundry includes enough clothes to keep a primitive village going for an entire year. By noon I'm ready for a padded cell. . . .
>
> [I]n the past sixty years we have come full circle and the American house-wife is again trapped in a squirrel cage. If the cage is now a plate-glass-and-broadloom ranch house or a convenient modern apartment, the situation is no less painful than when her grandmother sat over an embroidery hoop in her gilt-and-plush parlor and muttered angrily about women's rights.[42]

The postwar era was not quite as clear-cut as Friedan described. She played down evidence of women's public achievements and played up stories of claustrophobic domesticity.[43] She ignored the rapid increase in the number of married women entering the workforce: By 1960, 30 percent of white married women were working—almost double the proportion ten years before.[44] Nor was Friedan simply the frustrated middle-class housewife that she presented to the world. She had a long prehistory as a labor journalist and closet communist; early drafts of *The Feminine Mystique* were full of references to Marx and Engels that she cut out to make her polemic more palatable in the Cold War climate of the time.[45]

When all is said and done, however, Friedan's caricature still captured the ethos of the 1950s. Barely a third of college students in 1958 were female; back in 1920 the figure had been nearly half. The "G.I. Bill" was part of the explanation: Service veterans received subsidized education and they were overwhelmingly male. Women, it was said, dropped out of college in order to get their MRS degree and then worked on their PhT—Putting Hubbie Through. "We married what we wanted to *be*," the wife of a college administrator remarked. "If we wanted to be a lawyer or a doctor, we married one."[46]

Friedan's book inspired thousands of American women and made the author into an international celebrity. When pressures mounted to create a women's equivalent of the civil rights movement, she was the natural leader—not just because of her fame but because of her personality. As one colleague put it:

> She sweeps through meetings, telephone calls, dinners and speeches with frantic bursts of energy as if each day might be her last. Everything is in motion, not just her words, which come so fast she seems to ignore the necessity of breathing. Her hands gesticulate, wave, flail. Her eyes are deep, dark, charged, and violent as her language. Her nose is long, her hair, despite patient attention at the beauty parlor, often askew. Nothing fits the accepted model of beauty. Yet she exerts a powerful, haunting attractiveness—that special combustion that lights up a few rare individuals interacting with their audience.[47]

The new organization, formed in October 1966, was called NOW—the National Organization for Women. Deliberately "for" women, not "of," it aimed to include men, just as the early civil rights movement had included non-blacks. NOW's self-declared purpose was "to take action to bring women into full participation in the mainstream of American society now, exercising all privileges and responsibilities in equal partnership with men." NOW noted that "there is no civil rights movement to speak for women as there has been for Negroes and other victims of discrimination. The National Organization for Women must begin to speak."[48]

Organizations like NOW tended to be middle class and professional, campaigning for equal rights especially in the workplace. The Civil Rights Act of 1964 had included a ban on discrimination based on "sex" but, as with the affirmation of black equality, that remained largely a dead letter. In 1967 NOW picketed newspapers like the *New York Times* to end the practice of sex-segregated job ads—with the male section seeking high-status professionals in law, medicine, and accountancy while women were invited to apply for domestic, clerical, and "helping" positions such as teacher or librarian. Despite intensive campaigning, sex-segregated ads were not finally banned by the Supreme Court until 1973.

Those women who did make it into top-rank jobs found the cards stacked against them, despite the existence since 1963 of an Equal Pay Act. Edith Grimm, who became the first female vice-president of a leading Chicago department store, reckoned that the pay of the average woman executive was about half that of her male counterpart, even though she had to perform far better just to survive: "A woman who is determined to play a game [that is] so fixed had better be prepared to look like a girl, act like a lady, think like a man, and work like a dog."[49]

The campaign for equality with men in pay and workplace rights was the goal of one element of the new women's movement, but there was another, more radical element, campaigning not simply for women's rights but for women's liberation.

Some of its roots lay in SNCC, the student civil rights organization, where white women volunteers were appalled at the sexism that lurked within the crusade against racism. Two of them, Mary King and Casey Hayden, circulated a manifesto:

> Assumptions of male superiority are as widespread and deep-rooted and every much as crippling to the woman as the assumption of white supremacy are to the Negro. Consider why it is in SNCC that women who are competent, qualified, and experienced are automatically assigned to the "female" jobs such as: typing, desk work, telephone work, filing, library work, cooking, and the assistant kind of administrative work but rarely the "executive" kind. . . . [M]aybe sometime in the future the whole of the women in this movement will . . . start the slow process of changing values and ideas so that all of us gradually come to understand that this is no more a man's world than it is a white world.[50]

Many white women volunteers found themselves pressured to engage in interracial sex to prove their commitment to black-white equality. Stokely Carmichael, the black radical, asked, "What is the position of women in SNCC?" and then answered his question: "The position of women in SNCC is prone."[51]

Radical young women found sexism equally rampant in New Left organizations against imperialism and war. A popular slogan among men who burned their draft cards ran "Girls Say Yes to Guys Who Say No!" So, many female radicals concluded that equal rights were not the remedy; women had to liberate themselves totally from the patriarchal, "male chauvinist" assumptions that riddled even liberal America. A small but symbolic protest that hit the headlines was at the annual Miss America pageant in September 1968. Outside, feminists threw objects of female oppression such as bras, curlers, and high-heeled shoes into a "freedom trash can." They crowned a sheep Miss America, chanting "Ain't she sweet; making profits off her meat," and urged people to come back next year to "Don't Miss America."

Women's lib, like black radicalism, split into many factions, with diminishing overall appeal. The women's movement as a whole never gained much support in any event among the working class, for whom career aspirations were secondary to holding down a job and keeping the money coming into the home, or among black women, for whom race rather than gender remained the great American divide. Nor did it dramatically change the white suburbs: "[F]or the majority of American women, life at the end of the sixties was not markedly different from what it was at the beginning."[52] But there was a gradual growth of female consciousness: In 1962 two-thirds of American women said they did not consider themselves to be victims of discrimination; in 1974 two-thirds said they did.[53]

Probably the biggest women's issue of the 1960s was not political but personal, about gaining control of their bodies. In April 1967 *Time* magazine's cover story was subtitled "Freedom from Fear": "'The pill' is a miraculous tablet that . . . costs 1¼ cents to manufacture; a month's supply now sells for $2.00 retail. It is little more trouble to take on schedule than a daily vitamin. Yet in a mere six years it has changed and liberated the sex and family life of a large and still growing segment of the US population: eventually, it promises to do the same for much of the world."[54]

Women had practiced contraception for centuries but the Pill, based on synthetic hormones, was the first oral contraceptive. Used initially to treat menstrual disorders and infertility, it was marketed for birth control in 1960. At this time many U.S. states still had laws against contraception but these were struck down by the Supreme Court in 1965 and 1972. In these landmark decisions the Court affirmed, for the first time, a constitutional right to privacy: Both the concept and the Court's reasoning would have far-reaching implications (see Chapter 16).

Legal or not, the Pill was widely used in the 1960s: In the same 1967 *Time* article it was estimated that, of nearly 40 million American women currently capable of motherhood, one-seventh were using the Pill. As to what this signified, commentators were divided. Some saw it as a sign of sexual liberation, a new permissive society. According to Betty Friedan, "In the mysterious way of history, there was this convergence of technology that occurred just as women were ready to explode into personhood."[55] As America's colleges went co-educational, the issue of "sex on the Campus" became a popular topic for TV programs, which reported exchanges like this between a health official and a girl who came to get a prescription for the Pill:

> "How old are you?"
> "Twenty-one."
> "You have a particular man in mind?"
> "Well, yes, I do."
> "Have you ever stopped to think that you might someday want to marry
> a man who holds virginity in high regard?"
> "Yes. But I'm not at all sure I want to marry a man like that."[56]

But co-eds on campus were only a small proportion of American females. Most users of the Pill were married women seeking to control the size of their families or engaged couples who wanted premarital sex. Sociological surveys cast doubt on the idea that sexual habits fundamentally changed in the 1960s. "Promiscuity was not invented by the current college generation," declared *Life* magazine, "and the evidence indicates that it is no more common than it ever was. There has been much speculation that the Pill has accelerated the willingness to engage in sex. The studies all refute this." What had changed, it was argued, was not sexual behavior but the willingness to talk about it—and to do so without shame or guilt. One doctor remarked, "The presence of the Pill does not make people decide to have sex. It is after they decide to have sex that they go get the Pill."[57]

Although the women on the Pill grabbed the headlines, what caused more concern in the 1960s were those who were not on it. Just as black women were suspicious of women's lib, so they proved more resistant to contraception. Middle-class blacks such as Martin Luther King urged family planning as a way out of the ghetto, but black radicals argued that this was a form of "black genocide." "Our birth rate is the only thing we have," Charles Greenlee, a black doctor in Pittsburgh, exclaimed angrily. "If we keep on producing, they're going to have to either kill us or grant us full citizenship." Scary rumors swirled around the ghetto. A leader of the Planned Parenthood organization said, "Many Negro women have told our workers, 'There are two kinds of pills—one for white women and one for us . . . and the one for us causes sterilization.'" But other black women disagreed. A thirty-year-old mother in Cleveland said wearily, "I've heard all this talk about 'genocide' and such things. What the Black Power people want—well, that's their business and I guess there's nothing wrong with it. But I've had eight babies and two miscarriages, and honest to God, I just can't have no more. Birth control is my only salvation."[58]

The debate had become intense because birth control was now being pushed not just by charities but by the federal government. It had become a centerpiece of Washington's "war on poverty."

THE "WAR ON POVERTY"

In his first State of the Union message as president, in January 1964, Lyndon Johnson announced that his administration "here and now, declares unconditional war on poverty in America" and urged Congress and the country to join him. It would not be, Johnson warned, "a short or easy struggle, no single weapon or strategy will suffice, but we shall not rest until that war is won. The richest Nation on earth can afford to win it. We cannot afford to lose it. . . . It must be won in the field, in every private home, in every public office, from the courthouse to the White House."[59]

Johnson's language was striking. As the London *Sunday Times* noted, this "was not the most daring, but it was perhaps the most bellicose programme of social reform in history." This was to be a "war" on poverty. Federal funds were to be "fired in" to areas of poverty in what was officially called "the rifle-shot approach."[60]

Declaring war on the country's problems is a trait of American political discourse—witness Richard Nixon's "war on drugs" in 1971 or George W. Bush's "war on terror" in 2001.* But why wage war on poverty in 1964? The answer tells us a lot about 1960s America and about Lyndon Baines Johnson—one of the most remarkable and most flawed presidents of the twentieth century.

The United States always had an underclass of poor, but in the 1960s Americans rediscovered poverty. Pioneering the way was commentator Michael Harrington,

* And in 1936 President Franklin Roosevelt called his New Deal nothing less than "a war for the survival of democracy."

whose 1962 best-seller, *The Other America*, argued that the United States in the 1960s contained an "affluent society within its borders" but also "an underdeveloped nation." This "other America," said Harrington, "the America of poverty, is hidden today in a way that it never was before," because in the suburbs "it is easy to assume that ours is, indeed, an affluent society. . . . The other America does not contain the adventurous seeking a new life and land. It is populated by the failures, those driven from the land and bewildered by the city, by old people suddenly confronted by the torments of loneliness and poverty, and by minorities facing a wall of prejudice."[61]

During the Depression, the problem of poverty had seemed relatively simple: no jobs and low incomes. But in the 1960s Harrington and others discerned a whole "culture of poverty"—a set of interdependent problems that kept the poor in their place, going far beyond money to include housing, education, health, and racial prejudice.

In the 1930s America's leaders had addressed the problem of poverty because it was staring them in the face on every street corner. But in the early 1960s, as Harrington also said, poverty seemed remote: Suburban America was in a boom, not a depression, the campuses were quiet, and the ghettos had not yet started to burn. This was not a must-do issue but a can-do issue. America's elite, at the height of their technocratic optimism, saw the poor as the next problem to be solved. "The elimination of poverty is well within the means of Federal, state, and local governments," social scientists at the University of Michigan stated flatly in 1962. They estimated that the cost of raising every individual and family in the nation above the subsistence level would be about $10 billion a year—less than 2 percent of America's GNP, under 10 percent of tax revenues, and one-fifth of the annual defense budget.[62] So poverty could be solved—and should be solved because it was an affront to American values. Poverty, said economist John Kenneth Galbraith, was "not remarkable in India," but in the United States it was "a disgrace."[63]

John Kennedy had been genuinely concerned about the issue; in fact, he coined the term "war on poverty" in a speech in August 1960.[64] After five weeks campaigning in the coal-mining towns of West Virginia, he declared, "I shall never forget what I have seen." Kennedy spoke of "men, proud men, looking for work who cannot find it," of "people over 40 who are told that their services are no longer needed," and of young people "forced to leave the state for opportunities elsewhere." He pledged that "West Virginia will be on the top of my agenda at the White House."[65]

It was not, however. Kennedy, as we shall see, was preeminently a foreign policy president, preoccupied by the Cold War, not by fighting poverty. He did try to get Congress to pass bills on schools and health care for the elderly but made little progress. On education Kennedy faced particular obstacles because he was the nation's first Catholic president. The issue had become so rancorous in the 1960 election campaign—reviving the old canards that a papist president would owe primary allegiance to the pope—that Kennedy eventually had to face it head-on. He pledged his faith in "an America where the separation of church and state is absolute," a country "where religious intolerance will someday end." This, he said, was the kind of America "I fought for in the South Pacific, and the kind my brother died for in Europe. No one suggested then that we may have a 'divided loyalty,' that we did not believe in liberty."[66]

By 1960 the United States had moved on from the election of 1928, when Al Smith's Catholicism helped reduce him to abject defeat. Kennedy won the White House but the religious issue still dogged him there. His education bill did not extend federal funding to private schools because most of the latter were Catholic and he could not afford to risk any charge of favoritism. As a result the Catholic hierarchy and its supporters in Congress blocked the bill.

Aside from specific problems such as religion, there was an institutional block on Kennedy's reforms. Although the Democrats controlled the House and Senate, their majorities were narrow and effective power lay with a conservative coalition of both parties that had blocked reform since the waning of the New Deal. By November 1963 Kennedy had gained acceptance for less than a third of his legislative program.[67]

And then he was assassinated. Whether the man arrested as his killer, Lee Harvey Oswald, was guilty or innocent, a lone gunman or part of a larger conspiracy, obsessed Americans at the time and continues to provoke debate. What is unquestionable, however, is that the murder made Kennedy, like Lincoln in 1865, into a martyr. JFK, of course, had always seemed youthful and glamorous—in marked contrast with Lincoln's gauche public manner—yet his domestic record to date had been unimpressive and in foreign affairs (as we shall see in the next chapter) early disasters had only just been redeemed by his handling of the Cuban missile crisis. But assassination simplified everything, making Kennedy, like Lincoln, a symbol of his age.

This was partly the effect of his funeral, which had even more impact than Lincoln's (or FDR's) thanks to TV satellite broadcasting. Millions in America and around the world watched every movement of his beautiful widow, attired in black, and her two small children as they followed the coffin first to Washington's Catholic cathedral and then to Arlington National Cemetery—an apt apotheosis. But the Kennedy myth was also testimony to Jacqueline Kennedy's own legacy project, recorded by journalist Theodore White on the following weekend. As he pieced together her anguished, broken narrative, "She did not want Jack left to the historians." History, she kept saying, was what "those bitter old men write." She believed—and so did her husband, said White—"that history belongs to heroes; and heroes must not be forgotten."[68] At night before bed, she told White tearfully, Jack liked to play records, including one of the Broadway musical *Camelot*. This was the heroic image that fixated Jackie—King Arthur and the Knights of the Round Table, captured by lines from one of Jack's favorite songs: "Don't let it be forgot/that once there was a spot/for one brief shining moment/that was known as Camelot." And, she added, "it will never be that way again."[69]

Enter Lyndon Johnson. The son of a struggling Texas hill farmer, not of a Boston tycoon and U.S. ambassador to Britain. A graduate of Southwest Texas State Teachers' College, not of Harvard University. And the man whom Kennedy defeated for the Democratic nomination in 1960, giving him the vice-presidency as consolation prize. Now, in November 1963, Johnson stepped into a dead man's shoes.

LBJ's political cross was not Catholicism but being southern. Back in 1958, when Senator Johnson arrived for a meeting in the White House, a grinning Eisenhower gestured to the high-backed president's chair.

"You sit there."

"Oh, no. That's your chair, Mr. President."

"It'll be yours someday."

"No, I will never sit in that chair."

Since the Civil War no southerner apart from Woodrow Wilson had been president and LBJ doubted that things would change during his lifetime.[70]

Then, suddenly, Johnson got his chance and he was determined to use it well. Shrewdly he assumed the mantle of the slain president, telling Congress that "the ideas and the ideals which he so nobly represented must and will be translated into effective action . . . let us here highly resolve that John Fitzgerald Kennedy did not live—or die—in vain."[71] But in private Johnson had little time for Kennedy. He told one historian, "I am a Roosevelt New Dealer. As a matter of fact, to tell the truth, John F. Kennedy was a little too conservative to suit my taste. . . . No man knew less about Congress than John Kennedy," Johnson went on. "When he was young, he was always off to Boston or Florida for long weekends. . . . I never saw him eating with another congressman once. . . . He didn't have rapport with Congress."[72]

LBJ, by contrast, had lived and breathed Congress for thirty years, making his way up the House and then the Senate. A bear-like six foot three, he possessed legendary skills as a manipulator. According to one journalistic account of what was called The Treatment, it "could last ten minutes or four hours. . . . Its tone could be supplication, accusation, cajolery, exuberance, scorn, tears, complaint, the hint of threat. . . . Its velocity was breathtaking." Johnson would move in close, "his face a scant millimeter from his target, his eyes widening and narrowing, his eyebrows rising and falling. From his pockets poured clippings, memos, statistics. Mimicry, humor, and the genius of analogy made The Treatment an almost hypnotic experience and rendered the target stunned and helpless."[73]

But Kennedy's memory and the Johnson Treatment alone would not have been enough to get the reform program through Congress. The president benefited crucially from the election landslide of 1964. His Republican opponent, Senator Barry Goldwater, was an ardent anti-communist and a vehement critic of big government. So were many Americans, but Goldwater had a rare talent for alienating and alarming people, making statements such as:

- "The child has no right to an education. In most cases he will get along very well without it."
- "We must—ourselves—be prepared to undertake military operations against vulnerable Communist regimes."
- "Sometimes I think the country would be better off if we could just saw off the Eastern Seaboard and let it float out to sea."[74]

Goldwater fans had a slogan: "In Your Heart You Know He's Right." Democrats replied, "In Your Guts You Know He's Nuts."

In November 1964 Johnson gained a crushing victory, winning 61 percent of the popular vote—the largest share in U.S. political history to date. He was now president in his own right. Equally important, the Democrats chalked up two-to-one majorities in both the House and Senate—enough to break the stranglehold of the conservative coalition. So it was LBJ who mounted the war on poverty and pushed through what he called his Great Society program.

Education was a high priority. America's schools were funded by local taxes and state subsidies, but resources had failed to keep up with the baby boom. LBJ's Elementary and Secondary Education Act of 1965 was the first time that substantial federal funds had been allocated to schools to provide "compensatory education" for the poor. As a Protestant, Johnson was able to buy off the Catholics; as a southerner, he was able to overcome the fears of segregationists and states'-righters. In three months he turned into law ideas that Congress had debated for twenty years. Deliberately he signed the bill in the one-room schoolhouse in Texas where he'd been educated: "As a son of a tenant farmer, I know that education is the only valid passport from poverty. As a former teacher—and, I hope, a future one—I have great expectations of what this law will mean for all of our young people. As President of the United States, I believe deeply no law I have signed or will ever sign means more to the future of America."[75]

Next to be rammed through Congress was health-care reform. Once again Johnson the supreme lawmaker gave hostile interest groups The Treatment, particularly the powerful American Medical Association. When one union leader expressed his fears that the AMA wouldn't cooperate, Johnson asked if he'd ever fed chickens. No, was the puzzled reply. Well, said the president, using the pungent prose for which he was notorious, "Chickens are real dumb. They eat and eat and never stop. Why, they start shitting at the same time they're eating, and before you know it, they're knee-deep in their own shit. Well, the AMA's the same. They've been eating and eating non-stop and now they're knee deep in their own shit and everybody knows it. They won't be able to stop anything."[76]

Johnson was right about the AMA's unpopularity, which he exploited ruthlessly to drive through his reforms. Medicare provided health insurance for those over sixty-five, financed by payroll taxes on employers and employees. Medicaid legislated federal and state help for those of all ages with low incomes and inadequate health insurance. These were the biggest innovations in social welfare since Roosevelt's Social Security Act thirty years before. The poor and old no longer had to go without health care; the middle class did not have to choose between college education for their kids and medical care for their parents. In tune with LBJ's general approach of throwing money at problems, there was no effective control on costs and this would become a serious issue in the future, but in 1965 the positives seemed all-important.

Both education reform and Medicaid were aimed particularly at America's blacks. Racial issues, as we have seen, were also central to the Voting Rights Act. This, the third of Johnson's great social reforms of 1965, was signed into law in August. Together these new laws enshrined the rights revolution of the 1960s—the expanded commitment of the federal government to promote individual rights, particularly for marginal social groups.

When Professor William Leuchtenburg, premier historian of Roosevelt's New Deal, was given a special interview with LBJ in September 1965 he decided to ingratiate himself with an opening remark: "Mr. President, this has been a remarkable Congress. It is even arguable whether this isn't the most significant Congress ever." "No, it isn't," snapped Johnson. "It's not arguable." The president went on—using Leuchtenburg rather as Jackie Kennedy had treated Theodore White: "You can perform a great service, if you say that never before have the three independent branches been so productive. Never has the American system worked so effectively in producing quality legislation—and at a time when our system is under attack all over the world."[77]

Despite the hubris, this was true: LBJ's legislative accomplishments ranked with those of Teddy Roosevelt, Woodrow Wilson, and FDR—though they, like him, had been aided by a temporarily favorable political balance on Capitol Hill. Although in this monologue to Leuchtenburg the president kept eulogizing Roosevelt—"he was like a daddy to me"—he clearly thought himself FDR's superior as a master legislator. "In 1936 Roosevelt won by a landslide. But he was like the fellow who cut cordwood and sold it all at Christmas and then spent it all on firecrackers. It all went up with a bang."[78]

LBJ made clear his determination and confidence that *his* presidency would not go up in smoke. Hubris indeed. In 1968, four years after winning the biggest victory to date in U.S. presidential elections, Lyndon Johnson was so unpopular that he dared not run again for the White House.

15

THE IMPOTENCE OF OMNIPOTENCE

In 1952, Denis Brogan, a British scholar and commentator, warned of a widespread "illusion of omnipotence" in the United States—a belief "that the world must go the American way if the Americans want it strongly enough and give firm orders to their agents to see that it is done."[1] As we have seen, such self-confidence in American might and right was evident in the diplomacy of the 1950s and in the war on poverty during the 1960s, but this sense of righteous omnipotence was displayed above all in Vietnam. Yet that conflict eventually showed the limits of America's power: A nuclear arsenal for a third world war was not much use in third-world war and, for the globe's most precocious democracy, waging war abroad depended upon consent at home. The Vietnam War helped bring down two presidents (Lyndon Johnson and Richard Nixon) and seemed to suggest the impotence of American omnipotence.

But the signs were there already in the early 1960s in Cuba. That, Washington insiders joked, was a four-letter word for John and Bobby Kennedy.

CUBA—THE FOUR-LETTER WORD

Fidel Castro had gained power in Cuba in 1959, toppling a corrupt military regime that had ruled for much of the previous quarter-century. From 1898, when the United States seized Cuba from Spain, until 1934, the island was an American protectorate; after that it remained an economic colony. The United States dominated Cuba's trade and finance through control of its main industry, sugar, and also retained a naval base covering forty-five square miles at Guantánamo Bay at the southeastern end of the island. Castro did not start out as a Marxist, but his program of land reform threatened U.S. interests and Washington's hostility pushed him toward Moscow. Once Castro started taking aid from the USSR and allowed it to establish bases on the island, a collision with the United States was almost inevitable.

During President Eisenhower's last months in office the CIA formulated plans for an invasion of the island by Cuban exiles in the United States, which would supposedly trigger risings by the anti-Castro resistance. The director of the CIA predicted confidently that "the great mass of Cuban people" felt "the hour of decision is at hand" and that "the Castro regime is steadily losing popularity." It was generally believed, he said, "that the Cuban Army has been successfully penetrated by opposition groups and that it will not fight in the event of a showdown."[2]

The CIA plan disturbed John Kennedy when he entered the White House in January 1961. Less than five years earlier the United States had condemned the Soviet invasion of Hungary as an act of blatant, brutal imperialism and he did not want to do anything that would open America to a similar charge. "The minute I land one Marine, we're in this up to our necks," he told aides. "I can't get the United States into a war and then lose it, no matter what it takes. I'm not going to risk an American Hungary. And that's what it could be, a fucking slaughter."[3]

So Kennedy stripped the operation of all overt U.S. support, including air cover. This jeopardized the success of the plan but, on the other hand, he did not feel he could call a halt. In the 1960 election campaign he had blasted the Eisenhower administration for letting the Red tide flood across the globe: "In 1952 the Republicans ran on a program of rolling back the Iron Curtain in Eastern Europe. Today the Iron Curtain is 90 miles off the coast of the United States."[4] And CIA covert operations had won some spectacular triumphs under Eisenhower, notably toppling the leftist regime in Guatemala in 1954. As John Kennedy's brother Bobby put it later, "If he hadn't gone ahead with it, everybody would have said it showed he had no courage"; their line would be that "Eisenhower's people all said it would succeed, and you turned it down."[5]

So Kennedy allowed the Cuban operation to go ahead on April 17, 1961. But the Castro regime was not falling apart and the 1,400 Cuban exiles were killed or captured on the beaches of the Bay of Pigs. The U.S. chief of naval operations urged Kennedy to drop the mask and use American power, but the president wouldn't budge—no air strikes, even with unmarked planes, no naval support, not even a single destroyer. And so the "deniable plan" became an "undeniable fiasco"[6]— reducing Kennedy to tears of impotent rage. "He felt very strongly," Bobby Kennedy recalled, that the Bay of Pigs had "materially affected" both his standing as president and that of the United States around the world. "We were going to have a much harder role in providing leadership."[7] Bobby put it more angrily at the time to Kennedy's key advisers: "All you bright fellows have gotten the President into this, and if you don't do something now, my brother will be regarded as a paper tiger by the Russians."[8]

And it was not just the Bay of Pigs. A week before, the Soviet Union had trumped America by being first to put a man into space. Yuri Gagarin's face grinning out on TV screens and front pages all around the world was another damaging blow to American prestige. "In the eyes of the world," Vice-President Lyndon

Johnson warned, "first in space means first, period; second in space is second in everything."[9] Hitherto, Kennedy had not shown much interest in space but now he had no choice. On May 25, asking Congress for billions more for defense and foreign aid, he also declared that if America was to "win the battle that is now going on around the world between freedom and tyranny" it was time for "a great new American enterprise." He proposed that "this nation should commit itself to achieving the goal, before this decade is out, of landing a man on the moon and returning him safely to the earth."[10]

Eisenhower had refused to make space into a race but, after Gagarin and the Bay of Pigs, his beleaguered young successor saw no alternative. Yet the idea of landing a man on the moon by the end of the decade was just pie in the sky in 1961 and Kennedy's position worsened all through the summer. In June he met the Soviet leader, Nikita Khrushchev, in an ill-judged summit in Vienna. Kennedy, fiercely competitive, wanted to get the measure of his superpower opponent, but he let himself be sucked into a fruitless ideological argument. Khrushchev, old enough to be Kennedy's father, crowed to his aides that "this man is very inexperienced, even immature." By comparison, he added scathingly, Eisenhower "was a man of intelligence and vision."[11]

The president, shaken by Khrushchev's belligerent bluster, knew he had come off worse. He told a friendly journalist that the Vienna summit had been the "roughest thing in my life" and mused as to why it had happened. "I think he did it because of the Bay of Pigs. I think he thought that anyone who was so young and inexperienced as to get into that mess could be taken, and anyone who got into it, and didn't see it through, had no guts. So he just beat hell out of me. So I've got a terrible problem. If he thinks I'm inexperienced and have no guts, until we remove those ideas we won't get anywhere with him."[12]

One place to get tough was Berlin, where the Western allies still had a foothold deep in Soviet-controlled East Germany, but Kennedy did nothing to stop the East Germans building a wall across the city in August 1961 to prevent refugees fleeing to the West. The president joked grimly that "a wall is a hell of a lot better than a war,"[13] but many people in West Germany and across the world felt that he had failed to stand up for freedom.

Given the way in 1961 that the Soviets seemed to be running rings around the Americans, it is hardly surprising that Cuba became a four-letter word for the Kennedys. Yet the antagonism to Castro went beyond Cold War imperatives; it became a gut issue for the macho president and his brother, accustomed to winning. In January 1962 Bobby Kennedy told the CIA and other agencies that resolving the Castro problem was "the top priority in the United States Government—all else is secondary—no time, money, effort, or manpower is to be spared." He promised "full backing" from the White House.[14]

Prodded by Bobby, the CIA concocted various assassination plots, some bordering on the farcical, such as poisoned pens and exploding cigars. And the White

House authorized plans to stir up a revolt in Cuba to overthrow the government, this time organized and mounted by the CIA. The U.S. base at Guantánamo Bay became an important asset in these projects. In public during the summer of 1962 the Pentagon staged several amphibious exercises around the Caribbean—the last being openly billed as an invasion to topple a dictator named "Ortsac." That code word could be cracked by anyone able to read backwards.

The undisguised American threat to Cuba was one reason Khrushchev decided to reinforce the Soviet Union's foothold on America's doorstep. Given Kennedy's performance at Vienna, he also thought he would be able to get away with it. His language to American visitors in the summer of 1962 expressed his confidence that the Soviet Union was now the coming power. "It's been a long time since you could spank us like a little boy," he told Kennedy's interior secretary. "Now we can swat your ass." To the poet Robert Frost he was even more blunt about the fading power of the West, quoting Tolstoy's aphorism about sex in old age: "The desire is the same, it's the performance that's different."[15]

So Khrushchev decided to "throw a hedgehog down Uncle Sam's pants"—in plain language, to install medium-range nuclear missiles in Cuba.[16] During the summer of 1962 the CIA monitored the buildup of Soviet troops and equipment, but it was not until October 16 that spy-plane overflights yielded clear evidence of the missile bases. Presented with the photographic proof, Kennedy said his first instinct was "we're going to take out those missiles." As more evidence came in about additional missile sites, the joint chiefs of staff advised a full-scale invasion, but Kennedy baulked at that. "Invasions are tough, hazardous," he noted. If thousands of Americans got killed in Cuba, he feared he would be in "much more of a mess" than by simply taking out the bases. The president and his brother were also swayed by the ethical point made passionately by George Ball of the State Department: "[W]here we strike without warning, that's like Pearl Harbor. It's the kind of conduct that one might expect of the Soviet Union. It is not conduct that one expects of the United States." So the administration opted for something less than military action—a blockade of Cuba that showed toughness but gave Khrushchev room to back down.[17]

Kennedy's erratic psychology, macho yet insecure, had played a part in creating the Cuban crisis, but now he was now behaving with greater maturity. The issues were being thrashed out in extended seminars with his key advisers—an executive committee of the National Security Council known as Ex Comm. Their discussions built consensus, thoughtfully analyzed both U.S. interests, and also—as shown by Ball's intervention—affirmed national values. By contrast, Soviet policy was the product of an unstable dictator: Khrushchev had personally decided on the Cuban gamble and he implemented it with little discussion. Despite Washington's predilection for Cold War ideological hype, the way the Cuban missile crisis was handled did demonstrate the difference between "freedom" and "tyranny."

On October 22 the president went public, informing America and the world for the first time that the Soviets were installing nuclear missiles in Cuba and explaining the U.S. response: "To halt this offensive buildup, a strict quarantine on all offensive military equipment under shipment to Cuba is being initiated. All ships of any kind bound for Cuba from whatever nation or port will, if found to contain cargoes of offensive weapons, be turned back." Kennedy stated that it would be "the policy of this Nation to regard any nuclear missile launched from Cuba against any nation in the western hemisphere as an attack by the Soviet Union on the United States, requiring a full retaliatory response upon the Soviet Union."[18]

The American blockade of Cuba came into force at 10 A.M. on October 24. Ex Comm, monitoring events as they unfolded, was told that Soviet ships showed no signs of stopping and that two were within a few miles of the line. A few minutes later they learned that a Soviet submarine had positioned itself between the two ships. A U.S. destroyer moved in. In the Cabinet Room of the White House, "the danger and concern that we all felt hung like a cloud over us," Bobby Kennedy noted. "These few minutes were the time of greatest worry by the president. His hand went up to his face and covered his mouth and he closed his fist. His eyes were tense, almost gray, and we just looked at each other across the table. Was the world on the brink of a holocaust?"[19]

Then came news that the Russian ships had stopped dead in the water. Then that they had turned back. Secretary of State Dean Rusk murmured, "We're eyeball to eyeball and I think the other fellow just blinked."[20]

Yet one blink did not end the face-off. Even if no more missiles reached Cuba, the existing ones were still an affront that Kennedy could not tolerate—for reasons of national security, domestic politics, and international prestige. How to get them out? By the weekend Ex Comm and even the president were leaning toward military action. Contingency plans for air strikes and/or invasion were finalized and on Saturday, October 27 a U-2 spy-plane was shot down, killing its pilot.

Yet in this apparently inexorable countdown to war, Khrushchev now drew back, conscious that, if it came to a nuclear exchange, the USSR would be the certain loser. (We know now that the Americans could have launched around 4,000 nuclear warheads at the USSR, with considerable accuracy, whereas the Soviets had only 220, many of which had little chance of reaching their targets.[21]) In a long, rambling letter to Kennedy on October 26 the Soviet leader suggested that the two of them show "statesmanlike wisdom," telling Kennedy "we and you ought not now to pull on the ends of the rope in which you have tied the knot of war, because the more the two of us pull, the tighter that knot will be tied." Instead, "to untie that knot," he proposed that "we, for our part, will declare that our ships, bound for Cuba, will not carry any kind of armaments. You would declare that the United States will not invade Cuba with its forces and will not support any sort of forces which might intend to carry out an invasion of Cuba. Then the necessity for the presence of our military specialists in Cuba would disappear."[22]

The following day Khrushchev complicated matters by proposing publicly that, as part of a deal, the United States also publicly remove its own nuclear missiles from Turkey, just across the Black Sea from the Crimea. Kennedy was ready to do this but, after much debate, Ex Comm persuaded him to ignore this message and bargain on the basis of Khrushchev's initial proposal. Given the Soviet leader's evident loss of nerve, it seemed worth calling his bluff.

The American tactic worked and a deal was agreed. With Kennedy promising not to invade Cuba, the Soviets gradually withdrew their missiles and personnel. In parallel, Kennedy also pulled the U.S. missiles out of Turkey, but this was done in secret. So, although the president had acquiesced in the survival of the Castro regime, his bête noire, the overall impression around the world was that the Soviet Union had backed down and lost face. Among most Americans, the debacles of the Bay of Pigs, the Vienna summit, and the Berlin Wall were now forgotten or at least forgiven. Richard Rovere in the *New Yorker* said that Kennedy had achieved "perhaps the greatest personal diplomatic victory of any President in our history"; *Newsweek* reported that Kennedy's crisis management had given Americans "a deep sense of confidence in the temper of their President and the team he had working with him."[23]

In the summer of 1963 Kennedy paid a triumphant visit to western Europe, showing just how much his stock had risen since the fumbles of 1961. The rhetoric soared accordingly. Kennedy promised that "the United States is here on this continent to stay. So long as our presence is desired and required, our forces and commitments will remain." Americans, he declared, would "keep this free world free until the day comes, as Thomas Jefferson predicted it would, that the disease of liberty, which is catching, spreads throughout the world." The high point of his trip was a rapturous reception in West Berlin, where he hammered home the propaganda message of the Wall. "There are many people in the world who really don't understand, or say they don't, what is the great issue between the free world and the Communist world. Let them come to Berlin. There are some who say that communism is the wave of the future. Let them come to Berlin."[24]

This was heavy ideological stuff but Kennedy believed that his belated dominance in superpower relations also gave him a new flexibility. In January 1961 at his inauguration he had shown his concern to defuse the Cold War. "Let us never negotiate out of fear. But let us never fear to negotiate."[25] Until the Cuban missile crisis, Khrushchev had been tempted by Kennedy's apparent weakness. After the crisis, however, there was no danger of the president seeming to negotiate out of fear, so he was now ready to negotiate.

In the summer of 1963 the superpowers signed a treaty banning nuclear tests in the atmosphere—a small but significant step toward controlling what Kennedy had called "the dark powers of destruction unleashed by science." And he gave a major address about world peace, emphasizing that "as Americans, we find communism profoundly repugnant as a negation of personal freedom and dignity." But, he added, "we can still hail the Russian people for their many achievements—in science and space, in economic and industrial growth, in culture and in acts of courage," not least in World War II. So, the president declared, "if we cannot end now our differences, at least we can help make the world safe for diversity. For, in the final analysis, our most basic common link is that we all inhabit this small planet. We all breathe the same air. We all cherish our children's future. And we are all mortal."[26]

This speech, at the American University in Washington, received few plaudits at the time but it showed Kennedy at his most visionary. From a position of strength he reached out to the Russian people and, while not abandoning the Cold War, he talked the language of coexistence. The reference to making the world "safe for diversity" was a conscious reworking of Woodrow Wilson's call in 1917 to make the world "safe for democracy." That Wilsonian vision had been the categorical imperative for America's Cold War leaders, reflecting the country's Manichean worldview of good versus evil. It was reinforced by the absence of viable communist or even socialist parties in the United States at a time when much of the postwar world had lurched leftward. From that frame of reference almost all political radicals around the globe seemed at odds with America's conception of democracy. But now Kennedy was hinting that the United States—empowered by Cuba yet also chastened—could live with and in a pluralist world.

How Kennedy might have moved on from the rhetorical platform of his American University speech is one of the tantalizing what-ifs of history. But, as he observed, "we are all mortal"—and he was dead less than five months later. In any case, during his period of weakness, Kennedy had helped create a problem that would destroy his successor and, had he lived, would probably have undermined him as well—Vietnam.

VIETNAM—BATTLEGROUND OF FREEDOM

> All men are created equal. They are endowed by their Creator with certain inalienable rights, among these are Life, Liberty and the pursuit of Happiness.
>
> This immortal statement was made in the Declaration of Independence of the United States of America in 1776. In a broader sense, this means: All the peoples on earth are equal from birth; all the peoples have a right to live, to be happy and free.[27]

These words were written by Ho Chi Minh; they come from the beginning of Vietnam's Declaration of Independence from France in 1945. Ho was deliberately using America's celebrated rejection of British colonial rule to justify Vietnam's bid for freedom from French colonialism. But it would take Vietnam thirty years to win its independence, and its opponent most of that time was not Old World France but New World America.

Ho Chi Minh was a Marxist, but he led a broad-based nationalist movement, the Vietminh, in a war against hated French colonial rule. French Indochina had been overrun by the Japanese in 1940–1941 and the power vacuum when Japan surrendered at the end of World War II allowed Ho to establish a foothold before the French got back. In the late 1940s the Vietminh just about maintained its control of rural areas but after 1950 it received arms and supplies on a large scale from the new communist government in China. This tipped the balance and at home the French people gradually lost the will to fight. At the Geneva conference of 1954 Vietnam was divided in two at the 17th parallel. This was supposedly a temporary measure, paving the way for free elections in 1956, but these were never held because of American obstructionism.

The future of Vietnam after the French posed a classic ideological dilemma for the United States. On the one hand, there was America's historic antipathy toward European colonialism, dating back to 1776 and reiterated in 1954 by President Eisenhower to Winston Churchill: "Colonialism is on its way out as a relationship among peoples. The sole question is one of time and method. I think we should handle it so as to win adherents to Western aims." Ike told Churchill, as a leader of one of the colonial powers, "If you could say that twenty-five years from now, every last one of the colonies (excepting military bases) should have been offered a right to self-government and determination, you would electrify the world."[28]

On the other hand, Eisenhower was intensely worried about what would fill the vacuums left around the world by decolonization. Also in 1954 he told Churchill that if the French crumbled in Vietnam and "Indochina passes into the hands of the Communists, the ultimate effect on our and your global strategic position . . . throughout Asia and the Pacific could be disastrous." He found it "difficult to see how Thailand, Burma and Indonesia could be kept out of Communist hands. This we cannot afford. The threat to Malaya, Australia and New Zealand would be direct."[29]

Eisenhower famously depicted Asian states as a row of dominoes: The fall of one could easily topple all the others. That is why the Eisenhower administration blocked elections in Vietnam after the French pulled out. It feared that Ho Chi Minh, already running the North, would gain control of the whole country. So instead of elections for national unity the outcome, rather like that in Korea, was an American-backed regime in the South and the communist government in the North—each consolidating its position during the rest of the 1950s. From Hanoi, the northern capital, Ho rebuilt his economy, implemented land reform, and created a socialist state. His methods were brutal but—once the Catholic elite and peasantry had fled—the regime, with its nationalist credentials burnished in the long freedom struggle, enjoyed rice-roots support.

South Vietnam, by contrast, was an artificial state kept alive by massive transfusions of American aid; it was effectively a U.S. colony, though Washington balked at the hated word. Eisenhower poured over $1 billion of economic and military assistance into South Vietnam; by 1961 the country ranked fifth among all recipients of American aid. Its leader was Ngo Dinh Diem—a devout Catholic mandarin who was both anti-French and anti-communist. The Americans latched on to him because there seemed no one else, but Diem was not up to the job. "He was a short, broadly built man with a round face and a shock of black hair, who walked and moved jerkily," recalled one American observer. "He always dressed in white and looked as if he were made out of ivory. . . . A single question was likely to provoke a dissertation for an hour or more," because Diem was absorbed in himself and his own ideas. He lacked the charisma of Ho and had no blueprint for a modern, post-colonial state. Harking back to imperial Vietnam before the French, he blocked land reform, resting his rule on the big landlords and his own corrupt relatives.[30]

So South Vietnam was no advertisement for American ideals, but these ideological compromises seemed essential to prevent a communist takeover. Diem resisted Washington's pressure to reform his regime and by the end of the 1950s the internal opposition against him had mushroomed into a guerrilla uprising (the Vietcong) supported and orchestrated by North Vietnam.

This was the situation in Vietnam when John Kennedy became president in 1961. Although accepting an agreement with Moscow to make neighboring Laos a neutral, unified state, he rejected that line in Vietnam. After being humiliated by Khrushchev in Cuba, in outer space, and at the Vienna summit, he felt he had to take a stand somewhere, telling a friendly journalist, "now we have a problem in trying to make our power credible, and Vietnam looks like the place."[31] Kennedy had also long been an outspoken supporter of the Diem regime, declaiming in 1956 that "Vietnam represents the cornerstone of the Free World in Southeast Asia. . . . It is our offspring, we cannot abandon it."[32]

On the other hand, Kennedy rejected Pentagon pressure to introduce U.S. combat troops into South Vietnam. "They say it's necessary in order to restore confidence and maintain morale," he told an aide wryly. But "the troops will march in; the bands will play; the crowds will cheer; and in four days everyone will have forgotten. Then we will be told we have to send in more troops. It's like taking a drink. The effect wears off, and you have to take another."[33]

Instead, as became the pattern on Vietnam, Kennedy sought middle ground between the contending bureaucrats. In November 1961 he decided to increase American aid and "military advisers," effectively taking over direction of South Vietnam's war against the guerrillas, while keeping this as secret as possible. "Once in a while, Washington remembers there is a war on in Vietnam," a *New York Times* journalist commented in 1963. "But for long stretches, the war . . . fades from memory here, not because no one cares, but because the men who care most decided long ago to discuss it as little as possible."[34]

By the summer of 1963, however, America's covert war in Vietnam could not be kept off the front pages. A crackdown by Diem's Catholic clique against the Buddhist majority stirred up massive protests, including the shocking sight of Buddhist monks setting fire to themselves in the streets of the capital, Saigon. Diem and his regime were now a liability and Kennedy reluctantly accepted the advice of leading aides that the United States should signal support for a military coup. To the very end, the president wavered over both the ethics and the practicalities, but his ambassador in Saigon cabled home firmly:

> We are launched on a course from which there is no respectable turning back: the overthrow of the Diem government. There is no turning back in part because US prestige is already publicly committed to this end in large measure and will become more so as facts leak out. In a more fundamental sense, there is no turning back because there is no possibility, in my view, that the war can be won under a Diem administration, still less that Diem or any member of the family can govern the country in a way to gain the support of the people who count, i.e., the educated class in and out of government service, civil and military—not to mention the American people.[35]

After several false starts, the generals toppled Diem and then shot him and his brutal brother in the back of an armored personnel carrier. American support for the coup was an open secret; the U.S. ambassador was cheered in the streets of Saigon.[36] But Kennedy himself was shocked at the news, apparently imagining that regime change would occur peacefully. "I saw the President soon after," aide Arthur Schlesinger recalled. "He said that Diem had fought for his country for twenty years and that it should not have ended like this." Schlesinger found Kennedy "somber and shaken. I had not seen him so depressed since the Bay of Pigs. No doubt he realized that Vietnam was his great failure in foreign policy, and that he had never given it his full attention. . . . When he came into office, 2,000 American troops were in Vietnam. Now there were 16,000."[37] The president ordered another review of America's options in Vietnam, including the possibility of withdrawal, but he would never read it. Three weeks after the murder of Diem, John Kennedy was himself the victim of an assassin's bullet.

The coup in Saigon settled nothing. Six governments came and went between November 1963 and June 1965, while the military situation deteriorated and the Vietcong gained effective control of more than half of South Vietnam. Hanoi now stepped up the pressure, convinced the time was ripe for a major military offensive by the North linked to a general uprising in the South. By the end of 1964 regular North Vietnamese army units were infiltrating into the South and in February 1965 the Vietcong attacked a U.S. base at Pleiku, in the central highlands. Eight Americans were killed and over a hundred injured—the first large-scale U.S. casualties.

Pleiku brought to a head a great debate in Washington. In the first year of his presidency LBJ had focused on domestic problems—trying, like Kennedy, to keep Vietnam off the TV screens while increasing U.S. aid in secret. After his election victory in November 1964, Johnson wanted to concentrate on his Great Society programs against poverty and racism. Instead, he was forced to leave what he called "the woman I really loved" for "that bitch of a war on the other side of the world."[38]

In early 1965 National Security Adviser McGeorge Bundy and Defense Secretary Robert McNamara—both holdovers from Kennedy—told the president that they were "pretty well convinced that our current policy can lead only to disastrous defeat." They argued that "the underlying difficulties in Saigon arise from the spreading conviction there that the future is without hope for anti-Communists. . . . The Vietnamese know just as well as we do that the Viet Cong are gaining in the countryside. Meanwhile, they see the enormous power of the United States withheld, and they get little sense of firm and active US policy." Bundy and McNamara believed it was no longer possible to maintain the essentially passive policy so far adopted by Kennedy and Johnson of leaving the war to South Vietnam while providing discreet American support. They wanted "to use our military power in the Far East to force a change in Communist policy."[39]

Yet no one in Johnson's inner circle had a clear and credible idea of how to accomplish that goal. They advocated bombing the North not because this was expected to bring the enemy to its knees but rather desperately in order to show that the United States was doing something.[40] Johnson reluctantly agreed and the bombing began in March, using the attack on Pleiku as a pretext, but, as Kennedy had predicted, escalation was like alcohol—the effect wore off and more seemed to be required. In July Johnson succumbed to pressure from McNamara and the generals to introduce American troops into large-scale combat. On this schedule, there would be 175,000 U.S. soldiers in the country by the end of 1965, with the possibility of another 100,000 during the following year.

Bombing the North and introducing U.S. combat troops showed that the Vietnam War was being Americanized. It was ever harder to maintain the pretense that America was simply helping a free people defend itself against communist aggression. In June 1965 a new military government took power in Saigon; the prime minister, Nguyen Cao Ky, was a womanizing ex-airman who boasted Hitler as his hero "because he pulled his country together," but, said Ky, the situation was now so dire that "we need four or five Hitlers in Vietnam."[41]

There was an alternative to escalation, advocated by a few "doves" such as George Ball in the State Department, namely that America should cut its losses and seek a neutralized Vietnam. This was, however, rejected by Johnson and his inner circle. They believed that South Vietnam could not be allowed to fall, because the United States had invested too much in its survival. In a press conference in July 1965 Johnson rehearsed the familiar Cold War arguments about U.S. credibility, the global threat to national security, and the lessons of appeasement:

> If we are driven from the field in Viet-Nam, then no nation can ever again
> have the same confidence in American promises, or in American protection.
> In each land the forces of independence would be considerably weakened,

and an Asia so threatened by Communist domination would certainly im-
peril the security of the United States itself. . . . Nor would surrender in Viet-
Nam bring peace, because we learned from Hitler at Munich that success
only feeds the appetite of aggression. The battle would be renewed in one
country and then another country, bringing with it perhaps even larger and
crueler conflict, as we have learned from the lessons of history.[42]

Probably any U.S. president would have felt pushed to escalate the Vietnam War in
1965. Eisenhower was publicly urging Johnson on and, despite the assertions of
Kennedy intimates that he would have extricated the country from Vietnam in his
second term,[43] JFK had made the original commitments and shared the general
worldview.

The real difference between LBJ and his predecessors was probably over the politics of the policy rather than its principle. Bundy and McNamara coupled their
calls for escalation with requests that the president mobilize public consent by securing full congressional support and by increasing taxes to pay for the war.
Kennedy might have taken that route—his passion was foreign affairs, his self-
image was bound up with the Cold War, and he had the charisma and oratory to
rouse public opinion for a new crusade[44]—but Johnson's heart was at home. He
feared that, if he dramatized the crisis in Vietnam, conservatives in Congress, who
dominated the key committees, would use that to scuttle his reform agenda. "Those
damned conservatives," he fumed, "they don't want to help the poor and the Negroes but they're afraid to be against it." He feared "they'll take the war as their
weapon. . . . [T]hey'll say they're . . . not against the poor, but we have this job to do,
beating the Communists. We beat the Communists first, then we can look around
and maybe give something to the poor."[45]

Johnson therefore played down the escalation in Vietnam. He declined to announce the bombing campaign in public; the troop commitments were mentioned
in a midday press conference rather than a special message to Congress. Instead of
full political debate, he took refuge behind a congressional resolution, passed in
August 1964 at the time of naval incidents in the Gulf of Tonkin, authorizing the
president to take "all necessary measures to repel any armed attack against the
forces of the United States and to prevent further aggression."[46] The Gulf of Tonkin
resolution became Johnson's pretext for ever larger troop commitments without
further congressional endorsement. Equally significant was the subterfuge with
which he paid for the war. In 1965 and 1966 the president refused to ask Congress
for tax increases, fearful that this would "kill" his legislative program. Instead he
funded the escalation quietly through increased government borrowing.[47]

Yet LBJ's domestic bias did not signify lack of faith in what was at stake in Vietnam. On the contrary, Johnson—with supreme arrogance—believed that he could
abolish poverty and save Vietnam simultaneously. "I was determined to be a leader

of war and a leader of peace," he said later. "I wanted both, I believed in both, and I believed America had the resources to provide for both."[48] That was LBJ in a nutshell.

1968—PARALYSIS OF A PRESIDENT

The strategic bombing of North Vietnam had little effect. Factories were moved out of urban centers and fuel stocks quickly dispersed across the country. Using the network of trails along the jungle-clad mountain range inside neighboring Laos, supplies could be transported slowly but surely into South Vietnam, increasingly by truck but often on foot or by bicycle. And despite the pounding of B-52 bombers, wiping some small towns almost off the map, civilian morale held up. North Vietnam manufactured 20 million rudimentary bomb shelters—mostly pre-stressed concrete tubes five feet high for people to stand in—with the slogan "Call the shelter your second home."

A few American officials recognized the underlying problem. James Thomson of the NSC staff insisted that bombing "will not bring them to their knees or to the negotiating table. We could bomb them back to the stone age. They will disappear into the jungle and they will wait us out. Because they know something we know deep down, and they know that we know, which is that some day we're going to go home."[49]

As for the ground war in the South, American firepower was often irrelevant against an unconventional and elusive enemy who fought without tanks or air cover. Indeed, it was usually counterproductive, by sacrificing the advantage of surprise. According to a National Security memo in late 1968, "Three-fourths of the battles are at the enemy's choice of time, place, type, and duration. CIA notes that less than one percent of nearly two million Allied small unit operations conducted in the last two years resulted in contact with the enemy."[50] In such a shadowy war the prime criterion of success became the body count, whose rule of thumb was well known: "If it's dead and it's Vietnamese, it's Vietcong." Few U.S. soldiers knew the country or spoke its languages; they despised the locals as "gooks," "slants," or "dinks." Their fear and hatred were understandable, since villagers often passed on information for Vietcong ambushes or helped lay vicious anti-personnel landmines. "To us," one soldier recalled, "there were no friendly civilians, only ones who posed no immediate threat." Another said, "When you are trying to survive, there is no such thing as too much firepower."[51]

Of course, the United States could have taken the gloves off and bombed North Vietnam's supply lines from China and Russia but that would have risked an all-out war with the communist giants—as had happened with China in Korea in 1950. America's massive nuclear arsenal was now even less relevant. So being a superpower was not much use when fighting in Indochina.

While the war was not being won in Vietnam, Johnson was losing it at home. By the end of 1967 nearly half a million U.S. troops were in Vietnam and 16,000 had died,[52] yet this remained an undeclared war, with Johnson still fighting it under cover of the Gulf of Tonkin resolution. The president was slow to admit the failure of his guns-and-butter economic policy. Because of his determination to fund the war through borrowing rather than taxes, the government deficit rose from $1.6 billion in 1965 to $25.2 billion in 1968. Only in January 1967 did LBJ ask Congress for a modest tax surcharge, but the bill took eighteen months to pass because of his reluctance to placate conservatives by cutting domestic programs.[53] The result was rampant inflation and a falling dollar.

There was now a large and vocal anti-war movement, centered on students who did not want to be drafted as cannon fodder for Vietnam. Most days a tired and fractious Johnson could hear demonstrators outside the White House chanting, "Hey, hey, LBJ; how many kids have you killed today?" Liberals who had lauded Johnson in 1964–1965 for his Great Society legislation now denounced him as a killer and an imperialist. Particularly galling for LBJ was the vocal opposition of Martin Luther King, who in 1967 came out publicly against the "madness" of Vietnam.

A rising tide of liberal anger did not mean, however, that most of the country had turned against the war. The press still took its cue from positive official statements, while TV portrayed the war as a moral struggle between American goodies and North Vietnamese baddies. Fewer than a quarter of film reports from Southeast Asia in 1965–1967 showed actual combat, or even clips of dead or wounded. As in any war, the media did not want to seem blatantly unpatriotic; in the debate about Vietnam, "television was a follower rather than a leader."[54] What legitimized dissent was the growing argument among the political elite, articulated by senators such as J. William Fulbright. At the Pentagon, McNamara, architect of escalation, now had second thoughts and resigned. But even in November 1967 two-thirds of Americans felt that the main problem in Vietnam was that "the military has been handicapped by civilians who won't let them go all out."[55]

In public, Johnson kept accentuating the positives. "We are making progress," he insisted in November 1967. "We are inflicting greater losses than we are taking. . . . The fact that the population under free control has constantly risen, and that under Communist control has constantly gone down, is a very encouraging sign." Admitting "we have a lot to do yet," the president insisted that "overall, we are making progress."[56]

But on January 30, 1968, during the Vietnamese New Year holiday of Tet, Hanoi's regular army and Vietcong guerrillas mounted major assaults on cities and towns all over the South that, as Time magazine reported, "left Washington shocked and stunned—and with good reason. . . . To a capital lulled by repeated boasts that the military war was being won, the strength and duration of the Red offensive came as an unpleasant, even humiliating surprise." As Time said, "the mighty US suddenly seemed as impotent as a beached whale. Even those nations that normally delight in American embarrassment refrained from crowing openly."[57]

In fact, the Tet offensive proved a military disaster for the communists. Hoping to stir up a civilian uprising throughout the South, they ended up a few weeks later with most of the Vietcong leadership and activists dead or wounded. Henceforth the war would have to be fought largely by the North Vietnamese army. But at the diplomatic and psychological level, Tet was a triumph for Hanoi. TV pictures of fighting in the grounds of the U.S. embassy in Saigon gave the lie to Johnson's talk of "progress." The long battles in Hue and Khe Sanh kept the war in American living rooms for weeks. Photos of the South Vietnamese police chief calmly putting his gun to the head of a Vietcong captive and pulling the trigger were featured around the world. In the ruins of Ben Tre, a U.S. major delivered the notorious sentence, "It became necessary to destroy the town in order to save it." In February 1968, fewer than one-third of Americans believed they were making progress in Vietnam; by late March LBJ's approval rating for his handling of the war had dropped thirteen points to 26 percent.[58]

Shaken by Tet and tired of fighting with one hand tied behind their backs, the senior generals asked for another 200,000 troops; they would not say whether still more would be needed or predict how many years victory would take. This kind of scenario was politically impossible. Basically the war was stalemated: After Tet, the United States was unlikely to lose but there was no hope of victory on terms that the American people would accept.

Johnson was now exhausted and depressed, rarely able to sleep for long. At night, in his dressing gown, he would prowl around the situation room in the basement of the White House, desperate for the latest news. When he did nod off, he started dreaming again the dream he used to have in his Texan youth after seeing his aged grandmother—once a robust pioneer—sitting paralyzed by a stroke. He dreamed that he was in a big, straight chair in the middle of the great, open plains with a stampede of cattle coming toward him. He tried to move, but he couldn't. He cried for help, but no one came. In early 1968 Johnson said, "I felt that I was being chased on all sides by a giant stampede coming at me from all directions. . . . Vietnam . . . the inflationary economy . . . rioting blacks, demonstrating students, marching welfare mothers, squawking professors and hysterical reporters." LBJ ranted bitterly that "after thirty-seven years of public service, I deserved something more than being left alone in the middle of the plain, chased by stampedes on every side."[59]

In March 1968 Johnson dreamed an even creepier variant of the old nightmare. This time he imagined himself lying in a bed in the White House—except that the face was his but the thin, rigid body was that of Woodrow Wilson, paralyzed by a stroke in 1919 while campaigning for the League of Nations. Johnson would awake terrified, take a flashlight, and walk the dark corridors of the White House until he found Wilson's portrait. Stroking the canvas, he was able to persuade himself that Wilson was dead and that he, Lyndon Johnson, was still alive and moving.[60]

But there was little question now that LBJ was dead politically; his hopes of being elected for a second term had been buried. By March 1968, such was the mood that even Bobby Kennedy, Johnson's bête noire, had decided it was safe to challenge the president for the Democratic nomination.

Recognizing he needed a way out, Johnson asked his new defense secretary, Clark Clifford, to review the whole situation. Clifford summed up: "We are not sure that a conventional military victory, as commonly defined, can be achieved. . . . We seem to have gotten caught in a sinkhole. We put in more, they match it. . . . I see more and more fighting in sight with more and more casualties on the US side, and no end in sight."[61]

Johnson used Clifford's review to justify the change of policy he now accepted had to come. On March 31 the president addressed the nation on TV and radio: "Good evening, my fellow Americans." Millions of Johnson-haters braced themselves for another propaganda blitz about containing communism and making progress. Instead Johnson declared, "Tonight I want to speak to you of peace in Vietnam and Southeast Asia." Although insisting that American resolve remained firm, he said there was "no need to delay the talks that could bring an end to this long and this bloody war" and announced that America was "prepared to move immediately toward peace through negotiations." As a first step, he stated that the United States would stop bombing most of the North and at the end he slipped in some sentences he had kept up his sleeve until the very last minute. In order to concentrate on peace, LBJ said, "I shall not seek, and I will not accept, the nomination of my party for another term as your President."[62]

At the end of the speech, Johnson—to quote one aide—"bounded from his chair in the Oval Office to join his family in watching the television reviews. His shoulders temporarily lost their stoop. His air was that of a prisoner let free."[63] But his freedom was short lived. Four days later, on April 4, a white petty crook shot Martin Luther King on the balcony of a hotel in Memphis, Tennessee. "Everything we've gained in the last few days we're going to lose tonight," Johnson groaned on hearing the news. America's ghettos burned anew—Detroit, Cleveland, Chicago, and more than a hundred cities—with some of the worst violence in the capital itself. General William Westmoreland, back from Vietnam for official meetings, said that Washington "looked worse than Saigon did at the height of the Tet offensive." He joked that in 1814 the British had burned the city; this time Americans were doing it themselves.[64]

Then, two months later, on June 5, Bobby Kennedy was gunned down by a lone killer. Listening on the radio, LBJ stopped work in the Oval Office: "His head slumped way down between his knees as he listened, so low that those in front of the desk could barely see him. When it was over, he snapped the radio off, rose from his chair a stricken man, walked out of the French doors into the Rose Garden and stood there alone, silent."[65] Johnson's shock was genuine, but he must also have glimpsed how his presidency would now be remembered. "The bookends to his administration would be the two Kennedy assassinations, he reduced to a cipher and they elevated in the public imagination to the level of political demigods embodying the youth, vigor, and idealism of the nation."[66]

Ever the political alchemist, Johnson tried to extract good from evil. He used King's assassination to drive a fair housing law through Congress and, on the back of Bobby Kennedy's funeral, he urged again the tough gun-control law that he had been pressing since JFK's assassination. He told lawmakers, "On occasions before, I have spoken of the terrible toll inflicted on our people by firearms—750,000 Americans dead since the turn of the century. This is far more than have died at the hands of our enemies in all the wars we have fought. . . . Each year, in this country, guns are involved in more than 6,500 murders. This compares with 30 in England." He noted that "weapons of destruction can be purchased by mail as easily as baskets of fruit or cartons of cigarettes. We must eliminate the dangers of mail-order murder."[67]

Johnson wanted a radical law that banned the sale of firearms to minors and by mail, and also required the national registration of all guns. Although in the autumn he signed what he called "the most comprehensive gun control law ever signed in this Nation's history," he was disappointed at its gaps. Congress, lobbied intensively by the National Rifle Association, had rejected a national register of guns and also the licensing of those who carried them, even though there were now an estimated 160 million guns in America—in Johnson's words "more firearms than families." The president uttered a passionate but futile cry: "The voices that blocked these safeguards were not the voices of an aroused nation. They were the voices of a powerful lobby, a gun lobby, that has prevailed for the moment in an election year. But the key to effective crime control remains, in my judgment, effective gun control. And those of us who are really concerned about crime just must—somehow, someday—make our voices felt."[68]

This sense of failure pervaded the last months of Johnson's presidency. His attempts to negotiate peace in Vietnam got nowhere and his Democratic Party became polarized between pro-war and anti-war factions. The party convention in Chicago in August was one of the most notorious in American history. While the politicians slanged each other indoors, the streets and parks of Chicago attracted thousands of counterculture protestors, running the gamut from anti-war to free love. At their center were the Yippies, who offered a weeklong Festival of Life as antidote to what they called the Festival of Death in the convention hall. They even had their own candidate for president: a pig.

The Yippies' festive calendar for the week included:

- August 26 (am) Workshop in drug problems, underground communications, how to live free, guerrilla theater, self-defense, draft resistance, communes . . .
- August 26 (pm) Folksinging, barbecues, swimming, lovemaking . . .

- August 28 (am) Yippie Olympics. Miss Yippie Contest, Catch the Candidate, Pin the Tail on the Candidate, Pin the Rubber on the Pope and other normal healthy games.[69]

Mayor Richard Daley of Chicago had no intention of letting his city be polluted by such lewdness. He had already seen off Martin Luther King; now he deployed 12,000 police, backed by Illinois National Guardsmen armed with rifles, bazookas, and flamethrowers just in case the revolution really was at hand. Once again, it was all played out on television, as Daley's men clubbed the protestors and many innocent bystanders, including enraged journalists. How you reacted became a litmus test for Americans. Senator Abe Ribicoff of Connecticut denounced "those Gestapo tactics in the streets of Chicago," but Hubert Humphrey, the eventual Democratic candidate, had no time for Daley's critics: "I know what caused these demonstrations. They were planned, premeditated by certain people in this country that feel that all they have to do is riot and they'll get their way. . . . The obscenity, the profanity, the filth that was uttered night after night in front of the hotels was an insult to every woman, every daughter, indeed every human being. . . . Is it any wonder police had to take action?"[70]

Ribicoff spoke for millions who, in different ways, supported the rights revolution of the 1960s. But Humphrey was the voice of millions more who believed it had all gone too far, that America had been poisoned at home and abroad by an overdose of liberalism. Yet Humphrey was a Democrat desperately trying to salvage his chances of the presidency by reaching out to Middle America. The man who would benefit from the chaos of 1968 and start the conservative backlash was his Republican opponent, Richard Nixon.

VIETNAM—"PEACE WITH HONOR"?

In the 1950s Nixon had served as Eisenhower's vice-president but, after failing to win the White House in 1960 and the governorship of California two years later, he left politics, telling the media bitterly, "you won't have Nixon to kick around any more, because, gentlemen, this is my last press conference."[71] Yet Nixon had not abandoned his political ambitions and the chaos of 1968 played into his hands; appealing to America's "silent majority" as the ghettos burned and the campuses rioted, he finally reached the Oval Office.

During 1969 Nixon had some heady moments. In July the space program launched by Kennedy in 1961 finally paid off at a cost of $25 billion. Two American astronauts set foot on the moon, with Neil Armstrong uttering the carefully prepared words, "That's one small step for a man, one giant leap for mankind." Nixon muscled in on the action, calling it "the greatest week in the history of the world since the Creation."[72]

But nothing could obscure the president's overwhelming problem—the war in Vietnam, where Americans were dying at the rate of 200 a week at a cost of $30 billion a year. "I'm not going to end up like LBJ," Nixon told an aide, "holed up in the White House, afraid to show my face on the street. I'm going to stop that war. Fast." His initial hope was to bludgeon the communists to the negotiating table, by around-the-clock bombing of Vietcong sanctuaries in neighboring Cambodia. He wanted to unsettle Hanoi: "I call it the madman theory. . . . I want the North Vietnamese to believe I've reached the point where I might *do* anything to stop the war. We'll just slip the word to them that, 'for God's sake, you know Nixon is obsessed about communism. We can't restrain him when he's angry—and he has his hand on the nuclear button.'" Then, said Nixon, "Ho Chi Minh will be in Paris in two days begging for peace."[73]

But when Ho died in September 1969, the Paris peace talks were still deadlocked and Nixon, like Johnson, was immured in the White House by the encircling peace protestors, including the children of many of his leading advisers.

Bombing alone was clearly not enough, so Nixon also hoped to detach the Soviet Union from North Vietnam by what he called "linkage"—tying movement in one area of superpower relations, such as arms control, to progress on Vietnam. He told cabinet members that "the Soviet leaders should be brought to understand that they cannot expect to reap the benefits of cooperation in one area while seeking to take advantage of tension or confrontation elsewhere."[74]

Washington's leverage over Moscow had diminished, however. Determined never again to be humiliated as in the Cuban missile crisis of 1962, the Soviets had systematically built up their nuclear arsenal, especially land-based intercontinental missiles. The United States was still superior in nuclear-capable bombers and submarines but, overall by 1969, it enjoyed only a two-to-one advantage in the total number of launchers, compared with four-to-one in 1964—and the gap was shrinking every month.[75]

The best way to put pressure on both Hanoi and Moscow, Nixon realized, was to capitalize on the split between the communist giants, China and Russia, which brought them to the verge of war in 1969. This would not be easy, because the United States remained committed to the Chinese Nationalists who had retreated to the island of Taiwan at the end of the civil war in 1949—still acknowledging them as the legitimate government of China. Although this policy was now totally implausible, it had the backing of right-wing Republicans and the influential China lobby on Capitol Hill. Refusing to recognize "Red China" was a litmus test of Cold War orthodoxy.

Yet Nixon had come to the conclusion that an opening to China was now both necessary and possible. Necessary because of China's growing nuclear strength; possible because the xenophobic frenzy of the Cultural Revolution was playing itself out. Nixon argued that "we simply cannot afford to leave China forever outside the family of nations, there to nurture its fantasies, cherish its hates and threaten its neighbors." But the answer was not simply to drop America's guard because "the world cannot be safe until China changes." In the short run that meant "a creative counterpressure designed to persuade Peking that its interests can only be served by accepting the basic rules of international civility." In the long run, it meant "pulling China back into the world community—but as a great and progressing nation, not as the epicenter of world revolution."[76]

Pulling China back into the world community became a goal of Nixon's diplomacy. If Washington thawed relations with Beijing, he reckoned, that could pressure Russia on arms control and also help detach both the communist giants from North Vietnam. Diplomatic as much as military pressure was clearly required to get the peace he wanted—and also needed if he was to secure reelection in 1972.

Nixon was trying to play an intricate global chess game. He could not move all the pieces alone, yet he had the profoundest contempt for professional bureaucrats—particularly in the State Department. His secretary of state, former law partner William Rogers, was pure window dressing. The appointment that mattered was Nixon's new national security adviser—the Harvard professor Henry Kissinger.

Nixon and Kissinger seemed an unlikely pair: the reclusive, workaholic son of a California grocer and the sparkling Jewish intellectual, a childhood refugee from Hitler's Germany. Kissinger also had a sense of humor that Nixon conspicuously lacked, joking even about his own vanity with lines like, "I have been called indispensable and a miracle worker. I know, because I remember every word I say," and, "I have not faced such a distinguished audience since dining alone in the Hall of Mirrors."[77]

But, for all their differences, both men were essentially similar—ruthless, ambitious loners, deeply insecure about their image and their place in history. Kissinger found Nixon "very odd. . . . He didn't enjoy people. What I never understood was why he went into politics. . . . Isolation had become almost a spiritual necessity to this withdrawn . . . tormented man who insisted so on his loneliness and created so much of his torment." As for Kissinger, what particularly struck Nixon's aide John Ehrlichman were the nails bitten right down to the quick: "He cared desperately what people wrote and said about him" and "erected a protective façade that was part self-deprecating humor and part intellectual show-boating, but behind it he was devastated by press attacks on his professional competence."[78]

Almost paranoid about everyone else, each man was also deeply suspicious of the other. Yet Kissinger would have been nowhere without Nixon, while the president needed his brilliant adviser to implement his foreign policy. The crux, both agreed, was total secrecy—keeping diplomacy out of the feeble hands of the diplomats and away from the prying eyes and loud mouths of the media. So Kissinger developed a "backchannel" to the Soviet ambassador in Washington, using him for all important messages to Moscow, and thus bypassing the State Department. And it was Kissinger who in July 1971, after months of covert contacts via Pakistan, flew in secrecy into the Forbidden City of Beijing.

His trip was a success and Nixon used a deliberately low-key TV address to make the bombshell statement that the Chinese leadership had extended an invitation for him to visit China, which he had accepted "with pleasure." Nixon said that the aims of the meeting would be "to seek the normalization of relations between the two countries and also to exchange views on questions of concern to the two sides."[79]

Nixon's pioneering visit to China took place in February 1972, carefully timed for prime-time Sunday-evening TV back home. Just to be sure that Kissinger did not muscle in on the photo opportunity, burly secret-service aides blocked the aisle of Air Force One as the president strode down the steps, hand outstretched. Premier Zhou Enlai said later, "Your handshake came over the vastest ocean in the world—twenty-five years of no communication."[80]

The visit was an icebreaker, largely symbolic, but both sides understood that a settlement in Vietnam was essential for normalization of Sino-American relations. And Nixon always saw the China opening as one move in the larger global chess game. "We're doing the China thing to screw the Russians and help us in Vietnam," he told Kissinger, adding, "And maybe down the road to have some relations with China."[81]

As Nixon hoped, his trip to Beijing did loosen the logjam with Moscow. The Soviets' great fear was being isolated if their old enemy and their new one started cozying up. Again Kissinger acted as go-between, paving the way to a summit, and in May 1972 Richard Nixon touched down in Moscow. This time there was substance as well as symbolism, with a series of agreements on economics, social cooperation, and, above all, arms control. The superpowers agreed to a five-year freeze on new missiles—the first time they had tried to restrain the arms race—and a treaty limiting missile defense systems.

So, in three months in 1972, Nixon had overturned a quarter-century of Cold War history, becoming the first U.S. president to visit the capitals of international communism. Johnson had hoped to, but only a notorious commie-basher like Nixon could have avoided being outflanked on the right. Even so, he needed a master of the backchannel like Kissinger to set up the summits without premature press exposure.

These diplomatic triumphs boosted Nixon's chances of reelection in the autumn, but what really mattered was ending the war in Vietnam. Although Nixon had reduced the U.S. troop presence, his periodic escalations of the bombing had aroused far bigger protests than in Johnson's time. Publicly Nixon kept talking of "peace with honor," but secretly at the Moscow summit Kissinger indicated that the Americans mainly wanted a lull in the fighting so they could pull out without losing face. "We are willing to withdraw military forces," Kissinger told the Soviet foreign minister, Andrei Gromyko. "We are prepared to reduce aid if our opponents are willing to reduce aid. This would then leave the struggle to the Vietnamese. . . . All we ask is a degree of time so as to leave Vietnam for Americans in a better perspective. . . . [W]e will not leave in such a way that a Communist victory is guaranteed. However, we are prepared to leave so that a Communist victory is not excluded."[82]

Moscow, like Beijing, put pressure on Hanoi, while Washington arm-twisted its ally in Saigon to accept terms. In the autumn Kissinger unwisely predicted "peace is at hand," but his peace talks with the North Vietnamese failed to win the ultimate prize before voters went to the polls. In an election-eve broadcast, Nixon did his best to sound upbeat: "As you know, we have made a breakthrough in the negotiations which will lead to peace in Vietnam." He added that "there are still some details that I am insisting be worked out and nailed down because I want this not to be a temporary peace. . . . But I can say to you with complete confidence tonight that we will soon reach agreement on all the issues and bring this long and difficult war to an end."[83]

Nixon won a landslide victory, carrying every state except Massachusetts and winning 60 percent of the popular vote. But he was angry at Kissinger's failure to secure peace and also seething that his adviser seemed to be getting the credit for the diplomatic triumphs of 1972. News that *Time* magazine would give both of them jointly the coveted Man of the Year award sent Nixon into paroxysms of rage.

In mid-December, with talks stalled and Congress conveniently out of session, the president authorized a new wave of bombings of North Vietnam. *Time*—hastily rebalancing its Men of the Year issue to acknowledge continued failure in Vietnam—said that "the President's message to the enemy was as unmistakable as it was brutal . . . the biggest, bloodiest air strikes ever aimed at the North." Criticism from America's allies was intense. In Paris, *Le Monde* compared the bombing to the destruction of Guernica in the Spanish Civil War. In Britain the *Daily Mirror* commented, "The American resumption of the bombing of North Viet Nam has made the world recoil in revulsion."[84]

The so-called Christmas bombings did prove the finale—though not because they changed much of substance in Hanoi's position. Contrary to the press, the raids were aimed as much at persuading Saigon—by extracting some cosmetic concessions from the North and demonstrating America's will to keep defending South Vietnam if the peace terms were violated.[85]

On January 23, 1973, three days after being inaugurated for his second term, Richard Nixon told the American people that "we today have concluded an agreement to end the war and bring peace with honor in Vietnam and in Southeast Asia." A ceasefire, internationally supervised, would begin the following Saturday; within sixty days all American prisoners of war throughout Indochina would be released and all American forces withdrawn from South Vietnam. "The people of South Vietnam have been guaranteed the right to determine their own future, without outside interference," Nixon asserted, adding that the United States would "continue to recognize the Government of the Republic of Vietnam as the sole legitimate government of South Vietnam."[86]

Nixon did not mention that the agreement allowed North Vietnamese troops to remain in the South—hardly a sign of self-determination "without outside interference." As we shall see in the next chapter, it would be only a matter of time before South Vietnam, America's fake state, was overrun, but Nixon wanted a decent interval to save face. In the war for South Vietnam's freedom, 58,000 Americans had died and perhaps 2 million Vietnamese. The Christmas bombings were a sadly apt ending, because during the conflict the United States had dropped a greater tonnage of bombs on Vietnam than it used in the whole of World War II against Germany, Italy, and Japan.[87]

But at least Nixon had extricated America from the Vietnam quagmire. He was, it seemed, starting his second term with a clean slate and could look ahead to a second Russian summit and progress in normalizing relations with China. There was, however, a fly in the ointment that January—the trial in a Washington court of some rather unusual burglars.

WATERGATE AND THE IMPERIAL PRESIDENCY

Let's go back to the previous year, June 18, 1972. The *Washington Post* did not usually put local burglaries on its front page but this one, at the Watergate apartment complex on the Potomac river, was not run-of-the-mill: "Five men, one of whom said he is a former employee of the Central Intelligence Agency, were arrested at 2:30 a.m. yesterday in what authorities described as an elaborate plot to bug the offices of the Democratic National Committee here."[88]

The *Post* quickly linked the burglars and the large sums of money sloshing through their bank accounts to the Committee to Re-elect the President, unpopularly known as CREEP. But the White House insisted that the attempted bugging of the Democrats' HQ was the work of a few out-of-control political mavericks. At a press conference on August 29 Nixon stated categorically that, after a thorough internal investigation, "no one in the White House Staff, no one in this Administration, presently employed, was involved in this very bizarre incident." He added that "what really hurts in matters of this sort is not the fact that they occur, because overzealous people in campaigns do things that are wrong. What really hurts is if you try to cover it up."[89] Wise words. If only Nixon had heeded them.

Nixon probably did not know about Watergate in advance but he had fostered the climate that encouraged such actions. His siege mentality assumed that "they" were all out to get him: the Democrats, the press, the liberal establishment. As he said to Kissinger and other aides early in his presidency, "One day we will get them—we'll get them on the ground where we want them. And we'll stick our heels in, step on them hard and twist . . . right? Henry knows what I mean. Get them on the floor and step on them, crush them, show no mercy."[90]

So Nixon sanctioned break-ins and illegal wiretaps of opponents. Furious about the constant exposés of government policy, particularly on Vietnam, he also created a White House operation to plug the leaks, known as the Plumbers. And he was right at the center of the cover-up that followed the arrests at Watergate. Less than a week later, on June 23, he told aides to warn the FBI "don't go any further into this case, period," on the grounds that it affected national security.[91] The cover-up, organized by White House Counsel John Dean, kept the lid on things until after the November election, but in the New Year of 1973 it was blown off with a vengeance.

There were two detonators. The first was that Nixon's landslide victory the previous November had not been matched on Capitol Hill. The Democrats still controlled both Houses of Congress and they used their position to harry the president, particularly by appointing a special committee of the Senate to inquire into Watergate. The other detonator of publicity was that, despite White House pressure, the Watergate burglars and their immediate bosses were prosecuted. The trial ran from January to March 1973, in the full glare of the media, and at the end— faced with years as jailbirds—the ringleaders were ready to sing. The press, led by the *Washington Post*, followed up every lead, delighted to get back at the president— the hatred was mutual.

"There's no doubt about the seriousness of the problem," Dean told Nixon in a long and, as it proved, momentous conversation on March 21. "We have a cancer— within, close to the Presidency—that's growing, it's growing daily." This, said Dean, was because "we're being blackmailed" by the burglars and because "people are going to start perjuring themselves" to maintain the cover-up. Nixon's main concern was to keep the burglars quiet. He asked, "How much money do you need?" Dean reckoned $1 million over the next two years. "We could get that," Nixon responded. "And you could get it in cash. I know where it could be gotten."[92]

By the end of March, however, hush money was not enough. The press was claiming that culpability lay much higher, and Dean, seeing that he was being lined up as the next scapegoat, started talking to Watergate prosecutors. To save himself, Nixon accepted the resignation of his closest aides, Bob Haldeman and John Ehrlichman. The pressure was now getting to him—his hands were shaking, his breath often smelled of liquor—and he told Haldeman melodramatically, "You know, Bob, there's something I've never told anybody before, not even you. Every night since I've been President, every single night before I've gone to bed, I've knelt down on my knees beside my bed and prayed to God for guidance and help in this job. Last night before I went to bed, I knelt down and this time I prayed that I wouldn't wake up in the morning. I just couldn't face going on."[93]

Nixon was prone to self-pity and he loved melodrama. Even so, these words probably came from the heart. The most powerful man in the world—custodian of the nuclear codes that could exterminate millions—could not stop the wheels of justice and democracy gradually grinding him down. "I've trapped myself," he told

Haldeman on April 17, only three months after his second inaugural; as Dean observed, it was "a domino situation."[94]

Yet it was another fifteen months before the final domino would fall. A fighter all his life, Nixon waged a dogged rearguard action on two fronts—against the Senate Watergate committee, now in full cry with televised hearings, and against the independent special prosecutor, the appointment of whom he had been forced to concede because the Justice Department was implicated in the cover-up. Ironically, though, it was Nixon who sealed his own fate. In mid-July an aide admitted to the Watergate committee that Nixon had installed a voice-activated taping system to record his conversations. Such tapes were not unique—presidents back to Franklin Roosevelt, Democrat and Republican, had recorded some conversations—but Nixon had taken the practice much further, anxious to document his every word in readiness for eventual memoirs and also to protect himself against Kissinger, who often leaked distorted accounts of their conversations to the press.

All through the summer Nixon resisted the attempts of the Senate committee and the special prosecutor to subpoena the tapes. Watergate was now sapping not only his energy and health but also his political credibility. He had hoped to dispense with Kissinger—jealous of his cult status—but now needed his national security adviser to bolster the Nixon presidency. In fact, in September 1973, when William Rogers resigned as secretary of state—frustrated at being constantly bypassed—Nixon grudgingly appointed Kissinger to that post as well. For the rest of the beleaguered second term, Nixon's foreign policy was essentially Kissinger's.

No more so than in late October 1973 during the Arab-Israeli Yom Kippur War, which coincided with one of the most dramatic moments of Watergate. Nixon fired the attorney general and then his deputy, both of whom refused to sack the persistent special prosecutor, and there was a huge public outcry, with calls for the president to be impeached. Four days after this "Saturday Night Massacre," on the evening of October 24, intelligence reports suggested that the Kremlin might be about to send in Soviet forces to support Egypt. The White House responded by putting U.S. forces around the world on DefCon III—the highest level of defense readiness short of imminent attack.

Yet the decision was taken not by the president and commander-in-chief but by his secretary of state. Nixon was asleep and his entourage decided not to wake him. "Have you talked to the President?" White House chief of staff Al Haig asked. "No, I haven't," replied Kissinger. "He would just start charging around. . . . I don't think we should bother the President."[95] Whether Nixon was exhausted or drunk remains unclear. It is quite evident, however, that the president was becoming a liability for the presidency. Harried in one televised press conference by a battery of questions about the tapes, the cover-up, buggings, and his personal finances, he exclaimed that "people have got to know whether or not their President is a crook. Well, I am not a crook."[96] If a president needs to say that to the American people, he is as good as finished.

In a war of attrition over the winter Nixon was forced to release some of the tapes and further transcripts. Using this evidence, staff of the House Judiciary Committee (among them a young Yale law graduate named Hillary Rodham) prepared the case for impeachment. This constitutional provision for trying a president for "treason, bribery or other high crimes and misdemeanors" had been used only once before, unsuccessfully, against Andrew Johnson in 1868. But at the end of July 1974 the committee approved the articles of impeachment and the Supreme Court rejected Nixon's final effort to withhold subpoenaed tapes. Release of the so-called smoking-gun transcript from June 1972, when he tried to stop the FBI investigation into Watergate, sealed Nixon's fate. With Republican support in Congress hemorrhaging, he resigned on August 9, 1974, telling White House staff in a tearful, rambling farewell, "never be petty; always remember, others may hate you, but those who hate you don't win unless you hate them, and then you destroy yourself."[97] If Nixon had followed those precepts, he might have avoided self-destruction.

Much of the world watched in bemusement as the Watergate drama unfolded. It seemed incredible that the globe's most powerful leader could be toppled by what appeared to be a minor burglary and its cover-up. Certainly it made no sense in Beijing or Moscow, where far graver breaches of civil liberty were routine, legal accountability was negligible, and any political opposition inconceivable. "Too much freedom of expression," muttered Mao, who blamed Nixon's downfall on American "warmongers."[98] The Kremlin, likewise, assumed that the furor was part of a calculated counterattack on détente by American hard-liners.

Yet Watergate was no bizarre eccentricity. It was in fact symptomatic of the backchannel, backstabbing methods by which the Nixon presidency operated—methods that lay behind its foreign policy triumphs as much as its domestic scandals. The standard defense of Nixon is that bypassing Congress, bureaucracy, and the media was necessary for diplomatic success, because the U.S. political system, in which power is packaged out, deliberately frustrates vigorous executive leadership. "It is difficult for a President to make new departures through the system," Kissinger asserted. "No doubt Nixon went to extremes in trying to achieve dominance. . . . His administrative approach was weird and its human cost unattractive, yet history must also record the fundamental fact that major successes were achieved that had proved unattainable by conventional procedures."[99] There is some truth in this claim, but one could equally say that, through their secrecy and deception, Nixon and Kissinger failed to establish a strong domestic consensus beneath their policies. That lack of foundations, in turn, undermined their achievements—as we shall see in the next chapter.

The Nixon-Kissinger style was evident in the bloody overthrow of Salvador Allende, head of Chile's elected Marxist government. Fearful of another Cuba in the western hemisphere and anxious about U.S. business interests, the administration worked to depose Allende (whose reforms had wrecked the Chilean economy) while avoiding direct involvement. The CIA channeled millions of dollars to Allende's opponents and, after he was toppled in September 1973, Washington quickly endorsed the new and brutal military junta. The White House was exultant at the outcome: "[O]ur hand doesn't show on this one," Nixon exclaimed.[100]

In a best-seller, historian Arthur Schlesinger set Vietnam and Watergate in a longer perspective, as the apogee of what he called an "imperial presidency" that had grown throughout the Cold War. This, he said, was "essentially the creation of foreign policy. A combination of doctrines and emotions—belief in permanent and universal crisis, fear of communism, faith in the duty and the right of the United States to intervene swiftly in every part of the world—had brought about the unprecedented centralization of decisions over war and peace in the Presidency." But, Schlesinger went on, "as it overwhelmed the traditional separation of powers in foreign affairs, it began to aspire toward an equivalent centralization of power in the domestic polity." Together, he said, Vietnam and Watergate were "forcing Americans to think—harder than they had for more than a century—about the basic principles of government and the proper distribution of authority in a democratic republic."[101]

In November 1973 Nixon was reminded by a journalist of a story about Benjamin Franklin, who, when leaving the Constitutional Convention in 1787, was asked, "What have you given us, sir, a monarch or a republic?" Franklin answered, "A republic, sir, if you can keep it." The journalist asked Nixon whether, in the Watergate crisis, it would be possible to keep that republic. "Well," Nixon replied, "I would certainly not be standing here answering these questions unless I had a firm belief that we could keep the republic, that we must keep it, not only for ourselves but for the whole world."[102] Coming from him, those words sounded hollow, but in the end, republican democracy—however clumsy, volatile, and partisan—did bring down the imperial president.

As a nuclear power the United States was, if not omnipotent, at least preeminent: The Cuban missile crisis made that clear. But its nuclear arsenal was useable only as a last resort and at suicidal cost. It was not employed against North Vietnam, partly for fear of Soviet retaliation but also because this would have negated the supposed rationale of the whole U.S. war effort—to save the Vietnamese people from communism and give them their liberty.

Illusions of omnipotence also tainted America's ideology. The assumption that any society not narrowly conforming to American values was inimical to U.S. interests was unrealistic as well as hubristic. Kennedy, near the end of his life, had groped toward the idea of diversity but it was not until Nixon that the diplomacy of détente, of coexistence with communism, took root.

But these roots were shallow because Nixon felt he had to practice his diplomacy in defiance of democracy; likewise Johnson, who went around the back of Congress to wage war in Vietnam. Both leaders paid a heavy price. Although a global superpower, the United States was conducting foreign policy within an eighteenth-century constitution intended to restrain executive power. And much of the country's population still held a simplistic, parochial view of the outside world divided between goodies and baddies, which Cold War propaganda served only to reinforce. Ultimately the limits on American imperialism, for good and ill, were imposed by its politics and its people.

16

DÉTENTE AND DISCONTENT

The second half of the 1970s was especially stressful and perplexing for the American people. Nixon and Kissinger had hoped that détente would herald a new and more stable relationship with the Soviet Union. Instead America's political weakness after Watergate and Vietnam was treated by Moscow as an opportunity to expand in the third world; this prompted conservatives to demand a reassertion of U.S. power. At home the long postwar boom came to an end and there was a fierce backlash against the rights revolution of the previous decade. Issues such as abortion, women's rights, and school desegregation aroused intense feeling in the white suburbs. What made this backlash distinctive was that it mobilized, for the first time since the 1920s, evangelical Protestants as a political force.

It did not help that America's presidents in the later 1970s were hardly great leaders. Gerald Ford (1974–1977) was a caretaker figure replacing Nixon; Jimmy Carter (1977–1981) developed important new policies but lacked the skill or the political base to implement them. Yet, given the multiple discontents of the decade, even an able president would probably have floundered.

AMERICA IN RETREAT?

Vietnam and Watergate changed perceptions of America across much of the world. Books were published with titles like *The End of the American Era* and *The Retreat of American Power*. The latter was written by Henry Brandon, a veteran British correspondent in Washington, who reflected that the

> retreat from domination has been a very painful experience for all great powers throughout history. Now the United States is going through this searing and shattering experience, intensified in this case by the revulsion against the humiliation in Vietnam. Americans have always been proud, confident

and optimistic people. They have been taught to look upon American power
as close to absolute. They have placed a profound trust in all the values that
they have learned to identify as truly American. . . . [T]hey have also enjoyed
the certainty that economically they will always be richer than anybody else.

Brandon judged that "by the very nature of being American they have been taught
how to succeed, but not how to suffer failure."[1] And Gerald Ford was not the man
to get them going again.

Ford had come to prominence in October 1973 when Vice-President Spiro
Agnew had been forced to resign over charges of bribery and tax evasion. Richard
Nixon replaced Agnew with Ford, according to several insiders, because he cynically thought Congress would never impeach him knowing who would be his successor. Ford was diligent, affable but plodding—a veteran congressman of whom
one Republican colleague observed, "Jerry is popular because he is not a leader. If
he were a leader, he would not be popular."[2]

Ford did not prove to be the firewall that Nixon hoped but, once president, he
did try to damp down the flames. After succeeding Nixon in August 1974 Ford declared, "My fellow Americans, our long national nightmare is over. Our Constitution works; our great Republic is a government of laws and not of men. Here the
people rule."[3] The beneficent effect of Nixon's departure and Ford's evident decency were, however, almost immediately offset by the new president's announcement of a full pardon to Nixon. His aim was to draw a line under Watergate: "My
conscience tells me that only I, as President, have the constitutional power to firmly
shut and seal this book."[4]

Ford was probably right—and Nixon's acceptance of a pardon did imply some
admission of guilt—but the nation's wounds were too raw for early healing. After
the pardon Ford's Gallup Poll rating plunged in a month from 71 percent to 49
percent, the biggest-ever drop. A partial amnesty for Vietnam draft dodgers did little to assuage popular anger; many people suspected a prior deal in order to get
Nixon out of the White House. This belief was unwarranted but Ford's presidency
never fully recovered.[5]

Even a strong, credible president would have struggled in 1974, the year of the
first oil crisis. Ever since the 1950s the West's economic growth had depended on
cheap, secure supplies of oil, but then in 1973, as a weapon in the Arab-Israeli War,
the oil-exporting states raised prices dramatically and imposed an embargo on Israel's allies, notably the United States. Prices at America's pumps rose 50 percent
over the winter; at around sixty cents a gallon they were hardly crippling by today's
standards but to a country that assumed that cheap gas was an American birthright,
the oil crisis was a real shock. An analysis of public opinion in December 1973 detected "incipient signs of panic." People were said to believe that "the country has
run out of energy."[6]

This was nonsense, of course: Unlike western Europe, which imported nearly all its oil, in America domestic production satisfied two-thirds of the country's needs. But the other third came mostly from the Middle East and the price hike plus public panic created a crisis.

Time magazine reported in February 1974:

> Housewives in hair curlers knit sweaters at the wheels of their station wagons in the predawn blackness of Miami. . . . Young couples in Manhattan, armed with sandwiches and hot chocolate, invite friends along for an evening of gasoline shopping. Connecticut executives regale each other with lurid tales of mile-long queues and two-hour waits at the pump. Otherwise sane citizens are in the cold grip of the nation's newest obsession: gasoline fever. As supplies tighten in many parts of the country, people are wondering where their next gallon is coming from. . . . For millions of Americans, happiness is a full tank of gas.[7]

The pursuit of happiness was, of course, one of the fundamental rights enshrined in Jefferson's Declaration of Independence, but the oil crisis intensified debate about whether Americans had become too self-indulgent in their use of natural resources. The country's environmental movement, as we saw in Chapter 10, dated back to the late nineteenth century, but it became much more prominent during the 1960s. Best-selling books made an impact, among them Rachel Carson's *Silent Spring* (1962), whose exposé of the damage caused by pesticides led eventually to the banning of DDT, and *The Population Bomb* (1968) by Paul Ehrlich, which predicted a global Malthusian crisis as humanity exhausted nature's resources. During the 1960s membership of environmental groups such as the Sierra Club soared and in January 1969 there was huge media attention when an undersea oil blowout polluted hundreds of miles of the California coast around Santa Barbara. This disaster helped prompt the first Earth Day in April 1970, when several million Americans, many of them schoolchildren, participated in parades and teach-ins. Later that year Nixon, responding to the new mood, established the Environmental Protection Agency (EPA)—the first attempt to create a single federal body to regulate pollution.

The surge of environmentalism did have some effect on American attitudes toward the automobile. Emission standards were tightened and, after the oil crisis, car makers began producing new models with better fuel efficiency. But the majority of U.S. automobiles remained gas-guzzlers by European standards and the fuel crisis gradually abated, helped by new American sources of supply such as Alaska coming onstream. In any case, across much of America's hinterland, the car was the only way to get around; the policy of subsidizing roads rather than rail embodied in the Interstate Highway Act of 1956 (see Chapter 13) had almost destroyed the country's once-great passenger rail network. With petrol at the pump hardly taxed, most Americans outside the inner cities had little incentive to turn from private cars to public transport.

A more persistent problem than the fuel crisis was what economists called stagflation—a theoretically puzzling combination of stagnant growth and soaring inflation that lasted for the rest of the decade. The United States coped better than most developed countries, but 8 percent inflation and 7 percent unemployment were undoubtedly shocks to the system after the long postwar boom.

There were other structural changes. In 1971 the dollar had been forced off gold, and the world lurched into a new and uncertain era of floating exchange rates, which seemed another sign of American decline. Actually it was more accurate to see the period 1945–1970 as one of exaggerated U.S. hegemony, because the rest of the developed world had been slow to recover from the ravages of World War II. The dollar remained the world's prime reserve currency, though at a lower relative value after 1971, which made U.S. exports more competitive and helped the country achieve modest growth; but what struck most people was that the dollar no longer seemed Almighty.

Dramatizing the sense of decline was the endgame in Vietnam. Although Nixon had pulled out U.S. troops in 1973 as part of the peace agreement with North Vietnam, he still hoped to prop up South Vietnam for a decent interval with massive economic and military aid and by the threat of U.S. air power from bases nearby. But, as part of the reaction against the so-called imperial presidency, Congress slashed aid budgets and imposed the War Powers Act in November 1973. This prevented the president from using U.S. troops in combat for more than sixty days without congressional approval. The aim of the Act was to forestall undeclared wars such as Vietnam, which Johnson and Nixon waged under their authority as commander-in-chief without asking Congress for a formal declaration of war.

Such was the strength of feeling on Capitol Hill that the bill was passed over Nixon's veto. He had claimed it was unconstitutional and "would seriously undermine this Nation's ability to act decisively and convincingly in times of international crisis. As a result, the confidence of our allies in our ability to assist them could be diminished and the respect of our adversaries for our deterrent posture could decline."[8]

The cuts in aid and the War Powers Act dramatically reduced Nixon's ability to sustain South Vietnam. In any case, it had always been a corrupt and fragile state, held together by military rule—"not a country with an army but an army with a country," to quote one U.S. officer.[9] By 1974 a fifth of the civilian workforce was unemployed, inflation was running at 65 percent, and deserters were fleeing the army in droves. The North Vietnamese offensive in March 1975 administered the coup de grâce; their troops drove through places like Pleiku and Hué—which, seven years before, had been described as vital for the survival of the free world—and raced toward Saigon. The Americans evacuated personnel and dependants. Finally, amid torrential rain, helicopters landed on the roof of the U.S. embassy to pull out the ambassador and key staff. Many South Vietnamese, desperate to escape, had forced their way into the building and U.S. Marines used tear gas and rifle butts to hold back the mob screaming to be taken along. "Floor by floor," *Time* magazine reported, "the Marines withdrew toward the roof of the embassy with looters right behind them. Abandoned offices were transformed into junkyards of smashed typewriters and ransacked file cabinets. Even the bronze plaque with the names of the five American servicemen who died in the embassy during the 1968 Tet offensive was torn from the lobby wall."[10] The last chopper took off from the roof of the embassy just before 8 A.M. on April 30, 1975. At noon North Vietnamese tanks bulldozed the gates of the presidential palace and within minutes the Liberation Flag flew from the flagpole. The *Frankfurter Allgemeine Zeitung*, a leading German paper, printed a front-page editorial headlined "AMERICA—A HELPLESS GIANT."[11]

By the end of that summer the rest of Indochina, Laos and Cambodia, had also gone communist and a new front was opening up in the global Cold War as the Portuguese empire, the last relic of European imperialism, crumbled in southern Africa. In Guinea and Mozambique the aftermath of independence was relatively peaceful, because the guerrilla movements in both were largely united. Angola, by contrast, had three rival factions vying for control, each with different tribal roots, and it also boasted large mineral resources, including oil. The Americans got drawn in, using South African troops as proxies, while Moscow's front-line force comprised Cuban mercenaries backed by Soviet supplies and air transport. And it was the Soviet-backed Marxist guerrillas who triumphed in March 1976.

Henry Kissinger, retained by Ford as secretary of state, was deeply concerned about this Soviet-Cuban expansionary axis. "The United States must make it clear that Angola sets no precedent; this type of action will not be tolerated elsewhere," he declared. "If continued it would have serious consequences for any possibility of easing of relations with the Soviet Union." Angola, said Kissinger, "represents the first time that the Soviets have moved militarily at long distance to impose a regime of their choice" and also, he added, "the first time that the United States has failed to respond to Soviet military moves outside the immediate Soviet orbit."[12]

The Soviets would find out to their cost, like the Americans in Vietnam, that third-world states were not easily controlled, but in the mid-1970s the revolutions in Vietnam and Angola encouraged bullish optimism in Moscow—a sense that, to quote one senior Soviet official, "the world was turning in our direction."[13] In America, the communist successes provoked growing skepticism about the whole process of "détente" that Nixon and Kissinger had set in motion. That word means literally relaxation of tension—the Americans had expected that the Soviets would now draw back from trouble-making around the world—but the Kremlin read détente very differently. America's acceptance of nuclear parity and its evident international weakness in the post-Watergate era boosted hopes in Moscow that the world was now safe for revolutionary change, for exploiting postcolonial situations in Southeast Asia and Africa to extend Soviet influence. Kissinger warned grimly that détente could not "survive any more Angolas."[14]

In this atmosphere hopes waned for a further arms-control agreement between the superpowers to build on Nixon's achievements in 1972 and, with an election campaign looming in 1976, President Ford dropped the word "détente" from his speeches. He was now on the defensive against a strong right-wing challenge for the Republican nomination from Ronald Reagan, the former movie-actor and governor of California. Reagan damned U.S. foreign policy as "wandering without aim," citing Angola as a prime example. "If detente were the two-way street it's supposed to be, we could have told the Soviet Union to stop its trouble-making and leave Angola to the Angolans. But it didn't work out that way." Now, he said, "we are told Washington is dropping the word 'detente,' but keeping the policy. But whatever it's called, the policy is what's at fault." Reagan insisted that "peace does not come from weakness or from retreat. It comes from the restoration of American military superiority."[15]

In 1976 Reagan's bid for the presidency was not successful. Ford hung on to the Republican nomination, though he eventually lost the election to the Democrat Jimmy Carter. But Reagan spoke for millions of Americans who yearned, in his words, to "restore America" not only to preeminence abroad but also to sound values at home.

A CONSTITUTIONAL ABORTION

February 1970. Three women were talking earnestly in a pizza parlor in Dallas, Texas. Nothing unusual there, you might think, except that this conversation would echo all the way to the U.S. Supreme Court.

The three women in that pizzeria were Norma McCorvey and two lawyers. Norma was twenty-three; poor, divorced, and pregnant, she wanted an abortion, but that was a crime according to the law of Texas and indeed of most states in the Union. Many of these laws had been enacted in the mid-nineteenth century to protect women from back-street abortionists, but by the 1960s they were denounced by feminists as violating a woman's basic right to be in control of her body. To quote a best-seller from the Boston women's health collective titled *Our Bodies, Ourselves*: "One of our most fundamental rights as women is the right to choose whether and when to have children. Only when we are in control of that choice are we free to be all that we can be." The book acknowledged that birth control was "the single best tool for implementing this choice," but admitted that current methods were "just not effective enough for us always to avoid unwanted pregnancy. . . . So right now, for many of us, a second indispensable tool for taking control of our fertility is abortion."[16]

The rhetoric of women's rights tended to be a student and middle-class preserve, but there was another, grimmer side to abortion, noted by Shirley Chisholm, a black congresswoman from New York. Several young women had come to her after suffering permanent injuries at the hands of illegal abortionists. "Experience shows that pregnant women who feel they have compelling reasons for not having a baby, or another baby, will break the law, and even worse, risk injury and death, if they must to get one. Abortions will not be stopped," Chisholm warned. In her view the question was simply "what kind of abortions society wants women to have—clean, competent ones performed by licensed physicians or septic, dangerous ones done by incompetent practitioners."[17]

Like the women of whom Shirley Chisholm spoke, Norma McCorvey in the Dallas pizzeria had a very personal interest in abortion. By contrast, the two women lawyers talking with her were keen to advance women's rights and sought a test case to challenge whether the Texas anti-abortion law was constitutional. But the divide between them and Norma was not quite that stark because one of the lawyers, Sarah Weddington, had her own guilty secret. During law school she had driven into Mexico to get an illegal abortion. It turned out all right for Weddington, but she did not forget the nightmare—as she said years later, "my mouth goes dry as I put myself back in those days in Austin when my period was late."[18]

Weddington's experience of abortion and her difficulty in getting taken seriously by the Texas legal establishment, despite outstanding credentials, gave an edge of passion to this issue of principle. She and her colleague Linda Coffee obtained McCorvey's agreement to make her a test case, which they eventually appealed all the way to the U.S. Supreme Court. The case became known as *Roe v. Wade*—Henry Wade was the local district attorney in Texas who sought to uphold state law; Jane Roe was the legal pseudonym used to cloak the identity of Norma McCorvey.

As the case rose up the legal ladder, the two young women lawyers who had started it found themselves being muscled out by the men. Roy Lucas, a lawyer who had taken an interest in the case from early on, argued that he was better qualified to argue the issues in Washington. Lucas was a veteran campaigner against abortion laws, whose interest, like Weddington's, had personal roots—when in college he had flown to Puerto Rico with his then girlfriend, who there underwent a degrading back-street abortion.[19] He argued that he alone should present the case to the Supreme Court: "It has taken me virtually years to read and absorb everything which might be relevant to the case, and it would be wasteful to not make full use of this experience. You," he told Weddington rather patronizingly, "should be well-prepared on all of the issues in the case in the event that I go down in an airplane accident, but every maxim of appellate advocacy demands that the case be presented by one attorney, and that the attorney be the most thoroughly prepared. . . . I trust you will put the best interests of the cause over any personal desires in the matter."[20]

Lucas did not get his way, however. He was felt to have a combative courtroom style and, in any case, there was a deeper issue at stake. The whole argument was that women had a unique perspective on abortion and that they were making a long-delayed bid for full rights. This argument would be undercut if a man pleaded their case before the Supreme Court, so the women lawyers and their clients held the line. But it was a real risk. Weddington was just twenty-six, and this would be her first appearance before the Supreme Court. Three weeks before the case was to be heard, she phoned a colleague. "I'm going to argue the case," she told him, and then broke down in tears.[21]

Adding to the pressure was the Court's tight timetable: Although each side prepared lengthy written arguments, its lawyer had only thirty minutes to present an oral argument to the nine justices—the lengthy orations of the nineteenth century were a thing of the past. Sarah Weddington had to touch on a variety of legal and constitutional issues and also field questions from the justices, but she succeeded in getting across her central point: "[A] pregnancy to a woman is perhaps one of the most determinative aspects of her life. It disrupts her body. It disrupts her education. It disrupts her employment. And it often disrupts her entire family life." So, Weddington told the Court, this was "a matter which is of such fundamental and basic concern to the woman involved that she should be allowed to make the choice as to whether to continue or to terminate her pregnancy."[22]

Representing the state of Texas was Jay Floyd. In contrast to Weddington's calm, articulate presentation, Floyd spoke slowly and often haltingly; he was also flustered by the questions. On courtroom performance alone, the case would have gone against him; in any case the Texas statute, which dated from the 1850s, was hard to defend, allowing abortion only if the mother's life was in danger. But the Supreme Court did not reach a decision on that round of argument—two justices short because of recent resignations, it decided to rehear the case on October 11, 1972, when fully up to strength.

This time Sarah Weddington played down women's rights and emphasized the civil rights guaranteed each individual by the Constitution. Justice Harry Blackmun asked if her case therefore depended partly "on the proposition that the fetus has no constitutional rights." Weddington rephrased her point: "It depends on saying that the woman has a fundamental constitutional right; and that the State has not proved any compelling interest for regulation in the area. Even if the Court, at some point, determined the fetus to be entitled to constitutional protection, you would still get back into the weighting of one life against another." This gave Byron White, one of the new conservative justices, an opening: "That's what's involved in this case? Weighing one life against another?" Weddington quickly recovered: "No, Your Honor, I say that would be what would be involved, if the facts were different and the State could prove that there were a 'person' for the constitutional right." Potter Stewart interjected that "*if* it were established that an unborn fetus is a person, with the protection of the Fourteenth Amendment, you would have an almost impossible case, would you not?" Weddington conceded it would be "very difficult."[23]

This was the contention of the state of Texas, advanced by the opposing counsel, Robert Flowers, that "upon conception, we have a human being; a person, within the concept of the Constitution of the United States, and that of Texas, also." Justice Stewart asked how that issue should be decided: "Is it a legal question? A constitutional question? A medical question? A philosophical question? Or a religious question?" Flowers responded that "we feel that it could be best decided by a legislature, in view of the fact that they can bring before it the medical testimony— the actual people who do the research." White cut in. "So then it's basically a medical question?" Flowers said, "From a constitutional standpoint, no, sir. I think it's fairly and squarely before this Court." He added quietly, "We don't envy the Court for having to make this decision."[24]

The Supreme Court was indeed faced with an unenviable task. These two rounds of legal argument had set out many of the essential issues around which debate still revolves—a woman's right to control her body versus the right of the unborn child; whether the fetus could be considered a "person" with rights under the Constitution and, if so, at what point in pregnancy that personhood emerged; whether abortion should be adjudicated by the Supreme Court in the light of its interpretation of the U.S. Constitution, or whether the question were better left to democratic lawmakers attuned to the will of the people.

But, as Flowers said, at this moment in history the Court had to take a decision and in January 1973 it finally spoke out. By seven to two the justices—all male— upheld the appeal of Jane Roe and declared that the Texas anti-abortion statute was unconstitutional. This they did by reaffirming the constitutional "right to privacy" they had already discerned and developed in judgments over the previous decade. But the Court also went much further, setting out a framework for abortion by dividing pregnancies into three equal "trimesters." In the first third of a pregnancy, a woman needed only the consent of her doctor, but in the later two-thirds the state's interest in the potential life allowed it to impose ever tighter regulation over abortion.

The decision on *Roe v. Wade* proved doubly controversial—the Court was adjudicating on an issue of enormous moral and religious sensitivity, and it was also doing so via very arguable legal reasoning. The majority decision had been written by Justice Blackmun, a recent appointee for whom this was his first major drafting task. Blackmun, by general consent, did not do a very good job. He found it hard to get to the essentials and spent too much time on medical rather than constitutional issues. Since 1973 constitutional scholars, even those who agree with the decision, have enjoyed rewriting the Court's opinion as they believe it should have been reasoned.

Two justices dissented from both the decision and the reasoning—Byron White and William Rehnquist. They were not against some kinds of abortion, particularly where the health of the mother or of the fetus was in doubt, but were opposed to what seemed to them abortion on demand. As White put it in a fierce dissent in a related abortion case, "At the heart of the controversy in these cases are those recurring pregnancies that pose no danger whatsoever to the life or health of the mother but are, nevertheless, unwanted for any one or more of a variety of reasons—convenience, family planning, economics, dislike of children, the embarrassment of illegitimacy, etc." His colleagues, White said, had in effect stated that "during the period prior to the time the fetus becomes viable, the Constitution of the United States values the convenience, whim, or caprice of the putative mother more than the life or potential life of the fetus."

White was also sure that the Court had far exceeded its authority by offering such a broad reading of the Fourteenth Amendment of 1868, which had been intended to secure civil rights for former slaves:

> I find nothing in the language or history of the Constitution to support the Court's judgment. The Court simply fashions and announces a new constitutional right for pregnant mothers and, with scarcely any reason or authority for its action, invests that right with sufficient substance to override most existing state abortion statutes. The upshot is that the people and the legislatures of the fifty States are constitutionally disentitled to weigh the relative importance of the continued existence and development of the fetus, on the one hand, against a spectrum of possible impacts on the mother, on the other hand.

White condemned the judgment as "an improvident and extravagant exercise of the power of judicial review that the Constitution extends to this Court."[25]

Roe v. Wade in 1973 cast a long shadow. The Supreme Court's decision created a fault line in American society, around which the arguments for and against abortion would polarize—pro-choice versus pro-life. *Roe v. Wade* also became a litmus test in American politics, an identifying mark of whether one was liberal or conservative. Finally, the decision and the way it was written became a landmark in American constitutional law. The angry dissent from Byron White—about how the Court was exceeding its authority, stretching the Constitution, even acting as the maker of law rather than as its interpreter—set out claims around which conservatives would rally as their backlash against the rights revolution gathered momentum. So although millions of Americans applauded *Roe v. Wade* for making abortion constitutional, for millions more it seemed like a constitutional abortion.

THE "SILENT MAJORITY" FINDS ITS VOICE

Nixon and Watergate, it seemed, had almost destroyed the Republican Party. In 1974 only one-fifth of the electorate described itself as Republican; two-thirds of voters, when asked, could not think of anything good to say about the Party. "In ten years," predicted conservative activist Richard Viguerie gloomily, "there won't be a dozen people in the country calling themselves Republican."[26]

Viguerie could not have been more wrong. Only six years later America had a Republican president, one who came, moreover, from the far right of the party. Ronald Reagan tapped the discontent about America's perceived weakness abroad and moral decline at home, but his success had deeper political roots. It reflected a conservative revival that had been brewing since the supposedly liberal 1960s. Viguerie was one of the organizers, but this was really a grassroots response by those whom Nixon had called America's "Silent Majority." At its heart were issues of sex and race, underpinned by mounting opposition to big government telling them how to run their lives.

The backlash against feminism took the form of a defense of family values. One traditionalist, Connie Marshner, depicted the campaign for women's rights as "a drab, macho-feminism of hard-faced women" who were "determined to secure their places in the world, no matter whose bodies they have to climb over." Their position, she said, was utterly selfish: "A relationship which proves burdensome? Drop it! A husband whose needs cannot be conveniently met? Forget him! Children who may wake up in the middle of the night? No way!" In reality, Marshner claimed, women were innately "other-oriented . . . ordained by nature to spend themselves in meeting the needs of others. And women, far more than men, will transmit culture and values to the next generation."[27] As that last sentence suggests, the defense of traditionalism often had an undercurrent of female superiority— women as the glue holding family and therefore society together.

In the 1970s the campaign to save the American family centered on blocking the proposed Equal Rights Amendment, or ERA. The idea for such an amendment to the U.S. Constitution, affirming that equal rights should not be denied or abridged on grounds of sex, had been around since the end of World War I—to complete the campaign for women's suffrage. But although the ERA was introduced in every session of Congress from 1923 it got nowhere until the 1970s; then the fresh wind of women's liberation helped it sail through the House and the Senate in 1971–1972. All the ERA needed to become part of the Constitution was ratification by three-quarters of the state legislatures, thirty-eight out of the total fifty. Twenty-two states had approved the ERA by the end of 1972 and it appeared to be coasting, until Phyllis Schlafly came along.

On one level, Schlafly seemed like the archetypal homemaker. The wife of a successful lawyer in Alton, Illinois, just across the river from St. Louis, she spent most of the 1950s and 1960s raising her six children. But she did so in unconventional ways, feeding them porridge for breakfast and sending them to school with healthy lunches of organic peanut butter sandwiches on whole-wheat bread. Yet that did not make her a counterculture mom, for Schlafly and her husband were committed Catholics and fervent anti-communists. She threw herself into various activities for conservative and Republican causes, including running for Congress, but always emphasized the role that could be played by grassroots activists. One of her standard speeches was titled "The Big Things Are Done by Little People," starting with Christ choosing his disciples.

A suburban mother who felt fulfilled and who engaged in community life yet was angered by national politics, Schlafly was the counterexample to Betty Friedan's "concentration camp" homemaker in *The Feminine Mystique*. She spoke for thousands of similar women who had been mobilized by Barry Goldwater's presidential campaign in 1964 in grassroots organizations like "Mothers for a Moral America," insisting that "the time is past when women of the Republican Party are merely doorbell pushers."[28]

So, although many feminists regarded Schlafly with near hatred as a cynical opportunist—"I'd like to burn you at the stake," Friedan exploded during a debate in 1973[29]—she tapped deep into American society. Her campaign against the ERA did not deny continued discrimination against women, especially in employment, but argued that this could be addressed through existing legislation. Passing the ERA, Schlafly claimed, would deprive women of their freedom to be women and the laws that guaranteed this. Instead, the ERA would impose "a doctrinaire equality under which women must be treated the same as men." Schlafly asserted that it would "take away from girls their exemption from the draft and their legal protection against predatory males. It will take away from wives and mothers their right to be provided with a home and financial support from their husbands. It will take away from senior women their extra social security benefits. It will take away a woman's present *freedom of choice* to take a job—*or* to be a full-time wife and mother. In short, it will take away the right to be a woman."[30]

ERA supporters strenuously contested Schlafly's interpretation of what the amendment would do to women's rights, but they were slow to organize against her campaign. Schlafly's STOP ERA—where STOP cleverly stood for "Stop Taking Our Privileges"—did indeed halt the momentum for ratification in the mid-1970s. *Time* magazine described Schlafly as "feminine but forceful . . . a very liberated woman." When she campaigned against the ERA in Illinois in June 1978, she looked "crisp and composed in a red shirtwaist dress, red-white-and-blue scarf and frosted hair." She and 500 supporters brought legislators trademark loaves of home-baked bread—gifts from the bread makers, she liked to say, for the breadwinners. But, noted *Time*, "as she climbed onto a kitchen stool to address the cheering crowd, Schlafly the demure housewife turned into Schlafly the aggressive polemicist, warning that passage of the ERA would mean '[g]overnment-funded abortions, homosexual schoolteachers, women forced into military combat and men refusing to support their wives.'"[31]

By 1978 thirty-five states had approved the ERA, but that was three short of the threshold for ratification. Although Congress extended the deadline for ratification to June 1982, no more states followed suit. In fact, five legislatures voted to rescind their original approval.

Schlafly's opponents denounced her as a hypocrite—freed by a wealthy husband from the need to take paid employment and even to look after the home that she claimed was where women found fulfillment. (According to *Time*, she employed "a full-time housekeeper to care for her six-bedroom Tudor-style mansion overlooking the Mississippi River."[32]) Critics also noted that women who opposed the ERA were mainly married and white from comfortable business and professional families. What, they asked, of women who were poor, black, and often single parents? These people needed the federal government to stand up for their rights. For conservatives, however, the way that Uncle Sam was intruding into daily life was the real offense.

This is clear from one of the other grassroots movements of the 1970s—against the enforced racial integration of schools. The Supreme Court had declared segregated schools to be unconstitutional back in 1954 but had left it up to the localities to desegregate "with all deliberate speed." The result, across much of the South, was deliberate foot-dragging. In Atlanta, for instance, 90 percent of school-age blacks remained in segregated schools in 1968; local journalist Ralph McGill asked in exasperation, "Must a nation which has put a man into space still argue about where and whether a colored child shall go to school?"[33]

Eventually the Supreme Court intervened again. The case before it was against the School Board of New Kent County, near Richmond, Virginia. Although the population was about equally black and white and there was no residential segregation, one of the two schools in the county had always been white and the other black. To get around the requirement of integration, the School Board came up with a carefully titled "freedom-of-choice" plan whereby students chose each year which school they wished to attend. In the plan's three years of operation, no white student had opted for the "black" school and only 15 percent of black students had been admitted to the "white" school.

In May 1968, a few weeks after the riots following the murder of Martin Luther King, the Supreme Court finally put its foot down, adjudging the Kent County plan unacceptable as a "deliberate perpetuation of the unconstitutional dual system." The Court insisted that "the time for mere 'deliberate speed' has run out" and the School Board was told to formulate a new plan that would "convert promptly to a system without a 'white' school and a 'Negro' school, but just schools."[34] The Court pointed out that in Kent County the obvious remedy was "zoning"—in other words, assigning the students geographically to the school nearer their home—but that would not work in many areas of the South and most of the nation where blacks and whites tended to live in separate neighborhoods. If, as the Court had insisted in 1954, racially segregated education was unconstitutional, then more radical steps seemed essential and a path was blazed in 1969 by a federal judge in North Carolina.

The city of Charlotte, North Carolina, was predominantly black, whereas surrounding Mecklenburg County was largely white. So in order to achieve some kind
of racial balance, school boards started the large-scale busing of children from home
to school. The result was a massive backlash from the white suburban middle class.
A "Concerned Parents Association" mobilized opposition from previously apolit-
ical families who disliked the way, as they put it, the government was "messing with
our children." They made no overt reference to race but talked the language of rights
and opportunity, as in this comment from one father: "I am not opposed to integration in any way. But I was 'affluent' enough to buy a home near the school where
I wanted my children to go. And I pay taxes to pay for it. They can bring anyone they
like to that school, but I don't want my children taken away from here."[35]

Charlotte became a shop window for the nation, in both its busing plan and its
backlash. This took two forms: Many parents moved their children into private
schools while those who could not afford the fees moved out to suburbs beyond the
busing zones. "This is our home, and we love it," lamented one white parent in
Montgomery, Alabama. "We can't buy a house as good as this for the price of this
one but we are willing to make the sacrifice."[36]

Busing accelerated this phenomenon, known as "white flight." Urban whites
moved out to the suburbs, leaving the inner cities to blacks—with mixed consequences. On the one hand, white flight resulted in many more black elected officials:
In 1964 there were about 500 in the whole country, of whom only 25 lived in the
South. By 1980 there were 4,000 black elected officials—more than three-fifths of
them in the South—and major cities such as Cleveland, Detroit, and Atlanta had
black mayors.[37] White flight, as much as the 1965 Voting Rights Act, gave blacks
their political opportunity.

Yet the new black politicians were running inner cities whose tax base and revenues had been eroded by white flight and by the exodus of the black middle class.
This exacerbated the cities' social and economic problems, of which schooling was
central. Some black leaders began to question whether busing really helped. As one
black school superintendent in Durham, North Carolina, put it, "quality education—not integration—is the top priority."[38] Spurious equality seemed to be getting
in the way of educational quality—diverting scarce resources from textbooks and
teachers into expensive busing programs whose main result often seemed to be
long and exhausting journeys for the children.

The backlash against busing was not confined to the South. It was often more
fraught in big northern cities, where residential segregation was starker. In September 1974 court-ordered busing provoked uproar in "liberal" Boston. The city
prided itself on being the crucible of the American Revolution and of the movement to abolish slavery. But the liberals lived in the far suburbs, safely outside the
city limits; the schools being desegregated were in blue-collar areas like Irish-
American South Boston, which was now supposed to welcome black students from
Roxbury. Buses were stoned and fights broke out among the students. Hundreds of

policemen were deployed to guard schools, with police helicopters hovering over-head. "Boston should be ashamed," exclaimed Roy Wilkins, a black leader who vis-ited the city. "My gosh, in Hattiesburg, Mississippi, children, black and white, are playing football together and singing in the choir together. And they call Boston the cradle of abolitionism!"[39]

The backlash against busing was not nationally organized, unlike the anti-ERA movement, but it had similar roots. The so-called Silent Majority was finding its voice: One Boston anti-busing organization was called ROAR (Restore Our Alien-ated Rights). Another common thread was the conviction that the federal govern-ment and especially the courts were meddling unacceptably in the lives of families and communities. When God was brought into the frame as well, the result was a political earthquake.

BRINGING GOD BACK INTO POLITICS

In the 1960s the Reverend Jerry Falwell was adamant that preachers should keep out of politics. In March 1965 this up-and-coming evangelical pastor from Lynch-burg, in the heart of Virginia, gave a sermon entitled "Ministers and Marches" ques-tioning "the sincerity and non-violent intentions of some civil rights leaders such as Dr. Martin Luther King, Jr.," who, said Falwell "are known to have left-wing as-sociations. It is very obvious that the Communists, as they do in all parts of the world, are taking advantage of a tense situation in our land, and are exploiting every incident to bring about violence and bloodshed. . . . Believing the Bible as I do," as-serted Falwell, "I would find it impossible to stop preaching the pure saving Gospel of Jesus Christ and begin doing anything else—including the fighting of commu-nism or participating in the civil rights reform." Preachers, he stated categorically, "are not called to be politicians, but to be soul-winners."[40]

Fourteen years later, in May 1979, however, Falwell became the founder of one of the most powerful grassroots religious movements in American political history—the Moral Majority. Asked to explain the U-turn, Falwell would say he was forced into it by the situation in Washington: "I never thought the government would go so far afield, I never thought the politicians would be so untrustworthy, I never thought the courts would go so nuts to the left." Falwell claimed that the lack of involvement by Christians was "probably the reason why the country's in the mess it is. We have defaulted by failing to show up for the fight."[41]

Falwell's transformation was not quite so simple. In the 1960s, he did not feel en-thusiastic for the political cause of the day, civil rights—his church baptized its first black member only in 1971—but his basic point was accurate. Falwell himself and thousands of other American evangelical Protestants were mobilized politically by what they saw as the godless drift of American life. It was a gathering storm, brew-ing since the early 1960s. Many liberals were surprised by its vehemence but that was because they had failed to appreciate that evangelical Protestantism had not been killed off by the modern secular society.

Evangelicals slipped off the national radar after the Scopes trial of 1925, about the teaching of Darwinism in schools (see Chapter 11). Since that ill-fated campaign by William Jennings Bryan, Protestants who took a literalistic view of the Bible had kept out of the political limelight, but they remained a potent force in the American heartland. One sign of this was the growth of Bible colleges, which placed the teaching of Christian fundamentals ahead of all else—there were 144 of these by 1950, almost triple the figure twenty years before. Even more important were Christian radio ministers like Charles E. Fuller, whose nationwide *Old Fashioned Revival Hour* ran for more than thirty years from 1937.

The pastor who really brought evangelicalism into the national mainstream was Billy Graham, from North Carolina, who developed a revivalist movement known as Youth for Christ. With slogans like "Geared to the Times But Anchored to the Rock," Graham's rallies used the razzmatazz of popular culture—music, celebrities, quizzes, even magicians—but all building up to preaching by Graham himself. "We used every modern means to catch the attention of the unconverted," he said, "and then we punched them right between the eyes with the gospel."[42] Graham won the support of newspaper tycoon William Randolph Hearst, who liked his mix of patriotism and morality; Hearst told his journalists laconically to "puff Graham," and they did. Graham became a truly national figure in 1952 with a five-week crusade in Washington, D.C., ending up on the steps of the Capitol—the first-ever formal religious service to be held there. Unlike old-style fundamentalists, Graham and fellow evangelicals were more concerned with saving souls than maintaining theological purity, so they did not retreat into sectarianism but sought to build bridges with the mainstream denominations and American society as a whole.

Fascinated by politics, Graham became personally close to both Lyndon Johnson and Richard Nixon, but he ended up getting badly burned by Watergate. A loyal supporter of the embattled president, he was so appalled when he finally read the transcripts of the White House tapes that he wept and threw up. "I'd had a real love of him," Graham said later of Nixon. "He's always been very attentive to his friends, he never forgot a birthday. He seemed to love his country, love his children. . . . I'd thought he was a man of such great integrity." But then, said Graham, "the way it sounded in those tapes. . . . He was just suddenly somebody else." Chastened, Billy Graham warned fellow pastors in 1974 not to "identify the Gospel with any one political program or culture," admitting that "this has been my own danger." He also said in 1980 that in his earlier days he "tended to identify the Kingdom of God with the American way of life. I don't think like that now."[43]

But younger evangelicals saw the story of the 1960s and 1970s as a series of attempts to push God out of the American way of life. A major affront was the Supreme Court decisions in 1962 and 1963 to outlaw officially sponsored prayers, Bible reading, and recitation of the Lord's Prayer in schools. The cases had been brought by the American Jewish Congress as a violation of the First Amendment upholding the separation of church and state, but evangelicals were appalled. When the preacher Billy James Hargis heard about the Court's decision on school prayer, his son recalled how "my dad talked about how this was really the beginning of the end for America, that the country had turned its back on God, and that any country that did that couldn't stand."[44]

Hargis's anger was widely shared because acts of Christian worship were ingrained in American education. In 1962 roughly half the states had laws requiring or allowing Bible reading in schools and about a third of all school districts held daily devotional services. Not only were the Supreme Court's decisions flouted but millions of people, especially in the South, signed petitions for a constitutional amendment to protect school prayer. Many of the protestors were Catholic.[45]

Another simmering issue was school textbooks, which became a national cause célèbre in 1974 following events in an obscure part of West Virginia. Throughout America, textbooks for the coming year were approved by a local school board on the basis of teachers' recommendations but usually selected from a state-approved list if the schools wanted to get state money. In 1974 the board of Kanawha County, West Virginia, nodded through a list of some 300 language and literature books, only to raise the ire of Alice Moore, the wife of an evangelical minister, who had already campaigned against the sex-education program in schools as being anti-Christian and morally relativist. "Sweet Alice"—as she was known to friends and foes, though with different inflections—was an effective campaigner. At one public meeting she held up one of the books and declared, "We have a lot of people from the community sitting here who have no idea what we are talking about." She got a member of the textbook committee, reluctantly, to read out an example she had selected—a poem by e. e. cummings. Said Moore, "It was dealing with sexual intercourse and pretty explicitly. He read the poem, and there was a kind of stunned reaction. No one was saying anything. And then he said, 'Well, I think it's talking about sex.' And the whole room broke up in uproarious laughter. It was a great moment. I had made my point."[46]

Apart from sex, Alice Moore and her ilk objected to profanities, leftist leanings, and lack of patriotism. Their net was wide, taking in "improper" works such as the *Iliad*, *Paradise Lost*, and *Moby Dick*. In accordance with state directives to reflect the contributions of minorities to America, the official list also included black authors such as James Baldwin and Langston Hughes, but the critics were aggrieved at their use of "nonstandard English." Some of Moore's supporters were less subtle—"Get the nigger books out," they would chant. In September 1974 Moore organized a boycott of schools in the county and won the support of local coal miners, several thousand of whom went out on wildcat strikes. As tempers mounted, there were fights, stonings, and acts of arson; national conservative figures descended on West Virginia reinforced, less welcomely, by the Ku Klux Klan. After two months of upheaval a compromise was reached affirming most of the books but with two important provisos: No students would be required to use any that were objectionable to their parents on religious or moral grounds and future lists of textbooks would be screened by a committee in which parents heavily out-numbered teachers.

Many educators were appalled. "The case of Kanawha County is not an isolated instance," noted one English teacher. "The time has come for educators to deal with the motives underlying censorship and to anticipate problems before emotion rules out rational solutions. The alternative is to surrender control of the schools to the shrillest members of the community."[47] But Alice Moore and her supporters across the country saw the issue very differently. For them this was an affirmation not just of Christian values but of local democracy.

The growth of Christian academies was another sign of the swelling reaction. Although the main motive was clearly racist—these private schools were a response to school busing to effect racial integration—they also reflected the desire, evident in the culture wars of Kanawha County, to have a curriculum that parents could control, embodying what were deemed to be Christian values. Jerry Falwell de-fended the school that his church in Virginia set up in 1967 not as "a white-flight school" but as a response to the Supreme Court decisions on prayer: "[F]rom day one I made it clear that Lynchburg Christian Academy (and we had a college in mind at the time, and a seminary) would be for any and all who loved Christ and wanted to study under born-again teachers in a Christian environment with aca-demic excellence."[48]

By the late 1970s Falwell had become a nationally renowned figure, pushing the still-revered Billy Graham to the edge of the spotlight. His pastorate had mush-roomed with a megachurch, a vast youth program, and a TV ministry whose title, the *Old Time Gospel Hour*, echoed Fuller's pioneering radio broadcasts; his Bible college, up and running, was grandly renamed Liberty University. Like many evan-gelicals, Falwell was particularly concerned by the growing public profile of ho-mosexuals—reflected in many sex-education courses in schools and in the test cases being put to the courts. October 1979 saw the first national gay rights rally in Washington, D.C. In one mailing, Falwell told supporters that "gays were recently given permission to lay a wreath on the Tomb of the Unknown Soldier at Arling-ton Cemetery to honor any sexual deviants who served in the military. That's right," he added incredulously, "the gays were allowed to turn our Tomb of the Unknown Soldier into: THE TOMB OF THE UNKNOWN SODOMITE."[49]

So, by the late 1970s there was a slate of moral issues that offended significant sections of conservative Christian opinion in the American heartland. Washington-based groups like the Heritage Foundation and the Conservative Caucus saw an op-portunity to mobilize the grassroots Christians as a nationwide force. They were, in the words of one organizer, "the greatest tract of virgin political timber on the political landscape."[50]

In 1979 the logging finally began. Falwell was a crucial figure because of his national appeal. He was now speaking out on moral issues but remained skeptical that there were enough evangelicals to change the nation. "Listen," said the evangelical theologian and film-maker Francis Schaeffer, "God used the pagans to do his work in the Old Testament, so why don't you use the pagans to do your work now?" They developed a concept of "co-belligerency"—fighting specific causes alongside those with whom they did not totally agree.[51] This was a far cry from the narrow doctrinal purity espoused by old-style fundamentalists, particularly when the "pagans" were often Catholic—until recently, hate figures for evangelical Protestants. Abortion became the rallying point.

The Supreme Court decision in January 1973 on *Roe v. Wade* had made America, at a stroke, one of the most liberal countries in the non-communist West in its abortion laws. The Court had moved further and faster than even many supporters of reform had urged. Initially the issue was not a live one for evangelicals; it was Catholics who took the lead in opposing abortion and this automatically alienated many evangelicals. Only gradually were evangelicals persuaded to see abortion as part of a broader issue—the sanctity of human life, which was now threatened by the advance of secular humanism. Schaeffer's film and book *Whatever Happened to the Human Race?* helped make abortion into a "pro-life" issue for many evangelicals and in the congressional elections of 1978 conservative strategists, most of them Catholics, mounted successful campaigns to topple several prominent members of Congress, Republican as well as Democrat, who had favored abortion rights. This showed the political potential of "co-belligerency."

In May 1979 some of these conservative strategists—led by Catholic Paul Weyrich, who had founded the Heritage Foundation—visited Falwell in Lynchburg to enlist his help. In this meeting, at the local Holiday Inn, Weyrich made the initial pitch: "Out there is what you might call a moral majority—people who would agree on principles based on the Decalogue [the Ten Commandments], for example— but they have been separated by geographical and denominational differences and that has caused them to vote differently. The key to any kind of political impact is to get these people united in some way."

Falwell interrupted him: "Go back to what you said earlier. . . . You started out by saying there is something out there . . . what did you call that?"

Weyrich had to think for a moment. "Oh, I said there is a moral majority."

"That's it!" Falwell exclaimed. "That's the name of the organization."[52]

With Falwell's mass appeal and the organizing skills of men like Weyrich, the Moral Majority rapidly took off. Support from prominent evangelical pastors unlocked the large mailing lists of their congregations, which Richard Viguerie, a pioneer of direct-mailing, exploited to huge effect to raise funds and support. Among evangelicals there was a real sense of crisis. At a meeting of a dozen leading preachers in Dallas, Billy Graham declared, "I believe God has shown me that unless we have a change in America, we have a thousand days [left] as a free nation . . . three years." The others agreed. Charles Stanley, another prominent TV evangelist, put his hand firmly on the table: "I'll give my life to stop this. I'll give everything I've got to turn this country." Almost everyone said they would take a lead, with the big exception of Graham. "I cannot be publicly involved," he said sadly. "I can only pray. I've been burned so badly with the public relationships I've had. I can't afford it, but I care so much."[53]

Graham spoke from bitter experience, but his was an older generation. The younger enthusiasts were now engaged in a crusade. The Moral Majority took evangelical religion right into the heart of national politics in the election of 1980 and the passions unleashed were all the stronger because America had already had a born-again president—but one whom the Moral Majority regarded as a heretic.

"KEEPING FAITH"

Jimmy Carter struck a new note on his very first day as president. Having delivered his inaugural address, he left Capitol Hill in a long black limo. But suddenly the car ground to a halt; the president and his wife and family got out. Gradually the crowds began to realize this was a deliberate act. People gasped in astonishment—"They're walking, they're walking."

And so on January 20, 1977, Jimmy and Rosalynn Carter strolled hand in hand a mile up Pennsylvania Avenue to the White House. For Carter this, the first pedestrian inauguration, was a deeply symbolic act. Mindful of the angry demonstrators who had confronted recent presidents and vice-presidents over Vietnam and Watergate, he said he "wanted to provide a vivid demonstration of my confidence in the people as far as security was concerned, and I felt a simple walk would be a tangible indication of some reduction in the imperial status of the President and his family."[54]

Curbing the imperial presidency was to be an abiding theme of Carter's time in office, but equally important at the start was being accepted as a southerner. Carter grew up in the small town of Plains in Georgia, and inherited his father's peanut business, rising through local and state politics to become governor of Georgia from 1971 to 1975. Georgia was in the Deep South, the heartland of the Civil War Confederacy and more recently of massive resistance to racial integration. For this the region had been ostracized by the nation. Campaigning for the presidency, Carter sensed a new mood: "[W]e in the South were ready for reconciliation, to be accepted as equals, to rejoin the mainstream of American political life," and if the nation would choose as its leader someone from the Deep South "the bitterness of the past could be overcome." Even after his victory, however, Carter found that old habits died hard. When Rosalynn asked the White House cooks if they could prepare some favorite southern dishes, she was told, "Yes, Ma'am, we've been fixing that kind of food for the servants for a long time."[55]

Carter's most important characteristic was his evangelical Christianity. Raised a Southern Baptist, he had been confirmed in his faith in 1968 in a long conversation with his sister Ruth. According to Carter's wife, Rosalynn, he had been struck, he told Ruth, by a recent sermon in their church titled "If you were arrested for being a Christian, would there be enough evidence to convict you?" Rosalynn said that "the question had haunted him. And he had decided to put God first in his life, to search and always try to do His will." He had a long and intense discussion with Ruth and decided that "her much deeper religious life and convictions were what he wanted and needed." This, said Rosalynn, was "Jimmy's famous 'born again' experience—no flashing lights, no weeping, no trauma or emotional scene, just a quiet acceptance of God and God's will for his life."[56]

Carter's faith was central to his presidency in two ways. He wanted to translate his Christian principles into political action and also to implement his broader faith in America and the values it stood for. "Ours was the first society openly to define itself in terms of both spirituality and human liberty," he declared in his inaugural, delivered just a few months after the celebrations of the bicentennial of American independence. "The American dream endures. We must once again have full faith in our country—and in one another."[57]

Carter's unapologetic Christian faith won him support from many evangelicals. On the face of it, he might seem a natural ally of preachers like Falwell, but Carter became increasingly uncomfortable with the Moral Majority. For him the evidence that would "convict" him as a Christian guided him more to the left than to the right.

In part, this expressed his own personal views—particularly the desire for America to act less imperially abroad—but it also reflected political necessities. Carter had run as an avowed outsider, both from Washington and its insider politics, tarnished by Watergate, and also from the old guard of southern conservatives and northern labor who for years had controlled Democratic Party politics. The newly mobilized women's vote was therefore important to Carter but he had to avoid becoming labeled as too radical.

So Carter and his wife were firm supporters of the Equal Rights Amendment, but they couched their endorsement in balanced language. "I feel that it is especially important to explain that women like me support the ERA," said Rosalynn Carter. "I am a relatively traditional person. I enjoy my roles as wife, mother, partner and businesswoman. I care how I look—and what I think. I am not threatened by ERA. I feel freed by it."[58]

On the even more sensitive issue of abortion, Carter straddled the fence, declaring in 1976 that "I am personally opposed to abortion. . . . I am aware that abortion is the treatment for failed contraception, but I believe that the need for abortion services can be minimized by improved family planning services." On the other hand, Carter said he was against a constitutional amendment to alter the Supreme Court's decision in *Roe v. Wade* by prohibiting abortions or giving states the right to enact local options. And although Carter was also personally opposed to government spending for abortion services, he said that as president he would be "guided and bound by the courts."[59]

In adopting these positions Carter was trying to keep faith with his own pro-life values and avoid antagonizing feminists by stressing his fidelity to the law. In fact, however, he managed to offend both camps. The women's movement resented his block on federal funding to pay for abortions for poor women (so-called Medicaid abortions); pro-lifers were angered by his unwillingness to help overturn or bypass *Roe v. Wade*. This fence-sitting on abortion was typical of Carter's position on many sensitive issues as he tried to satisfy both the new Democrats and the old.

By 1980 Carter had alienated most of the evangelicals who had supported, or tolerated, his candidacy in 1976. At a meeting with Falwell and other ministers he gave what they considered an evasive response about abortion and then what the Reverend Tim LaHaye described as "some off-the-wall answer about that the Equal Rights Amendment was good for the family." Said LaHaye, "I knew when he said that that he was out to lunch. We had a man in the White House who professed to be a Christian, but didn't understand how un-Christian his administration was." After the meeting LaHaye stood and prayed: "God we have to get this man out of the White House and get someone in here who will be aggressive about bringing back traditional moral values." He discovered later that several others offered up much the same prayer.[60]

Many evangelicals—and most conservative Americans—were equally alienated by Carter's foreign policy. He insisted that the United States must transcend its Cold War fixation about the Soviet Union: "We can no longer separate the traditional issues of war and peace from the new global questions of justice, equity, and human rights," he argued. "We have reaffirmed America's commitment to human rights as a fundamental tenet of our foreign policy. . . . We want the world to know that our Nation stands for more than financial prosperity."[61] This commitment to human rights and freedom meant, for Carter, curbing America's own imperialism, and nothing offended conservatives more than his surrender, as they saw it, of the Panama Canal.

In 1903, as we saw in Chapter 10, the United States had signed a treaty with the government of Panama, giving America the right in perpetuity to build and operate a canal through the Isthmus of Panama. The Canal, opened in 1914, proved invaluable in both world wars, enabling the U.S. navy to move even its biggest ships quickly between the Atlantic and the Pacific. But the treaty had been negotiated under duress—as part of a deal recognizing Panama's breakaway from Colombia—and opposition to it grew in Panama, especially after Castro's Cuban revolution spurred others to stand up to Uncle Sam. Frequent anti-American riots and Washington's embarrassment at this overt relic of imperialism prompted successive U.S. administrations to consider renegotiating the 1903 agreement, but these new international realities were little understood or appreciated at home: In 1967 Lyndon

Johnson's proposed treaties met with vehement dissent on Capitol Hill. Nixon and Kissinger tried again in the early 1970s and it was essentially their negotiating position that was embodied in the two linked treaties that Carter signed in September 1977. These gave full control of the Canal to Panama at the end of 1999 but guaranteed the waterway's permanent neutrality for use by all nations and also the right of the United States to intervene should that neutrality be threatened.

So, although the Panama Canal Treaties reflected Carter's personal convictions, they embodied the long-standing policy of both Democratic and Republican administrations. The problem was the gulf between official perceptions and the wider public, who simply did not accept the apparently paradoxical argument about "giving up the Canal to save it"[62]—abandoning formal ownership in order to safeguard larger American economic interests. Opinion polls showed consistently that between two-thirds and three-quarters of Americans favored holding on to the Canal. On the other hand, this feeling was largely latent—until Ronald Reagan came along. Once again he served as a catalyst for the conservative reaction.

During his battle for the Republican nomination in 1976, Reagan told retirees in Florida that "State Department actions for several years now have suggested that they are intimidated by the propaganda of Panama's military dictator, Fidel Castro's good friend, Omar Torrijos." He said that America's diplomatic corps "apparently believes the hints regularly dispensed by the leftist Torrijos regime that the Canal will be sabotaged if we don't hand it over." How, asked Reagan, could the State Department "suggest we pay blackmail to this dictator, for blackmail is what it is. When it comes to the Canal, we built it, we paid for it, it's ours, and we should tell Torrijos and company that we're going to keep it."[63]

"We built it, we paid for it, it's ours." The retirees roared their delight. Reagan, a masterful speaker, was so taken aback that he lost his place. Realizing they had found an issue, his campaign managers played up Panama—shrewdly combining anti-leftism, national pride, and a gut appeal to basic property rights. The emotions that Reagan had tapped over Panama in the 1976 campaign were released in full flood when Carter submitted the Panama Treaties to the Senate. To become law, any treaty needs not a simply majority but the consent of two-thirds of the Senate, and over Panama that proved immensely difficult. New Right politicos including Weyrich and Viguerie orchestrated a shrewd campaign, coordinating groups such as "Keep Our Canal" in a media and mail blitz to put pressure on senators. The treaties were portrayed as an act of craven surrender to a Marxist bully. Giving up such a vital U.S. asset, declared Reagan, "would make about as much sense as it would for the U.S.S.R. to invite the U.S. Sixth Fleet to roam at will around the Black Sea."[64]

Carter eventually got the two Panama Treaties through the Senate in March and April 1978, winning plaudits abroad for his enlightened policy. "Carter is a 'god' in Latin America," declared one Brazilian newspaper. At home, supporters like the *Baltimore Sun* called ratification "a pivotal moment," signaling "a readiness by the

United States to face up to the realities of a post-colonial world." But victory came
at a massive cost for Carter, using up most of his credit on Capitol Hill and thereby
weakening leverage on the rest of his political agenda. He also failed to convince a
majority of the public—general opinion being that his administration was spineless
about U.S. interests. For its part, the New Right had found a foreign policy issue to
match abortion and school prayer. "Panama identified hundreds of thousands of
closet conservatives," said one activist: "[T]he issue did for conservatives what Vietnam did for liberals." Supporters of the Treaties proved vulnerable targets in the
congressional elections of 1978 and 1980.[65]

Carter, however, was unabashed, regarding Panama as one of the greatest
achievements of his presidency. He claimed that the administration had "stopped
the advance into Central America of those subversive groups who were using the
issue of so-called North American colonialism to gain a foothold in Panama" and
had also proved its commitment to freedom and human rights "by demonstrating
that, in a showdown, a great democracy will practice what it preaches."[66]

Carter had another big foreign policy success—brokering the March 1979
peace treaty between Egypt and Israel. Like Panama, this was both a reflection of
his Christian values and an attempt to address another issue neglected by previous U.S. administrations, namely the fate of the Palestinians whose homelands
had been occupied during successive Arab-Israeli wars. Carter had hoped to foster a larger Middle Eastern peace, including the Palestinians, but his ambitions
were frustrated by the obdurate Israeli prime minister, Menachem Begin, who
knew Israel had enormous support in the United States. Appalled by the Holocaust and admiring Israel as an oasis of democracy in a desert of Arab autocracy,
Americans and their leaders had given almost unconditional support to Israel, especially after the life-or-death wars of 1967 and 1973. By 1976 Israel had become
the largest annual recipient of U.S. foreign aid, most of it in the form of military
hardware.

The so-called Israel lobby was one of the most influential coalitions on Capitol
Hill. As Washington outsiders, Carter and his aides had failed to appreciate its
power: It was "not part of our Georgia and Southern political experience," one aide
told the president lamely. But Israel was also backed by Gentile conservatives, as a
Western bastion in the Middle East, and by the Christian right, whose reading of
the Bible led them to believe that Israel's capture of all of Jerusalem and the West
Bank in 1967 was part of a process that would lead to Christ's second coming. So
supportive of Israel was Jerry Falwell that in 1979 Begin gave him a private jet.[67]

The March 1979 treaty between Egypt and Israel was the culmination of intense
personal diplomacy by Carter, who devoted far more time and energy to the Middle East than any other U.S. president. This included a two-week summit at Camp
David, the presidential retreat in Maryland, and an intense flurry of shuttle diplomacy between the two rival capitals. Although less than Carter had hoped for, the
treaty was a landmark in the history of the modern Middle East. But again the price

was high, diverting Carter's energy from other issues, including relations with the Soviet Union.

Guidelines for a new arms-control agreement with Moscow had been agreed by Ford in 1974, but Carter, a zealot about nuclear weapons, sought more radical cuts, and this delayed a formal treaty until June 1979, more than halfway into his presidency, when his credibility was already weak on Capitol Hill. The SALT II treaty signed by Carter and Soviet leader Leonid Brezhnev in Vienna restricted each superpower to 2,250 nuclear launchers. Overall, the Americans retained a 50 percent advantage in the total number of strategic-range nuclear warheads, but this contrasted with a three-to-one advantage back in 1974, and the Pentagon was particularly concerned about the potency of Soviet heavy ICBMs, in which Moscow had a substantial advantage. One leading critic, Senator Henry Jackson, likened the Vienna summit to Munich in 1938, calling it "appeasement in its purest form."[68] The treaty's deficiencies, together with the growing anti-Soviet feeling on Capitol Hill, presaged a hard fight to secure Senate approval of the treaty. Rejection was looking likely in late 1979; following Moscow's Christmas invasion of Afghanistan it became a certainty.

The Soviets intervened in an attempt to restore order in a feuding client state on their own doorstep. What they got was a guerrilla war that would tie down the Red Army for most of the 1980s as Afghanistan became the Soviets' Vietnam, but this was not, of course, apparent in the New Year of 1980. Within days of the invasion Carter withdrew the SALT II treaty from Senate consideration and announced bans on grain exports to the USSR and on the sale of high-tech goods. He also suspended most cultural exchanges and called on U.S. athletes to boycott the 1980 Olympic Games in Moscow.

These measures represented a victory for Carter's hawkish national security adviser, Zbigniew Brzezinski, over Cyrus Vance, the pro-détente secretary of state. The president now seemed to have accepted Brzezinski's dictum that "you first have to be a Truman before you are a Wilson"—in other words, proving America's toughness before one could make peace.[69] In fact, Carter now became more fervent than his adviser in denouncing Moscow. He told an interviewer that the Soviet action in Afghanistan "has made a more dramatic change in my own opinion of what the Soviets' ultimate goals are than anything they've done in the previous time I've been in office"—a comment that sounded so naive that the White House kept it out of the public record.[70] He informed members of Congress that U.S. national security was "directly threatened" and said that, if unchecked, the Soviets might push on to the Persian Gulf and control "a major portion of the world's oil supplies." He insisted that this crisis was "the greatest threat to peace since the Second World War."[71]

Carter was genuinely shaken by the Soviet actions, but his response also reflected the need to play it tough against conservatives at home in his campaign for reelection in November. These perceptions of his weakness were accentuated by the hostage crisis in Teheran.

In Iran, as with Panama and Palestine, Carter was reaping the whirlwind sown by earlier U.S. policies—in this case, three decades of support for the increasingly repressive and corrupt regime of the shah of Iran, in order to protect Western oil supplies and contain the influence of the USSR, Iran's neighbor. In February 1979 the shah was toppled by massive strikes and protests and an Islamic republic was installed, run by Muslim clerics. In November student militants invaded the U.S. embassy in Teheran, seizing diplomats in defiance of international law, and the new regime exploited the situation to rally national opinion against America, the "Great Satan." Initially Carter had benefited from the hostage crisis, which helped him resist a challenge for the 1980 Democratic nomination from Senator Edward Kennedy, younger brother of the slain president. But as the months dragged on, the fate of the fifty-two U.S. hostages became a national obsession, holding hostage his own presidency.

Frustrated by fruitless negotiations, Carter and his inner circle tried to mount a daring rescue mission in April 1980—only to have it aborted in Iran with the loss of eight Americans. Although Carter later claimed, defensively, that this debacle was the result of "a strange series of mishaps—almost completely unpredictable," in fact the plan was high-risk and complex, with enormous likelihood of foul-ups. Its codename was Operation Eagle Claw but many Americans, not just conservatives, concluded that the country's talons had been humiliatingly blunted. In the last months of his presidency Carter worked around the clock to get the hostages out by diplomatic means. "I cannot deny," he wrote later, "that I was eager to resolve this crisis while I was still President in order to justify the decisions I had made during the preceding months." But gallingly the hostages were released into U.S. custody just minutes after his presidency ended at noon on January 20, 1981.[72]

Whether their release before the election the previous November would have made any difference to the result is debatable. Carter was by now perceived as a weak president and the continued combination of inflation and unemployment also hit Americans where it hurt most—their wallets. His challenger, Ronald Reagan, went for the jugular in their one-and-only televised debate, which attracted some of the highest viewing figures of the 1970s. Reagan's breezy faith in American power and rightness contrasted favorably with Carter's earnest command of detail, and the challenger asked devastatingly simple questions at the end that resonated with millions of Americans—suggesting that when they went to vote the following week, "it might be well if you would ask yourself, are you better off than you were four years ago? Is it easier for you to go and buy things in the stores than it was four years ago? Is there more or less unemployment in the country than there was four years ago? Is America as respected throughout the world as it was? Do you feel that our security is as safe, that we're as strong as we were four years ago?"[73]

Reagan's performance in that debate is widely credited with turning Carter's narrow lead into a Republican landslide. Winning all but six states with a margin of nearly 10 percent over Carter on the popular vote, Reagan inflicted the worst defeat for an incumbent president since Franklin Roosevelt had trounced Herbert Hoover in 1932 during the Great Depression.

Carter had many failings as a leader—tending to micromanage detail and failing to build close relations with Congress. He also had the misfortune to be elected on a tide of leftward resentment about Watergate, Vietnam, and the imperial presidency, only to become victim of a new surge to the right as Americans became disenchanted with what they considered the country's degeneracy and international decline. Yet Carter, to his credit, had addressed moral issues that his predecessors had ignored, particularly in foreign policy. Although these issues did not figure high on the agenda of the Reagan administration, the debate about human rights and America's imperialism would not go away.

17

REVOLUTION AND DEMOCRACY

The year 1981 began more than a decade of Republican ascendancy under Ronald Reagan (1981–1989) and then George H.W. Bush (1989–1993). Reagan seemed an archetypal conservative, turning the clock back on big government at home, but he proved bizarrely radical in foreign policy. What is more, his utopian vision, ending the Cold War, proved to be practical politics. This denouement owed something to Reagan's unlikely rapport with the new reformist Soviet leader, Mikhail Gorbachev; even more to fundamental economic and social changes sweeping the world in the 1980s, especially the information revolution based on computing and electronics that emanated from America. But it was Bush, Reagan's much more pragmatic successor, who presided over the most startling revolutions of all—the demise of the Soviet Union and the construction of an unprecedented international coalition to win the Gulf War of 1991. These were heady days for the United States, when economic regulation was being rolled back at home, democracy seemed the wave of the future, and what Bush called "a new world order" appeared to have dawned.

THE "REAGAN REVOLUTION"

The inauguration of January 1981 was the first to be held on the West Front of the U.S. Capitol, looking out to the Potomac river and on, as it were, to the heartland of America. For many of Ronald Reagan's fans, that seemed entirely apt because they expected him to restore their country to the core values that had made it great.

The new president's inaugural did not disappoint them: "We are a nation that has a government—not the other way around. And this makes us special among the nations of the Earth," he boldly declared. "Our government has no power except that granted it by the people." As Reagan said repeatedly, he believed government wasn't the answer, it was the problem. "It is no coincidence that our present troubles

parallel and are proportionate to the intervention and intrusion in our lives that result from unnecessary and excessive growth of government."[1]

In his youth Reagan had been a Democrat, fervently supporting Roosevelt and
the New Deal, but as his Hollywood career faded after World War II he moved far
to the right as a critic of big government and the Soviet menace. His simple, stark
belief in the superiority of American values made him ideal as General Electric's
roving company ambassador in the 1950s. This experience of public speaking all
over the country, much more than his Hollywood career, turned Reagan into the
"Great Communicator." He and wealthy conservative backers in California used it
as his springboard into politics, winning him two terms as governor of the state
between 1966 and 1974.

Despite his right-wing ardor, Reagan did not come across as a zealot or even as
a control freak, like Jimmy Carter. His greatest assets were a sunny smile and an ap-
proachable manner. "He probably spends two or three hours a day on real work,"
one aide admitted. "All he wants is to tell stories about his movie days."[2] Reagan
worked nine-to-five, regularly napped, rarely asked questions during briefings, and
spent the equivalent of almost a year of his eight-year presidency on his beloved
ranch in southern California. Yet critics were disarmed by the president's humor. "I
am concerned about what is happening in government," he told reporters, "and it's
caused me many a sleepless afternoon." And again: "It's true hard work never killed
anyone but I figure, why take the chance?"[3] Later it became known that his schedule was choreographed by his wife, Nancy, after consultation with her astrologer.
The White House chief of staff was obliged to keep a color-coded calendar on his
desk, with green for "good days," red for "bad days," and yellow for "iffy days."[4]

Reagan was mocked by his opponents as the "acting president," but his success
as a politician could not be denied. "I've known every president since Harry Truman," Tip O'Neill, the Democratic Speaker of the House, reflected, "and there's no
question in my mind that Ronald Reagan was the worst. He wasn't without leadership ability, but he lacked most of the management skills that a president needs."
Yet, admitted O'Neill, "with a prepared text he's the best public speaker I've ever
seen"—maybe, he thought, even better than Franklin Roosevelt and John Kennedy.[5]

Reagan's skills as the "Great Communicator" were vital to the enactment of his
1981 legislative agenda. The president was also helped by Republican victory in
the Senate (for the first time since the election of 1952) and by a narrowing of the
Democratic margin in the House. And when it mattered, he *would* work hard,
meeting and phoning individual members of Congress to woo their votes. According to O'Neill, his political adversary, "Some House members said they saw
more of him during his first four months in office than they saw of Jimmy Carter
during his entire four years. . . . According to what I heard, he instructed his people, 'Tell me who you want me to call and I'll take care of it.'" Said O'Neill ruefully,
"I would have given my right arm to hear those words of Jimmy Carter."[6] O'Neill
was an old pork-barrel Democrat from Massachusetts—exactly the sort of politico

Reagan blamed for bloated government. So the budget and tax bills that the president eventually got Congress to pass in the summer of 1981 were a defeat for all that O'Neill stood for. More than that, nearly fifty members of Congress from O'Neill's own Democratic Party defied their leader and supported the president. Reagan's persuasive charms and the enormous grassroots pressure this generated on lawmakers had an effect; so did the president's grace and courage after a near-fatal assassination attempt in March.

As a result Congress cut income tax rates by 25 percent over the next three years, with the top rate falling from 70 percent to 50 percent.* The budget bill slashed many of the programs that Reagan had campaigned against—in public assistance, food stamps, work training, and disability benefits. At the same time, it mandated a 10 percent increase in defense spending each year over the next five years. In a political system designed to impede radical change, these congressional victories evoked comparisons with the early New Deal and were dubbed the Reagan Revolution.

Cutting taxes while increasing defense spending presaged an unbalanced budget, yet Reagan placed his faith in what was called "supply-side economics"—the idea that lower tax rates would encourage greater enterprise and therefore higher tax revenues. Reagan conveyed the idea in his usual down-home manner. At the peak of his movie career at Warner Brothers, he said, "I was in the ninety-four percent tax bracket; that meant that after a certain point I received only six cents of each dollar I earned and the government . . . took such a big chunk of my earnings that after a while I began asking myself whether it was worth it to keep on taking work." Something was fundamentally wrong with a system like that, Reagan reflected. "If I decided to do one less picture, that meant other people at the studio in lower tax brackets wouldn't work as much either; the effect filtered down, and there were fewer total jobs." But, he went on, if "you reduce tax rates and allow people to spend or save more of what they earn, they'll be more industrious. . . . The result: more prosperity for all—and more revenue for the government. A few economists call this principle supply-side economics. I just call it common sense."[7]

It was not quite so simple, however. Reagan had wanted to prune the social security budget but found that this was a cut too far. Some 30 million elderly or disabled Americans were current beneficiaries; another 100 million workers expected to benefit when they retired. Social security was the most widely valued welfare legacy of the Roosevelt New Deal. Not even the Great Communicator could persuade politicians to ignore the overwhelming evidence of their mailbags; he had to treat social security as sacrosanct. Yet to do so was effectively to ring-fence nearly half of government spending from possible cuts—making a balanced budget impossible.

---

* In his second term, Reagan went even further: The Tax Reform Act of 1986 reduced the top rate of tax to 28 percent, the lowest level since 1931.

As spending exceeded revenue year after year, the budget deficit soared from $60 billion in 1980 to $220 billion in 1986 (well over 5 percent of GDP). During this period the national debt more than doubled from $749 billion to $1,746 billion.[8] Since Americans were poor savers by general Western standards, the deficit was mostly covered by borrowing from abroad, turning the United States within a few years from the world's greatest creditor nation into its largest debtor. Not only was this damaging to America's status, it was also a profound shift in the international financial system since World War II, which had relied on the export of U.S. capital.

David Stockman, Reagan's whiz-kid budget director, was caught at the center of this mess. For him it became a commentary not just on the power of pork-barrel politics but on the inertia of the whole U.S. political system: "Our Madisonian government of checks and balances, three branches, two legislative houses, and infinitely splintered power is conservative, not radical. It hugs powerfully to the history behind it. It shuffles into the future one step at a time. It cannot leap into revolutions without falling flat on its face." By 1982, confessed Stockman, "I knew that the Reagan Revolution was impossible—it was a metaphor with no anchor in political and economic reality."[9]

For other ardent Reaganites—the religious right—his presidency also proved disenchanting. In November 1980 Reverend Jerry Falwell, leader of the Moral Majority, had listened to the election results over the radio with his aide, Ed Dobson. It was, Dobson recalled, "one of those moments of 'Can you believe what we did?' I'll never forget that moment." Even the "most cynical" of the press were admitting that the religious right had at least "influenced" the election. "Others were saying we had swayed it. We chose to believe we had swayed it." Falwell called Reagan's election "my finest hour."[10]

Falwell and other evangelical ministers became regular visitors to the White House, but access did not translate into real influence. Reagan's inner circle, particularly Chief of Staff James Baker and his deputy, Michael Deaver, had set their sights on his reelection in 1984 and were convinced that close identification with the religious right would alienate centrist voters. So although Reagan met a group of anti-abortion activists in the Oval Office, this was a typical piece of gesture politics, not followed up by substantive action.

When Reagan had the chance to fill a vacancy on the Supreme Court, he wanted to honor his campaign pledge to appoint the first female justice. His staff came up with Sandra Day O'Connor, a lawyer and politician from Arizona, but the Moral Majority was most unhappy. John Conlan, an evangelical ex-congressman from Arizona, explained why: "Sandra is a wonderful girl, handsome and beautiful-looking, smart as a tack, Stanford Law graduate. But she comes from upper-class landed aristocracy—ranching family" and "has no religious orientation, she fought hard for the Equal Rights amendment, and very hard for the legalization of abortion when she was in the State Senate." Such was Reagan's momentum in 1981, however, that O'Connor's appointment sailed through the Senate.[11]

To appease the religious right, the White House did take action on prayer in schools. "Our forbears came not for gold, but mainly in search of God and the freedom to worship in their own way," Reagan told religious leaders in May 1982. "Our Pledge of Allegiance states that we are 'one nation under God,' and our currency bears the motto, 'In God We Trust.' . . . The morality and values such faith implies are deeply embedded in our national character." Yet, he went on, "in recent years, well-meaning Americans in the name of freedom have taken freedom away. For the sake of religious tolerance, they've forbidden religious practice in our public classrooms." How, the president asked, "can we hope to retain our freedom through the generations if we fail to teach our young that our liberty springs from an abiding faith in our Creator?" He announced that he would soon submit to Congress a proposal to "amend our Constitution to allow our children to pray in school. No one must ever be forced or coerced or pressured to take part in any religious exercise, but neither should the government forbid religious practice. The amendment we'll propose will restore the right to pray."[12]

Although the proposed constitutional amendment was submitted to Congress, it did not come to a vote until the spring of 1984 and then fell short of the requisite two-thirds majority. The White House did not put real weight behind the proposal and many of the religious right felt that this unlikely bid to amend the Constitution was offered as a sop to them instead of pushing issues like abortion.

In November 1984 Reagan was reelected by an even bigger margin than in 1980, winning forty-nine of the fifty states and all but 13 of the 538 electoral college votes. The only historically notable thing about the Democrats' campaign was that it registered another incremental gain for women: Geraldine Ferraro was the first female vice-presidential candidate to be selected by a major political party.

The administration's first-term strategy of avoiding religious controversy and concentrating on economic issues had paid dividends. Millions of Americans felt better off, including so-called Reagan Democrats—ssouthern whites and northern workers who had traditionally voted Democrat. The Reagan managers had performed brilliantly, providing almost every day throughout the first term a carefully crafted photo and speech opportunity that Reagan performed superbly and the media lapped up. "The whole thing was PR," complained one disenchanted White House press aide. "This was a PR outfit that became President and took over the country." Even Deaver admitted that Reagan "enjoyed the most generous treatment by the press of any President in the postwar era."[13]

As historian Robert Dallek has observed, it was "a peculiar fact of Reagan's personality that a man who is so much a product of a consumer culture should be so strong a proponent of rugged individualism and other traditional values."[14] But the consumer culture that shaped Reagan was Hollywood—or, more exactly, his personal version of Hollywood celebrating those heroic individualist virtues. And it was on the world stage, supremely, that the acting president was able to play the hero to truly dramatic effect.

REAGAN AND THE "EVIL EMPIRE"

Ronald Reagan had been openly critical of the process of détente with Moscow constructed by his fellow Republicans Nixon and Kissinger. After failing to win the Republican nomination in 1976, he told his son he had wanted to become president in order to sit down with Leonid Brezhnev, the Soviet leader, to negotiate another arms-control treaty. "I was going to listen to him for maybe twenty minutes, and then I was going to get up from my side of the table, walk around to the other side, and lean over and whisper in his ear, 'Nyet.' It's been a long time since they've heard 'nyet' from an American president."[15]

When Reagan finally entered the White House in 1981, he struck an almost belligerent note, helping to usher in what became known as the New Cold War. At his first press conference on January 29 he claimed that "so far détente's been a one-way street that the Soviet Union has used to pursue its own aims." Their professed goal was "the promotion of world revolution and a one-world Socialist or Communist state"; their leaders, he asserted, "have openly and publicly declared that the only morality they recognize is what will further their cause, meaning they reserve unto themselves the right to commit any crime, to lie, to cheat" in order to attain their goal.[16]

Two years later, in March 1983, speaking to the National Association of Evangelicals in Florida, the president denounced the Soviet Union as "an evil empire," in fact "the focus of evil in the modern world." He also prophesied that "communism is another sad, bizarre chapter in human history, whose last pages even now are being written." Although much of the text was drafted by an ultraconservative speechwriter, Anthony Dolan, and was couched in language that would appeal to his evangelical audience, the phrase "evil empire" was Reagan's own: He had regularly used it in the mid-1960s.[17]

Even more dramatically, on March 23, 1983, the president announced a program to develop a defensive system to intercept and destroy nuclear weapons. The White House called this the Strategic Defense Initiative (SDI), but critics dubbed the multibillion-dollar project "Star Wars," and the label stuck. To Moscow, and much of western Europe, SDI seemed to threaten an escalation of the arms race into space and, if it worked, America might be able to mount a nuclear strike on the "evil empire" without fear of retaliation.

There was, however, another side to Reagan, because this ardent anti-communist was also a fervent opponent of nuclear weapons. Reagan believed that the Cold War policy of deterrence based on MAD (mutually assured destruction) was exactly that. On July 31, 1979, a day he never forgot, he toured the command center in Colorado that would coordinate U.S. defenses in the event of a nuclear war. It was a vast underground city, carved out of the Rocky Mountains and protected by a steel door several feet thick, but when the commander was asked what would happen if a Soviet missile landed outside, he shrugged: "It would blow us away." Reagan was shocked that even the nerve center of America's defenses was defenseless. "We have spent all that money and have all that equipment, and there is nothing we can do to prevent a nuclear missile from hitting us," he reflected on the flight back to Los Angeles that night. "We should have some way of defending ourselves against nuclear missiles." The trip reinforced his desire to replace mutual destruction with mutual survival.[18]

In essence SDI was the president's own idea, which he sprang on an astounded State Department. Some Pentagon hawks backed the project as a way to strengthen America for a possible first strike on the Soviet Union, but Reagan was absolutely sincere in March 1983 when he said that his goal was to "render these nuclear weapons impotent and obsolete."[19] His closest advisers in the White House doubted that he would have been willing to launch America's nuclear arsenal even if the country were under attack.

Critics of SDI depicted the president as a Hollywood gun-toting cowboy, ready to shoot from the hip, but Reagan's self-image was very different. Throughout his life his mind kept returning to summers as a teenage lifeguard on the Rock river in Illinois. Enthroned on an elevated wooden chair commanding the beach, his tanned, well-toned body made him into a cult figure. On his own reckoning, he plucked seventy-seven people from near death in the river. The lifeguard became the abiding motif of Reagan's inner life—a savior, almost a superman.[20] He had, said Robert McFarlane, one of Reagan's aides, "enormous self-confidence in the ability of a single heroic figure to change history." Another aide, Frank Carlucci, felt that Reagan was "convinced he could change the 'evil empire' to a 'good empire' through force of persuasion."[21]

Here was the central paradox of the Reagan presidency—on the one hand, the tough Cold Warrior; on the other, the would-be crusader for peace. The Soviets found it hard to decide which was the real Reagan, and this was understandable because the president never resolved the conundrum himself. This confusion was reflected within his cabinet—in the bitter feuding between Defense Secretary Caspar Weinberger, a ferocious hawk, and Secretary of State George Shultz, who was ready to enter into dialogue with Moscow.

In Reagan's first term the Cold Warrior was uppermost, as he sought to boost U.S. defense spending, but after his reelection in 1984 the tone began to change. Nancy Reagan, his closest confidante, wanted her husband to go down in history as a peacemaker; more important, he finally had someone to talk to in Moscow because, after three sick and senile Soviet leaders had wheezed their way from the Kremlin to the grave in less than three years, the Politburo skipped a generation and elected the young and dynamic reformer Mikhail Gorbachev.

The two leaders met in Geneva, neutral territory, in November 1985. Hopes for the meeting were not high, because Gorbachev was demanding an end to SDI, on which the president was unyielding; they locked horns on the issue on the first day of their summit. Gorbachev was not impressed by Reagan's reliance on cue cards, and the president's attempts at humor were unthinkingly tactless—for instance, when he told Gorbachev one of his favorite jokes, about an American and a Russian who were debating the extent of freedom in their respective countries: "The American said he could walk into the Oval Office, pound his fist on the table, and say that he didn't like how President Reagan ran the United States. The Soviet citizen responded that he could do the same. He could walk into the Kremlin, pound his fist on the table, and say that he didn't like how President Reagan ran the United States."[22] Gorbachev was not amused.

Yet against the odds, the two men clicked. When matters got heated, Reagan suggested that they take time out and saunter down to a pool house by Lake Geneva. On the way they chatted about his movie career. Although they carried on arguing, the two men hit it off at a human level. By the end of day one they had, to the amazement of staffers, agreed to hold follow-up summits in Moscow and Washington. Waiting for their limos, they shook hands and locked eyes with real feeling. Gorbachev recalled a "spark of electric mutual trust which ignited between us, like a voltaic arc between two electric poles." Reagan, though less grandiloquent, was similarly impressed. "You could almost get to like the guy," he told an aide. "I keep telling myself I mustn't do it, because he could turn."[23]

The Geneva summit also began important behind-the-scenes negotiations on a broad range of issues between Soviet and American diplomats, adroitly managed by Secretary of State Shultz. But no significant progress was made on the all-important nuclear issue, so Reagan and Gorbachev met again in October 1986 at Reykjavik in Iceland. Their arguments were even more intense than at Geneva but the personal chemistry was again palpable and they made real breakthroughs. As the meeting neared its end the two men—often talking with no advisers and only their interpreters—were on the verge of a deal to dismantle most of their nuclear arsenals over ten years.

Reagan's dream seemed to be coming true, but the sticking point at Reykjavik was Gorbachev's fixation with Star Wars. He wanted Reagan to agree that all SDI research should be confined to the "laboratory"—for fear of giving America a real advantage if relations soured—but this the president would not do. As it became clear that this difference was fundamental, the final exchanges of the summit were raw and emotional.

"I want to ask you once more to change your viewpoint," said Reagan, "to do it as a favor to me so that we can go to the people as peacemakers."

"We cannot go along with what you propose," Gorbachev replied grimly. "If you will agree to banning tests in space, we will sign the document in two minutes."

Reagan did not relent. "It's too bad we have to part this way. We were so close to an agreement. I think you didn't want to achieve an agreement anyway. I'm very sorry."

"I am also very sorry it's happened this way," said Gorbachev quietly. "I wanted an agreement and did everything I could, if not more."

Reagan said, "I don't know when we'll ever have another chance like this and whether we will meet soon."

"I don't either," replied the Soviet leader.[24]

Dejection was written all over their faces as they left the summit. Despite the recriminations after Reykjavik, however, signs of convergence increased in the following months. As his advisers had long urged, Gorbachev dropped his attempts to link all progress on arms control with restrictions on SDI. This reflected his urgent need to reduce the arms burden on the flagging Soviet economy, but he was also reacting to new realities in the United States.

After the Republicans lost control of the Senate in the November 1986 midterm elections, it was clear that SDI was not going to enjoy the same lavish funding as before. And Reagan himself was also seriously weakened by the Iran-Contra affair, which surfaced a few weeks after Reykjavik and consumed public attention for months. It became public that National Security Council staffers had covertly sold arms to Iran, breaching U.S. law and policy, in the hope of securing release of American hostages in Lebanon, and had then used some of the profits for equally illegal support of the Contra anti-communist guerrillas in Nicaragua. At best, Reagan was shown to be an ineffectual manager; at worst, possibly an accomplice in a new Watergate. In consequence, the weakened administration needed a foreign policy success and it was responsive to Gorbachev's efforts to make real progress in arms control.

The logjam broke rapidly. In December 1987 Gorbachev visited Washington to sign a treaty on intermediate-range nuclear weapons, the first time the superpowers had ever cut their arsenals. The following May the president finally set foot on the soil of the country he had made a political career out of denouncing. Welcoming Reagan to Moscow, Gorbachev quoted an apt Russian proverb: "It is better to see once than to hear a hundred times."[25] The most poignant moment came as the two men strolled through Red Square. The president was asked whether he still thought the Soviet Union was an evil empire. "No," he replied firmly. "I was talking about another time, another era."[26]

Much had indeed changed since Reagan's notorious speech five years earlier, but the new dialogue among the leaders and their advisers was only part of the story. The thaw in the Cold War also reflected the major changes that Gorbachev had initiated in Soviet society and these, in turn, were driven by a technological revolution that America had unleashed on the world.

THE INFORMATION REVOLUTION

Time magazine commenced its ritual of nominating a "Man of the Year" back in 1927, to commemorate Charles Lindbergh's epic solo flight across the Atlantic. Over the years *Time*'s choices were eclectic—selecting Hitler (once) and Stalin (twice), broadening out into women (the young Queen Elizabeth) and groups (the astronauts who made the first moon landing). But for more than a half-century, *Time* stuck to human beings—that is, until the end of 1982, when its editors chose an inanimate object: the personal computer.

"In 1982 a cascade of computers beeped and blipped their way into the American office, the American school, the American home," *Time* enthused. "The 'information revolution' that futurists have long predicted has arrived, bringing with it the promise of dramatic changes in the way people live and work, perhaps even in the way they think. America will never be the same." And, "In a larger perspective, the entire world will never be the same."[27]

Hyperbolic as ever, on this occasion *Time* was entirely right. The PC would transform America and the world; it even played a part in ending the Cold War. The story of how it was developed sheds a revealing light on some fundamental differences between the United States and the Soviet Union.

Great Britain has fair claim to have pioneered the computer, with the wartime electronic calculator, Colossus, used to crack German ciphers by the code-breakers at Bletchley Park, but it was in the United States that computers made their home. In the 1950s they began to replace the old punched-cards system for data crunching in big organizations like the U.S. Census Bureau. In November 1952 a UNIVAC—an acronym for universal automatic computer—was the sensational centerpiece of CBS's presidential election coverage after it correctly predicted an Eisenhower landslide on the basis of very early results and even though opinion polls all suggested a close race.

These first computers were enormous, often filling up a large office. One, on display at IBM's headquarters in Manhattan, contained 23,000 relays and 13,000 vacuum tubes. "The machine in operation must have been the most spectacular in the world," said one visitor from overseas. "Thousands of neon lamps flashed on and off, relays and switches buzzed away." The *New Yorker* magazine offered readers this description: "The principal cerebral parts are tubes and wires behind glass panels, covering three walls of the room. Two hoppers, looking rather like oversized mailboxes, stand near the middle of the room. One is the 'in' hopper, into which the questions are inserted on punched cards or tapes; the other is the 'out' hopper, from which, if all goes well, the answer emerges."[28]

By the early 1960s, however, the circuits of thousands of fragile vacuum tubes (or valves) were replaced by magnetic-core memories and by transistors—solid materials like silicon that acted as semiconductors of electricity. These transistors, in turn, were then miniaturized on tiny chips.

Such dramatic innovations were a tribute to the skill of American engineers and the enterprise of U.S. business, but they also needed the patronage of Uncle Sam. Transistor technology was hugely attractive to the armed forces for reliable, lightweight communications systems in weapons, ships, planes, and missiles. Army Signal Corps engineers reported in 1952 during the Korean War, "In more normal times the military services would embark on only a modest program of 'transistorization,' leaving the broad general problem of the maximum utilization of these devices to the ingenuity of our industry and research institutions. Now, however, in this period of international tension the services consider the possible benefits of transistors to military equipments [*sic*] as sufficient to warrant substantial programs in this field."[29] The U.S. military provided much of the start-up research funding and also the main market. In 1960, despite the popular craze for transistor radios, the military was buying nearly half of total American production of semiconductors.[30]

Computers were equally important for national defense. After the Soviets had tested an atomic bomb in 1949, U.S. military planners were alarmed at American vulnerability to air attack. To coordinate information from radar all over the continent a vast computing system was needed—operating in real time, a few seconds, unlike the machines used for the Census Bureau. IBM won the contract to build and run the computers for the whole system, known as SAGE (Semi-Automatic Ground Environment). It had twenty-four regional centers, each with two megacomputers for insurance. Costing around $8 billion, SAGE was the largest and most expensive military project of the 1950s. Not only did it account for about half of IBM's computer sales during that decade, it also gave thousands of engineers and programmers their basic training in the business. "I worked harder to win that contract than I worked for any other sale in my life," said Tom Watson, Jr., the company's boss. "It was the Cold War that helped IBM make itself the king of the computer business."[31]

By the end of the 1960s IBM accounted for three-quarters of mainframe production across the world.[32] Western countries, America's allies, were able to buy U.S. technology, but Cold War legislation imposed tight controls on technology transfer from the United States across the iron curtain. The Soviets had to rely on industrial espionage to keep up—most of their computers were modeled on pirated IBM systems, several years out of date. In this vital high-tech battleground of the Cold War, communism was falling seriously behind capitalism.

The IBM computers of the 1960s—with integrated circuits and magnetic-core memories—were a far cry from the early dinosaurs, but they still looked like elephants in comparison with the modern laptop. Because of their size and cost, they were overwhelmingly built by big business for big business. In 1968 there were fewer than 70,000 computers in use in the whole United States.[33]

What made computers into *personal* machines was the application of chips not just to the circuitry but to the whole computing process through a microprocessor. The "computer-on-a-chip" was developed by Intel, a California spin-off company in what was already known as Silicon Valley—the high-tech conglomeration around Stanford University. Yet it took several years to move from concept to reality, and in *this* technological revolution the military played no part.

It was, in fact, a very anti-establishment revolution, born in the Californian youth culture of the Vietnam War era. Its leaders were mostly young computer enthusiasts who worked in the industry or in electronics. Many were influenced by the ideology of "computer liberation," intended to wrest communications out of the grip of corporations. The Homebrew Computer Club in Silicon Valley became a Mecca for enthusiasts keen to experiment with microprocessors. Soon dozens of tiny new computer firms were competing for the hobbyist market, but one company managed to turn the personal computer into a consumer product.

This was Apple, founded in its hometown of Cupertino, California, by Stephen Wozniak and Steve Jobs—two college dropouts with complementary talents— Wozniak being a brilliant nerd, Jobs a charismatic salesman. Their first Apple computers—not much more than crude circuit boards—were assembled in the Jobs family garage, but Jobs had the vision to imagine an Apple II with far greater appeal: a self-contained unit in a plastic case, with keyboard, screen, and printer that could be used for correspondence, accounts, and other household tasks. This Wozniak designed and Jobs launched in the spring of 1977, aided by the software packages for spreadsheets and word processing that were now coming onto the market.

Apple's motto was "one person—one computer," in line with Jobs's counterculture philosophy of democratizing computer power. Some in IBM thought it was all a bit of a joke—one insider scoffing, "Why on earth would you care about a personal computer? It has nothing to do with automation. It isn't a product for big companies that use 'real' computers."[34] But spreadsheet software suggested that the future of the PC lay in the office as much as in the home, so belatedly in August 1981 IBM entered the market with its own PC. The microprocessor was bought from Intel, setting the company on course for dominance in the market for chips, and the software operating system came from a small Seattle firm called Microsoft, whose founders, Bill Gates and Paul Allen, were another computer hobbyist duo who got started in business by designing software for the Apple II. Microsoft's new disk operating system (MS-DOS) was sold with every IBM machine—this was Bill Gates's big break.

IBM put the imprimatur of one of the world's top corporations on the personal computer; now it was no longer a hobbyist's toy. Between 1980 and 1982 sales of PCs quadrupled to 2.8 million a year—hence *Time* magazine's accolade.[35] Other companies rushed to produce "IBM-compatible" machines, most also being sold with MS-DOS, and in the process the U.S. computer market was transformed. In 1978 about three-quarters of sales were mainframes; by 1984, fewer than half.[36] The computer was moving from government and corporations into small businesses and the home. The information revolution had begun.

One sign of this revolution was in America's financial markets. On the New York Stock Exchange the volume of trading tripled during the 1960s; by the end of the decade the exchange had to close on Wednesday afternoons to allow firms to catch up on the paperwork. But the National Association of Securities Dealers Automated Quotations (NASDAQ), founded in 1971, used 20,000 miles of phone lines to link subscriber terminals to a central computing system that recorded prices, deals, and other information. The phones were replaced by computerized trading in 1983. By the mid-1980s NASDAQ had become the third-largest stock exchange in the world, and all competitors had to follow its computerized methods or go to the wall.[37]

The growth in stock trading was not, however, simply the result of new technologies. In 1975 Congress abolished the requirement of fixed-rate brokerage commissions. In preparation for over a decade, this reform was signed into law by President Ford, who insisted that, given the need for new capital investment, "we must be sure that laws and regulations written thirty or forty years ago do not unfairly interfere with the need for changes in our modern-day markets."[38] The arcanely titled Securities Acts Amendments of 1975 were known colloquially (and more aptly) as the May Day Revolution. Exploited by zealous traders such as Charles Schwab, they transformed the U.S. stock market. Uncompetitive firms disappeared; more profitable ones were bought up by corporate giants such as Sears Roebuck and American Express. Equally important was the entry of millions of ordinary Americans into the stock market in the years that followed. This was partly due to the slashing or total removal of commissions for small investors, but it also reflected a loosening of tax regulations in 1975 that allowed people to open individual retirement accounts (IRAs). This gave a huge boost to mutual funds, which invest on behalf of many investors in a range of stocks and bonds.

The 1970s also saw large-scale "deregulation" of transport and utilities, dismantling structures established by the progressives (see Chapter 10) and strengthened by New Dealers to make private oligopolies take account of public interests. Deregulation—more accurately the loosening of regulation—was inspired by neoclassical economists such as Milton Friedman but it enjoyed bipartisan support. Nixon and Ford opened up the railroad and trucking industries in the early 1970s; Carter pushed through the Airline Deregulation Act of 1978. Their overall aim was to allow new firms to enter key industries and give them greater flexibility in setting prices. In airlines this more competitive environment helped bring down established companies such as Eastern and Braniff and promoted new low-cost airlines such as People Express and, more durably, Southwest. In the 1990s, the deregulation wave surged on into the banking industry, with more problematic consequences as we shall see in the next chapter.

In the telecommunications sector, deregulation and new technologies combined with spectacular effect. Unlike most other countries the United States did not have a government-run phone network, but the American Telephone and Telegraph Company had enjoyed almost monopoly status since the 1930s. AT&T ran the only long-distance network, its Bell operating companies provided nearly all local services, its subsidiary Western Electric manufactured most of the phones, and its research arm, Bell Telephone Laboratories, developed the essential technologies. The survival of this leviathan was due to the Pentagon's desire for a single organization with all these capabilities at the beck and call of the U.S. government. In

1970 AT&T was the largest corporation in the world, with $53 billion in assets, $2.5 billion in net income, and over a million workers. Its nearest American rival, Standard Oil of New Jersey, had less than half its assets and income, and a mere 143,000 employees.[39]

During the 1970s, however, AT&T endured a long and bruising legal action by the Justice Department, applying stronger antitrust legislation. Eventually the company agreed to its own break-up. In 1984 AT&T divested itself of the local operating companies, retaining its long-distance market but in competition with several hundred other carriers. This settlement blew the telecommunications market wide open. At the same time the old reliance on landlines was becoming outmoded because of mobile phones linked to a cellular network of radio stations. Cellphones were pioneered by Motorola in 1983 and then rapidly refined in portability and in features such as text messaging. By 1992 half the world's 17 million phones were located in the United States—a platform for exponential global growth in the years that followed.[40]

The result of all these changes was economic rejuvenation. Back in the 1970s the United States seemed to be floundering. Industrial growth had stagnated, inflation was out of control, and the heavy industries on which the postwar boom had been based, such as cars and textiles, were no longer competitive against Asian competition. Parts of urban America seemed like a rustbelt. In the 1980s, however, new service industries, spearheaded by information technology (IT) and boosted by deregulation, seemed to signal a "postindustrial" society. Meanwhile, however, the Soviet Union remained a "heavy metal" society—locked in the smokestack industries of yesteryear. Behind the iron curtain, deregulation and the IT revolution were inconceivable. The Soviets had found it hard enough to keep up with mainframe computers; their anemic consumer economy offered no stimulus to PC development; and the cellphone explosion was totally impossible in a closed society. Information is power and, under communism, both were tightly controlled.

In computers and electronics the Soviet Union lagged behind European clients like Czechoslovakia and East Germany, yet even their pirated products did not compare with authentic Western versions that were now flooding into eastern Europe. "With these computers comes not only technology but also ideology," lamented one Czech computer designer. "Children might soon begin to believe that Western technology represents the peak and our technology is obsolete and bad." In ten years' time, he warned, "it will be too late to change our children. By then they will want to change us."[41]

So the PC and the information revolution posed a double challenge to the Soviet bloc—both economic and ideological. Moscow's Five-Year Plan of 1985 envisaged 1.3 million PCs in Soviet schoolrooms by 1995, but the Americans already had 3 million in 1985 and in any case the main Soviet PC, the Agat, was an inferior version of the crude and by now antiquated Apple II.[42]

Gorbachev was keenly aware of these problems and the U.S. secretary of state, George Shultz, played on his concern. Shultz—formerly a business leader and an academic economist—liked to conduct tutorials with Gorbachev and his entourage. "We have left the industrial age," he would say, "and have moved into what we might think of as the information age, in which we have to think of new ways of working, of making decisions. Closed and compartmentalized societies cannot take advantage of the information age," Shultz warned the Kremlin leaders. "People must be free to express themselves, move around, emigrate and travel if they want, challenge accepted ways without fear. Otherwise they can't take advantage of the opportunities available."[43]

Becoming part of the American-led information age was a major reason why Gorbachev was so anxious to forge a new relationship with the United States. Otherwise the USSR would be consigned to obsolescence. By the 1980s, in fact, the whole Soviet bloc was in "a race between computers and collapse."[44]

"TEAR DOWN THIS WALL"

In June 1987 Reagan stood in front of the historic Brandenburg Gate in the center of Berlin, but between him and the Gate ran the notorious wall dividing the city between West and East. "As long as this gate is closed, as long as this scar of a wall is permitted to stand," Reagan declaimed, "it is not the German question alone that remains open, but the question of freedom for all mankind." After the recent talk from Moscow about "reform and openness," the president said there was "one sign the Soviets can make that would be unmistakable, that would advance dramatically the cause of freedom and peace. . . . Mr. Gorbachev, open this gate! Mr. Gorbachev, tear down this wall!"[45]

This seemed like another of Reagan's grand gestures—naive, provocative, and utterly utopian. Except that, in little more than two years, the Wall was no more.

Since the North Atlantic Treaty of 1949 the United States had committed itself to the security of western Europe, keeping troops in Germany as a tripwire for massive nuclear retaliation should the Soviets ever thrust westward. The NATO Alliance had been seriously strained in the early 1980s by the deployment of new U.S. intermediate-range missiles—Cruise and Pershing—in response to the new Soviet SS-20s. This revived the anti-nuclear movements of the 1960s, with mass protests and sit-ins in Britain and West Germany; only the tenacity of the conservative leaders in London and Bonn, Margaret Thatcher and Helmut Kohl, ensured that the NATO deployments went ahead. But even their loyalty was strained by Reagan's SDI program, which threatened to destabilize the Alliance's strategy of nuclear deterrence while offering vast high-tech benefits to U.S. corporations. President François Mitterrand of France—the country that was always America's most prickly ally—proposed a rival European program that, he said, "would establish technological Europe without delay."[46]

By the late 1980s these tensions had eased. SDI was fading as a pressure point in transatlantic relations and the new Soviet readiness to negotiate resulted in the 1987 treaty removing all intermediate-range nuclear missiles from Europe. As NATO came back together, the Soviet bloc began to fall apart. The economic burdens of its outmoded command economy were becoming unsustainable and political protest mounted. Gorbachev's programs of *perestroika* (restructuring) and *glasnost* (openness) had struck a chord in the West, but many suspected it was all windy rhetoric. In January 1989 former secretary of state Henry Kissinger dismissed the Gorbachev reforms as "atmospherics."[47]

The year opened with a new U.S. president. George Bush had served two full terms as Reagan's vice-president; he was, in fact, the first incumbent vice-president to be elected to the White House since Martin Van Buren a century and a half before. Having been in Reagan's shadow for so long, Bush was keen to put his own stamp on foreign policy. In any case, he worried that Reagan, once a fierce Cold Warrior, had been carried away by the Gorbymania of the 1980s. A pragmatist, famously contemptuous of what he called "the vision thing," Bush had real problems with Reagan's big ideas like SDI. As a consummate insider—having held posts such as ambassador to the UN and director of the CIA—he also did not share Reagan's hopes of revolutionary change in international relations.

So Bush took his time on U.S.-Soviet relations, commissioning a comprehensive policy review to consider scenarios and priorities into the next century. Four months into his presidency Bush finally spoke out. "We are approaching the conclusion of an historic postwar struggle between two visions: one of tyranny and conflict and one of democracy and freedom." Bush said that his policy review showed that "forty years of perseverance have brought us a precious opportunity." Instead of seeking simply to contain Soviet expansion, he declared, "we seek the integration of the Soviet Union into the community of nations."[48]

The slogan "beyond containment" struck a new note, yet Bush had no substantive new policies to offer and he warned against the United States relaxing its guard in the face of Moscow's still "awesome" military capabilities. Essentially the president was waiting on events, but in the second half of 1989 those events were truly dramatic.

The Soviet bloc started to crack in strike-ridden Poland, where free elections produced a government led by non-communists; then in Hungary, long a semi-capitalist state, the communists started to share power. As the crisis deepened Gorbachev adhered to his new principles, stating, "What the Poles and Hungarians decide is their affair, but we will respect their decision whatever it is."[49] This pledge was in total contrast to his predecessors, who had sent in the Red Army to crush liberalization in Hungary in 1956 and Czechoslovakia in 1968. Gorbachev's green, or at least amber light for reform emboldened protestors in East Germany—Moscow's showcase state in eastern Europe. Its old guard was toppled and when the new leaders eased travel restrictions to the West, thousands of Berliners simply overwhelmed the Wall and its checkpoints on the night of November 9. It was they who tore down the Wall over the ensuing weeks—but that was possible only because Gorbachev did not stop them.

As the news from Berlin came in on November 9 Bush held an impromptu press conference in the Oval Office but he struck a very low-key note. Asked whether this was the end of the Iron Curtain, he replied, "Well, I don't think any single event is the end of what you might call the Iron Curtain, but clearly this is a long way from the harshest Iron Curtain days—a long way from that."

Did he ever imagine anything like this happening, particularly on his watch?

Well, said Bush, "we've imagined it, but I can't say that I foresaw this development at this stage."

The press corps was puzzled. "You don't seem elated," remarked Lesley Stahl of CBS. "I'm wondering if you're thinking of the problems."

Bush went on the defensive. "I am not an emotional kind of guy."

"Well," pressed Stahl, "how elated are you?"

Bush pulled out the emotional stops. "I'm very pleased."[50]

Commentators had a field day imagining what Reagan, the Great Communicator, would have made of such an opportunity.

Yet Bush was acutely conscious of the sensitivity of the situation. For decades a divided Berlin and a fractured Germany had seemed like facts of international life. The Wall, though tragic for Berliners, had been almost a blessing for the United States—stabilizing the Cold War's most dangerous fault line. Now suddenly the Wall was coming down; would that start a violent international earthquake? Gorbachev begged the president not to overreact, warning of "unforeseen consequences," and western European leaders such as Mitterrand and Thatcher—with keen memories of World War II—dreaded the prospect of a reunited Germany. Repeatedly Bush told his advisers, "I'm not going to dance on the Wall," but he did give a discreet lead, with momentous consequences.[51]

Bush had fought in the war, but as a navy pilot in the Pacific. He described himself as "less of a Europeanist, not dominated by history,"[52] and told the press openly, "I don't share the concern that some European countries have about a reunified Germany because I think Germany's commitment to and recognition of the importance of the [Atlantic] alliance is unshakable." Bush added, "I don't think we ought to be out pushing the concept of reunification, or setting timetables, or . . . making a lot of new pronouncements on this subject. It takes time. It takes a prudent evolution." But, he stressed that the issue was "so much more front and center" because of the "rapid changes that are taking place in East Germany." This interview—front-paged by the *New York Times* under the headline "Possibility of a Reunited Germany Is No Cause for Alarm, Bush Says"—sent a clear message to the Europeans.[53]

Initially Kohl, the West German chancellor, envisaged a five-year timetable for unification but, as East Germany fell apart, he and Bush stepped up the pace. The

State Department developed a so-called 2+4 framework—negotiations between the two Germanies with the involvement of the four postwar occupying powers, the United States, the USSR, Britain, and France—as a formula to ensure both progress and consensus. The president's main concern was that the new Germany should remain bonded to the West. This was agreed with Kohl at a summit at Camp David, the first time a German chancellor had been accorded that honor. Afterward Bush announced, "We share a common belief that a unified Germany should remain a full member of the North Atlantic Treaty Organization, including participation in its military structure. We agreed that U.S. military forces should remain stationed in the united Germany and elsewhere in Europe as a continuing guarantor of stability."[54]

On NATO membership, Gorbachev tried to resist. "You are a sailor," he told Bush. "You will understand that if one anchor is good, two anchors are better"—meaning that Germany should be a member of both NATO and the Warsaw Pact. But Gorbachev now had little clout, desperately tacking from one position to another to keep abreast of the winds of change. "If he is a man with a moving bottom line," remarked one State Department official, "then our policy should be to help him move where we want him to go."[55]

With Kohl and Bush shaping policy, the western European powers and even the Soviet Union had to fall into line. On October 3, 1990, East Germany was absorbed into the Federal Republic. Although people-power in Germany had been decisive, Bush's combination of initiative and caution helped ensure international consensus. By not "dancing on the Wall"—not rubbing Gorbachev's nose in the successive humiliations of the USSR—the president also made it easier for the embattled Soviet leader to cooperate. The new leadership in Moscow was anxious not to jeopardize its newly open relationship with the West, even if that meant losing its empire. Anyway, under Gorbachev's new thinking, that empire now seemed more like a millstone than an asset.

But as the Cold War came to a surprisingly peaceful end in Europe, it took a very different course in China. Since the end of the 1970s a reformist leadership in Beijing had gradually loosened the command economy, encouraging local enterprise and foreign investment. A decade of rapid growth boosted living standards but also aroused demands for democratic change, which were further emboldened by the crumbling of communism in Europe. Then in June 1989, party hardliners turned the troops on student demonstrators encamped in Beijing's historic Tiananmen Square, where they had erected a huge plaster-and-styrofoam Goddess of Democracy—modeled on the Statue of the Liberty. The precise death toll remains a matter of debate, but it did not matter, lamented one student, "whether the total number killed was one thousand or ten thousand. The point is that our government turned its guns on its people."[56]

Here was the great divide with 1989 in Europe. Despite the challenges to his authority, Gorbachev almost always refrained from using force against protestors in eastern Europe and the Soviet Union. The result was democracy but also disintegration. Deng Xiaoping and the Chinese gerontocrats spilled blood but kept hold of power. Having successfully blocked democratization in 1989, in the next decade they resumed their policy of growing out of the planned economy into what was called a "socialist market economy with Chinese characteristics." The contrast between Russia and China in 1989 would define U.S. relations with these two giants for decades to come.

Tiananmen Square—scarcely known outside China before June 1989—became a byword all over the world for government brutality, but the torrent of criticism left Bush in a quandary. Since Nixon's pioneering visit to China in 1972 and then Carter's decision in 1979 to normalize diplomatic relations—giving the People's Republic its long-demanded seat on the UN Security Council—the United States had been trying to draw communist China in from the cold. Bush himself had been part of the process, serving as U.S. special representative in Beijing in 1974–1975. So, as president, his response to Tiananmen Square was typically measured. On June 5 he told the media, "We deplore the decision to use force, and I now call on the Chinese leadership publicly, as I have in private channels, to avoid violence and to return to their previous policy of restraint. The demonstrators in Tiananmen Square were advocating basic human rights, including the freedom of expression, freedom of the press, freedom of association. These are goals we support around the world."[57]

The president announced certain sanctions including a freeze on weapons sales and a ban on all high-level exchanges between government officials, but all this was undercut entirely at the end of June when he sent his national security adviser, Brent Scowcroft, on a secret mission to Beijing, using an unmarked cargo plane to avoid detection. Scowcroft delivered a personal letter from Bush to Deng in which the president bent over backwards to avoid pointing the finger or seeming to interfere in Chinese affairs. His tone was almost begging: "Any statement that could be made from China . . . about peacefully resolving further disputes with protestors would be very well received here. Any clemency that could be shown the student demonstrators would be applauded worldwide. We must not let the aftermath of the tragic recent events undermine a vital relationship patiently built up over the past seventeen years."[58]

The first President George Bush was a pragmatist. In Germany he welcomed the fall of the Wall but kept Gorbachev onside. In China he lamented the repression of democracy but did not let it upset U.S. foreign policy. This preference for cautious consensus-building was to be demonstrated most of all during the greatest challenge of his presidency, in the sands of Kuwait.

"A NEW WORLD ORDER"

August 1988 finally saw a ceasefire in the Iran-Iraq War. The conflict that Iraq had begun in September 1980 had turned into the longest conventional war of the twentieth century. The dead and wounded exceeded 1 million; the cost ran to $1.2 billion.[59] Although the fighting ended, no peace was agreed and, less than two years later, on August 2, 1990, Iraq invaded and occupied its neighbor to the southeast, the emirate of Kuwait.

Faced with vast war debts and growing internal discontent, Saddam Hussein, the Iraqi dictator, reckoned that invading Kuwait was the best way to increase his regional power, enhance his oil revenues, and shore up domestic support. Personalities aside, Iraq—hacked by the British in 1921 out of the ruins of the Ottoman empire—was virtually landlocked, having only fifteen miles of coastline through which its exports (mostly oil) could flow into the Gulf. Territorial disputes with neighboring Iran and Kuwait were features of its national history.

So Iraqi warmaking in 1990 was the act of a fragile state as well as a megalomaniac leader, but it was possible only because the West had built up Saddam as a major power. From 1983, as the war against Iran went decisively against him, the United States and the Arab states, including Saudi Arabia and Kuwait, came to his aid to prevent victory for the Islamic revolutionaries in Teheran. In 1983–1984 Baghdad's trade with Washington was three times the value of its trade with Moscow, officially its main patron. Saddam was receiving top-quality U.S. intelligence as well as credits to build an oil pipeline to Jordan.[60] Britain and other NATO states helped further to expand Saddam's arsenal—often using a spurious distinction between military and nonmilitary equipment to sell machine tools, computers, and other manufactures he needed to build heavy weaponry. The lack of Western condemnation of Saddam's brutal methods of war in Iran (including the use of chemical weapons) encouraged him to expect similar indifference when he attacked Kuwait.

The outcry that greeted Saddam's attack—from Bush in Washington to Hosni Mubarak in Cairo—was partly anger at having been deceived and surprised, but there was far more at stake. Although Kuwait was an autocratic monarchy, it was also a small country brutally overwhelmed by a big neighbor. Within hours Iraq had been unanimously condemned by the fifteen-member UN Security Council; even Marxist Cuba supported the United States. Three days after the invasion, Bush got into a testy exchange with skeptical reporters. How could he prevent the installation of an Iraqi puppet government in Kuwait, journalists asked. "Just wait. Watch and learn," the president shot back. "I view very seriously our determination to reverse out this aggression. This will not stand. This will not stand, this aggression against Kuwait."[61]

By effectively promising to liberate Kuwait, the president was going against the firm advice of the chairman of the joint chiefs of staff, Colin Powell—the first black American to hold that post.[62] Bush had been goaded by the media, but he was also expressing a gut instinct, and what stuck in his gut was Hitler.

"Half a century ago, the world had the chance to stop a ruthless aggressor and missed it," he told a conference of war veterans later in August. "I pledge to you: We will not make that mistake again."[63] As reports of Saddam's atrocities in Kuwait kept coming in, the president's anger mounted: "We're dealing with Hitler revisited, a totalitarianism and a brutality that is naked and unprecedented in modern times. And that must not stand. We cannot talk about compromise when you have that kind of behavior going on this very minute. Embassies being starved, people being shot, women being raped—it is brutal. And I will continue to remind the rest of the world that this must not stand."[64]

By occupying Kuwait, Saddam had doubled his control over world oil reserves to 20 percent; if he also invaded Saudi Arabia and the United Arab Emirates, then the proportion would rise to over half. It is not clear that he planned to do so but, having been wrong-footed over Kuwait, U.S. policymakers lurched from complacency to alarm. Within days the Saudis had acceded to American pressure and asked for U.S. troops to help defend their kingdom. So began Operation Desert Shield.

General Powell and Secretary of State James Baker still hoped that international sanctions might be enough to persuade Saddam to pull out of Kuwait, but Bush and Brent Scowcroft, his national security adviser, were gearing up for war. On October 30, Powell gave a White House briefing on his recent trip to the Middle East, using a series of flip-charts to illustrate U.S. plans. He reported that the first phase of the mission was virtually accomplished. "We'll soon be in a position to defend Saudi Arabia." Flipping to the next page, Powell explained how America could "go on the offensive to kick the Iraqis out of Kuwait."

The president leaned forward—this was what he had been waiting to hear. When Powell had finished his exposition, Scowcroft asked, "What size force are we talking about?"

"We're approaching two hundred and fifty thousand for the defensive phase," Powell replied. "But if the President opts for this offensive, we'll need a hell of a lot more."

"How much more?" asked Scowcroft.

"Nearly double," responded Powell. He estimated it would require about two hundred thousand extra troops.

There were gasps around the room but the president did not flinch. Instead he asked, "Colin, are you sure that air alone won't do it?" Powell said he would be "the happiest soldier in the Army if the Iraqis turned tail when the bombs start falling," but he reminded the group that history indicated that air power alone was unlikely to prove decisive. "If we make the threat we have to mean it," he said firmly. "We have to be ready to go to war." Bush let the discussion run on for a few more minutes. Then he said laconically, "Okay, let's do it."[65]

The die had been cast, but Bush was still careful to proceed by consent. On November 29 the United States secured a resolution in the UN Security Council authorizing member-states to "use all necessary means to uphold and implement" previous resolutions about Kuwait and to "restore international peace and security in the area" if Iraq was not out of the country by January 15, 1991. This gave Bush the legitimacy he needed for war.

The following day the president praised what he called the "historic" UN resolution. His language about Saddam was now unrestrained: "We're dealing with a dangerous dictator all too willing to use force who has weapons of mass destruction and is seeking new ones and who desires to control one of the world's key resources—all at a time in history when the rules of the post-cold-war world are being written." But then Bush seemed to undercut all he had said—stating that he was ready to "go the extra mile for peace" by meeting the Iraqi foreign minister in Washington and sending Baker to see Saddam in Baghdad.[66]

Foreign allies were shocked: If Saddam was Hitler then this sounded like appeasement. The Saudi ambassador told Bush, "To you, sending Baker is goodwill; to Saddam, it suggests you're chicken."[67] But the president's priority was to make sure Congress and public opinion were fully behind him. Many Americans feared that this would be a long and bloody war—another Vietnam. To add to the sense of foreboding, that autumn PBS was running Ken Burns's blockbuster series on the American Civil War; its images of death and destruction were sobering reminders that real combat was not as clinical as a computer game. Bush needed to show Americans he had done everything possible to avoid bloodshed. Afterward Baker reckoned that the "extra mile" pledge was "decisive."[68]

This final diplomatic flurry got nowhere; Saddam had lost touch with reality. Even so, with the undeclared war in Vietnam in mind, Bush was at pains to obtain congressional approval, though the vote was close in the Senate. The White House offered various justifications for the impending war—from stopping Hitlerite aggression to securing Western oil, from safeguarding American jobs to denying Saddam a nuclear arsenal—but increasingly another slogan took precedence. As Bush told Americans on the day the war began in January 1991, "We have before us the opportunity to forge for ourselves and for future generations a new world order— a world where the rule of law, not the law of the jungle, governs the conduct of nations. When we are successful—and we will be—we have a real chance at this new world order, an order in which a credible United Nations can use its peacekeeping role to fulfill the promise and vision of the U.N.'s founders."[69]

The phrase "new world order" dated back to Woodrow Wilson at the end of World War I, but those hopes had been dashed by the failure of the League of Nations in the 1930s and then the impotence of the UN during the Cold War— paralyzed between the superpowers. In 1991, however, things were very different. Although the Soviet Union had been Saddam's staunch ally for decades, Gorbachev's foreign minister, Eduard Shevardnadze, stated bluntly when Saddam invaded Kuwait that his aggression was "inconsistent with the principles of new political thinking and, in fact, with the civilized relations between nations."[70] Despite sniping by Moscow hawks, Gorbachev proved a loyal supporter of Bush's war. Also unprecedented was the attitude of the French, who, since the mid-1960s, had refused to accept U.S.

military direction in NATO. Yet in January 1991 France placed its troops under U.S. command in Saudi Arabia, becoming, with Britain, a vital source of additional fighting power. Among the Arab states—not merely Egypt and Saudi Arabia, long-standing American allies—were supportive but also inveterate foes such as Syria.

So, when the defensive Operation Desert Shield became the offensive Desert Storm in mid-January 1991, it was a war waged by a unique international alliance. The mood in America, however, remained somber. Playing on these fears, Saddam promised "a second Vietnam" and the "mother of all battles."[71]

On January 17 the coalition began intensive bombing against Iraq's air defense and command systems, and then against similar targets in occupied Kuwait. Ground operations started five weeks later. The Allied commander, General H. Norman Schwarzkopf, controlled 540,000 U.S. troops and 250,000 from the Allies, of whom the Saudis comprised the largest contingent. Schwarzkopf planned a classic encirclement. Feint attacks north against Kuwait City would suck in the enemy, while the bulk of his U.S. armored and mechanized units, plus a British and a French division, would sweep hundreds of miles west and then east to cut off the Iraqi forces.

Execution was almost perfect. The ground war began on February 24 and lasted only 100 hours before Bush called a halt to avoid what seemed on TV to be a massacre. Later estimates range from 35,000 to 80,000 Iraqi dead. The coalition lost 240 killed in action, of whom 148 were Americans. Almost a quarter of the American dead, and over half the British, came from what was called "friendly fire." This caused an outcry though it was, in fact, a familiar feature of modern wars fought by long-range artillery and air power.[72]

Even so, the victory was spectacularly one-sided. "It's a proud day for America," exclaimed the president. "And, by God, we've kicked the Vietnam syndrome once and for all."[73] The United States had proved it could fight and win a major war—both on the battlefield and in living rooms at home. Much was also made of the new technologies of warfare. The flanking attack would have been impossible without the Pentagon's Global Positioning System to provide accurate navigation, and the bombing campaign featured computerized, satellite-guided missiles capable of turning down individual streets or going right into military bunkers. Admittedly, precision bombs constituted less than 10 percent of the tonnage dropped during the Gulf War, and their accuracy was only as good as the target intelligence; the Allies were also pounding a demoralized enemy in open, foreign terrain (unlike Vietnam). But air power had proved remarkably effective in the Gulf War and many saw the new "smart weapons" as heralding so-called technowars to come.[74]

For Bush, victory vindicated his new rhetoric. "Until now, the world we've known has been a world divided—a world of barbed wire and concrete block, conflict, and cold war. Now, we can see a new world coming into view. A world in which there is the very real prospect of a new world order."[75]

Diplomatically, however, the impact of the war was less definitive. Bush deliberately stopped fighting when Kuwait was liberated; he did not invade Iraq or seek to topple Saddam, though he hoped and assumed that after such a disaster there would be a coup in Iraq. In the aftermath, as Saddam recovered, there was much criticism of U.S. restraint, but Bush remained unrepentant. Defending his actions seven years later he argued that, in order to seek out and eliminate Saddam, "we would have been forced to occupy Baghdad and, in effect, rule Iraq. The coalition would instantly have collapsed." Furthermore, he went on, "we had been self-consciously trying to set a pattern for handling aggression in the post–Cold War world. Going in and occupying Iraq, thus unilaterally exceeding the United Nations mandate, would have destroyed the precedent of international response to aggression that we hoped to establish. Had we gone the invasion route, the United States could conceivably still be an occupying power in a bitterly hostile land."[76]

Written in 1998, those words sound sadly prescient today, yet Bush had himself sown the seeds of problems to come. Having gone out of his way to demonize Saddam as a new Hitler and to warn of his "weapons of mass destruction," the president helped to foster the impression that America had won the war but lost the peace. This left unfinished business for his successors—not least, of course, his own son.

That was in the future, however. In 1991 Bush could bask in the glow of his new world order and, by the end of the year, watch the final demise of the "evil empire" as the feuding republics finally broke up the Soviet Union. Joy was tinged with sadness at the demise of Mikhail Gorbachev, who had lost both his job and his country. On Christmas Day, just hours before the USSR ceased to exist, over the phone the two men had their final conversation as world leaders.

Bush, at Camp David with his family for the holiday, kept his emotions under control, but at the end he said, "And so, at this special time of year and at this historic time, we salute you and thank you for what you have done for world peace."

"Thank you, George," Gorbachev replied. "You have said to me many important things and I appreciate it."

"All the best to you, Mikhail."

"Goodbye."

Before he returned to hearth and family that Christmas evening, Bush reflected, "God, we're lucky in this country—we have so many blessings."[77]

18

PRIDE AND PREJUDICE

_____

The demise of the Soviet Union did not bring contentment for Americans. There was pride, yes, that America had seen off the "evil empire" and now seemed to reign supreme, but the end of the old enemy unleashed new passions at home. In the 1990s the balance of American politics lurched back and forth between right and left, while the culture wars over social values intensified with conservatives warning about the "multicultural" disintegration of American society. Prejudice was rampant on both sides. Then September 2001 saw the most-devastating-ever assault on American soil. President George W. Bush identified Islamic fundamentalism as the new evil against which America should define itself in the new century. Meanwhile the economy continued to boom, yet some of its foundations were shaky and this became dramatically clear in 2008. After the pride came the fall. So the presidential election that November was a summation of many of the themes of U.S. history over the past few decades.

SOLE SUPERPOWER, EDGY AMERICANS

After nearly a half-century of Cold War, the Soviet Union was no more, leaving the United States as unquestionably the world's only superpower. Russia was deeply resentful at the collapse of its empire, storing up problems for the future, but the break-up of the USSR into feuding national republics underlined the success of America's federal system. Whatever its faults, this had proved more effective at holding together a huge, fractious country than any comparably sized government on the planet—not just the Soviet Union but other vast countries like Canada, India, or Nigeria. And formerly closed societies seemed to be going democratic, with elections the name of the game across the old Soviet Union, eastern Europe, and the Balkans.

The conservative commentator Francis Fukuyama summed up the mood extravagantly by proposing that humanity had reached "the end of history." He suggested that "what we may be witnessing is not just the end of the Cold War, or the passing of a particular period of postwar history, but the end of history as such: that is, the end point of mankind's ideological evolution and the universalization of Western liberal democracy as the final form of human government. . . . [I]t is the ideal that will govern the world *in the long run*."[1]

Fukuyama's headline-grabbing claim was wrapped in neo-Hegelian jargon, but it did seem in the early 1990s that the world was going democratic. Yet, as we shall see, even at this heady moment the United States was having its own problems with democracy. The end of the Cold War made Americans edgy, not content.

George Bush Senior did not benefit politically from the Allied victory in Kuwait and the demise of the Soviet Union. That may seem surprising given the magnitude of those events, which deterred many prominent Democrats from challenging him in the election of 1992. But what mattered for most Americans in the early 1990s was a sharp and painful recession. Bush's Democratic opponent, Bill Clinton, formerly governor of Arkansas, focused on the economy and on the president's failure to honor his 1988 campaign promise: "Read My Lips—No New Taxes." Clinton's campaign manager stuck up on the wall of their "war room" a sign with just three lines on it:

- Change v. More of the Same
- The Economy, stupid
- Don't forget health care[2]

Clinton's victory marked a generational shift in U.S. politics—from the men of World War II to the "baby boomers." Also a sign of the times, the Clinton campaign featured his articulate lawyer wife, Hillary Rodham Clinton. Bill promised that, by electing him, voters would get "two for the price of one." The Clintons were, in fact, a remarkable political couple, ferociously ambitious and, despite Bill's notorious infidelities, deeply intertwined. He provided the political passion, she the focus and organization. "They're not whole without each other," said one close friend. The child of a broken home, Clinton was raised in Arkansas but went to Oxford as a Rhodes Scholar and then to Yale Law School, where he met Hillary. She came from a Republican, Methodist family in the Midwest; radicalized during her student years, she threw herself into Democratic politics. In the early 1970s Betsey Wright, who became one of Bill's closest aides, was, on her own admission, "less interested in Bill's political future than Hillary's. I was obsessed with how far Hillary might go, with her mixture of brilliance, ambition, and self-assuredness."[3] After much soul-searching Hillary moved to Arkansas, married Bill, and became a successful lawyer to pay the bills, but his political career was always a joint project—a point that is fundamental to their story.

In some ways, the 1992 campaign suggested the vitality of American democracy. Clinton—like an earlier southern governor, Jimmy Carter—demonstrated that a shrewd and determined outsider could topple even an incumbent president, positioning himself as a "New Democrat" not wedded to the party's traditional "tax and spend" policies. His party won the White House and also control of both houses of Congress, for the first time since Carter's victory in 1976. The Clinton years saw dramatic improvements on the economic front. In 1993 Clinton drove through a budget deal aimed at reducing the huge federal debt that had mushroomed during the Reagan years. The economy pulled out of the recession, posting steady growth at a time when Europe was struggling. The savage downsizing of old industries in the 1980s had boosted competitiveness and American business had capitalized more quickly and extensively than its rivals on the new information technologies. A sign of confidence was the spectacular rise in share values. The Dow Jones industrial average climbed from under 2,000 in 1987 to 4,000 in 1995 and doubled again by July 1997. In March 1999 it topped 10,000 for the first time. The booming economy and stock market resulted in larger tax revenues: In February 1998 Clinton was able to present Congress with a balanced budget for fiscal year 1999.[4]

The stock market boom partly reflected the inflated prices of IT stocks. This "dot com" bubble finally burst in March 2001, wiping out some major corporations such as WorldCom, the telecommunications giant. But the speculative tendency did not abate, shifting instead into housing. The boom was stimulated more generally by continued loosening of financial regulation, building on the reforms of 1975 (see Chapter 17). Of particular importance was the Financial Services Modernization Act of 1999. For some years bankers had been campaigning for an easing of the Glass-Steagall banking act of 1933, which, reacting to the Crash and Depression, erected rigid legal barriers between commercial and investment banks (see Chapter 12). In the global boom of the 1990s this seemed anachronistic and the 1999 Act, with bipartisan support, removed the barriers. From the medley of ensuing mergers emerged a more flexible industry known as financial services. Deregulation of its practices continued, with banks allowed to take increasing risks in the size of the assets they held against soaring debts and trades, and under Alan Greenspan, five-term chairman of the Federal Reserve from 1987 to 2006, interest rates were kept low, fuelling the boom in credit.

The information revolution was also gathering pace. Computer networks had been pioneered by the U.S. military but, thanks to the personal computer, they were now spinning off into American society as a whole. One benefit was in communication—electronic mail—but equally important was the mass of information being organized as of the late 1980s through the World Wide Web. This allowed users to move from a word or phrase highlighted on the screen (hypertext) to related information on computers all over the world. During 1992 the number of Internet sites surpassed 1 million. The Clinton administration wanted the riches of the Web to be available democratically to all Americans, Vice-President Al Gore declaring: "We must make sure that all children have access. . . . That's not the case now. 22 percent of white primary-school students have computers in their homes; less than 7 percent of African-American children do. We can't create a nation of information haves and have-nots. The on-ramps to the information superhighway must be accessible to all."[5]

Despite the positives, however, all did not seem well with American democracy. In the 1992 election Ross Perot, running as an independent, had won nearly 19 percent of the popular vote—the best showing by a third-party candidate since Theodore Roosevelt in 1912. This testified to grassroots alienation from the two main parties and the people who ran them. "The British aristocracy we drove out in our Revolution has been replaced by our own version," Perot warned, "a political nobility that is immune to the people's will"—what he called "the little group of Washington insiders, lobbyists and professional politicians who thought of the national government as their own private playground." But, Perot insisted, "[t]he people are owners of this country. Everyone in government, from the President of the United States to the newest employee in a small town, works for the people."[6]

Yet Perot was able to mount his populist campaign only because of his own private wealth as a Texas IT billionaire. The cost of running for president was increasing exponentially from a total of around $500 million in the campaign of 1992 to over $1 billion by 2004. Outsiders therefore needed their own resources, as Perot had, or else lavish support from insiders and interest groups—hardly what Jefferson and his generation would have regarded as the essence of republican values.

One problem was the length of the election campaign, dictated by the expensive sequence of state-by-state primaries that starts nearly a year before the November election. Primaries originated back in the 1910s as a progressive reform to open up party nominations to the people, but critics argued that in the age of the Internet other, cheaper ways could and should be found.

Alienation ran deep, it seemed. In 1996 voter turnout in the presidential election fell below 50 percent of those eligible for the first time since the 1920s. American civil society seemed to be in decline as well. Back in the 1830s the French observer Alexis de Tocqueville noted Americans' remarkable propensity for forming and joining associations—clubs, churches, and other groups that created a rich texture of community life. By the 1990s, however, sociologists detected a marked decline in churchgoing, union membership, and involvement in school PTAs, the American Red Cross, Boy Scouts, and fraternal societies.

Sociologist Robert Putnam summed up this trend: "The most whimsical yet discomfiting piece of evidence of social disengagement in contemporary America that I have discovered is this: more Americans are bowling today than ever before, but bowling in organized leagues has plummeted in the last decade or so." "Bowling alone" was Putnam's eye-catching metaphor for this disconcerting trend. He wrote that "in the established democracies, ironically, growing numbers of citizens are questioning the effectiveness of their public institutions at the very moment when liberal democracy has swept the battlefield, both ideologically and geopolitically."[7]

In tandem with this disengagement from community values, it seemed that Americans had become increasingly polarized by their culture wars over religious and social issues such as abortion and school prayer. The point was made dramatically in August 1992 by Pat Buchanan, who had challenged for the Republican nomination on the grounds that President Bush was too liberal. At the party's convention Buchanan, a former Reagan aide and traditionalist Catholic, made his peace with Bush while attempting to hijack the Republican campaign as a far-right crusade: "The agenda Clinton & Clinton would impose on America—abortion on demand . . . homosexual rights, discrimination against religious schools, women in combat—that's change, all right. But it is not the kind of change America wants. It is not the kind of change America needs. And it is not the kind of change we can tolerate in a nation that we still call God's country." Buchanan declared that "there is a religious war going on in our country for the soul of America. It is a cultural war, as critical to the kind of nation we will one day be as was the Cold War itself."[8] Conservative coolness for Bush significantly reduced Republican turnout on election day, and "culture wars" became a feature of American politics throughout the 1990s.

Washington infighting during the Clinton years became as vicious as in the Watergate era—but much more balanced, as the advantage ebbed and flowed from one side to the other. In his first couple of years the president held the initiative, making a dramatic attempt to reform health care. The United States was unique among major developed nations in having no universal system of health care provided via compulsory health insurance, taxation, or a mixture of both. Apart from government safety-net systems like Medicare, most Americans' health care derived from their employment package. Urging reform, the president told Congress, "Our health care is too uncertain and too expensive, too bureaucratic and too wasteful. It has too much fraud and too much greed." On any given day, he asserted, "over 37 million Americans, most of them working people and their little children, have no health insurance at all."[9] That was around 15 percent of the U.S. population.

Reforming health care would have challenged any president—in the past, both Truman and Nixon had tried and failed—but Clinton made serious mistakes along the way. He chose his wife to head a task force on the problem, just as when he targeted education as his priority in Arkansas in 1983. The choice was intended to demonstrate his personal commitment to reform, but she became a lightning rod for Republicans who dubbed the program HillaryCare. Her ideas, her role, even her hairstyle became topics of endless comment. Mrs. Clinton came up with an enormous sheaf of proposals, more than 1,300 pages, which the opposition easily blasted as hopelessly bureaucratic. The medical profession, the pharmaceutical companies, and the health insurance industry mounted a massive propaganda campaign, often deliberately distorted. But at root the Clintons failed to persuade millions of Americans, particularly small businesses, of the merits of their scheme of mandatory health insurance, paid for largely by employers. Without enough votes to get it through even a Democrat-controlled Congress, the president had to admit defeat in August 1994.

Later Hillary Clinton acknowledged her own mistakes: "Our proposal for reform was inherently complex—just like the health care problem itself—which made it a public relations nightmare. Virtually every interest group could find something objectionable in the plan." But she noted the concerted opposition from vested interests and also made a deeper point: "We were on the front lines of an increasingly hostile ideological conflict between centrist Democrats and a Republican Party that was swinging further and further to the right. At stake were American notions of government and democracy and the direction our country would take for years to come."[10]

The vehemence of the political struggle became clear in the midterm congressional elections of November 1994, when the Republicans regained the Senate and won control of the House for the first time in forty years. This stunning victory came on the back of a carefully orchestrated campaign by the Republican House leader, Newt Gingrich, who mobilized 367 Republican candidates behind his "Contract with America." This foresaw "the end of government that is too big, too intrusive, and too easy with the public's money" and its replacement by "a Congress that respects the values and shares the faith of the American family."[11]

In 1995 Gingrich, now Speaker of the newly elected House, pushed ahead with his legislative agenda to cut taxes and social programs. Although moderate Republicans in the Senate were more cautious, Gingrich was now on a collision course with Clinton and the fight became personal. Matters came to a head around Christmas when Gingrich proposed resolutions that would move welfare programs and Medicaid to the states. He trumpeted this as "the largest domestic decision" since the New Deal in 1933—"a fundamental change in the direction of government."[12] Pollsters assured Clinton that these proposals were too radical for the American people, and the president vetoed the Republicans' proposed budget for 1996. With neither side budging, the federal government effectively shut down for three weeks—national parks closed and 800,000 employees went without their December pay. In this face-off, the Republicans finally blinked, accepting Clinton's revised budget.

Personality and partisanship aside, the underlying issue here was the proper place of the federal government in American life—a debate that went back to the Founding Fathers but which had been reenergized by the New Right in recent years. On Capitol Hill the struggle, though bitter, remained within the political arena, but some Americans were ready to go further.

On April 19, 1995, a truck bomb exploded outside the main federal building in downtown Oklahoma City, killing 168 people—the worst act of terrorism in U.S. history to date. The perpetrator, eventually executed, was Timothy McVeigh—an alienated veteran obsessed with guns, computer games, and loathing for the federal government—but Clinton believed that the Oklahoma City bombing was symptomatic of more than the derangement of one young man:

> Anti-government paranoia had been building in America for years, as more and more people took the historical skepticism of Americans toward government to a level of outright hatred. This animus led to the rise of armed militia groups that rejected the legitimacy of federal authority and asserted the right to be a law unto themselves. The atmosphere of hostility was intensified by right-wing radio talk-show hosts, whose venomous rhetoric pervaded the airwaves daily, and by Web sites urging people to rise up against the government and offering practical assistance, including easy-to-follow instructions on how to make bombs.[13]

The lurch to extremism—on Capitol Hill or in Oklahoma City—probably helped Clinton seem more acceptable to the majority of Americans. His credibility was also strengthened by his capacity to act "presidentially" in foreign affairs.

The Bosnian civil war, involving Serbs, Croats, and Muslims, was the bloodiest of the conflicts in the former Yugoslavia. Peacekeepers from the United Nations and the European Union proved ineffectual—some British and French troops even being taken hostage by the Serbs. Clinton had been reluctant to get drawn in—his priorities were domestic and he had been badly bitten by an early foray in peacekeeping in 1993, when U.S. troops were killed in Somalia—but in August 1995, after a wave of Serb atrocities, he finally committed American air power. Two weeks of relentless NATO bombing brought the Serbs to the negotiating table; U.S. Assistant Secretary of State Richard Holbrooke then shipped the warring leaders off to an airbase at Dayton, Ohio, and banged their heads together until they signed an agreement effectively partitioning Bosnia.

For the Europeans this was a sobering reminder of American power. When Yugoslavia began to break up in 1991, they had claimed that "this is the hour of Europe"—anticipating that in the post–Cold War era, western Europe would no longer be so dependent on U.S. help in security matters. But, as Holbrooke put it, "for over half a century Europe had been unable to act as a unified power without American leadership," and the 1990s proved no different. The denouement of the Bosnian crisis underlined the supremacy of the United States as the world's sheriff and also helped Clinton's image.[14]

After the humiliation of 1994 and the revival of 1995, 1996 proved the year of the Comeback Kid—as Clinton dubbed himself. Having repositioned himself as a centrist against the extremes of liberalism and conservatism, the president pruned welfare and highlighted "family values" such as reducing youth crime and teenage pregnancies. His campaign for reelection was helped by the Republicans' choice of candidate Bob Dole—a veteran senator whose acerbic manner and age (seventy-three) both told against him. To appease Pat Buchanan, who had again been a vigorous contender for the nomination, Dole included an anti-abortion plank in the party platform. All this served to reinforce Clinton's claim to be the man of moderation. On a tide of economic recovery, Americans voted him back to the White House in November 1996 with a thumping majority.

The Republicans kept control of Congress, however, so partisan animosity did not abate. Indeed, it intensified because the Republicans were furious that "Slick Willie," as they called Clinton, had talked his way out of trouble and back into the White House. Congress had already managed to establish an "independent counsel" to investigate the Clintons' finances. When a panel of conservative judges appointed Kenneth Starr (Bush's solicitor general) to that post in 1994, the investigation developed a keen partisan edge. Clinton's Achilles' heel was his philandering sex life, as accusations and revelations over the years had made clear. Starr broadened his investigations to cover these and particularly Clinton's encounters with a young White House intern, Monica Lewinsky, about which he was given information and evidence.

The Lewinsky scandal surfaced in the press in January 1998. After several days of frenzied and salacious gossip, Clinton issued a formal denial. With his wife standing beside him, he declared, "I want to say one thing to the American people. I want you to listen to me. I'm going to say this again. I did not have sexual relations with that woman, Miss Lewinsky. I never told anybody to lie, not a single time—never. These allegations are false."[15]

The Lewinsky scandal engulfed America for months. Eventually, having been given immunity from prosecution, she handed Starr a semen-stained dress to back up her allegations that, on at least nine occasions in or near the Oval Office, she had oral sex with the president. Starr's pursuit of Clinton became a crusade inspired by a blend of political partisanship and moral revulsion—Starr came from the religious right. Eventually, on August 17, 1998, Clinton was forced to go on national TV to admit that he had misled the nation in January: "Indeed, I did have a relationship with Ms. Lewinsky that was not appropriate. In fact, it was wrong. It constituted a critical lapse in judgment and a personal failure on my part for which I am solely and completely responsible. . . . I know that my public comments and my silence about this matter gave a false impression. I misled people, including even my wife."[16]

But Clinton's belated penitence was too little, too late. Starr was now in full cry, delivering a 450-page report full of explicit detail to Congress in September. He stated that the president had made various "false statements" about his relationship with Lewinsky and delayed congressional and other inquiries. Starr concluded that all this "may constitute grounds for an impeachment."[17]

Republican leaders in the House gleefully seized their opportunity, proceeding to a trial of the president before the Senate. This was only the second impeachment in U.S. history, the first being the unsuccessful trial of Andrew Johnson in 1868.

But Starr and the Republicans were not backed by the bulk of the public. The president still enjoyed high ratings in opinion polls thanks to the economic boom, and many people found Starr's report sensationalist and prurient. "What in the heck are we doing, making this kind of near-pornographic material available on the Internet with the imprimatur of the US Congress?" asked Congressman James P. Moran of Virginia.[18] He was a Democrat, but many moderate Republicans shared his unease.

So impeachment failed to give congressional Republicans the bounce they hoped for in the 1998 midterm elections, prompting an exhausted Gingrich to resign as Speaker. It did not help the Republicans when he was revealed to have been conducting an affair with a congressional aide young enough to be his daughter. The arch impeacher was not, it seemed, a man of unimpeachable morals.

The outcome of Clinton's trial was never really in doubt because it required a two-thirds majority of the Senate to impeach a president and the Republicans held only 55 of the 100 seats. Nevertheless, the proceedings dragged on for more than a month, further humiliating Clinton, before the charges of perjury and obstructing justice were rejected on February 12, 1999.

Nobody emerged from the business with credit. Starr and the Republican leadership in the House had overreached themselves, pursuing a political vendetta. Yet Clinton had been revealed as an adulterer and a liar: Despite his achievements and his remarkable resilience, the scandal was an indelible stain on his reputation. Historian Joseph Ellis likened Monica Lewinsky to "a tin can that's tied to Clinton's tail that will rattle through the ages."[19]

The Lewinsky affair also raised yet more questions about America's political system. In a parliamentary democracy, critics argued, a prime minister who behaved in this way would have been quickly removed by his party, but America's separation of powers encouraged a ding-dong war between executive and legislature that paralyzed politics and damaged the country's image.

And there was worse to come. The election of November 2000 confirmed the intensity of America's culture wars and suggested that they could no longer be settled by political means.

The Republican candidate was George W. Bush, son of the former president and known in the family as "Dubya." Unlike his father, the younger Bush was a born-again Christian who opposed abortion in virtually all circumstances. His opponent was Al Gore, Jr., Clinton's vice-president, who favored abortion and gun control and was an enthusiast about the environment. So, although Bush promised a "compassionate conservatism," the clash between the two men seemed to embody America's cultural polarization. The outcome proved extremely close: On November 7 Gore beat Bush very narrowly on the popular vote, by about half a million, but the numbers that mattered were in the electoral college.

The decisive state was Florida, where after a recount Bush's majority was a bare 500 ballots over Gore out of a total of 5.8 million. At stake, given the winner-takes-all principle, were Florida's 25 electoral votes, so the result in Florida would swing the whole election. Gore demanded manual recounts in several counties and, with evidence of irregularities on both sides and the added interest that Bush's younger brother, Jeb, was governor of Florida, Democrats and Republicans took the issue to the courts and eventually to the very top. On December 12 the U.S. Supreme Court voted by five to four to overturn the Florida supreme court's decision to require a state-wide recount. Gore protested the judgment but conceded defeat.

The Court's decision provoked an outcry. Critics noted that the majority five had all been appointed by Republican presidents. Sandra Day O'Connor's notes to the chief justice routinely referred to the Republicans as "we" and "us."[20] Harvard law professor Alan Dershowitz even asserted that *Bush v. Gore* "may be ranked as the single most corrupt decision in Supreme Court history, because it is the only one that I know of where the majority justices decided as they did because of the personal identity and political affiliation of the litigants. This was cheating, and a violation of the judicial oath."[21]

Also noteworthy was the reasoning involved. The majority rested its case on a clause in the Fourteenth Amendment of 1868, which stipulated that no state should "deny to any person within its jurisdiction the equal protection of the laws." In the recent past this "equal protection" clause had been exploited by liberal justices to promote affirmative action for racial minorities, to the dismay of conservatives who considered it a federal erosion of states' rights. But it was these same conservatives who in 2000 invoked the clause to stop the Florida recount. Critics of the decision also noted the justices' remarkable caveat that "our consideration is limited to the present circumstances, for the problem of equal protection in election processes generally presents many complexities." Legal analyst Jeffrey Toobin translated that to mean that "the opinion did not reflect any general legal principles; rather the Court was acting only to assist a single individual—George W. Bush."[22]

The minority on the Court was vocal in its dissent. "Although we may never know with complete certainty the identity of the winner of this year's Presidential election," wrote Justice John Stevens, "the identity of the loser is perfectly clear. It is the Nation's confidence in the judge as an impartial guardian of the rule of law." Justice David Souter, the least political of the nine, kept his silence but was so ashamed of the decision that he seriously considered resigning. Both Stevens and Souter, incidentally, had been appointed by Republican presidents, but they were less partisan than the majority.[23]

Bush v. Gore was therefore a hugely problematic decision by the Supreme Court—paralleling *Roe v. Wade* on abortion in 1973. In that case liberals had stretched the Fourteenth Amendment to suit their wider political opinions; in 2000 the conservatives had done something similar. In each case a stinging dissent (by

White and now by Stevens) challenged the legal reasoning involved. In *Roe v. Wade*, however, the issue was a specific cultural value; in *Bush v. Gore* the Court was effectively deciding the presidential election. As one of the placards at Bush's inaugural put it, "THE PEOPLE HAVE SPOKEN—ALL FIVE OF THEM."

The election of 2000 therefore rounded off a decade in which American democracy had been under the microscope more comprehensively even than in the era of Watergate. Culture wars, adversarial politics, the separation of powers, the wisdom of having an electoral college, even the impartiality of the Supreme Court—all had become subjects of angry debate. While promoting democratic values as a global panacea, the United States found democracy hard to operate at home. "America has conquered the world," remarked BBC correspondent Gavin Esler, "and yet Americans have found little peace."[24]

MULTICULTURALISM OR DISINTEGRATION?

Eldrick Tont Woods is not the most promising name for a sports superstar. "Tiger" Woods sounds much better and that was how the twenty-one-year-old golfing prodigy hit the world's front pages in April 1997, wearing the fabled green jacket awarded to winners of the U.S. Masters. "We need a black in a green jacket," his father had told him, but Woods didn't like the "black" label. He invented the word "Cablinasian" to capture his intricate racial makeup—a mix of Caucasian, black, Indian, and Asian. His father, a retired army officer, was half African-American, a quarter Chinese, and a quarter Native American. His mother's ancestry was half Thai, a quarter Chinese, and a quarter Dutch.[25]

Tiger Woods embodied, in microcosm, the new multiculturalism that was redefining the United States in the 1990s. In the first two decades of the twentieth century mass immigration had been one of the most sensitive issues in politics, but the human tide was slowed dramatically by the imposition of quotas in the 1920s, by the Depression of the 1930s, and then by World War II. In 1965 a new Immigration Act abolished the national quotas that had privileged the countries of northwestern Europe, but President Lyndon Johnson played down the law's significance: "It will not reshape the structure of our daily lives, or really add importantly to either our wealth or our power." The Act would, said Johnson, merely correct "a cruel and enduring wrong in the conduct of the American Nation" by abolishing the discriminatory quotas and confirming the principle that "from this day forth those wishing to immigrate to America shall be admitted on the basis of their skills and their close relationship to those already here."[26]

Johnson was at pains to state that "the days of unlimited immigration are past." He assumed that the main beneficiaries of the 1965 Act would be people from southern and eastern Europe—the main victims of the 1920s quotas—and did not expect a flood of migrants. In fact, the last third of the century saw a dramatic surge in immigration—4.5 million in the 1970s, over 7 million in the 1980s, and 9 million in the 1990s, making that the peak decade of the century for migrants apart from the 1900s. By the year 2000 more than 10 percent of the U.S. population were foreign-born. What's more, again contrary to Johnson's expectations, the surge came not from Europe but from Asia and especially Latin America, marking a decisive shift in the pattern of U.S. immigration.

Mexico had never been subject to restrictions because of the need for farm labor; the earlier racist barriers to migrants from China, Japan, and Korea were dismantled in the 1940s and 1950s. Both Hispanics and Asians were able to profit from the 1965 Act because it opened the door to family members of permanent residents. This started what has been called a "chain migration of relatives."[27]

By 2000 12.5 percent of the U.S. population were of Hispanic origin—double the percentage of twenty years before. More Americans described themselves as Hispanic than African-American (12.3 percent). By far and away the most substantial group of Hispanics were Mexicans—over 7 percent of the U.S. population in 2000— but the official census figures failed to pick up thousands of illegal immigrants who flitted to and fro across the 2,000-mile frontier between Mexico and the United States. Despite the efforts of a so-called Border Patrol, this was virtually impossible to police.

Traditionally Mexicans had been a downtrodden minority in the United States. "Mexicans are restricted in the main to only the lowest kinds of labor," the Los Angeles police department reported during World War II. "They are discriminated against and have been heretofore barred from learning trades. . . . Discrimination and segregation . . . in certain restaurants, public swimming plunges, public parks, and even schools, cause resentment among Mexican people. . . . There are certain plunges where they are not allowed to swim, or else only one day of the week . . . signs [read] 'Tuesdays reserved for Negroes or Mexicans.'"[28]

Mexicans perceived such discrimination against a long background of mistreatment by the "Anglos," going back to the war of 1846–1848 when the United States stripped Mexico of much of its territory, including California. By the 1960s younger Mexican-Americans started talking of themselves as Chicanos—a badge of self-assertion similar to the shift from "Negro" to "black" among African-Americans. Mexicans were also at pains to distinguish themselves from blacks; activists spoke of being a "bronze people with a bronze culture" going back to the heyday of the Aztec empire.[29]

Hispanic America also had a substantial minority from the Caribbean archipelago of Puerto Rico, half of them living in New York City and most of the rest in San Francisco and Los Angeles. Unlike Mexicans, Puerto Ricans were often labeled "black" because of the long history of black slavery on the islands, but "mixed race" was a more accurate description for both groups. Like Tiger Woods they showed that the traditional racial categories, still used in the U.S. Census, bore little relationship to the new American reality.

"Hispanics" were not even a unified culture. Mexicans and Puerto Ricans shared little except the Spanish language and Roman Catholicism. And, to take the other big immigrant group of the 1990s, "Asians"—people of Chinese, Filipino, Japanese, and Korean background—had even less in common with each other in language, religion, and culture.

Those who adopted a positive view of these developments lauded the new "multiculturalism" of late-twentieth-century America. On Columbus Day in October 1998 President Bill Clinton declared, "Although both a dreamer and a visionary, Columbus—a son of Italy whose enterprise was funded by the Spanish crown—could never have foreseen the multicultural, multiracial Nation that would ultimately emerge in the New World he helped to discover. As we enter a new era, let us embrace Columbus' spirit of discovery and embrace as well the great diversity of cultures, religions, and ethnic traditions that we enjoy because so many have followed his course to this great land."[30]

But the wave of immigration, particularly from outside Europe, provoked anger on the political right. "Our country is undergoing the greatest invasion in its history, a migration of millions of illegal immigrants yearly from Mexico," fumed Pat Buchanan in 1992. "A nation that cannot control its own borders can scarcely call itself a state any longer."[31]

Much of the resentment was concentrated in Texas and California, states where Hispanics now amounted to a third of the population. In November 1994 a majority of Californians—voting along ethnic and class lines—approved Proposition 187, which denied public education and social services to illegal immigrants. "We have to defend ourselves against invaders," said Barbara Coe, a leader of the campaign for Proposition 187. "The militant Mexican-American groups want to take back California. Our children cannot get an education, because their classes are jammed with illegals. In many classes only 20 minutes of English is spoken an hour." But opponents noted that many illegals paid taxes and asked who else would pick the crops and wash the dishes for next to nothing. Historic resentments also surfaced. Proponents of 187 "have forgotten that this piece of land belonged to Mexico," said L.A. housewife Yolanda Rivera. "We are all immigrants—even the ones who came on the Mayflower. We all came to try to get ahead, and we all deserve that opportunity."[32]

California's Proposition 187 was eventually overturned, but it took almost five years and it encouraged similar ballots in other states. A related concern was the growth of Spanish as a semiofficial language in some areas—and also the proliferation of other languages used on government documents and websites. In 1983 the former California senator Samuel Hayakawa, a Japanese-American but also a professor of English, founded a movement dedicated to making English the official language of the United States. Bilingualism was fine for individuals, he argued, but not for a country, pointing to the experience of Belgium and Canada: "Language is a unifying instrument which binds people together. When people speak one language they become as one, they become a society." Hayakawa believed that the United States, "a land of immigrants from every corner of the world, has been strengthened and unified because its newcomers have historically chosen ultimately to forgo their native language for the English language."[33]

Hayakawa's movement, U.S. English, had considerable success. By 2000 at least twenty states had passed their own laws; a bill to make English the "official" national language passed the House in 1996, though not the Senate. The advisory board of U.S. English in the 1990s included respected figures such as the journalists Walter Cronkite and Alistair Cooke,[34] but its co-founder, Dr. John Tanton, a Michigan ophthalmologist, struck a more belligerent note, arguing that the real issue was sex: "In this society, will the present majority peaceably hand over its political power to a group that is simply more fertile? Can *homo contraceptivus* compete with *homo progenitivo* [sic] if our borders aren't controlled? . . . Perhaps this is the first instance in which those with their pants up are going to get caught by those with their pants down."[35] Tanton's diatribe echoed nativists of the past, who claimed that lesser breeds like the Irish or the Italians were simply outbreeding their betters.

The underlying issue, again reviving long-standing debates, was whether the United States could maintain its unity, adhere to its motto of *E Pluribus Unum*. Was not multiculturalism just a recipe for social disintegration? Historian Arthur Schlesinger warned against "the recent apotheosis of ethnicity, black, brown, red, yellow, white," arguing that "the cult of ethnicity exaggerates differences, intensifies resentments and antagonisms, and drives ever deeper the awful wedges between races and nationalities. The end-game is self-pity and self-ghettoization."[36]

Harvard political scientist Samuel Huntington went further: "Historically American national identity has been defined culturally by the heritage of Western civilization and politically by the principles of the American Creed, on which Americans overwhelmingly agree: liberty, democracy, individualism, equality before the law, constitutionalism, private property." But now, asserted Huntington, American multiculturalists "reject their country's cultural heritage . . . they wish to create a country of many civilizations, which is to say a country not belonging to any civilization and lacking a cultural core." History, he said, "shows that no country so constituted can long endure as a coherent society. A multicivilizational United States will not be the United States; it will be the United Nations."[37]

For Huntington, Mexican immigration posed the immediate threat to the coherence of the United States but, on a global scale, the clash of civilizations that really mattered in his view was that of Muslims against the West. To his critics, Huntington was simply reworking into a new cultural form the old rhetoric about separate, conflicting races. But his claim that the post–Cold War world was sliding toward an apocalyptic clash of civilizations hit home for many Americans in September 2001.

"AMERICA IS UNDER ATTACK"

"Everybody get ready to read the title of the story," called out the teacher.

"*The Pet Goat*," the kids chanted back.

For second-graders at the Emma E. Booker Elementary School in Sarasota, Florida, it was an unbelievable moment. The president of the United States was listening to them read.

For George W. Bush it was also an unbelievable moment. Sitting on a stool in the classroom, doing a photo-opportunity for the media, his face was frozen in suppressed shock.

"She played with her goat in her yard."

"Good job. Go on," said the teacher.

"But the goat did some things that made the girl's dad mad."

All the president could think about was what an aide had just whispered in his ear. "A second plane hit the second tower. America is under attack."[38]

George W. Bush had been in the White House for less than eight months and had not found them very easy. He was still tarnished by the way his narrow election victory had been decided by conservatives on the Supreme Court. He had made a number of strong decisions, evoking enthusiasm and abuse in equal measure—such as instituting a major tax cut and rejecting the Kyoto Protocol to reduce greenhouse gas emissions—but by the summer of 2001 his presidency seemed to be losing momentum at home.

Nor was he looking for action abroad. On foreign policy, his line was more cautious than that of the Clinton administration, which had become entangled in messy peacekeeping operations in Africa and the Balkans. In one of the election debates in 2000 Bush said he was worried about "over-committing our military around the world" and considered "this idea of nation building" to be "grandiose." Bush felt that "what we need to do is convince people who live in the lands they live in to build the nations." He rejected the idea of America providing "a kind of a nation-building corps," insisting that "our military is meant to fight and win war" and "when it gets overextended, morale drops." Bush promised he would be "judicious as to how to use the military. It needs to be in our vital interest, the mission needs to be clear, and the extra strategy obvious."[39]

But all this was before Tuesday, September 11, 2001. At 9:30 that morning, having extricated himself from the children and their goat, Bush spoke briefly to the media at the school in Florida: "Today we've had a national tragedy. Two airplanes have crashed into the World Trade Center in an apparent terrorist attack on our country." The president said he had ordered that "the full resources of the federal government go to help the victims and their families and to conduct a full-scale investigation to hunt down and to find those folks who committed this act. Terrorism against our Nation will not stand."[40]

"Find those folks." Bush sounded a bit overwhelmed, searching for ringing words. Commentators noted that his line about terrorism was an echo, conscious or not, of what his father had said eleven years before about Saddam Hussein: "This will not stand, this aggression against Kuwait."[41]

To many observers, in fact, "Dubya" seemed out of his depth in the White House. His verbal gaffes were notorious, his Texan cowboy image embarrassed many intellectuals, and he was widely assumed to be the tool of strong advisers. In reality, however, Bush was his own man. After a dissolute, often drunken youth, he became a born-again Christian and renounced alcohol—evidence of his strong willpower. As governor of Texas and as president of the United States, Bush delegated widely but made up his own mind—often in quick-fire decisions to cover his own ignorance of the issues.

The problem was that nothing could have prepared any president for 9/11; it was a day like no other in U.S. history. The nearest equivalent atrocity, Pearl Harbor—dubbed by Franklin Roosevelt "a day which will live in infamy"—took place 2,000 miles from the American mainland; the continental United States had been virtually unscarred by World War II. In 2001, by contrast, Bush was facing an assault of unknown dimensions on the heart of America's finance and government—two hijacked planes destroying the giant twin towers of the World Trade Center, another plowing into the Pentagon, and a fourth finally forced down by courageous passengers en route to the White House itself.

In the aftershock, Bush struggled to find his touch. It did not help that he was not allowed back into Washington until that evening, because of fears of more terrorist attacks. Then followed what *Time* magazine called "two days in which Bush blinked his way through TelePrompTered remarks like a schoolboy reciting his lessons. In one of those staged events that are designed to look candid but fail utterly, he paced behind his desk during a photo-op phone call with Mayor Rudy Giuliani [of New York], accepting the mayor's invitation to tour his city's wreckage. Bush looked like a nervous teenager making weekend plans."[42]

On Friday the president spoke at a special service at Washington National Cathedral, the eyes of the country upon him. It was an occasion for national solidarity, Democrats and Republicans together, but the loneliness of leadership was palpable. "Every history book tells us how war renders a President an island unto himself," *Time* reflected. After the president had delivered his homily, "Bush senior reached over to squeeze his son's hand, his eyes not looking at him but raised toward the heavens. Like few others," said *Time*, "he knows that the President is on his own."[43]

That afternoon, after the service, the president flew up to Manhattan for his first visit since the attacks. The Twin Towers had collapsed but the ruins were still on fire and staffers on the chopper flying into Manhattan sniffed the smell of burning twenty miles out. For Bush, the sight of the dark, smoking wasteland of Ground Zero left an indelible impression, one that he would recall as "very, very, very eerie" and "a nightmare, a living nightmare." The destruction was far worse than he had imagined, even from TV pictures, and he was also struck by the thirst for revenge among the crowd of rescue workers. One pointed to him and yelled out, "Don't let me down." Bush did not forget the man's face or his words. It was, he said, like being in "some ancient arena." The rescue workers began chanting "U-S-A, U-S-A, U-S-A."[44]

So George W. Bush was cast in the role of America's gladiator. His aides were utterly unprepared; they had no plans for a speech, no sound equipment in place— this was billed simply as a meeting with rescue workers. But clearly the president had to say something. Nearby was a charred fire truck that had been pulled out of the rubble. Bush was helped up on top of it and somebody found a white bullhorn.

"U-S-A! U-S-A! U-S-A!" the crowd kept shouting.

"Thank you all," said the president. "I want you all to know—"

"Can't hear you," someone shouted.

"I can't go any louder. I want you all to know that America today—America today is on bended knee in prayer for the people whose lives were lost here, for the workers who work here, for the families who mourn. This Nation stands with the good people of New York City and New Jersey and Connecticut as we mourn the loss of thousands of our citizens."

Another cry of "I can't hear you."

"I can hear you," Bush shouted back. "I can hear you. The rest of the world hears you. And the people who knocked these buildings down will hear all of us soon."

The chants rolled back: "U-S-A! U-S-A! U-S-A.!"[45]

At last the president of the United States had found his voice. New Yorkers did not want to be told that their nation was still "on bended knee." They wanted to hear that America's attackers would soon be punished for their crimes.

Over the weekend the president and his advisers evaluated the intelligence and planned their response. By now it was clear that the attacks had been conducted by al-Qaeda—a collection of radical Islamic fundamentalist cells headed by Osama bin Laden. It was also clear that al-Qaeda was being sheltered by the fundamentalist Taliban regime in Afghanistan. On September 20 Bush, now at his most presidential, spoke to a joint session of Congress. He touched on the remarkable wave of sympathy that had surged around the globe—"the sounds of our national anthem playing at Buckingham Palace, on the streets of Paris, and at Berlin's Brandenburg Gate." But his main message was for his fellow Americans: "Our grief has turned to anger and anger to resolution. Whether we bring our enemies to justice or bring justice to our enemies, justice will be done. . . . Our war on terror begins with Al Qaida, but it does not end there. It will not end until every terrorist group of global reach has been found, stopped, and defeated."[46]

The phrase "war on terror" was deliberately open-ended. A war, not merely a campaign; waged not against specific terrorist groups but against terror itself because "terror" threatened everything that America stood for. "They hate our freedoms—our freedom of religion, our freedom of speech, our freedom to vote and assemble and disagree with each other." Bush insisted that this was not just America's fight for America's freedom. "This is the world's fight. This is civilization's fight. This is the fight of all who believe in progress and pluralism, tolerance and freedom." He declared that "the course of this conflict is not known, yet its outcome is certain. Freedom and fear, justice and cruelty have always been at war, and we know that God is not neutral between them."[47]

Not only had Bush found his voice; he had identified a new enemy, a new evil against which America could define itself after the demise of the Soviet Union. The purveyors of terror, said the president, "are the heirs of all the murderous ideologies of the 20th century. By sacrificing human life to serve their radical visions, by abandoning every value except the will to power, they follow in the path of fascism and Nazism and totalitarianism."[48] He even spoke of the struggle as a "crusade"— a word quickly dropped because of its connotations in the Middle East but one that accurately reflected his feelings.[49]

Cynically, one might say that in September 2001 the Bush administration needed a focus, needed an enemy, but that does not do justice to the searing effect of 9/11 on public opinion and on the president himself—especially the sights, smells, and sounds in the arena of smoke and darkness that was Ground Zero. Although the death toll was eventually scaled down from tens of thousands to 3,000, this was by far the worst attack on American soil, directed at two of the country's most iconic buildings. The president's rhetoric, and, it seems, his worldview, became increasingly messianic; he talked of liberty as God's gift to humanity and himself as a divine mouthpiece. "I trust God speaks through me," he was reported as saying in July 2004. "Without that, I couldn't do my job."[50]

Yet passionate faith has its dangers in politics and in diplomacy: The terrorist attacks on September 11 drove Bush into Afghanistan, with the world's support, but it also impelled him into Iraq, where the story was very different.

IRAQ AND THE "AXIS OF EVIL"

On September 12, the day after the attacks, Bush spoke with his counterterrorism czar, Richard Clarke.

"Look, I know you have a lot to do and all," he muttered, "but I want you, as soon as you can, to go back over everything, everything. See if Saddam did this. See if he's linked in any way."

Clark was incredulous. "But, Mr. President, al-Qaeda did this." He had been hammering on for years about the threat from al-Qaeda.

"I know, I know, but . . . see if Saddam was involved. Just look. I want to know any shred. . . ."

"Absolutely," Clarke said, nodding "we will look . . . again. But, you know, we have looked several times for state sponsorship of al-Qaeda and not found any real linkages to Iraq. Iran plays a little, as does Pakistan, and Saudi Arabia, Yemen."

"Look into Iraq, Saddam," said Bush testily and moved on.[51]

In Clarke's personal view, this was totally wrongheaded. "Having been attacked by al-Qaeda," he said, "for us now to go bombing Iraq in response would be like our invading Mexico after the Japanese attacked us at Pearl Harbor."[52] But Iraq did become the administration's prime target after 9/11. This was a war born of obsession and sold by deception; for good or ill, it would dominate the Bush administration.

Against all expectations after the Gulf War of 1991, Saddam Hussein had clung on to power, to mounting concern in Washington. Saddam had used chemical weapons on Iran and on his own people; there was also evidence that he was working to develop nuclear weapons. But the efforts of the UN and its weapons inspectors to track down these programs got nowhere, as the Iraqis played cat and mouse, so in December 1998 America and Britain bombed Iraqi military installations. Iraq was therefore a problem by the time Bush entered the White House in January 2001, but not a major item on his agenda. What put it there was 9/11 and also the neo-cons.

The neo-conservatives were a disparate group—some of the older figures, such as Daniel Bell and Irving Kristol, were formerly left-leaning intellectuals who, like Ronald Reagan, had swung to the right in reaction against America's perceived failure to stand up to communism abroad and radicalism at home. The Republican ascendancy in the 1980s had seemed like a new dawn, but neo-cons became disillusioned, especially by the elder Bush and what was seen as his failure to finish the job in Iraq in 1991. In the late 1990s a younger generation of neo-cons—men such as Paul Wolfowitz, Richard Perle, and John Bolton—were thirsting for power in a new Republican administration and had a clear plan for what should be done.

Neo-cons shared an essentially black-and-white worldview that starkly pitted good against evil, with the United States leading the forces of good. They believed that military power was what mattered in the world and argued that the United States should exploit its "unipolar" advantage, without worrying about international institutions, especially the UN—derided as weak and corrupt—or even historic allies such as the western Europeans. "We no longer need them in the way that we once did," said Perle. "They are no longer vital to the defense of our interests in the world." Passionately for Israel and against militant Islam, the neo-cons saw the Middle East as America's prime battleground, with the Iraqi regime as enemy number one. "Toppling Saddam is the only outcome that can satisfy the vital US interest in a stable and secure Gulf region," asserted Wolfowitz.[53]

In 1998 leading neo-cons signed an open letter to President Clinton warning that "the policy of 'containment' of Saddam Hussein has been steadily eroding" and that "the only acceptable strategy is one that eliminates the possibility that Iraq will be able to use or threaten to use weapons of mass destruction. In the near term, this means a willingness to undertake military action as diplomacy is clearly failing. In the long term, it means removing Saddam Hussein and his regime from power. That now needs to become the aim of American foreign policy."[54]

When Bush became president in 2001, leading neo-con intellectuals secured prominent senior positions in the administration and most of the very top jobs went to those who shared their priorities. The incoming head of the Defense Department was Donald Rumsfeld, a bureaucratic bruiser who had also held the post under Ford in 1975–1977—making him at once the youngest and the oldest to hold the position in U.S. history. Vice-President Dick Cheney had been Bush Senior's defense secretary. Obsessed with the failure to finish off Saddam in 1991, he saw regime-change in Iraq as the easiest way to make a dramatic demonstration of U.S. power after 9/11. The main exception to the neo-con predominance was Secretary of State Colin Powell. Reflecting both his own inclinations and the institutional bias of the State Department, Powell believed in working with allies and using U.S. military power only in exceptional circumstances. But, as a former soldier, Powell was always hesitant to challenge his commander-in-chief.

The September 11 attacks gave the neo-cons their chance. Immediately Wolfowitz insisted that Iraq must have been behind the attacks—an idea that lodged with the president. Although it was pushed to one side during the invasion of Afghanistan and the search for Osama bin Laden, the president came back to it in early November 2001, asking Rumsfeld to update U.S. planning for a possible war against Iraq. The neo-cons were now in full cry, seeking to use the "war on terror" to deal once and for all with Saddam.

What made their argument persuasive within the administration was partly the sour taste left by 1991 and partly concerns about Israel and oil, but the impact of 9/11 was fundamental. This merciless and unprecedented attack on the United States had a searing effect. If terrorists could achieve that kind of damage with aircraft, what might they do with weapons of mass destruction? And which was the rogue state most likely to have such weapons? Answer—Islamic Iraq under its brutal dictator. The reasoning was hardly watertight, but this was an administration gripped by nightmares, not logic.

Neo-cons also kept sight of their constructive agenda for U.S. foreign policy in a unipolar world because 9/11 gave them the justification, otherwise lacking, to try to democratize the Middle East along American lines. Richard Perle articulated this vision: "I think there is a potential civic culture in Arab countries that can lead to democratic institutions and I think Iraq is probably the best place to put that proposition to the test because it's a sophisticated educated population that has suffered horribly under totalitarian rule." Perle argued that this goal was not just idealism but also realism—a policy suited to American interests because "the lesson of history is that democracies don't initiate wars of aggression."[55]

By Christmas 2001 the U.S.-led campaign had removed the Taliban from power in Afghanistan. Although bin Laden eluded capture and the Taliban would soon regroup as a powerful guerrilla force, the administration now widened its net in the "war on terror." In his State of the Union message in January 2002, the president identified North Korea, Iran, and Iraq as "an axis of evil, arming to threaten the peace of the world. By seeking weapons of mass destruction, these regimes pose a grave and growing danger." Bush pledged, "I will not wait on events while dangers gather. I will not stand by as peril draws closer and closer. The United States of America will not permit the world's most dangerous regimes to threaten us with the world's most destructive weapons."[56]

"Axis of evil" was the phrase that the world latched on to. "Axis" evoked Hitler and his allies in World War II; "evil" demonized Iraq, Iran, and North Korea as almost agents of the devil and, by echoing Reagan's warning about the "evil empire" in 1983, suggested that the "war on terror" was linearly descendant to the Cold War.

Of the trio of evil, Iraq was Bush's priority and the momentum for war built up inexorably in Washington. The main resistance came from Colin Powell at the State Department. Although increasingly marginalized—stuck "in the refrigerator," as he joked ruefully—the secretary of state still tried to argue the case against war and on August 5, 2002, he got a rare chance to do so at length and face-to-face. Powell reeled off his concerns to Bush: "You are going to be the proud owner of 25 million people. You will own all their hopes, aspirations, and problems." He warned that a war in Iraq would "suck the oxygen out of everything." It would define the president's first term. Powell also reminded Bush that Iraq had never been a real democracy, "so you need to understand that this is not going to be a walk in the woods," and he warned against the neo-cons' "go-it-alone" mentality: "It's nice to say we can do it unilaterally, except you can't . . . you need allies."[57]

Powell was largely responsible for persuading the president to use the United Nations—anathema to neo-cons—in the hope that this could force Saddam to abandon his weapons program, or at least lay the basis for an international coalition if it eventually came to war. Here was a fundamental clash between the traditional U.S. policy since 1941 of working with allies and the neo-cons' post–Cold War vision of unilateral power plays. But although Powell slowed the rush to war, he could not stop it.

In September 2002 the administration promulgated a new National Security Strategy, arguing that in the war on terror the United States had to move beyond traditional Cold War policies of containment and deterrence. "The greater the threat, the greater is the risk of inaction—and the more compelling the case for taking anticipatory action to defend ourselves, even if uncertainty remains as to the time and place of the enemy's attack. To forestall or prevent such hostile acts by our adversaries, the United States will, if necessary, act pre-emptively."[58]

Some historians argued that a strategy of unilateralism and preemption had roots deep in U.S. history, going back to the Monroe Doctrine of 1823,[59] but the "Bush Doctrine" of 2002 was certainly a break with America's recent Cold War past and with the multilateralism practiced by the president's own father in his war against Saddam in 1991. Although represented as a statement of considered global policy, the new strategy also served more immediately as justification for preemption against Iraq.

To help build the administration's case, the intelligence agencies were leaned on to massage the fragmentary and ambiguous evidence about Saddam's weapons programs into a clear-cut case for war. "Simply stated, there is no doubt that Saddam Hussein now has weapons of mass destruction," Vice-President Dick Cheney had the effrontery to tell the Veterans of Foreign Wars in August 2002. "There is no doubt he is amassing them to use against our friends, against our allies, and against us. And there is no doubt that his aggressive regional ambitions will lead him into future confrontations with his neighbors—confrontations that will involve both the weapons he has today, and the ones he will continue to develop with his oil wealth."[60]

Cheney, described by a close observer as having "a sense of mission so acute that it drove him to seek power without limit," dismissed fears that the United States was going to get mired in Iraq, as with Vietnam. Bullishly he told one skeptical Republican congressman, "[W]e have great information. They're going to welcome us. It'll be like the American army going through the streets of Paris [in 1944]. They're sitting there ready to form a new government. The people will be so happy with their freedoms that we'll probably back ourselves out of there within a month or so."[61]

The neo-cons were heavily reliant on Ahmad Chalabi, an Iraqi exile whom they were promoting as the future leader of Iraq. Chalabi (who had fled Iraq way back in 1958) and the dubious sources around him were the main conduits for intelligence about Saddam's weaponry and the state of Iraqi opinion. Not everyone in Washington agreed with the neo-con assessment that establishing democracy in Iraq would be a "cakewalk." The State Department and other agencies set out the potential pitfalls in a thirteen-volume report on the future of Iraq, using expertise in postwar planning going back to the democratization of Germany and Japan after 1945. But State was losing this argument as well, because Rumsfeld's office in the Pentagon, backed by Cheney, had seized charge of peacemaking as well as war fighting.

Powell's final humiliation was being set up to make the case for war at the UN. In what he later admitted was a "blot" on his record, he deployed in the most categorical terms what he claimed was the intelligence evidence: "My colleagues, every statement I make today is backed up by sources, solid sources. These are not assertions. What we're giving you are facts and conclusions based on solid intelligence." Powell stated as unvarnished fact that "we know that Saddam Hussein is determined to keep his weapons of mass destruction; he's determined to make more." Powell insisted that the United States could not "take the risk that he will not some day use these weapons at a time and a place and in the manner of his choosing."[62]

What followed is now a familiar story. Finally losing patience with the UN, the United States invaded Iraq on March 20, 2003. Britain's backing was useful militarily and invaluable diplomatically, providing a fig leaf of international support for naked

American power. Baghdad fell in less than three weeks and on May 1 President Bush flew dramatically onto the deck of the aircraft carrier *Abraham Lincoln* (off the California coast) to declare, "Major combat operations in Iraq have ended. In the battle of Iraq, the United States and our allies have prevailed." He thanked the American armed forces: "Because of you, our Nation is more secure. Because of you, the tyrant has fallen, and Iraq is free." Behind him a large banner proudly proclaimed "Mission Accomplished."[63]

Intended as a PR coup, this speech proved one of the biggest gaffes of the Bush presidency. Up to that date, 139 Americans had died in Iraq; by the end of 2006 the U.S. death toll of 3,000 exceeded that of 9/11.[64] Because of Rumsfeld's neglect of postwar planning, the demise of Saddam's regime created a huge power vacuum that was filled by rival insurgent groups that the United States could not control. And without police and security services, the country slid into anarchy. As images of looting filled the TV screens, Rumsfeld blustered defensively, "Stuff happens. It is untidy and freedom's untidy and free people are free to make mistakes and commit crimes and do bad things. They're also free to live their lives and do wonderful things. And that's what's going to happen here."[65]

Prince Bandar bin Sultan, the Saudi ambassador to Washington, warned that Iraq had been run for nearly a half-century by the Baath Party and the military: There was no budding democracy just waiting to bloom. Bandar advised the president to effect regime change slowly and incrementally: "Take the top echelon off because of their involvement and their bloody hands. But keep and maintain the integrity of the institutions. What you should do: announce all of the military report back to their barracks and keep, let's say, the colonels on down." Bandar urged treating the Iraqi intelligence and security services similarly: "Take off the top echelon and keep the second line and let them find those bad guys, because those bad guys will know how to find bad guys."[66]

But that advice was deemed "too Machiavellian" by the White House.[67] Bush stuck to his mantra, proclaimed on the deck of the *Abraham Lincoln*, that once the tyrant had fallen the people would be free. This, after all, was essentially the argument of the Declaration of Independence and Bush was a true believer in the American creed. As he declared in November 2003, "We've witnessed, in little over a generation, the swiftest advance of freedom in the 2,500-year story of democracy." He judged it "no accident that the rise of so many democracies took place in a time when the world's most influential nation was itself a democracy" and claimed that "liberty is both the plan of heaven for humanity and the best hope for progress here on Earth. . . . The advance of freedom is the calling of our time. It is the calling of our country. . . . And we believe that freedom, the freedom we prize, is not for us alone; it is the right and the capacity of all mankind."[68]

Bush remained unrepentant about Iraq, despite the long and bloody war and the failure to find weapons of mass destruction. The shambles did not cost him reelection but his poll ratings plummeted and, from early in his second term, he became a lame duck. A "surge" of troops in 2007 and a reduction in street violence allowed the administration to start withdrawing some U.S. troops; the focus now shifted to finding a plausible exit strategy to wind down a war that had cost more than 4,150 American lives and over $800 billion by the end of Bush's presidency. The lowest credible estimates for Iraqi dead ranged from 100,000 to 150,000 and, even with diminishing violence, the prospects remained remote for a stable democracy in this ethnically and religiously fractured country. Meanwhile, the diversion of resources and attention to Iraq away from the original war to stabilize Afghanistan seriously weakened the prospects of success there.

So, even if liberty is the "plan of heaven for humanity," turning that plan into reality did not prove as straightforward as Rumsfeld, Cheney, Perle, and Wolfowitz had implied. For many Americans the neo-cons had turned out to be con men. Freedom was indeed untidy, "stuff" unfortunately does happen, and Bush's successor would have to pick up the pieces.

ELECTION 2008: SYMBOLS AND SUBSTANCE

No U.S. election is routine but some are more dramatic than others, and 2008 was truly epic: full of sound and fury, signifying—everything. The candidates personified some of the great themes of America's past; the victor transformed the nature of campaigning and broke the biggest taboo of U.S. politics; but he entered the White House amid the gravest crisis of capitalism for seventy-five years.

The Republican candidate, Senator John McCain, was the son and grandson of U.S. admirals and a Vietnam veteran himself. Badly wounded, he spent more than five years as a prisoner of war, often beaten and tortured, yet this experience deepened his faith in his country and its values. "Nothing in life is more liberating than to fight for a cause larger than yourself," he wrote later, "something that encompasses you but is not defined by your existence alone." Of the Vietnam War, McCain said: "We should never let this one mistake, terrible though it was, color our perceptions forever of our country's purpose. We were a good country before Vietnam, and a good country after Vietnam. In all of history, you cannot find a better one."[69] Here was a man who embodied the imperial tradition of modern America—military service for country and cause in a global Cold War.

McCain's running mate was completely different, indeed almost implausible— Sarah Palin, the former beauty queen turned governor of Alaska. Palin was a mother of five, a self-styled "Bible-believing Christian," passionate about moose hunting and a lifelong member of the pro-gun National Rifle Association. Here were heartland American values—evangelical and libertarian—yet expressed with feminine bite. She told the Republican Party convention: "I had the privilege of living most of my life in a small town. I was just your average hockey mom and signed up for the PTA." After the applause died down, she continued: "I love those hockey moms. You know, they say the difference between a hockey mom and a pit bull? Lipstick."[70] Palin became an overnight sensation. She spoke to and for millions of conservative Americans, aroused by the culture wars of the 1980s and '90s against the onward march of secularism and big government.

On the Democratic side, Hillary Clinton stood for a different kind of liberty. Her roots lay in the feminism of the 1970s, as an educated professional woman seeking to carve out her own life as a lawyer. Actually Hillary had put her husband's career before her own but she was never allowed to forget her ill-considered response to a reporter back in 1992: "You know, I suppose I could have stayed home and baked cookies and had teas, but what I decided to do was have a profession, which I entered before my husband was in public life."[71] That line about cookies and teas stuck. To millions of Americans, Hillary became a symbol of assertive feminism, which her high-profile role in Bill's White House seemed to confirm. This was a tradition of liberty very different from that of Sarah Palin—intellectual women's lib, not down-home libertarian.

But 2008 was not to be Hillary's payback for years of standing by her man. Her rival for the Democratic nomination, Barack Obama, aged forty-six, was nearly fourteen years younger, making her seem like a dated member of the baby-boom generation. Obama was African-American, but of a most exotic sort—the son of a black man from Kenya and a white woman from Kansas, raised in Hawaii and Indonesia and trained at Harvard Law School before settling down in Chicago. As he said in March 2008:

> I have brothers, sisters, nieces, nephews, uncles and cousins, of every race and every hue, scattered across three continents, and for as long as I live, I will never forget that in no other country on Earth is my story even possible. It's a story that hasn't made me the most conventional candidate. But it is a story that has seared into my genetic makeup the idea that this nation is more than the sum of its parts—that out of many, we are truly one.[72]

It was this mixed background that made Obama fundamentally different from earlier generations of black activists who had grown up in the South—men such as Reverend Jesse Jackson, one of Martin Luther King's aides, who had bid for the Democratic nomination in the 1980s. The descendants of slaves, they still railed against the racism of white America, whereas Obama's strategy was more inclusive:

> [W]orking together we can move beyond some of our old racial wounds. . . . For the African-American community, that path means embracing the burdens of our past without becoming victims of our past. It means continuing to insist on a full measure of justice in every aspect of American life. But it also means binding our particular grievances—for better health care, and

better schools, and better jobs—to the larger aspirations of all Americans—
the white woman struggling to break the glass ceiling, the white man who's
been laid off, the immigrant trying to feed his family.[73]

Obama's inclusiveness was one reason why he ended up victorious: He proved
more successful at reaching out to all Americans, whereas McCain, Palin, and
Clinton—the martial patriot, the cultural conservative, and the feminist intellectual—
proved much narrower in their appeal. But his victory was also due to path-breaking
use of the Internet, capitalizing on the IT revolution that, as we have seen, had been
transforming American life since the 1980s. His campaign created its own social net-
working site, with help from Chris Hughes, co-founder of Facebook; this attracted
more than 1.5 million members. And Obama raised a record $600 million from more
than 3 million people, many of them donating online. One of the managers of Bill
Clinton's election victory in 1992 spoke admiringly of what Obama had done: "He's
run a campaign where he's used very modern tools, spoken to a new coalition, talked
about new issues, and along the way, he's reinvented the way campaigns are run. Compared to our 1992 campaign, this is like a multinational corporation versus a nonprofit organisation."[74]

A telling tribute—except that by November 2008 the whole U.S. economy
looked like a nonprofit organization, mired in its worst financial crisis since the
early 1930s. This was rooted in problems that had been growing for years. During
the decade since 1997 house prices more than doubled, encouraging many Americans to refinance their mortgages at more advantageous rates on the assumption
that property values would continue to rise. Millions of these people were actually
risky bets because their income levels, spending habits, and other debts made it
unlikely that they would keep up with repayments. To spread the risk, lenders bun-
dled up these "subprime" mortgages with other assets and sold them to banks in
America and beyond. But securitization, as this practice was known, spread the
bad debts through the financial system as a latent and hidden toxin, which was finally released in 2006–2007 when house prices started falling and interest rates
rose. Over a million U.S. mortgage-holders defaulted or got into difficulties with repayments, testing the reserves of even major finance houses and constraining the
lending between banks that was essential for day-to-day liquidity.

In mid-September 2008 the strain became overwhelming. The collapse of the investment bank Lehman Brothers (founded in 1850) represented the largest bankruptcy in U.S. history; other struggling financial giants either were bought up by
stronger rivals (the fate, for instance, of Merrill Lynch and Wachovia) or were bailed
out by the federal government (as with the American International Group—an insurance giant). Washington Mutual, the nation's largest savings bank, was taken
over completely by Uncle Sam. This was, of course, anathema to most Republicans
but the Bush administration, after considerable dithering, concluded that something close to a temporary takeover of much of the banking sector was imperative

to sort out the financial crisis, now overwhelming the stock market as well. The Dow Jones industrial average had fallen nearly 20 percent in a month from mid-September. Almost as alarming was its volatility: The downward slide was punctuated by spasmodic violent rallies, showing the panic and uncertainty among investors.

So U.S. Treasury Secretary Henry Paulson, a former Wall Street banker, proposed a bill giving him up to $700 billion with which to purchase toxic assets from the banks in order to promote liquidity and reassure investors. Initially drafted as almost a blank check to himself, Paulson's plan was heavily criticized on Capitol Hill as crony capitalism. But after being amended to provide greater scrutiny, curbs on executive pay and also sweeteners for the districts of skeptical members of Congress, it was passed into law at the beginning of October. To critics on the right this seemed like socialism on an unimaginable scale; on the left questions were asked about why a cabal of financial gamblers was being rescued by the American people at a cost of over $2,000 per head. There was also a clamor for tighter financial practices after the deregulation of the previous thirty years, but finding a balance between prudent supervision and the constriction of credit would not be easy. Beyond the financial specifics, the collapse seriously damaged America's credibility abroad. Pundit Francis Fukuyama, who in 1991 had trumpeted the Cold War triumph of U.S. capitalism and democracy as signaling "the end of history," was forced to admit: "It's hard to fathom just how badly these features of the American brand have been discredited."[75]

The mess would take years to sort out but its immediate political effect was to tilt the election campaign dramatically toward Obama. In such an alarming economic crisis jeopardizing jobs, savings, and pensions, the cultural symbolism represented by Palin seemed secondary to millions of Americans; TV interviews also found her out of her depth on major issues. McCain, despite his maverick image, was not able to distance himself from a financial meltdown that was widely blamed on a complacent Republican president and his Wall Street allies. Nor did McCain's own conduct inspire confidence, with erratic changes of course (including "suspending" his campaign for a few days to help refine the Paulson plan). By contrast, Obama's concerned calm seemed reassuring. The three presidential debates were not decisive but Obama—simply by holding his own—blunted McCain's charge that his young rival was not up to the job. As the election neared, McCain's organization creaked and crumbled, while Obama's well-organized volunteers got out the vote in key battleground states.

On November 4 Americans went to the polls in record numbers: The turnout of nearly 63 percent, unmatched since the 1960s, quelled talk of political apathy. Obama had energized millions, inspired by his message of hope after an administration that seemed to thrive on a mantra of terror. He won 365 electoral votes—202 more than McCain—and 52.9 percent of the popular vote—a six-point margin. With Democrats strengthening their hold over the House and Senate, this was victory on a par with Johnson's in 1964. That parallel was, of course, double-edged. Four years later, in 1968, Nixon won the White House in a Republican land-slide—a reminder that events can topple the most assured of leaders. Obama would inherit a daunting list of problems, topped by financial crisis and two botched wars. And under the surface lurked fears about whether he, even more than other presidents, would be the target of a crazy gunman.

Yet the essential point was breathtakingly simple: Obama was the first African-American to be elected president of the United States. Some black voters carried photographs of their parents and grandparents into the booths, as belated witnesses to history. America, though conceived in liberty, had been born in original sin. Even when slavery was finally abolished in the 1860s, racism continued to taint American life throughout the twentieth century. So Obama became cast almost as a messiah who would cancel out that sin and redeem the nation's historic promise. Such expectations were impossible but politics at its best is not mere pragmatism. As the president-elect declared in his victory speech: "If there is anyone out there who still doubts that America is a place where all things are possible; who still wonders if the dream of our founders is alive in our time; who still questions the power of our democracy, tonight is your answer."[76]

On January 20, 2009, Obama took the oath of office, addressing over a million jubilant supporters filling the Mall in Washington and billions more around the world. He could have made a triumphalist declaration as America's first black president; he might have spoken, like John Kennedy, about the torch having been passed to a new kind of American. But Obama, the apostle of inclusiveness, had not come to gloat; in any case, he didn't need to. Simply standing behind a podium bearing the seal of the President of the United States was enough. There was just one searing aside about how "a man whose father less than sixty years ago might not have been served at a local restaurant can now stand before you to take a most sacred oath." Whatever may be the fate of Obama and his presidency, merely by being inaugurated he had already booked his place in history.[77]

CONCLUSION

———————

"There has never been a time when the power of America was so necessary; or so misunderstood; or when, except in the most general sense, a study of history provides so little instruction for our present day." Thus British prime minister Tony Blair in July 2003.[1] Obviously I do not share Mr. Blair's belief in the irrelevance of history; if I did, I would not have written this book. Yet his comment is in some ways very American. "The youth of America is their oldest tradition," joked the playwright Oscar Wilde. "It has been going on now for three hundred years."[2] Wilde was writing in 1893; since then another century of youthfulness has passed.

In important respects the United States is actually an old country, with four centuries of European settlement and a native population that goes back thousands of years. America boasts the oldest written constitution in the world, if you leave aside the claims of San Marino—not quite in the same league. And, as I have tried to show throughout this book, its past keeps on reverberating in the present.

So, let me return to the three overarching themes I outlined at the start. How far do empire, liberty, and faith help us understand where the United States has come from and where it is going?

"We're not an imperial power," insisted George W. Bush in 2004. "We are a liberating power."[3] The president was articulating the familiar American self-conception, born of its break from the British empire back in 1776. Yet Thomas Jefferson, the author of the Declaration of Independence, had no problem embracing both those ideas; indeed, he proudly envisaged the United States as an "empire of liberty" or "for liberty."

Let us begin with liberty, the core American value, which was rooted in the colonial experience. Although Spain and France both gained early footholds on the North American continent—Spain in what is now Florida and New Mexico, France pushing down the Mississippi from its base in Canada to create Louisiana— by the late seventeenth century the English were far better established. Their colonies, unlike those of Spain and France, were largely left to themselves by the Crown, preoccupied by its long struggle with Parliament, and the colonists enjoyed much greater liberty than those of New France and New Spain—with extensive land ownership, broad religious freedom, and colonial assemblies based on a wide white male franchise. The English colonies also flourished economically, cashing in on the booming Atlantic trade network, exporting fish and timber from New England and especially tobacco, rice, and cotton from the South.

Yet the relative availability of cheap land meant that there was little incentive to work as wage-labor for others, so the English colonies faced a chronic labor shortage for most of the seventeenth century. Northern family farmers relied on their sons; southern planters used indentured servants who worked off the cost of their passage. But with the flow of migrants tailing off after the end of the English Civil Wars, the colonists turned to the forced labor of African slaves, especially to cultivate the booming cash crops of the South. So, forced black labor became essential to operating an economy that offered unusual liberties to whites. The distinction between freeman and slave became a fundamental dividing line in law and society.

In the last third of the seventeenth century the English colonies became more diverse with the inclusion of the Dutch in New York and the religious and ethnic pluralism of Pennsylvania. New waves of immigrants in the eighteenth century— from Scotland, Ulster, and the German states—made the colonies markedly less English in character, while the growth of cities like Boston, New York, and Philadelphia stimulated an urban consumer society and a thriving local press. These were all signs of a precocious maturity, at odds with a colonial status. The contradiction did not matter as long as London left the colonies alone but, after the Seven Years War eliminated France's rule over Canada and confirmed Britain in a vast North American empire, successive British ministries were determined to make the colonies pay their share.

Initially the protestors against British taxes demanded the rights and liberties of "freeborn Englishmen," especially that of no taxation without representation. But as the struggle intensified and London resorted to force, patriots in Virginia and Massachusetts pushed for full independence—on the grounds that the British Crown had become so tyrannical that the colonists had a right to form their own government. Just as freeman and slave became the great divide in society, so liberty versus tyranny came to define political discourse.

After winning independence in 1783, the founding generation tried to formulate these two polarities into a new ideology. In order to propitiate the South, they turned a blind eye to the existence of slavery, focusing mainly on the construction of a stronger national government that would nevertheless respect local liberties. The war for independence had been essentially a revolt by separate colonies; only the threat from Britain forced a modicum of cooperation. In 1787 the colonies agreed to replace the existing loose alliance of states by a federal government, but only with strict controls on its authority to prevent a repetition of British tyranny.

This government was created for certain specified purposes—notably foreign relations, borrowing and coining money, the promotion of trade, and administration of the vast, unsettled West. The real locus of politics was at the state level; when Jefferson spoke of an "empire" he meant an association of states.

The United States was therefore a reluctant union and, throughout its history, one of the fundamental struggles over liberty has been between the states and the federal government. To solidify support for the new nation, the Founders affirmed basic freedoms—including those of speech, religion, and a nuanced right to bear arms—and this Bill of Rights has been fundamental to subsequent debate. Yet it was not enough to restrain the centrifugal forces at play in the early decades of the republic, when the South, New England, and then the South again talked angrily about possible secession when national politics were not going its way. And when the South finally did break apart in 1861, it resorted to the language of 1776—claiming the right to form a new government because the existing regime had tyrannically overridden local liberties.

The Founders also developed a set of republican values, built on the axiom that government was a necessary evil. Given human ambition, they believed that the basic threat to liberty was the aggrandizing tendency of power. Those in power built up networks of clients—people who lacked economic freedom and were therefore dependent on others. For this reason, the Founders were not democrats: They wanted to reserve the franchise for property owners, those with a stake in society, rather than for the *demos*—the crowd of dependent wage-laborers—and they feared factions, parties, and the corrupting influence of a national debt. Republican values soon collided with the realities of governance—a debt proved essential, factions and parties inevitable—but the specter of corruption and the dread of dependence proved enduring republican principles.

By the 1830s the United States had become a democracy, at least for white males. Married women remained legally dependent and therefore outside politics, though from the 1840s some females campaigned actively to be granted the full range of American liberties. Blacks were entirely beyond the pale: Apart from the small and ambiguous group of "free Negroes" they were slaves and so ineligible for the rights of freemen. Although an abolitionist movement got going in the North and most northerners saw slavery as a moral evil, the focus of most northern animosity toward the South was the power of the slave owners.

The new Republican Party—picking up on the old republican ideology—proclaimed the exclusive right of freemen to settle in the West, not only to contain slavery but also to prevent the slave states from developing a stranglehold on national politics. Slave or free became the defining question for the Union and, when the South broke away in the name of liberty against tyranny, the North denied them that right in the name of America. The bloody Civil War affirmed a new sense of nationhood and resolved some long-standing debates: Slavery was unacceptable in the land of liberty, so, too, was the idea of secession. States could choose to join the Union but, once admitted, they could not break away. Yet the New South contained residues of the Old in the form of structural discrimination against blacks and an entrenched commitment to states' rights.

The growth of federal power was therefore a slow and uneven process—usually stimulated by external challenges like the British in the early years of the republic or by secession in 1861–1865. In the 1930s, the near-total collapse of the banking system and 25 percent unemployment justified a substantial expansion of federal manpower and spending, including the belated construction of a welfare state, and this expansion was accelerated by the demands of World War II and the Cold War. In all these cases, a sense of acute insecurity was required to override the state-centered localism that was the norm of American politics.

As the twentieth century progressed, federal power was utilized more ambitiously to tilt the social balance. During the New Deal, the Democrats rewrote the law to confirm the rights of labor unions to organize and strike. In the 1960s, a new generation of Democrats, responding to black militancy, finally employed federal power to force southern states to enfranchise black Americans and end legal segregation. Civil rights now trumped states' rights, and this gave a cue to other social groups, notably women and also homosexuals. Rights-talk became the dominant discourse of late twentieth-century politics—consumer rights, the right to privacy, prisoners' rights, the right to die.

This reflected a deeper shift in the language of liberty, previously largely a negative concept ("freedom from . . . "—usually from federal interference) but now increasingly positive in scope (freedom to do or to be something). Conservatives still resorted to the traditional discourse of states' rights—for instance, in their battle against school busing—but increasingly they accepted the rights revolution and asserted rights of the right, one might say, in opposition to those espoused by the left. When women claimed the right to abortion in the name of choice, for example, their adversaries affirmed the "right to life" of the unborn child.

Since the 1970s Americans have been so polarized over social issues that Congress has hesitated to legislate in sensitive areas. Into this vacuum has stepped the Supreme Court. In the nineteenth century the Court was usually an ardent defender of states' rights and limited government but, since the 1930s, it has taken a more permissive view of federal power, initially on economic issues but later on racial integration and eventually social mores. In particular, the Court has used the Fourteenth Amendment of 1868 affirming civil rights to articulate a whole range of personal rights; it has even pronounced on such vexed issues as abortion and gun ownership where Congress has stood back. The judicial activism of the Court, liberal or conservative in thrust depending on the current majority, has made it the center of controversy, especially after it adjudicated the 2000 presidential election, yet its enhanced role testifies to the difficulty that democratic politicians have faced in dealing with the rights revolution in an increasingly diverse society.

This diversity will become even greater in the future given recent demographic trends. The U.S. Census Bureau has projected that whites, two-thirds of the population in 2008, will constitute well under half the total by 2050—outnumbered by Hispanics, blacks, Asians, and other non-white groups. Except that, by then, the great divide between white and non-white that has color-coded U.S. history to date will have become meaningless because of intermixing. "Obama is 2050," declared one demographer. "Multiracial. Multi-ethnic."[4]

This anticipated melting pot is still some way off, however. In the meantime, it is the angry fragmentation of modern America that strikes many outside observers. Yet one could adopt a diametrically opposite perspective. What remains remarkable—in global terms—is how such a vast and complex mix of social groups has held together as a polity. The United States, with 300 million people, is far more coherent than other megacountries like India, Indonesia, or Pakistan, let alone the former USSR. China, even larger geographically, is held together by tight central control. The American miracle, often forgotten, is that for all the demonstrable failings of its political system, the federal structure imposed by the Founders on the reluctant states still provides a viable framework for a country the size of a continent, with a population three-fifths the size of the European (so-called) Union. Federalism, American-style, has provided a crucial expansion joint to prevent the political structure from becoming so rigid that it cracks apart. And it is federalism that helps us understand what Jefferson meant by referring to the United States as an *empire* of liberty.

In the nineteenth century the country's expansion westward across North America paralleled the expansion of Russia eastward across central Asia. The United States won the sprawling Ohio territory from Britain as the spoils of war in 1783; similarly Florida was wrested from Spain in the 1810s and the desert West as far as California from Mexico after victory in 1848. The vast Louisiana Purchase was extracted from Napoleon in 1803 after hard bargaining at the negotiating table.

A similar blend of war and diplomacy, of course, built up earlier empires. Nor were Americans unique in the way they treated the aboriginal inhabitants—concluding treaties with them as foreign and equal nations but then driving them off their guaranteed lands as westward expansion became relentless. From Ohio to Oklahoma and on to Wounded Knee.

Yet in several respects the American empire proved very different from the Russian. First of all, there was Jefferson's method for gradually bringing the colonies into the Union. From the start the new territories were granted their own democratic governments; when population crossed a certain numerical threshold the territories could apply for admission as states. Sometimes entry was delayed (Utah), sometimes it was done in a frantic rush (California), but in principle there was a steady escalator to full citizenship. Equally important, the local liberties guaranteed under American federalism gave state governments flexibility to develop economically in their own ways—for instance, when New York gambled on building the Erie Canal. On the other hand, the federal government retained immense powers over the unsettled West: Policy decisions such as land grants for railroads and homesteads for settlers fundamentally shaped western history. Empire and liberty were indeed intertwined.

Until the end of the Civil War the full potential of the West was negated by the struggle over slavery; after 1865, however, the country's new unity allowed industrialization to proceed apace. America's internal empire now spanned a whole continent—and one blessed with rich resources. It lacked the national divisions that frustrated Europe's economic integration and eventually dragged the Old World into two ruinous wars. So railroads and telegraphs drew together a truly national market, while the laissez-faire ethos allowed entrepreneurs to amass vast fortunes and create huge conglomerates without tight government regulation. A single market dominated by big business: Here were the distinctive foundations of America's economic dominance in the twentieth century.

Also important for industrial growth was the largely open door to migrants from Europe, who provided essential labor for America's industrial revolution. Cooped up in a small urbanized country this influx could have proved socially and politically explosive but that was not the American experience. In the United States the ethnic diversity of the immigrants defused class consciousness, the democratic franchise reduced the allure of political extremism, and the chance to move on from the slums to the suburbs, from east-coast cities into the American hinterland, gave immigrants, or at least their children, the prospect of advancement. The empire of liberty helped head off the challenge of socialism, which polarized European politics for much of the twentieth century.

So the United States was intrinsically an empire, albeit of a very distinctive character. As for *possessing* an empire, the temptation to seize and rule overseas colonies was relatively short lived. The Philippines and Hawaii, acquired during the jingoistic Spanish-American war of 1898, proved the exceptions, not the rule—though both of these possessions ensured that in 1941 the United States became the target of a Japanese attack that might have been avoided if the country had not been a Pacific power. In the early twentieth century the United States chose to extend its global reach through finance, commerce, and cultural aggrandizement—what we would now call "soft" power. But during the Cold War it developed a military nexus that now numbers some 750 bases in more than 130 countries and its defense spending amounts to over two-fifths of the world's total.[5] In some regions, particularly western Europe, this military presence has been by mutual agreement— "empire by invitation" or "hegemony by consent."[6] But elsewhere—for instance, in Central America or Indochina—the invitees have been, at most, a segment of the political elite, a group of imperial clients. At home the demands of the armed forces became a major factor in the domestic economy, prompting President Eisenhower's warning in 1961 about the influence of the military-industrial complex.

Major technological innovations such as transistors and computers would not have taken off without Uncle Sam as both investor and customer.

I therefore think it makes more sense to see the United States on a continuum with earlier imperial powers than to accept the doctrines of American exceptionalism—the idea that the United States is both historically unique and morally exemplary. On the other hand, that idea has shaped the form of America's power projection over-seas. Anti-imperialists were a powerful brake during the Spanish-American conflict over Cuba in 1898; in the twentieth century there was robust opposition to U.S. involvement in both world wars. Reiterating the warnings of Washington and Jefferson about entangling alliances, the proponents of hemisphere defense in 1917 and especially in 1941 warned that fighting in the battles of the Old World could undermine the liberties of the New. So the architects of America's Cold War strategy were at pains to justify overseas commitments as a way to contain Soviet imperialism rather than to create an American empire. The old script of liberty versus tyranny was adapted for the international stage, with the United States becoming the champion of the free market and the leader of the free world.

Yet in the post–Cold War world, the empire of liberty has metamorphosed again—from an "empire of production" to an "empire of consumption."[7] At the beginning of the twentieth century the United States displaced Britain as the preeminent industrial and financial power and this economic predominance made it the "arsenal of democracy" in World War II and the Cold War. Since the 1980s, however, the United States has run persistent deficits on its federal budget and on its payments with the rest of the world. The national debt, $3 trillion in 1990 after the profligacy of the Reagan presidency, exceeded the $10 trillion mark in the autumn of 2008. America also became a society of debtors: The subprime mortgage crisis that brought down the U.S. banking system in 2008 was symptomatic of a lifestyle in which consumption depended on credit. Since the beginning of the new century, household debt had doubled to a staggering $14 trillion; the average American home possesses thirteen credit cards. These soaring debts and deficits have been sustained only because of the willingness of other nations to invest in the United States—rather than the other way around as for most of the previous century.[8]

What does all this suggest for the future? The negative interpretation is that when an empire becomes a debtors' prison, it is definitely in decline. This seems to be the "lesson" of history from ancient Rome, Hapsburg Spain, and Great Britain since 1945 and it sounds especially minatory during a global economic recession. The optimistic interpretation is that such consumption and indebtedness reflect the increasingly open nature of the world economy: As foreigners invest in the United States, so American business is outsourcing employment and moving into services and IT. In other words, this is empire liberated by globalization rather than crippled with debt. Only time will tell which of these assessments is right but, in the meantime, Americans in 2009 could reasonably ask whether Islamic terrorists or

Wall Street fat cats had posed a bigger threat to their daily lives during the Bush-Cheney presidency.

The entangled stories of empire and liberty throw light on the American experience, but I have also argued that they need to be understood by reference to a third theme—faith. By this I mean both religious faith and, very much related, faith in the nation itself.

The colonies were predominantly Protestant, often fiercely so. The vehement anti-popery that characterized popular Protestantism in Britain was replicated across the Atlantic, from the embattled Puritanism of Massachusetts in the 1630s to New England's antipathy toward French Canada in the 1750s. Yet the Founders of the new nation balanced religious faith with a commitment to religious liberty: no established church and complete freedom of belief and worship for people of any faith or none at all. Legislation to this effect passed in individual states during the Revolutionary era was capped by the first article in the Bill of Rights, which, in Jefferson's famous phrase, built "a wall of separation between church and State."[9]

Here was a fundamental, enduring tension—between the principle of a secular state and the ideal of a godly people. A succession of evangelical revivals pulsated through America from the 1740s to the mid-nineteenth century, confirming American Protestantism as a Bible-based faith that demanded individual commitment and conversion. Evangelicalism spawned new denominations such as the Baptists and Methodists but, even more important, a profusion of sects that helped give American Protestantism its distinctively democratic ethos.

A religion of conversion implied an either/or worldview—good versus evil, the saved or the damned—and this inspired the crusades to redeem society that were also characteristic of nineteenth-century Protestant America. Drink was one demon—linked in the Protestant mind with papists—but the biggest crusade for northern radicals was eradicating slavery from the land of liberty. The eventual triumph of the Union in 1865 was taken as proof of what abolitionist William Lloyd Garrison hailed as "the resistless might of the Eternal Providence."[10] Although religion was used to offer a paternalist defense of slave-owning, nineteenth-century evangelicalism was predominantly a force for change and liberalization.

Evangelical Protestant values were, however, tested as never before in America's new urban, industrial age. The mass of immigrants from southern and eastern Europe were one threat—with Catholics still a particular bugbear, as the 1928 election showed, because of their perceived looseness about drink and the Sabbath (too much liberty) and their authoritarian hierarchy (not enough liberty). The mounting tide of secularism inspired religious conservatives to rally around the "fundamentals" of their biblical faith against secular values and also liberal Christianity. Moreover, Darwinism called into question the easy assumption that religion and science were simply different facets of a unified cosmic order. The notorious Scopes Trial of 1925 helped stereotype fundamentalism as a small-town, small-minded faith and drove evangelical Protestantism out of national politics for a half-century.

At the same time, however, the redemptive impulse was being elevated onto the international stage. It was evident in the movement for foreign missions, in which American funds and people (many of them women) played a disproportionate role. In 1900 there were maybe 5,000 American missionaries abroad; by the late 1970s ten times that number, and more than 100,000 today.[11] The redemptive theme was even more evident in the rhetoric of U.S. foreign policy—the global mission articulated by Woodrow Wilson to "make the world safe for democracy" and then the Manichean struggles against Nazism and communism. In fact, America's imperial outreach has been consistently justified through the language of faith as well as liberty. Communism was depicted as a godless society, an "evil" empire; it threatened to impose nothing less than "slavery" on subject nations, which was why containment and détente were always second-best for millions of Americans. Like Lincoln speaking of the United States in the 1850s, they did not believe it possible for the world to remain half-slave, half-free. This conception of foreign policy as an apocalyptic struggle reemerged after 9/11 as the Bush administration discerned new global threats from Islamic extremism and from an "axis of evil" brandishing weapons of mass destruction.

This self-image of the United States as a "Crusader State called to save the world"[12] was rooted in the evangelical worldview but usually eschewed overtly religious language. In domestic politics, however, that was not the case. Martin Luther King and his lieutenants drew repeatedly on biblical concepts and phrases to inspire blacks in the fight against discrimination—likening them to the children of Israel struggling from Egyptian bondage into the Promised Land. Although black radicals went on to embrace Marxist models, the mainstream southern civil rights movement was rooted in the evangelical tradition.

But so, too, in a different way, was the conservative backlash against the 1960s. White evangelicals in the South had kept to themselves since the 1920s, but the sexual revolution—the Pill, abortion, gay rights—seemed to portend a breakdown of family values. This in turn was taken to portend the wholesale secularization of society—an issue symbolized in the Supreme Court's ban (in the name of religious liberty) on prayer and Bible reading in schools. In a sense the South was being "Americanized," its culture eroded by the values of the rest of the nation. But in another way, parts of America were being "southernized" by the exodus of millions of people out of the South since World War II, particularly to the Midwest and California, providing grassroots support for Reagan in 1980. Southern preachers also played a disproportionate role in leading organizations such as the Moral Majority. In contrast with the religious dynamics of the nineteenth century, evangelicalism had now become a deeply conservative force in American politics and, again in contrast with the past, it was no longer fervently anti-papist because Catholics featured in the new religious right, both as followers and as leaders such as Phyllis Schlafly.

The recent "culture wars" suggest a deep polarization of American society, a struggle over the extent to which the United States should be a secular society or a Christian nation. Optimistic commentators note that most of the religious right still adhere to the Founders' radical principle of religious freedom, the separation of church and state. But pessimists fear that "the level of religious conflict appears to be rising and the historically unprecedented extent of religious freedom may be in some danger."[13] This argument is open and unresolved.

Historically, America has tended to fight its culture wars most fiercely during times of prosperity; economic recession concentrates hearts and minds on material issues. Yet the current polarization is as profound as at any time in the past. One might hazard a guess that here, too, Obama looks more like the American future than, say, Sarah Palin, but whether the recent evangelical revival is a durable trend or a last fling before European-style secularization really sets in, only time will tell. The outcome will also have implications for America's global role. History suggests that the decline of empires stems from loss of faith in the imperial mission as much as from financial and economic crisis. And America's distinctive empire has always been built on faith, not just power.

All this is, of course, a personal view of America's past. Other writers might privilege different themes but, to my mind, liberty, empire, and faith seem particularly illuminating. None is exclusive: I have tried to show how each is interwoven with the others and also shot through with paradox—the empire forged by anti-imperialists, the land of liberty that rested on slavery, the secular state energized by godly ambition. The result is a history that is rarely simple, often messy, and sometimes appalling; yet also full of surprises, frequently epic, and on occasion wonderfully uplifting. Above all, it's a history that matters if we want to get a bearing on where this youthful old country may be going in the future.

SUGGESTIONS FOR
FURTHER READING

The following abbreviations have been employed throughout the Further Reading and Notes sections:

AHR	*American Historical Review*
CUP	Cambridge University Press
CWH	*Civil War History*
DH	*Diplomatic History*
FRUS	U.S. Department of State, *Foreign Relations of the United States* (multivolumes, Washington, DC: U.S. Government Printing Office, 1861–)
JAH	*Journal of American History*
JER	*Journal of the Early Republic*
OUP	Oxford University Press
PPPUS	Public Papers of the Presidents of the United States—website at http://www.presidency.ucsb.edu/ws/
UNC	University of North Carolina
WMQ	*William and Mary Quarterly*

General

Other general histories include Hugh Brogan, *The Penguin History of the USA* 2nd ed. (London: Penguin, 2001)—a vivid and readable personal view—and Maldwyn A. Jones, *The Limits of Liberty: American History, 1607–1992* 2nd ed. (Oxford: OUP, 1995)—a superb textbook.

On some specific themes, see Michael P. Conzen, ed., *The Making of the American Landscape* (Boston: Unwin Hyman, 1990), David B. Danbom, *Born in the Country: A History of Rural America* (Baltimore: Johns Hopkins University Press, 1995), Mark A. Noll, *The Old Religion in a New World: The History of North American Christianity* (Grand Rapids, MI.: William B. Eerdmans, 2002), Elizabeth Frost and Kathryn Cullen-DuPont, *Women's Suffrage in America: An Eyewitness History* (New York: Facts on File, 1992), and Clyde A. Milner II, Carol A. O'Connor, and Martha A. Sandweiss, eds., *The Oxford*

History of the American West (New York: OUP, 1994). James M. McPherson, *"To the Best of My Ability": The American Presidents* (London: DK Publishing, 2004), offers vivid, illustrated vignettes, and Stephen Graubard, *The Presidents: The Transformation of the American Presidency from Theodore Roosevelt to George W. Bush* (London: Penguin, 2006), provides an incisive analysis of the twentieth century. Thomas G. Paterson et al., *American Foreign Relations: A History* (2 vols., 6th ed., New York: Wadsworth Publishing, 2004), is a readable textbook. For encyclopedic guidance on individual topics and themes see Peter J. Parish, ed., *A Reader's Guide to American History* (London: Fitzroy Dearborn, 1997).

1: Natives and Europeans

Alice Beck Kehoe, *America Before the European Invasions* (London: Longman, 2002), is a useful overview of native societies. For a lively and informed account of the scholarly debates see Charles C. Mann, *Ancient Americans: Rewriting the History of the New World* (London: Granta, 2005)—published in the United States as *1491: New Revelations of the Americas Before Columbus*. John D. Daniels, "The Indian Population of North America in 1492," *WMQ*, 3rd series, 49 (1992), pp. 298–320, provides a judicious guide to an intemperate but vital debate. See also Linda A. Newson, "The Demographic Collapse of Native Peoples of the Americas, 1492–1650," in Warwick Bray, ed., *The Meeting of Two Worlds: Europe and the Americas, 1492–1650* (Oxford: OUP, 1993), pp. 247–288, and, on the epidemics, Noble D. Cook, *Born to Die: Disease and New World Conquest, 1492–1650* (Cambridge: CUP, 1998).

On the colonial era in general, Alan Taylor, *American Colonies: The Settling of North America* (New York: Penguin, 2001), is a superb introduction, covering the various ethnic groups and making Indians and slaves central features of his narrative. J. H. Elliott, *Empires of the Atlantic World: Britain and Spain in America, 1492–1830* (London: Yale University Press, 2006), is a magisterial exercise in comparative history, ranging over all aspects of society and explaining the contrasting outcomes of British and American imperialism in the New World. See also Anthony Pagden, *Lords of All the World: Ideologies of Empire in Spain, Britain and France, c. 1500 to c. 1800* (New Haven: Yale University Press, 1995).

On the major colonial powers: David J. Weber, *The Spanish Frontier in North America* (New Haven: Yale University Press, 1992), is an informed, lucid, and lavishly illustrated overview of Spanish imperialism, with extensive notes and bibliography. See also his conceptual and historiographical article "Turner, the 'Boltonians,' and the Borderlands," *AHR*, 91 (1986), pp. 66–81. On the French, the best recent study is Gilles Havard and Cécile Vidal, *Histoire de l'Amérique Française* (Paris: Flammarion, 2003), but see also Richard White, *The Middle Ground: Indians, Empires, and Republics in the Great Lakes Region, 1660–1815* (Cambridge: CUP, 1991), where French colonialism is placed well in context and Turner's concept of the frontier is refined in the influential concept of the "middle ground." On the latter see also the forum in *WMQ*, 63/1 (Jan. 2006).

David Beers Quinn, ed., *New American World: A Documentary History of North America to 1612* (5 vols., New York: Arno Press, 1979), is an excellent collection of extracts from early travelers and explorers—Spanish, French, and English. Many such sources are also available in full on the Web: See, for instance, *American Journeys: Eyewitness Accounts of Early American Exploration and Settlement*—a digital library developed by the Wisconsin State Historical Society and others at http://www.americanjourneys.org/index.asp.

2: Empire and Liberties

Allan Kulikoff, *Tobacco and Slaves: The Development of Southern Cultures in the Chesa- peake, 1680–1800* (Chapel Hill: UNC Press, 1986), and Peter H. Wood, *Black Majority: Ne- groes in Colonial South Carolina from 1670 Through the Stono Rebellion* (New York: Alfred A. Knopf, 1974), remain central. For a short introduction to slavery see Betty Wood, *The Origins of American Slavery: Freedom and Bondage in the English Colonies* (New York: Hill & Wang, 1997), but the fundamental work is still Winthrop Jordan, *White over Black: Amer- ican Attitudes Toward the Negro, 1550–1812* (Baltimore: Pelican, 1969).

On the Puritan migration see Virginia DeJohn Anderson, *New England's Generation: The Great Migration and the Formation of Society and Culture in the Seventeenth Century* (Cambridge, CUP, 1991). The complexity and variety of Puritanism is stressed by David D. Hall, "Narrating Puritanism," in Harry S. Stout and D. G. Hart, eds., *New Directions in American Religious History* (New York: OUP, 1997), pp. 51–83. For women's experience see Laurel Thatcher Ulrich, *Good Wives: Image and Reality in the Lives of Women in Northern New England, 1650–1750* (New York: Alfred A. Knopf, 1982), and, for a suggestive case study of economic patterns, Daniel Vickers, *Farmers and Fishermen: Two Centuries of Work in Essex County, Massachusetts, 1630–1850* (Chapel Hill: UNC Press, 1994). On the theme of religious liberty consult Thomas J. Curry, *The First Freedoms: Church and State in America to the Passage of the First Amendment* (New York: OUP, 1986).

For the Dutch era see Jaap Jacobs, *New Netherland: A Dutch Colony in Seventeenth-Cen- tury America* (Leiden: Brill, 2005). Useful studies of New York and the Dutch legacy in- clude Robert C. Ritchie, *The Duke's Province: A Study of New York Politics and Society, 1664–1691* (Chapel Hill: UNC Press, 1977). On "ethnicization" and "Anglicization" see Joyce D. Goodfriend, *Before the Melting Pot: Society and Culture in Colonial New York City, 1664– 1730* (Princeton, NJ: Princeton University Press, 1992). The most recent study of Penn is Mary K. Geiter, *William Penn* (London: Longman, 2000)—a revisionist work that proba- bly underplays the genuine religious elements of Penn's politics. There are useful essays on the Dutch and Germans and on the "Scots-Irish" in Bernard Bailyn and Philip D. Morgan, eds., *Strangers Within the Realm: Cultural Margins of the First British Empire* (Chapel Hill: UNC Press, 1991). See also Aaron Spencer Fogleman, *Hopeful Journeys: German Immigra- tion, Settlement and Political Culture in Colonial America, 1717–1775* (Philadelphia: Uni- versity of Pennsylvania Press, 1996), and, generally, Wayne Bodle, "Themes and Directions in Middle Colonies Historiography, 1980–1994," *WMQ*, 51 (1994), pp. 355–388.

Debate on the Great Awakening was reopened by Jon Butler, "Enthusiasm Described and Decried: The Great Awakening as Interpretive Fiction," *JAH*, 69 (1982), pp. 305–325. For balanced assessments of the historiography see Allen C. Guelzo, "God's Designs: The Literature of the Colonial Revivals of Religion, 1735–1760," and Gordon S. Wood, "Reli- gion and the American Revolution," both in Harry S. Stout and D. G. Hart, eds., *New Di- rections in American Religious History* (New York: OUP, 1997), pp. 141–172 and 173–205. A valuable reinterpretation is Frank Lambert, *Inventing the "Great Awakening"* (Princeton, NJ: Princeton University Press, 1999). For a good short biography of Whitefield, consult Harry S. Stout, *Divine Dramatist: George Whitefield and the Rise of Modern Evangelicalism* (Grand Rapids, MI: William B. Eerdmans, 1991). On black evangelicalism see Sylvia Frey and Betty Wood, *Come Shouting to Zion: African-American Protestantism in the American South and British Caribbean to 1830* (Chapel Hill: UNC Press, 1998).

Fred Anderson, *Crucible of War: The Seven Years War and the Fate of Empire in British North America, 1754–1766* (London: Faber and Faber, 2000), is the standard study. For a revisionist, often caustic, view from the Indian side see Francis Jennings, *Empire of Fortune: Crowns, Colonies, and Tribes in the Seven Years War in America* (New York: W. W. Norton, 1988). Frank W. Brecher, *Losing a Continent: France's North American Policy, 1753–1763* (Westport, CN: Greenwood Press, 1998), traces the story from the vantage point of the defeated. Noel St. John Williams, *Redcoats Along the Hudson: The Struggle for British North America, 1754–1763* (London: Brassey's, 1997), is a readable military history, with a good deal on soldier life, while Fred Anderson, *A People's Army: Massachusetts Soldiers and Society in the Seven Years War* (Chapel Hill: UNC Press, 1984), is a case study of the colonial experience of war.

3: Independence and Republicanism

Gordon S. Wood, *The American Revolution: A History* (London: Phoenix, 2003), is short and celebratory. For a fuller account, see Robert Middlekauf, *The Glorious Cause: The American Revolution, 1763–1789* 2nd ed. (Oxford: OUP, 2005). A more critical view of the Revolutionary era, emphasizing its casualties, is offered by Gary B. Nash, *The Unknown American Revolution: The Unruly Birth of Democracy and the Struggle to Create America* (London: Pimlico, 2007). Richard B. Morris, *The Forging of the Union, 1781–1789* (New York: Harper & Row, 1987), remains a masterly overview of the "critical decade."

On the Founders see the studies by Joseph J. Ellis, especially *American Sphinx: The Character of Thomas Jefferson* (New York: Alfred A. Knopf, 1997), *His Excellency: George Washington* (New York: Vintage Books, 2005), and *Founding Brothers: The Revolutionary Generation* (New York: Vintage Books, 2000). On the meaning of 1776 see the contrasting readings by Gary Wills, *Inventing America: Jefferson's Declaration of Independence* (New York: Doubleday, 1978), Pauline Maier, *American Scripture, Making the Declaration of Independence* (New York: Vintage Books, 1998), and David Armitage, *The Declaration of Independence: A Global History* (Cambridge, MA: Harvard University Press, 2007). On the Constitution consult Jack N. Rakove, *Original Meanings: Politics and Ideas in the Making of the Constitution* (New York: Vintage Books, 1997). On the architecture of the new nation see C. M. Harris, "Washington's Gamble, L'Enfant's Dream: Politics, Design and the Founding of the National Capital," *WMQ*, 56 (1999), pp. 527–564. For the ideology of republicanism see Daniel T. Rodgers, "Republicanism: The Career of a Concept," *JAH*, 79 (1992), pp. 11–38, and the articles edited by Joyce Appleby in the *American Quarterly*, 37/4 (1985), special issue: "Republicanism in the History and Historiography of the United States."

4: Liberty and Security

On Jefferson's vision for America see Robert W. Tucker and David C. Hendrickson, *Empire of Liberty: The Statecraft of Thomas Jefferson* (New York: OUP, 1990), and Peter S. Onuf, *Jefferson's Empire: The Language of American Nationhood* (Charlottesville: University of Virginia Press, 2000). Karl-Friedrich Walling, *Republican Empire: Alexander Hamilton on War and Free Government* (Lawrence: University Press of Kansas, 1999), offers a spirited if not convincing defense of Hamilton against charges of Bonapartism. Andro Linklater, *Measuring America* (London: HarperCollins, 2003), is a readable, if unreferenced, survey of how the West was won, mapped, and settled. On the War of 1812, the standard account remains J.C.A. Stagg, *Mr. Madison's War: Politics, Diplomacy, and Warfare in the Early American Republic, 1783–1830* (Princeton, NJ: Princeton University Press, 1983).

On the female experience, two pioneering books remain central: Mary Beth Norton, *Liberty's Daughters: The Revolutionary Experience of American Women* (Ithaca, NY: Cornell University Press, 1980), and Linda K. Kerber, *Women of the Republic: Intellect and Ideology in Revolutionary America* (Chapel Hill: UNC Press, 1980). See also Judith Apter Klinghoffer and Lois Elkis, "'The Petticoat Electors': Women's Suffrage in New Jersey, 1776–1807," *JER*, 12 (1992), pp. 159–193. On blacks, Benjamin Quarles, *The Negro in the American Revolution* (Chapel Hill: UNC Press, 1961), remains basic, but also see Ira Berlin, *Many Thousands Gone: The First Two Centuries of Slavery in North America* (Cambridge, MA: Harvard University Press, 1998). For an overview on the other "victims" of the Revolutionary era, consult Colin Calloway, *The Revolution in Indian Country: Crisis and Diversity in Native American Communities* (Cambridge: CUP, 1995).

5: East and West

For an informed and readable overview of the politics of the period, based on recent scholarship, consult Sean Wilentz, *The Rise of American Democracy: Jefferson to Lincoln* (New York: W. W. Norton, 2005). Daniel Walker Howe, *What Hath God Wrought: The Transformation of America, 1815–1848* (New York: OUP, 2007), charts the country's prodigious development and celebrates the vision of the Whigs. H. W. Brands, *Andrew Jackson: His Life and Times* (New York: Anchor Books, 2005), offers a lively biography. On economic and social change both George Taylor Rogers, *The Transportation Revolution, 1815–1860* (New York: Rinehart & Co., 1951), and Ray Allen Billington, *Westward Expansion: A History of the American Frontier* 4th ed., (New York: Macmillan, 1974), remain essential.

On evangelicalism, see Nathan O. Hatch, *The Democratization of American Christianity* (New Haven, CT: Yale University Press, 1989), and Richard J. Carwardine, *Evangelicals and Politics in Antebellum America* (New Haven, CT: Yale University Press, 1993). Anthony F. C. Wallace, *The Long Bitter Trail: Andrew Jackson and the Indians* (New York: Hill & Wang, 1993), provides a good introduction to this sad saga. There are stimulating reevaluations of the frontier myth in Richard Slotkin, *Regeneration Through Violence: The Mythology of the American Frontier* (Middletown, CT: Wesleyan University Press, 1973), and David E. Nye, *America as Second Creation: Technology and Narratives of New Beginnings* (Cambridge, MA: MIT Press, 2003).

6: Slave or Free?

On 1850, the standard account is still Holman Hamilton, *Prologue to Conflict: The Crisis and Compromise of 1850* (Lexington: University Press of Kentucky, 1964), but see also the lively recent narrative by John C. Waugh, *On the Brink of Civil War: The Compromise of 1850 and How It Changed the Course of American History* (Wilmington, DE: Scholarly Resources, 2003). Michael F. Holt has distilled the wisdom of several vast books about the politics of the 1840s and 1850s into an incisive little overview: *The Fate of Their Country: Politicians, Slavery Extension, and the Coming of the Civil War* (New York: Hill & Wang, 2005). David M. Potter, with Don Fehrenbacher, *The Impending Crisis, 1848–1861* (New York: Harper Torchbooks, 1976), remains a classic.

On the South there are good introductions in Bruce Collins, *White Society in the Antebellum South* (London: Longman, 1985), and Eugene D. Genovese, *Roll, Jordan, Roll: The World the Slaves Made* (New York: Random House, 1974)—despite the author's since discarded Marxist framework. See also John B. Boles and Evelyn Thomas Nolen, eds., *Interpreting Southern History: Historiographical Essays in Honor of Sanford W. Higginbotham*

(Baton Rouge: Louisiana State University Press, 1987). On the contemporary debate about slavery and the "slave power" see Eric Foner, *Free Soil, Free Labor, Free Men: The Ideology of the Republican Party Before the Civil War* (New York: OUP, 1970), David Brion Davis, *The Slave Power Conspiracy and the Paranoid Style* (Baton Rouge: Louisiana State University Press, 1969), and David F. Ericson, *The Debate over Slavery: Antislavery and Proslavery Liberalism in Antebellum America* (New York: New York University Press, 2000).

Among the biographies of principal politicians, mention should be made of Robert W. Johannsen, *Stephen A. Douglas* (New York: OUP, 1973), David Herbert Donald, *Lincoln* (New York: Simon & Schuster, 1995)—a detailed biography—and the more analytical Richard Carwardine, *Lincoln: A Life of Purpose and Power* (New York: Random House, 2006). For a magisterial survey of the culture of the Old South, see Michael O'Brien, *Conjectures of Order: Intellectual Life in the American South, 1810–1860* (2 vols., Chapel Hill: UNC Press, 2004).

7: North and South

For an outstanding overview of the conflict, see James M. McPherson, *Battle Cry of Freedom: The American Civil War* (London: Penguin, 1990). The story is told vividly in Geoffrey C. Ward, with Ric Burns and Ken Burns, *The Civil War: An Illustrated History* (New York: Alfred A. Knopf, 1990). For the experience of combat and death see Gerald F. Linderman, *Embattled Courage: The Experience of Combat in the American Civil War* (New York: The Free Press, 1989), and Drew Gilpin Faust, *The Republic of Suffering: Death and the American Civil War* (New York: Alfred A. Knopf, 2008).

On the home front, Philip Shaw Paludan, *"A People's Contest": The Union and the Civil War, 1861–1865* (New York: Harper & Row, 1988), is very useful. For the human dimension see David Williams, *A People's History of the Civil War: Struggles for the Meaning of Freedom* (New York: The New Press, 2005), and the rich documentation in Henry Steele Commager and Erik Bruun, eds., *The Civil War Archive: The History of the Civil War in Documents* 2nd ed. (New York: Black Dog & Leventhal, 2000). Doris Kearns Goodwin, *Team of Rivals: The Political Genius of Abraham Lincoln* (New York: Simon & Schuster, 2005), has become a modern classic.

8: White and Black

On the impact of the war there are important contributions by Mark E. Neely, Jr., "Was the Civil War a Total War?" *CWH*, 37 (1991), pp. 5–28, Paul F. Paskoff, "Measures of War: A Quantitative Examination of the Civil War's Destructiveness in the Confederacy," *CWH*, 64 (2008), pp. 35–62, and Roger L. Ransom and Richard Sutch, *One Kind of Freedom: The Economic Consequences of Emancipation* 2nd ed. (New York: CUP, 2001). The best overall study of Reconstruction remains Eric Foner, *Reconstruction: America's Unfinished Revolution, 1863–1877* (New York: Harper & Row, 1988). See also Ira Berlin and Barbara J. Fields et al., *Slaves No More: Three Essays on Emancipation and the Civil War* (New York: CUP, 1992).

Most of the literature on the New South still engages with the arguments of C. Vann Woodward, especially his *Origins of the New South, 1877–1913* (Baton Rouge: Louisiana State University Press, 1951) and *The Strange Career of Jim Crow* (New York: OUP, 1955). For a useful update on the debates see Howard N. Rabinowitz, *The First New South, 1865–1920* (Arlington Heights, Ill.: Harlan Davidson, 1992), and John Herbert Roper, ed., *C.*

Vann Woodward: A Southern Historian and His Critics (Athens: University of Georgia Press, 1997). Among important recent monographs are Grace Elizabeth Hale, *Making Whiteness: The Culture of Segregation in the South, 1890–1940* (New York: Pantheon, 1998), and Michael Perman, *Struggle for Mastery: Disfranchisement in the South, 1888–1908* (Chapel Hill: UNC Press, 2001).

9: Capital and Labor

Glenn Porter, *The Rise of Big Business, 1860–1920* 2nd ed. (Arlington Heights, Ill.: Harlan Davidson, 1992), offers a short, clear introduction, although Samuel P. Hays, *The Response to Industrialism, 1885–1914* (Chicago: University of Chicago Press, 1957), remains useful. Among biographies of the tycoons see Ron Chernow, *Titan: The Life of John D. Rockefeller, Sr.* (Boston: Little, Brown, 1998), and David Nasaw, *Andrew Carnegie* (New York: Penguin, 2006). On management, the classic study is Alfred D. Chandler, Jr., *The Visible Hand: The Managerial Revolution in American Business* (Cambridge, MA: Harvard University Press, 1977); for a social history of the managers see Olivier Zunz, *Making America Corporate, 1870–1920* (Chicago: University of Chicago Press, 1990).

Richard H. Heindel, *The American Impact on Great Britain, 1898–1914: A Study of the United States in World History* (Philadelphia: University of Pennsylvania Press, 1940), covers a range of economic, social, and cultural themes not examined elsewhere. For an example of the British literature about the "American invasion," read W. T. Stead, *The Americanisation of the World, or The Trend of the Twentieth Century* (London: Review of Reviews, 1902).

Sarah Bradford Landau and Carl W. Condit, *Rise of the New York Skyscraper, 1865–1913* (New Haven, CT: Yale University Press, 1996), is an erudite, beautifully illustrated study of the buildings, the technology, and the public debate. On Sullivan the best biography is Robert Twombly, *Louis Sullivan: His Life and Work* (Chicago: University of Chicago Press, 1987).

Maldwyn Allen Jones, *American Immigration* (Chicago: University of Chicago Press, 1960), remains the best short study of this theme, but see also Roger Daniels, *Coming to America: A History of Immigration and Ethnicity in American Life* (New York: Harper Perennial, 2002), and Stephan Thernstrom, ed., *Harvard Encyclopedia of American Ethnic Groups* (Cambridge, MA: Harvard University Press, 1980). On attitudes to the immigrant, John Higham, *Strangers in the Land: Patterns of American Nativism, 1860–1925* (New Brunswick, NJ: Rutgers University Press, 1955), remains a classic. For more recent discussion see the articles by Russell A. Kazal, "Revisiting Assimilation: The Rise, Fall, and Reappraisal of a Concept in American Ethnic History," *AHR*, 100 (1995), pp. 437–471, Gary Gerstle, "Liberty, Coercion, and the Making of Americans," *JAH*, 84 (1997), pp. 524–558, and David Montgomery, "Racism, Immigrants, and Political Reform," *JAH*, 87 (2001), pp. 1253–1274.

10: Reform and Expansion

For recent overviews see Lewis L. Gould, *America in the Progressive Era, 1890–1914* (Harlow: Longman, 2001), Michael McGerr, *A Fierce Discontent: The Rise and Fall of the Progressive Movement in America, 1870–1920* (New York: The Free Press, 2003), and Maureen A. Flanagan, *America Reformed: Progressives and Progressivism, 1890s–1920s* (New York: OUP, 2007). On the politics of reform consult Lewis L. Gould, *Reform and Regulation: American Politics, 1900–1916* (New York: John Wiley & Sons, 1978), and, on T.R., Edmund Morris, *Theodore Rex* (London: HarperCollins, 2002).

Stephen Skowronek, *Building a New American State: The Expansion of National Administrative Capacities, 1877–1920* (New York: CUP, 1982), opens up the broader issues; likewise Richard Jensen, "Democracy, Republicanism and Efficiency: The Values of American Politics, 1885–1930," in Byron Shafer and Anthony Badger, eds., *Contesting Democracy: Substance and Structure in American Political History, 1775–2000* (Lawrence: University Press of Kansas, 2001), pp. 149–180.

On recreation see Douglas Brinkley, *Wheels for the World: Henry Ford, His Company, and a Century of Progress, 1903–2003* (New York: Viking, 2003), and Edward White, *Creating the National Pastime: Baseball Transforms Itself, 1903–1953* (Princeton, NJ: Princeton University Press, 1996), and on religion, George M. Marsden, *Fundamentalism and American Culture* 2nd ed. (Oxford: OUP, 2006).

On the West, Anne M. Butler and Michael J. Lansing, *The American West: A Concise History* (Oxford: Blackwell, 2008), is a short, recent introduction. See also the essays in Clyde A. Milner II, Carol A. O'Connor, and Martha A. Sandweiss, eds., *The Oxford History of the American West* (New York: OUP, 1994). On Buffalo Bill consult the excellent cultural history by Louis S. Warren, *Buffalo Bill's America: William Cody and the Wild West Show* (New York: Alfred A. Knopf, 2005). Samuel P. Hays, *Conservation and the Gospel of Efficiency: The Progressive Conservation Movement, 1890–1920* (Cambridge, MA: Harvard University Press, 1959), is still the standard text but Roderick Frazier Nash, *Wilderness and the American Mind* 4th ed. (New Haven, CT: Yale University Press, 2001), has become a classic since its first appearance in 1967.

David F. Trask, *The War with Spain in 1898* (New York: Macmillan, 1981), provides a detailed overview while Paul T. McCartney, *Power and Progress: American National Identity, the War of 1898, and the Rise of American Imperialism* (Baton Rouge: Louisiana State University Press, 2006), is a stimulating reinterpretation from the perspective of international cultural history. Brian McAllister Linn, *The Philippine War, 1899–1902* (Lawrence: University Press of Kansas, 2000), offers a judicious treatment of the military side. Lewis L. Gould, *The Presidency of William McKinley* (Lawrence: Regents Press of Kansas, 1980), remains a succinct and powerful critique of the idea that McKinley was a weak president. David McCullough, *The Path Between the Seas: The Creation of the Panama Canal, 1870–1914* (New York: Simon & Schuster, 1977), provides an epic narrative.

11: War and Peace

David M. Kennedy, *Over Here: The First World War and American Society* (New York: OUP, 1980), is still the best overview, but see also Robert H. Ferrell, *Woodrow Wilson and World War I, 1917–1921* (New York: Harper & Row, 1985). On the president, John A. Thompson, *Woodrow Wilson* (London: Longman, 2002), is a stimulating and accessible study, arguing against the historiographical grain that Wilson was a political pragmatist. On the League fight the best recent study is John Milton Cooper, Jr., *Breaking the Heart of the World: Woodrow Wilson and the Fight for the League of Nations* (New York: CUP, 2001), though I think he exaggerates the international significance of Wilson's failure.

Elizabeth Frost and Kathryn Cullen-DuPont, *Women's Suffrage in America: An Eyewitness History* (New York: Facts on File, 1992), provides an excellent overview from 1800 with extensive extracts from contemporary documents. The older study by Eleanor Flexner, *Century of Struggle: The Woman's Rights Movement in the United States* rev. ed. (Cambridge, MA: Harvard University Press, 1975), though very critical of direct action, remains useful. On what influenced Wilson see Sally Hunter Graham, "Woodrow Wilson, Alice Paul, and the Woman Suffrage Movement," *Political Science Quarterly*, 98 (1983–

1984), pp. 665–679. For recent essays see Jean H. Baker, ed., *Votes for Women: The Struggle for Suffrage Revisited* (New York: OUP, 2002), and also the useful overview article by Paula Baker, "The Domestication of Politics: Women and American Political Society, 1780–1920," *AHR*, 89 (1984), pp. 620–647. The Alice Paul Institute has a very useful website at http://www.alicepaul.org/alicepaul.htm.

Robert K. Murray, *Red Scare: A Study in National Hysteria, 1919–1920* (Minneapolis: University of Minnesota Press, 1955), is still the best overview, but see also Paul Avrich, *Sacco and Vanzetti: The Anarchist Background* (Princeton, NJ: Princeton University Press, 1991).

On the 1920s, William E. Leuchtenburg, *The Perils of Prosperity, 1914–1932* (Chicago: University of Chicago Press, 1958), is still a good short introduction. Lynn Dumenil, *The Modern Temper: American Culture and Society in the 1920s* (New York: Hill & Wang, 1995), reflects recent historiography, although weaker on more traditional themes such as the automobile and Prohibition. Lary May, *Screening Out the Past: The Birth of Mass Culture and the Motion Picture Industry* (Chicago: University of Chicago Press, 1983), is excellent, while Andrew Sinclair, *Prohibition: The Era of Excess* (London: Faber and Faber, 1962), remains the best overview of this subject. Ted Gioia, *The History of Jazz* (New York: OUP, 1997), is a useful introduction. Edward J. Larson, *Summer for the Gods: The Scopes Trial and America's Continuing Debate over Science and Religion* (New York: Basic Books, 1997), is superb on both the trial and its significance.

12: From Boom to Bomb

A vast but readable survey of the period is David M. Kennedy, *Freedom from Fear: The American People in Depression and War, 1929–1945* (Oxford: OUP, 1999). Eric Rauchway, *The Great Depression & the New Deal: A Very Short Introduction* (Oxford: OUP, 2008), provides exactly what the subtitle promises. Maury Klein, *Rainbow's End: The Crash of 1929* (New York: OUP, 2001), is a good recent overview. Michael A. Bernstein, *The Great Depression: Delayed Recovery and Economic Change in America, 1929–1939* (New York: CUP, 1987), focuses on deep structural changes in the economy, whereas Gene Smiley, *Rethinking the Great Depression* (Chicago: Ivan R. Dee, 2002), blames government interference in market economics. On some of the deeper cultural and economic roots of boom and bust see Roland Marchand, *Advertising the American Dream: Making Way for Modernity, 1920–1940* (Berkeley: University of California Press, 1985), and Martha L. Olney, *Buy Now, Pay Later: Advertising, Credit, and Consumer Durables in the 1920s* (Chapel Hill: UNC Press, 1991).

Anthony J. Badger, *The New Deal: The Depression Years, 1933–1940* (London: Macmillan, 1989), is the best one-volume study, though William E. Leuchtenburg, *Franklin D. Roosevelt and the New Deal, 1932–1940* (New York: Harper & Row, 1963), remains a classic. Alonzo L. Hamby, *For the Survival of Democracy: Franklin Roosevelt and the World Crisis of the 1930s* (New York: The Free Press, 2004), endeavors to set the New Deal in international context. For short biographies of the president consult Patrick Renshaw, *Franklin D. Roosevelt* (London: Longman, 2004), and Patrick J. Maney, *The Roosevelt Presence: The Life and Legacy of FDR* (Berkeley: University of California Press, 1998). On foreign policy see David Reynolds, *From Munich to Pearl Harbor: Roosevelt's America and the Origins of the Second World War* (Chicago: Ivan R. Dee, 2001), and, in more detail, Robert Dallek, *Franklin Roosevelt and American Foreign Policy, 1932–1945* (New York: OUP, 1979). On his personal "special relationship" see Warren F. Kimball, *Forged in War: Roosevelt, Churchill, and the Second World War* (New York: William Morrow, 1997).

John W. Jeffries, *Wartime America: The World War II Home Front* (Chicago: Ivan R. Dee, 1996), is a good overview. On the first family see Doris Kearns Goodwin, *No Ordinary Time: Franklin and Eleanor Roosevelt: The Home Front in World War II* (New York: Simon & Schuster, 1994); on race, Roger Daniels, *Prisoners Without Trial: Japanese Americans in World War II* (New York: Hill & Wang, 1993), and Daniel Kryder, *Divided Arsenal: Race and the American State During World War II* (Cambridge: CUP, 2000). Richard Rhodes, *The Making of the Atomic Bomb* (London: Penguin, 1986), is outstanding. For aspects of the American experience of the war abroad see Ronald H. Spector, *Eagle Against the Sun: The American War with Japan* (New York: Vintage Books, 1985), Carlo D'Este, *Decision in Normandy* (New York: Harper Perennial, 1991), Gerald F. Linderman, *The World Within War: America's Combat Experience in World War II* (New York: The Free Press, 1997), and David Reynolds, *Rich Relations: The American Occupation of Britain, 1942–1945* (London: HarperCollins, 1996).

13: Red or Dead?

Richard Crockatt, *The Fifty Years War: The United States and the Soviet Union in World Politics, 1941–1991* (London: Routledge, 1995), is a useful overview, but see more generally David Reynolds, *One World Divisible: A Global History Since 1945* (London: Penguin, 2000). For an excellent overview of U.S. history in the three decades after World War II see James T. Patterson, *Grand Expectations: The United States, 1945–1974* (New York: OUP, 1996). Christopher Andrew, *For the President's Eyes Only: Secret Intelligence and the American Presidency from Washington to Bush* (London: HarperCollins, 1995), is a readable and incisive analysis focusing on the Cold War.

David McCullough, *Truman* (New York: Simon & Schuster, 1992), is a popular biography; for a more skeptical view of his foreign policy see Arnold A. Offner, *Another Such Victory: President Truman and the Cold War, 1945–1953* (Stanford, CA: Stanford University Press, 2002). Michael J. Lacey, ed., *The Truman Presidency* (New York: CUP, 1989), contains some useful essays. On the Cold War from both sides—though with different interpretations—see John Lewis Gaddis, *We Now Know: Rethinking Cold War History* (Oxford: Clarendon Press, 1997), and Melvyn P. Leffler, *For the Soul of Mankind: The United States, the Soviet Union, and the Cold War* (New York: Hill & Wang, 2007). True to its title is the prize-winning study by Odd Arne Westad, *The Global Cold War: Third World Interventions and the Making of Our Times* (New York: CUP, 2005). Also see the stimulating article by Eduard Mark, "October or Thermidor? Interpretations of Stalinism and the Perception of Soviet Foreign Policy in the United States, 1927–1947," *AHR*, 94 (1989), pp. 937–962.

Kenneth T. Jackson, *Crabgrass Frontier: The Suburbanization of the United States* (New York: OUP, 1985), remains essential. An important recent study is Lizabeth Cohen, *A Consumer's Republic: The Politics of Mass Consumption in Postwar America* (New York: Alfred A. Knopf, 2003). On rights and benefits see Alan Brinkley, *The End of Reform: New Deal Liberalism in Recession and War* (New York: Alfred A. Knopf, 1995), Suzanne Mettler, *Soldiers to Citizens: The G.I. Bill and the Making of the Greatest Generation* (New York: OUP, 2005), and Cass Sunstein, *The Second Bill of Rights: FDR's Unfinished Revolution and Why We Need It More Than Ever* (New York: Basic Books, 2004). On women, William H. Chafe, *The Paradox of Change: American Women in the Twentieth Century* (New York: OUP, 1991), is still a good overview; more specifically see Elaine Tyler May, *Homeward Bound: American Families in the Cold War Era* (New York: Basic Books, 1988).

On the Red Scare see John Earl Haynes, *Red Scare or Red Menace? American Communism and Anticommunism in the Cold War Era* (Chicago: Ivan R. Dee, 1996), Allen Weinstein and Alexander Vassiliev, *The Haunted Wood: Soviet Espionage in America—the Stalin*

Era (New York: Random House, 1996), and, more generally, Stephen J. Whitfield, *The Culture of the Cold War* 2nd ed. (Baltimore: Johns Hopkins University Press, 1996).

On the Eisenhower era see Chester J. Pach, Jr., and Elmo Richardson, *The Presidency of Dwight D. Eisenhower* (Lawrence: University Press of Kansas, 1991), Günter Bischof and Stephen E. Ambrose, eds., *Eisenhower: A Centenary Assessment* (Baton Rouge: Louisiana State University Press, 1995), and David Halberstam, *The Fifties* (New York: Villard Books, 1993). On foreign policy, Robert Divine, *Eisenhower and the Cold War* (New York: OUP, 1981), and John Lewis Gaddis, *Strategies of Containment: A Critical Appraisal of Postwar American Security Policy* (New York: OUP, 1982), are still useful introductions. Among more recent works see Robert R. Bowie and Richard H. Immerman, *Waging Peace: How Eisenhower Shaped an Enduring Cold War Strategy* (New York: OUP, 1998), Shawn J. Parry-Giles, *The Rhetorical Presidency: Propaganda and the Cold War, 1945–1955* (Westport, CT: Praeger, 2002), and Kenneth Osgood, *Total Cold War: Eisenhower's Secret Propaganda Battle at Home and Abroad* (Lawrence: University Press of Kansas, 2006).

14: Rights and Riots

Adam Fairclough, *Better Day Coming: Blacks and Equality, 1890–2000* (New York: Penguin, 2002), is a succinct, readable overview. Among good introductions to the civil rights era see Harvard Sitkoff, *The Struggle for Black Equality, 1954–1980* (New York: Hill & Wang, 1981), and Juan Williams, *Eyes on the Prize: America's Civil Rights Years* (New York: Viking, 1987). For the broader context see David Goldfield, *Black, White, and Southern: Race Relations and Southern Culture, 1940 to the Present* (Baton Rouge: Louisiana State University Press, 1990). Adam Fairclough, *Martin Luther King* (London: Sphere, 1990), is a short, readable biography.

On women, aside from the general survey by Chafe, *The Paradox of Change* (see ch. 13), for more detailed studies consult Eugenia Kaledin, *Mothers and More: American Women in the Fifties* (Boston: Twayne, 1984), Blanche Linden-Wood and Carol Hurd Green, *Changing the Future: American Women in the 1960s* (New York: Twayne, 1993), and Kathleen C. Berkeley, *The Women's Liberation Movement in America* (Westport, CT: Greenwood Press, 1999). On contraception see Bernard Asbell, *The Pill: A Biography of the Drug That Changed the World* (New York: Random House, 1995).

15: The Impotence of Omnipotence

On Kennedy's foreign policy see Lawrence Freedman, *Kennedy's Wars: Berlin, Cuba, Laos, and Vietnam* (New York: OUP, 2000), Michael R. Beschloss, *The Crisis Years: Kennedy and Khrushchev, 1960–1963* (New York: HarperCollins, 1991), and Aleksandr Fursenko and Timothy Naftali, *"One Hell of a Gamble": Khrushchev, Castro and Kennedy, 1958–1964* (New York: W. W. Norton, 1997). Randall B. Woods, *LBJ: Architect of American Ambition* (Cambridge, MA: Harvard University Press, 2006), offers a good one-volume biography, while the older memoir-history by Doris Kearns, *Lyndon Johnson and the American Dream* (New York: Signet, 1977), is revealing.

On Vietnam, George C. Herring, *America's Longest War: The United States and Vietnam, 1950–1975* 2nd ed. (New York: Alfred A. Knopf, 1986), is still a good overview of the whole conflict; Robert S. McNamara, with Brian VanDeMark, *In Retrospect: The Tragedy and Lessons of Vietnam* (New York: Times Books, 1995), renders a sad postmortem and mea culpa. For detailed studies of key points see Fredrik Logevall, *Choosing War: The Lost Chance for*

Peace and the Escalation of War in Vietnam (Berkeley: University of California Press, 1999), and Larry Berman, *Lyndon Johnson's War: The Road to Stalemate in Vietnam* (New York: W. W. Norton, 1989).

Robert Dallek, *Nixon and Kissinger: Partners in Power* (London: Penguin, 2007), provides the best overview of this fascinating relationship. On their summitry see Margaret MacMillan, *Seize the Hour: When Nixon Met Mao* (London: John Murray, 2006), and David Reynolds, *Summits: Six Meetings That Shaped the Twentieth Century* (London: Penguin, 2007), ch. 5. For recent analysis see the essays in Fredrik Logevall and Andrew Preston, eds., *Nixon in the World: American Foreign Relations* (New York: OUP, 2008). On Nixon's downfall, Fred Emery, *Watergate: The Corruption and Fall of Richard Nixon* (London: Jonathan Cape, 1994), remains useful, but see also the rich sources available online, for instance the *Washington Post* special website on Watergate (Politics—Special Reports), at http://www.washingtonpost.com/wp-srv/politics/special/watergate/index.html and the growing number of White House tapes and transcripts on the Nixon Library website at http://nixon.archives.gov/forresearchers/find/tapes/index.php.

16: *Détente and Discontent*

Raymond Garthoff, *Détente and Confrontation: American-Soviet Relations from Nixon to Reagan* 2nd ed. (Washington, DC: The Brookings Institution, 1994), is vast and encyclopedic but full of excellent insights and lateral connections. On the larger global context see Odd Arne Westad, *The Global Cold War: Third World Interventions and the Making of Our Times* (Cambridge: CUP, 2005).

For an overview of the conservative reaction, see William C. Berman, *America's Right Turn: From Nixon to Clinton* 2nd ed. (Baltimore: Johns Hopkins University Press, 1998), and the useful essays in David Farber and Jeff Roche, eds., *The Conservative Sixties* (New York: Peter Lang, 2003). Donald T. Critchlow, *Phyllis Schlafly and Grassroots Conservatism: A Woman's Crusade* (Princeton, NJ: Princeton University Press, 2005), relates Schlafly to the deeper currents of social change in post-1960s America. On race and affirmative action consult J. Harvie Wilkinson III, *From Brown to Bakke: The Supreme Court and School Integration, 1954–1978* (New York: OUP, 1979), and, on the Moral Majority, William Martin, *With God on Our Side: The Rise of the Religious Right in America* (New York: Broadway Books, 1996). On abortion, see N.E.H. Hull and Peter Charles Hoffer, *Roe v. Wade: The Abortion Rights Controversy in American History* (Lawrence: University Press of Kansas, 2001).

The Carter presidency is covered in the narrative by Burton I. Kaufman and Scott Kaufman, *The Presidency of James Earl Carter, Jr.* 2nd ed. (Lawrence: University Press of Kansas, 2006), and more analytically by John Dumbrell, *The Carter Presidency: A Reevaluation* 2nd ed. (Manchester, UK: Manchester University Press, 1995). On foreign policy see Robert A. Strong, *Working in the World: Jimmy Carter and the Making of American Foreign Policy* (Baton Rouge: Louisiana State University Press, 2000), and George D. Moffett III, *The Limits of Victory: The Ratification of the Panama Canal Treaties* (Ithaca, NY: Cornell University Press, 1985).

17: *Revolution and Democracy*

Lou Cannon, *President Reagan: The Role of a Lifetime* (New York: Simon & Schuster, 1991), remains probably the best of the biographies, even though much new material has since appeared. Raymond L. Garthoff, *The Great Transition: American-Soviet Relations and the End of the Cold War* (Washington, DC: The Brookings Institution, 1994), is an exhaustive scholarly account of the decade 1981–1991 from Reagan's inauguration to the collapse of the USSR, drawing on American and Soviet sources. See also Don Oberdorfer, *From the Cold War to a New Era: The United States and the Soviet Union, 1983–91* 2nd ed. (Baltimore: Johns Hopkins University Press, 1998)—lively and insightful by a journalist who was at the center of events—and Robert Lettow, *Ronald Reagan and His Quest to Abolish Nuclear Weapons* (New York: Random House, 2005).

Michael R. Beschloss and Strobe Talbott, *At the Highest Levels: The Inside Story of the End of the Cold War* (Boston: Little, Brown, 1993), offers a journalistic insider account; see also Philip Zelikow and Condoleezza Rice, *Germany Unified and Europe Transformed: A Study in Statecraft* 2nd ed. (Cambridge, MA: Harvard University Press, 1997)—a mixture of memoir and scholarship. Lawrence Freedman and Efraim Karsh, *The Gulf Conflict, 1990–1991* (London: Faber and Faber, 1993), provides a solid overview; and Bob Woodward, *The Commanders* (New York: Simon & Schuster, 1991), his usual chatty account based on insider interviews. The view from the White House is set out in George Bush and Brent Scowcroft, *A World Transformed* (New York: Vintage Books, 1999).

Martin Campbell-Kelly and William Aspray, *Computer: A History of the Information Machine* (New York: Basic Books, 1996), is an outstanding overview—informed, clear, and readable. On IBM see Emerson W. Pugh, *Building IBM: Shaping an Industry and Its Technology* (Cambridge, MA: MIT Press, 1995); and on transistors, Ernest Braun and Stuart MacDonald, *Revolution in Miniature: The History and Impact of Semiconductor Electronics* 2nd ed. (Cambridge: CUP, 1982).

18: Pride and Prejudice

James T. Patterson, *Restless Giant: The United States from Watergate to Bush vs. Gore* (New York: OUP, 2005), surveys the last quarter of the twentieth century. For an overview of the Clinton era see William C. Berman, *From the Center to the Edge: The Politics and Policies of the Clinton Presidency* (Lanham, MD: Rowman & Littlefield, 2001). Nigel Hamilton's biography *Bill Clinton* (2 vols. to date, London: Arrow Books, 2004, 2008), has so far taken the story up to the election of 1996; Carl Bernstein, *A Woman in Charge: The Life of Hillary Rodham Clinton* (New York: Vintage Books, 2008), is detailed and perceptive, despite being couched as the chronicle of a president in waiting. A vivid account of the recent Supreme Court, based on extensive insider interviews, is Jeffrey Toobin, *The Nine: Inside the Secret World of the Supreme Court* (New York: Anchor Books, 2008). On ethnicity see the extended essay by David A. Hollinger, *Postethnic America: Beyond Multiculturalism* (New York: Basic Books, 1995).

The 9/11 Commission Report (New York: W. W. Norton, 2004), is surprisingly readable for so detailed and official a volume. On the neo-cons, Stefan Halper and Jonathan Clarke, *America Alone: The Neo-Conservatives and the Global Order* (Cambridge: CUP, 2004), provides a good introduction, while Thomas E. Ricks, *Fiasco: The American Military Adventure in Iraq* (London: Penguin, 2007), offers a detailed and damning account of what they hoped would be their finest hour. A powerful searchlight on the power behind Bush's throne is shed by Barton Gellman, *Angler: The Shadow Presidency of Dick Cheney* (London: Allen Lane, 2008). For recent assessments, from different angles, of America's place in the world, see Niall Ferguson, *Colossus: The Rise and Fall of the American Empire* (London: Penguin, 2005), Charles S. Maier, *Among Empires: American Ascendancy and Its Predecessors* (Cambridge, MA: Harvard University Press, 2006), and Kevin Phillips, *American Theocracy: The Perils and Politics of Radical Religion, Oil, and Borrowed Money in the 21st Century* (New York: Penguin, 2007).

NOTES

For a list of abbreviations used throughout this section see p. 479.

Introduction

1. For examples of recent discussion see Niall Ferguson, *Colossus: The Rise and Fall of the American Empire* (London: Penguin Books, 2005), and Charles S. Maier, *Among Empires: American Ascendancy and Its Predecessors* (Cambridge, MA: Harvard University Press, 2006).

2. See the fuller discussion in Chapter 4 of this volume.

3. Speech in Springfield, Illinois, 16 June 1858, quoted in Roy P. Basler, ed., *The Collected Works of Abraham Lincoln* (9 vols., New Brunswick, NJ: Rutgers University Press, 1953–1955), II, p. 462.

4. Quoted in Frank Lambert, *The Founding Fathers and the Place of Religion in America* (Princeton, NJ: Princeton University Press, 2003), p. 239.

5. For useful overviews see Mark A. Noll, *The Old Religion in a New World: The History of North American Christianity* (Grand Rapids, MI: William B. Eerdmans, 2002), and George M. Marsden, *Fundamentalism and American Culture* 2nd ed. (Oxford: OUP, 2006); also Nicholas Guyatt, *Providence and the Invention of the United States, 1607–1876* (New York: CUP, 2007).

6. This is a central theme of books such as Walter A. McDougall, *Promised Land, Crusader State: The American Encounter with the World Since 1776* (Boston: Houghton Mifflin, 1997), and Walter Russell Mead, *Special Providence: American Foreign Policy and How It Changed the World* (New York: Alfred A. Knopf, 2001).

1: Natives and Europeans

1. H. M. Brackenridge, *Views of Louisiana; Together with a Journal of a Voyage Up the Missouri River, in 1811* (Pittsburgh: Cramer, Spear & Eichbaum, 1814), p. 187.

2. "The Prairies" (1832), in William Cullen Bryant, *Poems* (Dessau: Katz, 1854).

3. Brackenridge, *Views of Louisiana*, p. 188.

4. Alan Taylor, *American Colonies: The Settling of North America* (New York: Penguin, 2001), p. 5.

5. See the review essay in *American Antiquity*, 3 (1943), pp. 304–307.

6. Letter to the Emperor, 31 Oct. 1520, in Hernán Cortés, *Letters from Mexico*, trans. and ed. Anthony Pagden (London: Yale University Press, 1986), p. 108.

7. Alice Beck Kehoe, *America Before the European Invasions* (London: Longman, 2002), p. 43.

8. Quoted in Frank McNitt, ed., *Navaho Expedition: Journal of a Military Reconnaissance from Santa Fe, New Mexico, to the Navaho Country Made in 1849 by Lieutenant James H. Simpson* (Norman: University of Oklahoma Press, 1964), pp. 36–37, 39, entry for 26 Aug. 1849.

9. Statement by Hopi leaders to the "Washington Chiefs," (1894), quoted in Kendrick Frazier, *People of Chaco: A Canyon and Its Culture*, 2nd ed. (New York: W. W. Norton, 1999), p. 15.

10. See the pioneering work of Alfred W. Crosby, Jr., *The Columbian Exchange: Biological and Cultural Consequences of 1492* (Westport, CT: Greenwood Press, 1972).

11. Roosevelt, address at Denver, Colorado, 12 Oct. 1936 (PPPUS website).

12. Entry in Columbus's diary, dated 16 Dec. 1492, quoted in Julius E. Olson and Edward G. Bourne, eds., *The Northmen, Columbus and Cabot, 985–1503* (New York: Charles Scribner's Sons, 1906), p. 182.

13. Quoted in Alan R. Sandstrom, *Corn Is Our Blood: Culture and Ethnic Identity in a Contemporary Aztec Indian Village* (Norman: University of Oklahoma Press, 1991), pp. 239–240.

14. Quoted in Redcliffe N. Salaman, *The History and Social Influence of the Potato*, rev. impression, ed. J. G. Hawkes (Cambridge: CUP, 1985), p. 106.

15. Warwick Bray, "Crop Plants and Cannibals: Early European Impressions of the New World," in Bray, ed., *The Meeting of Two Worlds: Europe and the Americas, 1492–1650* (Oxford: OUP, 1993), pp. 289–326, esp. pp. 290–302.

16. Excerpt from "A Counterblaste to Tobacco" (1604), in James Craigie, ed., *Minor Prose Works of James VI and I* (Edinburgh: Scottish Text Society, 1981), p. 99.

17. See the discussion in Charles C. Mann, *Ancient Americans: Rewriting the History of the New World* (London: Granta, 2005), appendix C.

18. Quoted in Noble David Cook, *Born to Die: Disease and New World Conquest, 1492–1650* (Cambridge: CUP, 1998), pp. 213–214.

19. John Winthrop to Sir Nathaniel Rich, May 22, 1634, in *The Winthrop Papers*, vol. III (Boston: Massachusetts Historical Society, 1943), p. 167.

20. David Henige, *Numbers from Nowhere: The American Indian Contact Population Debate* (Norman: University of Oklahoma Press, 1998), p. 10.

21. Taylor, *American Colonies*, p. 40. The most thorough analysis of estimates for the base-point, the eve of Columbus, is John D. Daniel, "The Indian Population of North America in 1492," *WMQ*, 49 (1992), pp. 298–320.

22. Francis Jennings, *The Invasion of America: Indians, Colonialism, and the Cant of Conquest* (Chapel Hill: UNC Press, 1975), p. 15.

23. Francis Jennings, *The Founders of America* (New York: W. W. Norton, 1993), p. 175.

24. J. H. Elliott, *Empires of the Atlantic World: Britain and Spain in America, 1492–1830* (London: Yale University Press, 2006), p. 262.

25. Ibid., p. 408.

26. Pedro Menéndez de Avilés to Philip II, 15 Oct. 1565, quoted in David Beers Quinn, ed., *New American World: A Documentary History of North America to 1612* (5 vols., New York: Arno Press, 1979), II, p. 398.

27. Pedro Menéndez Marqués to the president of the Casa de Contratación, 17 June 1586, quoted in Quinn, ed., *New American World*, V, p. 40.

28. Don Juan de Oñate to the viceroy of New Spain, 2 March 1599, quoted in Herbert Eugene Bolton, ed., *Spanish Exploration in the Southwest, 1542–1706* (New York: Charles Scribner's Sons, 1916), p. 219.

29. Oñate's deposition of testimony by Gerónimo Marqués, 29 Dec. 1598, in Quinn, *New American World*, V, p. 459.

30. Sentence (1599), quoted in George P. Hammond and Agapito Rey, eds., *Don Juan de Oñate: Colonizer of New Mexico, 1595–1628* (2 vols., Albuquerque: University of New Mexico Press, 1953), I, p. 477.

31. A point emphasized by, among others, Ramon Gutiérrez, *When Jesus Came, the Corn Mothers Went Away: Marriage, Sexuality and Power in New Mexico, 1500–1846* (Stanford: Stanford University Press, 1991), pp. 103–104.

32. Intelligence from Indian messengers, quoted in Andrew L. Knaut, *The Pueblo Revolt of 1680: Conquest and Resistance in Seventeenth-Century New Mexico* (Norman: University of Oklahoma Press, 1997), pp. 9–10.

33. Letter from Joseph de Zúñiga y Cerda (1704), quoted in David J. Weber, *The Spanish Frontier in North America* (New Haven, CT: Yale University Press, 1992), p. 171.

34. *Voyages of Samuel de Champlain*, trans. Charles Pomeroy Otis (2 vols., Boston: Prince Society, 1878), II, p. 184.

35. As developed in Richard White, *The Middle Ground: Indians, Empires, and Republics in the Great Lakes Region, 1660–1815* (Cambridge: CUP, 1991).

36. Denys Delage, *Bitter Feast: Amerindians and Europeans in Northeastern North America, 1600–1664* (Vancouver: University of British Columbia Press, 1993), p. 243.

37. Taylor, *American Colonies*, p. 368.

38. Narrative of La Salle's voyage down the Mississippi by Father Zenobrius Membré, in Isaac Joslin Cox, ed., *The Journeys of René Robert Cavelier, Sieur de La Salle* (2 vols., New York: Allerton Book Co., 1922), I, p. 137.

39. The journal of Henri Joutel, in Cox, *Journeys of La Salle*, II, p. 128.

40. Figures from Daniel H. Usner, *Indians, Settlers and Slaves in a Frontier Economy: The Lower Mississippi Valley Before 1783* (Chapel Hill: UNC Press, 1992), pp. 32, 41.

41. Letter of 10 Jan. 1722, in Charles E. O'Neill, ed., *Charlevoix's Louisiana: Selections from the History and the Journal* (Baton Rouge: Louisiana State University Press, 1977), pp. 155–156.

42. Unnamed governor-general in 1748, quoted in Taylor, *American Colonies*, p. 370.

2: Empire and Liberties

1. Captain John Smith, *The Generall Historie of Virginia, New England & the Summer Isles . . .* (London: printed by I.D. and I.H. for Michael Sparkes, 1624), book IV, pp. 105–106.

2. Quoted in Winthrop Jordan, *White over Black: American Attitudes Toward the Negro, 1550–1812* (Baltimore: Pelican, 1969), p. 71.

3. Alan Taylor, *American Colonies: The Settling of North America* (New York: Penguin, 2001), p. 142.

4. Peter H. Wood, *Black Majority: Negroes in Colonial South Carolina from 1670 Through the Stono Rebellion* (New York: Alfred A. Knopf, 1974), p. 152.

5. Warren M. Billings, ed., *The Old Dominion in the Seventeenth Century: A Documentary History of Virginia, 1606–89* (Chapel Hill: UNC Press, 1975), pp. 150, 152.

6. Quoted in Betty Wood, *The Origins of American Slavery: Freedom and Bondage in the English Colonies* (New York: Hill & Wang, 1997), p. 5.

7. 4th Anne, Oct. 1705, chap. XLIX, articles IV, XX, and XXXIV, printed in William Waller Hening, *The Statutes at Large; Being a Collection of All the Laws of Virginia, from*

the First Session of the Legislature, in the Year 1619 (Philadelphia, 1823), vol. III, pp. 447–462, available online at http://www.vagenweb.org/hening/.

8. As emphasized in Elliott, *Empires of the Atlantic World*, pp. 106–107, 134–135.

9. Wood, *Black Majority*, pp. 56–62.

10. "Account of the Negroe Insurrection in South Carolina" (Oct. 1739), in Mark M. Smith, ed., *Stono: Documenting and Interpreting a Southern Slave Revolt* (Columbia: University of South Carolina Press, 2005), pp. 13–15 at p. 15.

11. Report of 1 July 1741 in the Journals of the South Carolina Commons House of Assembly, quoted in Wood, *Black Majority*, p. 308.

12. Mills Lane, ed., *General Oglethorpe's Georgia: Colonial Letters, 1733–1743* (2 vols., Savannah, Ga.: The Beehive Press, 1975), I, p. xxxiv.

13. Benjamin Martyn, *Reasons for Establishing the Colony of Georgia* (1733), in Trevor R. Reese, ed., *The Most Delightful Country in the Universe: Promotional Literature of the Colony of Georgia, 1717–1734* (Savannah, Ga.: The Beehive Press, 1972), p. 183.

14. Petition of 9 Dec. 1738, in Lane, *Oglethorpe's Georgia*, II, p. 374.

15. Taylor, *American Colonies*, p. 243.

16. John Winthrop's autograph draft of "General Observations" (Aug. 1629), in *Winthrop Papers*, vol. II (Boston: Massachusetts Historical Society, 1931), p. 114.

17. Winthrop's reply to the answer made to the discourse about the negative vote, May 1643, in R. C. Winthrop, *Life and Letters of John Winthrop* (2 vols., Boston, 1869), II, p. 430.

18. *Winthrop Papers*, vol. II, pp. 294–295.

19. Francis J. Bremer, *John Winthrop: America's Forgotten Founding Father* (New York: OUP, 2003), pp. 174–175. See also Theodore Dwight Bozeman, "The Puritans' 'Errand into the Wilderness' Reconsidered," *New England Quarterly*, 59 (1986), pp. 232–251.

20. See Mary Beth Norton, *Founding Mothers and Fathers: Gendered Power and the Forming of American Society* (New York: Alfred A. Knopf, 1996).

21. Quoted in Frank Lambert, *The Founding Fathers and the Place of Religion in America* (Princeton, NJ: Princeton University Press, 2003), pp. 18–19.

22. John Winthrop, "A Short Story of the Rise, Reign, and Ruine of the Antinomians, Familists and Libertines" (1644), in David D. Hall, ed., *The Antinomian Controversy, 1636–1638: A Documentary History* 2nd ed. (Durham, NC: Duke University Press, 1990), pp. 199–310 at p. 263. The account given here follows Michael P. Winship, *The Times and Trials of Anne Hutchinson: Puritans Divided* (Lawrence: University Press of Kansas, 2005).

23. "In no other experience in the pre-modern world were women so completely in control or so firmly bonded," Laurel Thatcher Ulrich, *Good Wives: Image and Reality in the Lives of Women in Northern New England, 1650–1750* (New York: Alfred A. Knopf, 1982), p. 132.

24. Quoted in "A Report of the Trial of Mrs Anne Hutchinson Before the Church in Boston, March 1638," in Hall, *Antinomian Controversy*, pp. 349–387 at pp. 382–383.

25. "Examination," in Hall, *Antinomian Controversy*, pp. 336–337.

26. A point emphasized by Mark A. Noll, *America's God: From Jonathan Edwards to Abraham Lincoln* (Oxford: OUP, 2002), pp. 40–41.

27. Virginia DeJohn Anderson, *New England's Generation: The Great Migration and the Formation of Society and Culture in the Seventeenth Century* (Cambridge, CUP, 1991), esp. pp. 100–103.

28. Bremer, *Winthrop*, p. 314.

29. Daniel Vickers, *Farmers and Fishermen: Two Centuries of Work in Essex County, Massachusetts, 1630–1850* (Chapel Hill: UNC Press, 1994), ch. 2, quoting p. 82.

30. "Remonstrance," 5 Sept. 1664 new style, in E. B. O'Callaghan, ed., *Documents Relative to the Colonial History of the State of New York*, vol. II (Albany: Ward, Parsons & Co., 1858), pp. 248–250. See also Robert C. Ritchie, *The Duke's Province: A Study of New York Politics and Society, 1664–1691* (Chapel Hill: UNC Press, 1977), chs. 1–2.

31. There was a synagogue by 1695; Trinity Church, on the corner of Broadway and Wall Street, was built in 1697. See generally Joyce D. Goodfriend, *Before the Melting Pot: Society and Culture in Colonial New York City, 1664–1730* (Princeton, NJ: Princeton University Press, 1992).

32. Letters to James Harrison, 25 Aug. 1681, and Robert Turner, 5 March 1681, in Jean R. Soderlund, ed., *William Penn and the Founding of Pennsylvania, 1680–1684: A Documentary History* (Philadelphia: University of Pennsylvania Press, 1983), respectively docs. 19 and 12, quoting pp. 77 and 54–55.

33. "Laws agreed upon in England," 5 May 1682, in Soderlund, *William Penn*, doc. 30, quoting p. 132.

34. In the late 1720s Quakers of English and Welsh stock constituted 60 percent of Pennsylvania's population and a similar proportion of its assemblymen. David Hackett Fischer, *Albion's Seed: Four British Folkways in America* (New York: OUP, 1989), pp. 431–432.

35. Letter to the Indians, 18 Oct. 1681, in Soderlund, *William Penn*, doc 23, quoting p. 88. See also Francis Jennings, *The Ambiguous Iroquois Empire: The Covenant Chain Federation of Indian Tribes with Indian Colonies from Its Beginnings to the Lancaster Treaty of 1744* (New York: W. W. Norton, 1984), pp. 240–248.

36. C. A. Weslager, *The Delaware Indians: A History* (New Brunswick, NJ: Rutgers University Press, 1972), p. 166.

37. John J. McCusker and Russell R. Menard, *The Economy of British America, 1607–1789* (Chapel Hill: UNC Press, 1985), p. 54.

38. Figures and quotation from Taylor, *American Colonies*, pp. 314–318.

39. A. G. Roeber, "'The Origin of Whatever Is Not English Among Us': The Dutch-speaking and the German-speaking Peoples of Colonial British North America," in Bernard Bailyn and Philip D. Morgan, eds., *Strangers Within the Realm: Cultural Margins of the First British Empire* (Chapel Hill: UNC Press, 1991), pp. 220–283 at p. 244.

40. "A Writer in Inverness" reported in *South-Carolina Gazette*, 11 April 1774, quoted in Bernard Bailyn with Barbara DeWolfe, *Voyagers to the West: A Passage in the Peopling of America on the Eve of the Revolution* (New York: Alfred A. Knopf, 1987), p. 200, n. 33.

41. Carl Bridenbaugh, *Cities in Revolt: Urban Life in America, 1743–1776* (New York: Alfred A. Knopf, 1959), p. 5.

42. See list in Frank Lambert, *Inventing the "Great Awakening"* (Princeton, NJ: Princeton University Press, 1999), p. 115.

43. Herbert S. Klein, *The Atlantic Slave Trade* (Cambridge: CUP, 1999), pp. 208–209, estimates 256,000 for the period 1700–1780. Migration tailed off substantially once the Revolution began in 1776.

44. Olaudah Equiano, *The Interesting Narrative of the Life of Olaudah Equiano, or Gustavus Vassa, The African Written by Himself* (London, 1789), ch. 2, accessed as Project Gutenberg e-book 15399.

45. To borrow the title of the biography by Harry S. Stout, *Divine Dramatist: George Whitefield and the Rise of Modern Evangelicalism* (Grand Rapids, MI: William B. Eerdmans, 1991).

46. This and following quotations taken from the text printed in Michael J. Crawford, "The Spiritual Travels of Nathan Cole," *WMQ*, 33 (1976), pp. 89–126 at pp. 92–93.

47. See the essays by Allen C. Guelzo and Gordon S. Wood in Harry S. Stout and D. G. Hart, eds., *New Directions in American Religious History* (New York: OUP, 1997), chs. 5 and 6.

48. Contrary to earlier claims by Alan Heimert, for instance, that "what was awakened in 1740 was the spirit of American democracy." Alan Heimert and Perry Miller, eds., *The Great Awakening: Documents Illustrating the Crisis and Its Consequences* (Indianapolis: Bobbs-Merrill, 1967), p. lxi.

49. John Williams, journal, 10 May 1771, quoted in Rhys Isaac, *The Transformation of Virginia, 1740–1790* (Chapel Hill: UNC Press, 1982), pp. 162–163, 383. The episode probably occurred in late April 1771.

50. Isaac, *Transformation of Virginia*, p. 173.

51. Story and quotations from Sylvia Frey and Betty Wood, *Come Shouting to Zion: African American Protestantism in the American South and British Caribbean to 1830* (Chapel Hill: UNC Press, 1998), pp. 112–113.

52. As emphasized by Francis Jennings, *Empire of Fortune: Crowns, Colonies, and Tribes in the Seven Years War in America* (New York: W. W. Norton, 1988), pp. xv–xvi.

53. Quoted in Fred Anderson, *Crucible of War: The Seven Years War and the Fate of Empire in British North America, 1754–1766* (London: Faber and Faber, 2000), p. 67.

54. George Washington, biographical memorandum, c. 1786, in United States George Washington Bicentennial Commission, *The Writings of George Washington*, ed. John C. Fitzpatrick (39 vols., Washington, DC: U.S. Government Printing Office, 1931–1944), XXIX, p. 44.

55. Benjamin Franklin, *The Autobiography and Other Writings*, ed. K. Jesse Lemisch (New York: Signet Classics, 1961), p. 153.

56. Quotations from Gordon S. Wood, *The Americanization of Benjamin Franklin* (New York: Penguin, 2005), pp. 72–78.

57. *Boston Evening Post*, 12 June 1758, quoted in Tom Pocock, *Battle for Empire: The Very First World War, 1756–1763* (London: Michael O'Mara Books, 1998), p. 95.

58. Fred Anderson, *A People's Army: Massachusetts Soldiers and Society in the Seven Years War* (Chapel Hill: UNC Press, 1984), pp. 14–16.

59. F. E. Whitton, *Wolfe and North America* (London: Ernest Benn, 1929), p. 396.

60. Quoted in William Nester, *The First Global War: Britain, France, and the Fate of North America, 1756–1775* (Westport, CT: Praeger, 2000), p. 190.

61. Lesuire (1760) and Choiseul (1767) quoted in Robert and Isabelle Tombs, *That Sweet Enemy: The French and British from the Sun King to the Present* (London: William Heinemann, 2006), pp. 121, 136.

3: Independence and Republicanism

1. Charles Townshend, speech of 6 Feb. 1765, quoting from versions in *Proceedings and Debates of the British Parliaments Respecting North America, 1754–1783*, ed. R. C. Simmons and P.D.G. Thomas (5 vols., Millwood, NY: Kraus International Publications, 1982), II, pp. 13, 16.

2. Fred Anderson, *Crucible of War: The Seven Years War and the Fate of Empire in British North America, 1754–1766* (London: Faber and Faber, 2000), pp. 670–671.

3. "Sons of Liberty" popularized a term used by one of the few parliamentary critics of the Stamp Act, Isaac Barré, who, significantly, knew North America well: He served as Wolfe's adjutant general and lost an eye at Quebec.

4. Declaration of Rights and Grievances, 19 Oct. 1765, as printed in C. A. Weslager, *The Stamp Act Congress* (Newark: University of Delaware Press, 1976), pp. 200–201.

5. Anderson, *Crucible of War*, p. 703.

6. Quoted in Gordon S. Wood, *The American Revolution: A History* (London: Phoenix, 2005), pp. 34–35.

7. George III and Gage quoted in Ian R. Christie and Benjamin W. Labaree, *Empire or Independence, 1760–1776* (London: Phaidon, 1976), pp. 183–184.

8. George Washington to George William Fairfax, 10 June 1774, and to Bryan Fairfax, 24 Aug. 1774, quoted in W. W. Abbot and Dorothy Twohig, eds., *The Papers of George Washington, Colonial Series*, vol. X (Charlottesville: University of Virginia Press, 1995), pp. 96, 155. Washington's idiosyncratic punctuation has been amended to convey his sense.

9. *Diary and Autobiography of John Adams*, vol. II, *Diary, 1771–1781*, ed. L. H. Butterfield (Cambridge, MA: Belknap Press of Harvard University Press, 1961), p. 97, entry for 25 June 1774.

10. John Adams to James Warren, 25 June 1774, in *Papers of John Adams*, vol. II, *December 1773–April 1775*, ed. Robert J. Taylor et al. (Cambridge, MA: Belknap Press of Harvard University Press, 1977), pp. 99–100.

11. Speech of 22 March 1775, quoted in Edmund Burke, *Pre-Revolutionary Writings*, ed. Ian Harris (Cambridge: CUP, 1993), p. 266.

12. Account and quotations from Robert Middlekauf, *The Glorious Cause: The American Revolution, 1763–1789* 2nd ed. (New York: OUP, 2005), pp. 274–279.

13. Gage to Lord Dartmouth, 25 June 1775, in Christie and Labaree, *Empire or Independence*, p. 263.

14. Quoted in Pauline Maier, *From Resistance to Revolution: Colonial Radicals and the Development of American Opposition to Britain, 1765–1776* (London: Routledge & Kegan Paul, 1972), pp. 238–239.

15. Ibid., p. 238.

16. John Adams to Abigail Adams, 17 June, 1775, in *Adams Family Correspondence*, ed. L. H. Butterfield et al. (multi vols., Cambridge, MA: Belknap Press of Harvard University Press, 1963–), I, p. 216.

17. Quotations from Gary B. Nash, *The Unknown American Revolution: The Unruly Birth of Democracy and the Struggle to Create America* (London: Pimlico, 2007), pp. 201–202.

18. Pauline Maier, *American Scripture: Making the Declaration of Independence* (New York: Vintage Books, 1998), p. 41.

19. Ibid., p. 236.

20. Ibid., p. 237.

21. Ibid., pp. 120–122, 146–147, 239.

22. David McCullough, *John Adams* (New York: Touchstone, 2002), pp. 126–129.

23. John Adams to Abigail Adams, 3 July 1776, in *Adams Family Correspondence*, II, pp. 30–31. In Adams's opinion, the day to commemorate was 2 July, when the crucial vote was taken after his speech; for years he resented the attention focused on 4 July and thus on Jefferson's declaration.

24. Washington to the president of Congress, 8 Sept. 1776, in *The Writings of George Washington*, X, p. 28.

25. Washington to the president of Congress, 23 Dec. 1776, in *The Writings of George Washington*, X, pp. 192–193.

26. Quotations from Charles Royster, *A Revolutionary People at War: The Continental Army and the American Character, 1775–1783* (Chapel Hill: UNC Press, 1979), pp. 218–219.

27. Washington, general orders, 31 May 1778, in *The Writings of George Washington*, XI, p. 497.

28. See generally Elizabeth A. Fenn, *Pox Americana: The Great Smallpox Epidemic of 1775–82* (New York, 2001).

29. Quoted in Robert and Isabelle Tombs, *That Sweet Enemy: The French and the British from the Sun King to the Present* (London: William Heinemann, 2006), p. 159.

30. Joseph Plumb Martin, *A Narrative of a Revolutionary Soldier* (1830) (New York: Signet Classics, 2001), p. 157.

31. Ibid., pp. 206–207.

32. Benjamin Franklin to William Franklin, 16 Aug. 1784, quoted in Gordon S. Wood, *The Americanization of Benjamin Franklin* (New York: Penguin, 2005), p. 163.

33. John Adams to John Jay, 2 June 1785, quoted in Charles Francis Adams, ed., *The Works of John Adams* (10 vols., Boston: Little, Brown, 1851–1856), IV, pp. 256–257.

34. Thomas Jefferson, *Notes on the State of Virginia* (1787), ed. Thomas P. Abernethy (New York: Harper Torchbooks, 1964), query XIII, p. 113.

35. Wood, *American Revolution*, p. 144.

36. Madison's notes, 16 June 1787, in Max Farrand, ed., *The Records of the Federal Convention of 1787* (3 vols., New Haven, CT: Yale University Press, 1911), I, p. 250.

37. Gunning Bedford, 30 June 1787, printed in Farrand, *Records of the Federal Convention*, I, pp. 500–501.

38. Madison, 29 June 1787, printed in Farrand, *Records of the Federal Convention*, I, p. 476.

39. Gouverneur Morris, 8 Aug. 1787, printed in Farrand, *Records of the Federal Convention*, II, p. 222 (abbreviations in original have been spelled out).

40. U.S. Constitution, article I, section 8.

41. Federalist paper 51, in Alexander Hamilton, James Madison, and John Jay, *The Federalist* with *"Letters of Brutus,"* ed. Terence Ball (Cambridge: CUP, 2003), p. 252.

42. Charles Pinkney, 25 June 1787, in Farrand, *Records of the Federal Convention*, I, p. 398.

43. Federalist paper 10, in *The Federalist*, pp. 41, 43, 45.

44. Federalist paper 14, in *The Federalist*, p. 63.

45. Washington to Henry Knox, 1 April 1789, in W. W. Abbot et al., eds., *The Papers of George Washington: Presidential Series* (Charlottesville: University of Virginia Press, 1987–), II, p. 2.

46. Quotations from Abbot et al., *The Papers of George Washington: Presidential Series*, IV, pp. 77-78.

47. Marvin R. Zahniser, *Charles Cotesworth Pinckney, Founding Father* (Chapel Hill: UNC Press, 1967), p. 99.

48. Madison, 8 June 1789, *Annals of Congress*, 1st Congress, 1st session, p. 449.

49. Ibid., p. 451.

50. Jefferson, *Notes on the State of Virginia*, query XVII, p. 152.

51. Jefferson to Washington, 9 Sept. 1792, in *The Papers of Thomas Jefferson*, ed. Julian Boyd et al. (multi vols., Princeton: Princeton University Press, 1950–), XXIV, p. 358.

52. Alexander Hamilton, "Report on Manufactures," 5 Dec. 1791, in *The Papers of Alexander Hamilton*, ed. Harold C. Syrett (27 vols., New York: Columbia University Press, 1961–1987), X, p. 291.

53. Jefferson, *Notes on the State of Virginia*, query XIX, pp. 157–158.

54. Alexander Hamilton, "Report Relative to a Provision for the Support of the Public Credit," 9 Jan. 1790, in *The Papers of Alexander Hamilton*, VI, pp. 67–69.

55. Ibid., pp. 74, 78.

56. Benjamin Rush to James Madison, 18 Feb. 1790, in Charles F. Hobson and Robert A. Rutland, eds., *The Papers of James Madison*, vol. XIII (Charlottesville: University of Virginia Press, 1981), p. 46.

57. Madison, speech of 1 March 1790, in Hobson and Rutland, eds., *Papers of James Madison*, vol. XIII, p. 72.

58. Thomas B. Wait to George Thatcher, 21 Aug. 1788, quoted in Kenneth R. Bowling, *The Creation of Washington D.C.: The Idea and Location of the American Capital* (Fairfax, VA: George Mason University Press, 1991), p. xv, cf. p. 3.

59. Jefferson to Washington, 15 March 1784 and Washington to Jefferson, 29 March 1784, in *The Papers of Thomas Jefferson*, VII, pp. 26, 49.

60. Jefferson, note (1792?), in *The Papers of Thomas Jefferson*, XVII, pp. 206–207.

61. Jacob E. Cooke, "The Compromise of 1790," *WMQ*, 27 (1970), pp. 523–545, disputed the significance of the dinner, but he was questioned in Kenneth R. Bowling, "Dinner at Jefferson's: A Note on Jacob E. Cooke's 'The Compromise of 1790,'" published with Cooke's "Rebuttal" in *WMQ*, 28 (1971), pp. 629–648. On the related bargaining see also Norman K. Risjord, "The Compromise of 1790: New Evidence on the Dinner Table Bargain," *WMQ*, 33 (1976), pp. 309–314.

62. Jefferson to Washington, 9 Sept. 1792, in *The Papers of Thomas Jefferson*, XXIV, p. 352.

63. C. M. Harris, "Washington's Gamble, L'Enfant's Dream: Politics, Design and the Founding of the National Capital," *WMQ*, 56 (1999), pp. 527–564.

64. James Sterling Young, *The Washington Community, 1800–1828* (New York: Columbia University Press, 1966), pp. 22, 26.

65. Abigail Adams to Abigail Adams Smith, 21 Nov. 1800, in Charles Francis Adams, *Letters of Mrs Adams, the Wife of John Adams* (Boston: Little, Brown, 1840), quoting from pp. 433–434.

66. John Adams to Abigail Adams, 2 Nov. 1800, quoted in McCullough, *John Adams*, p. 551.

67. Young, *Washington Community*, pp. 28–30.

68. J. G. A. Pocock, *The Machiavellian Moment: Florentine Political Thought and the Atlantic Republican Tradition* (Princeton, NJ: Princeton University Press, 1975), p. 507.

69. Robert Hughes, *American Visions: The Epic History of Art in America* (London: The Harvill Press, 1997), pp. 69–70.

4: Liberty and Security

1. Quoted in Robert and Isabelle Tombs, *That Sweet Enemy: The French and the British from the Sun King to the Present* (London: William Heinemann, 2006), p. 238.

2. Washington, farewell address of 19 Sept. 1796 (PPPUS website).

3. Washington to Charles Carroll, 1 May 1796, in *The Writings of George Washington*, XXXVII, p. 30.

4. Washington, farewell address of 19 Sept. 1796 (PPPUS website).

5. Jefferson to William Short, 3 Jan. 1793, in *The Papers of Thomas Jefferson*, ed. Julian Boyd et al. (multi vols., Princeton, NJ: Princeton University Press, 1950–), XXV, p. 14.

6. Jefferson to Philip Mazzei, 24 April 1796, in *The Papers of Thomas Jefferson*, XXIX, p. 82. The text was published in somewhat garbled form, being a translation back into English from a French translation—see ibid., pp. 73–81.

7. Thomas M. Ray, "'Not One Cent for Tribute': The Public Addresses and American Popular Reaction to the XYZ Affair, 1798–9," *JER*, 3 (1983), pp. 389–412 at p. 390.

8. Karl-Friedrich Walling, *Republican Empire: Alexander Hamilton on War and Free Government* (Lawrence: University Press of Kansas, 1999), p. 234.

9. "An Act for the Punishment of Certain Crimes Against the United States," 14 July 1798, 5th Congress, 2nd session, ch. 74, 1 Stat. 596.

10. "Resolutions adopted by the Kentucky General Assembly," 10 Nov. 1798, in *The Papers of Thomas Jefferson*, XXX, p. 550.

11. Sermon on 4 July 1798, quoted by Robert M. S. McDonald, "Was There a Religious Revolution of 1800?" in James Horn, Jan Ellen Lewis, and Peter S. Onuf, eds., *The Revolution of 1800: Democracy, Race, and the New Republic* (Charlottesville: University of Virginia Press, 2002), pp. 173–198 at p. 173.

12. James A. Bayard to Richard Bassett, 17 Feb. 1801, quoted in James E. Lewis, Jr., "'What is to become of our Government?': The Revolutionary Potential of the Election of 1800," in Horn et al., eds., *Revolution of 1800*, pp. 3–29 at p. 21.

13. Jefferson, inaugural address of 4 March 1801 (PPPUS website). Note that Jefferson actually wrote "federalist" and "republican" in lower case (but he was always stingy with capital letters). Newspapers printed his rallying cry as "We are all Republicans, we are all Federalists." That was probably what he wanted to convey, even though he regarded the hard-core Federalists as inimical to his conception of federalism. See Merrill D. Peterson, *Thomas Jefferson and the New Nation* (New York: OUP, 1970), p. 656.

14. Peter Irons, *A People's History of the Supreme Court* 2nd ed. (New York: Penguin, 2006), pp. 108–111.

15. 5 U.S. 137 (1803); on the Marshall Court see Peter Charles Hoffer, Williamjames Hull Hoffer, and N.E.H. Hull, *The Supreme Court: An Essential History* (Lawrence: University Press of Kansas, 2007), ch. 3.

16. Jefferson (1820) quoted in Irons, *A People's History of the Supreme Court*, p. 110.

17. E.g., Thomas Jefferson to George Rogers Clark, 25 Dec. 1780, in *The Papers of Thomas Jefferson*, IV, pp. 237–238. See also Jefferson to Madison, 27 April 1809, in James Morton Smith, ed., *The Republic of Letters: The Correspondence Between Thomas Jefferson and James Madison, 1776–1826*, vol. III (New York: W. W. Norton, 1994), p. 1586, where he writes of having "such an empire for liberty as she has never surveyed since the creation."

18. Jefferson to Samuel Kercheval, 12 July 1816, in Peter S. Onuf, *Jefferson's Empire: The Language of American Nationhood* (Charlottesville: University of Virginia Press, 2000), p. 120.

19. Quoted in Patricia Nelson Limerick, *The Legacy of Conquest: The Unbroken Past of the American West* 2nd ed. (New York: W. W. Norton, 2006), pp. 78–79.

20. Quoted in Peterson, *Thomas Jefferson*, pp. 752–753, 760.

21. Ibid., p. 760.

22. Ibid., pp. 771, 773.

23. Statistics from U.S. Department of the Interior, Bureau of Land Management, *Public Land Statistics 2006*, table 1–1.

24. Walsingham's speech in the House of Lords, 17 Feb. 1783, quoted in Barbara Graymont, *The Iroquois in the American Revolution* (Syracuse, NY: Syracuse University Press, 1972), pp. 261–262.

25. Shelburne's speech quoted in Graymont, *The Iroquois in the American Revolution*, p. 262.

26. Jefferson to General Chastellux, 7 June 1785, in *The Papers of Thomas Jefferson*, VIII, p. 185.

27. Jefferson to William Henry Harrison (governor of Indiana Territory), 27 Feb. 1803, in Joyce Appleby and Terence Ball, eds., *Jefferson: Political Writings* (Cambridge: CUP, 1999), pp. 524–525.

28. Gary B. Nash, *The Unknown American Revolution: The Unruly Birth of Democracy and the Struggle to Create America* (London: Pimlico, 2007), p. 378.

29. William Henry Harrison to William Eustis, 7 Aug. 1811, in John Sugden, *Tecumseh: A Life* (London: Pimlico, 1999), p. 215.

30. Nash, *The Unknown American Revolution*, p. 282.

31. Quoted in ibid., p. 409.

32. Herbert S. Klein, *The Atlantic Slave Trade* (Cambridge: CUP, 1999), p. 210–211.

33. Angela Lakwete, *Inventing the Cotton Gin: Machine and Myth in Antebellum America* (Baltimore: Johns Hopkins University Press, 2003). For the heroic myth see Harold Evans, *They Made America. From the Steam Engine to the Search Engine: Two Centuries of Innovators* (New York: Back Bay Books, 2004), pp. 50–54.

34. John Adams to Thomas Jefferson, 21 Dec. 1819, in Lester J. Cappon, ed., *The Adams-Jefferson Letters* (Chapel Hill: UNC Press, 1959), p. 551. For the "black cloud" passage, see Adams to Jefferson, 3 Feb. 1821, ibid., p. 571.

35. Jefferson to Edward Coles, 25 Aug. 1814, in Appleby and Ball, *Jefferson: Political Writings*, p. 492.

36. For this see Ira Berlin, *Many Thousands Gone: The First Two Centuries of Slavery in North America* (Cambridge, MA: Harvard University Press, 1998), p. 224.

37. Jefferson to John Holmes, 22 April 1820, in Appleby and Ball, *Jefferson: Political Writings*, p. 496.

38. Abigail Adams to John Adams, 31 March 1776, in *Adams Family Correspondence*, I, p. 370.

39. Ibid.

40. Joseph Plumb Martin, *A Narrative of a Revolutionary Soldier* (New York: Signet Classics, 2001), p. 115.

41. Wilkinson letters quoted from Mary Beth Norton, *Liberty's Daughters: The Revolutionary Experience of American Women* (repr., Ithaca, NY: Cornell University Press, 1996), pp. 171–172, and Linda K. Kerber, *Women of the Republic: Intellect and Ideology in Revolutionary America* (Chapel Hill: UNC Press, 1980), p. 226.

42. Newark *Centinel of Freedom*, 18 Oct. 1797, quoted in Norton, *Liberty's Daughters*, p. 192.

43. William Griffith, commentary on the New Jersey Constitution, 1798, quoted in Norton, *Liberty's Daughters*, p. 192.

44. Newark *Centinel of Freedom*, 29 Dec. 1801, quoted in Judith Apter Klinghoffer and Lois Elkis, "'The Petticoat Electors': Women's Suffrage in New Jersey, 1776–1807," *JER*, 12 (1992), pp. 159–193 at p. 182.

45. Norton, *Liberty's Daughters*, p. 193.

46. For the full story see Ethel Armes, ed., *Nancy Shippen, Her Journal Book* (Philadelphia: J. B. Lippincott, 1935).

47. Murray and Adams quoted in Mary Beth Norton, *Liberty's Daughters*, pp. 247–248, 295.

48. Elizabeth Frost and Kathryn Cullen-DuPont, eds., *Women's Suffrage in America: An Eyewitness History* (New York: Facts on File, 1992), pp. 3–4.

49. Thomas Jefferson to Anne Willing Bingham, 11 May 1788, and to Albert Gallatin, 13 Jan. 1807, in Appleby and Ball, *Jefferson: Political Writings*, pp. 543, 545.

50. Nash, *The Unknown American Revolution*, p. 453.

51. Peterson, *Thomas Jefferson*, p. 398.

52. Quoted in Bradford Perkins, *Prologue to War: England and the United States, 1805–1812* (Berkeley: University of California Press, 1961), p. 163.

53. *Newburyport Herald*, 13 May 1808, quoted in Benjamin W. Labaree, *Patriots and Partisans: The Merchants of Newburyport, 1764–1815* 2nd ed. (New York: W. W. Norton, 1975), p. 154.

54. Quotations from Madison's message to Congress, 1 June 1812, in J.C.A. Stagg et al., eds., *The Papers of James Madison: Presidential Series*, vol. IV (Charlottesville: University of Virginia Press, 1999), pp. 432–438.

55. Jefferson to William Duane, 4 Aug. 1812, quoted in J.C.A. Stagg, *Mr. Madison's War: Politics, Diplomacy, and Warfare in the Early American Republic, 1783–1830* (Princeton, NJ: Princeton University Press, 1983), p. 5, n. 8.

56. Dolley Madison to Lucy Todd, 24 Aug. 1814, quoted in Virginia Moore, *The Madisons: A Biography* (New York: McGraw-Hill, 1979), pp. 315–316.

57. Dolley Madison to Lucy Todd, 24 Aug. 1814, quoted in Moore, *The Madisons*, p. 316.

58. Anthony S. Pitch, *The Burning of Washington: The British Invasion of 1814* (Annapolis, MD: Naval Institute Press, 1998), p. 117.

59. Quoted in Moore, *The Madisons*, p. 320.

60. Declaration by Federalists of Essex Country, Massachusetts, quoted in James M. Banner, Jr., *To the Hartford Convention: The Federalists and the Origins of Party Politics in Massachusetts, 1789–1815* (New York: Alfred A. Knopf, 1970), pp. 307–308.

61. Report of Hartford Convention, quoted in Banner, *To the Hartford Convention*, p. 339.

62. Adams's statement in cabinet on 7 Nov. 1823, quoted in Bradford Perkins, *Castlereagh and Adams: England and the United States, 1812–1823* (Berkeley: University of California Press, 1964), p. 334.

63. Monroe, annual message, 2 Dec. 1823 (PPPUS website).

5: East and West

1. Statistics from Maldwyn A. Jones, *The Limits of Liberty: American History, 1607–1992* (Oxford: OUP, 1992), p. 117.

2. Quoted in H. W. Brands, *Andrew Jackson: His Life and Times* (New York: Anchor Books, 2005), pp. 40–41.

3. Henry Clay to Francis P. Blair, 29 Jan. 1825, and to Francis T. Brooke, 28 Jan. 1825, in James F. Hopkins, ed., *The Papers of Henry Clay*, vol. IV (Lexington: University Press of Kentucky, 1972), pp. 47 and 45–46.

4. Andrew Jackson to John Donelson, 7 June 1829, in *Correspondence of Andrew Jackson*, ed. John Spencer Bassett (7 vols., Washington, DC: Carnegie Institution, 1926–1935), IV, p. 42.

5. Brands, *Andrew Jackson*, p. 412.

6. Thomas Hart Benton, speech of 20 Jan. 1832, in *Register of Debates*, 22nd Congress, 1st session, col. 141.

7. Quotations from his correspondence in Robert V. Remini, *Andrew Jackson and the Course of American Freedom, 1822–1832* (New York: Harper & Row, 1981), p. 366.

8. Jackson, veto message, 10 July 1832 (PPPUS website).

9. Ibid.

10. Biddle to Clay, 1 Aug. 1832, quoted in Remini, *Jackson and the Course of American Freedom*, p. 369.

11. Richard P. McCormick, "New Perspectives on Jacksonian Democracy," *AHR*, 65 (1960), pp. 288–301 at pp. 292–293.

12. Quotation from van Buren's *Autobiography* in Marc W. Kruman, "The Second Party System and the Transformation of Revolutionary Republicanism," *JER*, 12 (1999), pp. 509–537 at p. 521.

13. Quoted in Brands, *Andrew Jackson*, pp. 473–474.

14. Alexis de Tocqueville, *Democracy in America*, ed. J. P. Mayer (New York: Anchor Books, 1969), vol. II, part 3, ch. 12, pp. 600–603.

15. Boston statistics for 1833 from Edward Pessen, "The Egalitarian Myth and the American Social Reality: Wealth, Mobility and Equality in the 'Era of the Common Man,'" *AHR*, 76 (1971), pp. 989–1034 at pp. 1020–1021.

16. "The American Scholar" (31 Aug. 1837), in Robert E. Spiller, ed., *The Collected Works of Ralph Waldo Emerson*, vol. I (Cambridge, MA: Harvard University Press, 1971), pp. 52–70 at pp. 52, 69.

17. Leon Chai, *The Romantic Foundations of the American Renaissance* (Ithaca, NY: Cornell University Press, 1987), p. 6.

18. Quoted in F. O. Matthiessen, *American Renaissance: Art and Expression in the Age of Emerson and Whitman* (New York: OUP, 1941), p. 519—a classic of criticism that still holds its own.

19. Nathan O. Hatch, *The Democratization of American Christianity* (New Haven, CT: Yale University Press, 1989), p. 20.

20. Harrison Gray Otis (1836), quoted in Hatch, *Democratization of American Christianity*, p. 66.

21. Statistics from Mark Noll, *The Old Religion in a New World: The History of North American Christianity* (Grand Rapids, MI: William B. Eerdmans, 2002), pp. 61, 64, 66–67.

22. Tocqueville, *Democracy in America*, vol. I, part 2, ch. 9, p. 295.

23. Beecher, address in 1814, quoted in James W. Fraser, *Pedagogue for God's Kingdom: Lyman Beecher and the Second Great Awakening* (Lanham, MD: University Press of America, 1980), p. 25.

24. Tocqueville, *Democracy in America*, vol. II, part 2, ch. 5, p. 513.

25. Quoted in Barbara Leslie Epstein, *The Politics of Domesticity: Women, Evangelism and Temperance in Nineteenth-Century America* (Middletown, CT: Wesleyan University Press, 1981), p. 94. This incident took place in 1865.

26. Richard R. John, "Taking Sabbatarianism Seriously: The Postal System, the Sabbath, and the Transformation of American Political Culture," *JER*, 10 (1990), pp. 517–567.

27. Richard J. Carwardine, *Evangelicals and Politics in Antebellum America* (New Haven, CT: Yale University Press, 1993), pp. 20, 43–44.

28. The *Liberator*, 1 Jan. 1831, front page reprinted in Henry Mayer, *All on Fire: William Lloyd Garrison and the Abolition of Slavery* (New York: St Martin's Press, 1998), p. 111.

29. Richard Furman, "Exposition of the Views of the Baptists Relative to the Coloured Population in the United States," 24 Dec. 1822, reprinted in James A. Rogers, *Richard Furman: Life and Legacy* (Macon, GA: Mercer University Press, 1985), appendix B, quoting from p. 280.

30. Metaphor adapted from Sylvia R. Frey, *Water from the Rock: Black Resistance in a Revolutionary Age* (Princeton, NJ: Princeton University Press, 1991), p. 262.

31. Frey, *Water from the Rock*, p. 322.

32. Quoted in Elizabeth Frost and Kathryn Cullen-DuPont, eds., *Women's Suffrage in America: An Eyewitness History* (New York: Facts on File, 1992), p. 25.

33. Ibid., p. 29.

34. Ibid., pp. 359–361.

35. Adams (1802) in Robert Kagan, *Dangerous Nation* (New York: Random House, 2006), p. 85.

36. Michael Paul Rogin, *Fathers and Children: Andrew Jackson and the Subjugation of the American Indian* (New York: Alfred A. Knopf, 1975), pp. 188–189.

37. Jackson, first annual message to Congress, 8 Dec. 1829 (PPPUS website).

38. Ibid. Extracts about the Indians also published in Anthony F. C. Wallace, *The Long Bitter Trail: Andrew Jackson and the Indians* (New York: Hill & Wang, 1993), appendix A, pp. 121–124.

39. Congressman Henry R. Storrs (NY), quoted in Remini, *Jackson and the Course of American Freedom*, p. 261.

40. Frelinghuysen, speech on 9 April 1830, *Register of Debates*, 21st Congress, 1st session, p. 312.

41. Text of the Indian Removal Act, 28 May 1830, printed in Wallace, *Long Bitter Trail*, appendix B, pp. 125–128.

42. John Ross and other Cherokee Chiefs to the Delegation of Seneca Indians, 14 April 1834, in Gary E. Moulton, ed., *The Papers of Chief John Ross* (2 vols., Norman: University of Oklahoma Press, 1985), I, p. 285.

43. Marshall's majority opinion, 18 March 1831, in *The Cherokee Nation v. The State of Georgia*, 30 U.S. 1.

44. Quoted in Ronald N. Satz, *American Indian Policy in the Jacksonian Era* (Lincoln: University of Nebraska Press, 1975), p. 49.

45. Account by "A Native of Maine," in the *New York Observer*, 26 Jan. 1839, quoted in Grant Foreman, *Indian Removal: The Emigration of the Five Civilized Tribes of Indians* 2nd ed. (Norman: University of Oklahoma Press, 1953), pp. 306–307.

46. Wallace, *Long Bitter Trail*, pp. 93–94.

47. As estimated by Rogin, *Fathers and Children*, p. 4.

48. Morris Birkbeck, *Notes on a Journey in America* (London, 1818), quoted in Martin Ridge and Ray Allen Billington, eds., *America's Frontier Story: A Documentary History of Westward Expansion* (New York: Holt, Rinehart & Winston, 1969), pp. 274–275.

49. Walt Whitman "Song of the Broad-Axe" (1856).

50. Copybook verses, c. 1824, in Roy P. Basler, ed., *The Collected Works of Abraham Lincoln* (9 vols., New Brunswick, NJ: Rutgers University Press, 1953–1955), I, p. 1.

51. "The Significance of the Frontier in American Life" (1893), reprinted as Frederick Jackson Turner, *The Frontier in American History* (New York: Henry Holt, 1920), ch. 1, quoting pp. 2–3.

52. Advertisement originally in the *Augusta Chronicle* (1819), quoted in Richard Wade, *The Urban Frontier: Pioneer Life in Early Pittsburgh, Cincinnati, Lexington, Louisville, and St Louis* (Chicago: University of Chicago Press, 1959), pp. 32–33.

53. Speech of 4 Feb. 1817, in *Annals of Congress*, 14th Congress, 2nd session, column 854.

54. Stressed by George Taylor Rogers, *The Transportation Revolution, 1815–1860* (New York: Rinehart & Co., 1951), p. 33.

55. Thomas A. Janvier, "The Evolution of New York—Second Part," *Harper's New Monthly Magazine*, 87/517 (June 1893), pp. 15–29 at p. 28.

56. Cadwallader D. Colden, Memorial (1825), quoted in Ronald E. Shaw, *Canals for a Nation: The Canal Era in the United States, 1790–1860* (Lexington: University Press of Kentucky, 1990), p. 44.

57. Charles Dickens, *American Notes* (1842) (London: Granville Publishing, 1985), ch. 10, p. 134.

58. Quoted in John F. Stover, *History of the Baltimore and Ohio Railroad* (West Lafayette, IN: Purdue University Press, 1987), p. 27.

59. Rogers, *Transportation Revolution*, pp. 74, 79.

60. Quoted in Frederick Merk, *Manifest Destiny and Mission in American History: A Reinterpretation* (New York: Alfred A. Knopf, 1963), p. 51.

61. Rogers, *Transportation Revolution*, p. 79.

62. Douglas, letter of 17 Dec. 1853, quoted in Robert W. Johannsen, *Stephen A. Douglas* (New York: OUP, 1973), p. 399.

63. The two Lincoln journeys are described in John F. Stover, *Iron Road to the West: American Railroads in the 1850s* (New York: Columbia University Press, 1978), pp. 1–3.

64. Lincoln, speech at Lafayette, Indiana, 11 Feb. 1861, printed in Basler, *Collected Works of Abraham Lincoln*, IV, p. 192. The next paragraph quotes from the same speech.

6: Slave or Free?

1. Quoted in Frederick Merk, *Albert Gallatin and the Oregon Problem: A Study in Anglo-American Diplomacy* (Cambridge, MA: Harvard University Press, 1950), p. 13.

2. John L. O'Sullivan in the *Democratic Review*, July–Aug. 1845, reprinted in Martin Ridge and Ray Allen Billington, eds., *America's Frontier Story: A Documentary History of Westward Expansion* (New York: Holt, Rinehart & Winston, 1969), pp. 491–493.

3. Polk, inaugural address, 4 March 1845 (PPPUS website).

4. Manuel Eduardo de Gorostiza (1840), quoted in Gene M. Brack, *Mexico Views Manifest Destiny, 1821–1846: An Essay on the Origins of the Mexican War* (Albuquerque: University of New Mexico Press, 1975), pp. 96–97.

5. Polk, special message to Congress, 11 May 1846 (PPPUS website).

6. Conversation with Congressman James A. Black (SC), 4 Jan. 1846, as recorded in Milo Milton Quaife, ed., *The Diary of James K. Polk During His Presidency, 1845–1849*, vol. I (Chicago: A. C. McClure, 1910), p. 155.

7. Quoted in Charles Sellers, *James K. Polk: Continentalist, 1843–1846* (Princeton, NJ: Princeton University Press, 1966), p. 384.

8. Robert E. Lee to John Mackay, 2 Oct. 1847, quoted in Michael Fellman, *The Making of Robert E. Lee* (New York: Random House, 2000), pp. 57–58.

9. Quotations from a speech in the House of Representatives, 12 Jan. 1848, in Roy P. Basler, ed., *The Collected Works of Abraham Lincoln* (9 vols., New Brunswick, NJ: Rutgers University Press, 1953–1955), I, pp. 433, 439–440, 441–442.

10. Quoted in John W. Schroeder, *Mr. Polk's War: American Opposition and Dissent, 1846–1848* (Madison: University of Wisconsin Press, 1973), p. 117.

11. *William Clayton's Journal* (Salt Lake City: The Deseret News, 1921), pp. 308–309, entry for 22 July 1847.

12. John A. Sutter, "The Discovery of Gold in California," *Hutchings' California Magazine*, 2/5 (Nov. 1857), pp. 193–202 at pp. 194–195.

13. Walter Colton, diary entry for 20 June 1848, in Ridge and Billington, *America's Frontier Story*, pp. 531–532.

14. Washington correspondent of the *New York Herald*, 28 Feb. 1850, quoted in John C. Waugh, *On the Brink of Civil War: The Compromise of 1850 and How It Changed the Course of American History* (Wilmington, DE: Scholarly Resources, 2003), p. 85.

15. John C. Calhoun, speech of 4 March 1850, *Congressional Globe*, 31st Congress, 1st session, pp. 451, 453.

16. Daniel Webster, speech of 7 March 1850, *Congressional Globe*, 31st Congress, 1st session, appendix, pp. 269, 274, 276.

17. William H. Seward, speech of 11 March 1850, *Congressional Globe*, 31st Congress, 1st session, appendix, quoting from pp. 261–265.

18. Douglas, speech in Chicago, 23 Oct. 1850, printed in *Speeches of the Hon. Stephen A. Douglas* (New York: Jared W. Bell, 1851), p. 5.

19. Quoted in Waugh, *On the Brink of Civil War*, p. 187.

20. Moses Y. Beach, ed., *The Wealth and Biography of the Wealthy Citizens of the City of New York* 10th ed. (New York: New York Sun, 1846), title page and foreword.

21. Ibid., pp. 2, 26.

22. *New York Times*, 1 July 1859, quoted in Tyler Anbinder, "From Famine to Five Points: Lord Landsdowne's Irish Tenants Encounter North America's Most Notorious Slum," *AHR*, 107 (2002), pp. 351–387 at p. 373.

23. Details from Anbinder, "From Famine to Five Points," esp. pp. 351–353.

24. Bushnell quoted in Robert Dunne, *Antebellum Irish Immigration and Emerging Ideologies of "America": A Protestant Backlash* (Lewiston, NY: The Edwin Mellon Press, 2002), p. 87.

25. *Native American*, 7 May 1844, quoted in Michael Feldberg, *The Philadelphia Riots of 1844: A Study of Ethnic Conflict* (Westport, CT: Greenwood Press, 1975), p. 108.

26. Lyman Beecher, *A Plea for the West* (1835), quoted in Dunne, *Antebellum Irish Immigration*, p. 36.

27. D. B. Beck, editor of the *Maine Temperance Watchman*, quoted in Ian R. Tyrrell, *Sobering Up: From Temperance to Prohibition in Antebellum America, 1800–1860* (Westport, CT: Greenwood Press, 1979), p. 268.

28. Constitution of the State Council of Connecticut, 7 Sept. 1854, quoted in Tyler Anbinder, *Nativism and Slavery: The Northern Know Nothings and the Politics of the 1850s* (New York: OUP, 1992), p. 23.

29. Thomas R. Whitney, *A Defence of the American Policy as Opposed to the Encroachments of Foreign Influence and Especially to the Interference of the Papacy . . .* (New York: De Witt & Davenport, 1856), pp. 326–327.

30. Ibid., p. 126. See also Bruce Levine, "Conservatism, Nativism, and Slavery: Thomas R. Whitney and the Origins of the Know-Nothing Party," *JAH*, 88 (2001), pp. 455–488.

31. Bruce Collins, *White Society in the Antebellum South* (London: Longman, 1985), pp. 15–16; William Kauffman Scarborough, *Masters of the Big House: Elite Slaveholders of the Mid-Nineteenth-Century South* (Baton Rouge: Louisiana State University Press, 2003), pp. 12–13.

32. John L. Manning to "My Dearest Wife," 21 Sept. 1851, in Scarborough, *Masters of the Big House*, pp. 175, 188.

33. "Linda Brent," *Incidents in the Life of a Slave Girl, Written by Herself* (Boston: The Author, 1861), ch. 5. "Linda Brent" was Jacobs's pen name; her owner was given the pseudonym "Dr. Flint."

34. Josiah Henson, *Truth Stranger Than Fiction: Father Henson's Story of His Own Life* (Boston: John P. Jewett & Co., 1858), pp. 8, 18–19.

35. Ibid., pp. 94–95.

36. Ibid., pp. 96–100.

37. Ibid., pp. 126–127.

38. Harriet Beecher Stowe, *Uncle Tom's Cabin, or, Life Among the Lowly* (1852), ch. 45, reprinted in Harriet Beecher Stowe, *Three Novels* (New York: Library of America, 1982), pp. 510, 514.

39. Speech in Rochester, New York, 5 July 1852, as printed in David B. Cheesebrough, *Frederick Douglass: Oratory from Slavery* (Westport, CT: Greenwood Press, 1998), p. 118.

40. James H. Hammond, speech in the Senate, 4 March 1858, in *Congressional Globe*, 35th Congress, 1st session, p. 962. See also David F. Ericson, *The Debate over Slavery: Antislavery and Proslavery Liberalism in Antebellum America* (New York: New York University Press, 2000), pp. 141–145.

41. William Seward's *Autobiography*, quoted in Eric Foner, *Free Soil, Free Labor, Free Men: The Ideology of the Republican Party Before the Civil War* (New York: OUP, 1970), p. 41.

42. Carl Schurz, speech in 1860, quoted in Foner, *Free Soil, Free Labor, Free Men*, p. 72.

43. Robert Hughes, *American Visions: The Epic History of Art in America* (London: The Harvill Press, 1997), pp. 191–222.

44. Douglas speech to Senate, 12 Feb. 1850, *Congressional Globe*, 31st Congress, 1st session, p. 343.

45. Quoted in Robert W. Johannsen, *Stephen A. Douglas* (New York: OUP, 1973), p. 451.

46. Announcement of a Republican Party meeting in Buffalo, NY, May 1856, quoted in Michael F. Holt, *The Political Crisis of the 1850s* (New York: John Wiley & Sons, 1978), p. 197.

47. Seward speech to Senate, 25 May 1854, *Congressional Globe*, 33rd Congress, 1st session, appendix, p. 769.

48. Edward Bridgman to "Cousin Sidney," 25 and 28 May 1856, available online at http://www.pbs.org/wgbh/aia/part4/4h2953t.html, accessed 14 Oct. 2008.

49. Quoted in David Donald, *Charles Sumner and the Coming of the Civil War* (New York: Alfred A. Knopf, 1960), p. 295.

50. *Dred Scott v. Sandford*, 6 March 1857, 60 U.S. 393, esp. pp. 404, 407, 451.

51. Don E. Fehrenbacher, *The Dred Scott Case: Its Significance in American Law and Politics* (New York: OUP, 1978), p. 209.

52. Peter Charles Hoffer, Williamjames Hull Hoffer, and N. E. H Hull, *The Supreme Court: An Essential History* (Lawrence: University Press of Kansas, 2007), pp. 99–100.

53. Speech in Springfield, Illinois, 16 June 1858, in Basler, *Collected Works of Abraham Lincoln*, II, p. 462.

54. Quotations from David S. Reynolds, *John Brown, Abolitionist* (New York: Alfred A. Knopf, 2005), pp. 395, 397.

55. Emerson, lecture on "Courage," 8 Nov. 1859, in Reynolds, *John Brown*, p. 366.

56. Johnson, speech to Senate, 12 Dec. 1859, *Congressional Globe*, 36th Congress, 1st session, pp. 106–107.

7: North and South

1. Lincoln, inaugural address, 4 March 1861 (PPPUS website). The final conciliatory sentences were based on suggestions from his new secretary of state, William H. Seward—see David Herbert Donald, *Lincoln* (New York: Simon & Schuster, 1995), pp. 284–285.

2. Varina Davis, *Jefferson Davis: Ex-President of the Confederate States of America, A Memoir by His Wife* (2 vols., New York, 1890), II, pp. 18–19.

3. Isabella D. Martin and Myrta Lockett Avary, eds., *A Diary from Dixie, as Written by Mary Boykin Chesnut* (New York: Appleton & Co., 1905), p. 35, entry for 12 April 1861.

4. Ibid., p. 38, entry for 13 April 1861.

5. Robert E. Lee to Anne Marshall, 20 April 1861, in Capt. Robert E. Lee, *Recollections and Letters of General Robert E. Lee* (London: Archibald Constable & Co., 1904), p. 26.

6. Robert Hunt Rhodes, *All for the Union: The Civil War Diary and Letters of Elisha Hunt Rhodes* (New York: Vintage Books, 1992), pp. 3–4, 12–13.

7. Sam R. Watkins, *"Company Aytch": A Confederate Memoir of the Civil War* (New York: Touchstone, 1990), pp. 7–8.

8. Rhodes, *All for the Union*, p. 22.

9. William Howard Russell, *My Civil War Diary*, ed. Fletcher Pratt (London: Hamish Hamilton, 1954), pp. 232–233, entry for 22 July 1861.

10. Watkins, *"Company Aytch,"* p. 8.

11. Russell, *My Civil War Diary*, p. 240.

12. McClellan to his wife, July to Nov. 1861, quoted in James M. McPherson, *Battle Cry of Freedom: The American Civil War* (London: Penguin, 1990), pp. 359–360, 364–365.

13. Quoted in Geoffrey C. Ward, with Ric Burns and Ken Burns, *The Civil War: An Illustrated History* (New York: Alfred A. Knopf, 1990), p. 90.

14. "The Harrison's Bar Letter," 7 July 1862, in George B. McClellan, *McClellan's Own Story* (New York: Charles L. Webster & Co., 1887), p. 488.

15. Letter of 16 Feb. 1862, quoted from Ulysses S. Grant, *Personal Memoirs of U. S. Grant* (London: Penguin, 1999), p. 167.

16. Watkins, *"Company Aytch,"* p. 27.

17. Ibid., p. 11.

18. McClellan to Lincoln, 20 April 1862, quoted in Stephen W. Sears, *To the Gates of Richmond: The Peninsula Campaign* (New York: Ticknor & Fields, 1992), p. 57.

19. *The Times*, 19 July 1862, quoted in D. P. Crook, *The North, the South, and the Powers, 1861–1865* (New York: John Wiley & Sons, 1974), p. 218.

20. Lee to Davis, 8 Sept. 1862, in McPherson, *Battle Cry of Freedom*, p. 535.

21. Palmerston to Russell, 22 Oct. 1862, quoted in Crook, *The North, the South, and the Powers*, p. 242.

22. Lincoln, first annual message, 3 Dec. 1861 (PPPUS website).

23. David Williams, *A People's History of the Civil War: Struggles for the Meaning of Freedom* (New York: The New Press, 2005), pp. 327, 332.

24. *Douglass' Monthly*, July 1861; McPherson, *Battle Cry of Freedom*, p. 354.

25. Preliminary Emancipation Proclamation, 22 Sept. 1862, and Emancipation Proclamation, 1 Jan. 1863 (PPPUS website).

26. Jefferson Davis, Presidential Message to the Congress of the CSA, 12 Jan. 1863, in *Journals of the Congress of the Confederate States of America, 1861–1865*, vol. III (Washington, DC: U.S. Government Printing Office, 1904), p. 13.

27. Resolution of the Illinois state legislature, 7 Jan. 1863, quoted in Henry Steele Commager and Erik Bruun, eds., *The Civil War Archive: The History of the Civil War in Documents* 2nd ed. (New York: Black Dog & Leventhal, 2000), p. 579.

28. *Douglass' Monthly*, Aug. 1863, quoted in McPherson, *Battle Cry of Freedom*, p. 564.

29. Quoted in Ward, *The Civil War*, p. 248.

30. James H. Gooding to Lincoln, 28 Sept. 1863, in Commager and Bruun, *The Civil War Archive*, p. 550.

31. [Dora Richards Miller], "A Woman's Diary of the Siege of Vicksburg," *Century Magazine*, 1885, pp. 767–775, entry of 20 March 1863.

32. Anonymous note of 28 June 1863, quoted in A. A. Hoehling, ed., *Vicksburg: 47 Days of Siege* (Englewood Cliffs, NJ: Prentice-Hall, 1969), pp. 241–242.

33. Letter of 4 July 1863, quoted in William S. McFeely, *Grant* (New York: W. W. Norton, 1981), p. 137.

34. James Longstreet, "Lee's Right Wing at Gettysburg," in Robert U. Underwood and Clarence C. Buel, eds., *Battles and Leaders of the Civil War* (4 vols., New York: Century, 1884–1888), III, pp. 339–354 at p. 339.

35. Ibid., p. 343.

36. Frank A. Haskell, *The Battle of Gettysburg*, ed. Bruce Catton (London: Eyre & Spottiswoode, 1959), pp. 97–98.

37. Quoted in Longstreet, "Lee's Right Wing at Gettysburg," p. 347.

38. Lincoln, address at the dedication of the National Cemetery at Gettysburg, 19 Nov. 1863 (PPPUS website).

39. The point is made by McPherson, *Battle Cry of Freedom*, p. 859.

40. Donald, *Lincoln*, pp. 405–406.

41. Watkins, *"Company Aytch,"* pp. 31–32.

42. Quoted in Philip Shaw Paludan, *"A People's Contest": The Union and the Civil War, 1861–1865* (New York: Harper & Row, 1988), p. 190.

43. Anna Dickinson, "What Answer?" (Boston, 1868), quoted in Commager and Bruun, *The Civil War Archive*, p. 482.

44. General Horace Porter, *Campaigning with Grant* (1897) (New York: Da Capo Reprint, 1986), pp. 174–175.

45. Grant, *Personal Memoirs*, p. 477.

46. Quoted in Arthur M. Schlesinger, Jr., ed., *History of American Presidential Elections, 1789–1968* (4 vols., New York: Chelsea House, 1971), II, p. 1179.

47. Donald, *Lincoln*, p. 529.

48. Joseph E. Brown to Alexander H. Stephens, 1 Sept. 1862, in Commager and Bruun, *The Civil War Archive*, pp. 517–518.

49. George Cary Eggleston, "Notes on Cold Harbor," in Underwood and Buel, *Battles and Leaders of the Civil War*, IV, pp. 230–232 at p. 231.

50. William Tecumseh Sherman, *Memoirs of General W. T. Sherman*, vol. 2 (New York: Library of America, 1990), ch. 19, pp. 600–601.

51. Eliza Frances Andrews, *The War-Time Journal of a Georgia Girl, 1864–1865* (New York: Appleton & Co., 1908), p. 32.

52. Martin and Avary, *A Diary from Dixie*, p. 327, entries for 21 and 24 Sept. 1864.

53. Ann K. Blomquist and Robert A. Taylor, eds., *This Cruel War: The Civil War Letters of Grant and Malinda Taylor, 1862–1865* (Macon, GA: Mercer University Press, 2000), pp. 322–323.

54. Williams, *A People's History of the Civil War*, p. 374.

55. Lee to Andrew Hunter, 11 Jan. 1865, in *The War of the Rebellion: A Compilation of the Official Records of the Union and Confederate Armies*, series 4, vol. III (Washington, DC: U.S. Government Printing Office, 1900), pp. 1012–1013.

56. General Howell Cobb to James A Seddon (secretary of war), 8 Jan. 1865, in *The War of the Rebellion*, pp. 1009–1010.

57. Lincoln, second inaugural address, 4 March 1865 (PPPUS website).

58. Lincoln to Fanny McCullough, 23 Dec. 1862, in Roy P. Basler, ed., *The Collected Works of Abraham Lincoln* (9 vols., New Brunswick, NJ: Rutgers University Press, 1953–1955), VI, pp. 17–18.

59. Quoted in Richard Carwardine, *Lincoln: A Life of Purpose and Power* (New York: Vintage Books, 2006), p. 314.

60. Diary of Frances Calden de la Barca Hunt, 3–4 April 1865, quoted in Emmy E. Werner, *Reluctant Witnesses: Children's Voices from the Civil War* (Boulder, CO: Westview Press, 1998), pp. 135–136.

61. Donald, *Lincoln*, pp. 576, 682; McPherson, *Battle Cry of Freedom*, pp. 846–847.

62. Quoted in Douglas Southall Freeman, *R. E. Lee: A Biography* (4 vols., New York: Charles Scribner's Sons, 1934–1935), IV, p. 120.

63. Quotations here and below from General Horace Porter, "The Surrender at Appomattox Court House," in Underwood and Buel, *Battles and Leaders of the Civil War*, IV, pp. 729–746 at pp. 739–744.

64. Joshua Lawrence Chamberlain, *The Passing of the Armies: An Account of the Final Campaign of the Army of the Potomac, Based upon Personal Reminiscences of the Fifth Army Corps* (New York: G. P. Putnam's Sons, 1915), pp. 260–261.

65. Donald, *Lincoln*, p. 593.

66. Gideon Welles, *Diary of Gideon Welles: Secretary of the Navy Under Lincoln and Johnson* (3 vols., Boston: Houghton Mifflin, 1911), II, pp. 286–287.

67. His exact words are contested, but I follow Donald, *Lincoln*, pp. 599, 686.

68. Quoted in Barry Schwartz, *Abraham Lincoln and the Forge of National Memory* (Chicago: University of Chicago Press, 2000), p. 53.

8: White and Black

1. Quoted in Emmy E. Werner, *Reluctant Witnesses: Children's Voices from the Civil War* (Boulder, CO: Westview Press, 1998), pp. 142–143.

2. Maris A. Vinovskis, ed., *Towards a Social History of the American Civil War: Exploratory Essays* (New York: CUP, 1990), p. 7; Eric Foner, *Reconstruction: America's Unfinished Revolution, 1863–1877* (New York: Harper & Row, 1988), p. 125.

3. Quoted in Myrta Lockett Avary, *Dixie After the War* (London: Doubleday, Page, 1906), p. 155.

4. For a recent cliometric evaluation see Paul F. Paskoff, "Measures of War: A Quantitative Examination of the Civil War's Destructiveness in the Confederacy," *CWH*, 64 (2008), pp. 35–62.

5. Quoted in Foner, *Reconstruction*, p. 9.

6. Frederick Douglass, *Life and Times of Frederick Douglass, His Early Life as a Slave, His Escape from Bondage, and His Complete History to the Present Time* (Hartford, CT: Park Publishing Co., 1881), p. 385.

7. Isabella D. Martin and Myrta Lockett Avary, eds., *A Diary from Dixie, as Written by Mary Boykin Chesnut* (New York: Appleton & Co. 1905), pp. 379, 380, and 384, entries for 19 and 22 April and 2 May 1865.

8. C. Vann Woodward and Elisabeth Muhlenfield, eds., *The Private Mary Chesnut: The Unpublished Civil War Diaries* (New York: OUP, 1984), p. 243, entry for 13 May 1865.

9. Richard Taylor, *Destruction and Reconstruction: Personal Experiences of the Late War* (New York: Appleton & Co., 1879), pp. 242–243.

10. Johnson, interview with G. L. Stearns, 3 Oct. 1865, in Walter L. Fleming, ed., *Documentary History of Reconstruction: Political, Military, Social, Religious, Educational and Industrial, 1865–1906* (2 vols., New York: Cleveland Clark, 1906), I, p. 117.

11. Johnson, special message to the Senate, 18 Dec. 1865 (PPPUS website).

12. Stevens, speech of 18 Dec. 1865, in Fleming, *Documentary History of Reconstruction*, I, pp. 147–149.

13. Stevens, speeches of 10 March 1866 and 3 Jan. 1867, in Fleming, *Documentary History of Reconstruction*, I, pp. 150–151.

14. Johnson, veto message of Civil Rights Act, 27 March 1866 (PPPUS website).

15. Foner, *Reconstruction*, p. 255.

16. Sumner's written opinion on the impeachment of President Johnson, 1868, in Fleming, *Documentary History of Reconstruction*, I, p. 470.

17. James S. Pike, *The Prostrate South: South Carolina Under Negro Government* (New York: Appleton & Co., 1874), p. 15.

18. Ibid., pp. 13, 17–21.

19. S. S. Greene, speaking at the NTA annual conference in 1865, in Fleming, *Documentary History of Reconstruction*, II, pp. 171–172.

20. Report of General John C. Robinson and J. W. Alvord (1866), quoted in Fleming, *Documentary History of Reconstruction*, II, p. 182.

21. Report of the Congressional Investigating Committee, 1872, in Fleming, *Documentary History of Reconstruction*, II, p. 39.

22. *New York Times*, 26 Dec. 1878, p. 1.

23. Detail and quotations in this paragraph from *New York Times*, 26 Dec. 1878, p. 1.

24. Ben Johnson, Slave Narrative, in Henry Steele Commager and Erik Bruun, eds., *The Civil War Archive: The History of the Civil War in Documents* 2nd ed. (New York: Black Dog & Leventhal, 2000), pp. 802–803.

25. Avary, *Dixie After the War*, pp. 370–371.

26. Henry Adams (Louisiana), in Senate Report (1876), quoted in Foner, *Reconstruction*, p. 582.

27. *The Nation*, 5 April 1877, quoted in Foner, *Reconstruction*, p. 582.

28. For the speech of 22 Dec. 1886, see Joel Chandler Harris, *Life of Henry W. Grady, Including His Writings and Speeches* (New York: Cassell, 1890), pp. 83–93.

29. John Wilber Jenkins, *James B. Duke: Master Builder* (New York: George H. Doran, 1927), pp. 66, 68, 77—generally ch. 5.

30. Jenkins, *James B. Duke*, pp. 53–54.

31. [Anon.], *Independent Magazine*, c. 1900, reprinted in Commager and Bruun, *The Civil War Archive*, pp. 806–809.

32. Ibid.

33. Speech at Atlanta, 18 Sept. 1895, in Louis R. Harlan, ed., *The Booker T. Washington Papers*, vol. III (Urbana: University of Illinois Press, 1974), pp. 583–587.

34. W.E.B. Du Bois, *The Souls of Black Folk* (1903) (New York: Fawcett, 1961), pp. 48–49.

35. Stephen B. Oates, *Let the Trumpet Sound: The Life of Martin Luther King, Jr.* (New York: Mentor Books, 1982), pp. 2–3. King changed his name and that of his son from Mike to Martin Luther in 1934, five years after Jr.'s birth.

36. W.E.B. Du Bois, *Darkwater: Voices from Within the Veil* (New York: Harcourt, Brace & Co., 1921), pp. 229–230.

37. *Plessy v. Ferguson*, 163 U.S. 537 (1896), p. 550—majority opinion delivered by Mr. Justice Henry Billings Brown, 18 May 1896.

38. *Plessy v. Ferguson*, 163 U.S. 537 (1896), p. 551.

39. Quoted in Stuart Anderson, *Race and Rapprochement: Anglo-Saxonism and Anglo-American Relations* (London: Associated University Press, 1981), p. 34.

40. Grace Elizabeth Hale, *Making Whiteness: The Culture of Segregation in the South, 1890–1940* (New York: Pantheon, 1998), p. 284.

41. Quotations from Mark DeWolfe Howe, ed., *Touched with Fire: Civil War Letters and Diary of Oliver Wendell Holmes, Jr., 1861–1864* (Cambridge, MA: Harvard University Press, 1946), respectively pp. 79, 23.

42. Douglas Southall Freeman, *R. E. Lee: A Biography* (4 vols., New York: Charles Scribner's Sons, 1934–1935), IV, p. 436.

43. Memorial Day oration, 30 May 1884, Keene, New Hampshire, in Mark DeWolfe Howe, ed., *The Occasional Speeches of Justice Oliver Wendell Holmes* (Cambridge, MA: Harvard University Press, 1962), quoting pp. 6, 8, 13, 15.

44. Gerald F. Linderman, *Embattled Courage: The Experience of Combat in the American Civil War* (New York: The Free Press, 1989), p. 275.

45. Vinovskis, *Towards a Social History of the American Civil War*, pp. 21–23, 172.

46. 1890 Georgia publication quoted in Linderman, *Embattled Courage*, p. 290.

47. Bruce Catton, "The Day the Civil War Ended: Gettysburg, Fifty Years After," *American Heritage*, 29/4 (June–July 1978), available online at http://www.americanheritage.com/articles/magazine/ah/1978/4/1978_4_56.shtml, accessed 14 Oct. 2008.

48. Ibid.

49. Quoted in Richard Gray, *A History of American Literature* (Oxford: Blackwell, 2004), p. 448.

50. William Faulkner, *Intruder in the Dust* (London: Chatto & Windus, 1949), ch. 9, pp. 194–195.

51. Malcolm X, with the assistance of Alex Haley, *The Autobiography of Malcolm X* (London: Penguin, 1968), p. 113.

52. James M. McPherson, *Battle Cry of Freedom: The American Civil War* (London: Penguin, 1990), pp. 859–860.

9: Capital and Labor

1. Michel Chevalier, "La Guerre et la crise européenne," *Revue des Deux Mondes*, 1 June 1866, pp. 784–785.

2. Upton Sinclair, *The Jungle* (London: William Heinemann, 1906), p. 246.

3. Ibid., p. 247.

4. Peter Krass, *Carnegie* (Hoboken, NJ: John Wiley & Sons, 2002), p. 25.

5. "The Road to Business Success: A Talk to Young Men," at the Curry Commercial College, Pittsburgh, 23 June 1885, reprinted in Andrew Carnegie, *The Empire of Business* (London: Harper & Brothers, 1902), pp. 3–18 at pp. 4, 10–11, 13, 17.

6. Andrew Carnegie, "Wealth," *North American Review*, 391 (June 1889), pp. 653–664. It was retitled "The Gospel of Wealth" at Gladstone's suggestion.

7. Charles Perrow, *Organizing America: Wealth, Power, and the Origins of Corporate Capitalism* (Princeton, NJ: Princeton University Press, 2002), p. 227.

8. "The Fate of the Salaried Man," *Independent* (New York), 20 Aug. 1903, pp. 2002–2003, quoted in Olivier Zunz, *Making America Corporate, 1870–1920* (Chicago: University of Chicago Press, 1990), p. 12.

9. Andrew Carnegie to W. E. Gladstone, 7 Feb. 1890, quoted in David Nasaw, *Andrew Carnegie* (New York: Penguin, 2006), pp. 338–339.

10. Derek Howse, *Greenwich Time and the Discovery of the Longitude* (Oxford: OUP, 1980), p. 120.

11. William F. Allen, "Report on Standard Time," 11 April 1883, quoted in Nathaniel Allen, "The Times They Are A-Changing: The Influence of Railroad Technology on the Adoption of Standard Time Zones in 1883," *The History Teacher*, 33 (2000), pp. 241–256 at p. 246.

12. *Indianapolis Sentinel*, 21 Nov. 1883, quoted in Allen, "The Times They Are A-Changing," pp. 247, 250.

13. E. D. McCafferty, *Henry J. Heinz: A Biography* (New York: B. Orr Press, 1923), pp. 147–148.

14. Ron Chernow, *Titan: The Life of John D. Rockefeller, Sr.* (Boston: Little, Brown, 1998), p. 675; Daniel Yergin, *The Prize: The Epic Quest for Oil, Money, and Power* (New York: Touchstone, 1992), pp. 57, 79–80.

15. "Report of the Committee on the Machinery of the United States of America," 23 Aug. 1854, in Nathan Rosenberg, ed., *The American System of Manufactures* (Edinburgh: Edinburgh University Press, 1969), at p. 122.

16. Nils William Olsson, ed., *A Pioneer in Northwest America, 1841–58: The Memoirs of Gustaf Unonius* (2 vols., Minneapolis, Swedish Pioneer Historical Society, 1950–1960), II, p. 185.

17. Statistics from Paul Kennedy, *The Rise and Fall of the Great Powers: Economic Change and Military Conflict from 1500 to 2000* (London: Unwin Hyman, 1988), pp. 199–202, 243.

18. Quoted in T. C. Barker and Michael Robbins, *A History of London Transport*, vol. II (London: George Allen & Unwin, 1974), pp. 61, 63.

19. F. A. Mackenzie, *The American Invaders* (London: Grant Richards, 1902), pp. 142–143.

20. W. T. Stead, *The Americanisation of the World, or The Trend of the Twentieth Century* (London: Review of Reviews, 1902), preface and p. 19.

21. Richard W. Davis, "'We Are All Americans Now!' Anglo-American Marriages in the Later Nineteenth Century," *Proceedings of the American Philosophical Society*, 135/2 (1991), pp. 140–199, esp. pp. 144–145, 156, 160.

22. Leon Edel, in his Afterword to Henry James, *The American* (1877) (New York: Signet Classics, 1963), p. 331.

23. Louis Sullivan, "The Tall Office Building Artistically Considered" (1896), in Robert Twombly, ed., *Louis Sullivan: The Public Papers* (Chicago: University of Chicago Press, 1988), pp. 103–112 at p. 108.

24. Dorothy Norman, *Alfred Stieglitz: An American Seer* (Millerton, NY: Aperture, 1973), p. 45.

25. *Engineering Record*, 19 Nov. 1910, p. 563, quoted in Sarah Bradford Landau and Carl W. Condit, *Rise of the New York Skyscraper, 1865–1913* (New Haven, CT: Yale University Press, 1996), p. 381.

26. *New York Times*, 25 April 1913, p. 20.

27. Henry Adams, *The Education of Henry Adams: An Autobiography* (Boston: Massachusetts Historical Society, 1918), p. 499.

28. Sinclair, *The Jungle*, pp. 27–28.

29. Jacob A. Riis, *How the Other Half Lives: Studies Among the Tenements of New York* (New York: Charles Scribner's Sons, 1890; repr. Dover Publishing, 1971), p. 17.

30. Paul U. Kellogg, ed., *The Pittsburgh District: Civic Frontage* (New York: Russell Sage Foundation, 1914), pp. 3–4.

31. David B. Danbom, *Born in the Country: A History of Rural America* (Baltimore: Johns Hopkins University Press, 1995), ch. 7, esp. pp. 132, 152–154.

32. Quoted in John D. Hicks, *The Populist Revolt: A History of the Farmers' Alliance and the People's Party* (Minneapolis: University of Minnesota Press, 1931), p. 132.

33. Ibid., p. 160.

34. Speech of 9 July 1896, printed in *Official Proceedings of the Democratic National Convention Held in Chicago, Illinois, July 7, 8, 9, 10, and 11, 1896* (Logansport, Ind.: Wilson, Humphreys & Co., 1896), pp. 226–234.

35. *Washington Post*, 7 July 1894, p. 1.

36. Speech of 16 May 1894, quoted in Almont Lindsey, *The Pullman Strike: The Story of a Unique Experiment and of a Great Labor Upheaval* (Chicago: University of Chicago Press, 1942), p. 124.

37. New York *World*, 4 July 1894, p. 4.

38. Speech of 22 Nov. 1895, reprinted in Eugene V. Debs, *Debs: His Life, Writings, and Speeches* (Chicago: Charles H. Kerr, 1908), pp. 327–344.

39. Quoted in Harold C. Livesay, *Samuel Gompers and Organized Labor in America* (Boston: Little, Brown, 1978), p. 112.

40. Werner Sombart, *Why Is There No Socialism in the United States?* (1906), trans. Patricia M. Hocking and C. T. Husbands (London: Macmillan, 1976), pp. 105–106.

41. Peter Morton Coan, *Ellis Island Interviews in Their Own Words* (New York: Checkmark Books, 1997), pp. 277–278.

42. Coan, *Ellis Island Interviews*, p. 278.

43. Ibid., respectively pp. 42–43, 40.

44. Maldwyn Allen Jones, *American Immigration* (Chicago: University of Chicago Press, 1960), pp. 177–179.

45. Robert F. Foerster, *The Italian Emigration of Our Times* (Cambridge, MA: Harvard University Press, 1919), p. 32.

46. Jacob A. Riis, *How the Other Half Lives: Studies Among the Tenements of New York* (1901) (New York: Dover Publishing, 1971), p. 19.

47. Quoted in Carl Wittke, *We Who Built America: The Saga of the Immigrant* (Cleveland: Case Western Reserve University Press, 1967), p. 445.

48. Constitution of the Immigration Restriction League (1894).

49. Cleveland, veto message, 2 March 1897 (PPPUS website).

50. Francis A. Walker, "Restriction of Immigration," *Atlantic Monthly*, 77/464 (June 1896), pp. 822–829 at p. 828.

51. Madison Grant, *The Passing of the Great Race, or The Racial Basis of European History* (London: Bell, 1917), pp. 47, 198.

52. Finley Peter Dunne, *Observations by Mr Dooley* (London: William Heinemann, 1903), pp. 50–51.

53. Riis, *How the Other Half Lives* (1971), p. 19.

10: Reform and Expansion

1. H. G. Wells, *The Future in America: A Search After Realities* (New York & London: Harper & Brothers, 1906), p. 153.

2. William L. Riordon, ed., *Plunkitt of Tammany Hall* (New York: McLure, Philips & Co., 1905), pp. 46, 47, 51–52.

3. Ibid., pp. 4, 34.

4. Lincoln Steffens, *The Shame of the Cities* (London: William Heinemann, 1904), pp. 6–8.

5. Frank Norris, *The Octopus: A Story of California* (London: Grant Richards, 1901), pp. 288–289.

6. Quoted in George E. Mowry, *The California Progressives* (Berkeley: University of California Press, 1951), pp. 120, 126.

7. Olivier Zunz, *Making America Corporate, 1870–1920* (Chicago: University of Chicago Press, 1990), p. 95.

8. *New York Times*, 26 March 1911, p. 1.

9. Stephen Skowronek, *Building a New American State: The Expansion of National Administrative Capacities, 1877–1920* (New York: CUP, 1982), p. 8.

10. James Bryce, *The American Commonwealth*, vol. I, 5th ed. (New York: Macmillan, 1910), ch. 8, pp. 78, 80.

11. Irwin Hood Hoover, *Forty-Two Years in the White House* (London: Williams & Norgate, 1935), pp. 28–29.

12. Quoted in Edmund Morris, *Theodore Rex* (London: HarperCollins, 2002), p. 81.

13. Theodore Roosevelt, *An Autobiography* (London: Macmillan, 1913), pp. 462–463.

14. Theodore Roosevelt, fifth annual message, 5 Dec. 1905 (PPPUS website).

15. Lewis L. Gould, *Reform and Regulation: American Politics, 1900–1916* (New York: John Wiley & Sons, 1978), p. 62.

16. Address of 17 June 1912, reprinted in *The Works of Theodore Roosevelt*, ed. Hermann Hagedorn (20 vols., New York: Charles Scribner's Sons, 1926), XVII, pp. 204–231.

17. Woodrow Wilson, *Congressional Government: A Study in American Politics* (Boston: Houghton Mifflin, 1885), pp. 281, 284–285, 332–333.

18. *Atlanta Constitution*, 18 July 1919, quoted in Steven A. Riees, *Touching Base: Professional Baseball and American Culture in the Progressive Era* (Westport, CT: Greenwood Press, 1980), p. 25.

19. *New York Times*, 6 April 1913, Sports Section, p. S1.

20. Announcement quoted in Henry Ford, with Samuel Crowther, *My Life and Work* (London: William Heinemann, 1922), p. 73.

21. Ibid., p. 72.

22. Douglas Brinkley, *Wheels for the World: Henry Ford, His Company, and a Century of Progress, 1903–2003* (New York: Viking, 2003), p. 130.

23. Charles E. Sorensen, with Samuel T. Williamson, *Forty Years with Ford* (London: Jonathan Cape, 1957), p. 117.

24. Ibid., pp. 130–131.

25. From twelve hours and twenty-eight minutes to ninety-three minutes are the precise times quoted in Henry Ford, *My Life and Work*, pp. 81–82.

26. Press release of 5 Jan. 1914, quoted in Brinkley, *Wheels for the World*, p. 130. The idea is generally said to have originated with Ford's general manager, James Couzens.

27. Jane Addams, *Twenty Years at Hull-House, with Autobiographical Notes* (New York: Macmillan, 1912), pp. 123–124.

28. Walter Rauschenbusch, *Christianizing the Social Order* (New York: Macmillan, 1912), pp. 177–179.

29. Reuben A. Torry et al., eds., *The Fundamentals: A Testimony to the Truth* (4 vols., Los Angeles: The Bible Institute of Los Angeles, 1917).

30. George M. Marsden, *Fundamentalism and American Culture* 2nd ed. (Oxford: OUP, 2006), p. 119.

31. See Turner's famous 1893 paper, "The Significance of the Frontier in American History," reprinted in Frederick Jackson Turner, *The Frontier in American History* (New York: Henry Holt, 1920), quoting from p. 1.

32. Malcolm Bradbury, *The Modern American Novel* (Oxford: OUP, 1984), p. 4.

33. *New York Times*, 23 April 1889, p. 1.

34. Ibid.

35. *Harper's Weekly*, 18 May 1889, p. 391.

36. Queen Victoria's diary, quoted in Robert A. Carter, *Buffalo Bill Cody: The Man behind the Legend* (New York: John Wiley & Sons, 2000), p. 313.

37. Carter, *Buffalo Bill Cody*, p. 313.

38. "Custer's Fate Illustrated," *New York Times*, 4 Jan. 1887, p. 4.

39. Louis S. Warren, *Buffalo Bill's America: William Cody and the Wild West Show* (New York: Alfred A. Knopf, 2005), p. 274.

40. Ibid., p. 276.

41. Robert Hughes, *American Visions: The Epic History of Art in America* (London: The Harvill Press, 1997), p. 203.

42. 30 USC, 21–22, 17 Stat. 32, 1 March 1872.

43. 16 USC 431–433, reprinted in Ronald F. Lee, *The Story of the Antiquities Act* (Washington, DC: National Park Service, revised e-edition, 2001), appendix A, available online at http://www.nps.gov/archeology/PUBS/LEE/Index.htm.

44. Theodore Roosevelt, annual message, 3 Dec. 1907 (PPPUS website).

45. Quotations from Roderick Frazier Nash, *Wilderness and the American Mind* 4th ed. (New Haven, CT: Yale University Press, 2001), p. 161.

46. New York *World*, 16 Feb. 1898, early edition, quoted in Charles H. Brown, *The Correspondents' War: Journalists in the Spanish-American War* (New York: Charles Scribner's Sons, 1967), p. 120.

47. Quoted in Brown, *The Correspondents' War*, p. 121.

48. Quoted in Robert B. Edgerton, *"Remember the Maine, To Hell with Spain": America's 1898 Adventure in Imperialism* (Lewiston, ME: The Edwin Meller Press, 2004), p. 46.

49. Official Report of the Naval Court of Inquiry into the loss of the Battleship MAINE, 21 March 1898, available online at http://www.spanamwar.com/mainerpt.htm.

50. Quoted in Hermann Hagedorn, *Leonard Wood: A Biography* (2 vols., New York: Harper & Brothers, 1931), I, p. 141.

51. Edmund Morris, *The Rise of Theodore Roosevelt* (New York: The Modern Library, 2001), pp. 627, 638.

52. McKinley, Message to Congress, 11 April 1898, in U.S. Department of State, *Papers Relating to the Foreign Relations of the United States, 1898* (Washington, DC: U.S. Government Printing Office, 1901), pp. 750–760 at pp. 757–758, 759.

53. *Chicago Tribune*, 7 May 1898, 4.30 a.m. extra, quoted in Brown, *The Correspondents' War*, p. 198.

54. Brown, *The Correspondents' War*, p. 185n.

55. *Washington Post*, 2 June 1898, quoted in Thomas G. Paterson, J. Garry Clifford, and Kenneth J. Hagan, *American Foreign Policy: A History to 1914* 2nd ed. (Lexington, MA: D. C. Heath & Co., 1983), p. 213.

56. Quotations from Paul T. McCartney, *Power and Progress: American National Identity, the War of 1898, and the Rise of American Imperialism* (Baton Rouge: Louisiana State University Press, 2006), p. 140.

57. Text of the Platt Amendment of 1901 (which replaced the Teller Amendment), from C. I. Bevans, ed., *Treaties and Other International Agreements of the United States of America, 1776–1949*, vol. VIII (Washington, DC: U.S. Government Printing Office, 1971), pp. 1116–1117.

58. Carl Schurz, Address on "American Imperialism" (4 Jan. 1899), in Ray Ginger, ed., *The Nationalizing of American Life, 1877–1900* (New York: The Free Press, 1965), pp. 305–306.

59. Gen. James F. Rusling, "Interview with President McKinley," *The Christian Advocate*, 22 Jan. 1903, pp. 137–138, quoted in Ginger, *The Nationalizing of American Life*, p. 282. On

the credibility of the source see Lewis L. Gould, *The Presidency of William McKinley* (Lawrence: Regents Press of Kansas, 1980), pp. 140–142.

60. Edgerton, *"Remember the Maine, To Hell with Spain,"* p. 102. For a balanced treatment of Samar and the war as a whole see Brian McAllister Linn, *The Philippine War, 1899–1902* (Lawrence: University Press of Kansas, 2000).

61. See, for instance, Thomas Bender, *A Nation Among Nations: America's Place in World History* (New York: Hill & Wang, 2006), pp. 223–224.

62. Lowell (1899), quoted in Walter L. Williams, "United States Indian Policy and the Debate over Philippines Annexation: Implications for the Origins of American Imperialism," *JAH*, 66 (1980), pp. 810–831 at p. 817.

63. Theodore Roosevelt, fourth annual message, 6 Dec. 1904 (PPPUS website).

64. A point stressed by Frederick W. Marks III, *Velvet on Iron: The Diplomacy of Theodore Roosevelt* (Lincoln: University of Nebraska Press, 1979), pp. 97–98.

65. Quotations from H. W. Brands, *T. R.: The Last Romantic* (New York: Basic Books, 1997), pp. 487–488.

66. Details from David McCullough, *The Path Between the Seas: The Creation of the Panama Canal, 1870–1914* (New York: Simon & Schuster, 1977), pp. 608–611.

11: War and Peace

1. Woodrow Wilson, "An Appeal to the American People," 18 Aug. 1914, in *The Papers of Woodrow Wilson*, ed. Arthur S. Link et al. (69 vols., Princeton, NJ: Princeton University Press, 1966–1994), XXX, pp. 393–394.

2. Ibid.

3. David Dimbleby and David Reynolds, *An Ocean Apart: The Relationship Between Britain and America in the Twentieth Century* (London: Hodder & Stoughton, 1988), p. 46.

4. *New York American*, 8 Aug. 1914, quoted in Jeffrey J. Safford, *Wilsonian Maritime Diplomacy, 1913–1921* (New Brunswick, NJ: Rutgers University Press, 1978), p. 38.

5. George Henderson (1994 interview) quoted in David Ramsay, *Lusitania: Saga and Myth* (London: Chatham Publishing, 2001), pp. 1–2.

6. *The Times*, 10 May 1915, quoted in Ramsay, *Lusitania*, p. 97.

7. Edith Bolling Galt Wilson, *Memoirs of Mrs Woodrow Wilson* (London: Putnam, 1939), p. 72.

8. "Address in Philadelphia to Newly-Naturalized Citizens," 10 May 1915, *Papers of Woodrow Wilson*, XXXIII, pp. 147–150.

9. Wilson to Edith Bolling Galt, 10 May 1914, *Papers of Woodrow Wilson*, XXXIII, pp. 160–161.

10. Theodore Roosevelt to Archie Roosevelt, 19 May 1915, quoted in H. W. Brands, *T. R.: The Last Romantic* (New York: Basic Books, 1997), p. 756.

11. First *Lusitania* note, 12 May 1915, *Papers of Woodrow Wilson*, XXXIII, pp. 174–178.

12. Wilson to Col. Edward House, 23 July 1916, *Papers of Woodrow Wilson*, XXXVII, p. 467.

13. Reginald McKenna, "Our Financial Position in America," 24 Oct. 1916, Cabinet Papers CAB 24/2, G-87 (The National Archives, Kew, Surrey).

14. Wilson, note of 18 Dec. 1916, *Papers of Woodrow Wilson*, XL, pp. 273–276.

15. Address to a Joint Session of Congress, 2 April 1917, *Papers of Woodrow Wilson*, XLI, pp. 519–527, quoting pp. 521–522, 525.

16. Wilson, *Memoirs of Mrs Woodrow Wilson*, p. 159.

17. Wilson to House, 21 July 1917, *Papers of Woodrow Wilson*, XLIII, p. 238.

18. David M. Kennedy, *Over Here: The First World War and American Society* (New York: OUP, 1980), p. 254.

19. George Creel, "Four Million Citizen Defenders: What Universal Training Means in Dollars, Duty, and Defense," *Everybody's Magazine*, 36 (Jan.–June 1917), at pp. 551, 553.

20. Kennedy, *Over Here*, pp. 17–18.

21. Robert Blake, ed., *The Private Papers of Douglas Haig, 1914–1919* (London: Eyre & Spottiswoode, 1952), p. 307, 1 May 1918.

22. William L. Langer (1965), quoted in Kennedy, *Over Here*, pp. 184–185.

23. Albert Ridge quoted in Merle Miller, *Plain Speaking: An Oral Biography of Harry S. Truman* (London: Victor Gollancz, 1974), p. 95.

24. Quotations from David McCullough, *Truman* (New York: Simon & Schuster, 1992), pp. 117–118.

25. Leaflet published by the Women's Anti-Suffrage Association of Massachusetts, quoted in Aileen S. Kraditor, *The Ideas of the Woman Suffrage Movement, 1890–1920* rev. ed. (New York: W. W. Norton, 1981), pp. 24–25.

26. Quotations from Doris Stevens, *Jailed for Freedom* (New York: Boni & Liveright, 1920), pp. 80, 84, 124, 139.

27. Ibid., p. 100.

28. Ibid., p. 108.

29. Ibid., p. 110.

30. Appeal to the Senate, 30 Sept. 1918, quoted in Elizabeth Frost and Kathryn Cullen-DuPont, eds., *Women's Suffrage in America: An Eyewitness History* (New York: Facts on File, 1992), pp. 406–407.

31. McCullough, *Truman*, pp. 128–129, 134.

32. Wilson, address to Congress, 8 Jan. 1918, in *Papers Relating to the Foreign Relations of the United States, 1918: Supplement I, The World War* (2 vols., Washington, DC: U.S. Government Printing Office, 1933), I, pp. 15–16.

33. Quoted in Lloyd C. Gardner, *Safe for Democracy: The Anglo-American Response to Revolution, 1918–1923* (New York: OUP, 1984), pp. 2–3.

34. Frank Cobb to Woodrow Wilson, 4 Nov. 1918, in Charles Seymour, ed., *The Intimate Papers of Colonel House* (4 vols., London: Ernest Benn, 1926–1928), IV, pp. 219–220.

35. Woodrow Wilson to Senator Key Pittman, 18 Nov. 1918, *Papers of Woodrow Wilson*, LIII, p. 116.

36. Wilson, *Memoirs of Mrs Woodrow Wilson*, p. 269.

37. Quoted in Daniel Smith, *The Great Departure: The United States and World War I, 1914–1920* (New York: John Wiley & Sons, 1965), p. 109.

38. House, diary, in Seymour, *Intimate Papers of Colonel House*, IV, p. 405, entry for 23 March 1919.

39. J. M. Keynes to Florence Keynes, 14 May 1919, in Elizabeth Johnson, ed., *The Collected Writings of John Maynard Keynes*, vol. 16 (London: Macmillan, 1971), p. 458.

40. *Philadelphia Irish Press*, 24 May 1919, quoted in Joseph P. O'Grady, ed., *The Immigrants' Influence on Wilson's Peace Policies* (Lexington: University Press of Kentucky, 1971), p. 77.

41. Hardwick quoted in John Milton Cooper, Jr., *Breaking the Heart of the World: Woodrow Wilson and the Fight for the League of Nations* (New York: CUP, 2001), p. 61.

42. Lodge, speech in the Senate, 12 Aug. 1919, quoted in Smith, *Great Departure*, p. 185.

43. Wilson, 19 Aug. 1919, quoted in Lloyd E. Ambrosius, *Woodrow Wilson and the American Diplomatic Tradition: The Treaty Fight in Perspective* (New York: CUP, 1987), p. 165.

44. Woodrow Wilson, *War and Peace: Presidential Messages, Addresses and Public Papers, 1917–1924*, ed. Ray Stannard Baker and William E. Dodd (2 vols., New York: Harper & Brothers, 1927), I, p. 640 (St Louis, 5 Sept. 1919), and II, p. 52, 212 (Sioux Falls, 8 Sept. and Portland, 15 Sept.).

45. Figures from Thomas A. Bailey, *Woodrow Wilson and the Great Betrayal* (Chicago: Quadrangle, 1963), p. 114.

46. Wilson, *Memoirs of Mrs Woodrow Wilson*, p. 331, quoting from the president's speech in Tacoma, Washington.

47. Irwin Hood Hoover, *Forty-Two Years in the White House* (London: Williams & Norgate, 1935), p. 103.

48. Stanley Coben, *A. Mitchell Palmer: Politician* (New York: Columbia University Press, 1963), p. 196.

49. Letters of Dec. 1915 and Feb. 1916 quoted in Brands, *T. R.: The Last Romantic*, pp. 762–763.

50. Debs, speech at Canton, Ohio, 16 June 1918, available online at http://www.marxists.org/archive/debs/works/1918/canton.htm, accessed 6 Oct. 2008.

51. Robert K. Murray, *Red Scare: A Study in National Hysteria, 1919–1920* (Minneapolis: University of Minnesota Press, 1955), p. 53.

52. Quoted in John Higham, *Strangers in the Land: Patterns of American Nativism, 1860–1925* 2nd ed. (New York: Atheneum, 1975), p. 226.

53. Quoted in Paul Avrich, *Sacco and Vanzetti: The Anarchist Background* (Princeton, NJ: Princeton University Press, 1991), p. 137.

54. Murray, *Red Scare*, p. 71.

55. Sgt. Burlinghame, quoted in Avrich, *Sacco and Vanzetti*, pp. 153–154.

56. Avrich, *Sacco and Vanzetti*, pp. 174–175.

57. Quoted in Higham, *Strangers in the Land*, p. 228.

58. Quoted in Avrich, *Sacco and Vanzetti*, p. 177.

59. Quoted in Higham, *Strangers in the Land*, p. 306.

60. Speech by Senator Ellison DuRant Smith, 9 April 1924, *Congressional Record*, 68th Congress, 1st session (Washington, DC: U.S. Government Printing Office, 1924), LXV, pp. 5961–5962.

61. Billy Sunday quoted in Andrew Sinclair, *Prohibition: The Era of Excess* (London: Faber and Faber, 1962), p. 82.

62. Quoted in James H. Timberlake, *Prohibition and the Progressive Movement* (Cambridge, MA: Harvard University Press, 1963), p. 179.

63. Anti-Saloon League, press statement, 15 Jan. 1920, quoted in Charles Merz, *The Dry Decade* new ed. (Seattle: University of Washington Press, 1969), p. 51.

64. Fox (1912) quoted in Lary May, *Screening Out the Past: The Birth of Mass Culture and the Motion Picture Industry* (Chicago: University of Chicago Press, 1983), pp. 152–153.

65. Statistics from May, *Screening Out the Past*, p. 164, and Richard Koszarski, *An Evening's Entertainment: The Age of the Silent Feature Picture, 1915–1928* (New York: Charles Scribner's Sons, 1990), p. 26.

66. Undated clipping quoted in May, *Screening Out the Past*, p. 171.

67. Jack H. Mendelson and Nancy K. Mello, *Alcohol: Use and Abuse in America* (Boston: Little, Brown, 1985), p. 86.

68. Quoted in Sinclair, *Prohibition*, p. 240.

69. Armstrong, unpublished manuscript (1954), quoted in Thomas Brothers, ed., *Louis Armstrong in His Own Words: Selected Writings* (New York: OUP, 1999), p. 74.

70. Quoted in Kenneth L. Kusmer, *A Ghetto Takes Shape: Black Cleveland, 1870–1930* (Urbana: University of Illinois Press, 1976), p. 158.

71. *Challenge Magazine*, quoted in John Hope Franklin, *From Slavery to Freedom: A History of Negro Americans* 5th ed. (New York: Alfred A. Knopf, 1980), p. 351.

72. Franklin, *From Slavery to Freedom*, p. 346.

73. U.S. Department of Commerce, *Statistical Abstract of the United States, 1921* (Washington: U.S. Government Printing Office, 1922), tables 33 and 35.

74. Richard Lingeman, *Sinclair Lewis: Rebel from Main Street* (New York: Random House, 2002), pp. 156–157.

75. Sinclair Lewis, *Main Street: The Story of Carol Kennicott*, ed. Malcolm Bradbury (Harmondsworth: Penguin, 1985), ch. 22, section III, p. 247.

76. Quotations from Edward J. Larson, *Summer for the Gods: The Scopes Trial and America's Continuing Debate over Science and Religion* (New York: Basic Books, 1997), pp. 41–45.

77. For an online transcript of the trial (20 July 1925) see http://personal.uncc.edu/jmarks/Darrow.html, accessed 6 Oct. 2008.

78. Quoted in William E. Leuchtenburg, *The Perils of Prosperity, 1914–1932* (Chicago: University of Chicago Press, 1958), p. 90.

79. Coolidge, address to the American Society of Newspaper Editors, Washington, DC, 17 Jan. 1925 (PPPUS website).

80. Coolidge, inaugural address, 4 March 1925 (PPPUS website).

81. David Cannadine, *Mellon: An American Life* (London: Penguin, 2006), p. 318.

82. Robert A. Slayton, *Empire Statesman: The Rise and Redemption of Al Smith* (New York: The Free Press, 2001), pp. ix–x.

12: From Boom to Bomb

1. Herbert Hoover, inaugural address, 4 March 1929 (PPPUS website).

2. FDR to Hugh Gibson, 2 Jan. 1920, quoted in Arthur M. Schlesinger, Jr., *The Crisis of the Old Order* (Boston: Houghton Mifflin, 1957), p. 82.

3. Speech in Des Moines, Iowa, 6 Sept. 1919, in Woodrow Wilson, *War and Peace: Presidential Messages, Addresses, and Public Papers, 1917–1924*, ed. Ray Stannard Baker and William E. Dodd (2 vols., New York: Harper & Brothers, 1927), II, p. 18.

4. Mira Wilkins, *The Maturing of Multinational Enterprise: American Business Abroad from 1914 to 1970* (Cambridge, MA: Harvard University Press, 1974), pp. 29–30.

5. Charles P. Kindleberger, *The World in Depression, 1929–1939* (Berkeley: University of California Press, 1973), p. 56.

6. Frank Costigliola, *Awkward Dominion: American Political, Economic, and Cultural Relations with Europe, 1919–1933* (Ithaca, NY: Cornell University Press, 1984), p. 142.

7. Josef Stalin, *Problems of Leninism*, quoted in Hans Rogger, "Amerikanism and the Economic Development of Russia," *Comparative Studies in Society and History*, 23 (1981), pp. 382–420 at p. 387.

8. Sinclair Lewis, *Babbitt* (1922) (London: Jonathan Cape, 1968), pp. 154–155.

9. F. Scott Fitzgerald, *The Great Gatsby* (Harmondsworth: Penguin, 1974), pp. 186–188.

10. Charles F. Kettering (1930), quoted in Maury Klein, *Rainbow's End: The Crash of 1929* (Oxford: OUP, 2001), p. 255.

11. See Martha L. Olney, *Buy Now, Pay Later: Advertising, Credit, and Consumer Durables in the 1920s* (Chapel Hill: UNC Press, 1991), pp. 86–91.

12. Quoted in Klein, *Rainbow's End*, p. 124.

13. Kenneth Goode (1926), quoted in Roland Marchand, *Advertising the American Dream: Making Way for Modernity, 1920–1940* (Berkeley: University of California Press, 1985), p. 160.

14. Jim Potter, *The American Economy Between the Wars* (London: Macmillan, 1974), pp. 55, 69, 74–75.

15. David M. Kennedy, *Freedom from Fear: The American People in Depression and War, 1929–1945* (Oxford: OUP, 1999), p. 38.

16. Frederick Lewis Allen, *Only Yesterday: An Informal History of the 1920s* (New York: Perennial Library, 1964), p. 273.

17. John Kenneth Galbraith, *The Great Crash, 1929* (London: Hamish Hamilton, 1955), pp. 82–83.

18. Eric Rauchway, *The Great Depression & the New Deal: A Very Short Introduction* (Oxford: OUP, 2008), p. 19.

19. Rauchway, *The Great Depression*, p. 30.

20. Marriner Eccles, quoted in Amity Shlaes, *The Forgotten Man: A New History of the Great Depression* (London: Jonathan Cape, 2007), pp. 105–106.

21. Kindleberger, *World in Depression*, p. 292.

22. Martha Gellhorn, "Report on Massachusetts," 30 Nov. 1934, quoted in John F. Bauman and Thomas H. Coode, *In the Eye of the Great Depression: New Deal Reporters and the Agony of the American People* (DeKalb: Northern Illinois University Press, 1988), pp. 74–75.

23. Quoted in Charles C. Alexander, *Nationalism in American Thought, 1930–1945* (Chicago: Rand McNally, 1969), p. 2.

24. E. J. Sullivan, "The 1932nd Psalm," printed in Robert S. McElvaine, ed., *Down and Out in the Great Depression: Letters from the "Forgotten Man"* (Chapel Hill: UNC Press, 1983), p. 34.

25. MacArthur press conference, 28 July 1932, quoted in D. Clayton James, *The Years of MacArthur*, vol. I, *1880–1941* (Boston: Houghton Mifflin, 1970), pp. 403–404.

26. Quoted in Schlesinger, *Crisis of the Old Order*, p. 265.

27. Walter Lippmann, "The Peculiar Weakness of Mr. Hoover," *Harper's Magazine*, 161 (June 1930), pp. 1–7, quoting pp. 2, 3, 6–7.

28. "Governor Roosevelt's Candidacy" (8 Jan. 1932), reprinted in Walter Lippmann, *Interpretations, 1931–1932*, ed. Allan Nevins (London: George Allen & Unwin, 1932), pp. 261–262.

29. Roosevelt, inaugural address, 4 March 1933 (PPPUS website).

30. Eliot Janeway, interview, quoted in Doris Kearns Goodwin, *No Ordinary Time: Franklin and Eleanor Roosevelt: The Home Front in World War II* (New York: Simon & Schuster, 1994), p. 17.

31. Patrick Renshaw, *Franklin D. Roosevelt* (London: Longman, 2004), p. 54.

32. Quoted in Schlesinger, *Crisis of the Old Order*, p. 406.

33. William E. Leuchtenburg, *Franklin D. Roosevelt and the New Deal, 1932–1940* (New York: Harper & Row, 1963), pp. 43–44.

34. Quoted in Anthony J. Badger, *FDR: The First Hundred Days* (New York: Hill & Wang, 2008), p. 40.

35. Leuchtenburg, *Roosevelt and the New Deal*, p. 44.

36. Roosevelt, first Fireside Chat, 12 March 1933 (PPPUS website).

37. Speech of 22 May 1932, in *The Public Papers and Addresses of Franklin D. Roosevelt*, ed. Samuel I. Rosenman (13 vols., New York: Random House, 1938–1950), I, p. 646.

38. Quoted in Arthur M. Schlesinger, Jr., *The Politics of Upheaval* (Boston: Houghton Mifflin, 1960), pp. 65–66.

39. Transcript of Reagan interviewed by David McCullough, 1 Dec. 1981, quoted in William E. Leuchtenburg, *In the Shadow of FDR: From Harry Truman to Ronald Reagan* (Ithaca, NY: Cornell University Press, 1983), p. 214. Also statistics from Anthony J. Badger, *The New Deal: The Depression Years, 1933–1940* (London: Macmillan, 1989), p. 203.

40. Quoted in Leuchtenburg, *Roosevelt and the New Deal*, p. 131.

41. Quoted in Arthur M. Schlesinger, Jr., *The Coming of the New Deal* (Boston: Houghton Mifflin, 1959), pp. 308–309.

42. James T. Patterson, *America's Struggle Against Poverty, 1900–1980* (Cambridge, MA: Harvard University Press, 1981), pp. 76–77.

43. Beverly Smith (1939) quoted in J. Joseph Huthmacher, *Senator Robert F. Wagner and the Rise of Urban Liberalism* (New York: Atheneum, 1971), p. 115.

44. D. Clayton Brown, *Electricity for Rural America: The Fight for the REA* (Westport, CT: Greenwood Press, 1980), pp. xiii–xiv, 69, 113.

45. Senator Lewis Schwellenbach of Washington state, 15 July 1938, quoted in Jason Scott Smith, *Building New Deal Liberalism: The Political Economy of Public Works, 1933–1956* (Cambridge: CUP, 2006), pp. 120–121.

46. Quoted in Gerald D. Nash, *The Great Depression and World War II: Organizing America, 1933–1945* (New York: St Martin's Press, 1979), p. 66.

47. Quoted in Leuchtenburg, *Roosevelt and the New Deal*, p. 192.

48. Roosevelt, speech in Philadelphia, 27 June 1936 (PPPUS website).

49. Quoted in William E. Leuchtenburg, *The Supreme Court Reborn: The Constitutional Revolution in the Age of Roosevelt* (New York: OUP, 1995), p. 121.

50. Roosevelt, message to Congress, 5 Feb. 1937 (PPPUS website).

51. William Allen White to Felix Frankfurter, 23 March 1937, quoted in Leuchtenburg, *Roosevelt and the New Deal*, p. 235.

52. Hughes quoted in Peter Irons, *A People's History of the Supreme Court* (New York: Penguin, 2006), p. 322.

53. See Milton Derber and Edwin Young, eds., *Labor and the New Deal* (Madison: University of Wisconsin Press, 1957), pp. 3, 31–32.

54. Susan Rosenthal, interview with Genora (Johnson) Dollinger, 1995, available online at http://www.historyisaweapon.com/defcon1/dollflint.html, accessed 7 Oct. 2008.

55. For the *Collier's* story see the categorical assertions in John Guenther, *Roosevelt in Retrospect* (London: Hamish Hamilton, 1950), p. 335.

56. Quoted in Cushing Strout, *The American Image of the Old World* (New York: Harper & Row, 1963), p. 205.

57. Roosevelt, address at Chautauqua, New York, 14 Aug. 1936 (PPPUS website).

58. Roosevelt to Roger B. Merriman, 15 Feb. 1939, President's Secretary's File 46: Great Britain, 1939 (Franklin D. Roosevelt Library, Hyde Park, NY).

59. Roosevelt, annual message, 4 Jan. 1939 (PPPUS website).

60. Roosevelt, Fireside Chat, 3 Sept. 1939 (PPPUS website).

61. Quoted in Wayne S. Cole, *Roosevelt and the Isolationists, 1932-1945* (Lincoln: University of Nebraska Press, 1983), p. 328.

62. For references see David Reynolds, *The Creation of the Anglo-American Alliance, 1937–1941: A Study in Competitive Co-operation* (London: Europa, 1981), pp. 112, 114.

63. Roosevelt, written message to Congress, 3 Sept. 1940 (PPPUS website).

64. Cole, *Roosevelt and the Isolationists*, p. 378, and generally J. Garry Clifford and Samuel R. Spencer, Jr., *The First Peacetime Draft* (Lawrence: University Press of Kansas, 1986).

65. Willkie, speech in Baltimore, 30 Oct. 1940, quoted in Robert A. Divine, *Foreign Policy and US Presidential Elections, 1940–1948* (New York: New Viewpoints, 1974), p. 80.

66. Roosevelt, speech in Boston, 30 Oct. 1940 (PPPUS website).

67. Roosevelt, annual message, 6 Jan. 1941 (PPPUS website).

68. Roosevelt, press conference, 17 Dec. 1940 (PPPUS website).

69. Wayne S. Cole, *America First: The Battle Against Intervention, 1940–1941* (Madison: University of Wisconsin Press, 1953), p. 30.

70. Quoted in Charles A. Beard, *President Roosevelt and the Coming of War, 1941* (New Haven, CT: Yale University Press, 1948), pp. 67–68.

71. Lindbergh, testimony to House hearings, 23 Jan. 1941, quoted in William L. Langer and S. Everett Gleason, *The Undeclared War, 1940–1941* (New York: Harper & Brothers, 1953), p. 269.

72. Quotations from Reynolds, *Creation of the Anglo-American Alliance*, pp. 155, 161.

73. Robert E. Sherwood, *Roosevelt and Hopkins: An Intimate History* (New York: Harper & Brothers, 1948), p. 227.

74. British War Cabinet minutes, 19 Aug. 1941, CAB 65/19, WM 84 (41) 1, confidential annex (The National Archives, Kew, Surrey).

75. Alistair Cooke, *Alistair Cooke's American Journey: Life on the Home Front in the Second World War* (London: Penguin, 2006), p. 6.

76. Ed Sheehan, quoted in Stanley Weintraub, *Long Day's Journey into War: December 7, 1941* (New York: Truman Talley, 1991), p. 206.

77. Cooke, *American Journey*, pp. 13–14.

78. Roosevelt, address to Congress, 8 Dec. 1941 (PPPUS website).

79. For a good discussion, see Richard J. Aldrich, *Intelligence and the War Against Japan* (Cambridge: Cambridge University Press, 2000), ch. 5.

80. Quoted in Richard R. Lingeman, *Don't You Know There's a War On? The American Home Front, 1941–1945* (New York: Capricorn Books, 1976), p. 26.

81. Walter Lippmann, "The Fifth Column on the Coast," syndicated press article, 12 Feb. 1942, quoted in Roger Daniels, *Prisoners Without Trial: Japanese Americans in World War II* (New York: Hill & Wang, 1993), p. 45.

82. Quoted in Daniels, *Prisoners Without Trial*, p. 65.

83. Opinion by Mr. Justice Murphy in the Hirabayashi case, June 1943, 320 U.S. 81 (1943). Despite his reservation Murphy was persuaded to offer a concurrence not, as originally intended, a dissent.

84. Quoted in Eric Larrabee, *Commander in Chief: Franklin Delano Roosevelt, His Lieutenants, and Their War* (New York: Touchstone, 1987), p. 177; see also Horst Boog et al., *Germany and the Second World War*, vol. VI (Oxford: Clarendon Press, 2001), pp. 377, 379.

85. Quoted in Richard Polenberg, *War and Society: The United States, 1941–1945* (New York: J. P. Lippincott, 1972), pp. 11–12.

86. Lingeman, *Don't You Know There's A War On?* p. 65.

87. Quoted in Cooke, *American Journey*, p. 58.

88. Winston S. Churchill, *The Second World War* (6 vols., London: Cassell, 1948–1954), III, p. 540, recalling a remark made by Sir Edward Grey.

89. Mark H. Leff, "The Politics of Sacrifice on the American Home Front in World War II," *JAH*, 77 (1991), pp. 1296–1318 at p. 1296.

90. Robert Higgs, "Wartime Prosperity? A Reassessment of the US Economy in the 1940s," *Journal of Economic History*, 52 (1992), pp. 41–60 at pp. 42–43.

91. Dos Passos, quoted in Lingeman, *Don't You Know There's a War On?* p. 75.

92. A total of 12 million people—John W. Jeffries, *Wartime America: The World War II Home Front* (Chicago: Ivan R. Dee, 1996), p. 71.

93. Polenberg, *War and Society*, p. 128.

94. Marshall to Stimson, 1 Dec. 1941, in Bernard C. Nalty and Morris J. MacGregor, eds., *Blacks in the Military: Essential Documents* (Wilmington, DE: Scholarly Resources, 1981), pp. 114–115.

95. National Association for the Advancement of Colored People Board of Directors, 8 Dec. 1941, quoted in Alan M. Osur, *Blacks in the Army Air Forces During World War II* (Washington, DC: Office of Air Force History, 1977), p. 11.

96. Lloyd L. Brown (1973), quoted in John Morton Blum, *V Was for Victory: Politics and American Culture During World War II* (New York: Harvest/HBJ, 1977), pp. 190–191.

97. Albert C. Wedemeyer, *Wedemeyer Reports!* (New York: Henry Holt, 1958), p. 192.

98. Harry C. Butcher, *My Three Years with Eisenhower* (New York: Simon & Schuster, 1948), pp. 268–269, entry for 23 Feb. 1943.

99. Stimson to Roosevelt, 10 Aug. 1943, quoted in Henry L. Stimson and McGeorge Bundy, *On Active Service in War and Peace* (London: Hutchinson, 1948), pp. 228–229.

100. Churchill to Smuts, 3 Dec. 1944, in Churchill, *The Second World War*, VI, p. 233.

101. Quoted in David Reynolds, *Rich Relations: The American Occupation of Britain, 1942–1945* (London: HarperCollins, 1996), pp. 443–444.

102. Alan S. Milward, *War, Economy and Society, 1939–1945* (Berkeley: University of California Press, 1979), p. 67.

103. Cooke, *American Journey*, p. 161.

104. Kenneth D. Nichols quoted in Richard Rhodes, *The Making of the Atomic Bomb* (London: Penguin, 1986), p. 426.

105. James Conant quoted in Rhodes, *Making of the Atomic Bomb*, p. 407.

106. Bohr quoted in Rhodes, *Making of the Atomic Bomb*, p. 500.

107. Millard Lampell, "The Lonesome Train," quoted in Lingeman, *Don't You Know There's a War On?* p. 353.

108. Quoted in Rhodes, *Making of the Atomic Bomb*, p. 676.

109. Quoted in Christopher Thorne, *Allies of a Kind: The United States, Britain and the War Against Japan* (London: Hamish Hamilton, 1978), p. 503.

110. Steve McConnell quoted in Studs Terkel, *The Good War: An Oral History of World War Two* (London: Hamish Hamilton, 1985), p. 584.

13: Red or Dead?

1. *Life*, 29 March 1943, quoting pp. 20, 29, 23 and 40.

2. Roosevelt to Churchill, 18 March 1942, in Warren F. Kimball, ed., *Churchill and Roosevelt: Their Complete Correspondence* (3 vols., Princeton, NJ: Princeton University Press, 1984), I, p. 421.

3. Quentin Reynolds, *The Curtain Rises* (London: Cassell, 1944), pp. 43, 139.

4. Quoted in Ivo Banac, ed., *The Diary of Georgi Dimitrov, 1933–1949* (New Haven, CT: Yale University Press, 2003), pp. 338, 372, entries for 28 Jan. and 7 June 1945.

5. Quoted in Walter Isaacson and Evan Thomas, *The Wise Men: Six Friends and the World They Made* (New York: Simon & Schuster, 1986), p. 338.

6. JCS 1769/1, report by Joint Strategic Survey Committee, 29 April 1947, reprinted in Thomas H. Etzold and John L. Gaddis, eds., *Containment: Documents on American Policy and Strategy, 1945–1950* (New York: Columbia University Press, 1978), p. 73.

7. Quoted in Thomas G. Paterson, *On Every Front: The Making of the Cold War* (New York: W. W. Norton, 1979), pp. 72–73.

8. *Time*, 24 Feb. 1947, p. 30.

9. Truman, special message to Congress, 12 March 1947 (PPPUS website).

10. Hoover Commission, Feb. 1947, quoted in Robert A. Pollard, *Economic Security and the Origins of the Cold War, 1945–1950* (New York: Columbia University Press, 1985), p. 140.

11. Charles E. Bohlen, *Witness to History, 1929–1969* (New York: W. W. Norton, 1973), p. 263.

12. Marshall, speech of 28 April 1947, quoted in Forrest C. Pogue, *George C. Marshall: Statesman, 1945–1959* (New York: Penguin, 1989), p. 200.

13. Marshall, speech of 5 June 1947, reprinted in *Department of State Bulletin*, 15 June 1957, pp. 1159–1160.

14. David Reynolds, *One World Divisible: A Global History Since 1945* (London: Penguin, 2000), p. 29.

15. Quoted in Robert J. Donovan, *Conflict and Crisis: The Presidency of Harry S. Truman, 1945–1948* (New York: W. W. Norton, 1977), p. 359.

16. Clay to Gen. Stephen J. Chamberlin, 5 March 1948, in Jean Edward Smith, ed., *The Papers of General Lucius D. Clay: Germany, 1945–1949* (2 vols., Bloomington: Indiana University Press, 1974), II, p. 568.

17. Truman, special message to the Congress on the threat to the freedom of Europe, 17 March 1948 (PPPUS website).

18. Clay to Gen. Charles Gailey, 13 June 1948, in Smith, *Papers of General Lucius D. Clay*, II, p. 677.

19. Marshall to Douglas, 28 June 1948, in U.S. Department of State, *Foreign Relations of the United States* (multi vols., Washington, DC: U.S. Government Printing Office, 1861–), 1948, vol. II, pp. 930–931.

20. Quoted in D. M. Giangreco and Robert E. Griffin, *Airbridge to Berlin—The Berlin Crisis of 1948, Its Origins and Aftermath* (Novato, CA: Presidio, 1988)—section on "The Chocolate Flyer" on Harry S Truman Library website at http://www.trumanlibrary.org/whistlestop/BERLIN_A/CHOCOLAT.HTM, accessed 7 Oct. 2008.

21. Quoted in Dennis L. Bark and David R. Gress, *A History of West Germany* (2 vols., 2nd ed., Oxford: Blackwell, 1993), I, p. 216.

22. Truman, address, 4 April 1949 (PPPUS website).

23. Arthur H. Vandenberg, Jr., *The Private Papers of Senator Arthur Vandenberg* (London: Victor Gollancz, 1953), pp. 477–478, 552–553, letters of 18 March 1949 and 5 Jan. 1950.

24. Truman, diary entry 21 July 1947, quoted in U.S. National Archives & Records Administration, Press Release, 10 July 2003; see also "Truman Wrote of '48 Offer to Eisenhower," *New York Times*, 11 July 2003, and Donovan, *Conflict and Crisis*, p. 338. Truman was particularly afraid that General Douglas MacArthur might decide to seek the Republican nomination.

25. Rear platform remarks, Dodge City, Kansas, 16 June 1948, 7.30 a.m. (PPPUS website).

26. Truman, statement of 23 Sept. 1949 (PPPUS website).

27. CIA report, 1 July 1949, quoted in David Holloway, *Stalin and the Bomb: The Soviet Union and Atomic Energy, 1939–1956* (New Haven, CT: Yale University Press, 1994), p. 220.

28. NSC 48/1, 23–30 Dec. 1949, in Etzold and Gaddis, *Containment*, doc. 33, quoting pp. 253, 259.

29. NSC 68, 14 April 1950, in Etzold and Gaddis, *Containment*, doc. 52, quoting pp. 385, 387.

30. "Creed for Women Realtors," Aug. 1950, quoted in Jeffrey M. Hornstein, *A Nation of Realtors: A Cultural History of the Twentieth-Century American Middle Class* (Durham, NC: Duke University Press, 2005), p. 188.

31. Kenneth T. Jackson, *Crabgrass Frontier: The Suburbanization of the United States* (New York: OUP, 1985), p. 232.

32. *Time*, 3 July 1950, cover story.

33. Quoted in Jackson, *Crabgrass Frontier*, p. 231.

34. Lewis Mumford, *The City in History: Its Origins, Its Transformation, and Its Prospects* (London: Secker & Warburg, 1961), p. 486.

35. Stephen E. Ambrose, *Eisenhower* (2 vols., New York: Simon & Schuster, 1983–1984), II, p. 250.

36. Quoted in Jackson, *Crabgrass Frontier*, p. 265.

37. Eisenhower, special message to Congress, 22 Feb. 1955 (PPPUS website).

38. Reynolds, *One World Divisible*, p. 156, and generally Mark H. Rose, *Interstate: Express Highway Politics, 1941–1956* (Lawrence: Regents Press of Kansas, 1979).

39. *Time*, 3 July 1950, cover story.

40. Davis R. B. Ross, *Preparing for Ulysses: Politics and Veterans During World War II* (New York: Columbia University Press, 1969), p. 124.

41. Roosevelt, State of the Union Address, 11 Jan. 1944 (PPPUS website).

42. Ibid.

43. Robert Nathan (1944), quoted in Lizabeth Cohen, *A Consumer's Republic: The Politics of Mass Consumption in Postwar America* (New York: Alfred A. Knopf, 2003), p. 116.

44. James T. Patterson, *Grand Expectations: The United States, 1945–1974* (New York: OUP, 1996), p. 61; Rosalind Rosenberg, *Divided Lives: American Women in the Twentieth Century* (New York: Hill & Wang, 1992), p. 144.

45. James T. Patterson, *America's Struggle Against Poverty, 1900–1980* (Cambridge, MA: Harvard University Press, 1981), pp. 79–80.

46. Elizabeth Borgwardt, *A New Deal for the World: America's Vision for Human Rights* (Cambridge, MA: Harvard University Press, 2005), pp. 136–139.

47. Quoted in David Halberstam, *The Fifties* (New York: Villard Books, 1993), p. 141.

48. Harry S. Truman, *Memoirs* (2 vols., New York: Signet, 1965), II, p. 378.

49. Ibid., pp. 378–379.

50. Truman, statement on the situation in Korea, 27 June 1950 (PPPUS website).

51. Taft, speech of 28 June 1950, quoted in Robert J. Donovan, *Tumultuous Years: The Presidency of Harry S. Truman, 1949–1953* (New York: W. W. Norton, 1982), p. 220.

52. Quoted in Max Hastings, *The Korean War* (London: Michael Joseph, 1987), pp. 194, 210–211.

53. Thomas C. Reeves, *The Life and Times of Joe McCarthy: A Biography* (New York: Stein and Day, 1982), p. 224.

54. Interview with Edward Olsen (1976), quoted in Edwin R. Bayley, *Joe McCarthy and the Press* (New York: Pantheon, 1981), pp. 29–30.

55. Memo, 12 May 1945, quoted in Robert H. Ferrell, ed., *Off the Record: The Private Papers of Harry S. Truman* (New York: Penguin, 1982), p. 22.

56. Quoted in David Caute, *The Dancer Defects: The Struggle for Cultural Supremacy During the Cold War* (Oxford: OUP, 2003), p. 166.

57. Quoted in Patterson, *Grand Expectations*, p. 185.

58. Truman, press conference, 30 Nov. 1950 (PPPUS website).

59. Letter of 20 March 1951, in William Manchester, *American Caesar: Douglas MacArthur, 1880–1964* (New York: Dell, 1979), p. 764.

60. Manchester, *American Caesar*, pp. 793–794.

61. Speech of 19 April 1951, in Manchester, *American Caesar*, pp. 790–791.

62. U.S. Congress, Senate, Committees on Armed Services and Foreign Relations, *Military Situation in the Far East* (Washington, DC: U.S. Government Printing Office, 1951), p. 732 (15 May 1951).

63. Speech to the American Legion, Madison Square Garden, New York, 25 Aug. 1952, quoted in *Time*, 1 Sept. 1952.

64. John Foster Dulles, "The Evolution of Foreign Policy," Address to the Council on Foreign Relations, New York, in Department of State, Press Release No. 81 (12 Jan. 1954).

65. Capt. William B. Moore, U.S. navy, memo dated 18 March 1954, of briefing at SAC HQ, Omaha, Nebraska, 15 March 1954, printed in David Alan Rosenberg, "'A Smoking Radiating Ruin at the End of Two Hours': Documents on American Plans for Nuclear War with the Soviet Union, 1954–1955," *International Security*, 6 (1981/2), pp. 3–38 at pp. 25, 27.

66. J. H. Doolittle et al., "Report on the Covert Activities of the Central Intelligence Agency, 30 Sept. 1954," pp. 6–7, copy in CIA Electronic Reading Room at http://www.foia.cia.gov/.

67. Recollections of David Atlee Phillips, quoted in John Ranelagh, *The Agency: The Rise and Decline of the CIA* (London: Sceptre, 1988), pp. 267–268.

68. Patterson, *Grand Expectations*, p. 348.

69. Rosser Reeves quoted in William E. Leuchtenburg, *A Troubled Feast: American Society Since 1945* (Boston: Little, Brown, 1973), p. 68.

70. Chester H. Liebs, *Main Street to Miracle Mile: American Roadside Architecture* (Boston: Little, Brown, 1985), pp. 125 and 131 (quotation from Aug. 1951).

71. Quoted in Albert Goodman, *Elvis* (London: Allen Lane, 1981), p. 110.

72. *The Times* (London), 15 Sept. 1956, p. 4.

73. Quoted in Richard F. Kuisel, *Seducing the French: The Dilemma of Americanization* (Berkeley: University of California Press, 1993), p. 63.

74. Quoted in Serge Guilbaut, *How New York Stole the Idea of Modern Art: Abstract Impressionism, Freedom, and the Cold War*, trans. Arthur Goldhammer (Chicago: University of Chicago Press, 1983), p. 172.

75. Kitchen debate, 24 July 1959, abbreviated text available online at http://www.teachingamericanhistory.org/library/index.asp?document=176, accessed 7 Oct. 2008.

76. G. Mennen Williams quoted in Robert S. Dudney, "When Sputnik Shocked the World," *Air Force Magazine*, 90/10 (Oct. 2007), pp. 42–47 at p. 46.

77. Lawrence G. Derthick (1958) quoted in Barbara B. Clowse, *Brainpower for the Cold War: The Sputnik Crisis and National Defense Act of 1958* (Westport, CT: Greenwood Press, 1981), p. 113.

78. Quoted in Daniel J. Kevles, *The Physicists: The History of a Scientific Community in Modern America* (New York: Alfred A. Knopf, 1978), pp. 384–385.

79. Quoted in Stuart W. Leslie, *The Cold War and American Science: The Military-Industrial Complex at MIT and Stanford* (New York: Columbia University Press, 1993), p. 14.

80. Johnson, statement of 25 Nov. 1957, quoted in Clowse, *Brainpower for the Cold War*, p. 59.

81. Walter A. McDougall, *The Heavens and the Earth: A Political History of the Space Age* (New York: Basic Books, 1985), p. 154.

82. Eisenhower, State of the Union Address, 9 Jan. 1958 (PPPUS website).

83. Daniel Yergin, *The Prize: The Epic Quest for Oil, Money, and Power* (New York: Touchstone, 1992), pp. 569–574, 665–666, quoting from p. 570.

84. Eisenhower, farewell address on radio and TV, 17 Jan. 1961 (PPPUS website).

85. See Charles Griffin, "New Light on Eisenhower's Farewell Address," *Presidential Studies Quarterly*, 22 (1992), pp. 469–479.

14: Rights and Riots

1. U.S. Supreme Court, *Brown v. Board of Education*, 347 U.S. 483 (1954)—opinion delivered by Chief Justice Warren.

2. Quoted in Juan Williams, *Eyes on the Prize: America's Civil Rights Years* (New York: Viking, 1987), p. 35.

3. Quoted in Clayborne Carson et al., eds., *The Eyes on the Prize Civil Rights Reader* (New York: Penguin, 1991), pp. 83–84, 93.

4. Quoted in Richard Kluger, *Simple Justice: The History of Brown v. Board of Education and Black America's Struggle for Equality* (New York: Vintage Books, 1977), p. 734.

5. Quoted in Harvard Sitkoff, *The Struggle for Black Equality, 1954–1980* (New York: Hill & Wang, 1981), p. 25.

6. Quoted in Howell Raines, *My Soul Is Rested: Movement Days in the Deep South Remembered* (London: Penguin, 1983), p. 41.

7. Joe Azbell, "Negro Rule in Boycott Is to Walk," *Montgomery Advertiser*, 5 Dec. 1955, p. 1, available online at http://www.montgomeryboycott.com/, accessed 7 Oct. 2008.

8. Stephen B. Oates, *Let the Trumpet Sound: The Life of Martin Luther King, Jr.* (New York: Mentor, 1985), pp. 67–68.

9. Ibid., p. 100.

10. Quoted in Williams, *Eyes on the Prize*, p. 116.

11. Ibid., p. 117.

12. Ibid., pp. 132–133.

13. Quoted in Carson et al., *Eyes on the Prize Civil Rights Reader*, p. 120.

14. Quoted in Williams, *Eyes on the Prize*, p. 139; cf. David Armstrong, *The Rise of the International Organization: A Short History* (London: Macmillan, 1982), p. 60.

15. Quoted in Raines, *My Soul Is Rested*, p. 109.

16. Quoted in Williams, *Eyes on the Prize*, p. 147.

17. Raymond Arsenault, *Freedom Riders: 1961 and the Struggle for Racial Justice* (New York: OUP, 2006), p. 7.

18. Quotations from ibid., pp. 6, 272, and 275.

19. Quoted in Carson et al., *Eyes on the Prize Civil Rights Reader*, p. 155.

20. Adam Fairclough, *Better Day Coming: Blacks and Equality, 1890–2000* (New York: Penguin, 2002), p. 276.

21. Johnson, remarks to civil rights leaders, 29 April 1964 (PPPUS website); Randall B. Woods, *LBJ: Architect of American Ambition* (Cambridge, MA: Harvard University Press, 2006), p. 472.

22. Quoted in Carol Mueller, "Ella Baker and the Origins of 'Participatory Democracy,'" in Vicki L. Crawford et al., eds., *Women in the Civil Rights Movement: Trailblazers and Torchbearers, 1941–1965* (Brooklyn: Carlson Publishing, 1990), pp. 51–70 at p. 64.

23. Specimen form posted on http://www.crmvet.org/info/lithome.htm, accessed 8 Oct. 2008.

24. Quoted in Williams, *Eyes on the Prize*, p. 254.

25. Ibid., p. 279.

26. Johnson, special message to Congress, "The American Promise," 15 March 1965 (PPPUS website).

27. Ibid.

28. Report of the Governor's Commission on the Los Angeles Riots, 2 Dec. 1965, section 3, "The Crisis—An Overview," available online at http://www.usc.edu/libraries/archives/cityinstress/mccone/contents.html, accessed 8 Oct. 2008.

29. Quoted in Fairclough, *Better Day Coming*, p. 297.

30. Quoted in Oates, *Let the Trumpet Sound*, p. 367.

31. Quoted in Carson et al., *Eyes on the Prize Civil Rights Reader*, p. 292.

32. Quoted in Oates, *Let the Trumpet Sound*, p. 399.

33. Ibid., p. 399.

34. Carson et al., *Eyes on the Prize Civil Rights Reader*, p. 281.

35. Quoted in Fairclough, *Better Day Coming*, p. 313.

36. Quoted in Carson et al., *Eyes on the Prize Civil Rights Reader*, pp. 346–347.

37. John H. Johnson (1964), quoted in Lizabeth Cohen, *A Consumer's Republic: The Politics of Mass Consumption in Postwar America* (New York: Alfred A. Knopf, 2003), p. 325.

38. Quoted in Carson et al., *Eyes on the Prize Civil Rights Reader*, pp. 443–444.

39. "Black Complaint," *Time*, 25 Oct. 1968.

40. "The American Woman," *Saturday Evening Post*, 22–29 Dec. 1962, p. 32.

41. Betty Friedan, *The Feminine Mystique* (New York: W. W. Norton, 1963), pp. 305, 307–308.

42. Quoted in ibid., p. 28.

43. See Joanna Meyerowitz, "Beyond the Feminine Mystique: A Reassessment of Postwar Mass Culture, 1946–1958," *JAH*, 79 (1993), pp. 1455–1482, esp. pp. 1479–1480.

44. Lynn Y. Weiner, *From Working Girl to Working Mother: The Female Labor Force in the United States, 1820–1980* (Chapel Hill: UNC Press, 1985), p. 89.

45. Daniel Horowitz, *Betty Friedan and the Making of The Feminine Mystique: The American Left, the Cold War, and Modern Feminism* (Amherst: University of Massachusetts Press, 1998), esp. pp. 201–202, 206; cf. Joanne Boucher, "Betty Friedan and the Radical Past of Liberal Feminism," *New Politics*, new series, 9/3 (Summer 2003), available online at http://www.wpunj.edu/~newpol/issue35/boucher35.htm, accessed 8 Oct. 2008.

46. Quoted in Eugenia Kaledin, *Mothers and More: American Women in the Fifties* (Boston: Twayne, 1984), pp. 43 and 53.

47. Horowitz, *Betty Friedan*, pp. 229–230.

48. NOW, Statement of Purpose, Oct. 1966, printed in Kathleen C. Berkeley, *The Women's Liberation Movement in America* (Westport, CT: Greenwood Press, 1999), pp. 159–160.

49. Quoted in Blanche Linden-Wood and Carol Hurd Green, *Changing the Future: American Women in the 1960s* (New York: Twayne, 1993), p. 109.

50. SNCC Position Paper, Nov. 1964, printed in Berkeley, *Women's Liberation Movement*, pp. 157–158.

51. Quoted in Berkeley, *Women's Liberation Movement*, p. 42.

52. Linden-Wood and Green, *Changing the Future*, p. xvii.

53. William H. Chafe, *The Paradox of Change: American Women in the Twentieth Century* (New York: OUP, 1991), p. 211.

54. "Contraception: Freedom from Fear," *Time*, 7 April 1967, p. 78.

55. Quoted in Bernard Asbell, *The Pill: A Biography of the Drug That Changed the World* (New York: Random House, 1995), p. 180.

56. Steven M. Spencer, "The Birth Control Revolution," *Saturday Evening Post*, 15 Jan. 1966, p. 66.

57. Quoted in Asbell, *The Pill*, p. 198.

58. Quotations from Mary Smith, "Birth Control and the Negro Woman," *Ebony*, March 1968, pp. 29–37 at pp. 30, 31, and 34.

59. Johnson, State of the Union Address, 8 Jan. 1964 (PPPUS website).

60. Quoted in William E. Leuchtenburg, *A Troubled Feast: American Society Since 1945* (Boston: Little, Brown, 1973), p. 138.

61. Michael Harrington, *The Other America: Poverty in the United States* (Baltimore: Penguin, 1963), quoting from pp. 10, 12, 17, and 155.

62. James T. Patterson, *America's Struggle Against Poverty, 1900–1980* (Cambridge, MA: Harvard University Press, 1981), p. 113—a book on which this section draws heavily.

63. John Kenneth Galbraith, *The Affluent Society* (London: Hamish Hamilton, 1958), p. 259.

64. Patterson, *America's Struggle Against Poverty*, p. 126.

65. Quoted in Robert Dallek, *John F. Kennedy: An Unfinished Life, 1917–1963* (London: Penguin, 2003), p. 254.

66. John F. Kennedy, address to the Greater Houston Ministerial Association, 12 Sept. 1960, John F. Kennedy Library website (http://www.jfklibrary.org/)—Reference, Speeches.

67. Leuchtenburg, *A Troubled Feast*, p. 134.

68. Theodore H. White, *In Search of History: A Personal Adventure* (New York: Warner Books, 1981), esp. pp. 675, 677–678.

69. Quoted in "For President Kennedy: An Epilogue," *Life*, 6 Dec. 1963, p. 159.

70. Tom Wicker, *JFK and LBJ: The Influence of Personality upon Politics* (Baltimore: Penguin, 1969), pp. 151–152.

71. Johnson, address to a joint session of Congress, 27 Nov. 1963 (PPPUS website).

72. Interview of 22 Sept. 1965, in William E. Leuchtenburg, "A Visit with LBJ," *American Heritage*, 41/4 (May–June 1990), pp. 47–64.

73. Rowland Evans and Robert Novak (1966) quoted in Woods, *LBJ: Architect of American Ambition*, p. 262.

74. Quoted in James T. Patterson, *Grand Expectations: The United States, 1945–1974* (New York: OUP, 1996), p. 558.

75. Johnson, remarks at Johnson City, Texas, 11 April 1965 (PPPUS website).

76. Woods, *LBJ: Architect of American Ambition*, p. 572.

77. Leuchtenburg, "A Visit with LBJ."

78. Ibid.

15: The Impotence of Omnipotence

1. "The Illusion of American Omnipotence," in D. W. Brogan, *American Aspects* (London: Hamish Hamilton, 1964), ch. 2 at pp. 9, 13.

2. Richard Bissell at meeting of 4 April 1961, in Richard Reeves, *President Kennedy: Profile of Power* (New York: Touchstone, 1994), pp. 80–81.

3. Michael R. Beschloss, *The Crisis Years: Kennedy and Khrushchev, 1960–1963* (New York: HarperCollins, 1991), p. 114.

4. Kent M. Beck, "Necessary Lies, Hidden Truths: Cuba in the 1960 Campaign," *DH*, 8 (1984), pp. 37–60 at p. 45.

5. Arthur M. Schlesinger, Jr., *Robert F. Kennedy and His Times* (New York: Ballantine Books, 1978), p. 477.

6. Lawrence Freedman, *Kennedy's Wars: Berlin, Cuba, Laos, and Vietnam* (New York: OUP, 2000), pp. 129, 133, 139.

7. Schlesinger, *Robert F. Kennedy*, p. 480.

8. Reeves, *President Kennedy*, p. 95.

9. Walter A. McDougall, *The Heavens and the Earth: A Political History of the Space Age* (New York: Basic Books, 1985), p. 320.

10. Kennedy, special message to Congress, 25 May 1961 (PPPUS website).

11. Oleg Troyanovsky, "The Making of Soviet Foreign Policy," in William Taubman et al., eds., *Nikita Khrushchev* (New Haven, CT: Yale University Press, 2000), ch. 9 at p. 231.

12. David Halberstam, *The Best and the Brightest* (New York: Fawcett Crest, 1973), pp. 96–97.

13. Beschloss, *Crisis Years*, pp. 278–279.

14. Richard Helms, memo of meeting with Robert Kennedy, 19 Jan. 1962, in *FRUS 1961–1963*, vol. XI, doc. 292.

15. Ernest R. May and Philip D. Zelikow, eds., *The Kennedy Tapes: Inside the White House During the Cuban Missile Crisis* (Cambridge, MA: Harvard University Press, 1997), p. 39.

16. William Taubman, *Khrushchev: The Man and His Era* (New York: W. W. Norton, 2003), p. 541.

17. Quotations from May and Zelikow, *The Kennedy Tapes*, pp. 71, 139, 152.

18. Kennedy, radio and TV address, 22 Oct. 1962 (PPPUS website).

19. Schlesinger, *Robert F. Kennedy*, p. 554.

20. May and Zelikow, *The Kennedy Tapes*, p. 358.

21. Steven J. Zaloga, *Target America: The Soviet Union and the Strategic Arms Race, 1945–1964* (Novato, CA: Presidio, 1993), p. 213.

22. Khrushchev to Kennedy, 26 Oct. 1962, in *FRUS 1961–1963*, vol. VI, doc. 65.

23. Both quoted in Beschloss, *Crisis Years*, p. 568.

24. Kennedy, addresses at Bonn-Cologne airport and at the Rathaus in Bonn, 23 June 1963, and at the Rathaus in West Berlin, 26 June 1963 (PPPUS website).

25. Kennedy, inaugural address, 20 Jan. 1961 (PPPUS website).

26. Kennedy, speech at the American University, 10 June 1963 (PPPUS website).

27. Declaration of Independence of the Democratic Republic of Vietnam, 2 Sept. 1945, printed in David Armitage, *The Declaration of Independence: A Global History* (Cambridge, MA: Harvard University Press, 2007), p. 231.

28. Eisenhower to Churchill, 22 July 1954, PREM 11/1074 (The National Archives, Kew, Surrey).

29. Eisenhower to Churchill, 4 April 1954, PREM 11/1074.

30. George C. Herring, *America's Longest War: The United States and Vietnam, 1950–1975* 2nd ed. (New York: Alfred A. Knopf, 1986), pp. 49, 57.

31. Halberstam, *The Best and the Brightest*, p. 97. Possibly Kennedy did not use those exact words—see David Kaiser, *American Tragedy: Kennedy, Johnson, and the Origins of the*

Vietnam War (Cambridge, MA: Harvard University Press, 2000), pp. 101–102—but they do seem to have been his sentiments.

32. Herring, *America's Longest War*, p. 43.

33. Arthur M. Schlesinger, Jr., *A Thousand Days: John F. Kennedy in the White House* (New York: Fawcett, 1971), p. 505.

34. Max Frankel, 3 July 1963, quoted in Robert Dallek, *John F. Kennedy: An Unfinished Life, 1917–1963* (London: Penguin, 2003), pp. 669–670.

35. Cable from Ambassador Lodge, 29 Aug. 1963, in *FRUS 1961–1963*, vol. IV, doc. 12.

36. Halberstam, *The Best and the Brightest*, p. 355.

37. Schlesinger, *A Thousand Days*, pp. 909–910.

38. Doris Kearns, *Lyndon Johnson and the American Dream* (New York: Signet, 1977), p. 263.

39. Bundy to Johnson, memo, 27 Jan. 1965, in Robert S. McNamara, with Brian Van-DeMark, *In Retrospect: The Tragedy and Lessons of Vietnam* (New York: Times Books, 1995), pp. 167–168.

40. The skepticism of the inner circle even as it advocated escalation is emphasized in Fredrik Logevall, *Choosing War: The Lost Chance for Peace and the Escalation of War in Vietnam* (Berkeley: University of California Press, 1999), p. 271.

41. Quotations from Brian VanDeMark, *Into the Quagmire: Lyndon Johnson and the Escalation of the Vietnam War* (New York: OUP, 1991), p. 149.

42. Johnson, press conference, 28 July 1965 (PPPUS website).

43. E.g., Schlesinger, *Robert F. Kennedy*, p. 780; McNamara, *In Retrospect*, pp. 96–97.

44. See Robert Dallek, "Lyndon Johnson and Vietnam: The Making of Tragedy," *DH*, 20 (1996), pp. 147–162.

45. Halberstam, *The Best and the Brightest*, pp. 614–615.

46. *FRUS, Vietnam, 1964*, p. 664.

47. See VanDeMark, *Into the Quagmire*, p. 180.

48. Kearns, *Lyndon Johnson and the American Dream*, p. 296.

49. Quoted in Logevall, *Choosing War*, p. 274.

50. James William Gibson, *The Perfect War: Technowar in Vietnam* (Boston: The Atlantic Monthly Press, 1986), p. 109.

51. Eric M. Bergerud, *The Dynamics of Defeat: The Vietnam War in Hau Nghia Province* (Boulder, CO: Westview Press, 1991), pp. 171, 175.

52. Figures from McNamara, *In Retrospect*, p. 321.

53. On this see Vaughn Davis Bornet, *The Presidency of Lyndon B. Johnson* (Lawrence: University Press of Kansas, 1983), pp. 240–245.

54. Daniel G. Hallin, *The "Uncensored War": The Media and Vietnam* (New York: OUP, 1986), pp. 129–130, 163 (quotation).

55. Larry Berman, *Lyndon Johnson's War: The Road to Stalemate in Vietnam* (New York: W. W. Norton, 1989), p. 121.

56. Johnson, press conference, 17 Nov. 1967 (PPPUS website).

57. "Double Trouble," *Time*, 9 Feb. 1968.

58. Hallin, *The "Uncensored War,"* pp. 167–174.

59. Kearns, *Lyndon Johnson and the American Dream*, pp. 34 and 359 (quotation).

60. Kearns, *Lyndon Johnson and the American Dream*, p. 358.

61. Robert Dallek, *Flawed Giant: Lyndon Johnson and His Times, 1961–1973* (New York: OUP, 1998), p. 509.

62. Johnson, address to the nation, 31 March 1968 (PPPUS website).

63. Dallek, *Flawed Giant*, pp. 529–530.

64. Randall B. Woods, *LBJ: Architect of American Ambition* (Cambridge, MA: Harvard University Press, 2006), pp. 838–839.

65. Hugh Sidey (1971) quoted in Dallek, *Flawed Giant*, p. 548.

66. Woods, *LBJ: Architect of American Ambition*, p. 846.

67. Johnson, letter to the Senate and the House, 6 June 1968 (PPPUS website).

68. Johnson, remarks on signing the Gun Control Act, 22 Oct. 1968 (PPPUS website).

69. Mark Kurlansky, *1968: The Year That Rocked the World* (New York: Random House, 2005), pp. 273–274.

70. Ibid., pp. 283, 285.

71. Stephen E. Ambrose, *Nixon* (3 vols., New York, 1987–1991), I, p. 671.

72. Nixon, remarks to Apollo 11 astronauts (PPPUS website).

73. Quotations in this paragraph from Walter Isaacson, *Kissinger: A Biography* (New York: Simon & Schuster, 1992), pp. 160, 163–164.

74. Nixon to Laird and Rogers, 4 Feb. 1969, *FRUS 1969–1976*, vol. I, doc. 10.

75. David Holloway, *The Soviet Union and the Arms Race* 2nd ed. (New Haven, CT: Yale University Press, 1984), pp. 58–59.

76. Richard M. Nixon, "Asia After Viet Nam," *Foreign Affairs*, 46/1 (Oct. 1967), pp. 111–125 at pp. 121, 123.

77. Isaacson, *Kissinger*, p. 193.

78. Quotations in this paragraph from Robert Dallek, *Nixon and Kissinger: Partners in Power* (London: Penguin, 2007), pp. 93–94.

79. Nixon, address, 15 July 1971 (PPPUS website).

80. Richard M. Nixon, *The Memoirs of Richard Nixon* (London: Arrow, 1979), p. 560.

81. White House tape, 22 July 1971, in *FRUS 1969–1976*, vol. XVII, p. 459, note 2. Conscious of the taping system, Nixon sometimes spoke for the historical record. Even so, these comments seem an accurate reflection of his approach.

82. Kissinger-Gromyko conversation, 27 May 1972, in *FRUS 1969–1976*, vol. XIV, doc. 290, quoting from pp. 1161, 1162, 1168.

83. Nixon, remarks on election eve, 6 Nov. 1972 (PPPUS website).

84. Quoted in "More Bombs Than Ever," *Time*, 1 Jan. 1973.

85. See, e.g., Isaacson, *Kissinger*, pp. 483–484.

86. Nixon, radio address, 23 Jan. 1973 (PPPUS website).

87. James P. Harrison, "History's Heaviest Bombing," in Jayne S. Werner and Luu Doan Huynh, eds., *The Vietnam War: Vietnamese and American Perspectives* (Armonk, NY: M. E. Sharpe, 1993), ch. 7, esp. pp. 133–134.

88. *Washington Post*, 18 June 1972, p. A1.

89. Nixon, news conference, 29 Aug. 1972 (PPPUS website).

90. Ambrose, *Nixon*, II, p. 660.

91. Transcript of Haldeman-Nixon meeting, 23 July 1972, p. 8, Nixon Library website (http://www.nixonlibraryfoundation.org/)—White House Tapes—Watergate Trial Conversations at http://nixon.archives.gov/forresearchers/find/tapes/watergate/trial/transcripts.php, accessed 8 Oct. 2008.

92. Transcript of Nixon-Dean-Haldeman meeting, 21 March 1973, pp. 5, 33–34.

93. Ambrose, *Nixon*, III, p. 133.

94. Fred Emery, *Watergate: The Corruption and Fall of Richard Nixon* (London: Jonathan Cape, 1994), p. 334.

95. Dallek, *Nixon and Kissinger*, p. 530.

96. Nixon, Q&A session at the Annual Convention of the Associated Press Managing Editors Association, Orlando, Florida, 17 Nov. 1973 (PPPUS website).

97. Nixon, remarks on leaving the White House, 9 Aug. 1974 (PPPUS website).

98. Ross Terrill, *Mao: A Biography* 2nd ed. (New York: Touchstone, 1993), p. 428.

99. Henry Kissinger, *White House Years* (London: Phoenix, 2000), pp. 840–841.

100. Dallek, *Nixon and Kissinger*, pp. 511–512.

101. Arthur M. Schlesinger, Jr., *The Imperial Presidency* (New York: Popular Library Edition, 1974), pp. 205, 447.

102. Nixon, Q&A session at the Annual Convention of the Associated Press Managing Editors Association, Orlando, Florida, 17 Nov. 1973 (PPPUS website).

16: Détente and Discontent

1. Henry Brandon, *The Retreat of American Power* (New York: Delta, 1974), pp. 2–3.

2. Quoted in Stephen E. Ambrose, *Nixon* (3 vols., New York, 1987–1991), III, p. 238.

3. Ford, remarks on taking the oath of office, 9 Aug. 1974 (PPPUS website).

4. Ford, remarks on signing the pardon, 8 Sept. 1974 (PPPUS website).

5. Ambrose, *Nixon*, III, pp. 461–462.

6. Report for the president by Daniel Yankelovich, in Daniel Yergin, *The Prize: The Epic Quest for Oil, Money and Power* (New York: Touchstone, 1992), p. 618.

7. "Gas Fever: Happiness Is a Full Tank," *Time,* 18 Feb. 1974.

8. Nixon, veto message, 24 Oct. 1973 (PPPUS website).

9. Quoted anonymously in Arnold R. Isaacs, *Without Honor: Defeat in Vietnam and Cambodia* (Baltimore: Johns Hopkins University Press, 1983), p. 102.

10. "Last Chopper Out of Saigon," *Time,* 12 May 1975.

11. Shown to the president himself. See Gerald R. Ford, *A Time to Heal* (London: W. H. Allen, 1979), p. 275.

12. Public statements in Jan. and Feb. 1976, quoted in Raymond Garthoff, *Détente and Confrontation: American-Soviet Relations from Nixon to Reagan* 2nd ed. (Washington, DC: The Brookings Institution, 1994), p. 580.

13. Karen Brutents, quoted in Odd Arne Westad, *The Global Cold War: Third World Interventions and the Making of Our Times* (Cambridge: CUP, 2005), p. 241.

14. Quoted in Garthoff, *Détente and Confrontation*, pp. 580–581.

15. Reagan speech, "To Restore America," 31 March 1976, text on PBS American Experience website at http://www.pbs.org/wgbh/amex/reagan/filmmore/reference/primary/restore.html, accessed 9 Oct. 2008.

16. The Boston Women's Health Collective, *Our Bodies, Ourselves: A Book by and for Women* 2nd ed. (New York: Simon & Schuster, 1979), p. 216.

17. Shirley Chisholm, *Unbought and Unbossed* (Boston: Houghton Mifflin, 1970), pp. 113–114.

18. Sarah Weddington, *A Question of Choice* (New York: Penguin, 1993), p. 12.

19. David J. Garrow, *Liberty and Sexuality: The Right to Privacy and the Making of Roe v. Wade* 2nd ed. (Berkeley: University of California Press, 1998), pp. 335–337.

20. Lucas to Weddington, 7 Nov. 1971, in Garrow, *Liberty and Sexuality*, pp. 514–515.

21. Garrow, *Liberty and Sexuality*, p. 517.

22. Sarah Weddington, oral argument, 13 Dec. 1971, in *Roe v. Wade,* 410 U.S. 113 (1973) on the Oyez Project, available online at http://www.oyez.org/cases/1970-1979/1971/1971_70_18/argument/, accessed 9 October 2008.

23. Sarah Weddington, oral argument, 11 Oct. 1972, *Roe v. Wade*, in N.E.H. Hull, Williamjames Hoffer and Peter Charles Hoffer, eds., *The Abortion Rights Controversy in*

America: A Legal Reader (Chapel Hill: UNC Press, 2004), p. 141; cf. Garrow, *Liberty and Sexuality*, pp. 568–569.

24. Robert Flowers, oral argument, 11 Oct. 1972, *Roe v. Wade*, in Hull et al., *The Abortion Rights Controversy*, p. 141; cf. Garrow, *Liberty and Sexuality*, pp. 569–570.

25. Mr. Justice White, dissenting opinion in *Doe v. Bolton*, 22 Jan. 1973, 410 U.S. 179 (1973).

26. John Micklethwait and Adrian Wooldridge, *The Right Nation: Conservative Power in America* (London: Penguin, 2005), p. 71.

27. Marshner quoted in William H. Chafe, *The Paradox of Change: American Women in the Twentieth Century* (New York: OUP, 1991), p. 217.

28. Donald T. Critchlow, "Conservatism Reconsidered: Phyllis Schlafly and Grassroots Conservatism," in David Farber and Jeff Roche, eds., *The Conservative Sixties* (New York: Peter Lang, 2003), pp. 108–126 at p. 119.

29. Donald T. Critchlow, *Phyllis Schlafly and Grassroots Conservatism: A Woman's Crusade* (Princeton, NJ: Princeton University Press, 2005), p. 12.

30. The Phyllis Schlafly Report, 6 (Nov. 1972), in Kathleen C. Berkeley, *The Women's Liberation Movement in America* (Westport, CT: Greenwood Press, 1999), doc. 9, quoting pp. 172, 174; original emphasis.

31. "Anti-ERA Evangelist Wins Again," *Time*, 3 July 1978.

32. Ibid.

33. Quoted in David Goldfield, *Black, White, and Southern: Race Relations and Southern Culture, 1940 to the Present* (Baton Rouge: Louisiana State University Press, 1990), p. 257.

34. *Green v. County School Board of New Kent County*, Virginia, 391 U.S. 430 (1968), decided 27 May 1968.

35. Matthew D. Lassiter, *The Silent Majority: Suburban Politics in the Sunbelt South* (Princeton, NJ: Princeton University Press, 2006), p. 140.

36. Goldfield, *Black, White, and Southern*, pp. 260–261.

37. Adam Fairclough, *Better Day Coming: Blacks and Equality, 1890–2000* (New York: Penguin, 2002), pp. 325–326.

38. Cleveland Hammond, quoted in Goldfield, *Black, White, and Southern*, p. 264.

39. Quoted in "Boston: Led by Children," *Time*, 7 Oct. 1974.

40. Falwell, Sermon of 21 March, 1965, quoted in William Martin, *With God on Our Side: The Rise of the Religious Right in America* (New York: Broadway Books, 1996), pp. 69–70.

41. Martin, *With God on Our Side*, p. 70.

42. William Martin, *The Billy Graham Story: A Prophet with Honour* (London: Hutchinson, 1991), p. 93.

43. Ibid., pp. 431–432, 472.

44. Martin, *With God on Our Side*, p. 78.

45. Jonathan Zimmerman, *Whose America? Culture Wars in the Public Schools* (Cambridge, MA: Harvard University Press, 2002), pp. 163–164, 174–175.

46. Martin, *With God on Our Side*, p. 122.

47. Quoted in Lester L. Langley, "What Happened in Kanawha County," *English Journal*, 64/5 (May 1975), pp. 7–9 at p. 9.

48. Martin, *With God on Our Side*, p. 71.

49. Mailing of 14 Aug. 1980, quoted in Martin, *With God on Our Side*, p. 205.

50. Morton Blackwell, quoted in Martin, *With God on Our Side*, p. 191.

51. Martin, *With God on Our Side*, p. 197.

52. Ibid., p. 200.

53. Ibid., p. 206.

54. Jimmy Carter, *Keeping Faith: Memoirs of a President* (New York: Bantam, 1982), p. 18.

55. Ibid., pp. 22, 24.

56. Rosalynn Carter, *First Lady from Plains* (Boston: Houghton Mifflin, 1984), p. 48.

57. Jimmy Carter, inaugural address, 20 Jan. 1977 (PPPUS website).

58. Rosalynn Carter, quoted in John Dumbrell, *The Carter Presidency: A Re-evaluation* 2nd ed. (Manchester, UK: Manchester University Press, 1995), p. 75.

59. Letter of Feb. 1976, quoted in Dumbrell, *The Carter Presidency*, p. 71.

60. Martin, *With God on Our Side*, p. 189.

61. Carter, address at Notre Dame University, 22 May 1977 (PPPUS website).

62. Title of an editorial in *Newsday*, 12 Aug., 1977, p. 17.

63. Quoted in Jules Witcover, *Marathon: The Pursuit of the Presidency, 1972–1976* (New York: Viking, 1977), p. 402.

64. Quoted in George D. Moffett III, *The Limits of Victory: The Ratification of the Panama Canal Treaties* (Ithaca, NY: Cornell University Press, 1985), p. 172.

65. Quotations from Moffett, *Limits of Victory*, pp. 176, 203.

66. Carter, *Keeping Faith*, p. 184.

67. See John J. Mearsheimer and Stephen M. Walt, *The Israel Lobby and US Foreign Policy* (London: Allen Lane, 2007), esp. pp. 26 and 135. Quotation from aide Hamilton Jordan in David Reynolds, *Summits: Six Meetings That Shaped the Twentieth Century* (London: Penguin, 2007), p. 273.

68. Quoted in Dumbrell, *The Carter Presidency*, p. 185.

69. Zbigniew Brzezinski, *Power and Principle: Memoirs of a National Security Adviser* (London: Weidenfeld & Nicolson, 1983), p. 520.

70. Garthoff, *Détente and Confrontation*, pp. 1059–1060.

71. Carter, briefing for members of Congress, 8 Jan. 1980 (PPPUS website).

72. Quotations from Carter, *Keeping Faith*, pp. 3–4, 518. For a succinct evaluation of the rescue plan see Robert A. Strong, *Working in the World: Jimmy Carter and the Making of American Foreign Policy* (Baton Rouge: Louisiana State University Press, 2000), ch. 9.

73. Carter/Reagan presidential debate, Cleveland, Ohio, 28 Oct. 1980 (PPPUS website).

17: Revolution and Democracy

1. Ronald Reagan, inaugural address, 20 Jan. 1981 (PPPUS website).

2. Robert Dallek, *Ronald Reagan: The Politics of Symbolism* (Cambridge, MA: Harvard University Press, 1984), p. 12.

3. Quoted in James T. Patterson, *Restless Giant: The United States from Watergate to Bush vs. Gore* (New York: OUP, 2005), p. 160.

4. Donald Regan, *From Wall Street to Washington* (New York: Harcourt Brace Jovanovich, 1988), p. 4.

5. Tip O'Neill, with William Novak, *Man of the House: The Life and Political Memoirs of Speaker Tip O'Neill* (New York: Random House, 1987), pp. 360, 363.

6. Ibid., p. 341.

7. Ronald Reagan, *An American Life* (New York: Simon & Schuster, 1990), pp. 231–232.

8. Joseph Hogan, "The Federal Budget in the Reagan Era," in Hogan, ed., *The Reagan Years: The Record in Presidential Leadership* (Manchester, UK: Manchester University Press, 1990), ch. 10 at pp. 231–232.

9. David A. Stockman, *The Triumph of Politics: The Crisis in American Government and How It Affects the World* (New York: Avon Books, 1987), pp. 9, 14.

10. William Martin, *With God on Our Side: The Rise of the Religious Right in America* (New York: Broadway Books, 1996), p. 220.

11. Martin, *With God on Our Side*, pp. 227.

12. Reagan, remarks at White House ceremony, 6 May 1982 (PPPUS website).

13. Mark Hertsgaard, *On Bended Knee: The Press and the Reagan Presidency* (New York: Farrar, Straus and Giroux, 1988), pp. 4 (Deaver) and 6 (Leslie Janka, White House press aide).

14. Dallek, *Reagan*, p. 13.

15. Peter Schweizer, *Reagan's War: The Epic Story of His Forty-Year Struggle and His Final Triumph over Communism* (New York, 2002), p. 91.

16. Reagan, news conference, 29 Jan. 1981 (PPPUS website).

17. Reagan, address to National Association of Evangelicals, Orlando, Florida, 8 March 1983 (PPPUS website); cf. Don Oberdorfer, *From the Cold War to a New Era: The United States and the Soviet Union, 1983–91* 2nd ed. (Baltimore: Johns Hopkins University Press, 1998), p. 23, and Robert Lettow, *Ronald Reagan and His Quest to Abolish Nuclear Weapons* (New York: Random House, 2005), p. 17.

18. Martin Anderson, *Revolution: The Reagan Legacy* 2nd ed. (Stanford, CA: Hoover Institution Press, 1990), pp. 82–83.

19. Reagan, address to National Association of Evangelicals, 8 March 1983; Lettow, *Reagan and His Quest*, pp. 35, 133.

20. Even when Alzheimer's clouded his memory in the final years, Reagan kept coming back to that story: Edmund Morris, *Dutch: A Memoir of Ronald Reagan* (New York, 1999), p. 667; Michael Deaver, *A Different Drummer: My Thirty Years with Ronald Reagan* (New York: HarperCollins, 2003), pp. 21–22.

21. Oberdorfer, *From the Cold War to a New Era*, p. 22 (McFarlane); Carlucci is quoted in William Wohlforth, ed., *Witnesses to the End of the Cold War* (Baltimore: Johns Hopkins University Press, 1996), p. 46. Both men served as national security adviser.

22. Reagan recalled the story afterward for NATO leaders, 21 Nov. 1985, transcript, 13; copy in Robert E. Linhard papers, box 92178: Geneva summit records (4)—Ronald Reagan Library, Simi Valley, California.

23. Quotations from David Reynolds, *Summits: Six Meetings That Shaped the Twentieth Century* (London: Penguin, 2007), p. 347.

24. Soviet transcript of fourth Gorbachev-Reagan conversation, 12 Oct. 1986, reprinted in FBIS-USR-93-121, 20 Sept. 1993, p. 8—available in the National Security Archive, Reykjavik File, doc. 16, at http://www.gwu.edu/~nsarchiv/NSAEBB/NSAEBB203/index.htm, accessed 9 Oct. 2008.

25. Gorbachev's remarks at the opening ceremony, 29 May 1988, in *USSR-USA Summit: Moscow, May 29—June 2, 1988—Documents and Materials* (Moscow: Novosti Press Agency, 1988), p. 30.

26. Joseph G. Whelan, *The Moscow Summit, 1988: Reagan and Gorbachev in Negotiation* (Boulder, CO: Westview Press, 1990), p. 41.

27. "Machine of the Year," *Time*, 3 Jan. 1983, p. 4.

28. Quotations from Martin Campbell-Kelly and William Aspray, *Computer: A History of the Information Machine* (New York: Basic Books, 1996), pp. 115–116.

29. Quoted in Thomas J. Misa, "Military Needs., Commercial Realities, and the Development of the Transistor, 1948–1958," in Merritt Roe Smith, ed., *Military Enterprise and Technological Change* (Cambridge, MA: MIT Press, 1985), pp. 253–287 at p. 273.

30. As measured by value. See Ernest Braun and Stuart MacDonald, *Revolution in Miniature: The History and Impact of Semiconductor Electronics* 2nd ed. (Cambridge: CUP, 1982), pp. 80–81.

31. Thomas J. Watson, Jr., and Richard Petre, *Father and Son, & Co.: My Life at IBM and Beyond* (London: Bantam, 1990), quoting respectively pp. 232, 230.

32. Campbell-Kelly and Aspray, *Computer*, p. 147.

33. Braun and MacDonald, *Revolution in Miniature*, p. 99.

34. Campbell-Kelly and Aspray, *Computer*, p. 256.

35. Figures from *Time*, 3 Jan. 1983, p. 4.

36. Kenneth Flamm, *Creating the Computer: Government, Industry, and High Technology* (Washington, DC: The Brookings Institution, 1988), p. 238.

37. Adrian Hamilton, *The Financial Revolution: The Big Bang Worldwide* (New York: Viking, 1986), pp. 42–45, 118.

38. Ford, statement on signing the Securities Acts Amendments, 6 June 1975 (PPPUS website).

39. Peter Temin, with Louis Galambos, *The Fall of the Bell System: A Study in Prices and Profits* (Cambridge: CUP, 1987), p. 10.

40. A. Jagoda and M. de Villepin, *Mobile Communications*, trans. J.C.C. Nelson (New York: John Wiley, 1993), pp. 80–81.

41. Karen Dawisha, *Eastern Europe, Gorbachev and Reform: The Great Challenge* 2nd ed. (Cambridge: CUP, 1990), p. 160.

42. Richard W. Judy, "Computing in the USSR: A Comment," *Soviet Economy*, 2 (1986), pp. 355–367 at pp. 362–363.

43. George P. Shultz, *Turmoil and Triumph: My Years as Secretary of State* (New York: Charles Scribner's Sons, 1993), p. 591.

44. Charles S. Maier, *Dissolution: The Crisis of Communism and the End of East Germany* (Princeton, NJ: Princeton University Press, 1997), p. 73. Maier was writing about East Germany but his argument applies more generally.

45. Reagan, remarks at the Brandenburg Gate, 12 June 1987 (PPPUS website).

46. Quoted in Gisèle Charzat, *La militarization intégrale* (Paris: L'Herne, 1986), p. 145.

47. Michael R. Beschloss and Strobe Talbott, *At the Highest Levels: The Inside Story of the End of the Cold War* (Boston: Little, Brown, 1993), p. 105.

48. Bush, remarks at Texas A&M commencement, College Station, Texas, 12 May 1989 (PPPUS website).

49. Quoted in R. J. Crampton, *Eastern Europe in the Twentieth Century* (London: Routledge, 1994), p. 408.

50. Bush, press conference, 9 Nov. 1990 (PPPUS website).

51. George Bush and Brent Scowcroft, *A World Transformed* (New York: Vintage Books, 1999), pp. 149–150; Beschloss and Talbott, *At the Highest Levels*, p. 135.

52. Philip Zelikow and Condoleezza Rice, *Germany Unified and Europe Transformed: A Study in Statecraft* 2nd ed. (Cambridge, MA: Harvard University Press, 1997), p. 28.

53. *New York Times*, 25 Oct. 1989, pp. 1, 12.

54. Joint news conference, 25 Feb. 1990, quoted in Zelikow and Rice, *Germany Unified and Europe Transformed*, p. 216.

54. Beschloss and Talbott, *At the Highest Levels*, p. 219.

55. Ibid., p. 219 (Gorbachev); Raymond L. Garthoff, *The Great Transition: American-Soviet Relations and the End of the Cold War* (Washington, DC: The Brookings Institution, 1994), p. 410.

56. James Lull, *China Turned On: Television, Reform and Resistance* (London: Routledge, 1991), p. 193.

57. Bush, news conference, 5 June 1989 (PPPUS website).

58. Bush and Scowcroft, *A World Transformed*, pp. 102, 105.

59. Dilip Hiro, *The Longest War: The Iran-Iraq Military Conflict* (London: Paladin, 1990), pp. 1, 250–251.

60. Hiro, *The Longest War*, pp. 159–160.

61. Bush, exchange with Reporters, 5 Aug. 1990 (PPPUS website).

62. Bob Woodward, *The Commanders* (New York: Simon & Schuster, 1991), p. 260.

63. Bush, remarks at the annual conference of Veterans of Foreign Wars, Baltimore, 20 Aug. 1990 (PPPUS website).

64. Bush, speech in Manchester, NH, 23 Oct. 1990 (PPPUS website).

65. Colin Powell, with Joseph E. Persico, *My American Journey* (New York: Ballantine Books, 1996), pp. 475–476.

66. Bush, news conference, 30 Nov. 1990 (PPPUS website).

67. Quoted in Woodward, *The Commanders*, p. 336.

68. James A. Baker III, with Thomas M. DeFrank, *The Politics of Diplomacy: Revolution, War and Peace, 1989–1992* (New York: G. P. Putnam's Sons, 1995), p. 344.

69. Bush, address to the nation, 16 Jan. 1991 (PPPUS website).

70. Quoted in Baker, *Politics of Diplomacy*, p. 2.

71. Lawrence Freedman and Efraim Karsh, *The Gulf Conflict, 1990–1991* (London: Faber and Faber, 1993), p. 282.

72. Freedman and Karsh, *The Gulf Conflict*, p. 408.

73. Bush, remarks to the American Legislative Exchange Council, 1 March 1991 (PPPUS website).

74. Edward Luttwak, "The Air War," in Alex Danchev and Dan Keohane, eds., *International Perspectives on the Gulf Conflict, 1990–1991* (London: Macmillan, 1994), ch. 10.

75. Bush, address before a joint session of the Congress, 6 March 1991 (PPPUS website).

76. Bush and Scowcroft, *A World Transformed*, p. 489.

77. Ibid., p. 561.

18: Pride and Prejudice

1. Francis Fukuyama, "The End of History?" *The National Interest* (Summer 1989), pp. 3–18 at p. 4; original emphasis.

2. Sign by James Carville quoted in Bill Clinton, *My Life* (London: Arrow, 2005), p. 425.

3. Quoted in Carl Bernstein, *A Woman in Charge: The Life of Hillary Rodham Clinton* (New York: Vintage Books, 2008), quoting from pp. 117, 87.

4. David Reynolds, *One World Divisible: A Global History Since 1945* (London: Penguin, 2000), p. 645.

5. Reynolds, *One World Divisible*, p. 515; Gore, speech to National Association of Black-Owned Broadcasters convention, Sept. 1994, accessed on 15 April 2009 at http://192.211.16.13/curricular/Tacoma/info1.htm.

6. Ross Perot, *United We Stand: How We Can Take Back Our Country* (New York: Hyperion, 1992), pp. 24, 112.

7. Robert D. Putnam, "Bowling Alone: America's Declining Social Capital" (1995), reprinted in Larry Diamond and Marc F. Plattner, eds., *The Global Resurgence of Democracy* 2nd ed. (Baltimore: Johns Hopkins University Press, 1996), pp. 290–304 at pp. 295, 302.

8. Pat Buchanan, speech at the Republican National Convention, Houston, Texas, 17 Aug. 1992, on the Patrick J. Buchanan official website at http://www.buchanan.org/pa-92-0817-rnc.html, accessed 10 Oct. 2008.

9. Clinton, address to Congress, 22 Sept. 1993 (PPPUS website).

10. Hillary Rodham Clinton, *Living History* (London: Headline, 2004), p. 230.

11. "Contract with America," unveiled 27 Sept. 1994, printed in Ed Gillespie and Bob Schellhas, eds., *Contract with America* (New York: Times Books, 1994), pp. 7–12.

12. William C. Berman, *From the Center to the Edge: The Politics and Policies of the Clinton Presidency* (Lanham, MD: Rowman & Littlefield, 2001), p. 55.

13. Clinton, *My Life*, p. 651.

14. Richard Holbrooke, *To End a War* (New York: Random House, 1998), p. 28.

15. Clinton, ending his statement on the After-School Child Care Initiative, 26 Jan. 1998 (PPPUS website).

16. Clinton, address to the nation, 17 Aug. 1998 (PPPUS website).

17. Referral to the U.S. House of Representatives by the Office of the Independent Council, 9 Sept. 1998, Grounds for Impeachment, F, Summary.

18. Quoted in the *Washington Post* edition of *The Starr Report* (New York: Public Affairs, 1998), p. xi.

19. Quoted in Berman, *From the Center to the Edge*, p. 94.

20. Jeffrey Toobin, *The Nine: Inside the Secret World of the Supreme Court* (New York: Anchor Books, 2008), p. 165.

21. Alan Dershowitz, *Supreme Injustice: How the Supreme Court Hijacked Election 2000* (New York: OUP, 2001), p. 174.

22. *Bush v. Gore*, 531 U.S. 98 (2000), 12 Dec. 2000, Opinion, section IIB; Toobin, *The Nine*, p. 203.

23. *Bush v. Gore*, 531 U.S. 98 (2000), 12 Dec. 2000, dissent by Justice Stevens; Toobin, *The Nine*, pp. 207–208; Peter Irons, *A People's History of the Supreme Court* 2nd ed. (New York: Penguin Books, 2006), pp. 513–514.

24. Gavin Esler, *The United States of Anger* (London: Penguin, 1998), p. 7.

25. *International Herald Tribune*, 24 April 1997, p. 3.

26. Lyndon Johnson, remarks at Ellis Island, 3 Oct. 1965 (PPPUS website).

27. Roger Daniels, *Coming to America: A History of Immigration and Ethnicity in American Life* 2nd ed. (New York: Harper Perennial, 2002), esp. pp. 343, 410.

28. Capt. E. Durand Ayres, quoted in Daniels, *Coming to America*, p. 315.

29. David C. Gutiérrez, *Walls and Mirrors: Mexican Americans, Mexican Immigrants, and the Politics of Ethnicity* (Berkeley: University of California Press, 1995), pp. 184–185.

30. Clinton, proclamation for Columbus Day, 9 Oct. 1998 (PPPUS website).

31. Quoted in James T. Patterson, *Restless Giant: The United States from Watergate to Bush vs. Gore* (New York: OUP, 2005), p. 292.

32. Margot Hornblower, "Making and Breaking Law," *Time*, 21 Nov. 1994.

33. Senator Samuel I. Hayakawa, speech, 13 Aug. 1982, U.S. English website at http://www.us-english.org/view/26, accessed 10 Oct. 2008.

34. Daniels, *Coming to America*, p. 398.

35. Ibid., p. 399.

36. Schlesinger (1991) quoted in Gutiérrez, *Walls and Mirrors*, p. 213.

37. Samuel P. Huntington, *The Clash of Civilizations and the Remaking of World Order* (New York: Simon & Schuster, 1996), pp. 305–306.

38. Robert Draper, *Dead Certain* (New York: The Free Press, 2008), pp. 135–136.

39. Bush, presidential debate in Winston-Salem, North Carolina, 11 Oct. 2000 (PPPUS website).

40. Bush, remarks in Sarasota, Florida, 11 Sept. 2001 (PPPUS website).

41. Bush (Sr.), exchange with reporters, 5 Aug. 1990 (PPPUS website).

42. Margaret Carlson, "A President Finds His Voice," *Time*, 24 Sept. 2001.

43. Ibid.

44. Bob Woodward, *Bush at War* (London: Pocket Books, 2003), p. 69.

45. Bush, remarks at the World Trade Center site, 14 Sept. 2001 (PPPUS website).

46. Bush, speech to joint session of Congress, 20 Sept. 2001 (PPPUS website).

47. Ibid.

48. Ibid.

49. Bush, remarks on arrival at White House, 16 Sept. 2001 (PPPUS website).

50. Kevin Phillips, *American Theocracy: The Perils and Politics of Radical Religion, Oil, and Borrowed Money in the 21st Century* (New York: Penguin, 2007), pp. 207–208, quoting from a Pennsylvania newspaper, the *Lancaster New Era*, 16 July 2004, about Bush's meeting with an Amish community.

51. Richard A. Clarke, *Against All Enemies: Inside America's War on Terror* (New York: The Free Press, 2004), p. 32.

52. Ibid., pp. 30–31.

53. Quoted in Stefan Halper and Jonathan Clarke, *America Alone: The Neo-Conservatives and the Global Order* (Cambridge: CUP, 2004), pp, 11, 95, 148.

54. Open letter to President Clinton, 26 Jan. 1998, signed by, among others Bolton, Perle, Rumsfeld and Wolfowitz; online at Project for a New American Century website http://www.newamericancentury.org/iraqclintonletter.htm, accessed 10 Oct. 2008.

55. *Think Tank, with Ben Wattenberg* (PBS TV program), episode titled "Richard Perle: The Making of a Neoconservative," broadcast 14 Nov. 2002, transcript available online at http://www.pbs.org/thinktank/transcript1017.html, accessed 10 Oct 2008.

56. Bush, State of the Union Address, 29 Jan. 2002 (PPPUS website).

57. Quoted in Bob Woodward, *Plan of Attack* (New York: Simon & Schuster, 2004), p. 151.

58. *The National Security Strategy of the United States of America*, Sept. 2002, p. 15— copy available online at http://www.whitehouse.gov/nsc/nss/2002/, accessed 10 Oct. 2008.

59. For instance, John Lewis Gaddis, *Surprise, Security, and the American Experience* (Cambridge, MA: Harvard University Press, 2004), esp. ch. 2; Melvyn P. Leffler, "9/11 and the Past and Future of American Foreign Policy," *International Affairs*, 79 (2003), pp. 1045–1063, esp. pp. 1050–1053.

60. Cheney, speech to Veterans of Foreign Wars Convention, 26 Aug. 2002, available online at http://www.whitehouse.gov/news/releases/2002/08/20020826.html, accessed 10 Oct. 2008.

61. Cheney to Dick Armey, the House Majority Leader, as quoted in Draper, *Dead Certain*, p. 178. The observer was journalist Barton Gellman in his study *Angler: The Shadow Presidency of Dick Cheney* (London: Allen Lane, 2008), p. 390.

62. Powell, address to the UN, 5 Feb. 2003, available online at http://www.whitehouse.gov/news/releases/2003/02/20030205-1.html, accessed 10 Oct 2008.

63. Bush, address to the nation from the USS *Abraham Lincoln*, 1 May 2003 (PPPUS website).

64. U.S. Defense Department, OSD statistics at http://siadapp.dmdc.osd.mil/personnel/CASUALTY/OIF-Total-by-month.pdf, accessed 10 Oct 2008.

65. Rumsfeld, press conference, 12 April 2003, available online at http://www.cnn .com/2003/US/04/11/sprj.irq.pentagon/, accessed 10 Oct 2008.

66. Quoted in Bob Woodward, *State of Denial* (New York: Simon & Schuster, 2006), p. 163.

67. Woodward, *State of Denial*, p. 163.

68. Bush, remarks on the 20th Anniversary of the National Endowment for Democracy, 6 Nov. 2003 (PPPUS website).

69. John McCain, with Mark Salter, *Faith of My Fathers* (New York: Random House, 1999), pp. 346, 348.

70. *New York Times*, 3 Sept. 2008.

71. Quoted in Clinton, *Living History*, p. 109.

72. Barack Obama, "A More Perfect Union," Philadelphia, 18 March 2008, available online at http://my.barackobama.com/page/content/hisownwords/, accessed 15 April 2009.

73. Obama, "A More Perfect Union."

74. Simon Rosenberg, quoted in Gordon Rayner, "How the Internet Helped Propel Barack Obama to the White House," *Daily Telegraph* (London), 6 Nov. 2008.

75. Francis Fukuyama," The Damage to Brand USA Needs Urgent Repair," *The Times*, 14 Oct. 2008, p. 26.

76. Barack Obama, victory speech in Chicago, 4 Nov. 2008 (PPPUS website).

77. Obama, inaugural address, 20 Jan. 2009 (PPPUS website).

Conclusion

1. Blair, speech to the U.S. Congress, 18 July 2003, Ten Downing Street website at http://www.number10.gov.uk/Page4220, accessed 10 Oct. 2008. This official text does not include an impromptu reference to history made by Blair: "Actually, you know, my middle son was studying 18th-century history and the American War of Independence, and he said to me the other day, 'You know, Lord North, Dad, he was the British prime minister who lost us America. So just think, however many mistakes you'll make, you'll never make one that bad.'" See http://edition.cnn.com/2003/US/07/17/blair.transcript/, accessed 10 Oct. 2008.

2. Lord Illingworth in "A Woman of No Importance," *The Complete Works of Oscar Wilde* (London: Collins, 1968), p. 436.

3. Bush, news conference, 13 April 2004 (PPPUS website).

4. James Bone, "Whites Outnumbered in a Generation as Immigrants Change the Face of America," *The Times*, 15 Aug. 2008, p. 33, quoting demographer William Frey of the Brookings Institution in Washington.

5. Niall Ferguson, *Colossus: The Rise and Fall of the American Empire* (London: Penguin, 2005), p. 16.

6. Geir Lundestad, "Empire by Invitation? The United States and Western Europe, 1945–1952," *Journal of Peace Research*, 23 (1986), pp. 263–277; John Lewis Gaddis, *Surprise, Security, and the American Experience* (Cambridge, MA: Harvard University Press, 2004), p. 77.

7. See the discussion in Charles S. Maier, *Among Empires: American Ascendancy and Its Predecessors* (Cambridge, MA: Harvard University Press, 2006), ch. 6, esp. pp. 255, 260.

8. Statistics from Fareed Zakaria, "There Is a Silver Lining," *Newsweek*, 20 Oct. 2008.

9. Letter of 1 Jan. 1802 in Joyce Appleby and Terence Ball, eds., *Jefferson: Political Writings* (Cambridge: CUP, 1999), pp. 396–397.

10. Quoted in Nicholas Guyatt, *Providence and the Invention of the United States, 1607–1876* (New York: CUP, 2007), p. 310.

11. Walter Russell Mead, *Special Providence: American Foreign Policy and How It Changed the World* (New York: Alfred A. Knopf, 2001), p. 142.

12. Walter A. McDougall, *Promised Land, Crusader State: The American Encounter with the World Since 1776* (Boston: Houghton Mifflin, 1997), p. 5.

13. William Martin, *With God on Our Side: The Rise of the Religious Right in America* (New York: Broadway Books, 1996), p. 170; for the optimistic view see George M. Marsden, *Fundamentalism and American Culture* 2nd ed. (Oxford: OUP, 2006), pp. 250–251.

ACKNOWLEDGMENTS

Although triggered by my work in writing and presenting a radio series for the BBC, this book reflects an engagement with America that goes back more than three decades. It was Jonathan Steinberg, an immensely gifted teacher, who introduced me to U.S. history as an undergraduate at Cambridge and encouraged me to apply for graduate fellowships in the United States. The year I consequently spent at Harvard was a life-changing experience from which I developed a lasting respect for the dynamism and openness of America. This came partly through the people I met and the things I learned during the academic year, but even more from travelling across the United States the following summer. Ten thousand miles on a Greyhound bus, staying mostly in people's homes, introduced me to the "real" America. Coincidentally but memorably I ended my journey in front of the White House the morning Richard Nixon resigned.

As a result I became fascinated by the United States and the contrasts with Europe, a fascination that was intensified by working on a doctorate. I remain grateful to the late Frank Freidel of Harvard for introducing me to the era of Franklin Roosevelt and to the beauty and archival riches of the Roosevelt Library in Hyde Park, New York. From those years have flowed a succession of visits and journeys, including memorable visiting appointments at the Charles Warren Center at Harvard, the University of Nebraska, Lincoln, and the University of Oklahoma, Norman.

At Cambridge University I have benefited from the expectation that academics will teach outside their own narrow specialisms: Years of supervising undergraduates on American history since 1750 laid the foundations for this book. Under the leadership of Tony Badger, Cambridge is now one of the best places outside the United States to study U.S. history. I have drawn on Tony's work and on that of colleagues Betty Wood, Michael O'Brien, John Thompson, and Andrew Preston in writing this book. I am particularly indebted to John for reading the manuscript with his usual acute eye. To the History Faculty and to colleagues at Christ's College, my continued thanks for stimulating and supportive working environments.

In researching this book I have been struck by how much primary material is now available in reliable form on the Internet but, as with other projects, I could not have managed without the resources of Cambridge University Library. Many of the recent books that I used bear a bookplate indicating their purchase from the resources of the Mark Kaplanoff Fund—named for a historian of nineteenth-century America who died tragically young but who left a munificent legacy to the Library.

My thanks to my British and American editors, Stuart Proffitt and Lara Heimert. Lara's colleagues at Basic Books, Kay Mariea and Christine Arden, did a superb job in turning the manuscript into a finished volume. The maps were drawn by Howard Cooke. Throughout the process my agent Peter Robinson has been a tower of strength.

More personally, I remain indebted to brother-in-law, David Ray, and Robin Hazard Ray for their endless hospitality in Boston; to my son, Jim, for being Jim; and above all to my wife, Margaret—the most important encounter of my initial year at Harvard and, since then, my abiding support. She read the draft with characteristic engagement and also helped dig out some of the research material. This is a book about her country; we have lived its recent history together. I dedicate the book to her; also to Jim as he explores his American roots and to his Bostonian cousins—Ellie, Lucy, and Maddy Ray—now spreading their wings across the empire of liberty.

Cambridge, England
Mirror Lake, New Hampshire
June 2009

INDEX

Abolitionism, abolitionists, 85, 106, 138, 144, 167, 191, 403, 471

Abortion, 181, 389, 394–398, 407, 409–410, 421, 445, 448, 450–451, 472

Acheson, Dean, 309

Adams, Abigail, 51, 53, 71, 86–87, 90

Adams, Henry, 208

Adams, John
    independence and, 49, 51–54, 57–59
    as president, 71, 75–78, 81, 92, 97, 208
    slavery and, 86
    women's rights and, 86–87, 89, 90

Adams, John Quincy, 97, 109, 208

Addams, Jane, 231

Affirmative action, 181, 190

Afghanistan, 413, 457, 458, 460, 464

African-Americans, 15, 84–86, 188–189, 190–191, 298–299

Agnew, Spiro, 390

Agriculture, 8–9, 67, 109, 169, 187, 210–214, 249, 285

Alaska, 333, 464

Ali, Muhammad, 349–350

Alien and Sedition Acts, 75, 93

Allende, Salvador, 386–387

Al-Qaeda, 457, 458

America First, 292–293

American Civil Liberties Union (ACLU), 245

American Dream, 133, 278, 347, 409

American Federation of Labor (AFL), 213–214

American Jewish Congress, 405

American Medical Association (AMA), 359

American Party, 135–136

American Railway Union, 212, 213

American Revolution
    beginning of, 49–54
    Bunker Hill, Battle of and, 50
    Concord, Battle of and, 50, 57
    Declaration of Independence and, 45, 52–54, 57
    Lexington, Battle of and, 49–50, 57
    Saratoga, Battle of and, 55–57
    slavery and, 53
    Treaty of Paris (1783) and, 57
    Valley Forge, winter at and, 54–55
    victory, 54–58
    Yorktown, Battle of and, 57

American Temperance Society, 105, 111

American West
    Columbus, Christopher and, 8
    evangelicalism and, 103–109
    politics and, 95
    slavery and, 130–132
    values of, 113–117
    Wild West myth and, 232–237

Americanism, 260–265

Amherst, Sir Jeffrey, 10

Anderson, Robert, 152–153

Anglicanism, Anglicans, 28, 38, 66

Anti-federalists, 62, 64–65, 66, 74, 78

Anti-semitism, xvi, 347

Arbenz, Jacobo, 328

Armas, Castillo, 328

Arms control, 379–381, 394, 413, 422, 425

Arms race, 246, 256, 333, 381, 422

Armstrong, Louis, 266–267

Armstrong, Neil, 378

Arthur, Chester, 225

Articles of Confederation, 58–59, 60
Astor, John Jacob, 118, 132
AT&T (American Telephone and
        Telegraph Company), 429–430
Atomic bomb, 302–303, 310, 325, 332, 427
Automobiles, 230–231, 275–276, 319

Baker, James, 420, 437, 438
Ball, George, 363, 371
Bank of the United States, 98–99, 101, 117,
        228
Baptists, 38, 39, 107
Baseball, 229–230
Bay of Pigs, 362–363, 366, 370
Bayard, James, 77
Beach, Moses, 132, 133
Beauregard, Pierre, 152–153
Beecher, Lyman, 104, 134
Benton, Thomas Hart, 98–99, 124
Berlin, Irving, 216
Bessemer, Henry, 198
Biddle, Nicholas, 98–99, 101
Bierstadt, Albert, 235–236
Big business, 197–201, 212, 224, 225, 227,
        228, 253, 289, 297, 427
Bill of Rights, 65, 66, 320
Bin Laden, Osama, 457, 460
Biological warfare, 10, 11
Birth control, 354–355
Birth of a Nation (film), 195
Black Panther movement, 348–349
Blackmun, Harry, 396, 397
Blacks. _See_ African-Americans
Blair, Tony, 469
Bohlen, Charles, 312
Bohr, Niels, 302
Bolshevism, 257, 261, 307
Bolton, John, 459
Bonus March (1932), 279, 320
Booth, John Wilkes, 144, 174–175
Boston, Mass., 3, 5, 12, 26, 29, 35, 38, 46,
        48, 50, 71, 102, 402–403
Bow, Clara, 265, 266–267
Brackenridge, Henry, 3–4
Braddock, Edward, 40–42, 55, 198
Bradley, Omar, 326
Brady, Tom, 337
Brandon, Henry, 389–390
Brezezinski, Zbigniew, 413

Brezhnev, Leonid, 413, 422
Brooks, Louise, 265
Brooks, Preston, 141
Brown, John, 141, 143–144, 161, 174
Brown, Joseph, 168–169
Brown, Lloyd, 299
_Brown et al. v. Board of Education of
        Topeka et. al._, 336–338
Bryan, William Jennings, 211–212, 249,
        268, 269, 404
Bryant, William Cullen, 4
Bryce, James, 225–226
Buchanan, James, 143
Buchanan, Pat, 445, 448, 453
Buckner, Simon Bolivar, 156–157
Buffalo Bill's Wild West show, 234–235
Bundy, McGeorge, 371, 372
Burgoyne, John, 55
Burke, Edmund, 1, 49
Burr, Aaron, 77
Bush, George H. W., 417, 442
        collapse of communism and, 432–435,
            440
        Gulf War of 1991 and, 435–440
Bush, George W.
        election of 2000 and, 449–451
        Iraq War of 2003 and, 457–464
        on liberty, 305, 463–464, 469
        war on terror and, 355, 441, 449–451
Bush Doctrine, 461
Bush v. Gore, 450–451
Bushnell, Horace, 134
Byrd, William, 35

Cahokia, 4–7, 17
Calhoun, John C., 91, 117, 130, 131
California, 125–132, 140, 223–224, 279,
        453
Calvinism, Calvinists, 28, 102
Campbell, Alexander, 103
Canning, George, 94
Capone, Al, 266
Carlucci, Frank, 423
Carmichael, Stokely, 348, 353
Carnegie, Andrew, 166–167, 198, 199,
        201–202, 203, 208, 214, 222
Carroll, Charles, 119
Carson, Rachel, 391
Carter, Jimmy, 389, 394, 408–415, 418, 443

foreign policy and, 410–414
religion and, 409–410
Carter, Rosalynn, 408, 409
Cartier, Jacques, 15
Castro, Fidel, 361–367, 411
Catholicism, Catholics, 16, 22, 27, 28, 33,
    95, 101, 132–136, 356–357
Central Intelligence Agency (CIA), 315,
    327–328, 346, 362–364, 386
Chalabi, Ahmad, 463
Chamberlain, Joshua, 174
Chamberlain, Neville, 290
Champlain, Samuel de, 15–16
Chaplin, Charlie, 324–325
Charles I, King, 22, 27
Charles II, King, 23, 31, 33
Charlevoix, Pierre de, 18
Chase, Samuel, 77
Cheney, Dick, 460, 463
Chernow, Ron, 204
Cherokee Indians, 109–110, 112–113
Chevalier, Michel, 101, 147, 197
Chicago, Ill., 206–210, 212, 347–348
Chicago race riots (1919), 267
Chicago World's Fair (1893), 210, 212
China, 315, 322–323, 379–381
Chinese-Americans, 217, 453
Choiseul, Duc de, 43
Churchill, Winston, 290, 293, 297,
    300–301, 309, 312, 368
Civil Rights Act (1866), 180, 181
Civil Rights Act (1964), 344, 352
Civil rights movement, 255, 336, 472
    Black power and, 346–350
    bus boycott and, 338–340
    Reconstruction and, 177
    Supreme Court, U.S. and, 336, 472
    Voting Rights Act (1965), 344–346
Civil War, U.S., 76, 150–151(map), 171,
    471–472
    Antietam, battle of and, 159, 160
    Atlanta, burning of and, 169–170
    Bull Run, battle of and, 154–155
    campaigns of 1861, 149–155
    Cold Harbor campaign and, 167–168
    commemoration of, 191–196
    conscription and, 166–167
    end of, 173–174
    Fort Donelson, battle of and, 156–157

Fort Sumter, battle of and, 152–153
    Fort Wagner, battle of and, 161–162
    Gettysburg, battle of and, 163–166,
        193
    origins of, 136–145
    Seven Days battle and, 158
    Sharpsburg, battle of and, 159
    Shiloh, battle of and, 156–157
    slavery and, 159–160, 171, 177
    Vicksburg, battle of and, 162–163
Clay, Henry, 91, 97, 99, 131
Clay, Lucius, 313
Clayton, William, 128
Clemenceau, Georges, 257
Cleveland, Grover, 212, 217, 227
Clinton, Bill, 442–449, 453, 459
    election campaign of 1992, 442–443,
        466
    health care and, 445–446
    impeachment and, 182, 448–449
Clinton, DeWitt, 117–118, 120
Clinton, Hillary Rodham, 386, 442,
    445–446, 465, 466
Cockburn, George, 91, 92
Cody, William F., 234–235
Cold War, 12, 308(map), 474, 475
    beginning of, 310–312
    Communism and, 312
    Cuba and, 361–366
    education and, 331–332
    Eisenhower, Dwight D. and, 326–328,
        331–334
    end of, 431–434, 442
    home ownership and, 317–321
    Korean War and, 321–323, 325–326
    McCarthyism and, 323–325
    Nixon, Richard and, 330–331
    popular culture and, 329–331
    Reagan, Ronald and, 417, 422–425,
        431–432
    Soviet Union and, 307, 310–312
    Truman, Harry and, 321–326
    See also Communism
Colden, Cadwallader, 118
Cole, Nathan, 37–38
Colonial America, 94
    Columbian exchange and, 7–11
    currency and, 15
    disease and, 16, 21, 36

Colonial America *(continued)*
  early history of, 21–44
  founding of, 3–7
  France and, 15–19
  Indians and, 23, 32, 34, 39–44
  middle colonies and, 21, 31–34, 35
  New England and, 26–31, 35, 38
  newspapers in, 35–36
  religion and, 22, 25, 26–31, 37–39
  Seven Years War (1756–1763) and,
    39–44
  slavery and, 21–26, 30–31, 36–37, 51
  South and, 21–26, 35
  Spain and, 11–15, 43
  taxation and, 28
  voting rights and, 22, 24, 28
  women and, 29
Colton, Walter, 129
Columbian exchange, 7–11
Columbus, Christopher, 3, 7–11, 214
Communications revolution, 120,
  429–430
Communism, 274, 290
  China and, 315, 322–323
  Cold War and, 312
  McCarthyism and, 323–325
  Red Scare of 1919 and, 261–263, 307
  Truman, Harry and, 323–324
  See also Cold War
Compromise of 1790, 70
Compromise of 1820, 70
Compromise of 1850, 70, 132, 136, 138,
  140, 144
Confederate States of America, 144, 152,
  159, 160, 183
Congregationalism, 30, 66, 102, 104, 106,
  192
Connecticut, 59, 89, 93
Connor, Eugene "Bull," 343, 348
Conscription, 166–167, 251, 291, 298, 313
Conservation, 236–237
Conservatism, conservatives, 399
  compassionate, 449
  neo-, 459–460, 463
Constitution, U.S.
  abortion and, 421
  Bank of the United States and, 99
  Bill of Rights, 320
  Bill of Rights and, 65, 66

Constitutional Convention (1787)
  and, 58–63
Eighteenth Amendment, 264
Equal Rights Amendment (ERA),
  399–401, 409
First Amendment, 66, 405
Fourteenth Amendment, 181, 182,
  190, 396–398, 450
immigration and, 217
impeachment and, 77
necessary and proper clause of, 61, 99
Nineteenth Amendment, 255
people and, 100
prayer in schools and, 421
privacy, right to and, 354
religion and, 66
Second Amendment, 65
Seventeenth Amendment, 223
slavery and, 60–61, 131, 142–143, 160,
  172
Supreme Court, U.S. and, 61, 63,
  64–65, 78, 336
Tenth Amendment, 65–66
Thirteenth Amendment, 172
Virginia Plan and, 59–60
women and, 89
Constitutional Convention (1787), 58–63,
  228
Contraception, 354–355
Contract with America, 446
Cooke, Alistair, 294–295, 297, 302, 454
Coolidge, Calvin, 270
Cooper, James Fenimore, 111
Cornell, Ezra, 200
Cornwallis, Lord, 56, 57
Coronado, Francisco Vásquez de, 12
Cortés, Hernán, 6, 11–12, 13
Crocker, Charles, 223
Cromwell, Oliver, 32
Cronkite, Walter, 454
Cuba, 40, 221, 226, 236–242, 361–367, 475
Cuban missile crisis, 357, 363–366, 387
Culture wars, xvi, 441, 445, 451, 465, 478
Custer, George, 174, 234, 235

Daley, Richard, 348, 378
Dallek, Robert, 421
Darrow, Clarence, 269
Darwinism, 191, 218, 245, 268–270, 404,
  476

Davis, Jefferson, 152, 160–161, 168
De Soto, Hernando, 12, 22
Dean, John, 384–385
Deaver, Michael, 420, 421
Debs, Eugene, 212, 213, 214, 261
Declaration of Independence, 45, 52–54, 57, 63, 65, 79, 81, 87, 99, 106, 108, 119
Declaration of Rights and Sentiments (1848), 1, 108
Deere, John, 115
Democracy, 22, 27, 61, 134, 147
    Founding Fathers and, 100, 223
    Jackson, Andrew and, 95, 97–103
    liberty and, 102
    people and, 62
    religion and, 101, 104
    representative, 100
    voting rights and, 136
Democracy in America (Tocqueville), 101–102
Democratic Party, Democrats, 8, 105–106, 132, 136
    Jackson, Andrew and, 100–101
    Korean War and, 327
    League of Nations and, 258
    Reagan, Ronald and, 421
    slavery and, 140, 141, 144
Deng Xiaoping, 435
Depression of 1890s, 210–214, 216–217
Dershowitz, Alan, 450
Détente, 393–394, 413, 422
Dewey, George, 239
DeWitt, John, 295
Dickens, Charles, 119
Dickinson, Anna, 167
Dickinson, John, 46, 51, 53
Diem, Ngo Dinh, 369–370
District of Columbia. *See* Washington, D.C.
Dobson, Ed, 420
Dole, Bob, 448
Dos Passos, John, 298
Douglas, Stephen, 120, 131–132, 140–142, 143, 144
Douglass, Frederick, 138, 161, 178
Draft, 166–167, 251, 291, 298, 313
Drake, Francis, 13
Dred Scott v. Sandford, 142–143, 181
Du Bois, W.E.B., 189, 190

Duke, James Buchanan, 187, 200, 205
Dulles, Allen, 328
Dulles, John Foster, 327
Dumore, John M., 50
Dunne, Finley Peter, 218
Dutch settlers, 16, 21, 31–32, 34, 59

Edison, Thomas, 200
Education, 320
    African-Americans and, 188–189
    Cold War and, 331–332
    Darwinism and, 245, 268–270
    immigration and, 134–135, 453
    Industrial Revolution and, 199–200
    Johnson, Lyndon B. and, 359
    Kennedy, John F. and, 356–357
    prayer in schools and, 404–405, 421, 477–478
    religion and, 106, 405–406
    segregation and, 336–338, 339–340, 401–403
    slavery, abolition of and, 183
Ehrlich, Paul, 391
Ehrlichman, John, 380–381, 384
Eisenhower, Dwight D.
    civil rights and, 336, 338, 339
    Cold War and, 307, 319, 326–328, 331–334
    as soldier, 300, 315, 319, 326
    Vietnam and, 368–369, 372
Elections
    presidential election of 1800, 76–77
    presidential election of 1828, 97–98
    presidential election of 1832, 99–101
    presidential election of 1844, 125–126
    presidential election of 1860, 144
    presidential election of 1864, 168, 170
    presidential election of 1868, 182
    presidential election of 1876, 185–186
    presidential election of 1896, 212
    presidential election of 1912, 227–228
    presidential election of 1928, 270–271, 357
    presidential election of 1932, 280
    presidential election of 1936, 286, 287
    presidential election of 1940, 291–292
    presidential election of 1948, 315–316
    presidential election of 1952, 326–327
    presidential election of 1960, 356–357
    presidential election of 1964, 358–359

Elections *(continued)*
　presidential election of 1968, 360, 376,
　　377–378
　presidential election of 1972, 382, 384
　presidential election of 1976, 394
　presidential election of 1980, 414–415
　presidential election of 1992, 442
　presidential election of 1996, 447–448
　presidential election of 2000, 449–451
　presidential election of 2008, 464–468
Ellis, Joseph, 449
Emancipation Proclamation, 160–161,
　166
Emerson, Ralph Waldo, 102, 103, 112, 128,
　144
Empire, America as, xiii–xv, 79–82,
　123–128, 240–242, 473–476
Engels, Friedrich, 351
Enlightenment, 63
Environmentalism, 9, 391–392
Equal Rights Amendment (ERA),
　399–401, 409
Erie Canal, 117–119, 120, 243, 474
European Union, 473
Evangelicalism, 37–39, 95, 103–109, 135,
　403–408
Evolution, 232, 245, 404

Falwell, Jerry, 403, 406–407, 409, 410, 411,
　420
Farming. *See* Agriculture
Faulkner, William, 194
Federal Bureau of Investigation (FBI), 65,
　263, 307, 324, 349, 386
Federal Reserve, 228, 276, 277, 281
Federal Trade Commission, 228
The Federalist, 62–63
Federalist Party, Federalists, 62, 74–78, 81,
　88, 93
The Feminine Mystique (Friedan), 351,
　400
Feminism, feminists, 181, 394, 399, 410,
　465
Ferraro, Geraldine, 421
Financial crisis of 2008, 466–467
Fitzgerald, F. Scott, 275
Florida, 10, 13–14, 15, 18, 24–25, 94
Forbes, James, 42
Ford, Gerald, 389, 390–391, 394, 429

Ford, Henry, 230–231, 232, 275, 302, 318
Founding Fathers, 49, 63, 71–72, 89, 109
　Bill of Rights and, 65
　Constitution, U.S. and, 62
　democracy and, 100, 223
　slavery and, 86, 142, 166
　Supreme Court, U.S. and, 78
France
　American Revolution and, 45, 54–58
　Colonial America and, 11, 15–19
　French Revolution and, 74–75
　Seven Years War (1756–1763) and,
　　39–44, 45
Frankfurter, Felix, 263
Franklin, Benjamin, 35–36, 41, 57, 387
Freedom
　of assembly, 66
　of choice, 400
　of conscience, 28
　of press, 66, 320
　of religion, 26–31, 66, 104, 292, 320
　of speech, 66, 292, 320
　See also liberty
Freedom Riders, 341–342
Freeman, Elizabeth, 84
Free-Soil party, Free-soilers, 141
Frelinghuysen, Theodore, 111
French and Indian Wars. *See* Seven Years
　　War (1756–1763)
French Huguenots, 12, 32
French Revolution, 73, 74–75
Freund, Ernst, 263
Friedan, Betty, 350–352, 354, 400
Friedman, Milton, 429
Frost, Robert, 363
Fuchs, Klaus, 324
Fukuyama, Francis, 442, 467
Fulbright, J. William, 374
Fundamentalism, 232, 270, 476–477
Furman, Richard, 107, 108

Gagarin, Yuri, 362–363
Gage, Thomas, 48, 50
Galbraith, John Kenneth, 356
Gandhi, Mahatma, 341
Garrison, William Lloyd, 106–107, 108,
　476
Gates, Bill, 428
Gates, Horatio, 55

George III, King, 45, 48, 51, 53, 58, 64, 100
Georgia, 25–26, 39, 85, 110
Germany, Germans, 21, 34, 36, 95, 106
Gettysburg Address, 165–166, 337
G.I. Bill (Serviceman's Readjustment Act), 320, 351
Gingrich, Newt, 446, 449
Giuliani, Rudy, 456
Gladstone, William Ewart, 201–202, 246
Godwyn, Morgan, 24, 29
Gold, 110, 129–130, 282
Gold standard, 211–212, 277, 392
Goldwater, Barry, 358–359, 400
Goldwyn, Sam, 216, 265–266
Gompers, Samuel, 213–214, 263
Gone with the Wind (film), 136, 195
Gorbachev, Mikhail, 417, 423–425, 431–435, 440
Gore, Al, 444, 449–451
Grady, Henry W., 186–187, 189
Graham, Billy, 38, 404, 406–408
Grant, Ulysses S., 127, 156–158, 162–163, 167, 172, 173, 182
Great Awakening, 37, 104
Great Britain
    American imperialism of, 11, 12, 18, 21–44
    American independence and, 45–58
    Civil War, U.S. and, 158, 159
    religious freedom in, 27
    Seven Years War (1756–1763) and, 21, 39–44
    slavery and, 158
    War of 1812 and, 91–94
    World War I and, 251–6, 258–60
    World War II and, 289–293, 299–301
Great Depression, 259, 273, 277–280, 280–286, 298
Great Society, 370–371, 374
Greenspan, Alan, 443
Griffith, D.W., 195
Grimké, Angelina and Sarah, 108, 181
Gromyko, Andrei, 381–382
Gulf War of 1991, 417, 435–440, 459

Haig, Douglas, 252
Haldeman, H.R. "Bob," 384–385
Hamilton, Alexander, 56, 62–63, 66–70, 75, 77, 81, 98

Hammond, James, 139
Harding, Warren G., 270
Hardy, Thomas, 194
Harrington, Michael, 355–356
Harrison, William Henry, 83, 100
Hartford Convention (1814), 93
Hawthorne, Nathaniel, 102–103
Hayakawa, Samuel, 453–454
Hayden, Casey, 353
Hayes, Rutherford B., 186, 225
Health care, 320, 359–360, 445–446
Hearst, William Randolph, 236–237, 243, 404
Heinz, H.J., 203, 205, 208
Hemingway, Ernest, 288–289
Higgins, Elizabeth, 211
Hispanic Americans, 452–454
Hiss, Alger, 324
Hitler, Adolf, 218, 247, 280, 286, 307
    analogies with, 311, 438, 461
    World War II and, 289, 290, 292–295, 300, 310, 324
Ho Chi Minh, 367–368, 379
Hoff, Maxie, 266
Holbrooke, Richard, 447
Holmes, Ogden, 85
Holmes, Oliver Wendell, 192–193
Homosexuality, 181, 350, 406, 445
Hoover, Herbert, 200, 273, 276–280
Hoover, J. Edgar, 263, 324, 325
Hopkins, Harry, 310
House Committee on Un-American Activities (HUAC), 324
Howe, Lord George, 42
Hughes, Charles Evans, 287
Hughes, Chris, 466
Humphrey, Hubert, 378
Huntington, Samuel, 454
Hussein, Saddam, 435–440, 456, 459–460, 463, 464
Hutchinson, Anne, 28–30, 38
Hutchinson, Thomas, 46, 48
Hydrogen bomb, 315

IBM, 427, 428
Immigration, 132–136, 245
    Chinese, 217
    colonial America and, 35
    Industrial Revolution and, 214–219

Immigration *(continued)*
    mid-nineteenth century, 132–136
    multiculturalism and, 451–454
    racism and, 217
    religion and, 132–136, 263–265
    World War II and, 296
Impeachment, 77, 181–182, 448–449
Indians, 1, 109–113
    agriculture and, 8–9
    America, discovery of and, 3–7, 7–11
    colonial America and, 23, 32, 34,
        39–44
    disease and, 10–11, 23
    environmentalism and, 9
    France's American imperialism and,
        15–16
    Jackson, Andrew and, 110–113
    Revolutionary era and, 82–84
    rights revolution and, 350
    Seven Years War (1756–1763) and,
        39–44
    Spain's New World empire and, 11–14
    Supreme Court, U.S. and, 112
    Trail of Tears and, 113
    westward expansion and, 72, 95
    Wild West and, 232–237
Industrial Revolution, 197
    antitrust legislation and, 204
    big business and, 197–201, 224
    cities and, 206–210, 212, 221–222
    depression of 1890s and, 210–214
    diet and, 203
    education and, 199–200
    electrical revolution and, 200–201
    immigration and, 214–219
    mass production and, 204–205
    politics and, 221–227
    railroads and, 201–203, 223
    steel industry and, 198–199
Information revolution, 417, 425–431,
    443–444, 466
Internet, 443–444, 466
Intolerable Acts, 48, 51
Iran hostage crisis, 413–414
Iran-Contra affair, 425
Iran-Iraq War, 435–436, 460–461
Iraq, 435–440, 458–464
Irish, 21, 34, 95, 106, 132–134, 218–219,
    245, 258, 270

Iron Curtain, 362, 427, 430, 433
Islam, 349–350

Jackson, Andrew, 94, 125, 136, 142, 185,
    228
    as president, 95, 97–100, 110–113
Jackson, Henry, 413
Jackson, Jesse, 465
James, Henry, 206
James I, King, 9
Japanese-Americans, 217, 296, 453
Jazz Age, 265–271, 275
Jefferson, Thomas, 75–78, 89, 90, 97, 101,
    106, 245
    America's capital and, 70
    Constitution, U.S. and, 58, 59, 61, 66
    Declaration of Independence and, 52,
        57
    empire of liberty of, xiii, 72, 78–82,
        82–86
    French Revolution and, 74–75
    Hamilton, Alexander financial plan
        and, 66–68, 70
    Indians and, 82–84, 109
    Kentucky and Virginia Resolutions
        and, 76
    Louisiana Purchase and, 81–82,
        85–86, 94, 126, 128, 159, 243
    slavery and, 84–86
Jews, 28, 32, 107, 217, 265, 347
Jobs, Steve, 428
Johnson, Andrew, 144, 179–182, 386
Johnson, Hiram, 223
Johnson, Lyndon B., 196, 332, 335
    civil rights movement and, 343–344
    education and, 359
    Great Society and, 359, 370–371, 374
    Vietnam War and, 361, 367–378
    War on Poverty and, 358–360
Judiciary. *See* Supreme Court, U.S.
The Jungle (Sinclair), 197–198

Kansas-Nebraska Act (1854), 140–142
Kennedy, Edward, 414
Kennedy, Jacqueline, 357–358, 360
Kennedy, John F., 192, 335, 342, 343,
    356–358
    Cold War and, 361–367
    Vietnam and, 369–370, 372

Kennedy, Robert F., 342, 362, 363, 376–377
Keynes, John Maynard, 258
Khrushchev, Nikita, 330–331, 333, 363–365
King, Martin Luther, Jr., 355, 376–378, 403
    civil rights movement and, 190, 232, 341–343, 345–348, 477
    Montgomery bus boycott and, 336–339
King, Martin Luther, Sr., 189, 190
Kissinger, Henry, 380–381, 383, 385, 386, 393
Know Nothings, 135–136, 140
Kohl, Helmut, 431, 433–434
Korean War, 321–323, 325–326
Kristol, Irving, 459
Ku Klux Klan (KKK), 184–185, 195, 267, 271, 339, 343, 405

La Salle, René-Robert Cavelier, Sieur de, 17, 18, 22
League of Nations, 256–260, 274, 438
Lee, Robert E., 127, 153, 157–158, 170–171, 172–174, 177, 197
    Gettysburg and, 163–165, 167
Lend-Lease, 292–293, 297, 309
Lenin, Vladimir, 307
Lévis, François Gaston de, 43
Levitt, Bill and Alfred, 318, 320
Lewinsky, Monica, 448–449
Lewis, Sinclair, 268, 274–275
Libertarianism, Libertarians, 72, 225, 227, 282
Liberty, xi–xiii, 1, 346, 469–473
    Christianity and, 106, 463, 476–477
    in colonial America, 21–44, 469–470
    democracy and, 102
    rights revolution and, 335–360
    slavery and, 19
    See also freedom, empire, Jefferson
Lincoln, Abraham, 115–116, 121, 141, 143, 144, 168, 259, 316
    assassination of, 174–175, 178, 179
    Civil War, U.S. and, 149, 152–175
    Gettysburg Address and, 165–166, 337
    slavery and, 149, 152, 159–160, 173
Lindbergh, Charles, 293, 425
Lippmann, Walter, 279, 280, 295

Livingston, Henry, 89
Livingston, Robert, 81, 82
Lloyd George, David, 257
Lodge, Henry Cabot, 217, 218, 258–259
Long, Huey, 282
Longstreet, James, 163, 164
Louis XIV, King, 17, 32
Louis XV, King, 43
Louisiana Purchase, 81–82, 85–86, 94, 126, 128, 159, 243
Lowell, A. Lawrence, 217
Lusitania, 247–249

MacArthur, Douglas, 279, 323, 325–326
Madison, James, 59–62, 65, 69, 70, 91–93, 97, 98, 117
Malcolm X, 195
Manifest destiny, 125, 128
Mao Zedong, 247, 315, 386
Marbury v. Madison, 78, 142
Marshall, George, 296, 299, 312, 313
Marshall, John, 78, 99, 112, 129, 142
Marshall, Thurgood, 336
Martin, Joseph, 55–56, 87, 325
Marx, Karl, 213, 351
Marxism, 197, 348
Massachusetts, 11, 27–29, 30–31, 34, 38, 51, 58, 59, 62, 89, 93
McCain, John, 464, 466, 467
McCarthy, Joseph, 323–325
McClellan, George B., 155–156, 158, 159, 168
McFarlane, Robert, 423
McKinley, William, 212, 226, 238–239, 240
McLean, John, 142
McLean, Wilmer, 173, 174
McNamara, Robert, 371, 372, 374
Medicaid, 359–360, 410, 446
Medicare, 359
Mellon, Andrew, 270
Melting pot, 21, 34, 245, 473
Melville, Herman, 103
Methodism, Methodists, 38, 39, 104, 107
Mexican-American War, 123–128, 452
Mexican-Americans, 452–454
Missouri Compromise of 1820, 86, 123, 130, 140
Mitchell, Margaret, 195
Mitterrand, François, 431, 433

Monroe, James, 81, 82, 94, 97, 242
Monroe Doctrine, 94, 126, 257, 461
Montcalm, Marquis de, 42–43
Moral Majority, 403, 407–408, 409
Morgan, J.P., 166–167, 199, 205, 222, 249, 262, 274
Mormonism, Mormons, 95, 128–129
Mubarak, Hosni, 436
Multiculturalism, 451–454
Munich Agreement, 289, 290

Napoleon Bonaparte, 74, 81, 97, 158, 165
Napoleonic Wars, 81, 90
National Aeronautics and Space Agency (NASA), 331
National Association for the Advancement of Colored People (NAACP), 336
National Association of Securities Dealers Automated Quotations (NASDAQ), 428–429
National Rifle Association (NRA), 377, 464
Native Americans. *See* Indians
Nazism, 290, 292, 312, 458
New Deal, 280–286, 472
     Agricultural Adjustment Act, 287
     Banking Act, 281
     federal deposit insurance and, 282
     Glass-Steagall Act, 282
     National Industrial Recovery Act, 287
     National Labor Relations Act (Wagner Act), 284, 287–288
     Public Works Administration, 285
     Rural Electrification Administration (REA), 284–285
     Social Security and, 282–283, 287
     Tennessee Valley Authority (TVA), 285
     Works Progress Administration, 282
New England, 16, 18, 21, 26–31, 35, 38, 66, 102
New Mexico, 6, 13–14, 15, 16, 18, 80, 129, 130–131
New York, 21, 32, 51, 53, 63, 118–119
New York City, N.Y., 71, 206–208, 224–225, 270–271
New York draft riots (1863), 167
New York Stock Exchange, 276, 428

New York Times, 133, 184, 224, 233, 235, 352
Nicholls, Richard, 31, 32
Niebuhr, Reinhold, 305
Nitze, Paul, 315–316
Nixon, Richard, 324, 355
     China visit of, 379–381
     Cold War and, 330–331
     imperial presidency and, 386–387
     Moscow visit of, 330–331, 333
     Vietnam War and, 361, 378–383
     Watergate and, 384–386, 390
North Atlantic Treaty, 314–316, 431
North Atlantic Treaty Organization (NATO), 326, 431, 434, 439
Northwest Ordinance of 1787, 79, 80, 84
Nuclear weapons, 327, 379, 413, 422–424

Obama, Barack, 465–468, 473, 478
O'Connor, Sandra Day, 420, 450
Oil crisis (1974), 390–392
Oklahoma city bombing (1995), 446–447
Oñate, Don Juan de, 13–14
O'Neill, Tip, 418–419
Operation Desert Shield, 437, 439
Operation Desert Storm, 439
Operation Plain Fare, 314
Operation Vittles, 314
Oppenheimer, Robert, 303
O'Sullivan, John L., 119–120, 125
Oswald, Lee Harvey, 357
The Other America (Harrington), 356

Palin, Sarah, 464–465, 466, 467, 478
Panama Canal, 242–243, 410–412
Parks, Rosa, 338, 345
Pearl Harbor, 294–296, 297, 303, 315, 332, 364, 456, 459
Pennsylvania, 21, 32–34, 35–36, 38, 40, 51, 58–60, 62, 84, 89
Pennsylvania Gazette, 35
People's Party, Populists, 211
Perle, Richard, 459, 460
Perot, Ross, 444
Pershing, John J., 252
Philadelphia, Pa., 33–35, 38, 49, 52, 54, 67, 69, 71, 163
Philanthropy, 199–200, 204, 222
Philippines, 40, 221, 239–241, 294

Pickett, George, 163–164, 193
Pinckney, Charles, 62, 65
Pitt, William, 42, 43, 45
Pittsburgh, Pa., 42, 209–210
Planned Parenthood, 355
Pledge of Allegiance, 421
Plessy v. Ferguson, 190, 336
Plunkitt, George Washington, 222, 225
Polk, James K., 125–128
The Population Bomb (Ehrlich), 391
Poverty, War on, 355–360
Powell, Colin, 436, 437, 460, 461, 463
Presbyterianism, Presbyterians, 104, 105
Press, freedom of, 66, 320
Progressivism, progressives
    economy and, 221
    politics and, 221–225
    religion and, 231–232
    Roosevelt, Theodore and, 225–229
    Wilson, Woodrow and, 228–229
Prohibition, 135, 245, 264–265, 266, 267,
    268, 270–271, 282
Protestantism, Protestants, 37–39, 66, 95,
    101, 476–477
    Catholics and, 132–136, 356–357
    colonial America and, 12, 22, 25, 27,
        30, 32
    evangelical, 103–109, 111, 132–136,
        268–270, 403–408
    post-Revolution, 38
Puritanism, Puritans, 12, 21, 26, 27–31, 38,
    102, 271
Putnam, Robert, 444–445

Railroads, 95, 119–121, 201–203, 223
Reagan, Nancy, 418, 423
Reagan, Ronald, 282, 305, 394, 399, 411
    Cold War and, 417, 422–425, 431–432
    economic agenda of, 418–420
    Election of 1980 and, 414–415
    Iran-Contra affair and, 425
    missile defense and, 422–424
    Reagan Revolution and, 417–421
Reconstruction, 177–186
Red Scare of 1919, 261–263, 307
Rehnquist, William, 397–398
Religion, 25
    colonial America and, 26–31, 37–39
    Constitution, U.S. and, xv, 66

democracy and, 101, 104
education and, 104, 106, 405–406
empire and, xvii, 16, 477
evangelicalism and, 37–39, 103–109
freedom of, 26–31, 66, 104, 292, 320
immigration and, 132–136
progressivism and, 231–232
slavery and, 24, 39, 106–108, 170
Religious Right, 420–421
Republican Party, Republicans,
    in 1790s and 1800s, 74, 76, 77, 78, 81
    hegemony in early 20th century, 212,
        228
    Reconstruction and, 179–180,
        182–186
    secession and, 141–142, 144, 149,
        471
Republicanism, 45, 72, 101, 471
Rights revolution
    civil rights movement and, 336–350,
        472
    freedom and, 335–336
    homosexuality and, 336, 350
    Native Americans and, 350
    women and, 336, 350–355
Riis, Jacob, 208, 216, 218
Riots
    Chicago race riots (1919), 267
    Detroit riots (1943), 299
    New York draft riots (1863), 167
    Philadelphia riots (1844), 134
    Watts riots (1965), 346–347
Rockefeller, John D., 166–167, 199–200,
    204, 222, 227, 262
Roe v. Wade, 395–398, 407, 409–410,
    450–451
Rogers, William, 379–381, 385
Roosevelt, Franklin D., 90
    Columbus Day and, 8, 9
    Great Depression and, 259, 273, 280
    New Deal and, 273, 280–286, 287
    Soviet Union and, 307, 309
    Supreme Court, U.S. and, 286–288
    World War II and, 273, 288–291,
        292–297
Roosevelt, Theodore, 225–229, 248, 261
    conservation and, 236–237
    imperialism and, 237–239, 242–243
Roosevelt Corollary, 242, 257

Rumsfeld, Donald, 460, 463, 464
Rush, Benjamin, 69, 90

Santa Anna, Antonio de, 124
Schlafly, Phyllis, 399–401, 478
Schlesinger, Arthur, 370, 387, 454
Schwarzkopf, H. Norman, 439
Scopes "monkey" trial, 268–269, 404,
     476–477
Scowcroft, Brent, 435, 437
Secession, 93, 130, 132, 144, 149, 152–153,
     177
Segregation, 190–191
     black protests and, 340–346
     busing and, 401–402
     in schools, 336–338, 339–340,
        401–403
     World War II and, 299, 301
Seneca Falls Convention, 108–109
September 11, 225, 441, 455–457, 460
Serviceman's Readjustment Act (G.I. Bill),
     320, 351
Seven Years War (1756–1763), 39–44, 45
Seward, William H., 131, 139, 141, 143
Sherman, William Tecumseh, 169–170,
     186–187, 194
Shultz, George, 423, 431
"Silent Majority," 398–403
Silent Spring (Carson), 391
Silver, 12, 211–212
Sinclair, Upton, 197–198, 208
Slavery, 19, 72, 102
     abolition of, 149, 159–160, 177
     American Revolution and, 53
     American West and, 130–132
     Civil War, U.S. and, 136–145, 149, 152,
        171, 177
     colonial America and, 21–26, 30–31,
        36–37, 51
     Compromise of 1850 and, 70, 132,
        136, 138, 140, 144
     Constitution, U.S. and, 60–61, 131,
        142–143, 160, 172
     Declaration of Independence and, 106
     Founding Fathers and, 166
     indentured servitude vs., 23–25, 31
     Kansas-Nebraska Act (1854) and,
        140–142
     Mexican-American War and, 124
     religion and, 24, 39, 106–108, 137, 170

     slave insurrections and, 24–25
     slave power and, 139–140, 142, 143
     slave trade and, 36–37, 53, 60–61, 84–85
     Supreme Court, U.S. and, 142, 181
     westward expansion and, 72, 80,
        84–86, 123
     women and, 108, 181
Smith, Al, 225, 270–271, 285–286, 357
Smith, Joseph, 103, 128
Social Security, 282–283, 419
Socialism, 197, 213, 214, 216
Souter, David, 450
South
     colonial America and, 21–26, 35
     Constitution, U.S. and, 60–61
     evangelicalism and, 107, 269–270,
        403–405
     liberty and slavery in, 21–26
     "New South" and, 186–191
     Reconstruction and, 177–186
     re-emergence of, 191, 408, 477
     secession and, 130, 144, 149, 152–153
     slavery and, 130–131, 160
     westward expansion and, 128
     See also African-Americans, civil
        rights movement
Southern Christian Leadership
        Conference (SCLC), 339, 341, 347
Soviet Union, 12, 274, 307
     atomic test (1949), 315
     Berlin blockade and, 313–314
     China and, 315,
     Cold War and, 307, 310–312
     collapse of, 417, 431–435, 440
     Cuba and, 361–367
     détente and, 393–394
     North Atlantic Treaty and, 314–316
     Reagan, Ronald and, 422–425
     space program of, 331–332, 362–363
     Truman, Harry and, 310–316
     World War II and, 307, 309
Space program, 331–332, 362–363, 378
Spain
     Colonial America and,, 11–15, 43
     Seven Years War (1756–1763) and, 43
     Spanish-American War of 1898 and,
        236–242, 474, 475
Spako, Theodore, 214–216
Spanish-American War of 1898, 236–242,
     474, 475

Sputnik II, 331–332
St. Valentine's Day Massacre, 266
Stagflation, 392
Stahl, Lesley, 433
Stalin, Josef, 247, 274, 309, 312, 313, 314, 324
Stamp Act of 1765, 46, 47, 48
Standard time zones, 202–203
Stanford, Leland, 200, 223
Stanton, Elizabeth Cady, 108, 181
Starr, Kenneth, 448, 449
States' rights, 61, 66, 76, 106, 177, 194, 339, 346
Stimson, Henry, 297, 300
Stock market crash of 1929, 276–277
Stowe, Harriet Beecher, 138, 177
Strategic Defense Initiative (SDI), 422–425
Strickland, William, 9
Strikes
    Pullman Strike (1894), 212–213
    sit-down, 288
    United Auto Workers strike (1937), 288
Student Non-Violent Coordinating
        Committee (SNCC), 341
Stuyvesant, Peter, 31–32
Suburban living, 317–321
Sumner, Charles, 141–142, 182
Supreme Court, U.S.
    abortion and, 395–398, 407, 409–410, 450–451
    antitrust legislation and, 204
    Bank of the United States and, 99
    civil rights movement and, 336–338, 472
    Constitution, U.S. and, 61, 63, 64–65, 77, 78, 336
    contraception and, 354
    Election of 2000 and, 450–451
    Indians and, 112
    judical activism and, 142–143
    judicial review and, 78, 287
    prayer in schools and, 404–405, 477–478
    Roosevelt, Franklin D. and, 286–288
    segregation and, 190, 339, 401
    slavery and, 142, 181

Taft, Robert, 292–293, 322
Taft, William Howard, 227–228

Tammany Hall political machine, 222, 225, 241, 270, 284
Taney, Roger, 142, 144
Taylor, Richard, 179
Tecumseh, 83–84
Tefft, Benjamin Franklin, 106
Television, 328–329
Teller, Edward, 331
Teller Amendment, 240
Terrorism, 74, 446–447, 455–457
    See also War on Terror
Texas, 15, 17, 18, 124–127
Thanksgiving, 3
Thatcher, Margaret, 431, 433
Thirty Years War, 27
Thoreau, Henry David, 102–103
Tocqueville, Alexis de, 1, 101, 104–105, 444
Tolstoy, Leo, 363
Townshend Duties, 47
Trail of Tears, 113
Transcendentalism, 102, 103
Treaty of Guadalupe Hidalgo, 127–128, 129
Treaty of Paris (1783), 57
Triangle factory fire (New York), 224–225, 284
Truman, Harry, 303, 307, 310–316, 321–326, 418
    World War I and, 252, 255, 303
Truman Doctrine, 311–312
Turner, Frederick Jackson, 116, 232
Tuskegee Institute, 188–189
Twain, Mark, 233
Tyler, John, 125–126

Uncle Tom's Cabin (Stowe), 138
Underground Railroad, 138
Unitarianism, 102
United Auto Workers (UAW), 288
United Nations (UN), 322, 335, 349, 437–438, 454, 461, 463
Universal Declaration of Human Rights, 335

Van Buren, Martin, 100, 101, 432
Vesey, Denmark, 107–108
Vietnam War, 335
    Eisenhower, Dwight D. and, 368–369, 372

Vietnam War *(continued)*
    Gulf of Tonkin resolution and, 372,
        374
    Johnson, Lyndon B. and, 361, 367–378
    Kennedy, John F. and, 369–370, 372
    Nixon, Richard and, 361, 378–383
    Tet offensive and, 374–375, 393
    War Powers Act (1973) and, 392–393
Viguerie, Richard, 399, 407
Virginia, 3, 21–24, 26, 40, 51, 58, 59–60, 68,
        114, 153
Voting rights
    colonial America and, 22, 24, 28, 33
    democracy and, 136
    westward expansion and, 80
    women and, 87–88, 108–109, 245,
        252–255
Voting Rights Act (1965), 344–346, 360,
        402

War of 1812, 91–93, 97, 117
War of the Spanish Succession, 14
War on Poverty, 355–360
War on Terror, 355, 457–464
War Powers Act (1973), 392
Warren, Earl, 336–337
Warsaw pact, 434
Washington, Booker T., 188–189, 339
Washington, D.C., 69–70, 72, 91–92, 94,
        154, 163, 376
Washington, George, 59, 70, 79, 90, 91–92,
        97, 227, 245, 291
    American Revolution and, 48, 50,
        54–56
    as America's first president, 64, 66
    foreign policy and, 74, 75
    Seven Years War (1756–1763) and, 40,
        41
    slavery and, 48
Watergate, 384–386, 390
Weapons of mass destruction (WMDs),
        438, 440, 463, 477
Wells, H.G., 221
West. *See* American West
Westward expansion, 96(map)
    Indians and, 72, 82–84, 95
    Jefferson, Thomas and, 78–82
    Louisiana Purchase and, 81–82, 85–86
    Mexican-American War and, 123–128

North v. South and, 128
    railroads and, 95
    slavery and, 72, 80, 84–86, 123
Whig Party, Whigs, 100–101, 105–106,
        125, 127, 132, 136, 140
White, Byron, 396, 397–398
White, Hugh, 47
White, Theodore, 357, 360
White, William Allen, 271, 287
White supremacy, 192, 267
Whitefield, George, 37–38, 39, 104
Whitman, Walt, 103, 114
Whitney, Eli, 85
Whitney, Thomas, 136
Wild West, 232–237
Wilde, Oscar, 469
Wilhelm II, Kaiser, 253
Wilmot proviso, 130
Wilson, Woodrow, 208, 212, 228–229, 253,
        270, 274, 293
    League of Nations and, 255–60, 438
    World War I and, 147, 245–251, 477
Winthrop, John, 11, 26–28, 38, 109
Women
    colonial America and, 29
    in combat, 445
    Constitution, U.S. and, 89
    contraception and, 354–355
    Equal Rights Amendment (ERA) and,
        399–401
    evangelical revivals and, 105
    Founding Fathers and, 72
    Industrial Revolution and, 208
    Revolutionary era and, 86–90
    rights revolution and, 350–355
    slavery and, 108, 181
    voting rights and, 87–88, 108–109,
        245, 252–255
    World War I and, 252–255
Woods, Tiger, 451, 452
Woolworth Building, 207–208
World War I, 251–255
    Americanism and, 260–265
    beginning of, 243
    end of, 255–260
    German U-boat campaign and,
        248–250
    immigration and, 263–265
    U.S. entry into, 245–251

women and, 252–255
Zimmermann Telegram and, 250
World War II, 298–304
African-Americans and, 298–299, 301
atomic bomb and, 302–303
Battle of the Bulge, 300
Japanese-Americans and, 296
Lend-Lease and, 292–293, 297, 309
Midway, battle of and, 297, 303
Normandy invasion and, 300

Pearl Harbor and, 294–296, 303, 315, 332, 364, 456, 459
Roosevelt, Franklin D. and, 273, 288–291, 292–297
U. S. entry into, 292–297
Wozniak, Stephen, 428

Young, Brigham, 128, 129, 132

Zhou Enlai, 381